THE NINTH
Garfield
Fat Cat 3-Pack

Jim Davis

The Random House Publishing Group • New York

A Ballantine Book
Published by The Random House Publishing Group

www.ballantinebooks.com

Library of Congress Catalog Card Number: 98-96212

ISBN 0-345-42903-6

Manufactured in the United States of America

First Edition: September 1998

20 19 18 17 16 15 14 13 12 11

Garfield

hits the big time

BY: JIM DAVIS

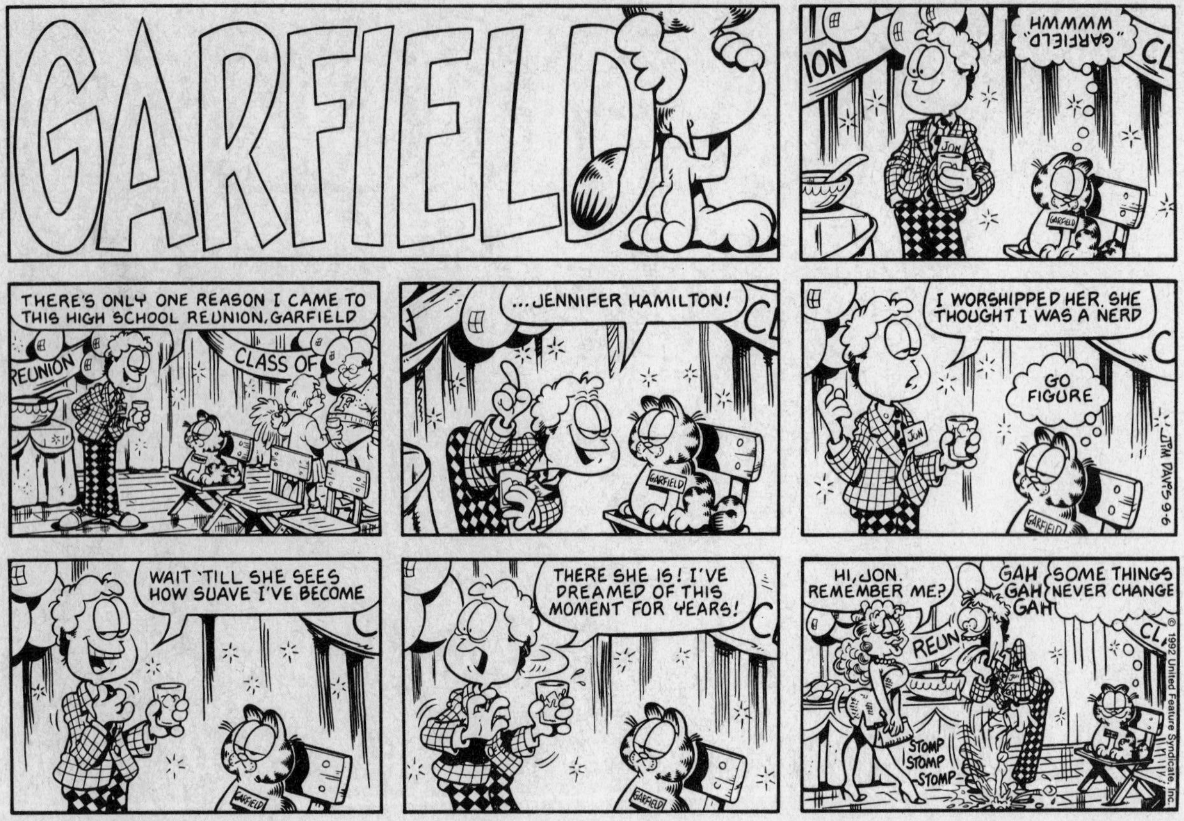
GARFIELD
"GARFIELD" WWWWH
ION
CL
JON
GARFIELD
THERE'S ONLY ONE REASON I CAME TO THIS HIGH SCHOOL REUNION, GARFIELD
REUNION
CLASS OF
...JENNIFER HAMILTON!
I WORSHIPPED HER. SHE THOUGHT I WAS A NERD
GO FIGURE
JIM DAVIS 9-6
WAIT 'TILL SHE SEES HOW SUAVE I'VE BECOME
THERE SHE IS! I'VE DREAMED OF THIS MOMENT FOR YEARS!
HI, JON. REMEMBER ME?
GAH GAH GAH
SOME THINGS NEVER CHANGE
REUN
STOMP STOMP STOMP
© 1992 United Feature Syndicate, Inc.

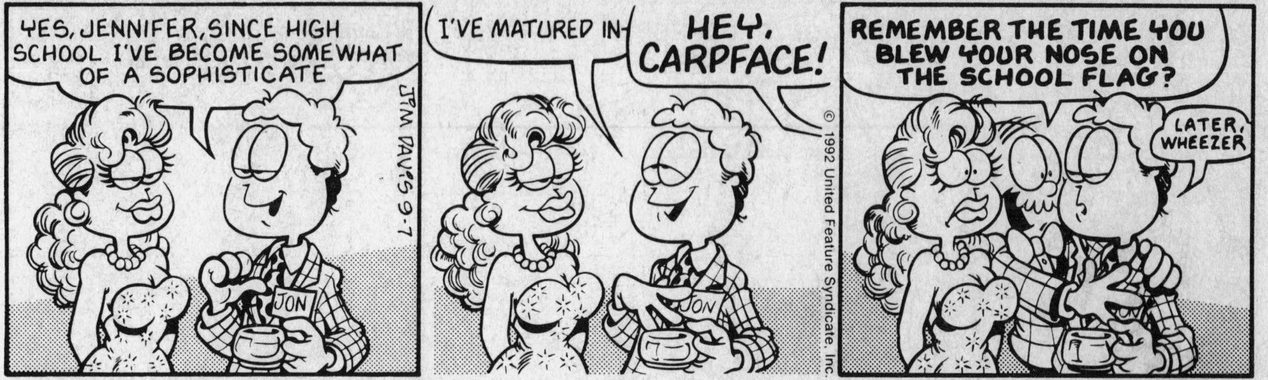
YES, JENNIFER, SINCE HIGH SCHOOL I'VE BECOME SOMEWHAT OF A SOPHISTICATE
JIM DAVIS 9-7
I'VE MATURED IN-
HEY, CARPFACE!
© 1992 United Feature Syndicate, Inc.
REMEMBER THE TIME YOU BLEW YOUR NOSE ON THE SCHOOL FLAG?
LATER, WHEEZER

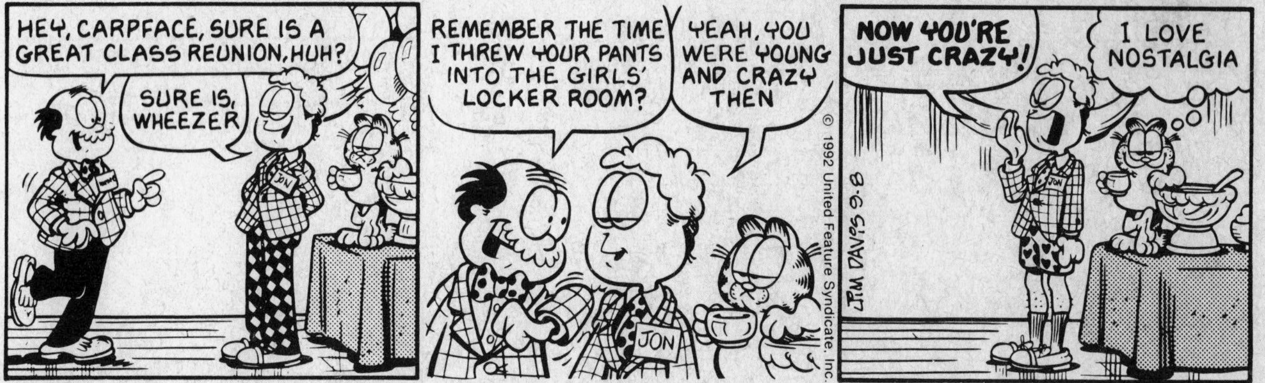
HEY, CARPFACE, SURE IS A GREAT CLASS REUNION, HUH?
SURE IS, WHEEZER
REMEMBER THE TIME I THREW YOUR PANTS INTO THE GIRLS' LOCKER ROOM?
YEAH, YOU WERE YOUNG AND CRAZY THEN
© 1992 United Feature Syndicate, Inc.
JIM DAVIS 9-8
NOW YOU'RE JUST CRAZY!
I LOVE NOSTALGIA

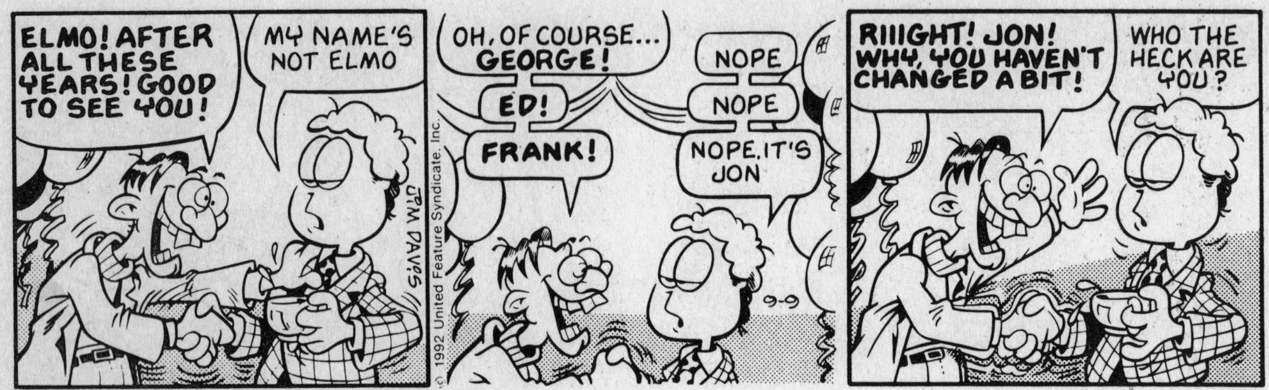
ELMO! AFTER ALL THESE YEARS! GOOD TO SEE YOU!
MY NAME'S NOT ELMO
JIM DAVIS
© 1992 United Feature Syndicate, Inc.
OH, OF COURSE... GEORGE!
NOPE
ED!
NOPE
FRANK!
NOPE. IT'S JON
9-9
RIIIGHT! JON! WHY, YOU HAVEN'T CHANGED A BIT!
WHO THE HECK ARE YOU?

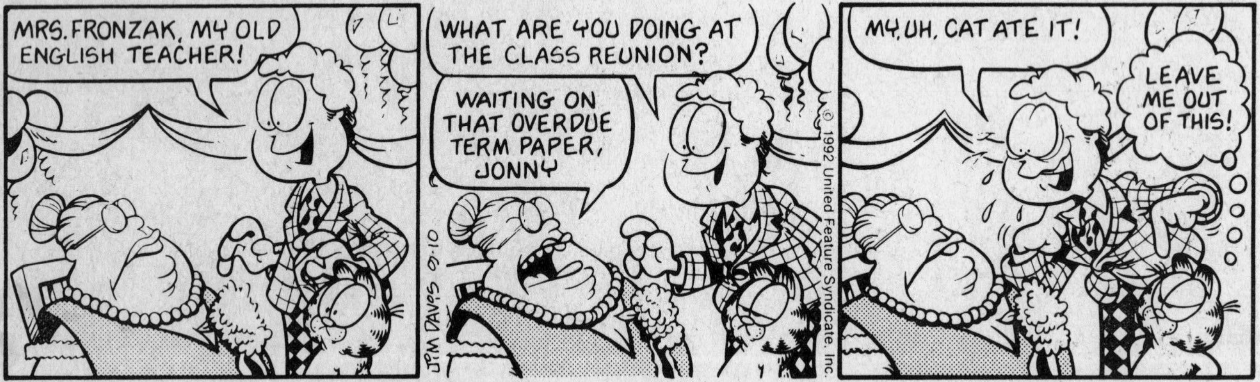
MRS. FRONZAK, MY OLD ENGLISH TEACHER!
WHAT ARE YOU DOING AT THE CLASS REUNION?
WAITING ON THAT OVERDUE TERM PAPER, JONNY
JIM DAVIS 9-10
© 1992 United Feature Syndicate, Inc.
MY, UH, CAT ATE IT!
LEAVE ME OUT OF THIS!

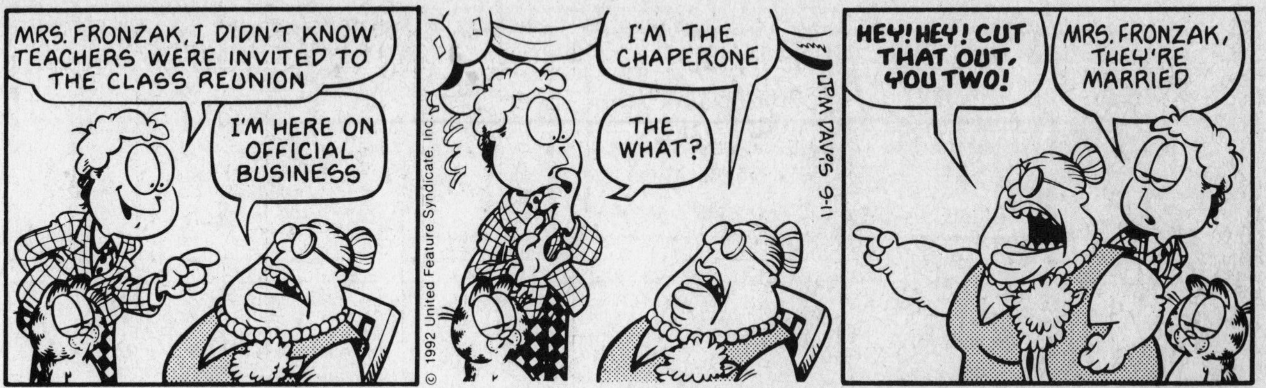
MRS. FRONZAK, I DIDN'T KNOW TEACHERS WERE INVITED TO THE CLASS REUNION
I'M HERE ON OFFICIAL BUSINESS
© 1992 United Feature Syndicate, Inc.
I'M THE CHAPERONE
THE WHAT?
JIM DAVIS 9-11
HEY! HEY! CUT THAT OUT, YOU TWO!
MRS. FRONZAK, THEY'RE MARRIED

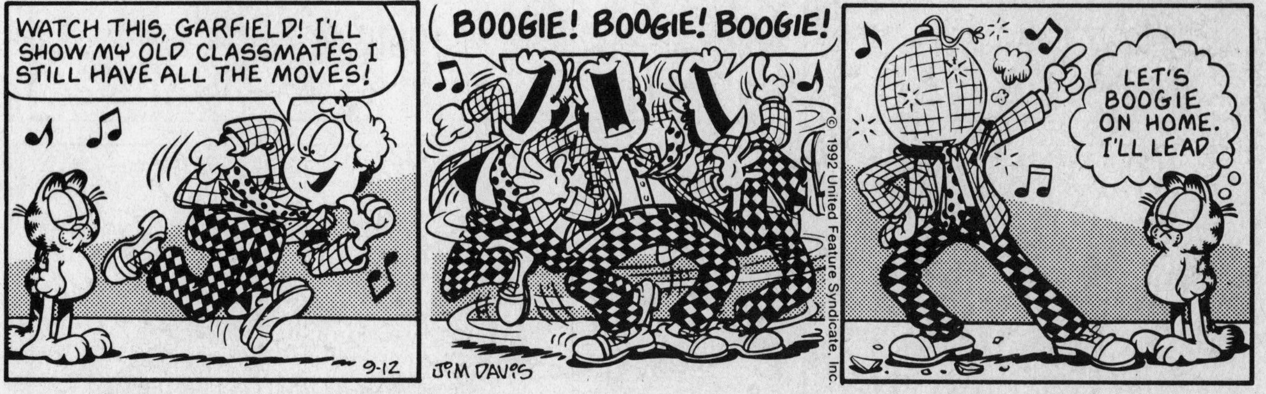
WATCH THIS, GARFIELD! I'LL SHOW MY OLD CLASSMATES I STILL HAVE ALL THE MOVES!
9-12
BOOGIE! BOOGIE! BOOGIE!
JIM DAVIS
© 1992 United Feature Syndicate, Inc.
LET'S BOOGIE ON HOME. I'LL LEAD

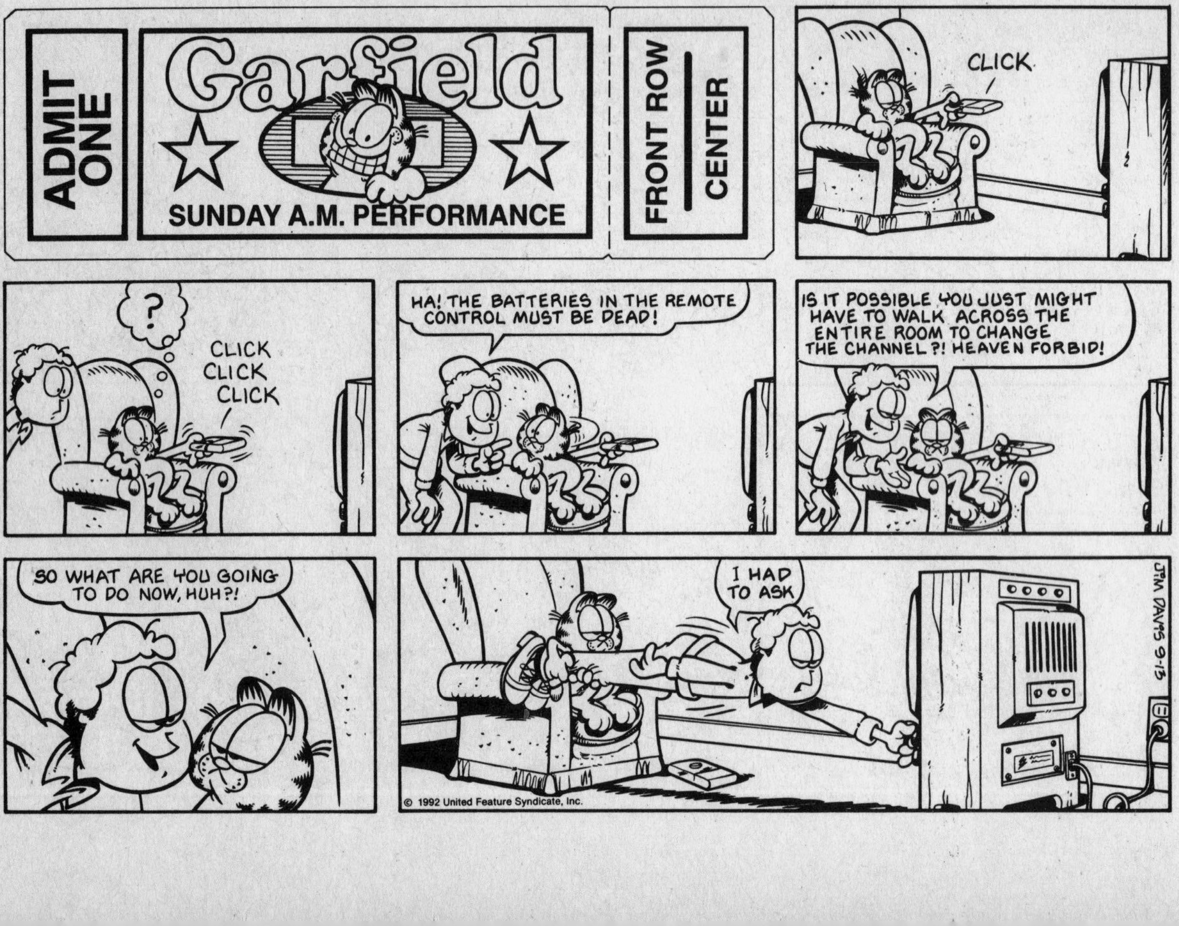
ADMIT ONE
Garfield
SUNDAY A.M. PERFORMANCE
FRONT ROW
CENTER
CLICK
?
CLICK
CLICK
CLICK
HA! THE BATTERIES IN THE REMOTE CONTROL MUST BE DEAD!
IS IT POSSIBLE YOU JUST MIGHT HAVE TO WALK ACROSS THE ENTIRE ROOM TO CHANGE THE CHANNEL?! HEAVEN FORBID!
SO WHAT ARE YOU GOING TO DO NOW, HUH?!
I HAD TO ASK
JIM DAVIS 9-13
© 1992 United Feature Syndicate, Inc.

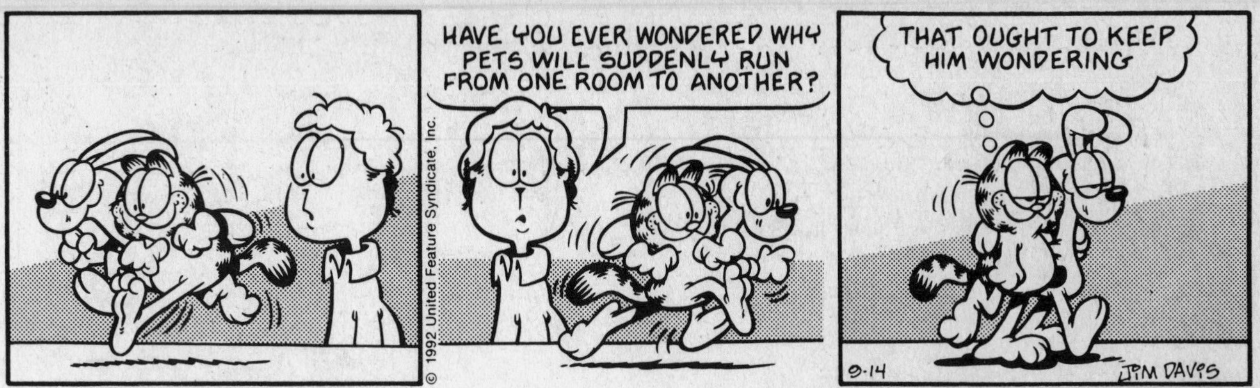
HAVE YOU EVER WONDERED WHY PETS WILL SUDDENLY RUN FROM ONE ROOM TO ANOTHER?
© 1992 United Feature Syndicate, Inc.
THAT OUGHT TO KEEP HIM WONDERING
9-14
JIM DAVIS

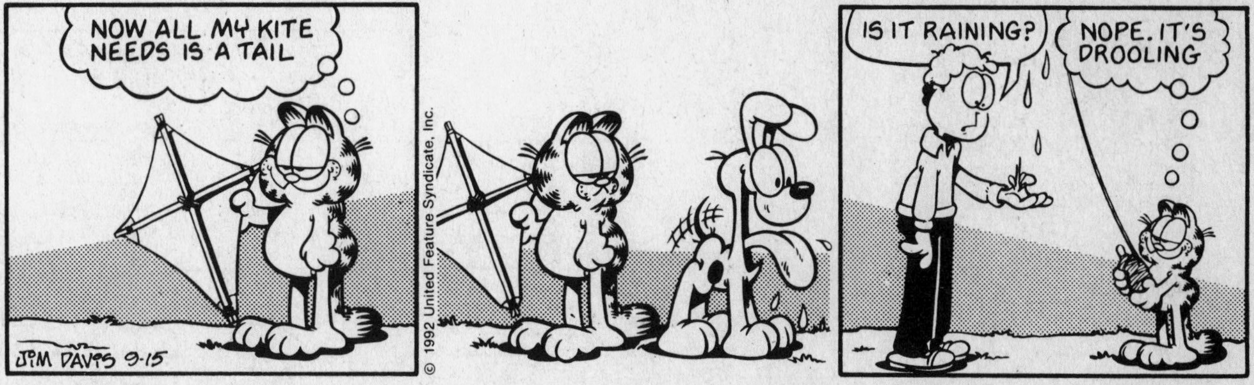
NOW ALL MY KITE NEEDS IS A TAIL
JIM DAVIS 9-15
© 1992 United Feature Syndicate, Inc.
IS IT RAINING?
NOPE. IT'S DROOLING

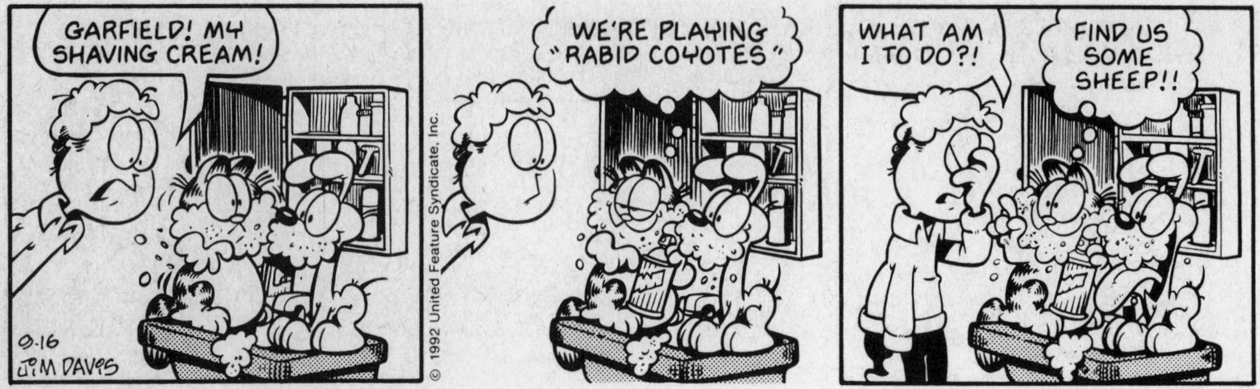
GARFIELD! MY SHAVING CREAM!
WE'RE PLAYING "RABID COYOTES"
WHAT AM I TO DO?!
FIND US SOME SHEEP!!
9-16
JIM DAVIS

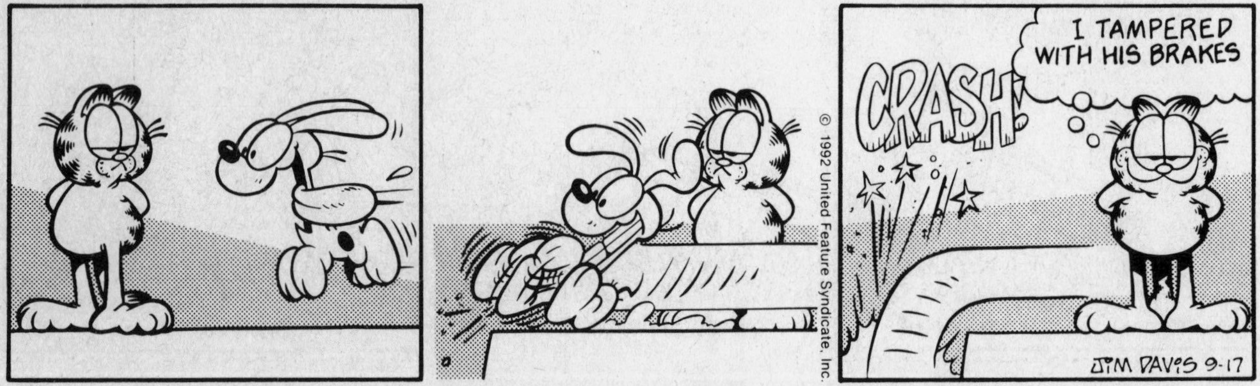
CRASH!
I TAMPERED WITH HIS BRAKES
JIM DAVIS 9-17

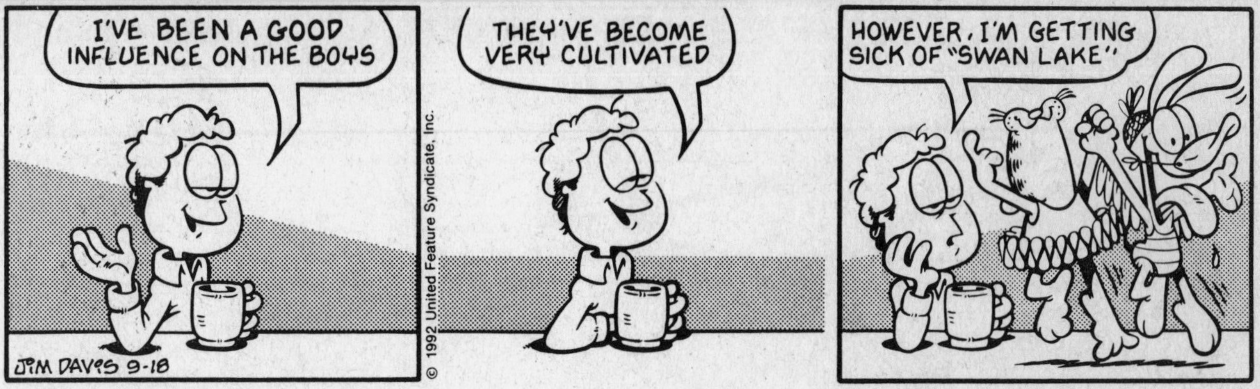
I'VE BEEN A GOOD INFLUENCE ON THE BOYS
JIM DAVIS 9-18
© 1992 United Feature Syndicate, Inc.
THEY'VE BECOME VERY CULTIVATED
HOWEVER, I'M GETTING SICK OF "SWAN LAKE"

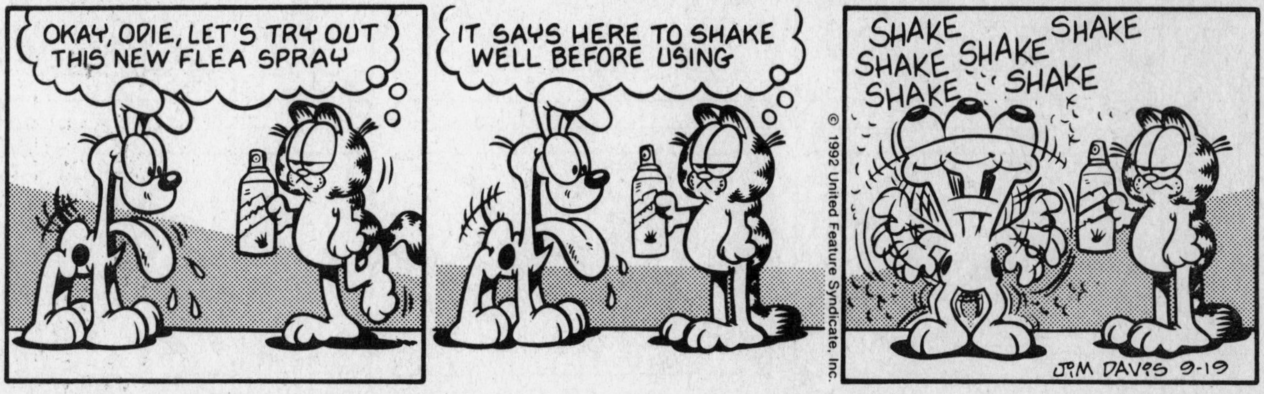
OKAY, ODIE, LET'S TRY OUT THIS NEW FLEA SPRAY
IT SAYS HERE TO SHAKE WELL BEFORE USING
© 1992 United Feature Syndicate, Inc.
SHAKE SHAKE
SHAKE SHAKE
SHAKE SHAKE
SHAKE
JIM DAVIS 9-19

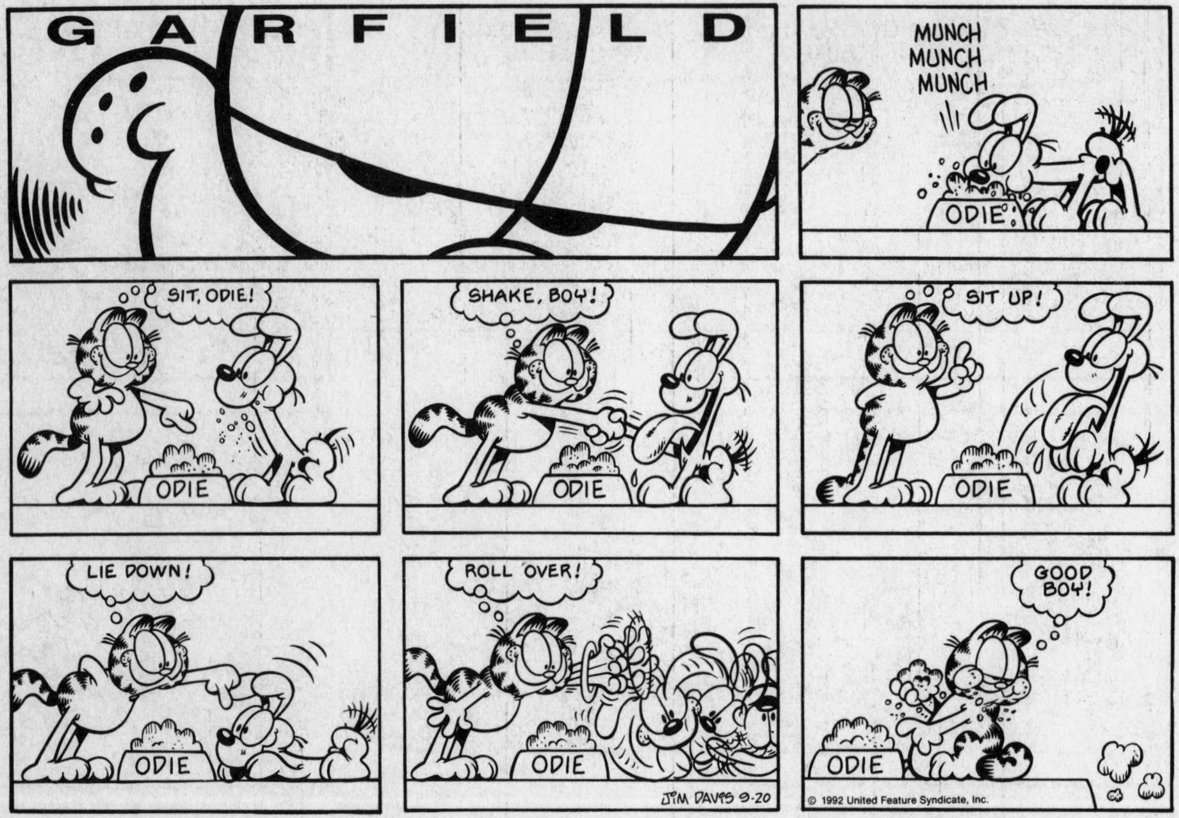
GARFIELD
MUNCH MUNCH MUNCH
ODIE
SIT, ODIE!
ODIE
SHAKE, BOY!
ODIE
SIT UP!
ODIE
LIE DOWN!
ODIE
ROLL OVER!
ODIE
JIM DAVIS 9-20
GOOD BOY!
ODIE
© 1992 United Feature Syndicate, Inc.

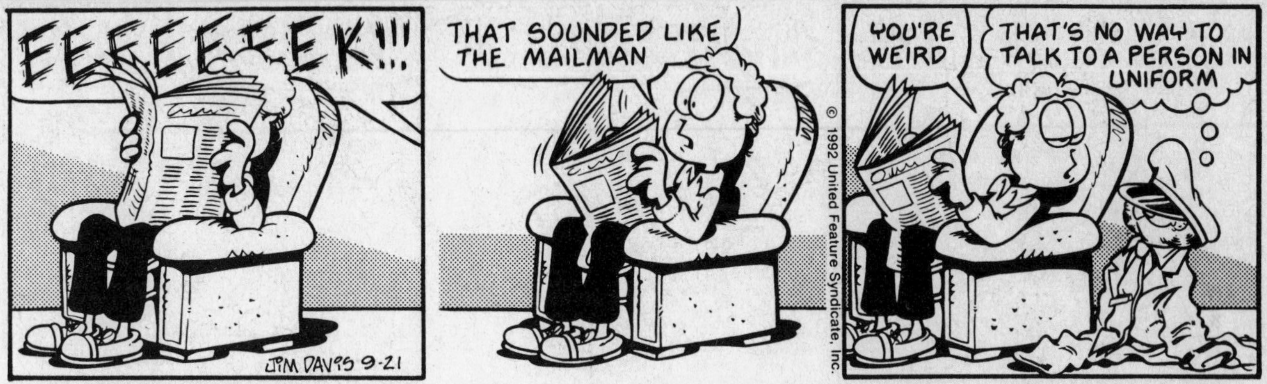
EEEEEEEK!!!
JIM DAVIS 9-21
THAT SOUNDED LIKE THE MAILMAN
© 1992 United Feature Syndicate, Inc.
YOU'RE WEIRD
THAT'S NO WAY TO TALK TO A PERSON IN UNIFORM

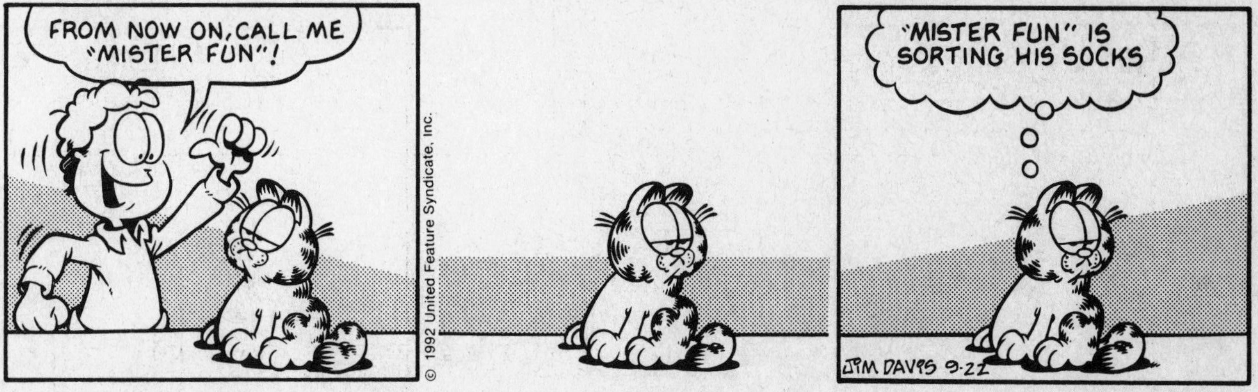
FROM NOW ON, CALL ME "MISTER FUN"!
© 1992 United Feature Syndicate, Inc.
"MISTER FUN" IS SORTING HIS SOCKS
JIM DAVIS 9-22

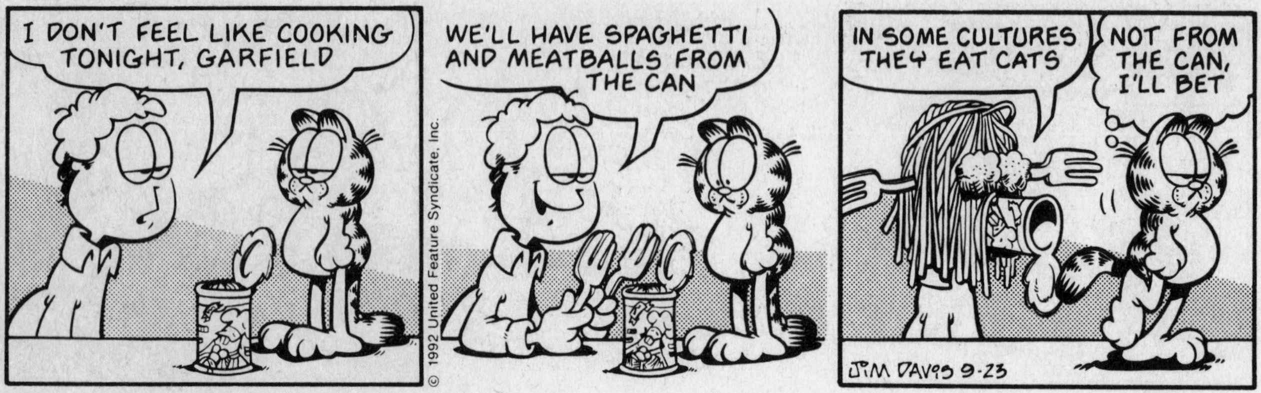
I DON'T FEEL LIKE COOKING TONIGHT, GARFIELD
WE'LL HAVE SPAGHETTI AND MEATBALLS FROM THE CAN
IN SOME CULTURES THEY EAT CATS
NOT FROM THE CAN, I'LL BET
JIM DAVIS 9-23
© 1992 United Feature Syndicate, Inc.

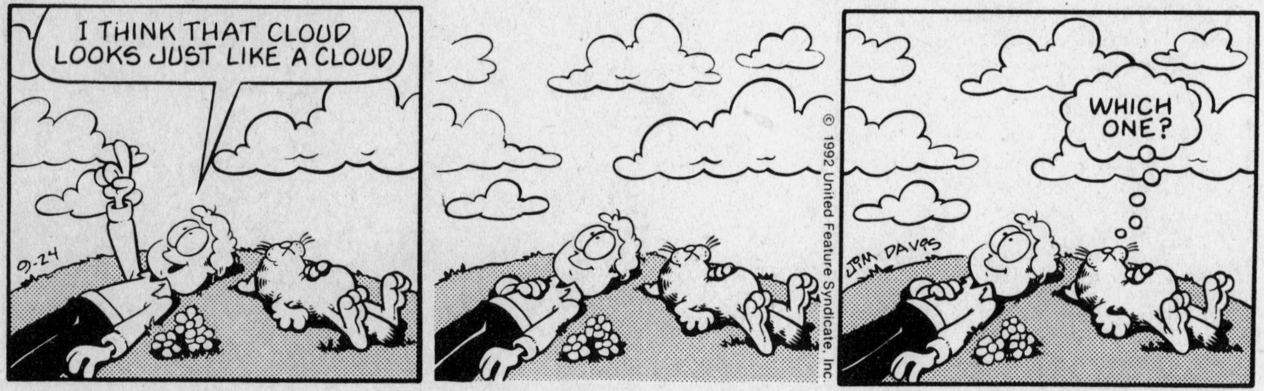
I THINK THAT CLOUD LOOKS JUST LIKE A CLOUD
9-24
WHICH ONE?
JIM DAVIS
© 1992 United Feature Syndicate, Inc.

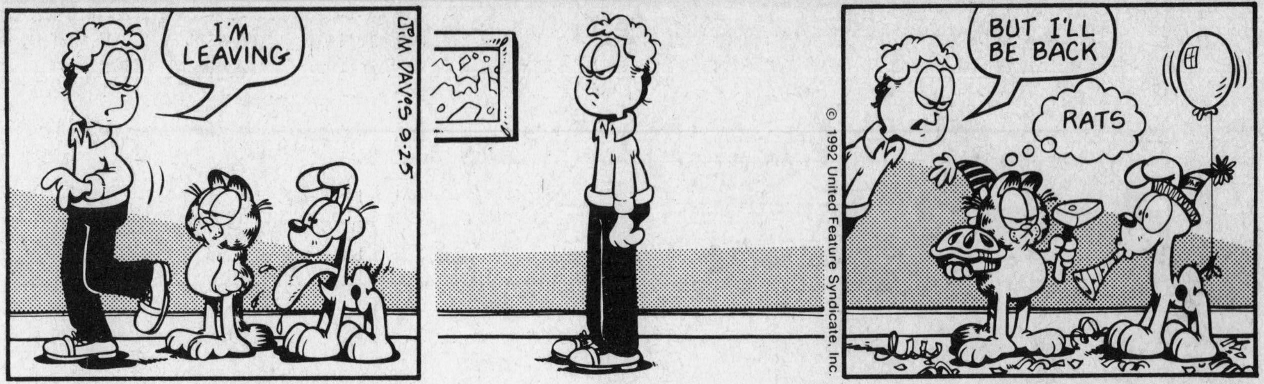
I'M LEAVING
JIM DAVIS 9-25
BUT I'LL BE BACK
RATS
© 1992 United Feature Syndicate, Inc.

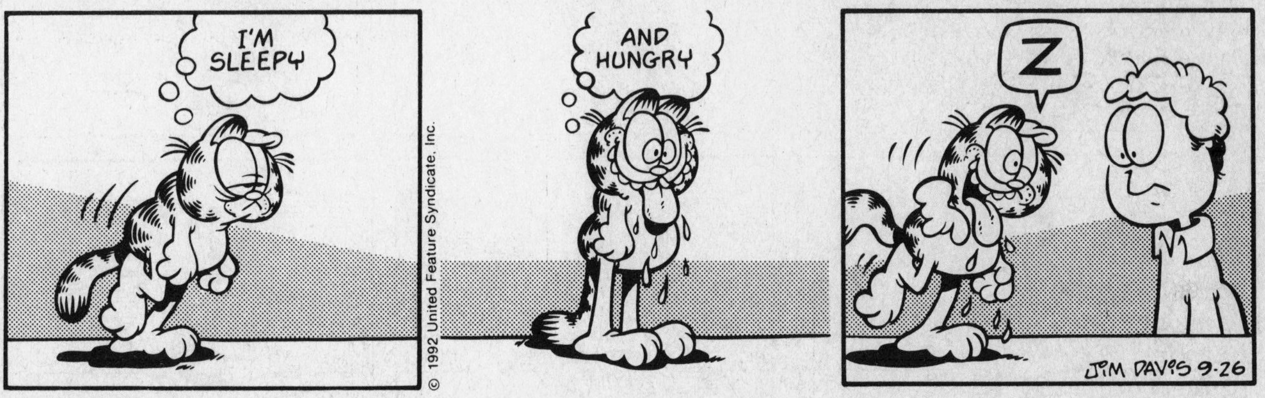
I'M SLEEPY
© 1992 United Feature Syndicate, Inc.
AND HUNGRY
Z
JIM DAVIS 9-26

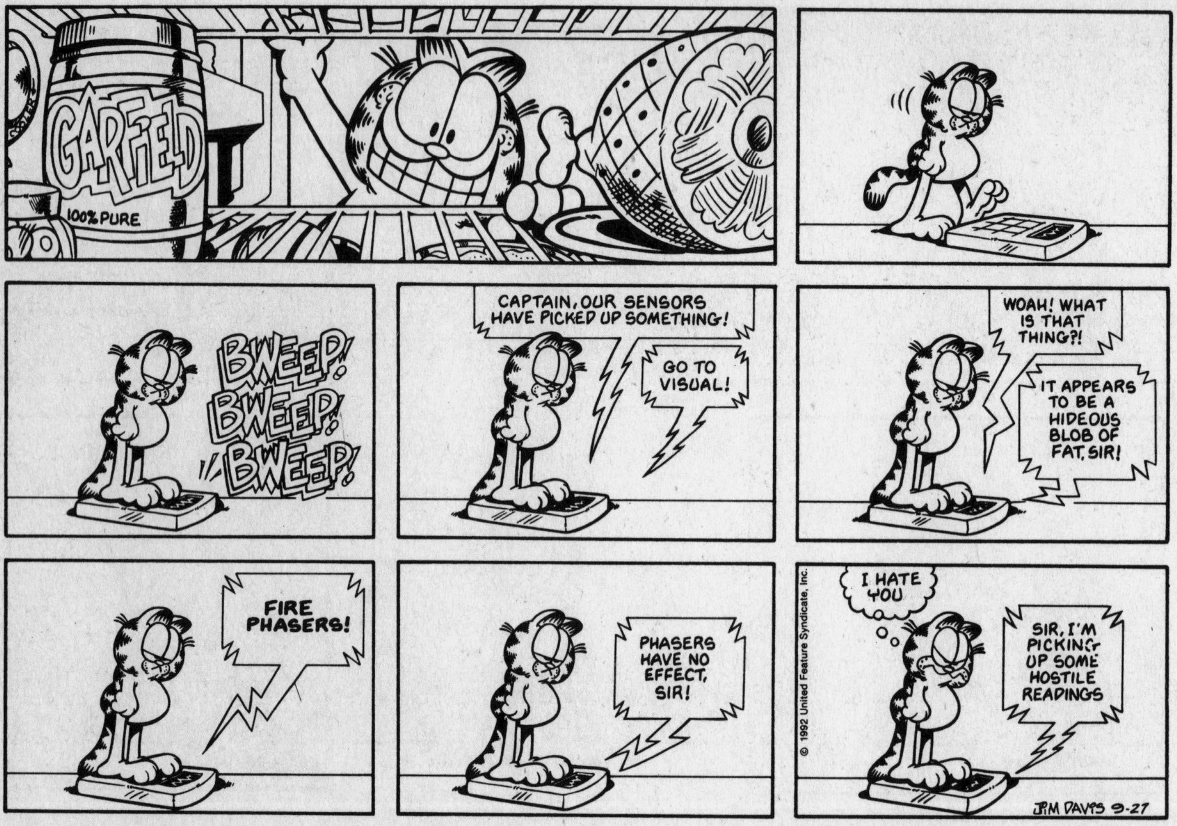
GARFIELD
100% PURE
BWEEP! BWEEP! BWEEP!
CAPTAIN, OUR SENSORS HAVE PICKED UP SOMETHING!
GO TO VISUAL!
WOAH! WHAT IS THAT THING?!
IT APPEARS TO BE A HIDEOUS BLOB OF FAT, SIR!
FIRE PHASERS!
PHASERS HAVE NO EFFECT, SIR!
I HATE YOU
SIR, I'M PICKING UP SOME HOSTILE READINGS
© 1992 United Feature Syndicate, Inc.
JIM DAVIS 9-27

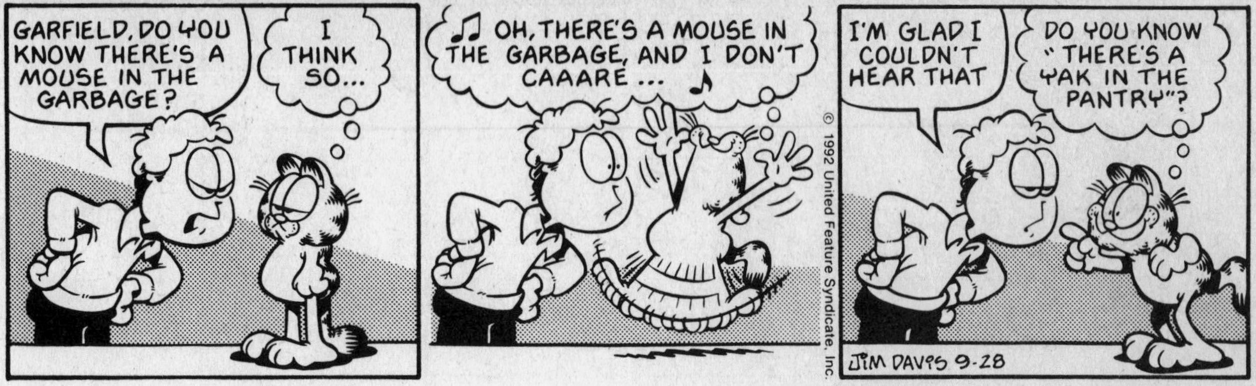
GARFIELD, DO YOU KNOW THERE'S A MOUSE IN THE GARBAGE?
I THINK SO...
OH, THERE'S A MOUSE IN THE GARBAGE, AND I DON'T CAAARE ...
I'M GLAD I COULDN'T HEAR THAT
DO YOU KNOW "THERE'S A YAK IN THE PANTRY"?
© 1992 United Feature Syndicate, Inc.
JIM DAVIS 9-28

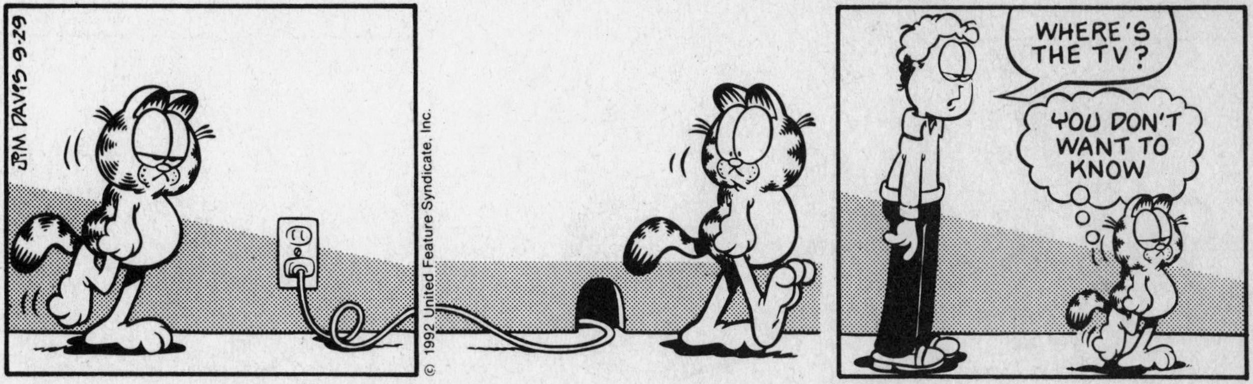
JIM DAVIS 9-29
© 1992 United Feature Syndicate, Inc.
WHERE'S THE TV?
YOU DON'T WANT TO KNOW

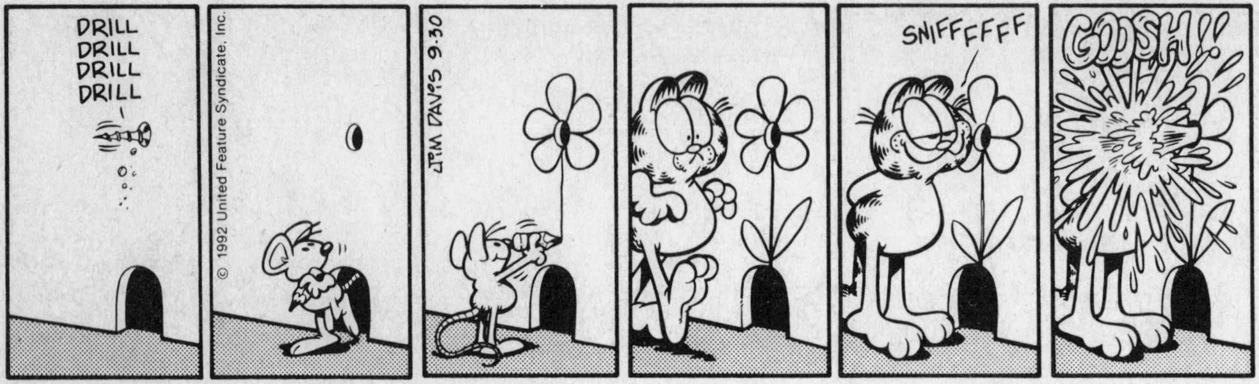
DRILL
DRILL
DRILL
DRILL
© 1992 United Feature Syndicate, Inc.
JIM DAVIS 9-30
SNIFFFFFF
GOOSH!!

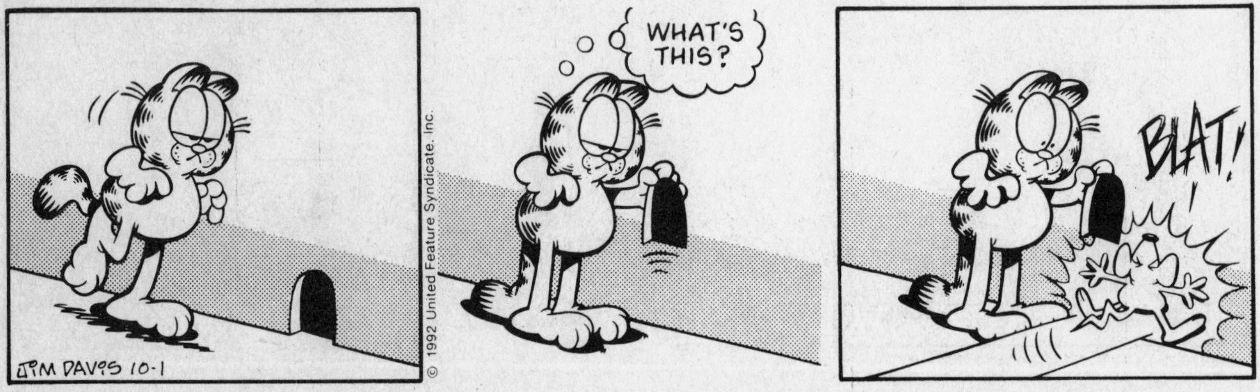
JIM DAVIS 10-1
© 1992 United Feature Syndicate, Inc.
WHAT'S THIS?
BLAT!

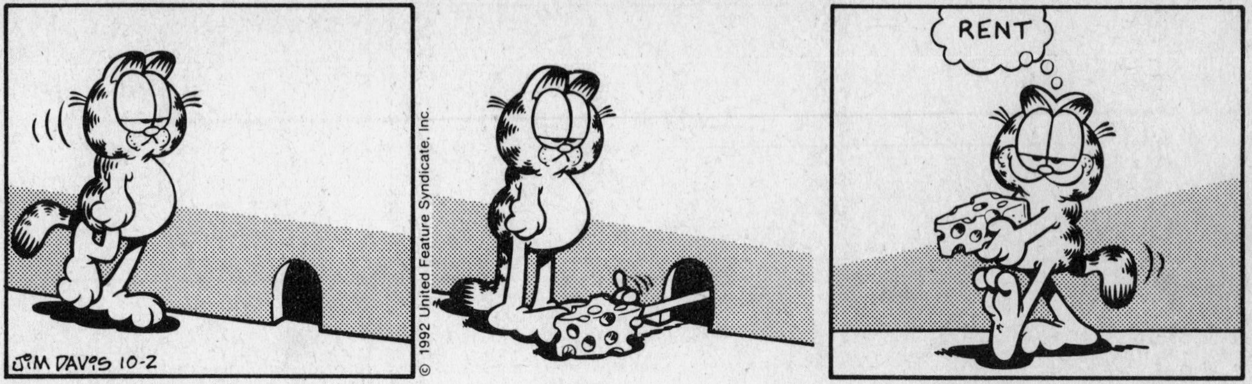
JIM DAVIS 10-2
© 1992 United Feature Syndicate, Inc.
RENT

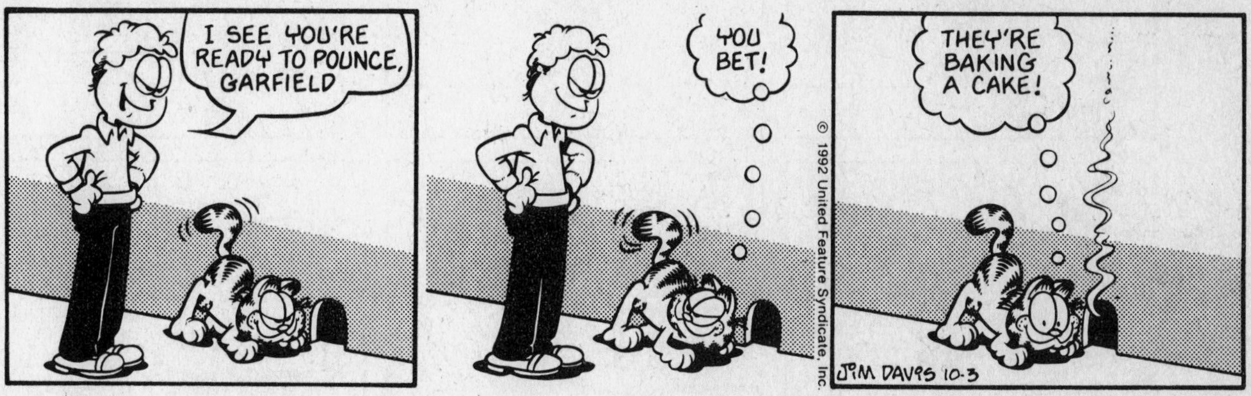
I SEE YOU'RE READY TO POUNCE, GARFIELD
YOU BET!
© 1992 United Feature Syndicate, Inc.
THEY'RE BAKING A CAKE!
JIM DAVIS 10-3

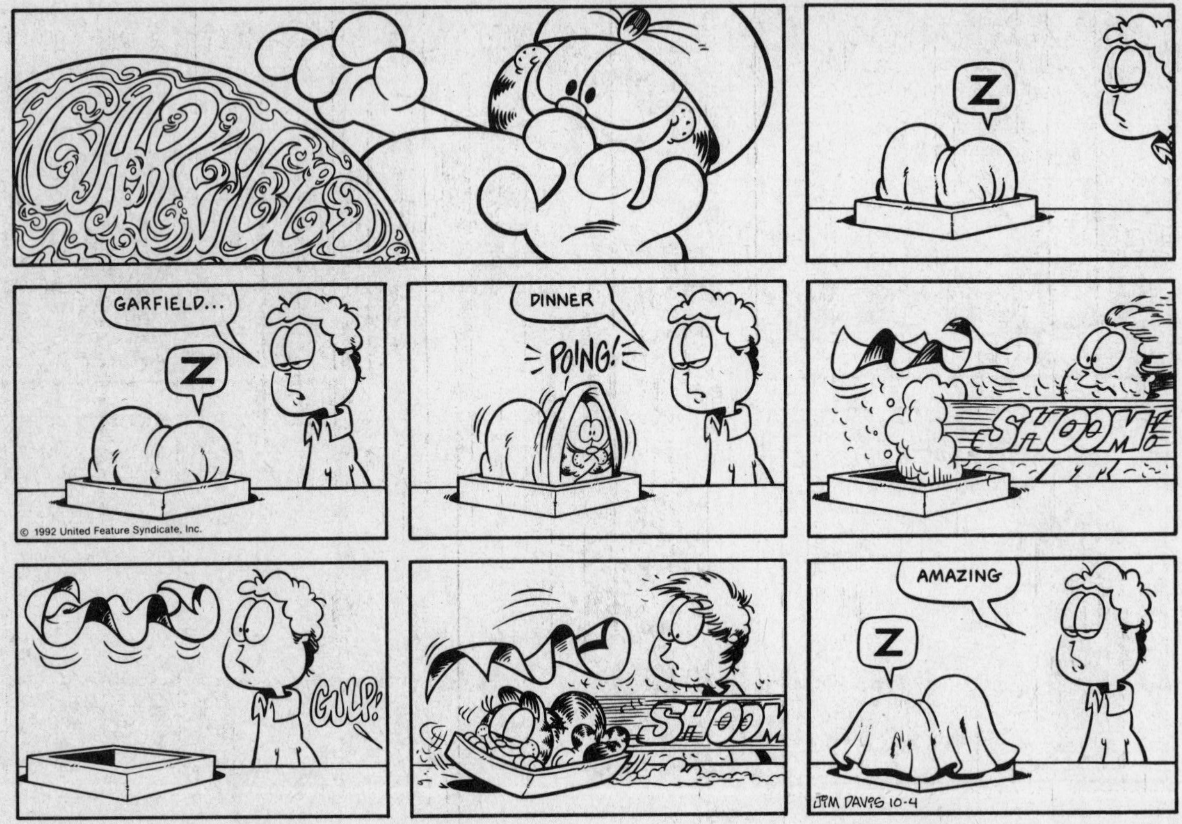
Z
GARFIELD...
Z
DINNER
POING!
SHOOM!
GULP!
SHOOM
AMAZING
Z
JIM DAVIS 10-4
© 1992 United Feature Syndicate, Inc.

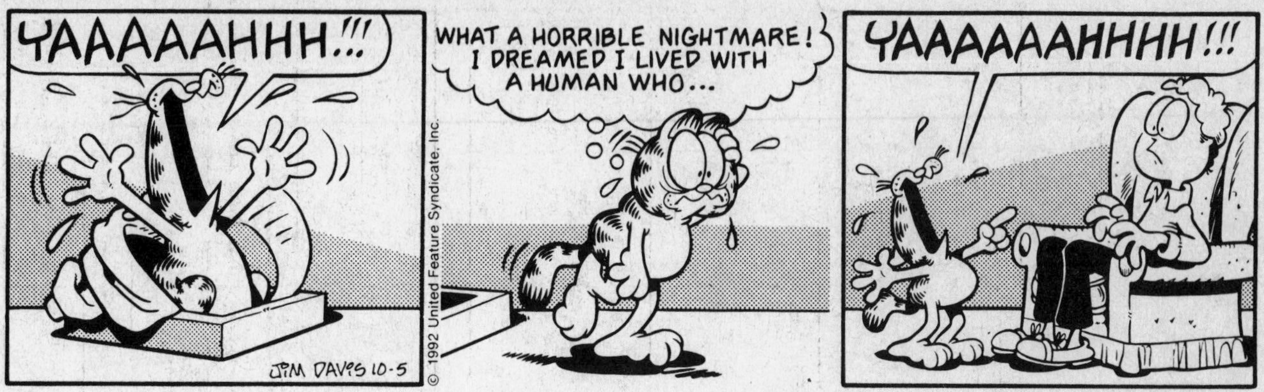
YAAAAAHHH!!!
WHAT A HORRIBLE NIGHTMARE! I DREAMED I LIVED WITH A HUMAN WHO...
YAAAAAAHHHH!!!
JIM DAVIS 10-5
© 1992 United Feature Syndicate, Inc.

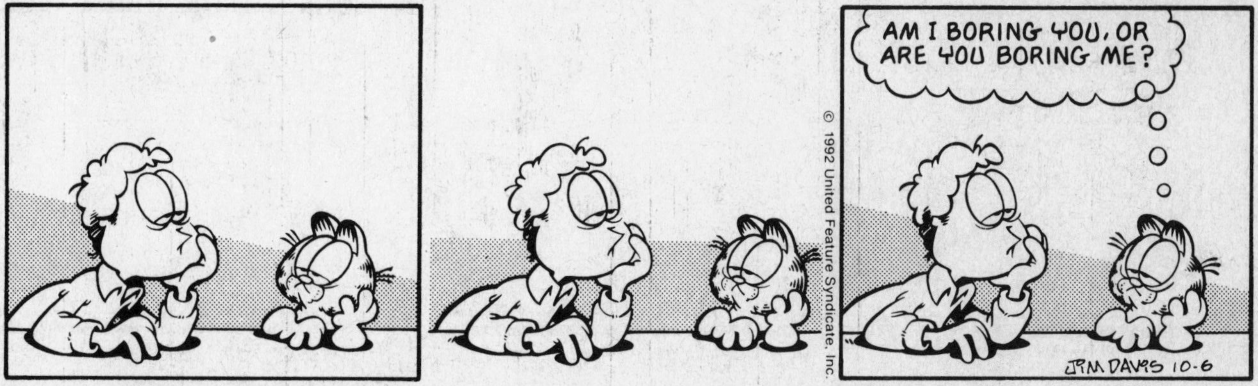
AM I BORING YOU, OR ARE YOU BORING ME?
JIM DAVIS 10-6
© 1992 United Feature Syndicate, Inc.

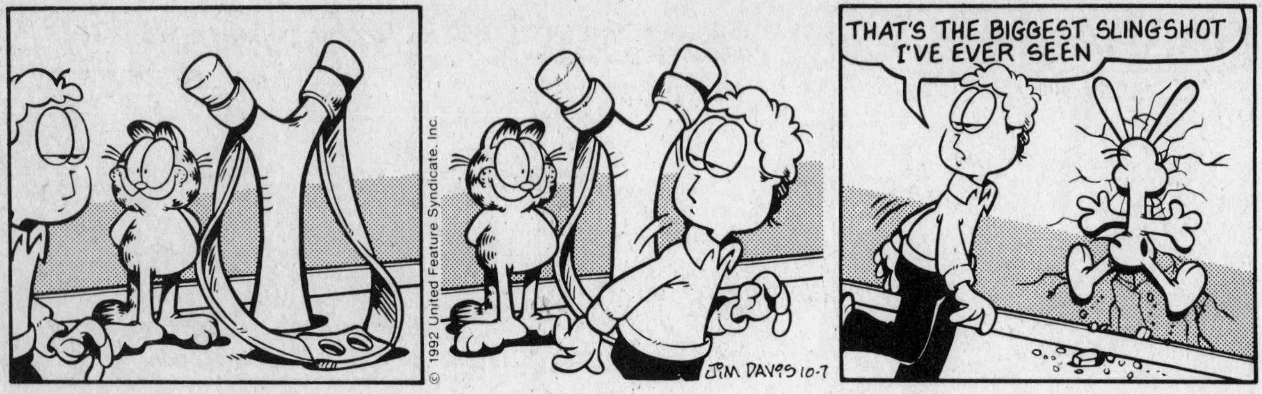
© 1992 United Feature Syndicate, Inc.
JIM DAVIS 10-7
THAT'S THE BIGGEST SLINGSHOT I'VE EVER SEEN

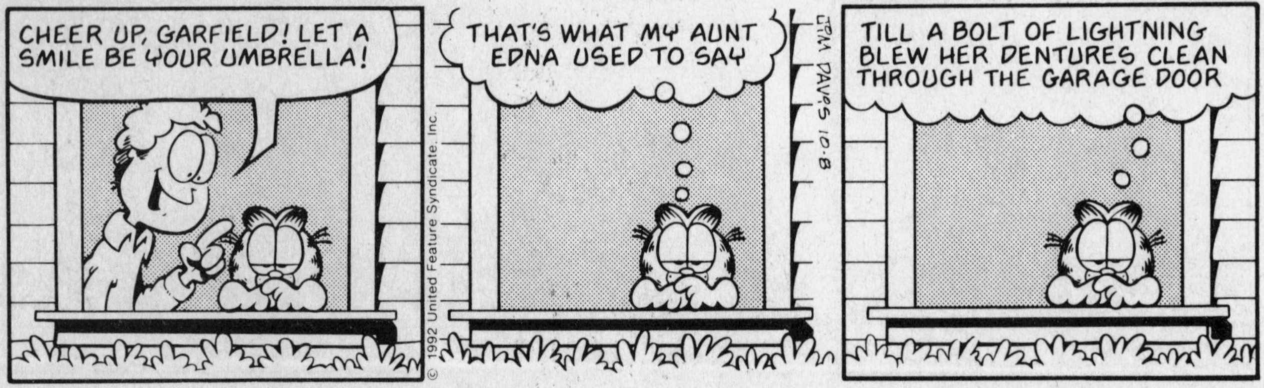
CHEER UP, GARFIELD! LET A SMILE BE YOUR UMBRELLA!
© 1992 United Feature Syndicate, Inc.
THAT'S WHAT MY AUNT EDNA USED TO SAY
JIM DAVIS 10-8
TILL A BOLT OF LIGHTNING BLEW HER DENTURES CLEAN THROUGH THE GARAGE DOOR

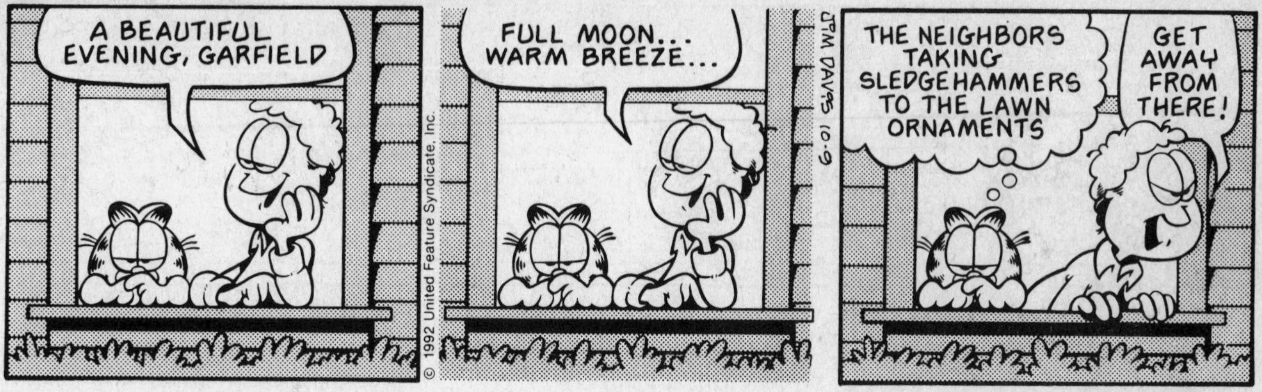
A BEAUTIFUL EVENING, GARFIELD
© 1992 United Feature Syndicate, Inc.
FULL MOON... WARM BREEZE...
JIM DAVIS 10-9
THE NEIGHBORS TAKING SLEDGEHAMMERS TO THE LAWN ORNAMENTS
GET AWAY FROM THERE!

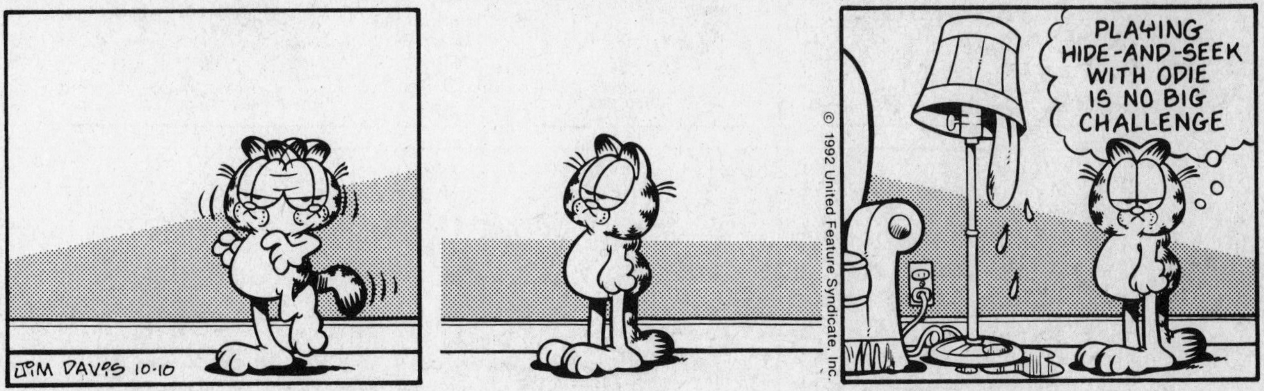
JIM DAVIS 10-10
© 1992 United Feature Syndicate, Inc.
PLAYING HIDE-AND-SEEK WITH ODIE IS NO BIG CHALLENGE

OF COURSE

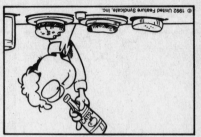

© 1992 United Feature Syndicate, Inc.

POMP POMP POMP POMP POMP POMP POMP POMP POMP POMP POMP

POMP POMP POMP

SHAKE SHAKE

NOW THAT'S A RECLINER

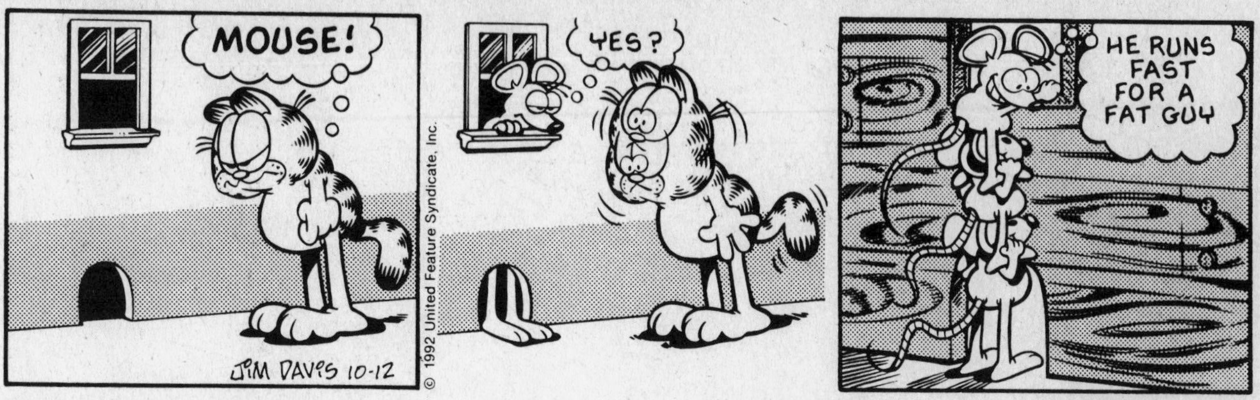
MOUSE!
JIM DAVIS 10-12
© 1992 United Feature Syndicate, Inc.
YES?
HE RUNS FAST FOR A FAT GUY

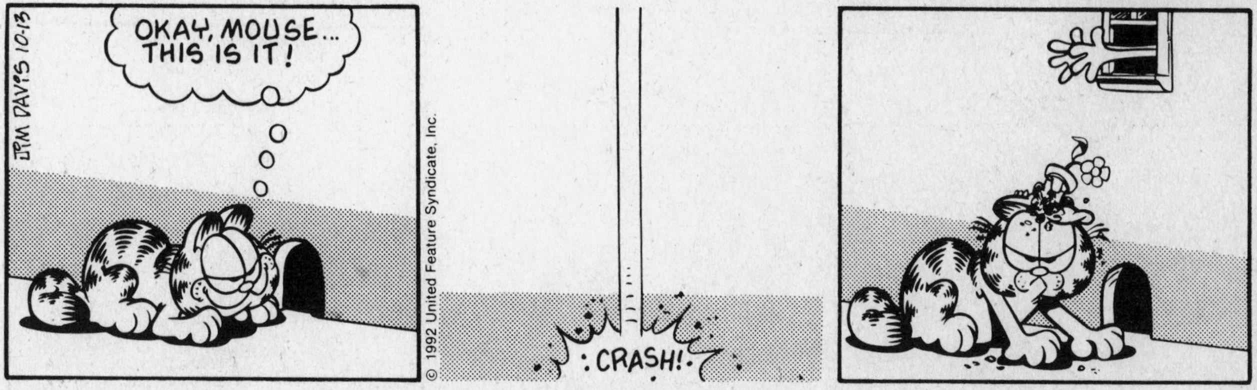
JIM DAVIS 10-13
OKAY, MOUSE... THIS IS IT!
© 1992 United Feature Syndicate, Inc.
CRASH!

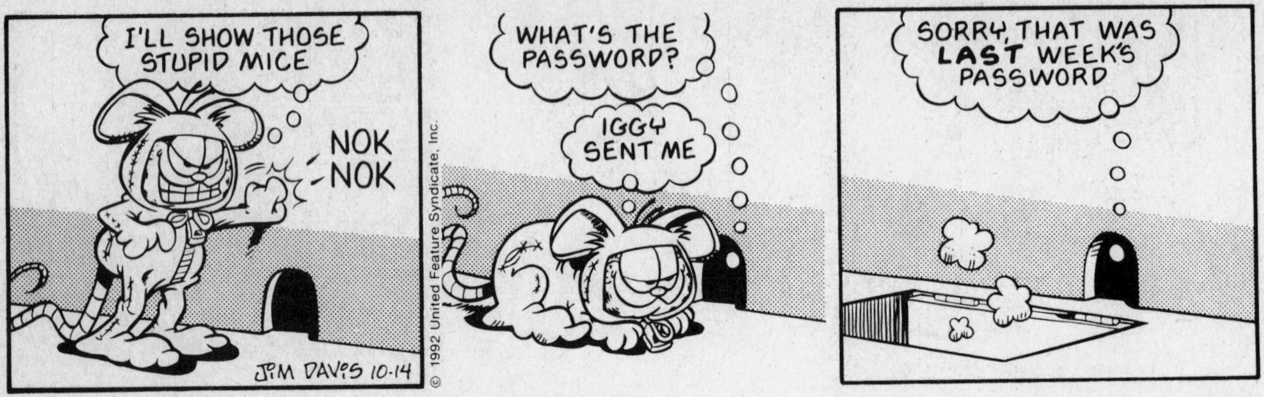
I'LL SHOW THOSE STUPID MICE
NOK NOK
JIM DAVIS 10-14
© 1992 United Feature Syndicate, Inc.
WHAT'S THE PASSWORD?
IGGY SENT ME
SORRY, THAT WAS **LAST** WEEK'S PASSWORD

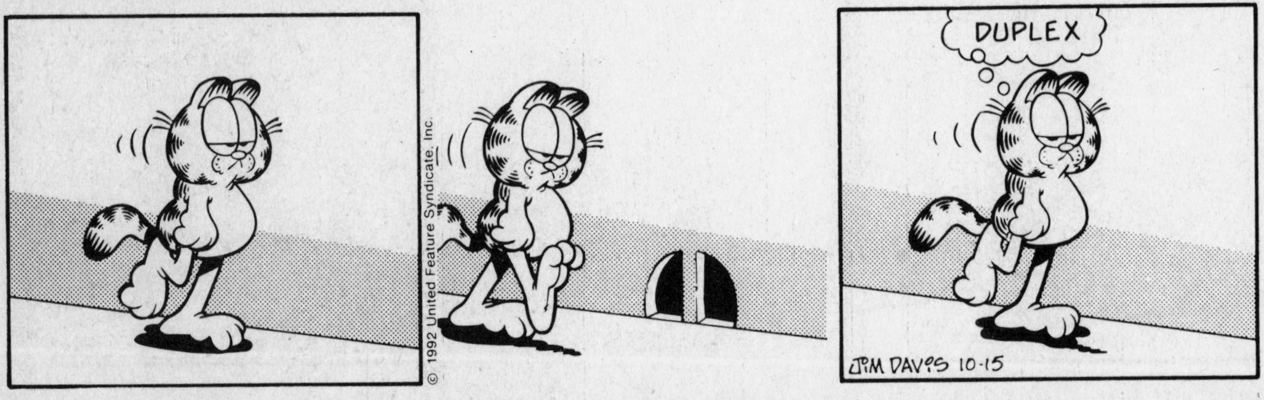
© 1992 United Feature Syndicate, Inc.
DUPLEX
JIM DAVIS 10-15

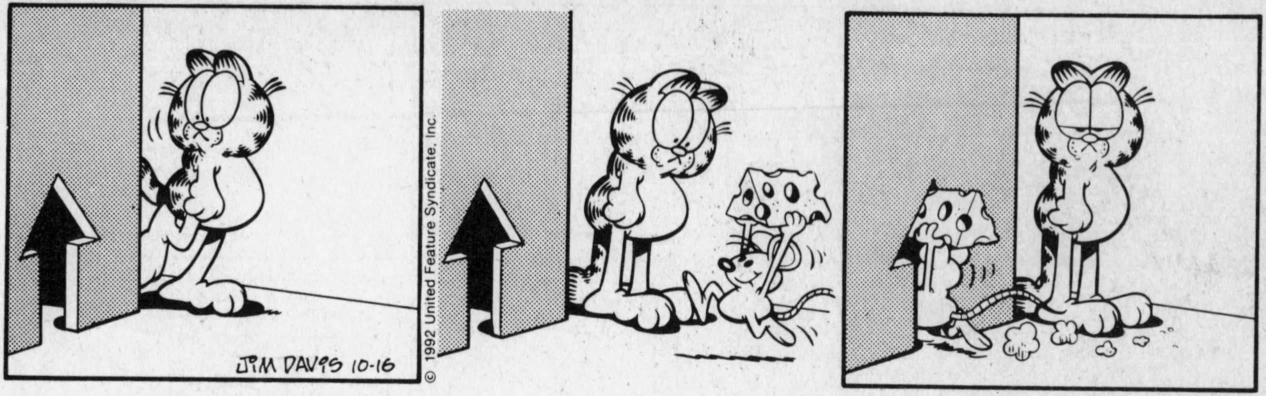
JIM DAVIS 10-16
© 1992 United Feature Syndicate, Inc.

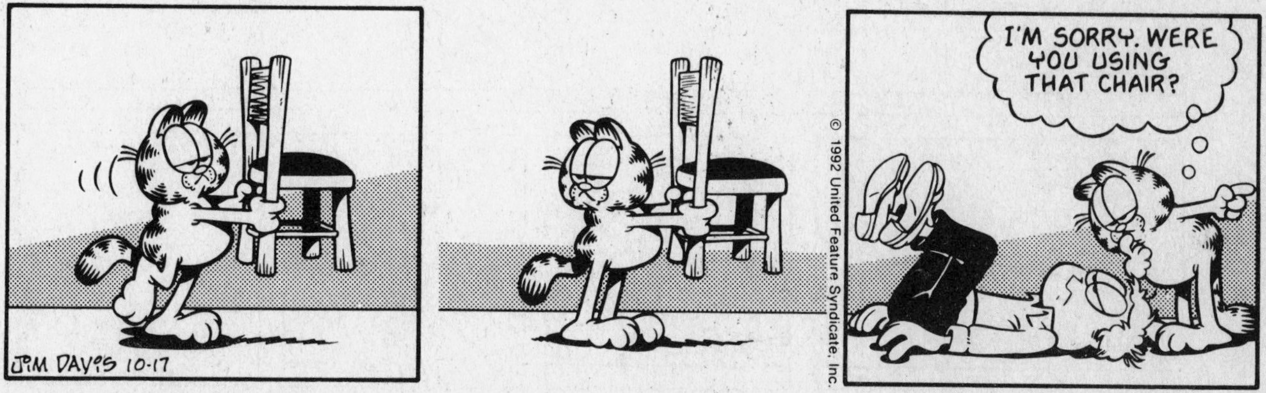
JIM DAVIS 10-17
© 1992 United Feature Syndicate, Inc.
I'M SORRY. WERE YOU USING THAT CHAIR?

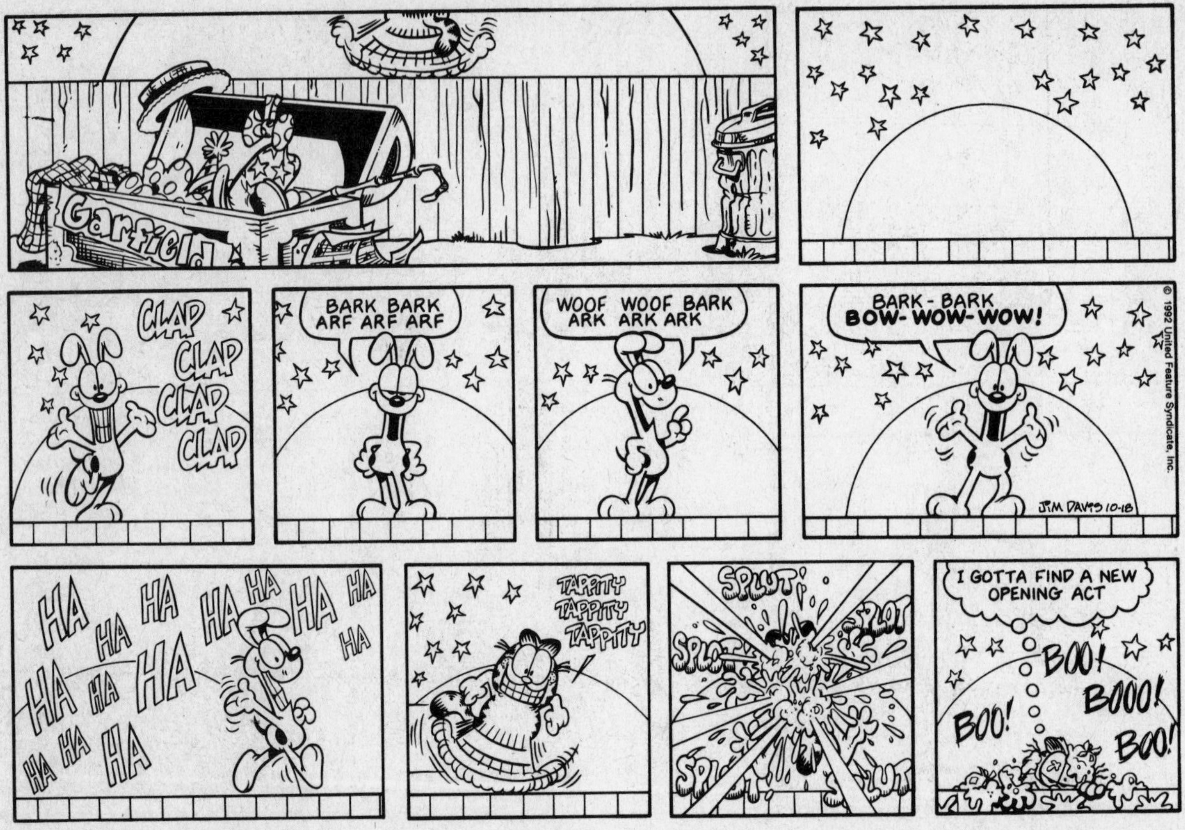
Garfield
CLAP CLAP CLAP CLAP
BARK BARK ARF ARF ARF
WOOF WOOF BARK ARK ARK ARK
BARK - BARK BOW-WOW-WOW!
JIM DAVIS 10-18
© 1992 United Feature Syndicate, Inc.
HA HA HA HA HA HA HA HA HA HA HA HA HA HA HA HA
TAPPITY TAPPITY TAPPITY
SPLUT! SPLOT SPLUT! SPLUT SPLUT
I GOTTA FIND A NEW OPENING ACT
BOO! BOOO! BOO! BOO!

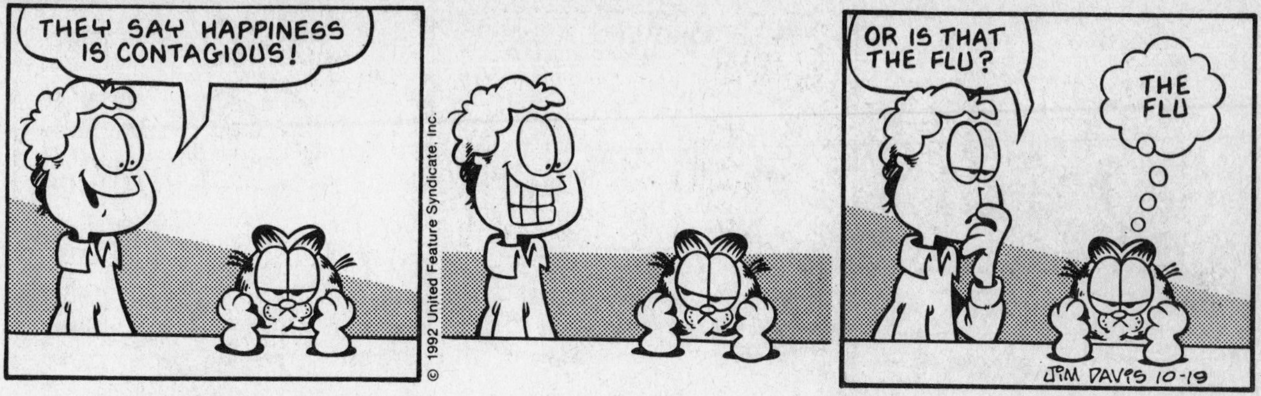
THEY SAY HAPPINESS IS CONTAGIOUS!
© 1992 United Feature Syndicate, Inc.
OR IS THAT THE FLU?
THE FLU
JIM DAVIS 10-19

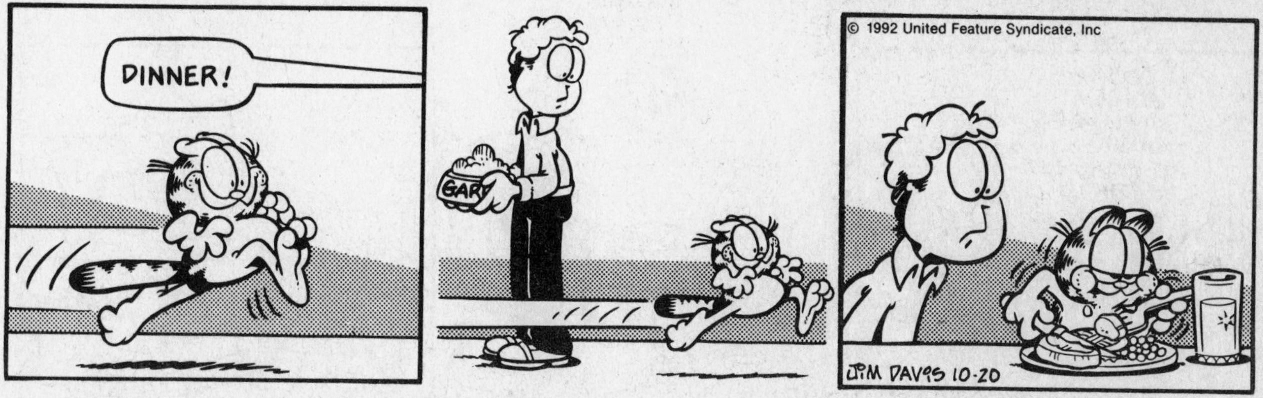
DINNER!
GAR
© 1992 United Feature Syndicate, Inc
JIM DAVIS 10-20

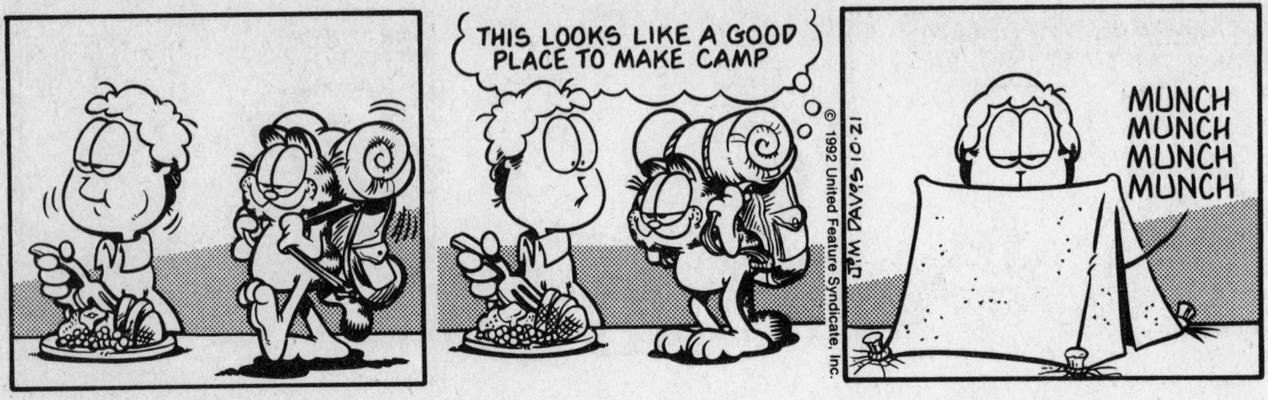
THIS LOOKS LIKE A GOOD PLACE TO MAKE CAMP
© 1992 United Feature Syndicate, Inc.
JIM DAVIS 10-21
MUNCH
MUNCH
MUNCH
MUNCH

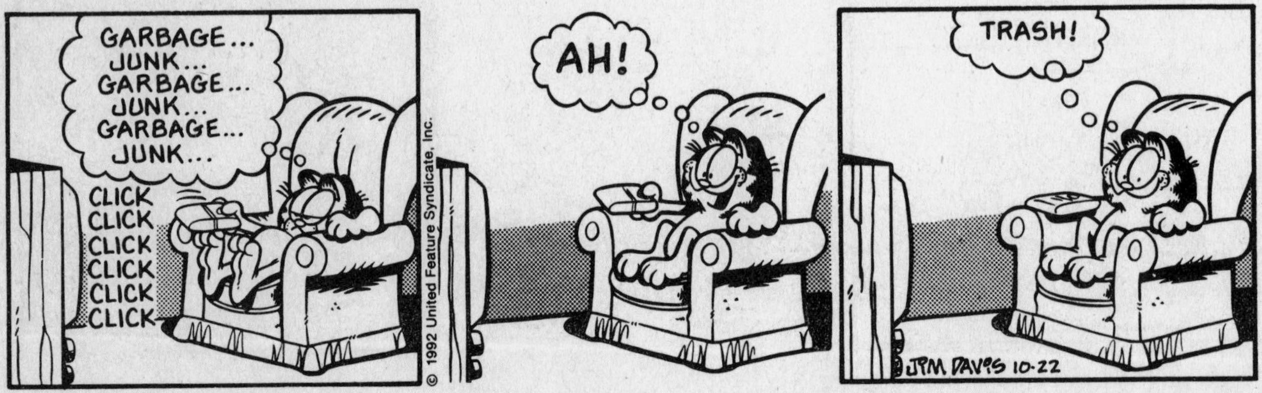
GARBAGE... JUNK... GARBAGE... JUNK... GARBAGE... JUNK...
CLICK
CLICK
CLICK
CLICK
CLICK
CLICK
© 1992 United Feature Syndicate, Inc.
AH!
TRASH!
JIM DAVIS 10-22

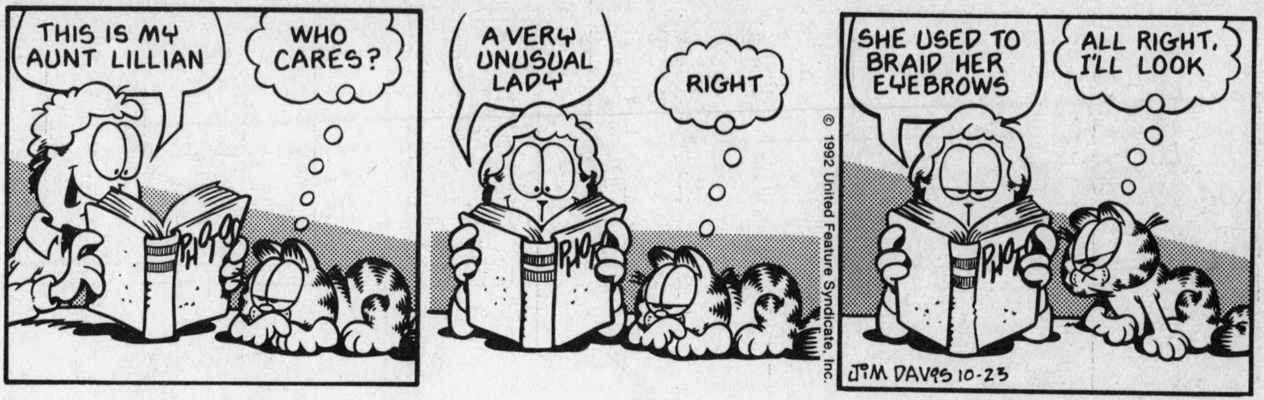
THIS IS MY AUNT LILLIAN
WHO CARES?
A VERY UNUSUAL LADY
RIGHT
SHE USED TO BRAID HER EYEBROWS
ALL RIGHT, I'LL LOOK
© 1992 United Feature Syndicate, Inc.
JIM DAVIS 10-23

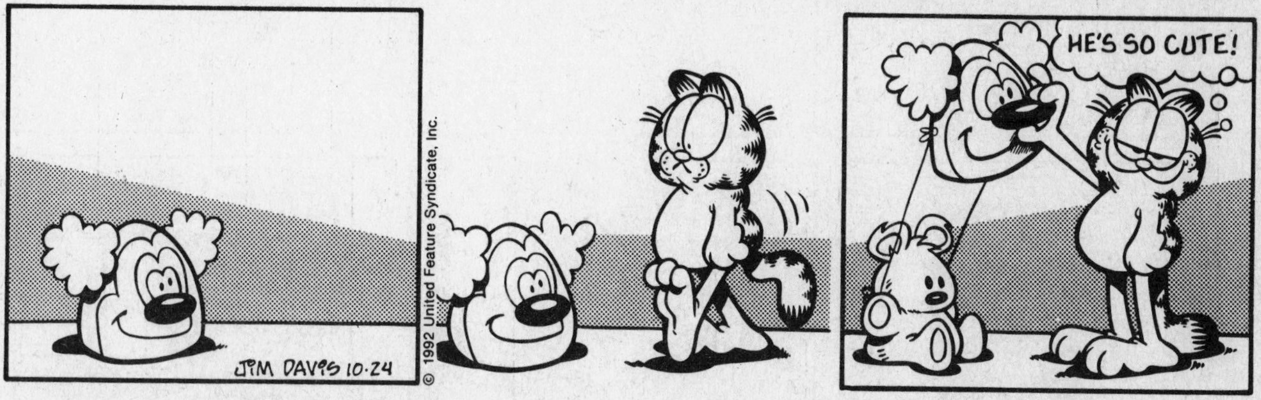
JIM DAVIS 10-24
© 1992 United Feature Syndicate, Inc.
HE'S SO CUTE!

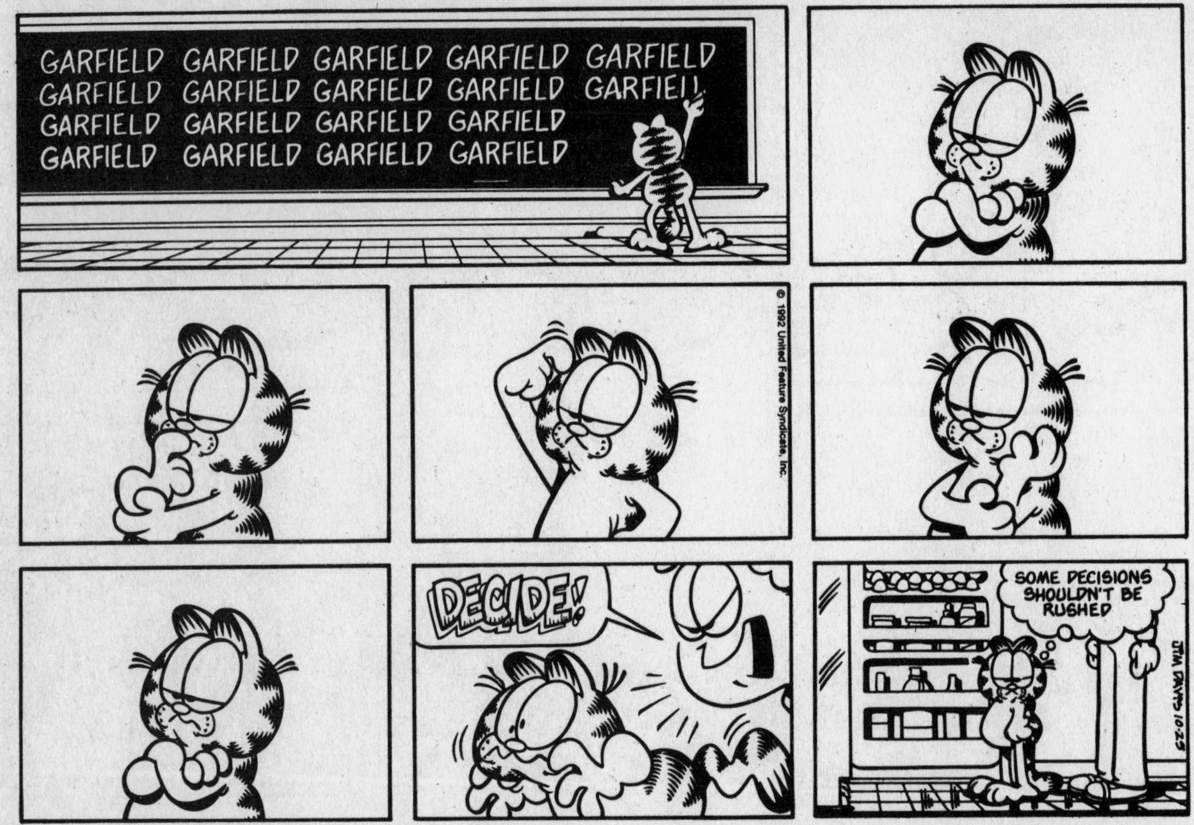
GARFIELD GARFIELD GARFIELD GARFIELD GARFIELD
GARFIELD GARFIELD GARFIELD GARFIELD GARFIEL
GARFIELD GARFIELD GARFIELD GARFIELD
GARFIELD GARFIELD GARFIELD GARFIELD
© 1992 United Feature Syndicate, Inc.
DECIDE!
SOME DECISIONS SHOULDN'T BE RUSHED
JIM DAVIS 10-25

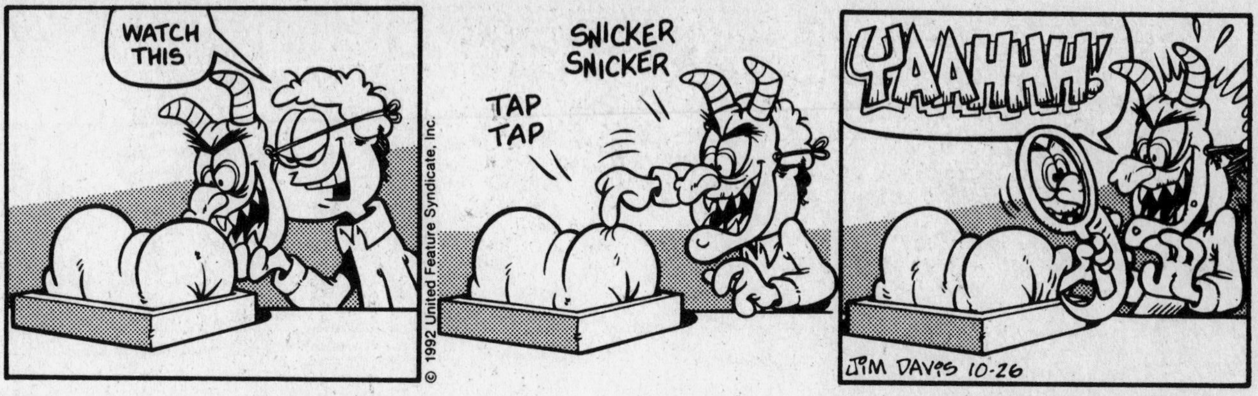
WATCH THIS
TAP TAP
SNICKER SNICKER
YAAHHH!
© 1992 United Feature Syndicate, Inc.
JIM DAVIS 10-26

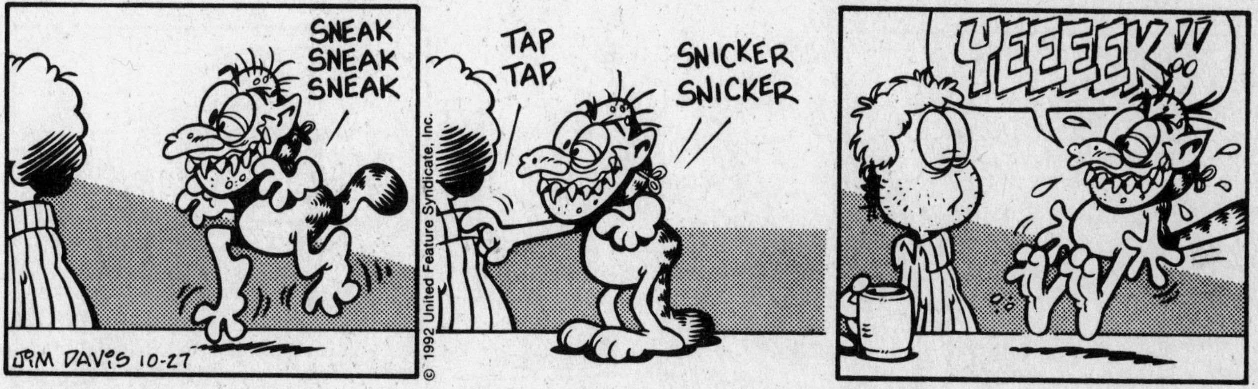
SNEAK SNEAK SNEAK
TAP TAP
SNICKER SNICKER
YEEEEK!!
© 1992 United Feature Syndicate, Inc.
JIM DAVIS 10-27

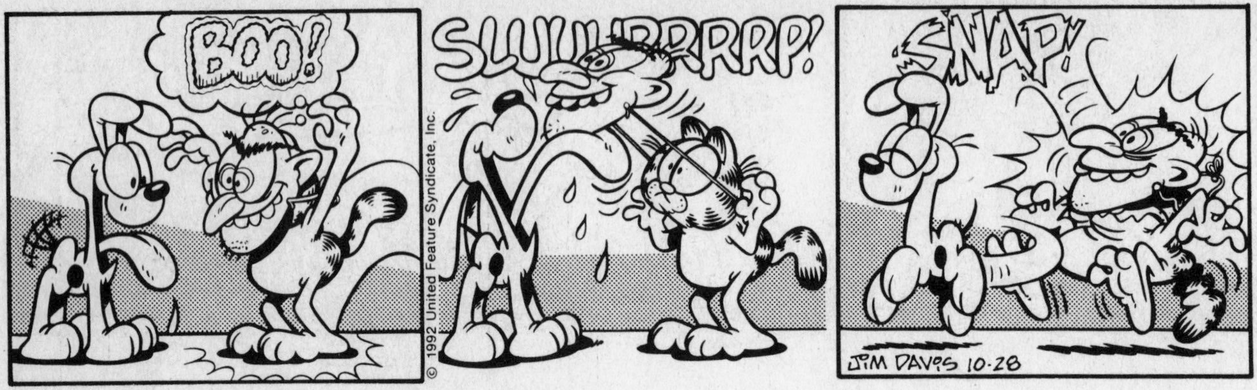
BOO!
SLUUUURRRRP!
SNAP!
JIM DAVIS 10-28
© 1992 United Feature Syndicate, Inc.

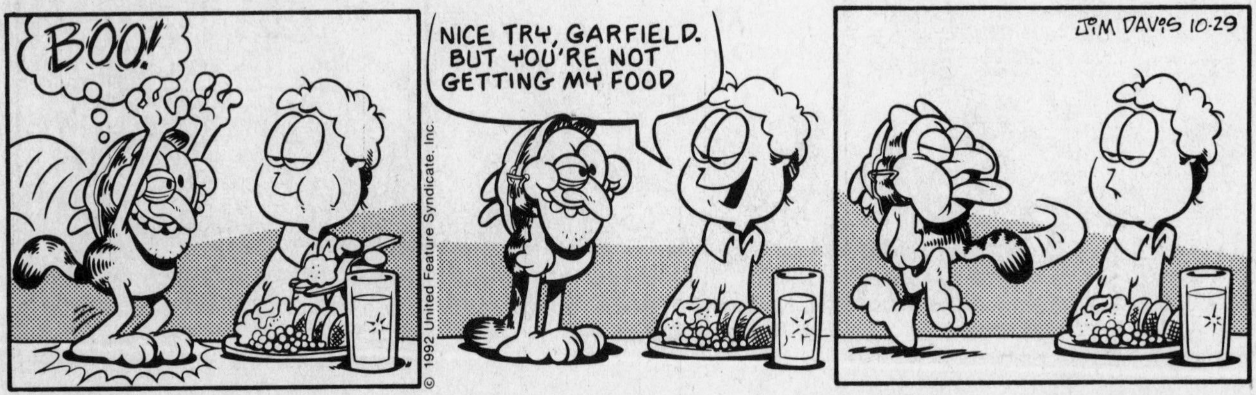
BOO!
NICE TRY, GARFIELD. BUT YOU'RE NOT GETTING MY FOOD
JIM DAVIS 10-29
© 1992 United Feature Syndicate, Inc.

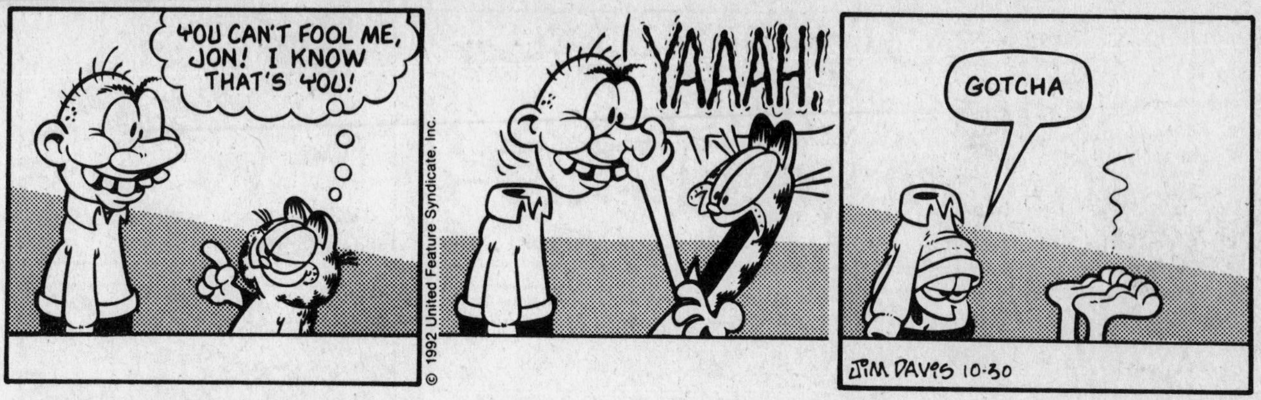
YOU CAN'T FOOL ME, JON! I KNOW THAT'S YOU!
YAAAH!
GOTCHA
© 1992 United Feature Syndicate, Inc.
JIM DAVIS 10-30

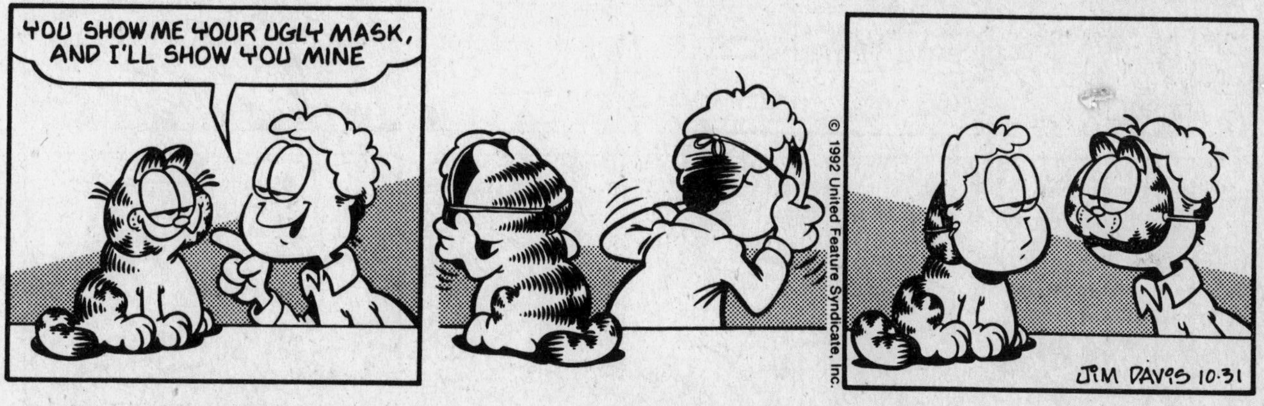
YOU SHOW ME YOUR UGLY MASK, AND I'LL SHOW YOU MINE
© 1992 United Feature Syndicate, Inc.
JIM DAVIS 10-31

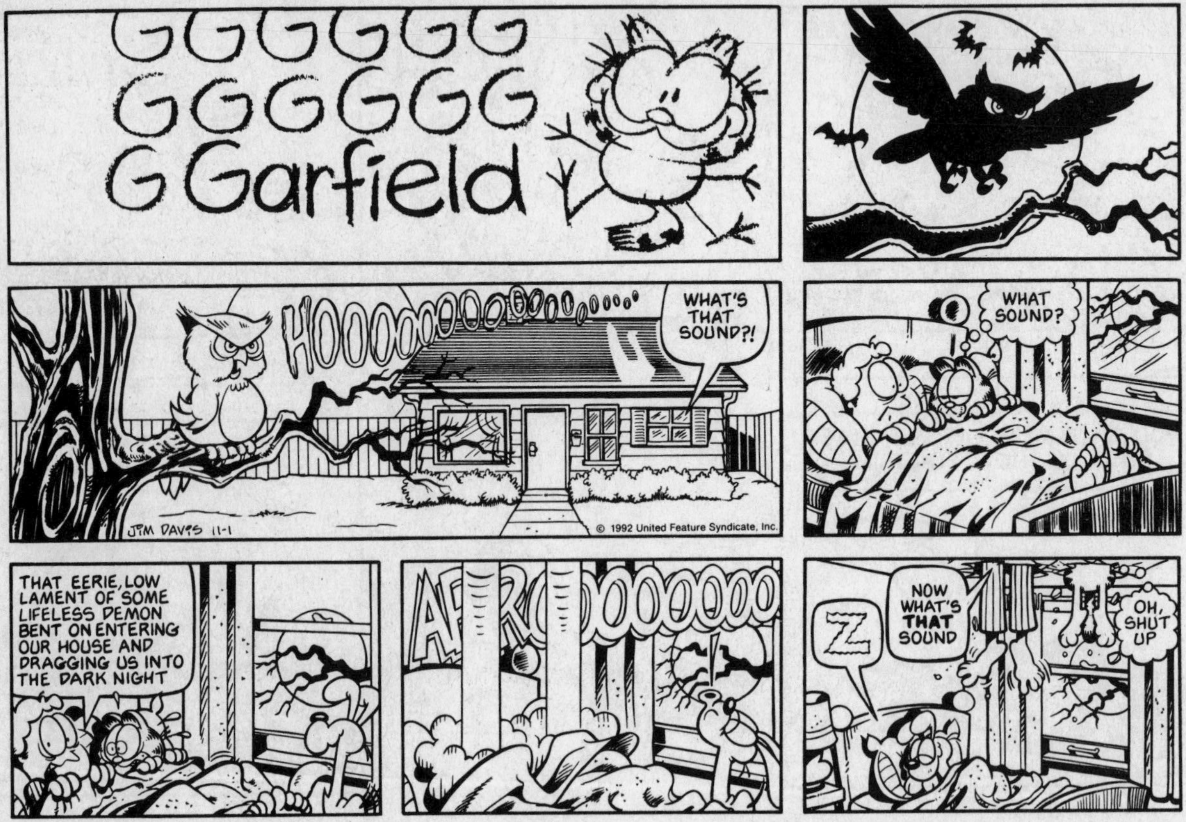
GGGGGG
GGGGGG
G Garfield
HOOOOOOOOOOOOOOOOoooo
WHAT'S THAT SOUND?!
JIM DAVIS 11-1
© 1992 United Feature Syndicate, Inc.
WHAT SOUND?
THAT EERIE, LOW LAMENT OF SOME LIFELESS DEMON BENT ON ENTERING OUR HOUSE AND DRAGGING US INTO THE DARK NIGHT
ARROOOOOOOO
Z
NOW WHAT'S THAT SOUND
OH, SHUT UP

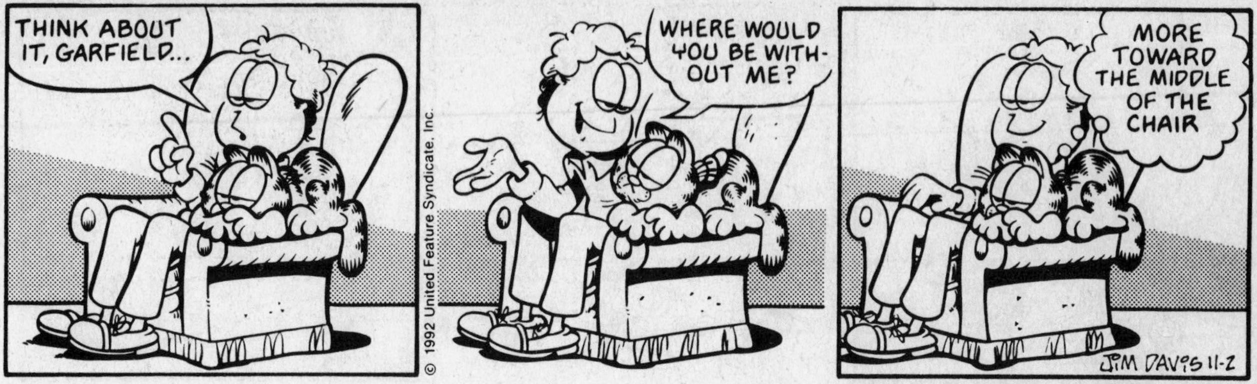
THINK ABOUT IT, GARFIELD...
WHERE WOULD YOU BE WITH-OUT ME?
MORE TOWARD THE MIDDLE OF THE CHAIR
JIM DAVIS 11-2
© 1992 United Feature Syndicate, Inc.

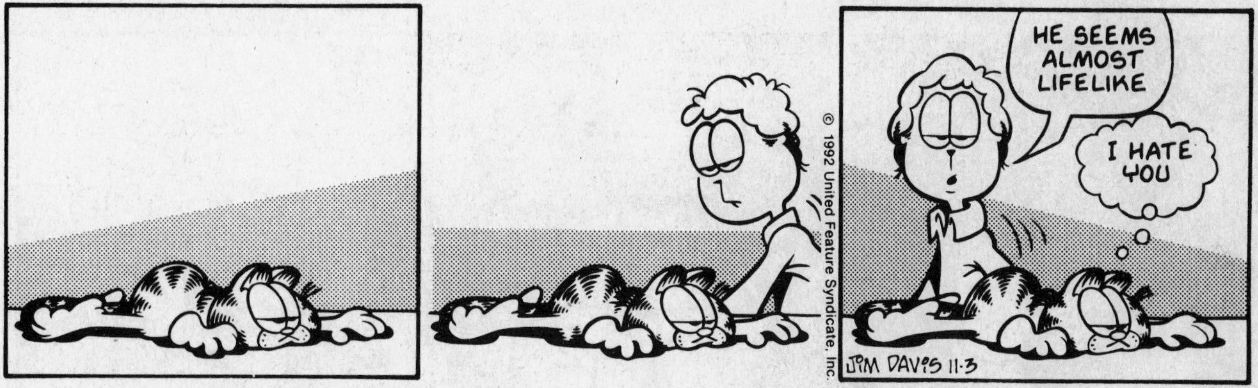
HE SEEMS ALMOST LIFELIKE
I HATE YOU
JIM DAVIS 11-3
© 1992 United Feature Syndicate, Inc.

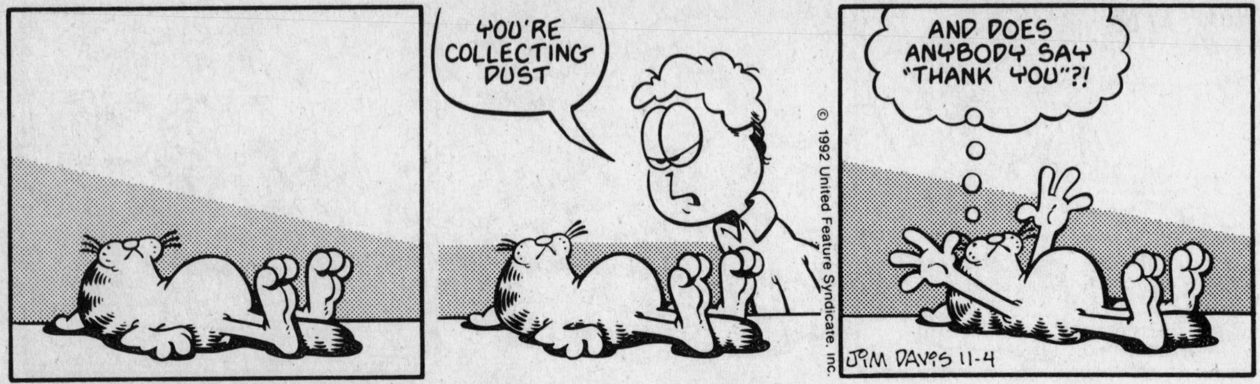
YOU'RE COLLECTING DUST
AND DOES ANYBODY SAY "THANK YOU"?!
JIM DAVIS 11-4
© 1992 United Feature Syndicate, Inc.

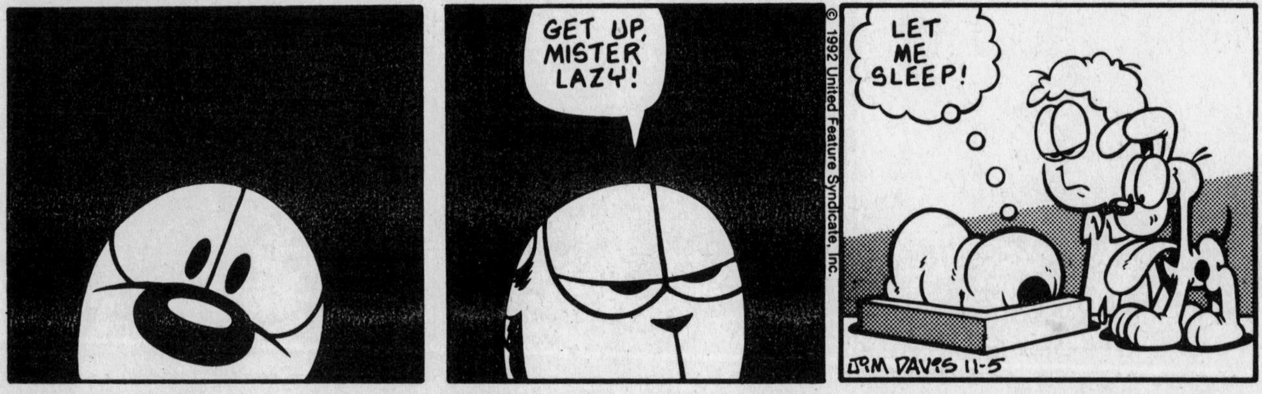
GET UP, MISTER LAZY!
LET ME SLEEP!
JIM DAVIS 11-5
© 1992 United Feature Syndicate, Inc.

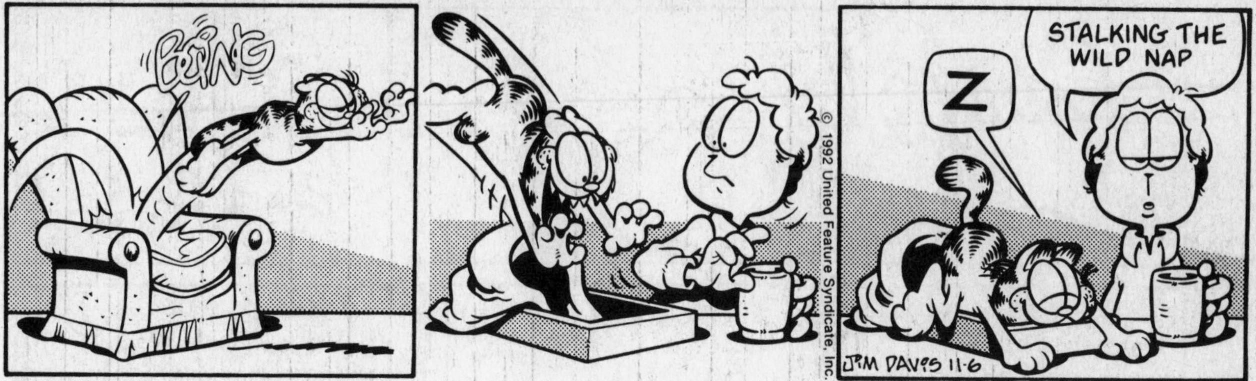
BOING
Z
STALKING THE WILD NAP
© 1992 United Feature Syndicate, Inc.
JIM DAVIS 11-6

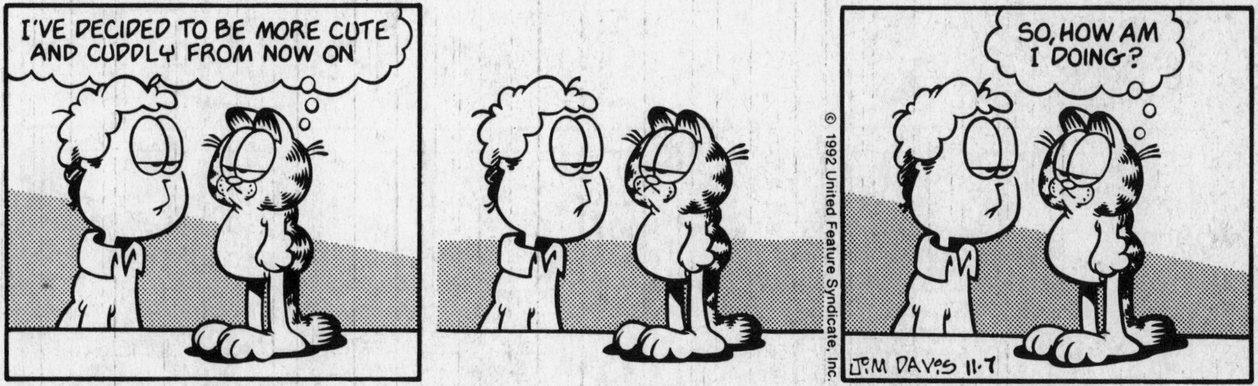
I'VE DECIDED TO BE MORE CUTE AND CUDDLY FROM NOW ON
SO, HOW AM I DOING?
© 1992 United Feature Syndicate, Inc.
JIM DAVIS 11-7

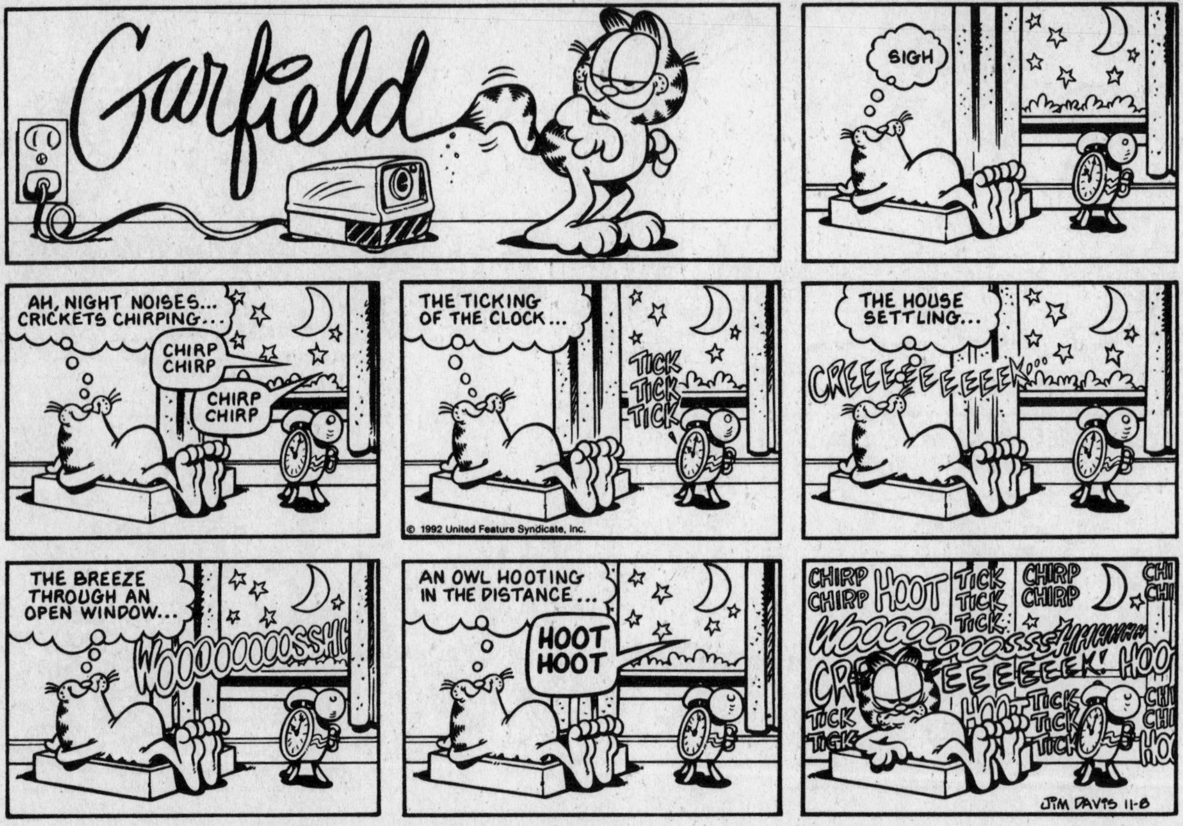
Garfield
SIGH
AH, NIGHT NOISES... CRICKETS CHIRPING...
CHIRP CHIRP
CHIRP CHIRP
THE TICKING OF THE CLOCK...
TICK TICK TICK
© 1992 United Feature Syndicate, Inc.
THE HOUSE SETTLING...
CREEEEEEEEEEK...
THE BREEZE THROUGH AN OPEN WINDOW...
WOOOOOOOOOSSHH
AN OWL HOOTING IN THE DISTANCE...
HOOT HOOT
CHIRP CHIRP
HOOT
TICK TICK TICK
CHIRP CHIRP
WOOOOOOOOOSSSHHHHHHH
CREEEEEEEEK!
HOO
JIM DAVIS 11-8

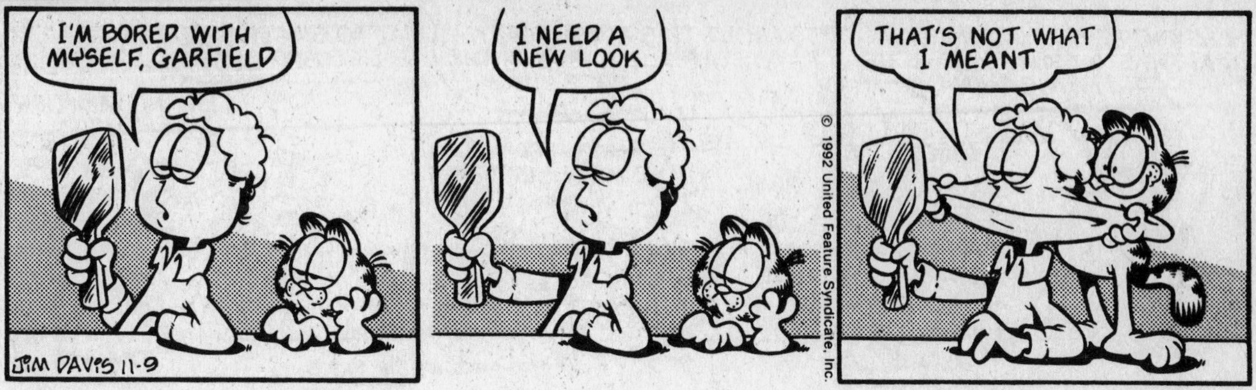
I'M BORED WITH MYSELF, GARFIELD
JIM DAVIS 11-9
I NEED A NEW LOOK
THAT'S NOT WHAT I MEANT
© 1992 United Feature Syndicate, Inc.

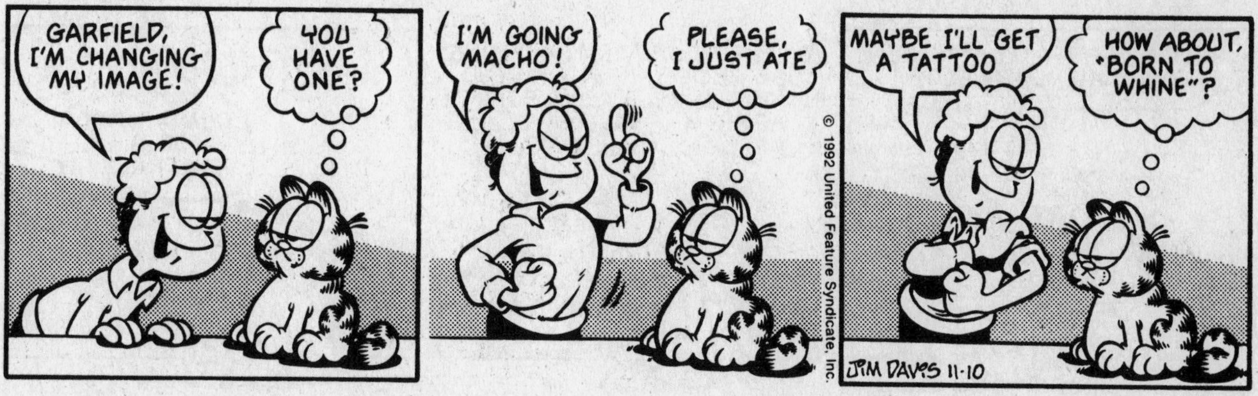
GARFIELD, I'M CHANGING MY IMAGE!
YOU HAVE ONE?
I'M GOING MACHO!
PLEASE, I JUST ATE
MAYBE I'LL GET A TATTOO
HOW ABOUT, "BORN TO WHINE"?
JIM DAVIS 11-10
© 1992 United Feature Syndicate, Inc.

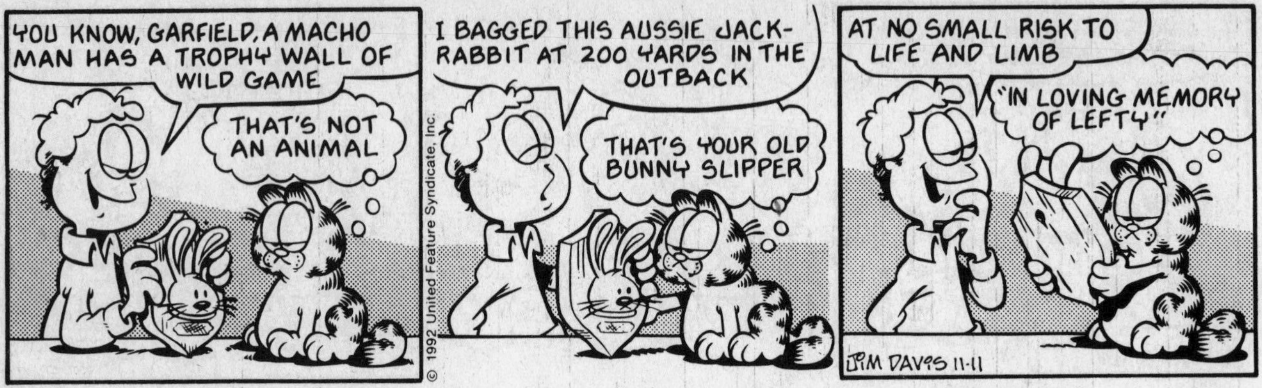
YOU KNOW, GARFIELD, A MACHO MAN HAS A TROPHY WALL OF WILD GAME
THAT'S NOT AN ANIMAL
I BAGGED THIS AUSSIE JACK-RABBIT AT 200 YARDS IN THE OUTBACK
THAT'S YOUR OLD BUNNY SLIPPER
AT NO SMALL RISK TO LIFE AND LIMB
"IN LOVING MEMORY OF LEFTY"
JIM DAVIS 11-11

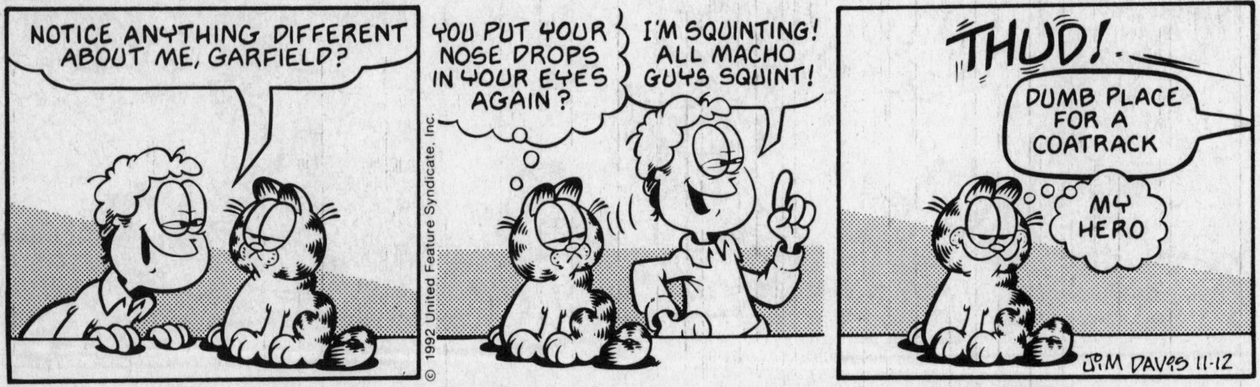
NOTICE ANYTHING DIFFERENT ABOUT ME, GARFIELD?
YOU PUT YOUR NOSE DROPS IN YOUR EYES AGAIN?
I'M SQUINTING! ALL MACHO GUYS SQUINT!
THUD!
DUMB PLACE FOR A COATRACK
MY HERO
JIM DAVIS 11-12

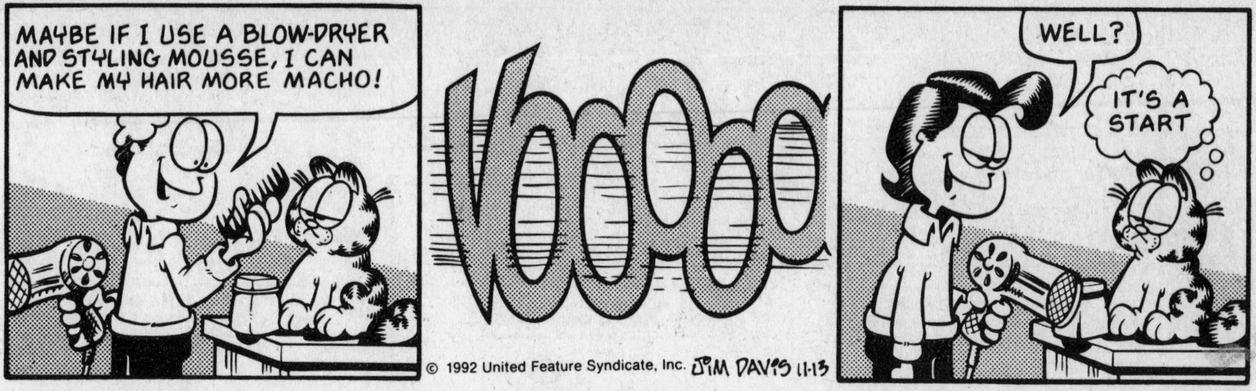
MAYBE IF I USE A BLOW-DRYER AND STYLING MOUSSE, I CAN MAKE MY HAIR MORE MACHO!
VOOOOO
WELL?
IT'S A START
© 1992 United Feature Syndicate, Inc.
JIM DAVIS 11-13

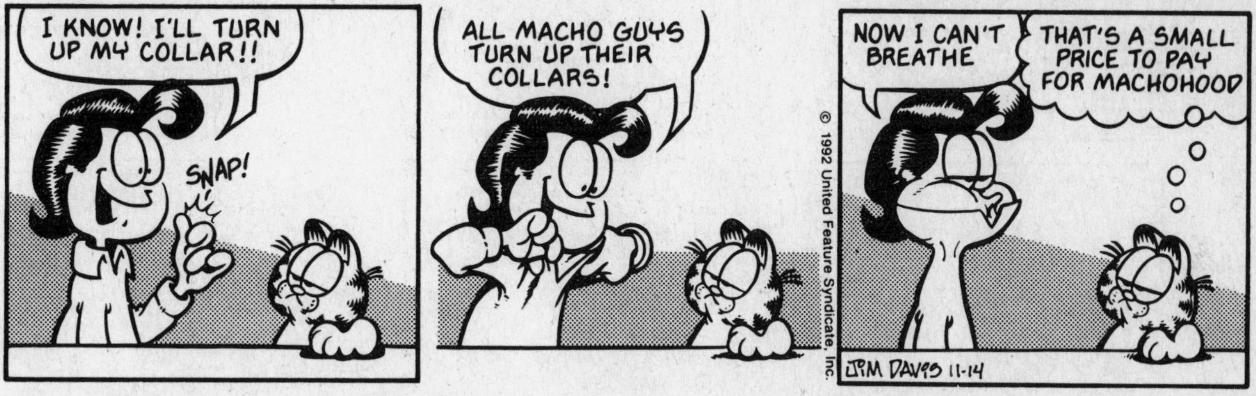
I KNOW! I'LL TURN UP MY COLLAR!!
SNAP!
ALL MACHO GUYS TURN UP THEIR COLLARS!
NOW I CAN'T BREATHE
THAT'S A SMALL PRICE TO PAY FOR MACHOHOOD
© 1992 United Feature Syndicate, Inc.
JIM DAVIS 11-14

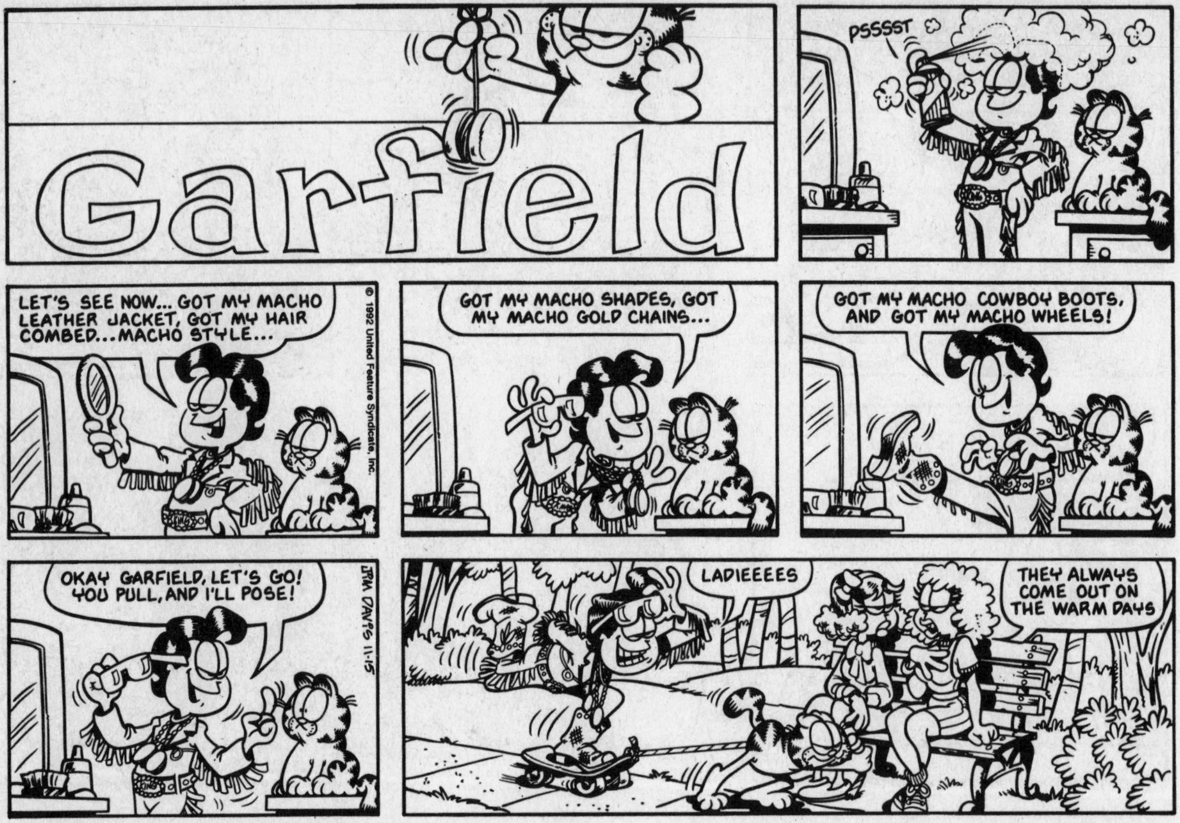
Garfield
PSSSST
LET'S SEE NOW... GOT MY MACHO LEATHER JACKET, GOT MY HAIR COMBED...MACHO STYLE...
© 1992 United Feature Syndicate, Inc.
GOT MY MACHO SHADES, GOT MY MACHO GOLD CHAINS...
GOT MY MACHO COWBOY BOOTS, AND GOT MY MACHO WHEELS!
OKAY GARFIELD, LET'S GO! YOU PULL, AND I'LL POSE!
JPM DAVIS 11-15
LADIEEEES
THEY ALWAYS COME OUT ON THE WARM DAYS

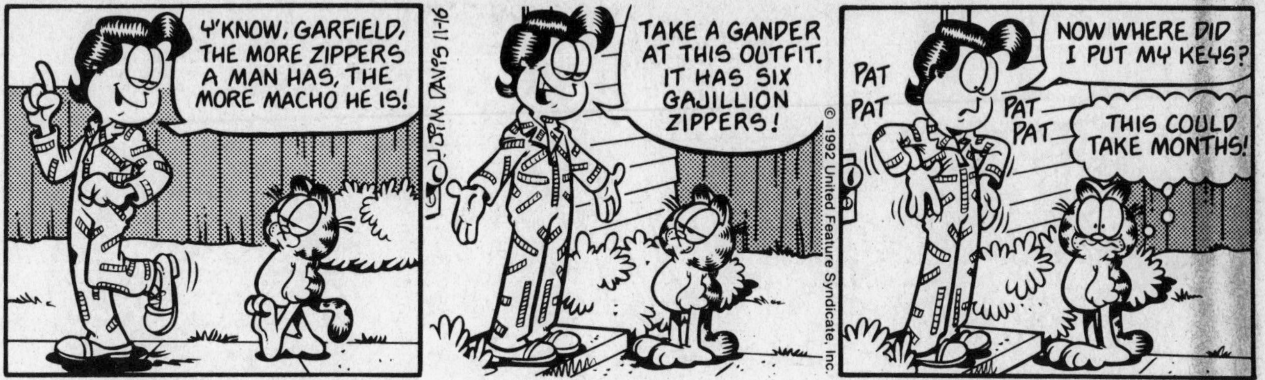
Y'KNOW, GARFIELD, THE MORE ZIPPERS A MAN HAS, THE MORE MACHO HE IS!
JIM DAVIS 11-16
TAKE A GANDER AT THIS OUTFIT. IT HAS SIX GAJILLION ZIPPERS!
© 1992 United Feature Syndicate, Inc.
PAT PAT
NOW WHERE DID I PUT MY KEYS?
PAT PAT
THIS COULD TAKE MONTHS!

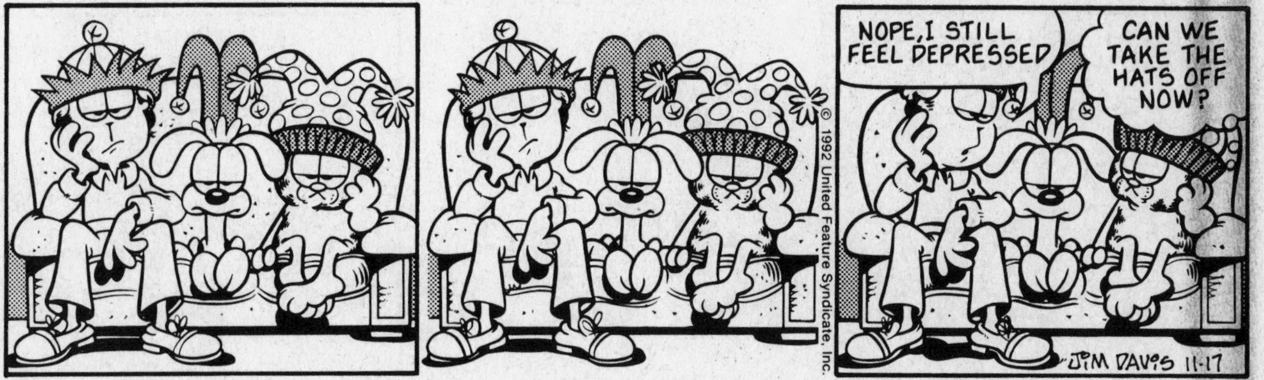
© 1992 United Feature Syndicate, Inc.
NOPE, I STILL FEEL DEPRESSED
CAN WE TAKE THE HATS OFF NOW?
JIM DAVIS 11-17

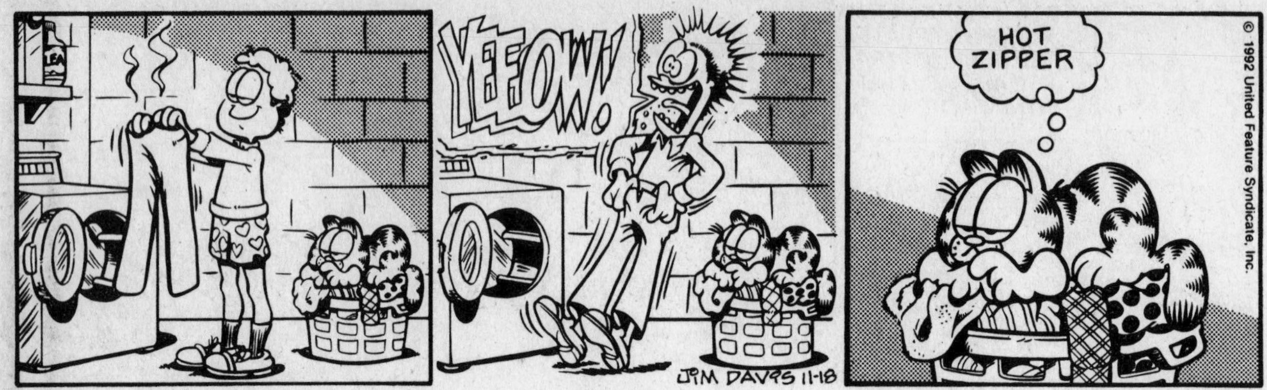
YEEOW!
HOT ZIPPER
JIM DAVIS 11-18
© 1992 United Feature Syndicate, Inc.

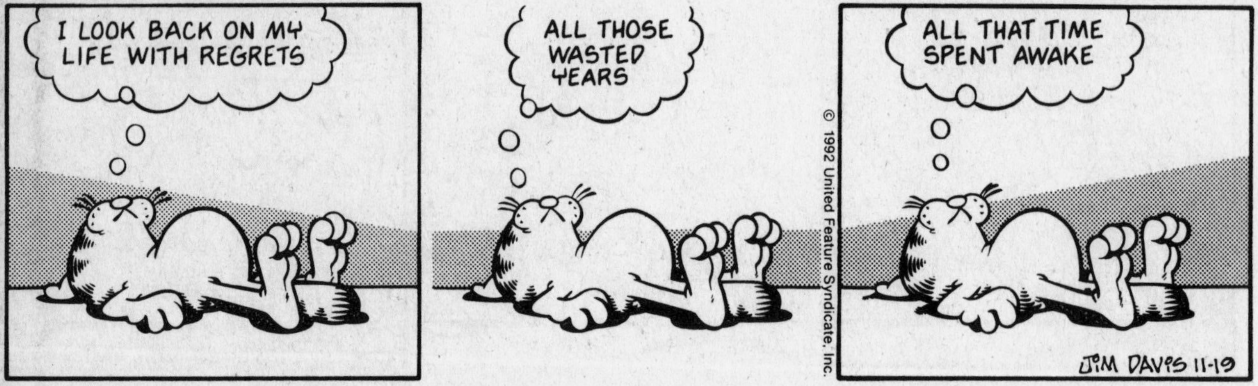
I LOOK BACK ON MY LIFE WITH REGRETS
ALL THOSE WASTED YEARS
ALL THAT TIME SPENT AWAKE
JIM DAVIS 11-19
© 1992 United Feature Syndicate, Inc.

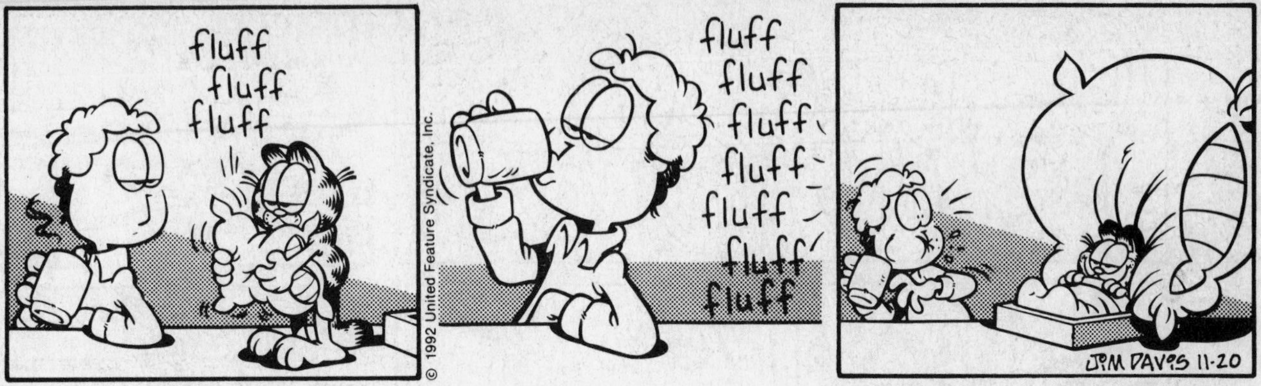
fluff fluff fluff
© 1992 United Feature Syndicate, Inc.
fluff fluff fluff fluff fluff fluff fluff
JIM DAVIS 11-20

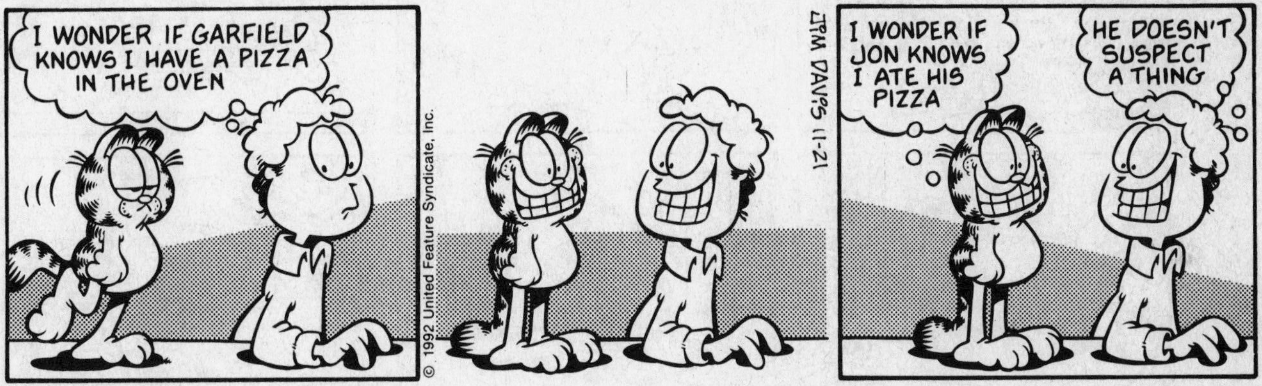
I WONDER IF GARFIELD KNOWS I HAVE A PIZZA IN THE OVEN
© 1992 United Feature Syndicate, Inc.
JIM DAVIS 11-21
I WONDER IF JON KNOWS I ATE HIS PIZZA
HE DOESN'T SUSPECT A THING

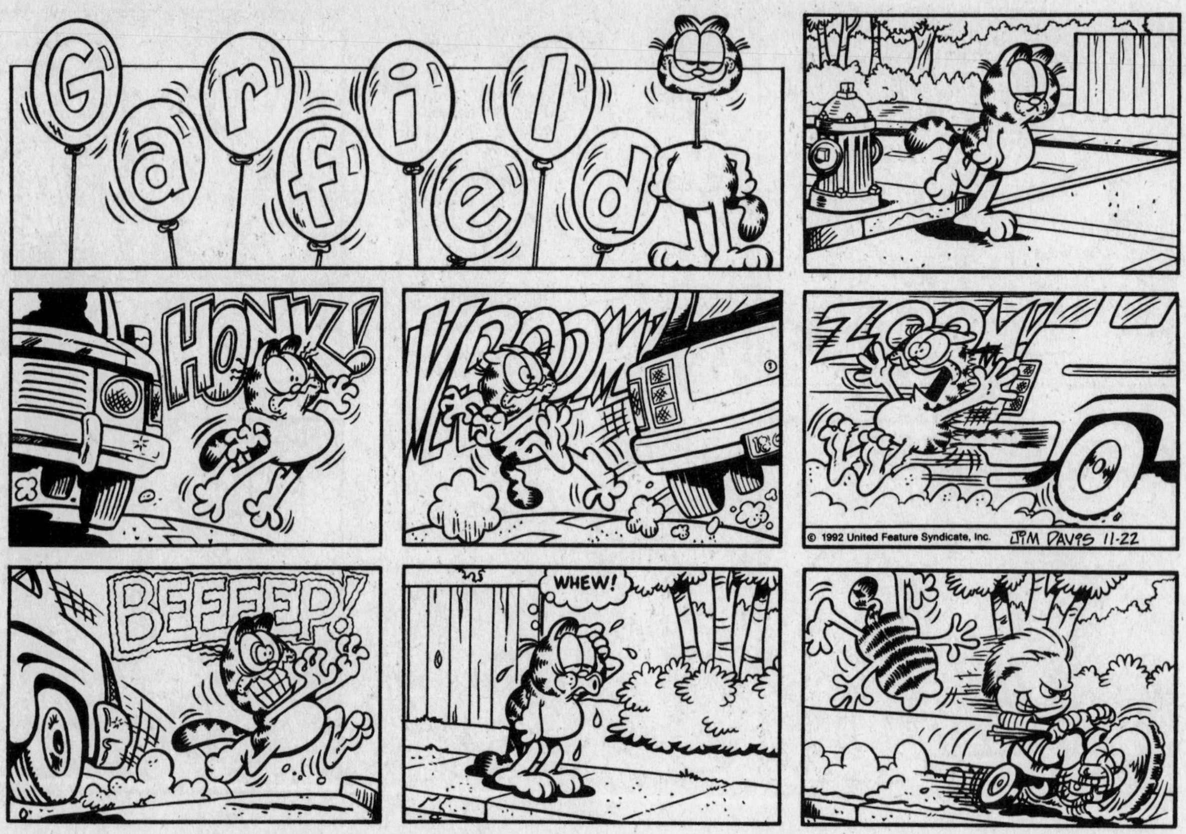
Garfield
HONK!
VROOOM
ZOOOM
© 1992 United Feature Syndicate, Inc.
JIM DAVIS 11-22
BEEEEP!
WHEW!

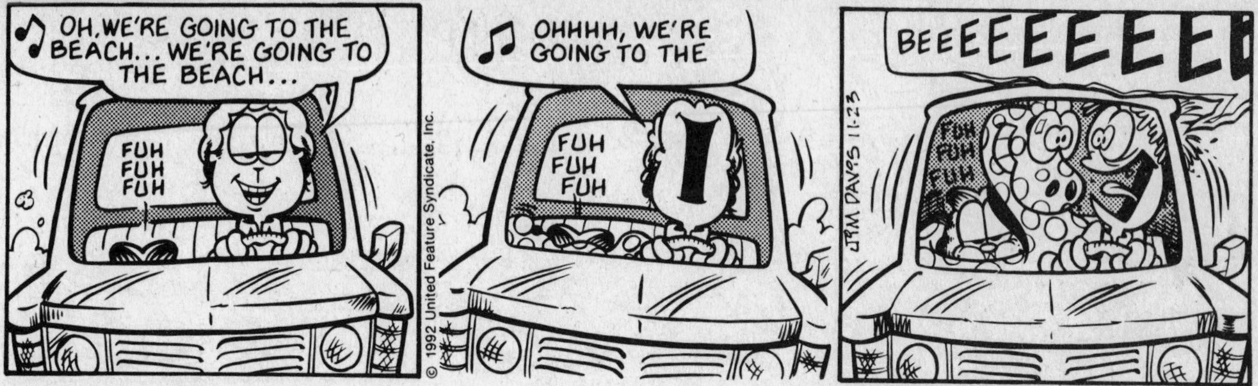
OH, WE'RE GOING TO THE BEACH... WE'RE GOING TO THE BEACH...
FUH FUH FUH
© 1992 United Feature Syndicate, Inc.
OHHHH, WE'RE GOING TO THE
FUH FUH FUH
BEEEEEEEEE
FUH FUH FUH
JIM DAVIS 11-23

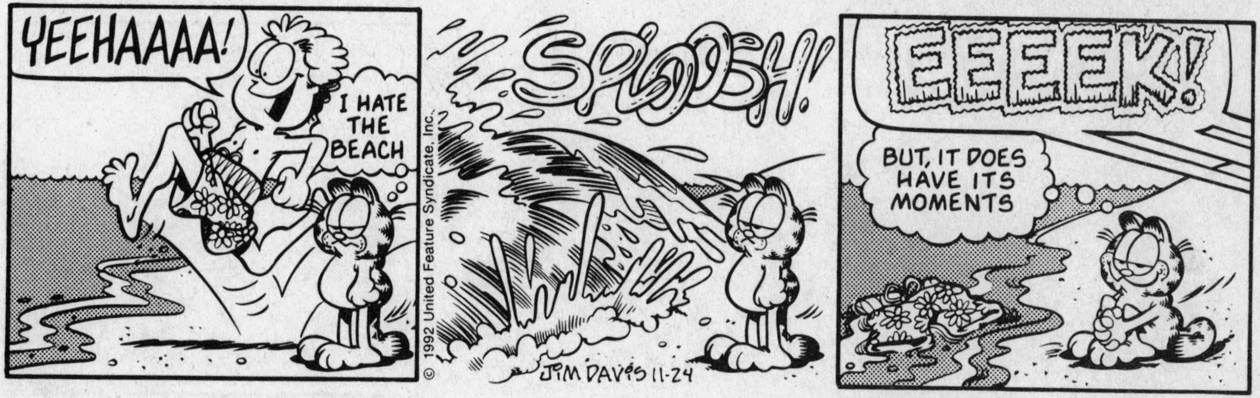
YEEHAAAA!
I HATE THE BEACH
© 1992 United Feature Syndicate, Inc.
SPLOOSH!
JIM DAVIS 11-24
EEEEK!
BUT, IT DOES HAVE ITS MOMENTS

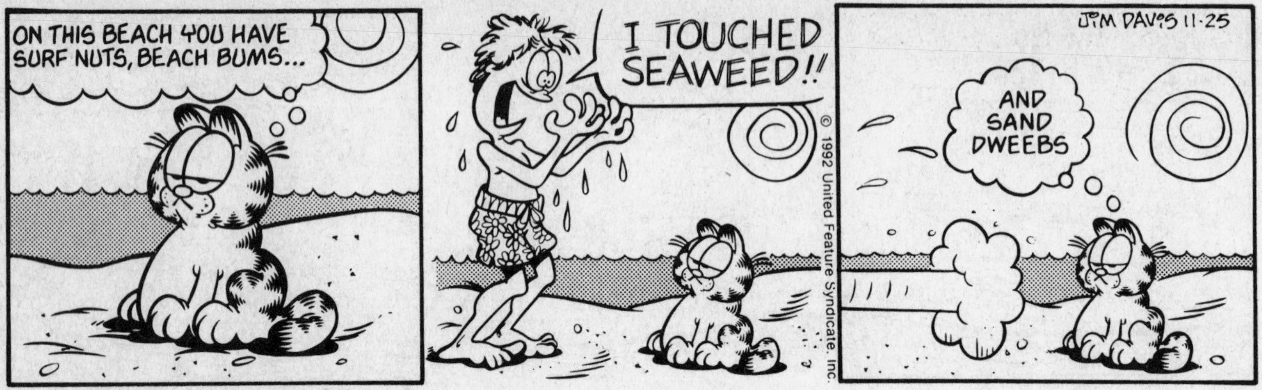
ON THIS BEACH YOU HAVE SURF NUTS, BEACH BUMS...
I TOUCHED SEAWEED!!
AND SAND DWEEBS
JIM DAVIS 11-25
© 1992 United Feature Syndicate, Inc.

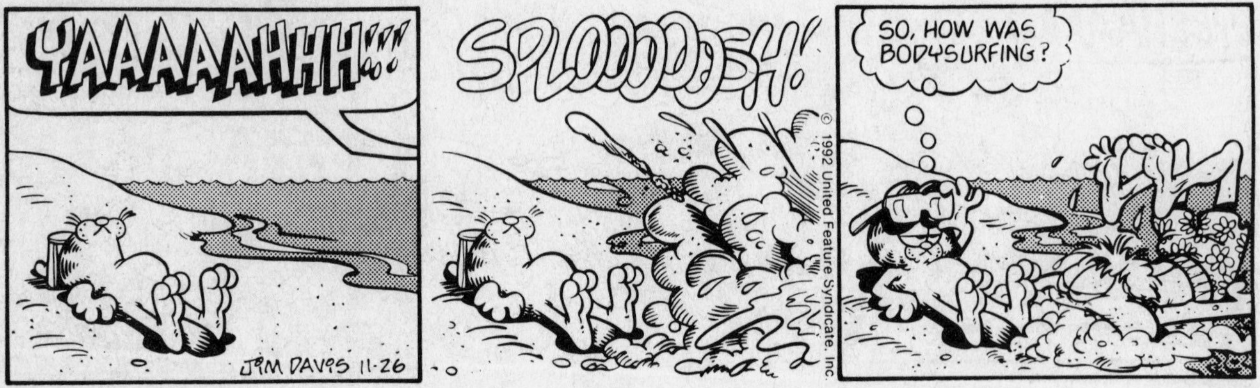
YAAAAAHHH!!!
SPLOOOOOSH!
SO, HOW WAS BODYSURFING?
JIM DAVIS 11-26
© 1992 United Feature Syndicate, Inc.

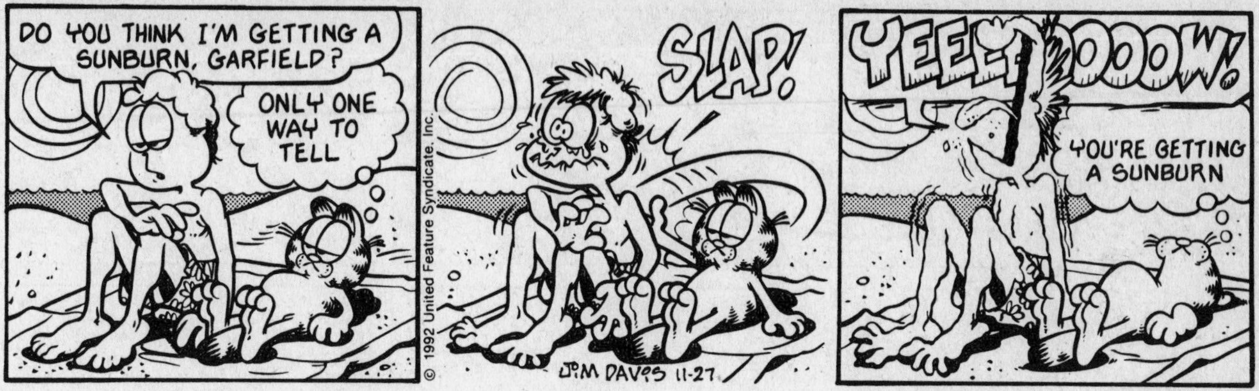
DO YOU THINK I'M GETTING A SUNBURN, GARFIELD?
ONLY ONE WAY TO TELL
SLAP!
© 1992 United Feature Syndicate, Inc.
JIM DAVIS 11-27
YEEEOOOOW!
YOU'RE GETTING A SUNBURN

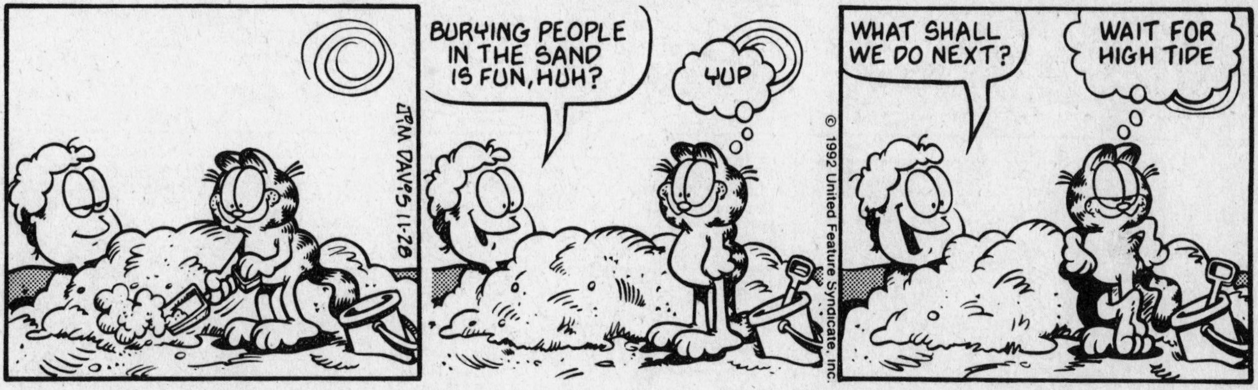
JIM DAVIS 11-28
BURYING PEOPLE IN THE SAND IS FUN, HUH?
YUP
© 1992 United Feature Syndicate, Inc.
WHAT SHALL WE DO NEXT?
WAIT FOR HIGH TIDE

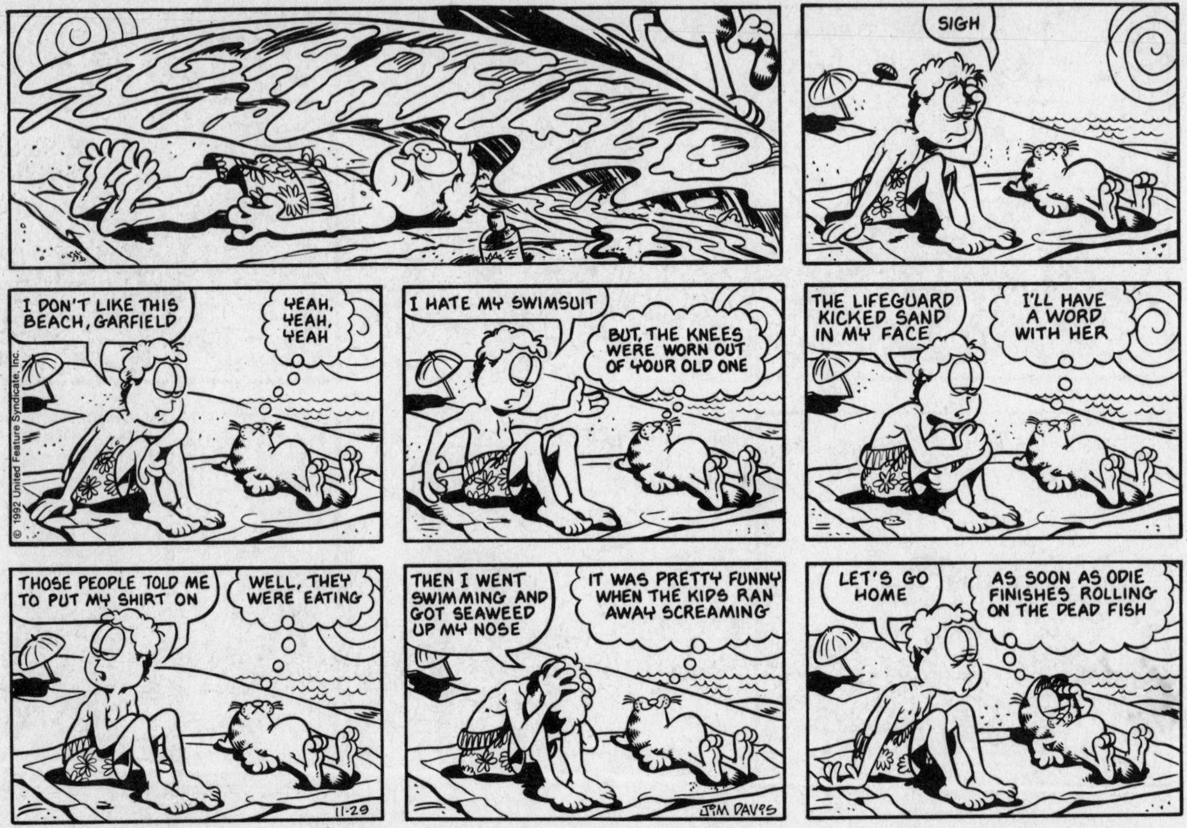

SIGH
I DON'T LIKE THIS BEACH, GARFIELD
YEAH, YEAH, YEAH
I HATE MY SWIMSUIT
BUT, THE KNEES WERE WORN OUT OF YOUR OLD ONE
THE LIFEGUARD KICKED SAND IN MY FACE
I'LL HAVE A WORD WITH HER
© 1992 United Feature Syndicate, Inc.
THOSE PEOPLE TOLD ME TO PUT MY SHIRT ON
WELL, THEY WERE EATING
11-29
THEN I WENT SWIMMING AND GOT SEAWEED UP MY NOSE
IT WAS PRETTY FUNNY WHEN THE KIDS RAN AWAY SCREAMING
JIM DAVIS
LET'S GO HOME
AS SOON AS ODIE FINISHES ROLLING ON THE DEAD FISH

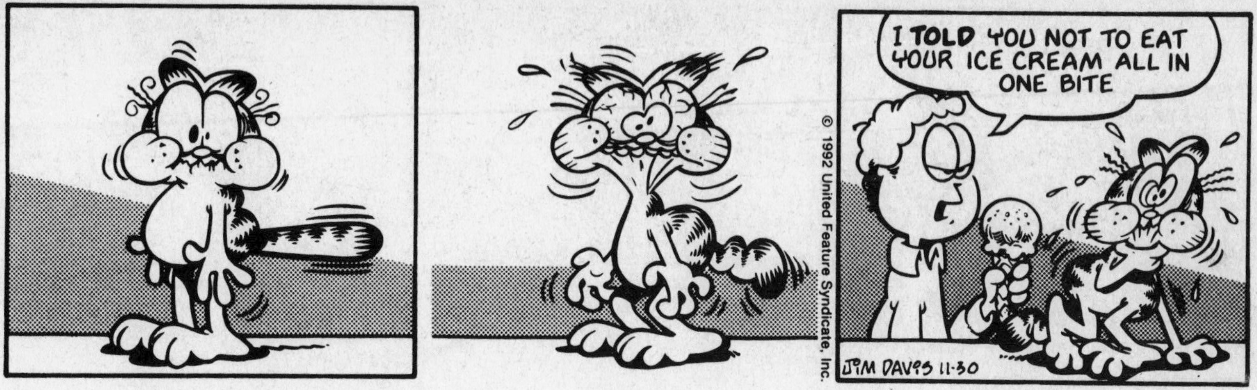
© 1992 United Feature Syndicate, Inc.
I TOLD YOU NOT TO EAT YOUR ICE CREAM ALL IN ONE BITE
JIM DAVIS 11-30

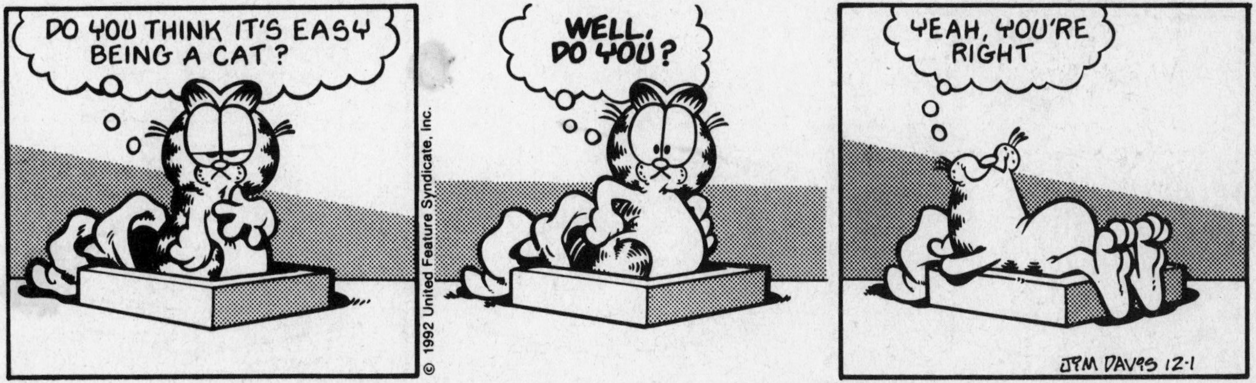
DO YOU THINK IT'S EASY BEING A CAT?
© 1992 United Feature Syndicate, Inc.
WELL, DO YOU?
YEAH, YOU'RE RIGHT
JIM DAVIS 12-1

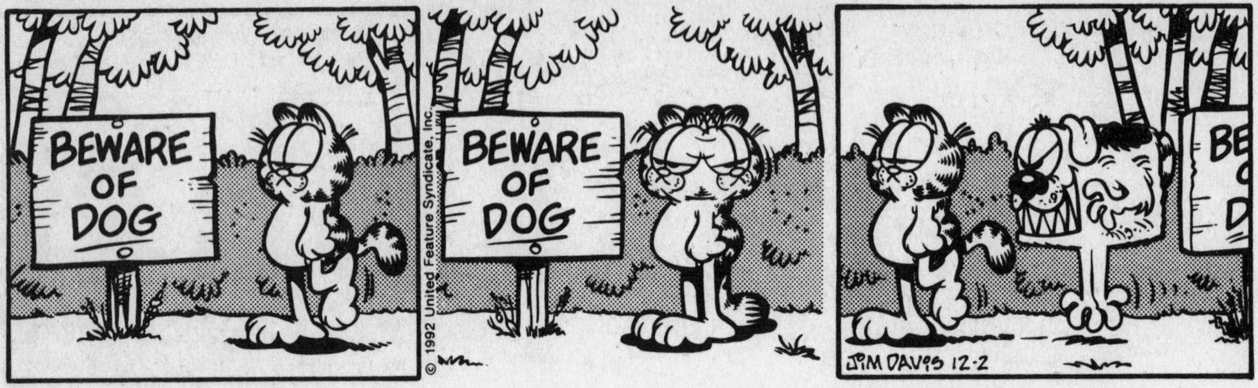
BEWARE OF DOG
BEWARE OF DOG
© 1992 United Feature Syndicate, Inc.
JIM DAVIS 12-2

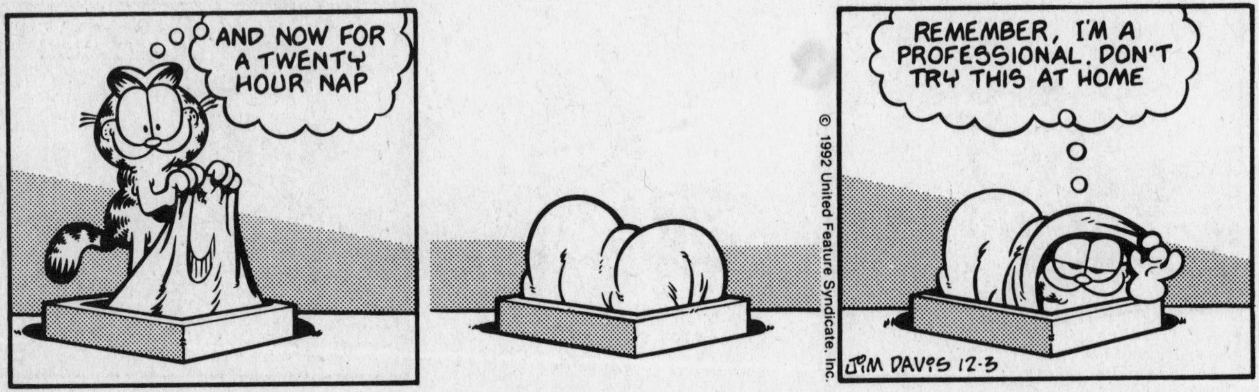
AND NOW FOR A TWENTY HOUR NAP
REMEMBER, I'M A PROFESSIONAL. DON'T TRY THIS AT HOME
© 1992 United Feature Syndicate, Inc.
JIM DAVIS 12-3

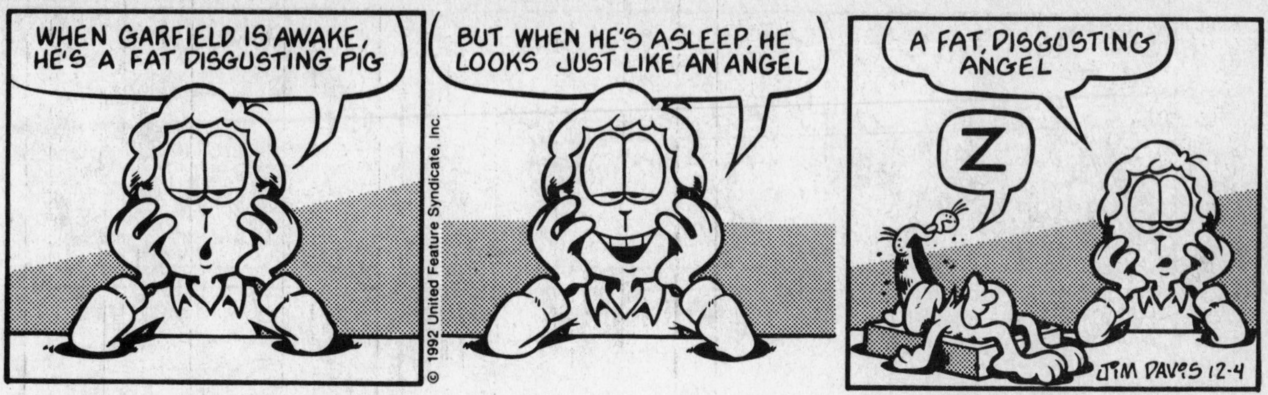
WHEN GARFIELD IS AWAKE, HE'S A FAT DISGUSTING PIG
BUT WHEN HE'S ASLEEP, HE LOOKS JUST LIKE AN ANGEL
A FAT, DISGUSTING ANGEL
Z
© 1992 United Feature Syndicate, Inc.
JIM DAVIS 12-4

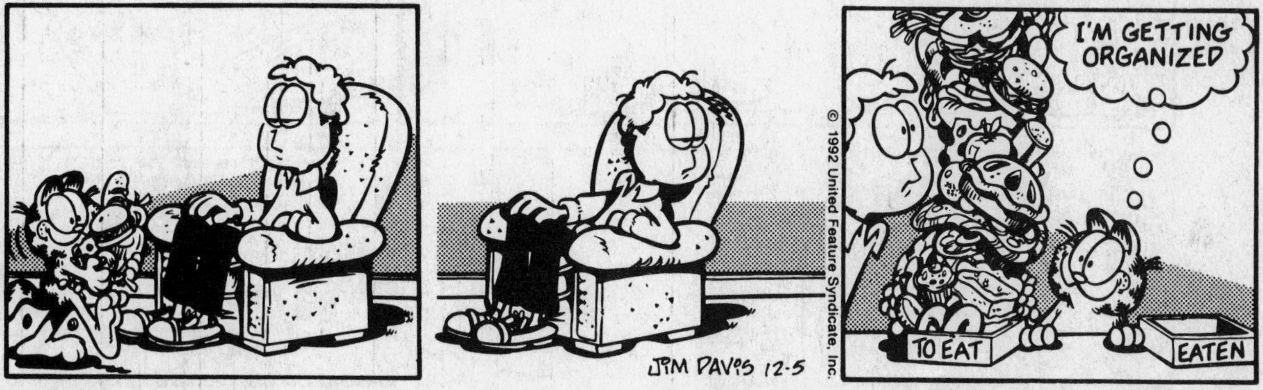
I'M GETTING ORGANIZED
TO EAT
EATEN
© 1992 United Feature Syndicate, Inc.
JIM DAVIS 12-5

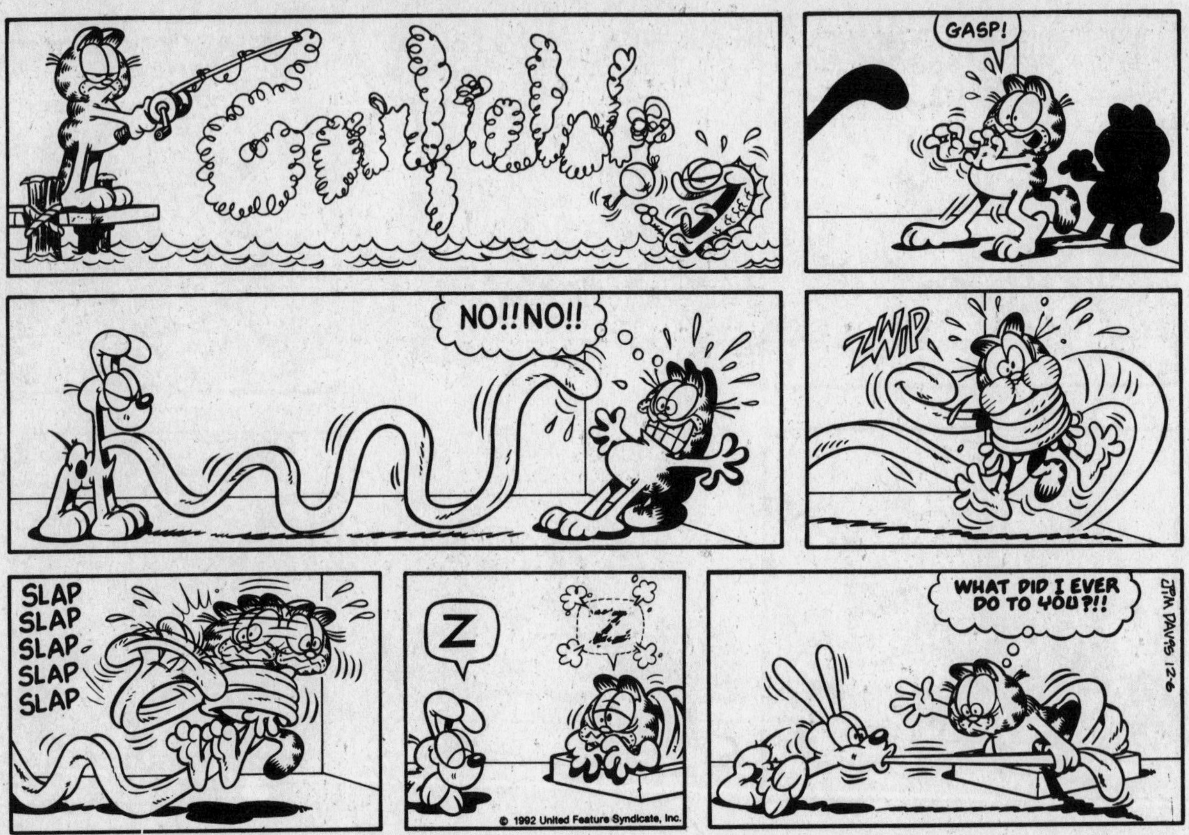

Garfield
GASP!
NO!!NO!!
ZWIP
SLAP
SLAP
SLAP
SLAP
SLAP
Z
Z
© 1992 United Feature Syndicate, Inc.
WHAT DID I EVER DO TO YOU?!!
JIM DAVIS 12-6

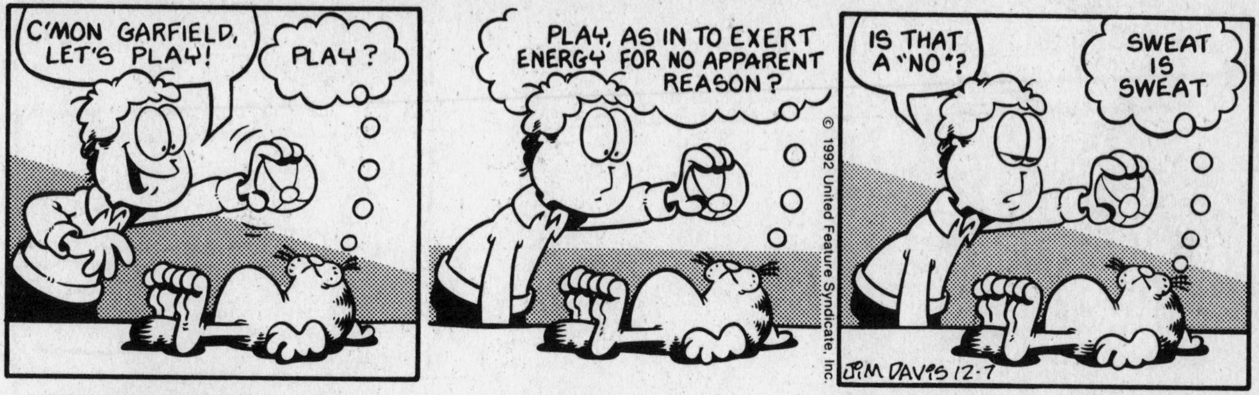
C'MON GARFIELD, LET'S PLAY!
PLAY?
PLAY, AS IN TO EXERT ENERGY FOR NO APPARENT REASON?
© 1992 United Feature Syndicate, Inc.
IS THAT A "NO"?
SWEAT IS SWEAT
JIM DAVIS 12-7

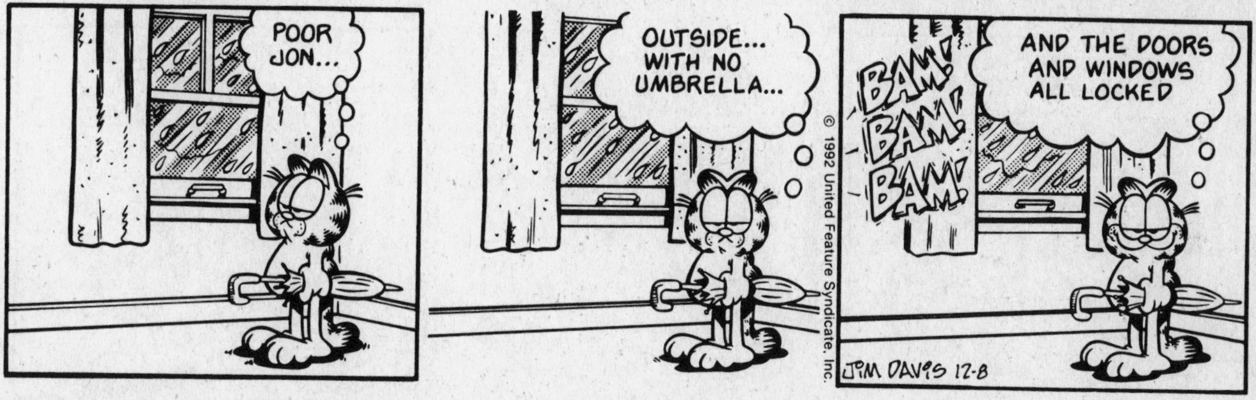
POOR JON...
OUTSIDE... WITH NO UMBRELLA...
© 1992 United Feature Syndicate, Inc.
BAM! BAM! BAM!
AND THE DOORS AND WINDOWS ALL LOCKED
JIM DAVIS 12-8

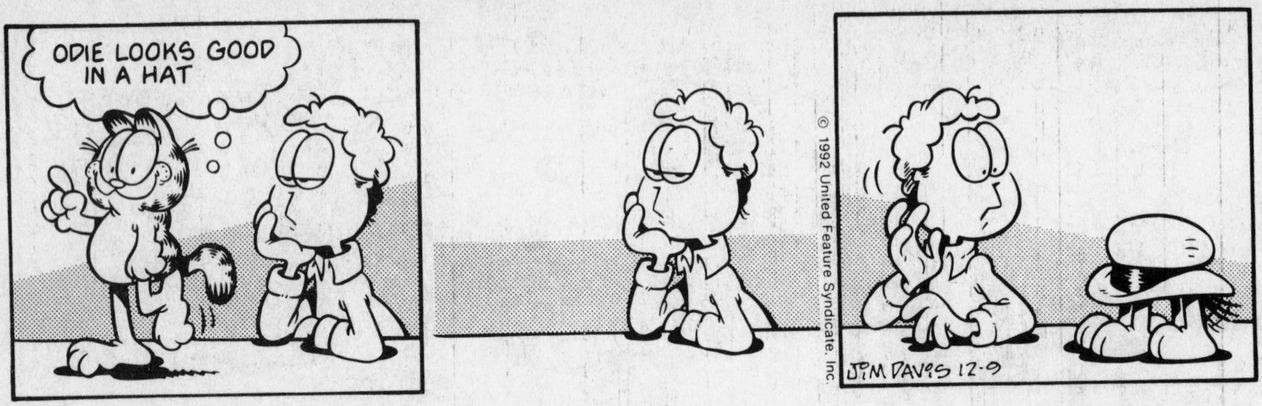
ODIE LOOKS GOOD IN A HAT
JIM DAVIS 12-9
© 1992 United Feature Syndicate, Inc.

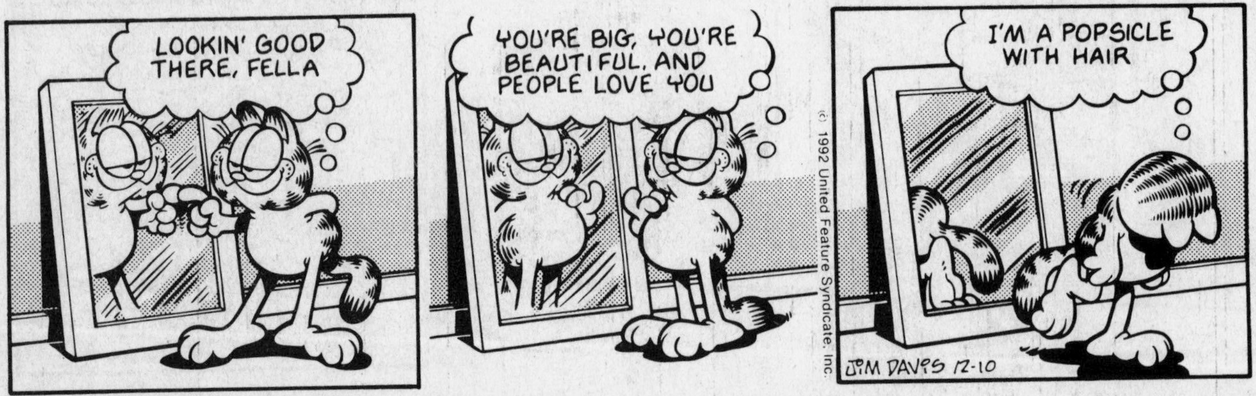
LOOKIN' GOOD THERE, FELLA
YOU'RE BIG, YOU'RE BEAUTIFUL, AND PEOPLE LOVE YOU
I'M A POPSICLE WITH HAIR
JIM DAVIS 12-10
(c) 1992 United Feature Syndicate, Inc.

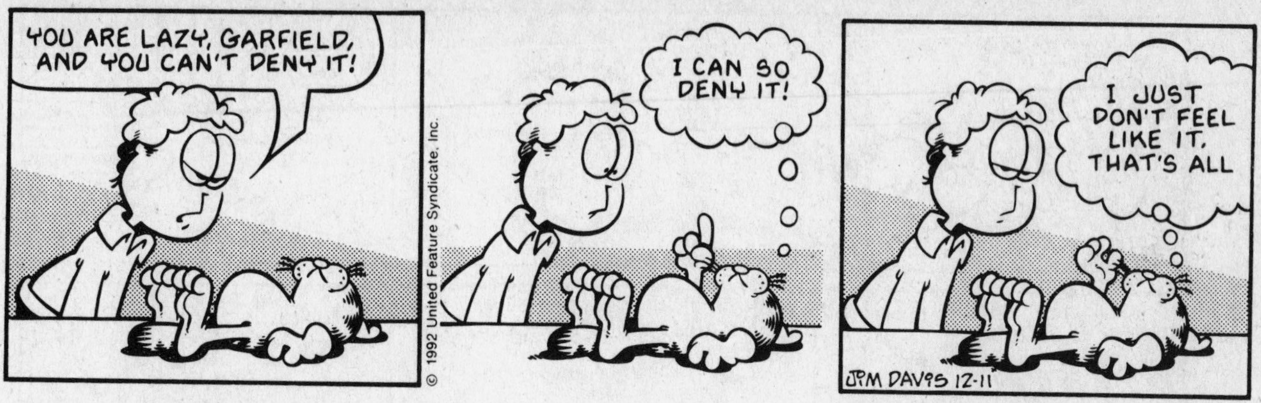
YOU ARE LAZY, GARFIELD, AND YOU CAN'T DENY IT!
I CAN SO DENY IT!
I JUST DON'T FEEL LIKE IT, THAT'S ALL
JIM DAVIS 12-11

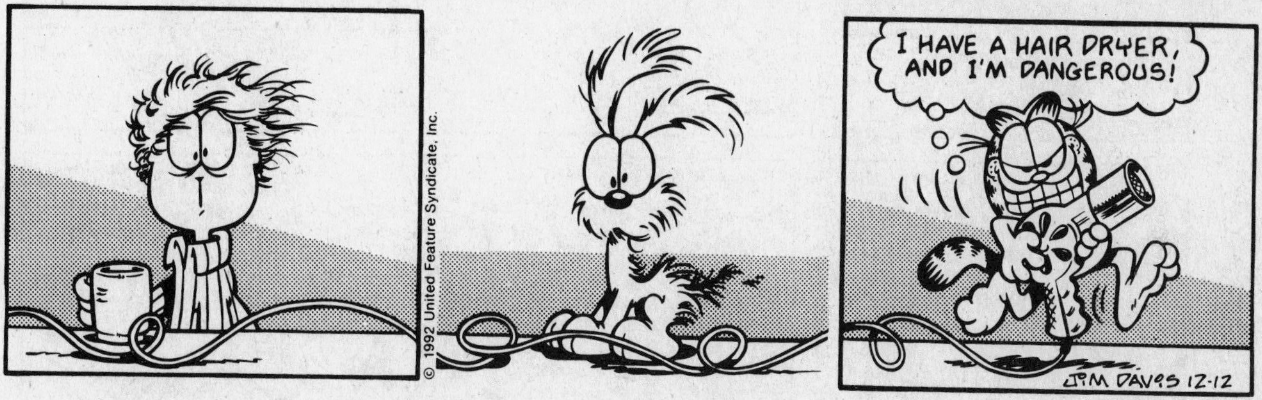
I HAVE A HAIR DRYER, AND I'M DANGEROUS!
JIM DAVIS 12-12

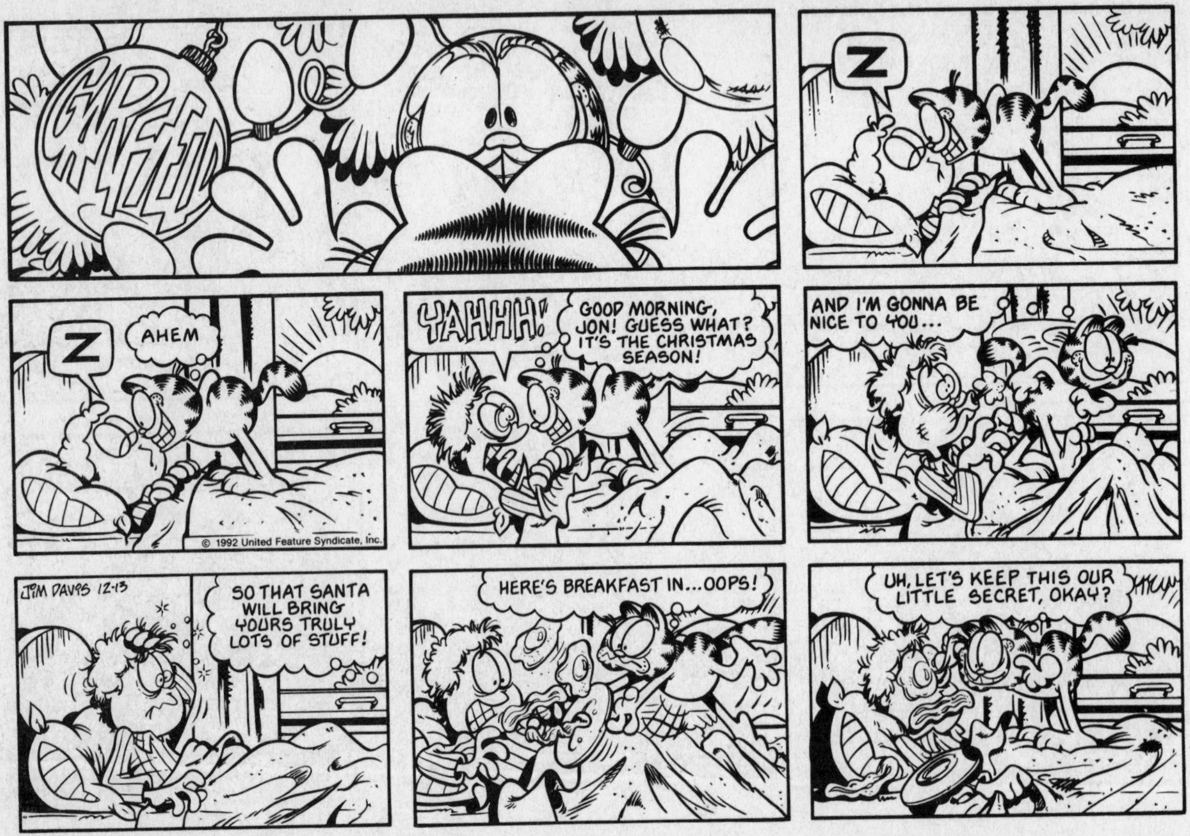
GARFIELD
Z
Z
AHEM
YAHHH!
GOOD MORNING, JON! GUESS WHAT? IT'S THE CHRISTMAS SEASON!
AND I'M GONNA BE NICE TO YOU...
SO THAT SANTA WILL BRING YOURS TRULY LOTS OF STUFF!
HERE'S BREAKFAST IN...OOPS!
UH, LET'S KEEP THIS OUR LITTLE SECRET, OKAY?
© 1992 United Feature Syndicate, Inc.
JIM DAVIS 12-13

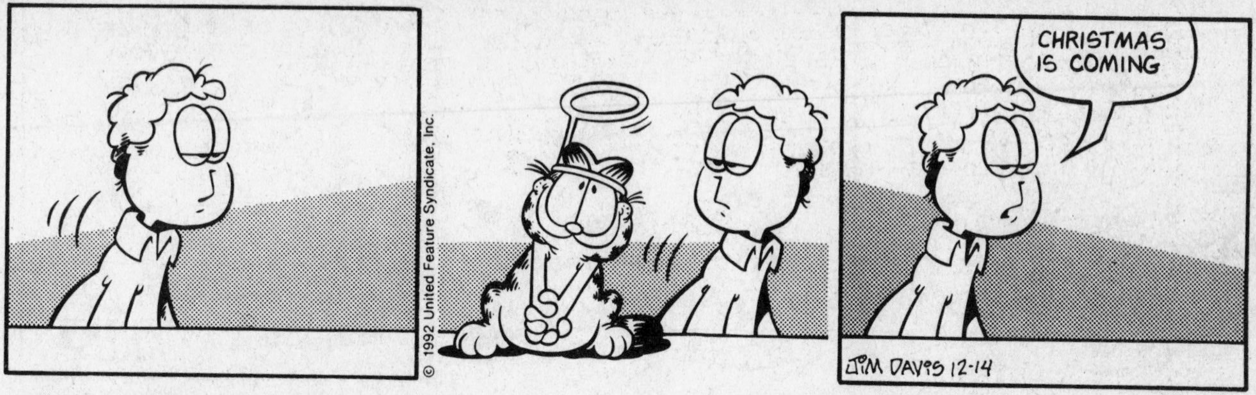
© 1992 United Feature Syndicate, Inc.
CHRISTMAS IS COMING
JIM DAVIS 12-14

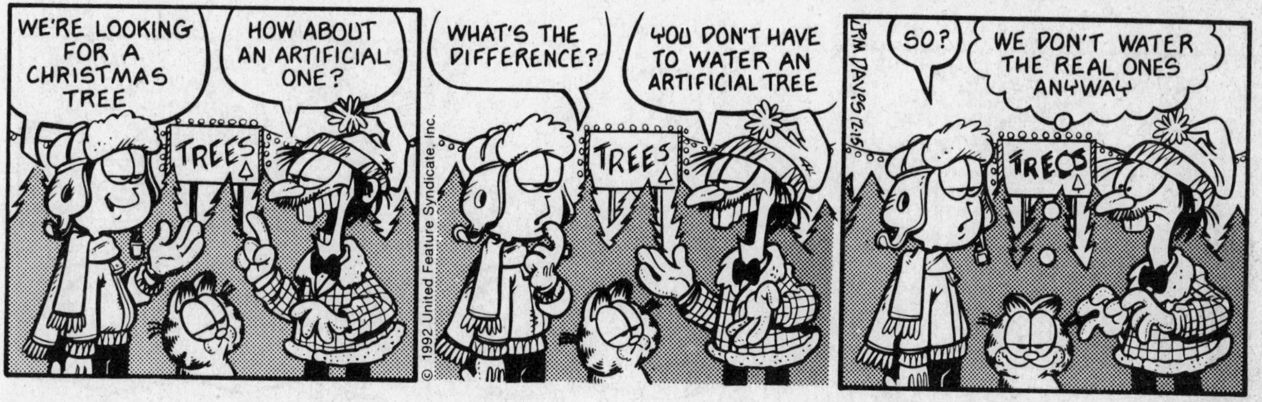
WE'RE LOOKING FOR A CHRISTMAS TREE
HOW ABOUT AN ARTIFICIAL ONE?
TREES
© 1992 United Feature Syndicate, Inc.
WHAT'S THE DIFFERENCE?
YOU DON'T HAVE TO WATER AN ARTIFICIAL TREE
TREES
JIM DAVIS 12-15
SO?
WE DON'T WATER THE REAL ONES ANYWAY
TREES

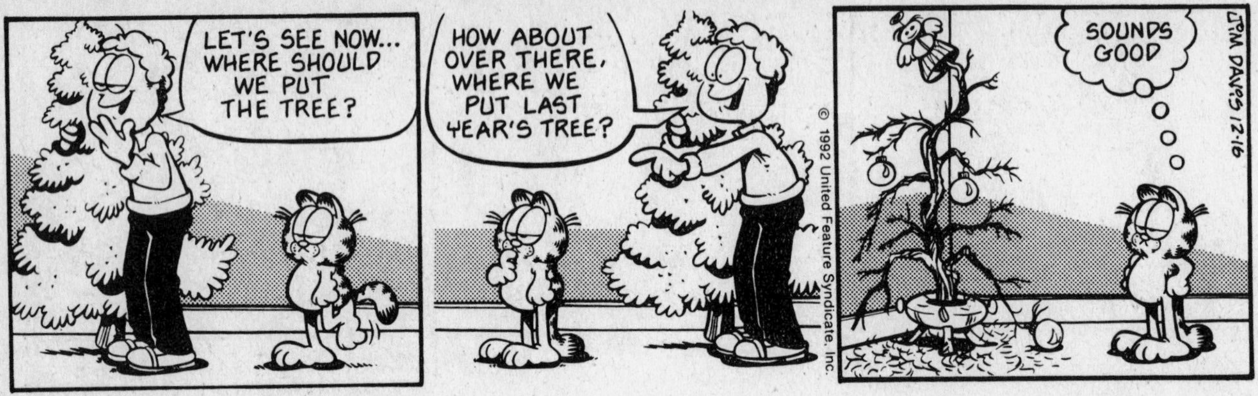
LET'S SEE NOW... WHERE SHOULD WE PUT THE TREE?
HOW ABOUT OVER THERE, WHERE WE PUT LAST YEAR'S TREE?
SOUNDS GOOD
JIM DAVIS 12·16
© 1992 United Feature Syndicate, Inc.

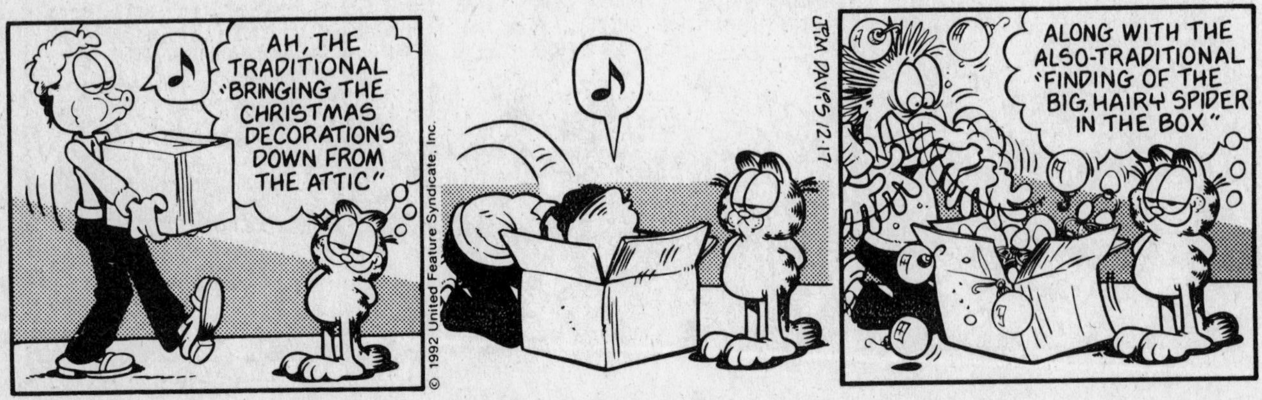
♪
AH, THE TRADITIONAL "BRINGING THE CHRISTMAS DECORATIONS DOWN FROM THE ATTIC"
♪
ALONG WITH THE ALSO-TRADITIONAL "FINDING OF THE BIG, HAIRY SPIDER IN THE BOX"
JIM DAVIS 12·17
© 1992 United Feature Syndicate, Inc.

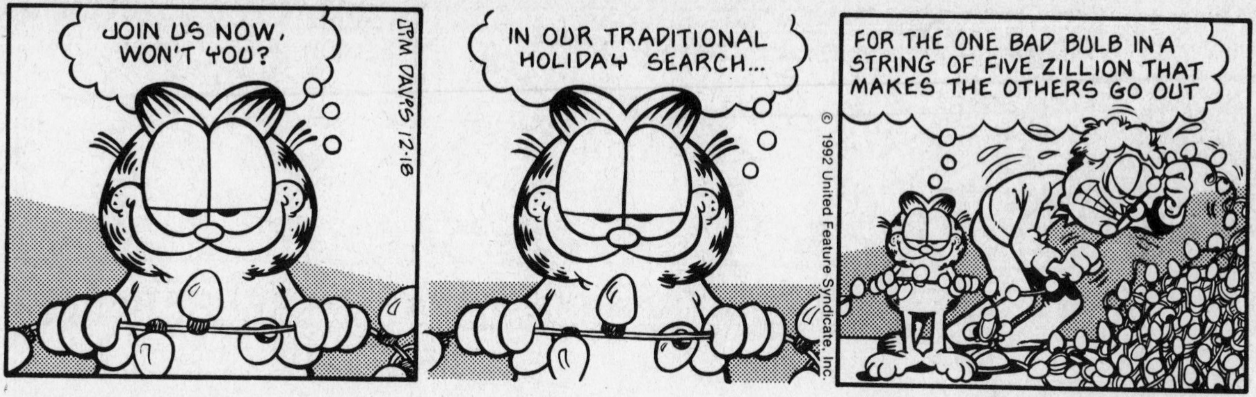
JOIN US NOW, WON'T YOU?
JPM DAVPS 12-18
IN OUR TRADITIONAL HOLIDAY SEARCH...
© 1992 United Feature Syndicate, Inc.
FOR THE ONE BAD BULB IN A STRING OF FIVE ZILLION THAT MAKES THE OTHERS GO OUT

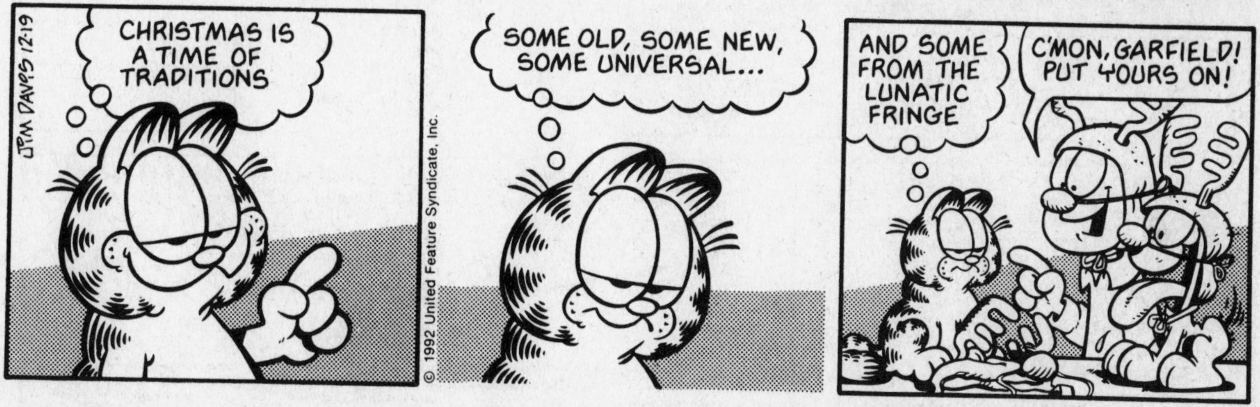
JPM DAVPS 12-19
CHRISTMAS IS A TIME OF TRADITIONS
© 1992 United Feature Syndicate, Inc.
SOME OLD, SOME NEW, SOME UNIVERSAL...
AND SOME FROM THE LUNATIC FRINGE
C'MON, GARFIELD! PUT YOURS ON!

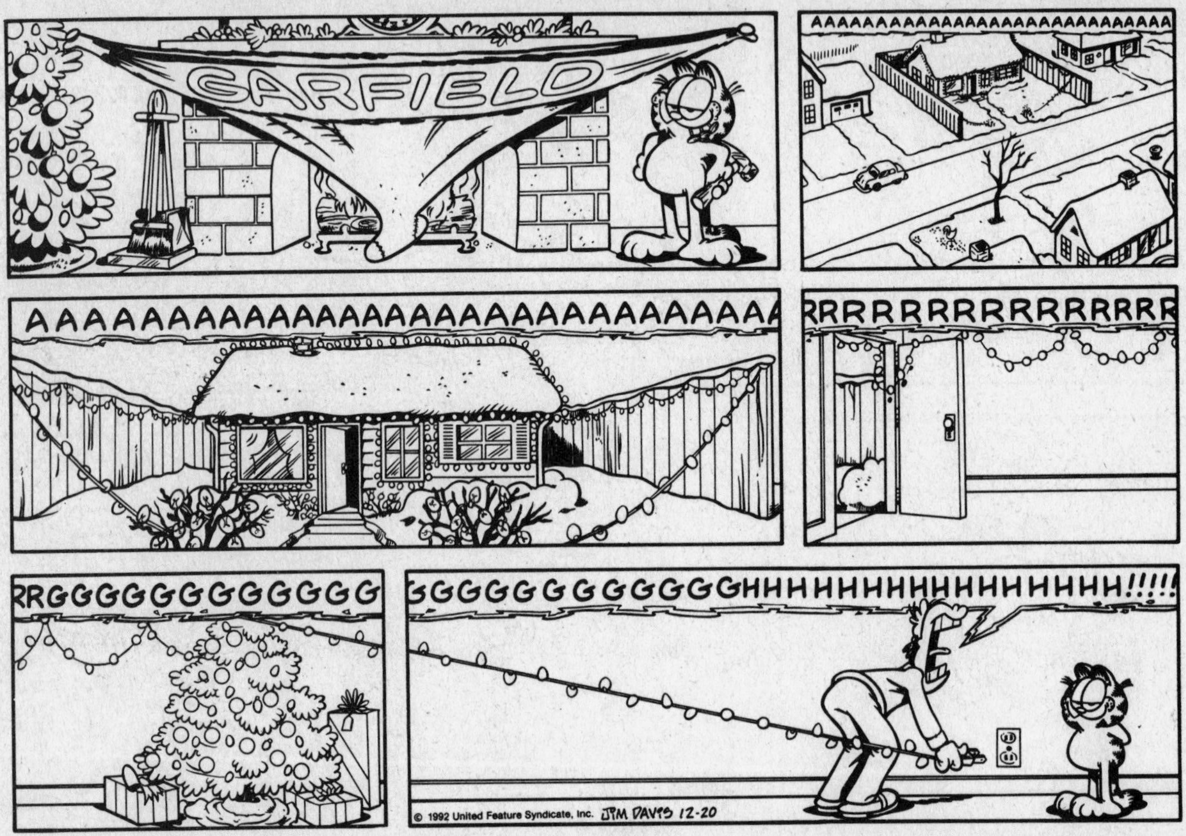
GARFIELD
AAAAAAAAAAAAAAAAAAAAAAAAAAAAA
AAAAAAAAAAAAAAAAAAAAAAAAAAAA
RRRRRRRRRRRRRR
RRGGGGGGGGGGGG
GGGGGGGGGGGGHHHHHHHHHHHHHHHH!!!!!
© 1992 United Feature Syndicate, Inc. JIM DAVIS 12-20

The Garfield Birthday Gallery

1978

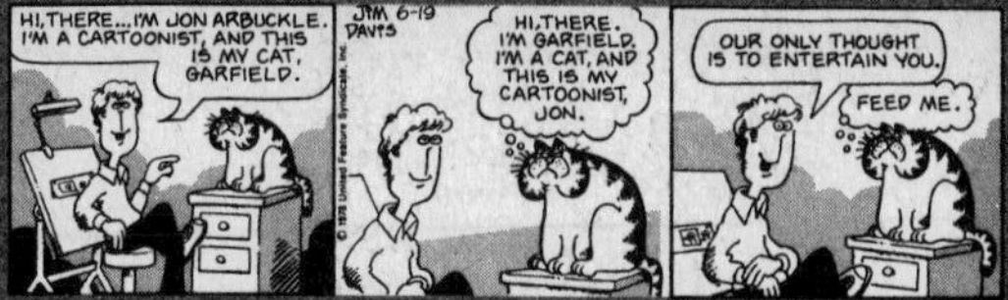
HI, THERE... I'M JON ARBUCKLE. I'M A CARTOONIST, AND THIS IS MY CAT, GARFIELD.
JIM DAVIS 6-19
HI, THERE. I'M GARFIELD. I'M A CAT, AND THIS IS MY CARTOONIST, JON.
OUR ONLY THOUGHT IS TO ENTERTAIN YOU.
FEED ME.

1979

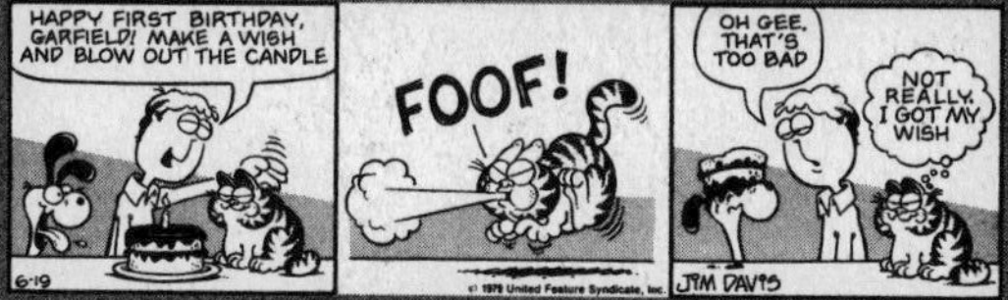
HAPPY FIRST BIRTHDAY, GARFIELD! MAKE A WISH AND BLOW OUT THE CANDLE
6-19
FOOF!
© 1979 United Feature Syndicate, Inc.
OH GEE. THAT'S TOO BAD
NOT REALLY. I GOT MY WISH
JIM DAVIS

1980

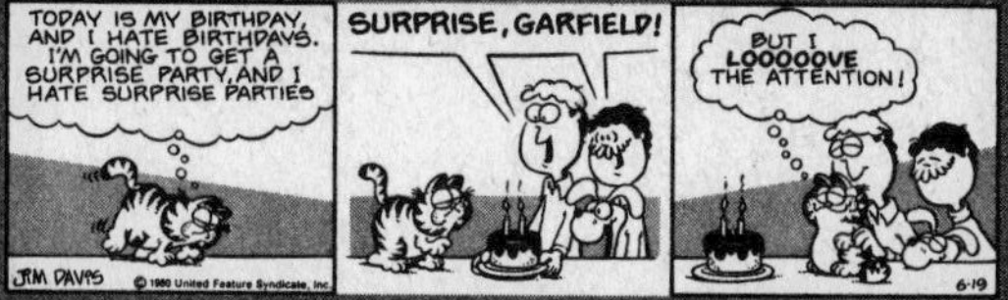
TODAY IS MY BIRTHDAY, AND I HATE BIRTHDAYS. I'M GOING TO GET A SURPRISE PARTY, AND I HATE SURPRISE PARTIES
JIM DAVIS
© 1980 United Feature Syndicate, Inc.
SURPRISE, GARFIELD!
BUT I LOOOOOVE THE ATTENTION!
6-19

1981

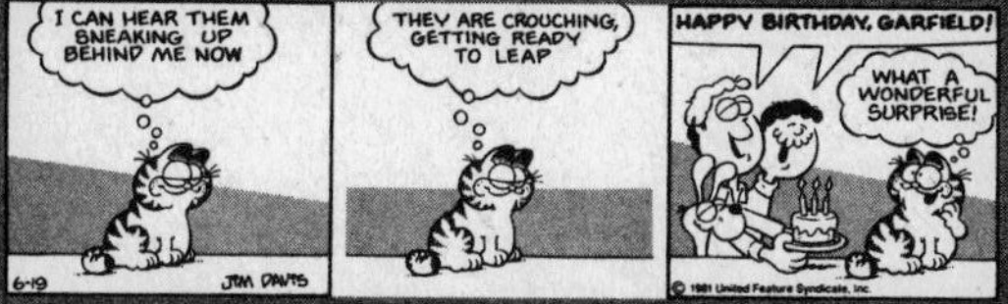
I CAN HEAR THEM SNEAKING UP BEHIND ME NOW
6-19
JIM DAVIS
THEY ARE CROUCHING, GETTING READY TO LEAP
HAPPY BIRTHDAY, GARFIELD!
WHAT A WONDERFUL SURPRISE!
© 1981 United Feature Syndicate, Inc.

1982

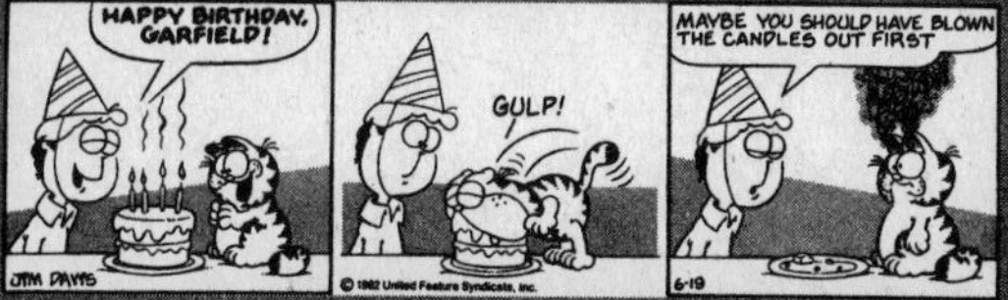
HAPPY BIRTHDAY, GARFIELD!
JIM DAVIS
GULP!
© 1982 United Feature Syndicate, Inc.
MAYBE YOU SHOULD HAVE BLOWN THE CANDLES OUT FIRST
6-19

1983

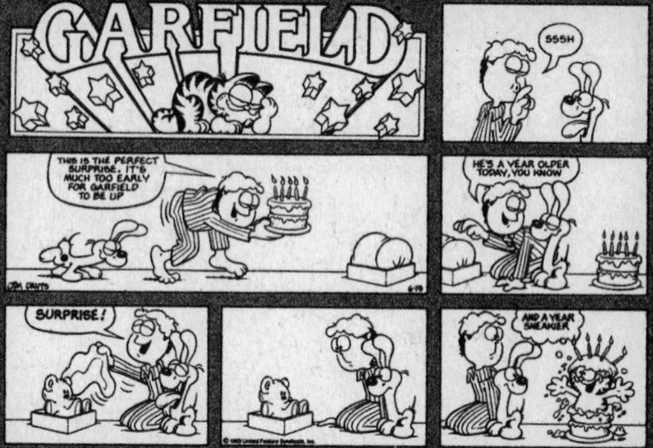
GARFIELD
SSSH
THIS IS THE PERFECT SURPRISE. IT'S MUCH TOO EARLY FOR GARFIELD TO BE UP
JIM DAVIS
6-19
HE'S A YEAR OLDER TODAY, YOU KNOW
SURPRISE!
AND A YEAR SNEAKIER

1984

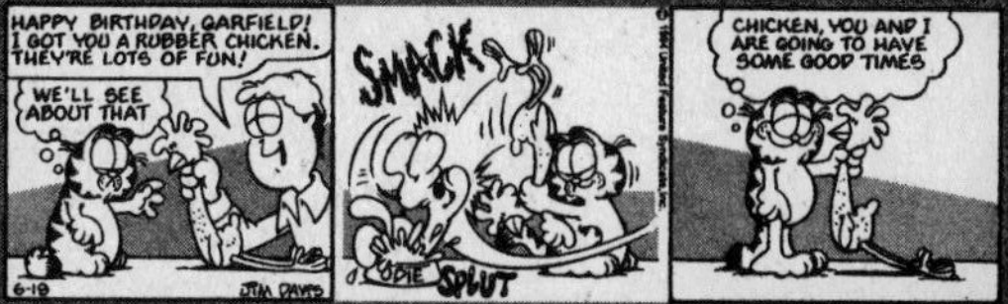
HAPPY BIRTHDAY, GARFIELD! I GOT YOU A RUBBER CHICKEN. THEY'RE LOTS OF FUN!
WE'LL SEE ABOUT THAT
6-19
JIM DAVIS
SMACK
SPLUT
ODIE
CHICKEN, YOU AND I ARE GOING TO HAVE SOME GOOD TIMES

1985

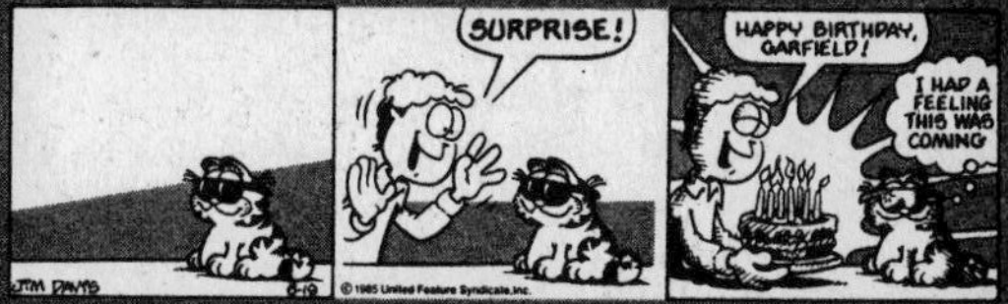
JIM DAVIS
6-19
SURPRISE!
© 1985 United Feature Syndicate, Inc.
HAPPY BIRTHDAY, GARFIELD!
I HAD A FEELING THIS WAS COMING

1986

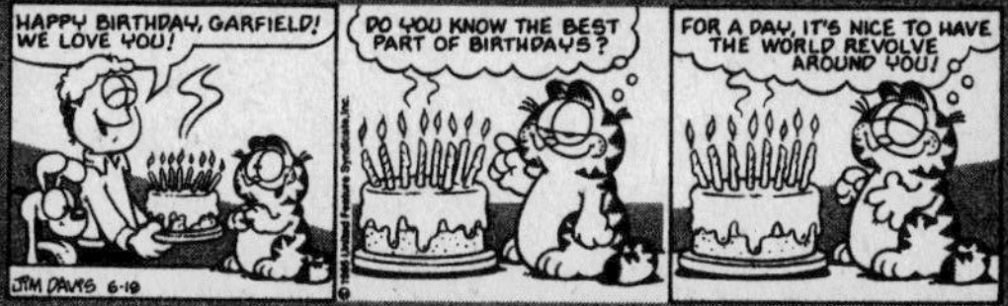
HAPPY BIRTHDAY, GARFIELD! WE LOVE YOU!
JIM DAVIS 6-19
DO YOU KNOW THE BEST PART OF BIRTHDAYS?
FOR A DAY, IT'S NICE TO HAVE THE WORLD REVOLVE AROUND YOU!

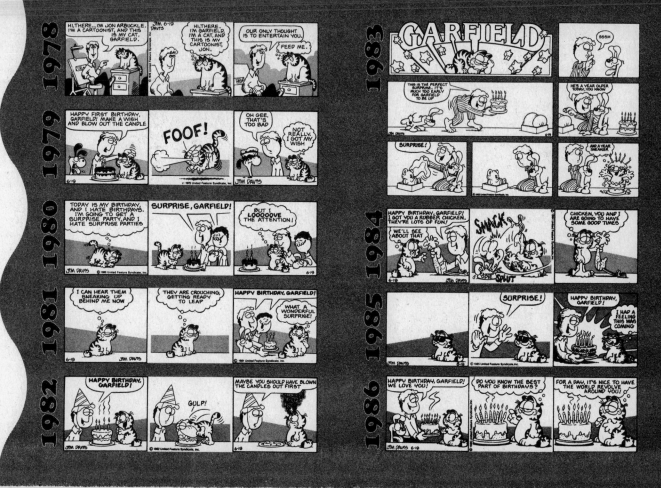

1987

HAPPY BIRTHDAY, GARFIELD!!
THAT SURE IS A LOT OF CANDLES
OH WELL, I SHOULD BE HAPPY TO HAVE A BIRTHDAY, I GUESS
FFFFF
AS OPPOSED TO THE ALTERNATIVE
JIM DAVIS 6-19

1988

HAPPY 10TH BIRTHDAY,
GARFIELD!
IF YOU BROUGHT ME PRESENTS YOU MAY STAY
HEY, GARFIELD, I JUST RAN ACROSS THE OLD FAMILY ALBUM
HO BOY
OUR ONLY THOUGHT IS TO ENTERTAIN YOU.
FEED ME.
SHOW ME A GOOD MOUSER, AND I'LL SHOW YOU A CAT WITH BAD BREATH.
WE'RE INSEPARABLE. AREN'T WE, GARFIELD?
YOU'RE STANDING ON MY TAIL
WHEN I WANT IN, I WANT IN NOW
IT'S NOT THE VALLEYS IN LIFE I DREAD SO MUCH AS THE DIPS
DO IT TO ME NOW MONDAY! GET IT OVER WITH!
WHEN THERE'S NAPPING TO DO AROUND HERE, I'LL DO IT
YOU'VE REALLY CHANGED IN TEN YEARS, GARFIELD
FEED ME
ALBUM
HAPPY 10TH BIRTHDAY, BUDDY, JIM DAVIS

1989

OKAY, I'LL BE THE BIRTHDAY CAT, AND YOU BE THE CAKE:
HAPPY BIRTHDAY TO ME, HAPPY BIRTHDAY TO MEEE, HAPPY BIRTHDAY DEAR GARFIELD, HAPPY BIRTHDAY TOOO MEEE!
FOOF!
JIM DAVIS 6-19

1990

HAPPY BIRTHDAY, GARFIELD!
DO THESE GUYS KNOW ME, OR DO THESE GUYS KNOW ME?
JIM DAVIS 6-19

1991

HAPPY BIRTHDAY, GARFIELD! WHAT WOULD YOU LIKE TO DO TODAY?
OH, CONSIDERING MY AGE, NOT MUCH
GULP!
PERHAPS A NIBBLE AND A NAP
CLICK CLICKETY CLICKETY CLICK
JIM DAVIS 6-19

1992

HAPPY BIRTHDAY, GARFIELD! READY FOR YOUR CAKE?
JUST A MINUTE!
OKAY!
BRING THAT SUCKER ON!
JIM DAVIS 6-19

1993

HAPPY BIRTHDAY, GARFIELD!
AH, YES. 'TIS TRUE I HAVE TRAVERSED FIFTEEN NOTABLE YEARS WITHIN THIS MORTAL COIL. THIS AUSPICIOUS OCCASION CALLS FOR AN APPROPRIATE ACKNOWLEDGEMENT
FEED ME!
6-19 JIM DAVIS

Feast your eyes
on the Garfield Birthday Gallery. The famished feline
has been perfecting the art of eating for fifteen years now. That's
a bellyful of laughs and lasagna. And rest assured that the Picasso of cats will
continue to color your world with fun for many years to come.

CELEBRATING 15 Fabulous Years!
1978·1993

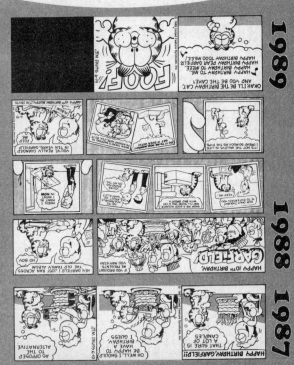

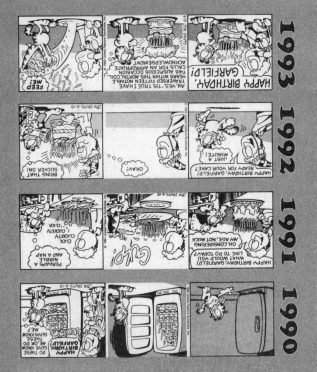

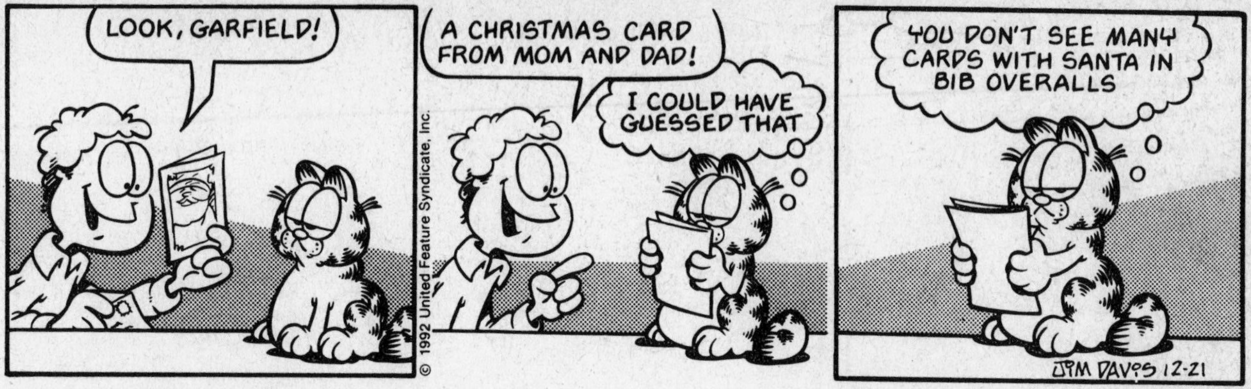
LOOK, GARFIELD!
A CHRISTMAS CARD FROM MOM AND DAD!
I COULD HAVE GUESSED THAT
YOU DON'T SEE MANY CARDS WITH SANTA IN BIB OVERALLS
© 1992 United Feature Syndicate, Inc.
JIM DAVIS 12-21

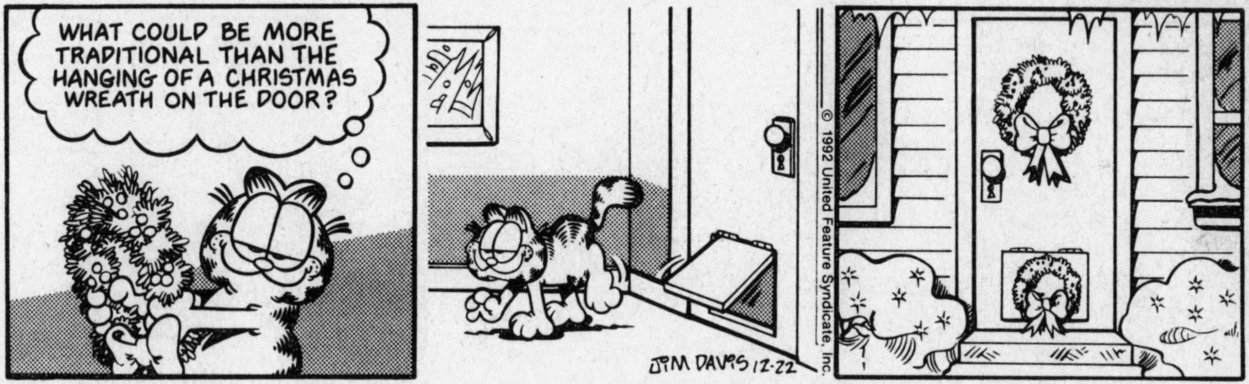
WHAT COULD BE MORE TRADITIONAL THAN THE HANGING OF A CHRISTMAS WREATH ON THE DOOR?
© 1992 United Feature Syndicate, Inc.
JIM DAVIS 12-22

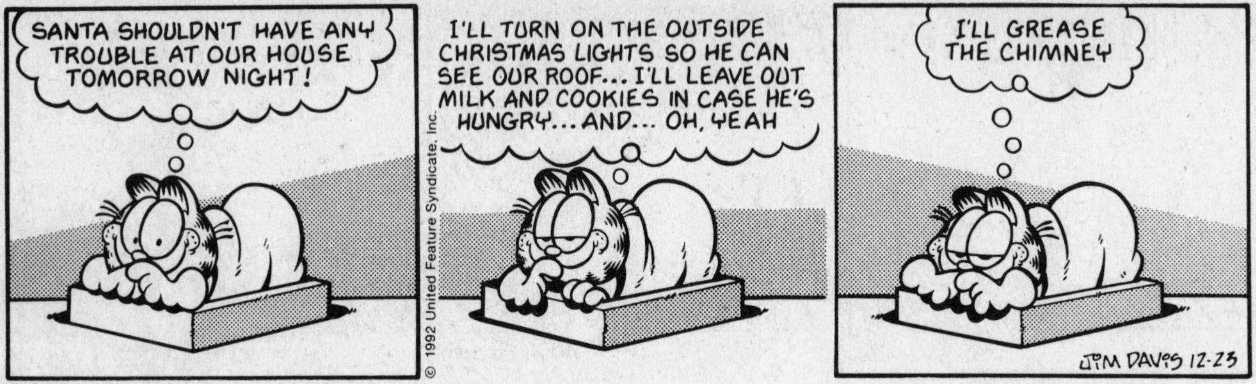
SANTA SHOULDN'T HAVE ANY TROUBLE AT OUR HOUSE TOMORROW NIGHT!
I'LL TURN ON THE OUTSIDE CHRISTMAS LIGHTS SO HE CAN SEE OUR ROOF... I'LL LEAVE OUT MILK AND COOKIES IN CASE HE'S HUNGRY... AND... OH, YEAH
I'LL GREASE THE CHIMNEY
JIM DAVIS 12-23
© 1992 United Feature Syndicate, Inc.

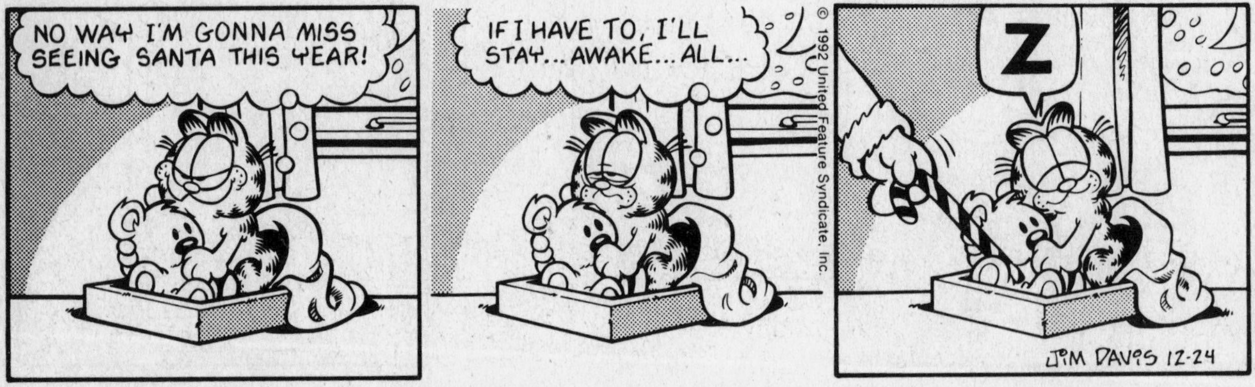
NO WAY I'M GONNA MISS SEEING SANTA THIS YEAR!
IF I HAVE TO, I'LL STAY... AWAKE... ALL...
Z
JIM DAVIS 12-24
© 1992 United Feature Syndicate, Inc.

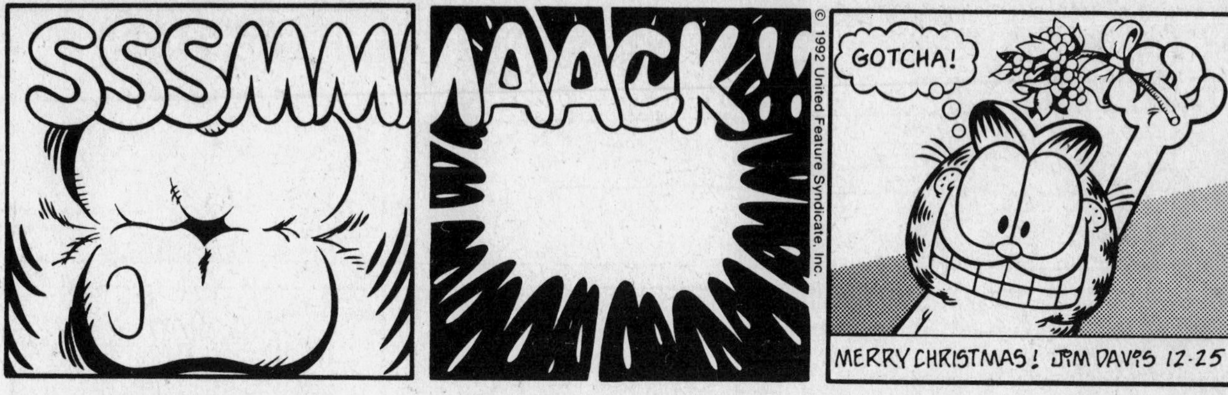
SSSMMMAACK!!
© 1992 United Feature Syndicate, Inc.
GOTCHA!
MERRY CHRISTMAS! JIM DAVIS 12-25

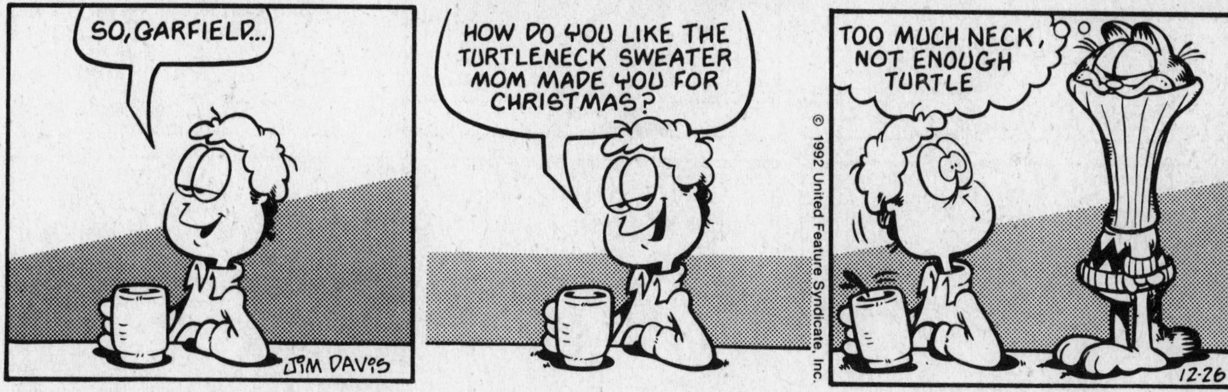
SO, GARFIELD...
JIM DAVIS
HOW DO YOU LIKE THE TURTLENECK SWEATER MOM MADE YOU FOR CHRISTMAS?
© 1992 United Feature Syndicate, Inc.
TOO MUCH NECK, NOT ENOUGH TURTLE
12-26

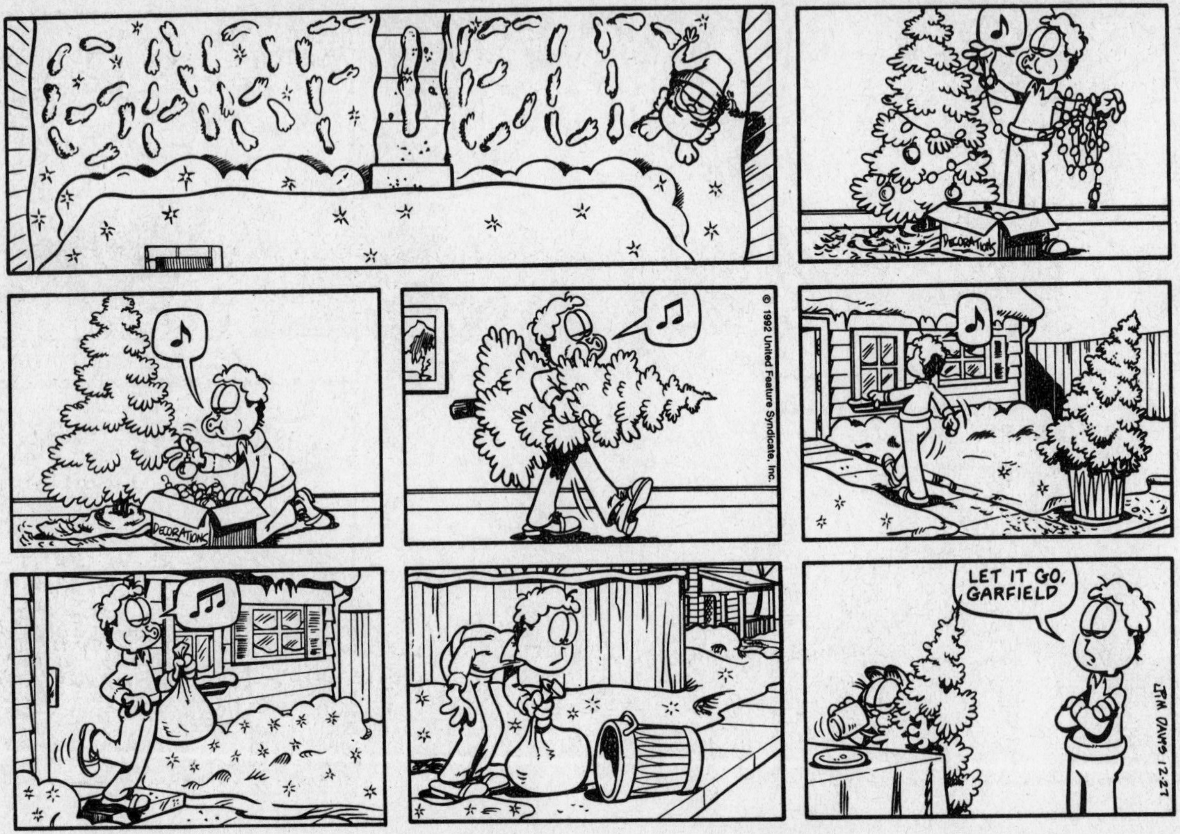
DECORATIONS
DECORATIONS
© 1992 United Feature Syndicate, Inc.
LET IT GO, GARFIELD
JIM DAVIS 12-27

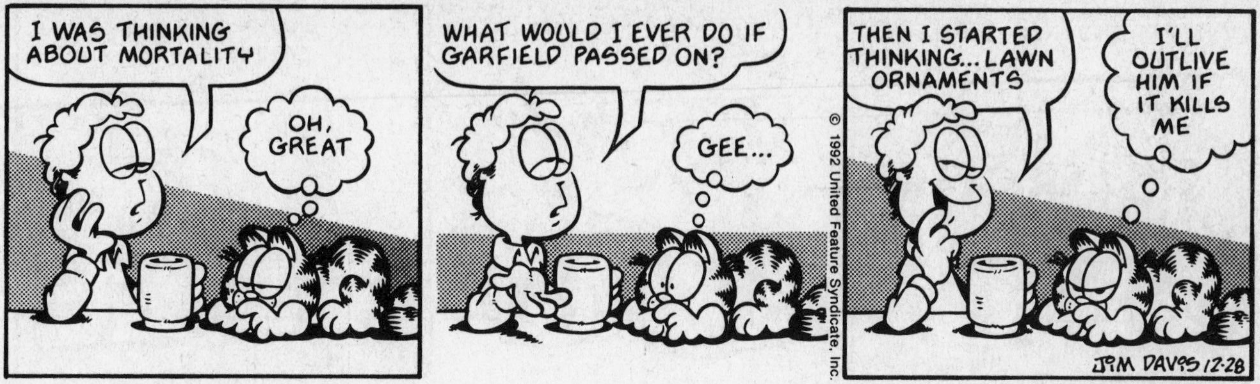
I WAS THINKING ABOUT MORTALITY
OH, GREAT
WHAT WOULD I EVER DO IF GARFIELD PASSED ON?
GEE...
© 1992 United Feature Syndicate, Inc.
THEN I STARTED THINKING... LAWN ORNAMENTS
I'LL OUTLIVE HIM IF IT KILLS ME
JIM DAVIS 12-28

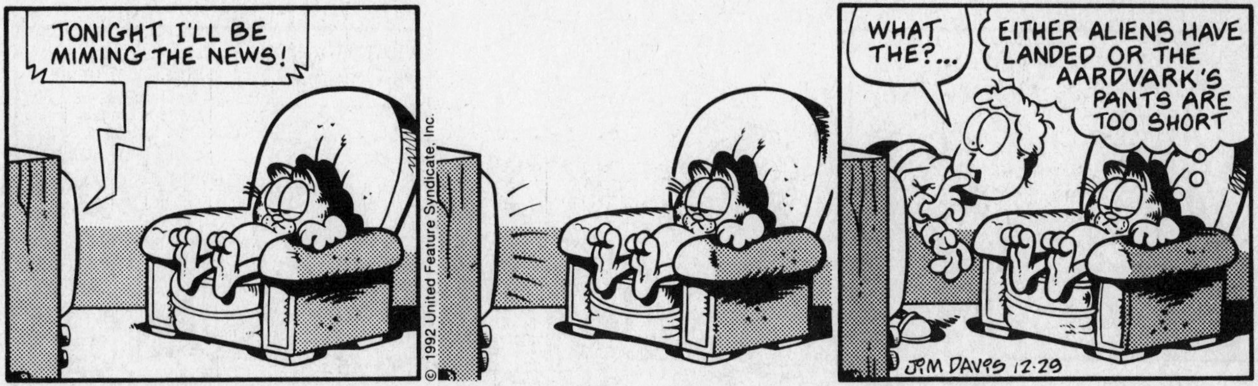
TONIGHT I'LL BE MIMING THE NEWS!
© 1992 United Feature Syndicate, Inc.
WHAT THE?...
EITHER ALIENS HAVE LANDED OR THE AARDVARK'S PANTS ARE TOO SHORT
JIM DAVIS 12-29

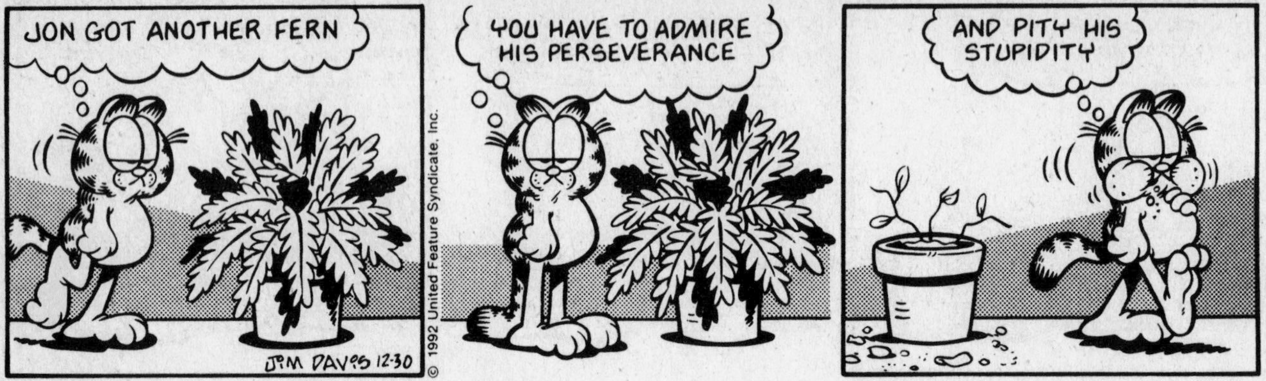
JON GOT ANOTHER FERN
JIM DAVIS 12-30
© 1992 United Feature Syndicate, Inc.
YOU HAVE TO ADMIRE HIS PERSEVERANCE
AND PITY HIS STUPIDITY

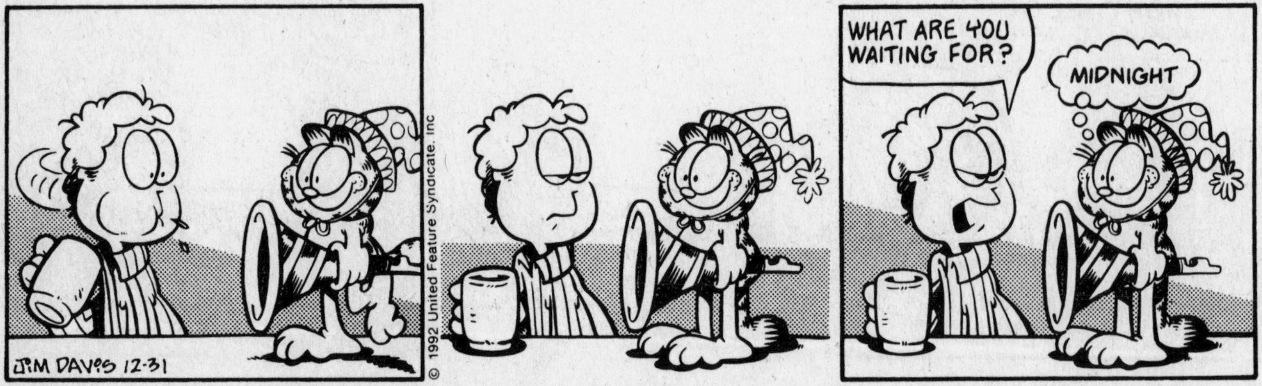
JIM DAVIS 12-31
© 1992 United Feature Syndicate, Inc.
WHAT ARE YOU WAITING FOR?
MIDNIGHT

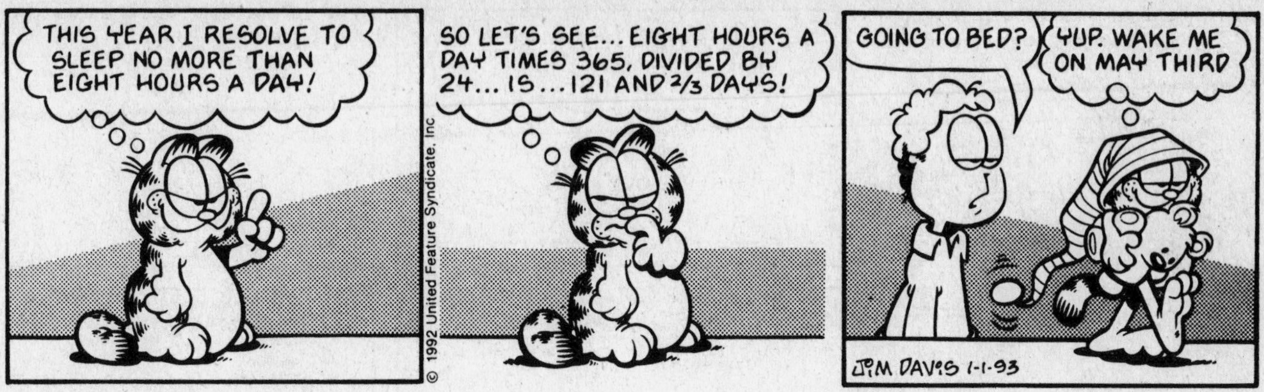
THIS YEAR I RESOLVE TO SLEEP NO MORE THAN EIGHT HOURS A DAY!
SO LET'S SEE... EIGHT HOURS A DAY TIMES 365, DIVIDED BY 24... IS... 121 AND 2/3 DAYS!
GOING TO BED?
YUP. WAKE ME ON MAY THIRD
JIM DAVIS 1-1-93
© 1992 United Feature Syndicate, Inc.

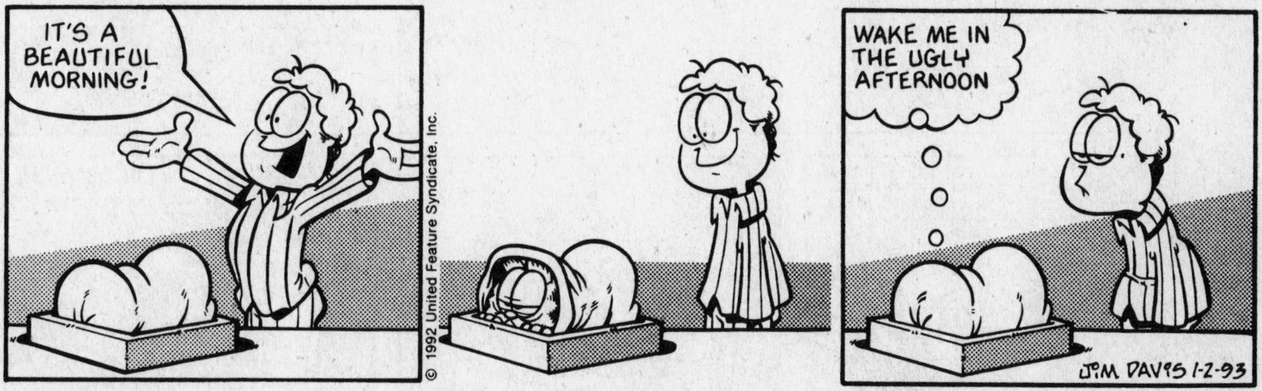
IT'S A BEAUTIFUL MORNING!
WAKE ME IN THE UGLY AFTERNOON
JIM DAVIS 1-2-93
© 1992 United Feature Syndicate, Inc.

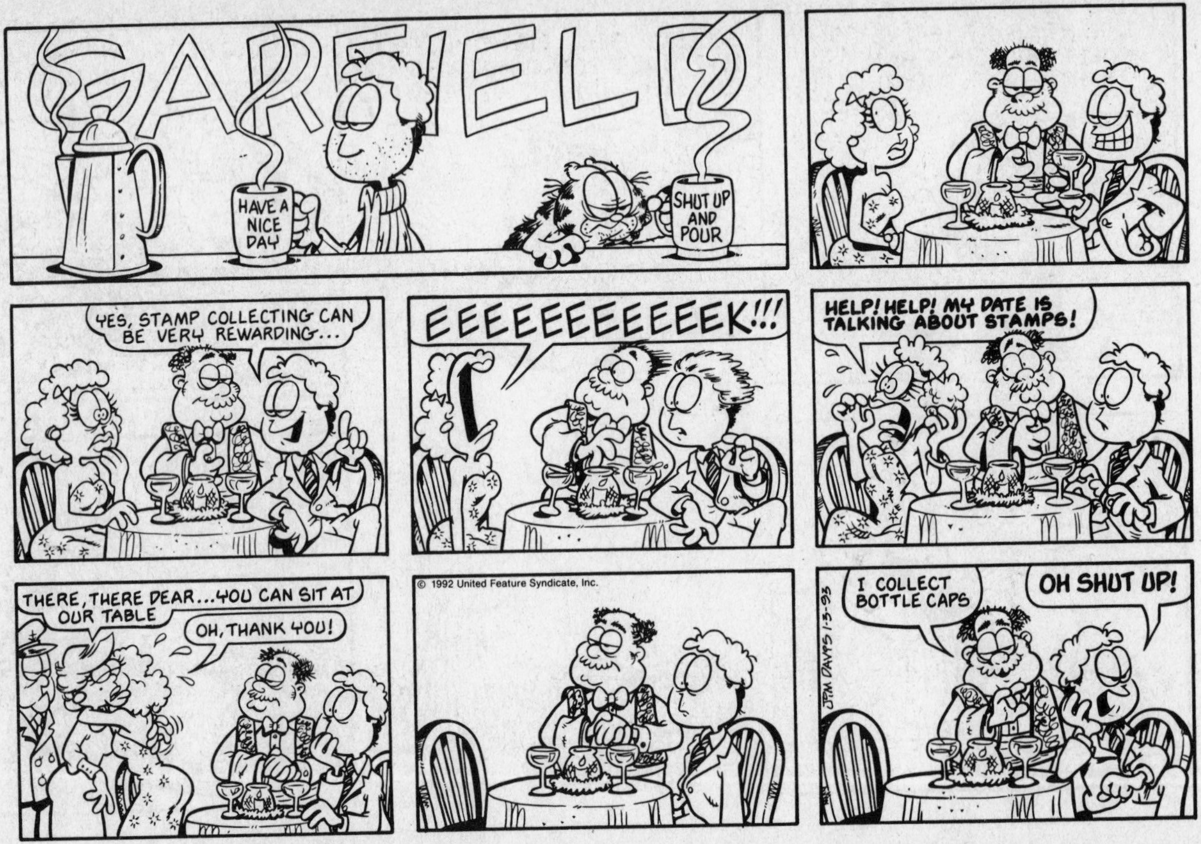
GARFIELD
HAVE A NICE DAY
SHUT UP AND POUR
YES, STAMP COLLECTING CAN BE VERY REWARDING...
EEEEEEEEEEEEK!!!
HELP! HELP! MY DATE IS TALKING ABOUT STAMPS!
THERE, THERE DEAR...YOU CAN SIT AT OUR TABLE
OH, THANK YOU!
© 1992 United Feature Syndicate, Inc.
JPM DAVIS 1-3-93
I COLLECT BOTTLE CAPS
OH SHUT UP!

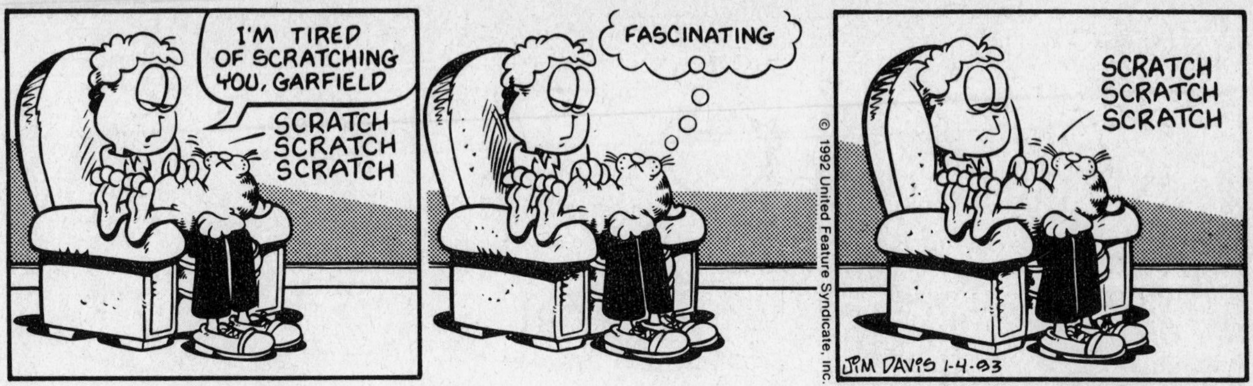
I'M TIRED OF SCRATCHING YOU, GARFIELD
SCRATCH SCRATCH SCRATCH
FASCINATING
SCRATCH SCRATCH SCRATCH
JIM DAVIS 1-4-93
© 1992 United Feature Syndicate, Inc.

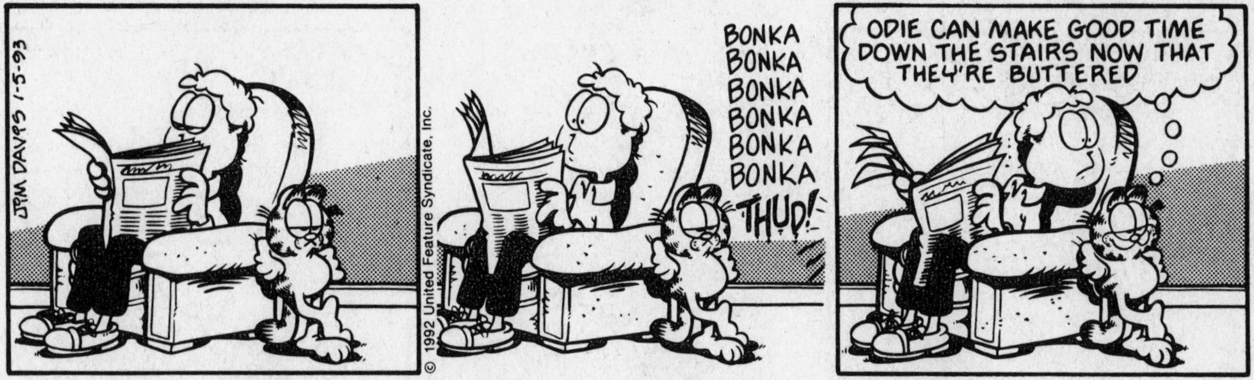
JIM DAVIS 1-5-93
© 1992 United Feature Syndicate, Inc.
BONKA BONKA BONKA BONKA BONKA BONKA
THUD!
ODIE CAN MAKE GOOD TIME DOWN THE STAIRS NOW THAT THEY'RE BUTTERED

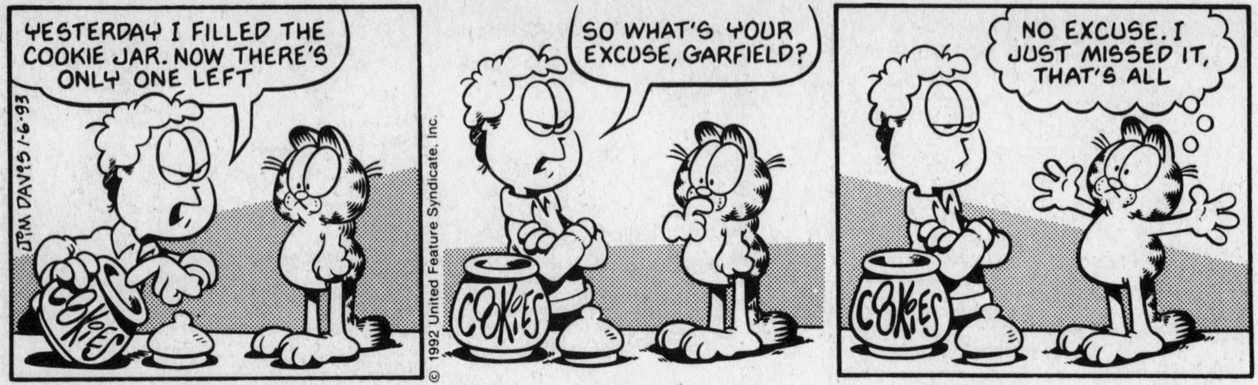
YESTERDAY I FILLED THE COOKIE JAR. NOW THERE'S ONLY ONE LEFT
JIM DAVIS 1-6-93
COOKIES
© 1992 United Feature Syndicate, Inc.
SO WHAT'S YOUR EXCUSE, GARFIELD?
NO EXCUSE. I JUST MISSED IT, THAT'S ALL

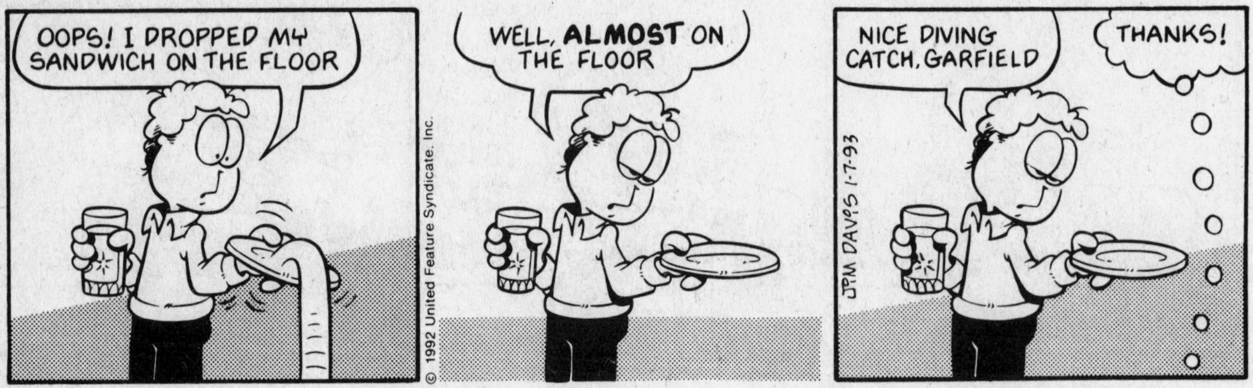
OOPS! I DROPPED MY SANDWICH ON THE FLOOR
© 1992 United Feature Syndicate, Inc.
WELL, ALMOST ON THE FLOOR
JIM DAVIS 1-7-93
NICE DIVING CATCH, GARFIELD
THANKS!

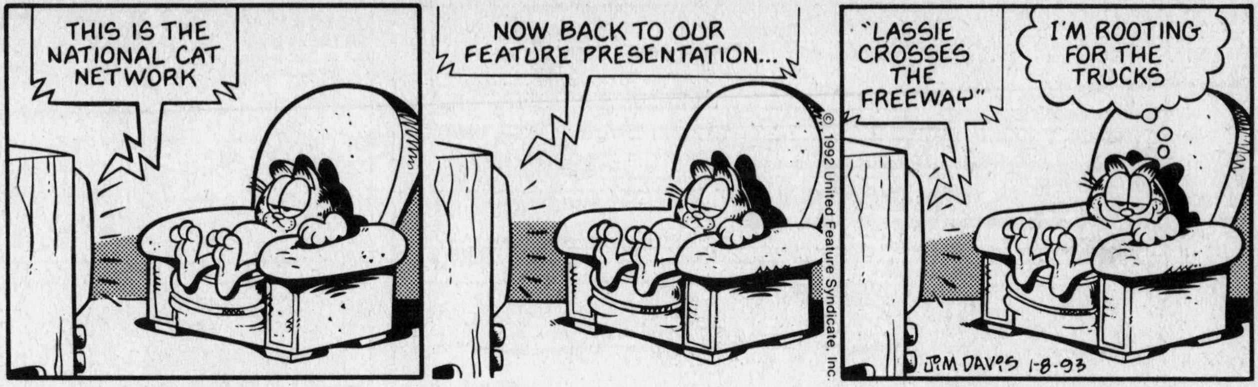
THIS IS THE NATIONAL CAT NETWORK
NOW BACK TO OUR FEATURE PRESENTATION...
"LASSIE CROSSES THE FREEWAY"
I'M ROOTING FOR THE TRUCKS
JIM DAVIS 1-8-93

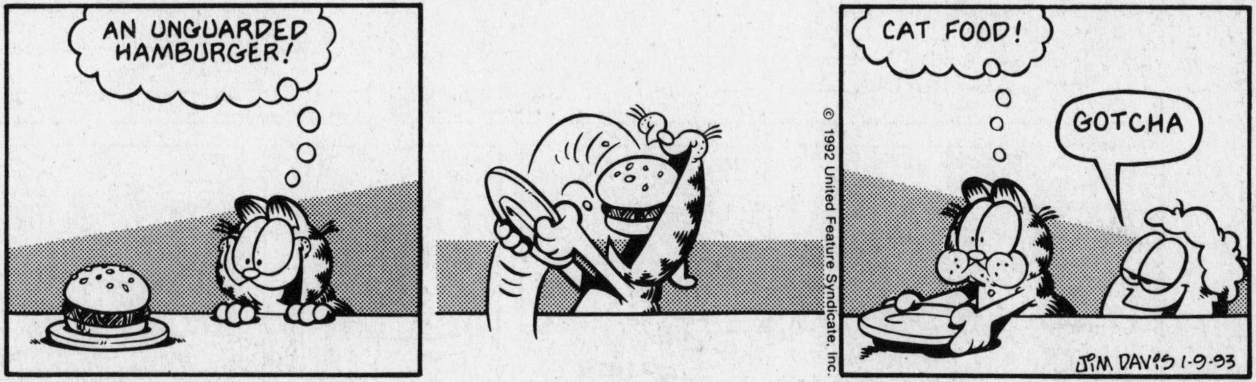
AN UNGUARDED HAMBURGER!
CAT FOOD!
GOTCHA
JIM DAVIS 1-9-93

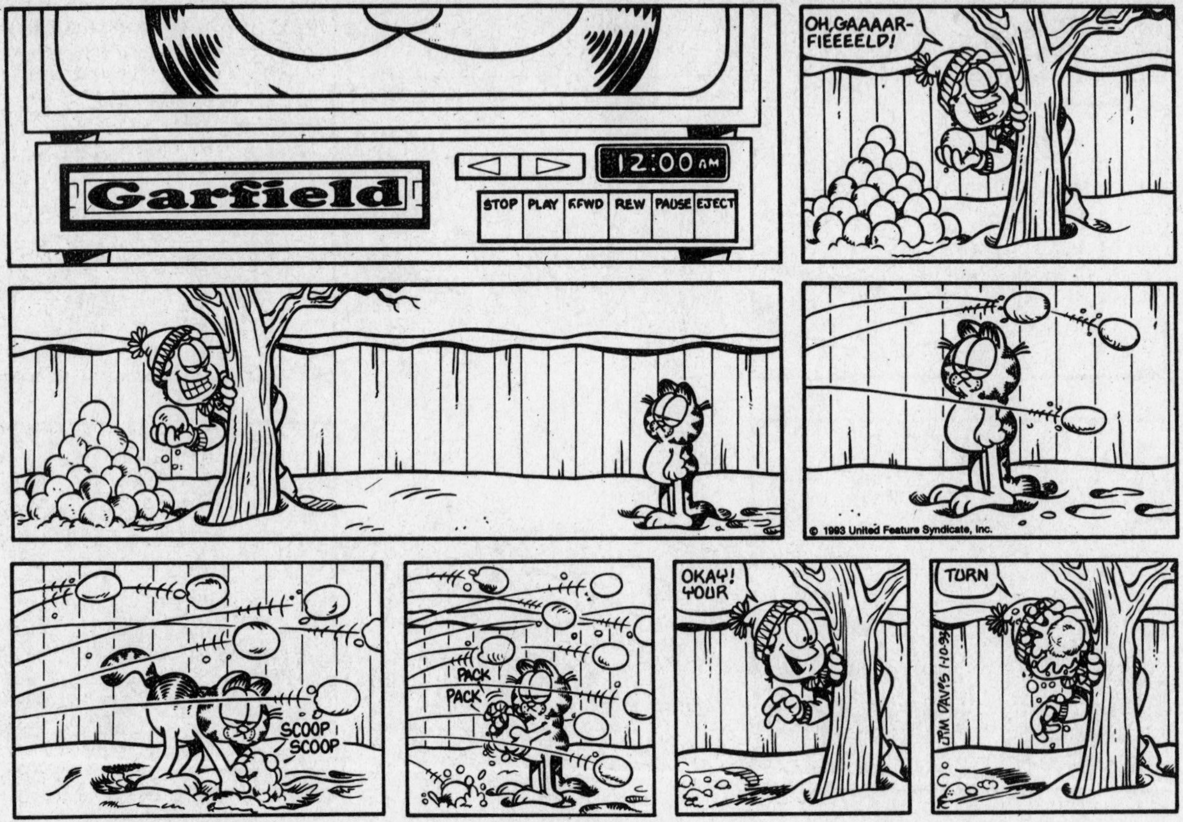
Garfield
12:00 AM
STOP PLAY FFWD REW PAUSE EJECT
OH, GAAAAR-FIEEEELD!
© 1993 United Feature Syndicate, Inc.
SCOOP SCOOP
PACK PACK
OKAY! YOUR
TURN
JIM DAVIS 1-10-93

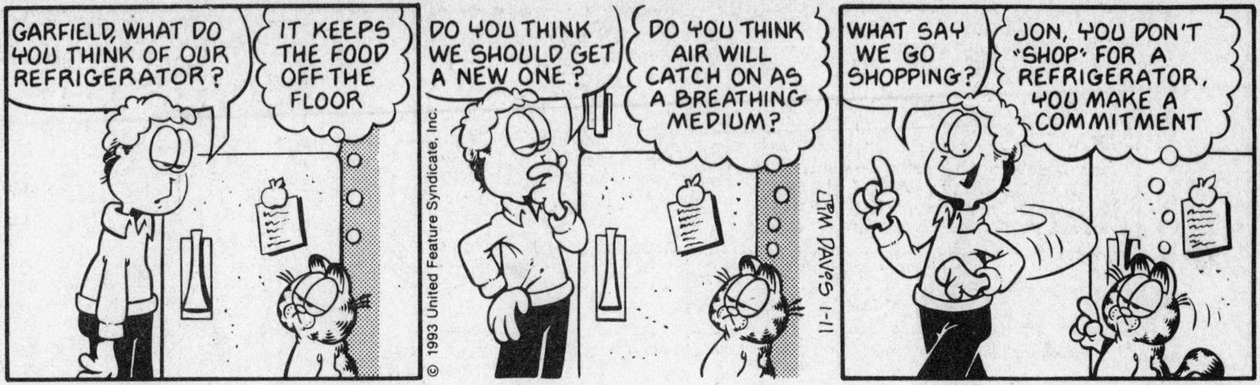

GARFIELD, WHAT DO YOU THINK OF OUR REFRIGERATOR?
IT KEEPS THE FOOD OFF THE FLOOR
DO YOU THINK WE SHOULD GET A NEW ONE?
DO YOU THINK AIR WILL CATCH ON AS A BREATHING MEDIUM?
© 1993 United Feature Syndicate, Inc.
JIM DAVIS 1-11
WHAT SAY WE GO SHOPPING?
JON, YOU DON'T "SHOP" FOR A REFRIGERATOR, YOU MAKE A COMMITMENT

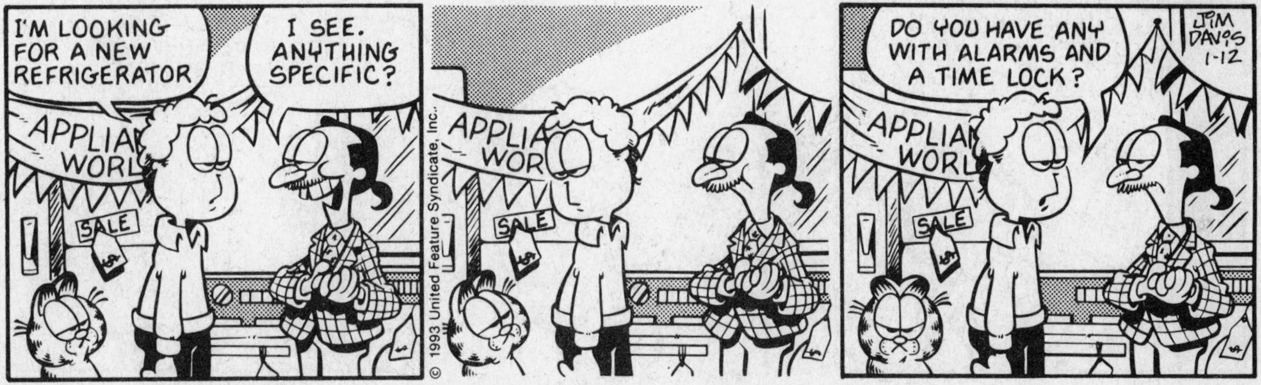

I'M LOOKING FOR A NEW REFRIGERATOR
I SEE. ANYTHING SPECIFIC?
APPLIA
WORL
SALE
© 1993 United Feature Syndicate, Inc.
DO YOU HAVE ANY WITH ALARMS AND A TIME LOCK?
JIM DAVIS 1-12

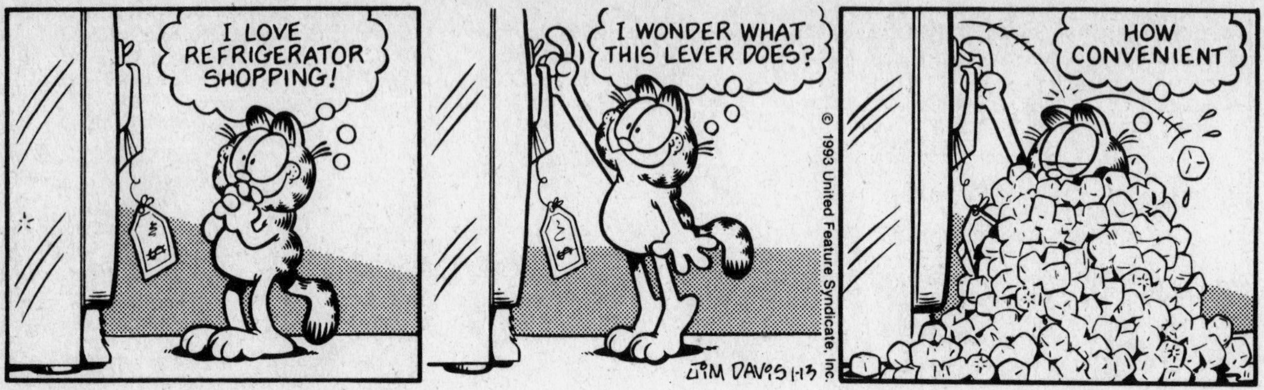
I LOVE REFRIGERATOR SHOPPING!
I WONDER WHAT THIS LEVER DOES?
HOW CONVENIENT
JIM DAVIS 1-13
© 1993 United Feature Syndicate, Inc.

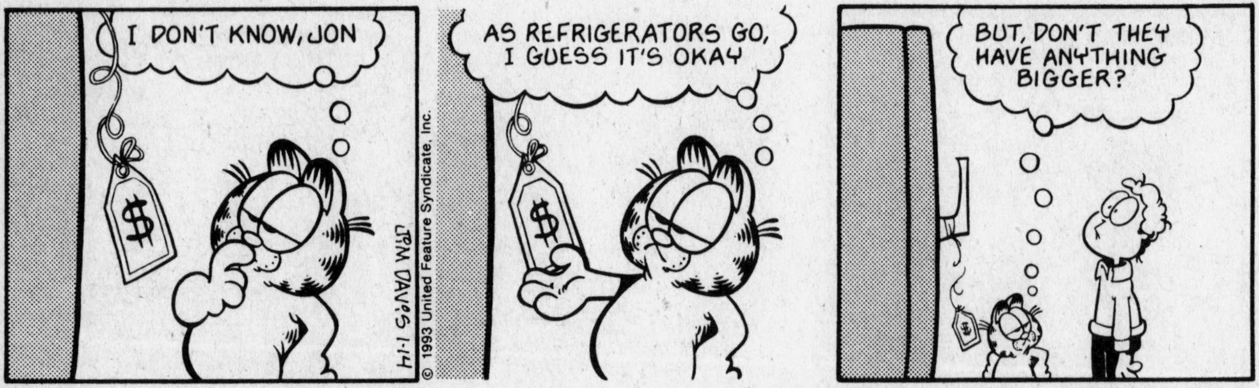
I DON'T KNOW, JON
AS REFRIGERATORS GO, I GUESS IT'S OKAY
BUT, DON'T THEY HAVE ANYTHING BIGGER?
JIM DAVIS 1-14
© 1993 United Feature Syndicate, Inc.

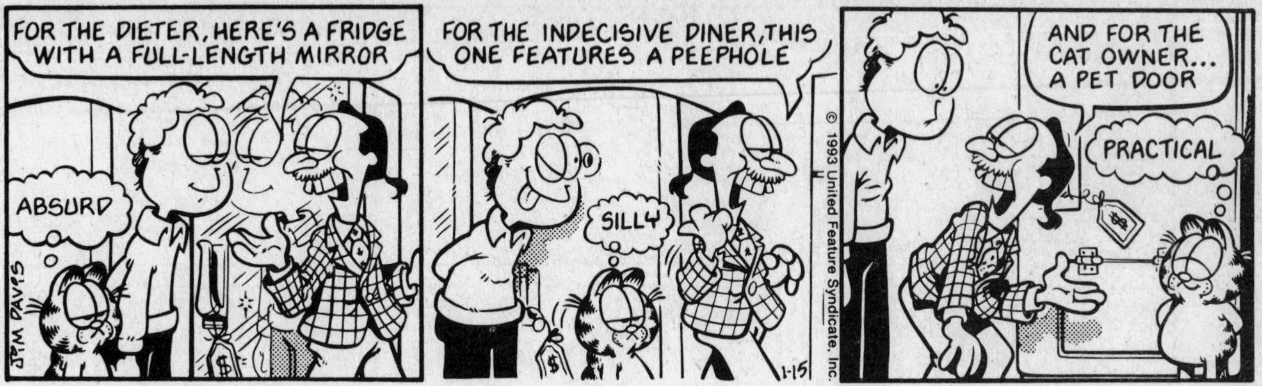
FOR THE DIETER, HERE'S A FRIDGE WITH A FULL-LENGTH MIRROR
ABSURD
JIM DAVIS
FOR THE INDECISIVE DINER, THIS ONE FEATURES A PEEPHOLE
SILLY
1-15
© 1993 United Feature Syndicate, Inc.
AND FOR THE CAT OWNER... A PET DOOR
PRACTICAL

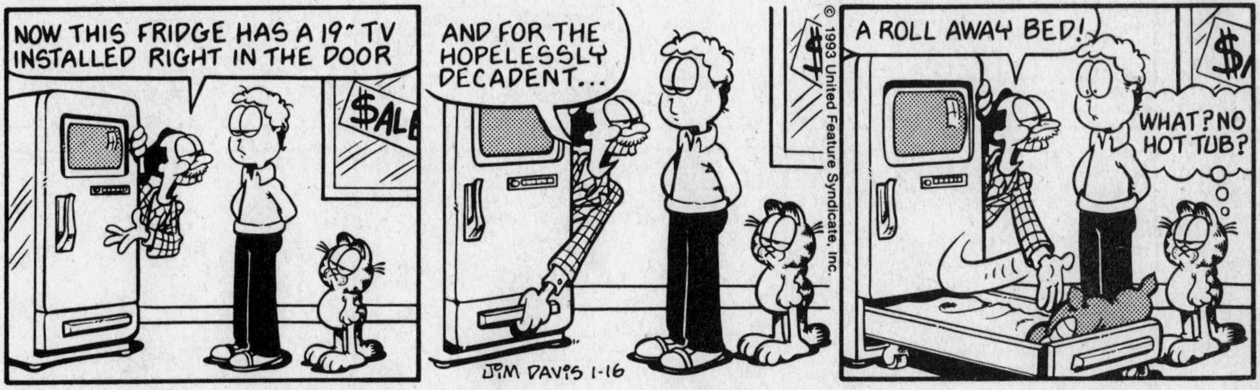
NOW THIS FRIDGE HAS A 19" TV INSTALLED RIGHT IN THE DOOR
$ALE
AND FOR THE HOPELESSLY DECADENT...
JIM DAVIS 1-16
© 1993 United Feature Syndicate, Inc.
A ROLL AWAY BED!
WHAT? NO HOT TUB?

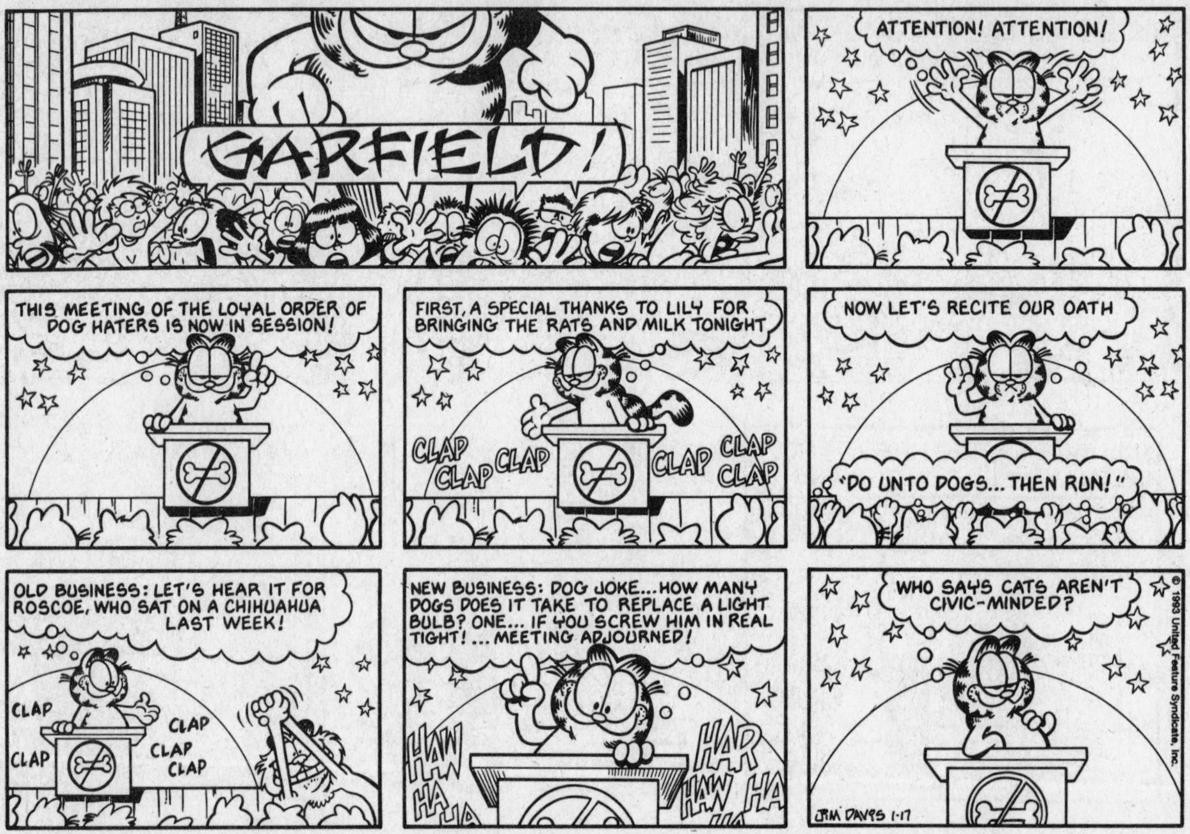
GARFIELD!
ATTENTION! ATTENTION!
THIS MEETING OF THE LOYAL ORDER OF DOG HATERS IS NOW IN SESSION!
FIRST, A SPECIAL THANKS TO LILY FOR BRINGING THE RATS AND MILK TONIGHT
CLAP CLAP CLAP CLAP CLAP CLAP
NOW LET'S RECITE OUR OATH
"DO UNTO DOGS... THEN RUN!"
OLD BUSINESS: LET'S HEAR IT FOR ROSCOE, WHO SAT ON A CHIHUAHUA LAST WEEK!
CLAP CLAP CLAP CLAP CLAP
NEW BUSINESS: DOG JOKE... HOW MANY DOGS DOES IT TAKE TO REPLACE A LIGHT BULB? ONE... IF YOU SCREW HIM IN REAL TIGHT! ... MEETING ADJOURNED!
HAW HA HAR HAW HA
WHO SAYS CATS AREN'T CIVIC-MINDED?
JIM DAVIS 1-17
© 1993 United Feature Syndicate, Inc.

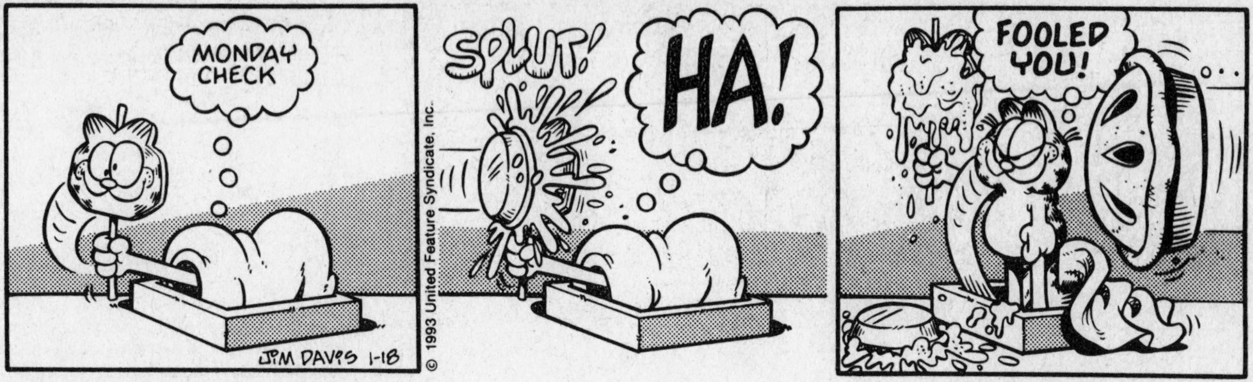
MONDAY CHECK
JIM DAVIS 1-18
© 1993 United Feature Syndicate, Inc.
SPLUT!
HA!
FOOLED YOU!
O . . .

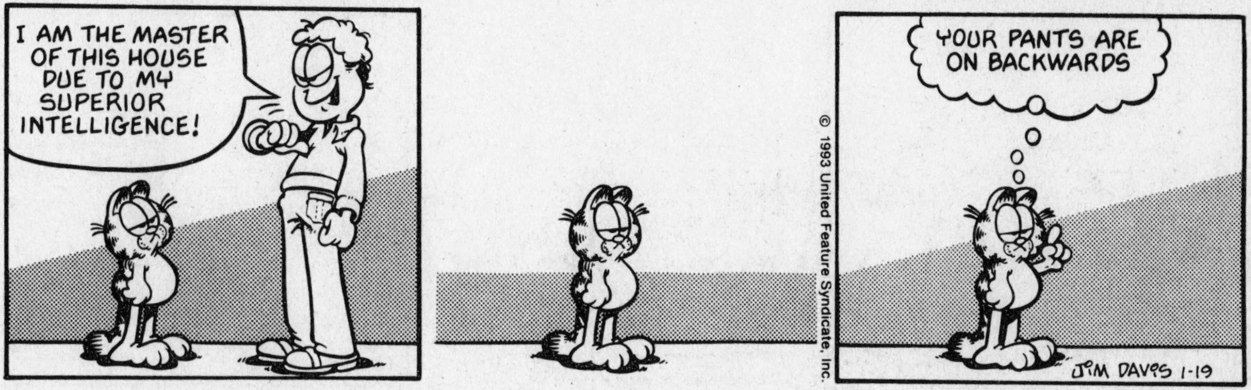
I AM THE MASTER OF THIS HOUSE DUE TO MY SUPERIOR INTELLIGENCE!
© 1993 United Feature Syndicate, Inc.
YOUR PANTS ARE ON BACKWARDS
JIM DAVIS 1-19

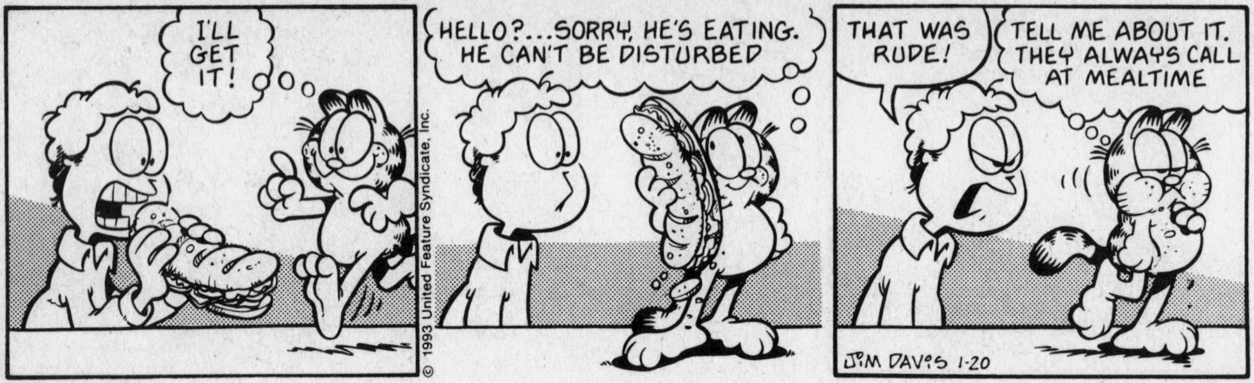
I'LL GET IT!
HELLO?...SORRY, HE'S EATING. HE CAN'T BE DISTURBED
THAT WAS RUDE!
TELL ME ABOUT IT. THEY ALWAYS CALL AT MEALTIME
JIM DAVIS 1-20
© 1993 United Feature Syndicate, Inc.

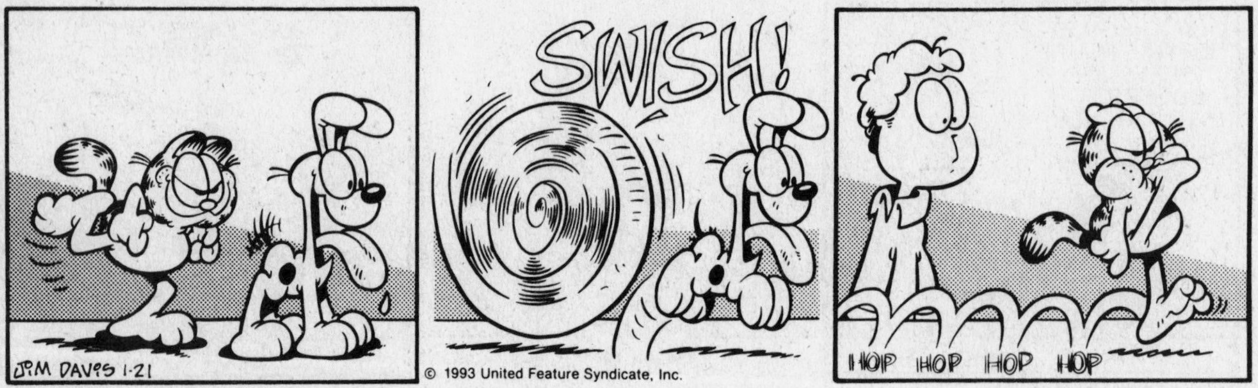
JIM DAVIS 1-21
SWISH!
HOP HOP HOP HOP
© 1993 United Feature Syndicate, Inc.

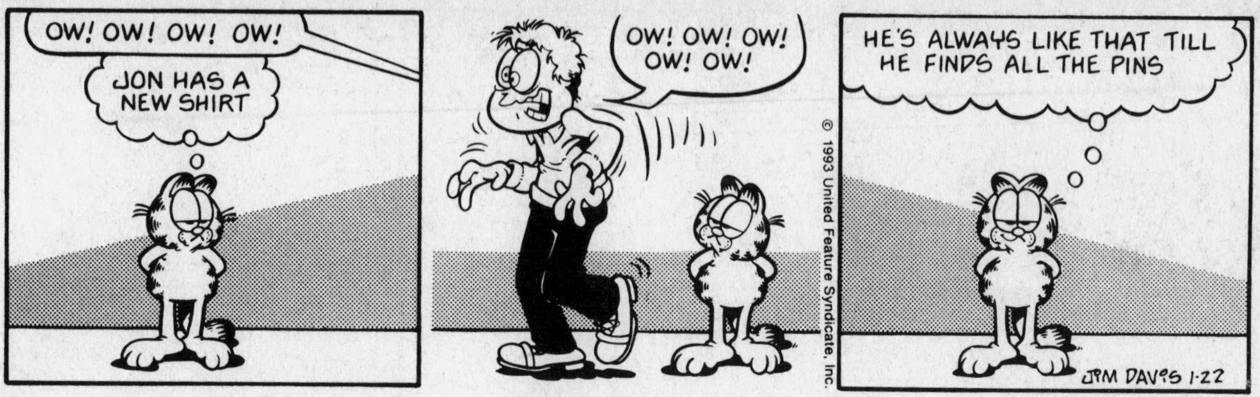
OW! OW! OW! OW!
JON HAS A NEW SHIRT
OW! OW! OW! OW! OW!
HE'S ALWAYS LIKE THAT TILL HE FINDS ALL THE PINS
JPM DAVPS 1-22
© 1993 United Feature Syndicate, Inc.

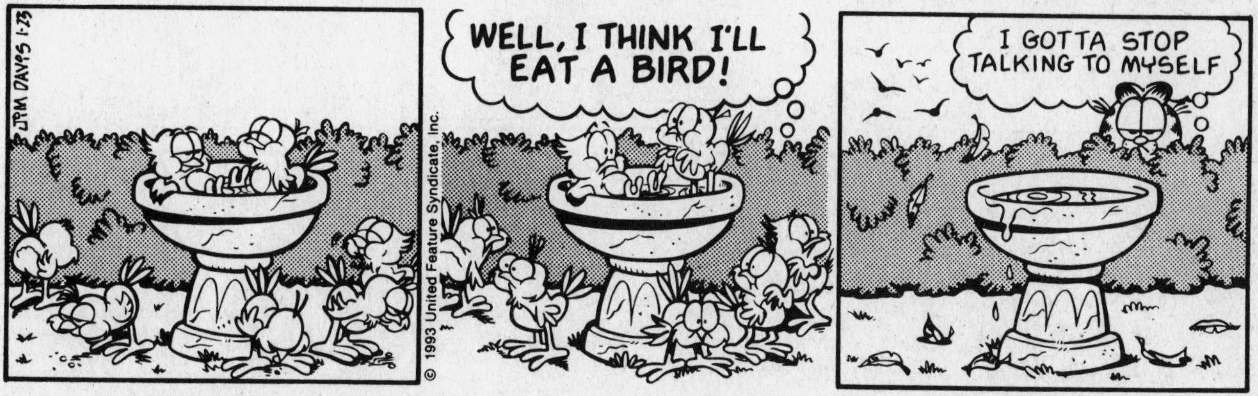
JPM DAVPS 1-23
© 1993 United Feature Syndicate, Inc.
WELL, I THINK I'LL EAT A BIRD!
I GOTTA STOP TALKING TO MYSELF

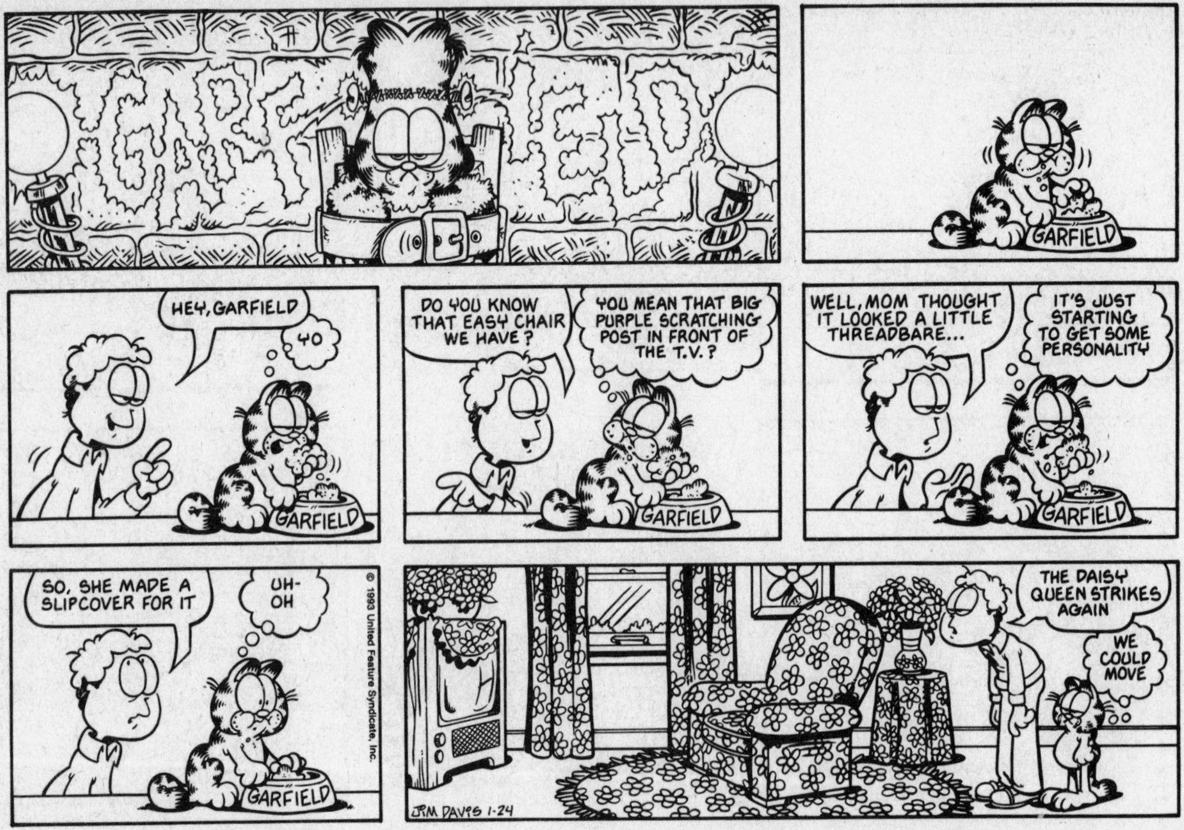
GARFIELD
GARFIELD
HEY, GARFIELD
YO
GARFIELD
DO YOU KNOW THAT EASY CHAIR WE HAVE?
YOU MEAN THAT BIG PURPLE SCRATCHING POST IN FRONT OF THE T.V.?
GARFIELD
WELL, MOM THOUGHT IT LOOKED A LITTLE THREADBARE...
IT'S JUST STARTING TO GET SOME PERSONALITY
GARFIELD
SO, SHE MADE A SLIPCOVER FOR IT
UH-OH
GARFIELD
© 1993 United Feature Syndicate, Inc.
THE DAISY QUEEN STRIKES AGAIN
WE COULD MOVE
JIM DAVIS 1-24

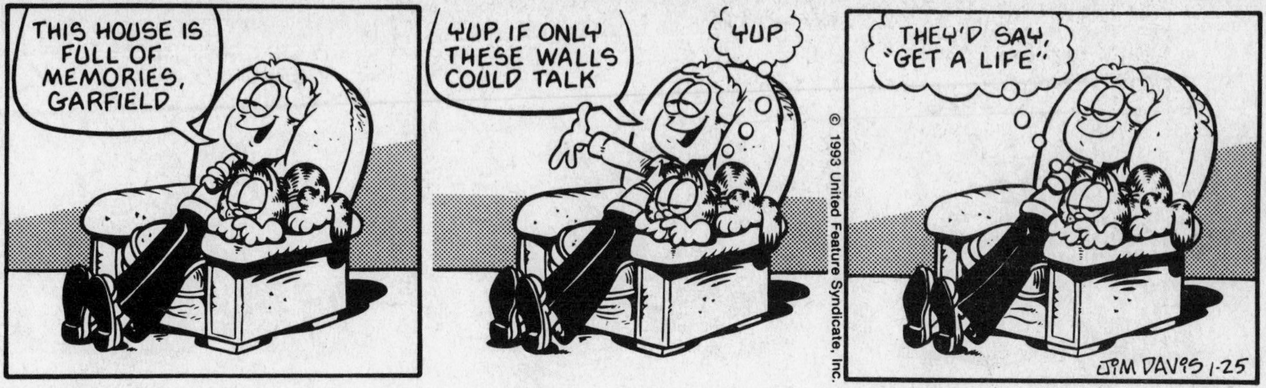
THIS HOUSE IS FULL OF MEMORIES, GARFIELD
YUP, IF ONLY THESE WALLS COULD TALK
YUP
THEY'D SAY, "GET A LIFE"
JIM DAVIS 1-25

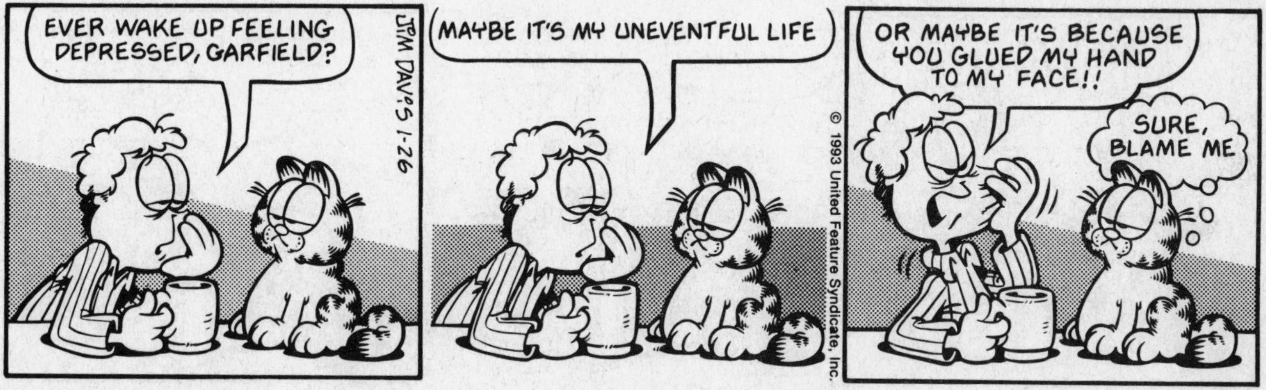
EVER WAKE UP FEELING DEPRESSED, GARFIELD?
JIM DAVIS 1-26
MAYBE IT'S MY UNEVENTFUL LIFE
OR MAYBE IT'S BECAUSE YOU GLUED MY HAND TO MY FACE!!
SURE, BLAME ME

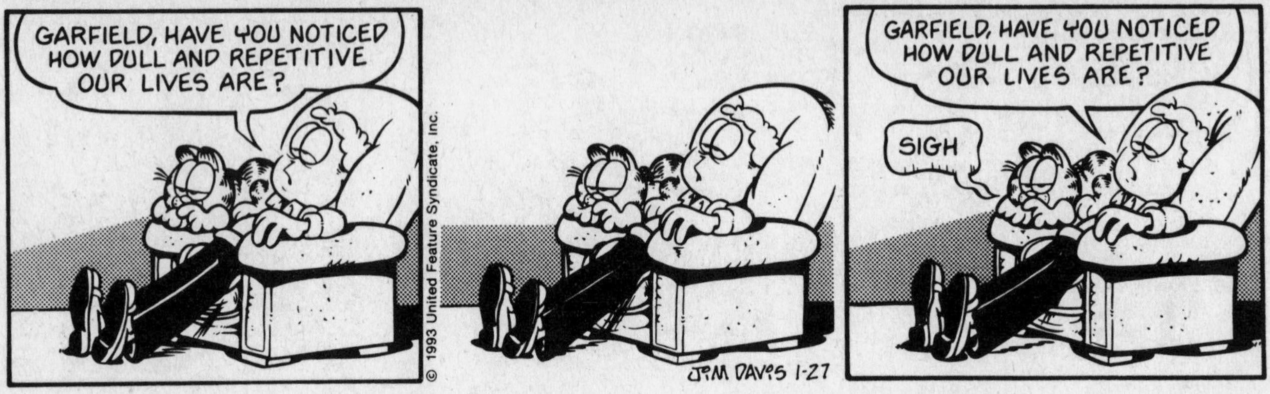
GARFIELD, HAVE YOU NOTICED HOW DULL AND REPETITIVE OUR LIVES ARE?
© 1993 United Feature Syndicate, Inc.
JIM DAVIS 1-27
GARFIELD, HAVE YOU NOTICED HOW DULL AND REPETITIVE OUR LIVES ARE?
SIGH

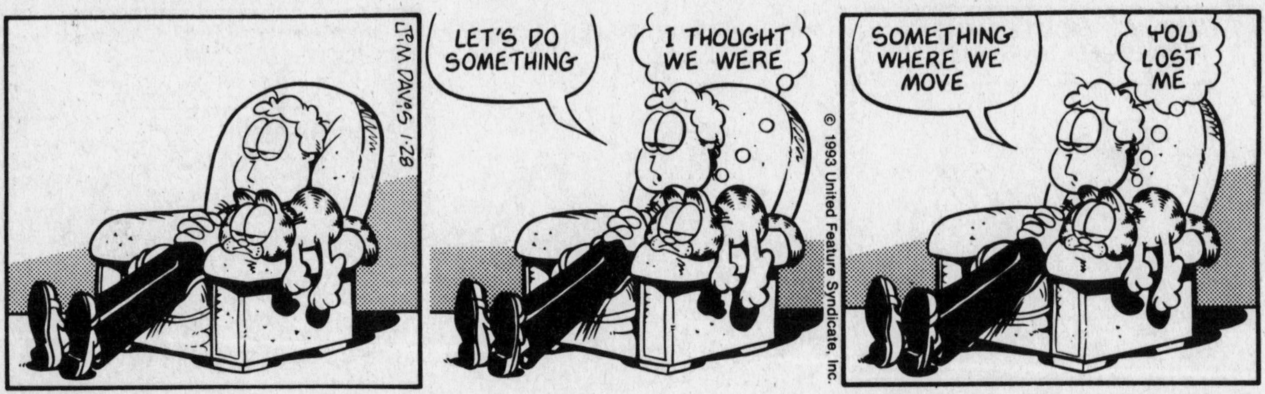
JIM DAVIS 1-28
LET'S DO SOMETHING
I THOUGHT WE WERE
© 1993 United Feature Syndicate, Inc.
SOMETHING WHERE WE MOVE
YOU LOST ME

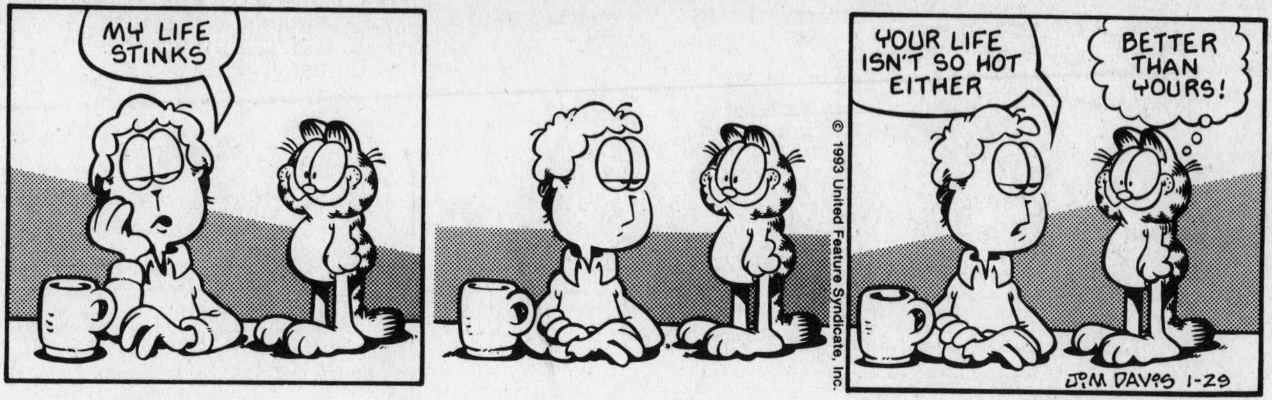
MY LIFE STINKS
YOUR LIFE ISN'T SO HOT EITHER
BETTER THAN YOURS!
© 1993 United Feature Syndicate, Inc.
JIM DAVIS 1-29

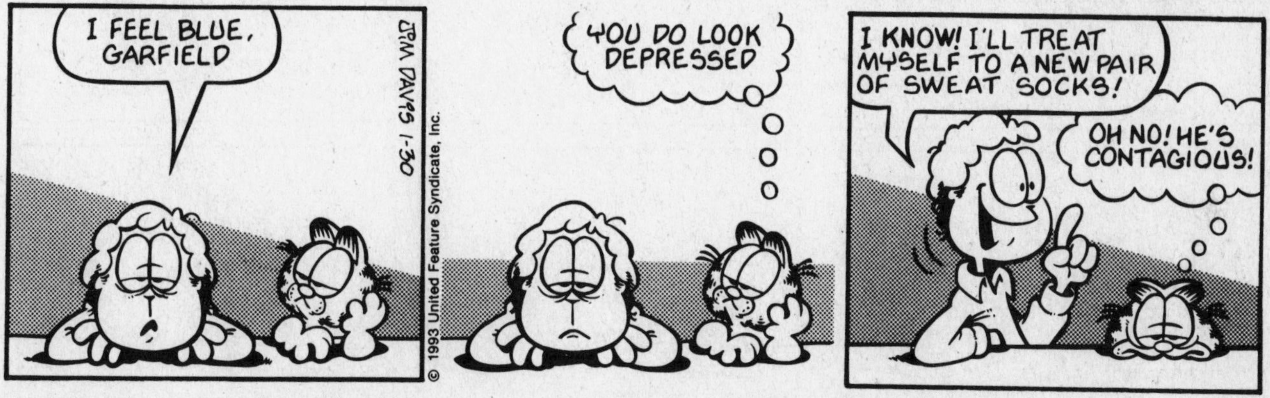
I FEEL BLUE, GARFIELD
JIM DAVIS 1-30
© 1993 United Feature Syndicate, Inc.
YOU DO LOOK DEPRESSED
I KNOW! I'LL TREAT MYSELF TO A NEW PAIR OF SWEAT SOCKS!
OH NO! HE'S CONTAGIOUS!

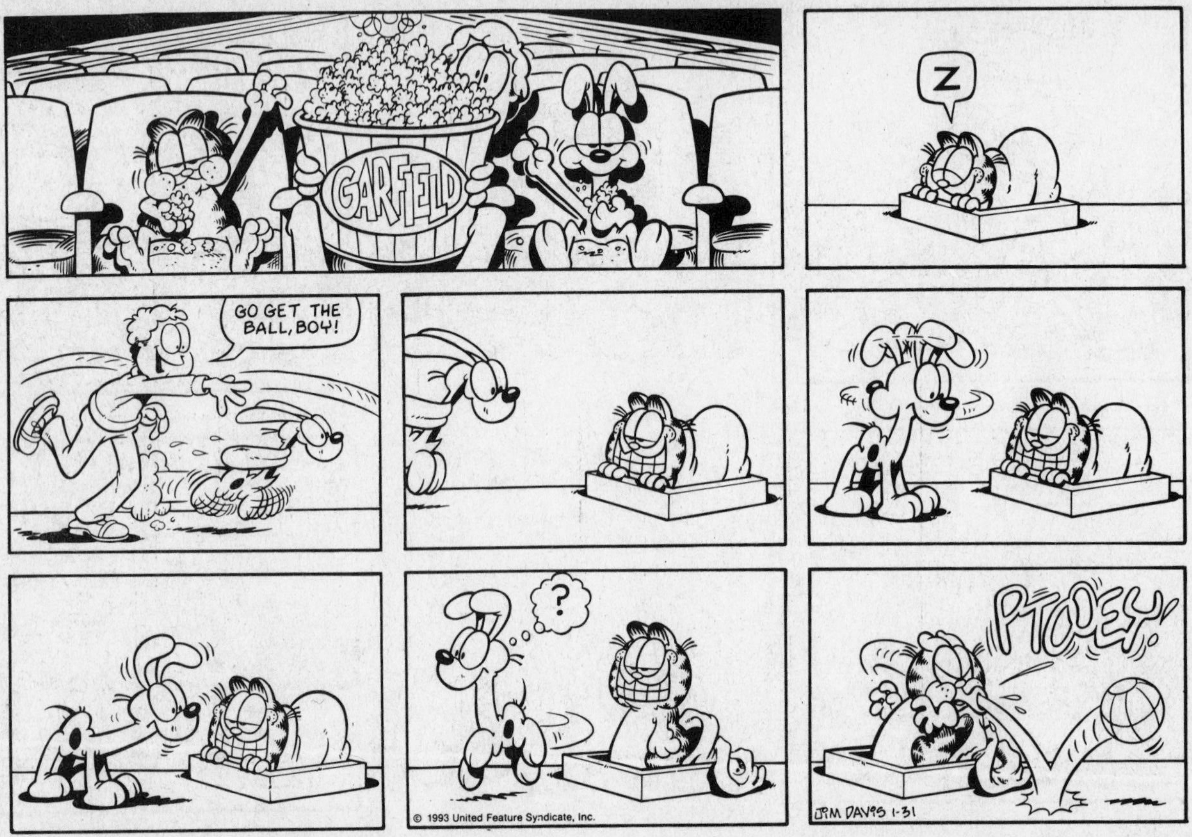
GARFIELD
Z
GO GET THE BALL, BOY!
?
PTOOEY!
© 1993 United Feature Syndicate, Inc.
JIM DAVIS 1-31

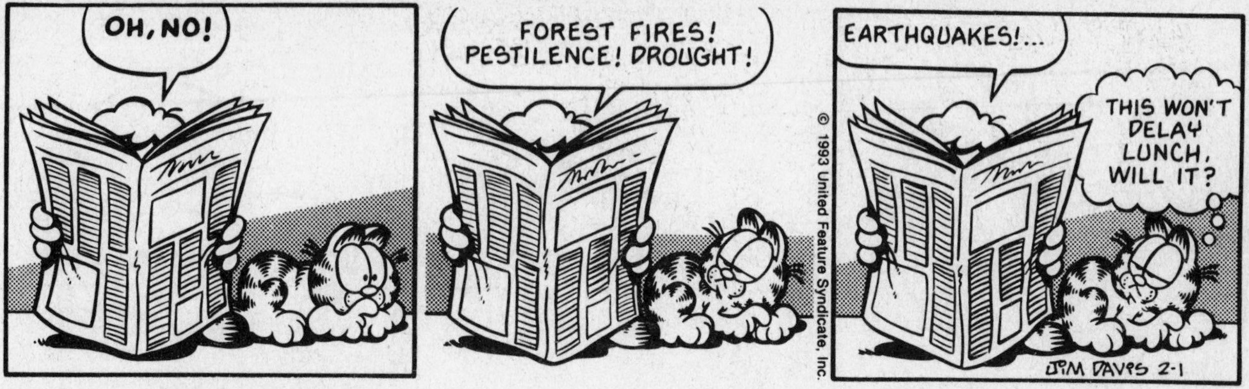
OH, NO!
FOREST FIRES! PESTILENCE! DROUGHT!
© 1993 United Feature Syndicate, Inc.
EARTHQUAKES!...
THIS WON'T DELAY LUNCH, WILL IT?
JIM DAVIS 2-1

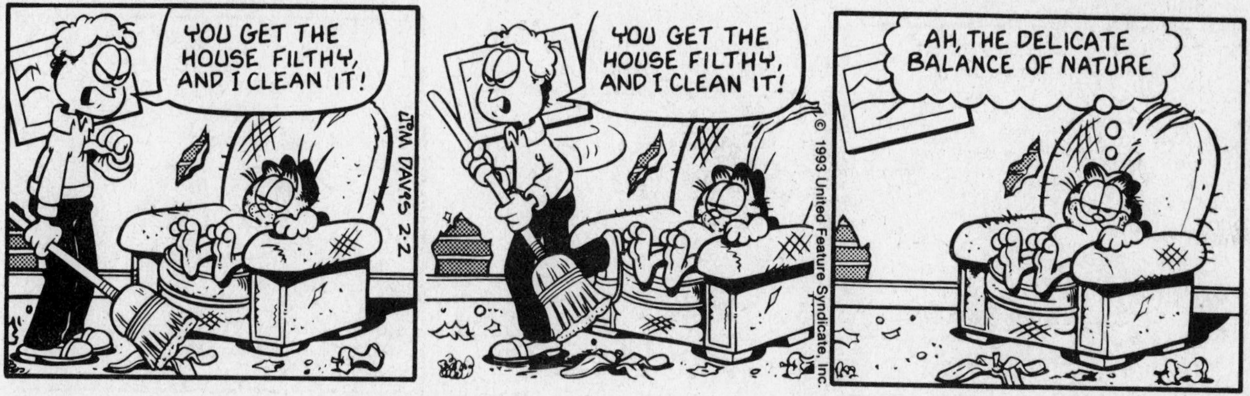
YOU GET THE HOUSE FILTHY, AND I CLEAN IT!
JIM DAVIS 2-2
YOU GET THE HOUSE FILTHY, AND I CLEAN IT!
© 1993 United Feature Syndicate, Inc.
AH, THE DELICATE BALANCE OF NATURE

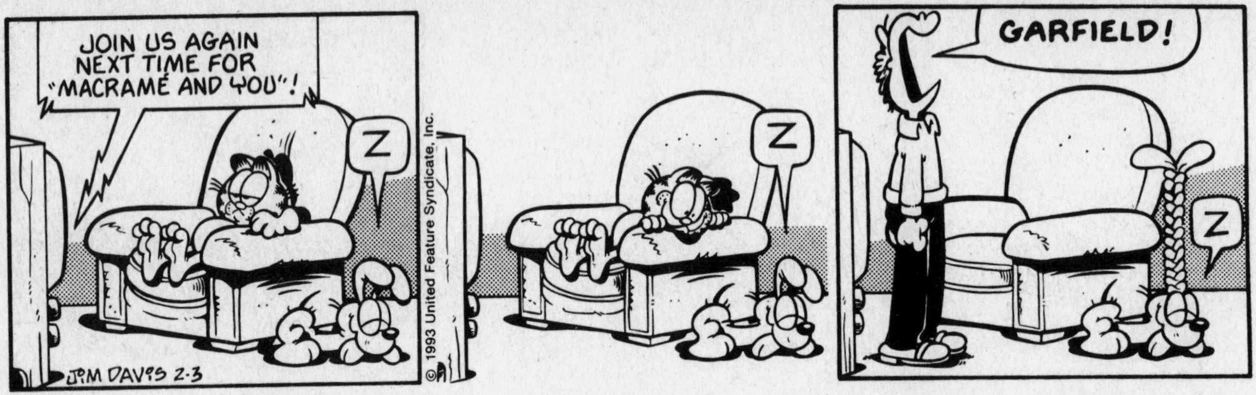
JOIN US AGAIN NEXT TIME FOR "MACRAMÉ AND YOU"!
Z
Z
GARFIELD!
Z
JIM DAVIS 2-3
© 1993 United Feature Syndicate, Inc.

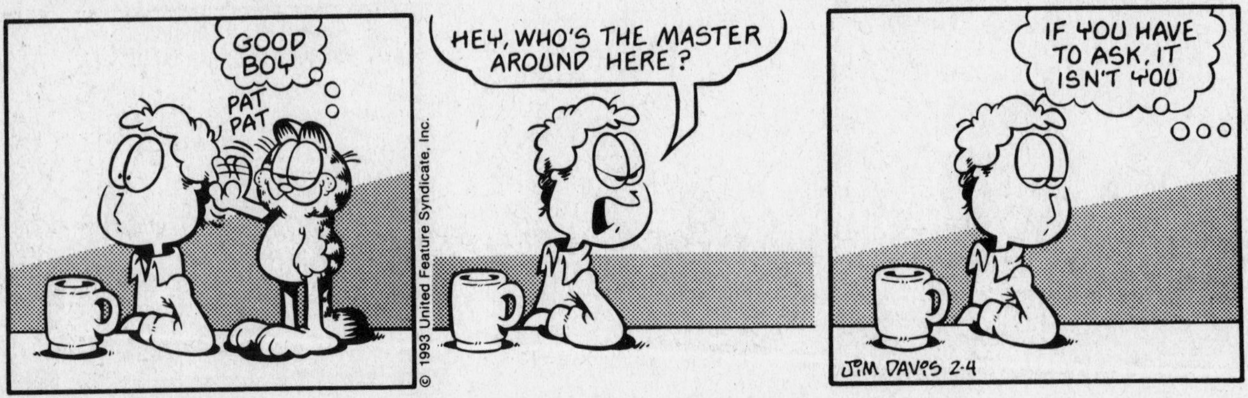
GOOD BOY
PAT PAT
HEY, WHO'S THE MASTER AROUND HERE?
IF YOU HAVE TO ASK, IT ISN'T YOU
JIM DAVIS 2-4
© 1993 United Feature Syndicate, Inc.

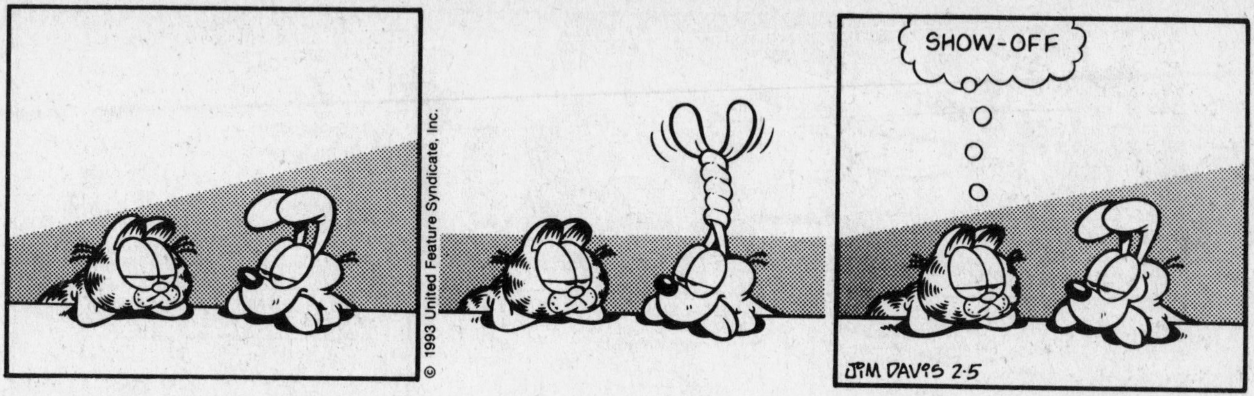
© 1993 United Feature Syndicate, Inc.
SHOW-OFF
JIM DAVIS 2-5

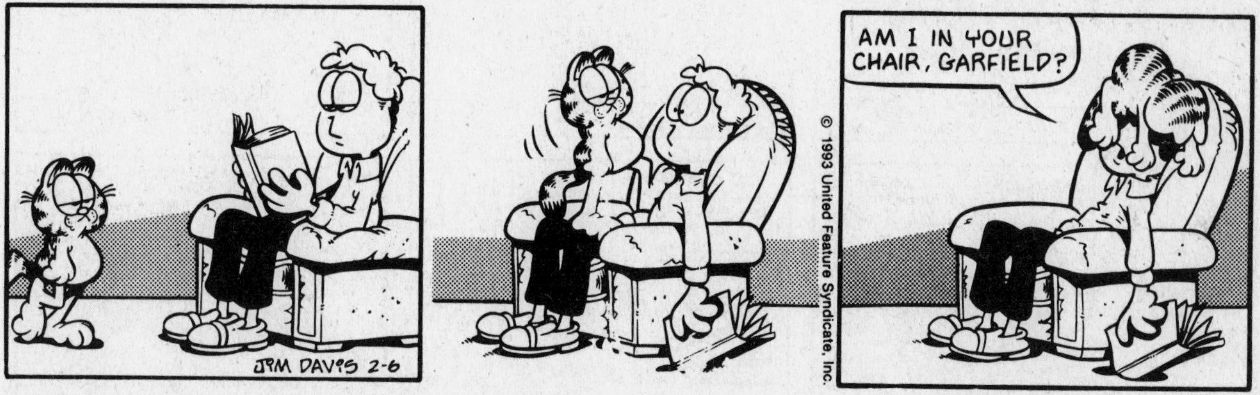
JIM DAVIS 2-6
© 1993 United Feature Syndicate, Inc.
AM I IN YOUR CHAIR, GARFIELD?

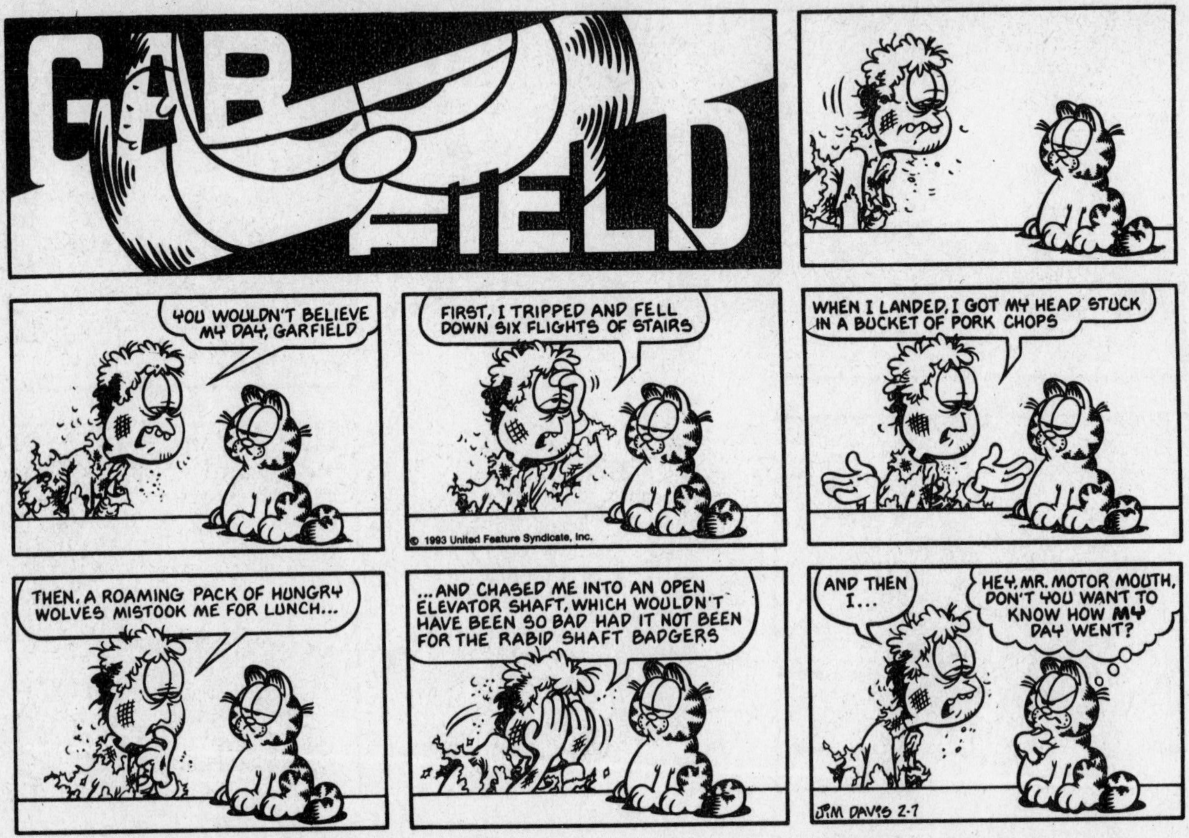
GARFIELD
YOU WOULDN'T BELIEVE MY DAY, GARFIELD
FIRST, I TRIPPED AND FELL DOWN SIX FLIGHTS OF STAIRS
© 1993 United Feature Syndicate, Inc.
WHEN I LANDED, I GOT MY HEAD STUCK IN A BUCKET OF PORK CHOPS
THEN, A ROAMING PACK OF HUNGRY WOLVES MISTOOK ME FOR LUNCH...
...AND CHASED ME INTO AN OPEN ELEVATOR SHAFT, WHICH WOULDN'T HAVE BEEN SO BAD HAD IT NOT BEEN FOR THE RABID SHAFT BADGERS
AND THEN I...
HEY, MR. MOTOR MOUTH, DON'T YOU WANT TO KNOW HOW MY DAY WENT?
JIM DAVIS 2-7

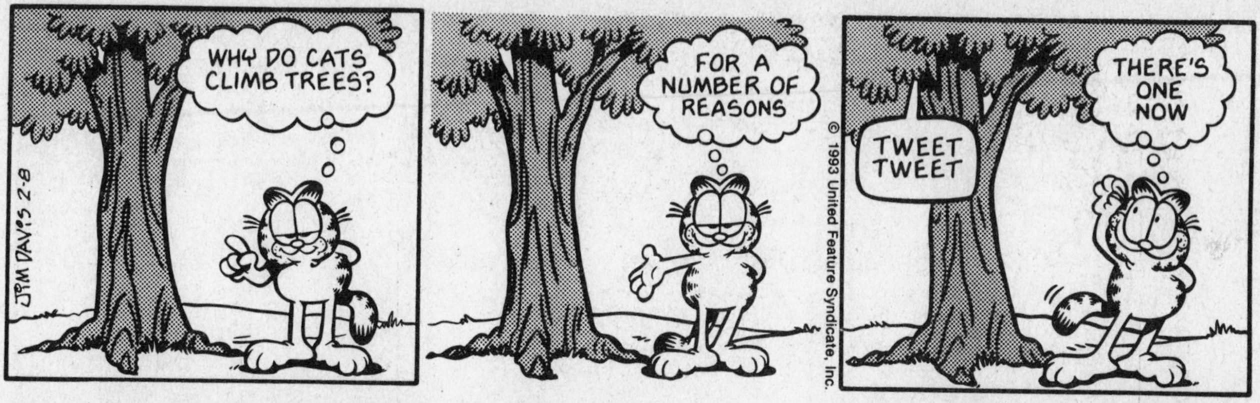
JIM DAVIS 2-8
WHY DO CATS CLIMB TREES?
FOR A NUMBER OF REASONS
© 1993 United Feature Syndicate, Inc.
TWEET TWEET
THERE'S ONE NOW

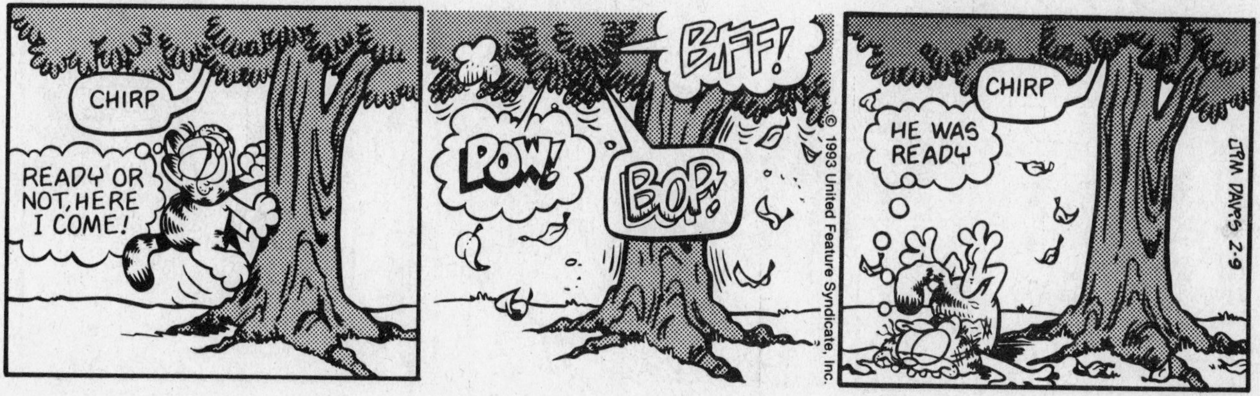
CHIRP
READY OR NOT, HERE I COME!
BIFF!
POW!
BOP!
© 1993 United Feature Syndicate, Inc.
CHIRP
HE WAS READY
JIM DAVIS 2-9

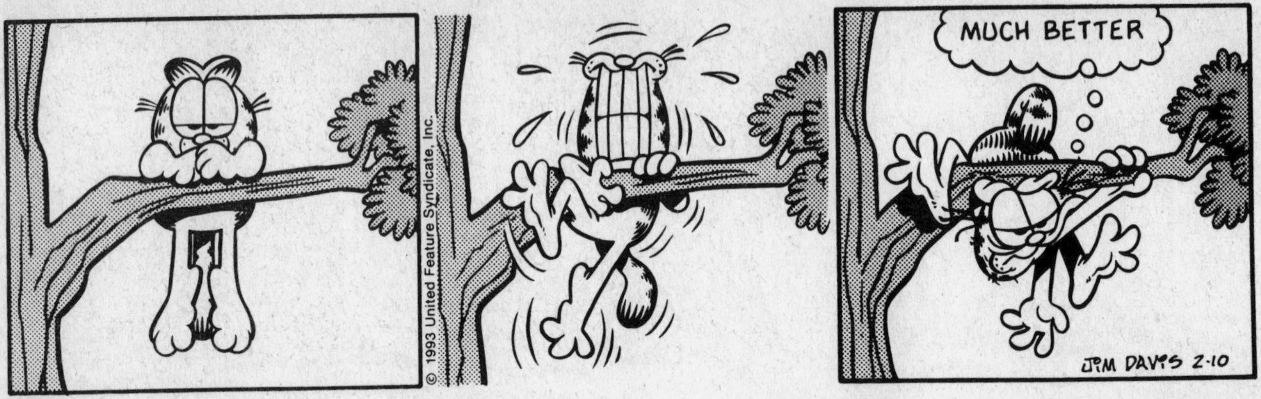
© 1993 United Feature Syndicate, Inc.
MUCH BETTER
JIM DAVIS 2-10

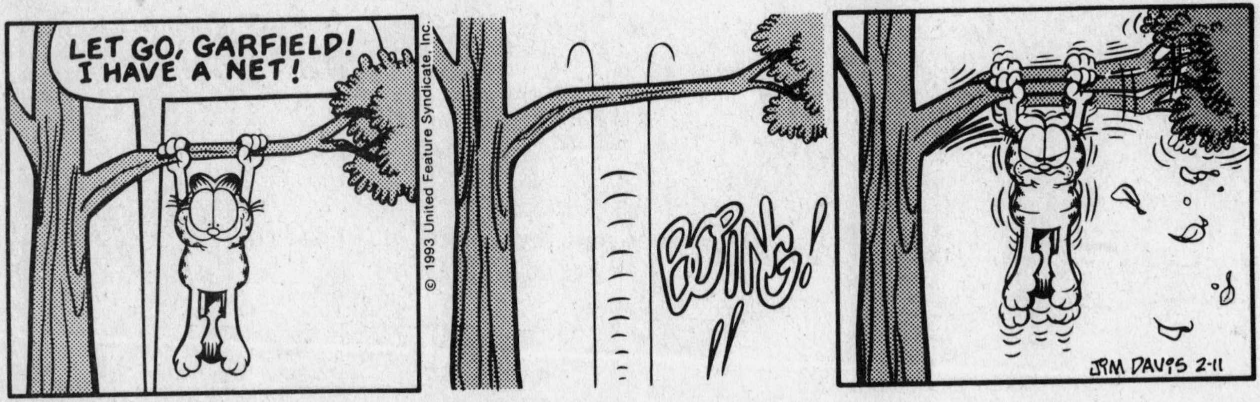
LET GO, GARFIELD! I HAVE A NET!
© 1993 United Feature Syndicate, Inc.
BOING!
JIM DAVIS 2-11

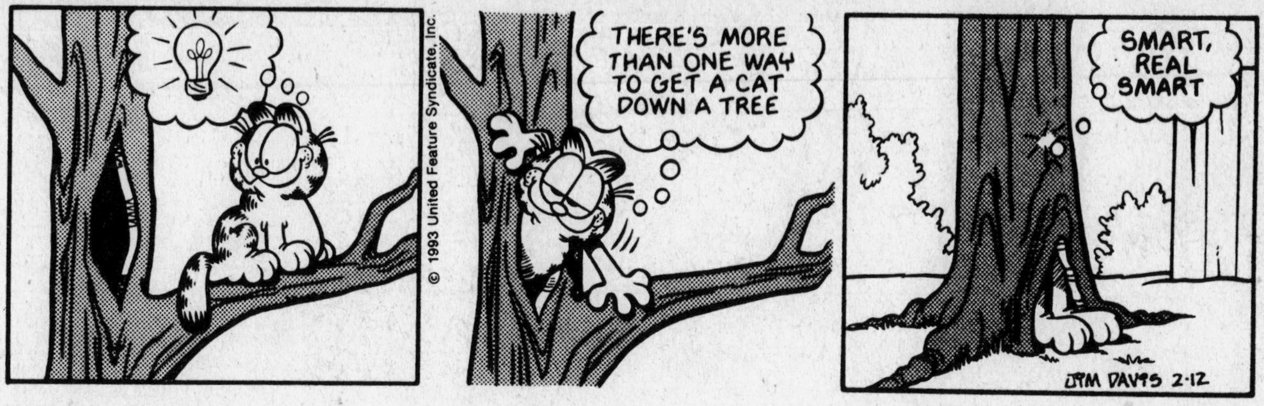

THERE'S MORE THAN ONE WAY TO GET A CAT DOWN A TREE
SMART, REAL SMART
JIM DAVIS 2-12
© 1993 United Feature Syndicate, Inc.

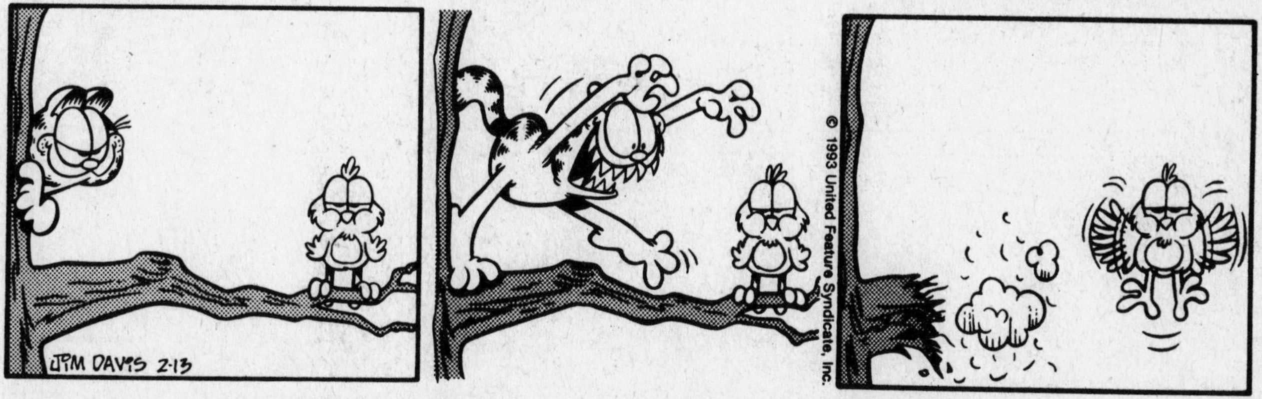

JIM DAVIS 2-13
© 1993 United Feature Syndicate, Inc.

GARFIELD
ODIE
ODIE
CONGRATULATIONS, ODIEEE!!!
ODIE
YOU HAVE JUST WON AN ALL EXPENSES PAID VACATION TO THE BACKYARD!
ODIE
FIRST, A PHOTO FOR THE PRESS
CLICK
ODIE
BON VOYAGE, YOU LUCKY PUP! SEND A POSTCARD!
ODIE
© 1993 United Feature Syndicate, Inc.
JIM DAVIS 2-14

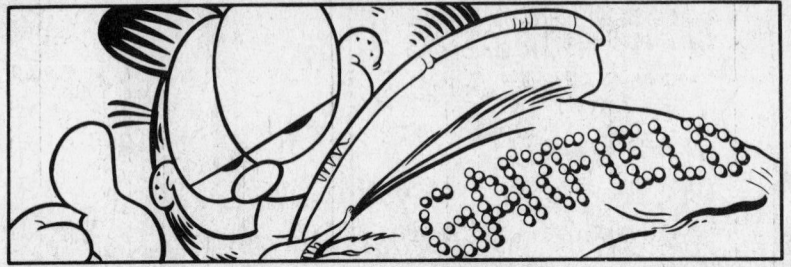

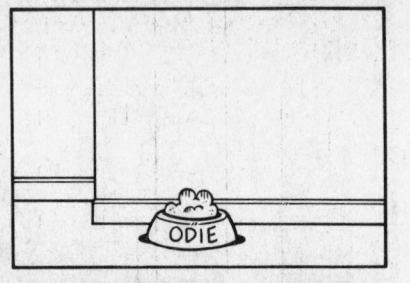

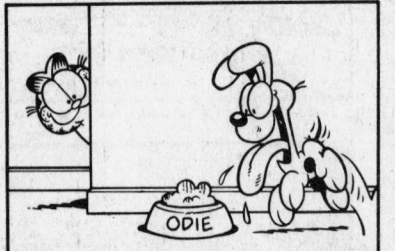

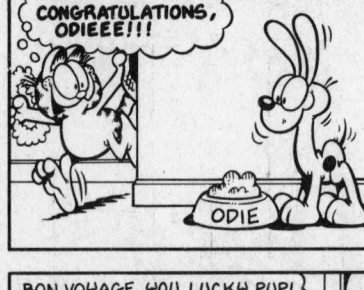

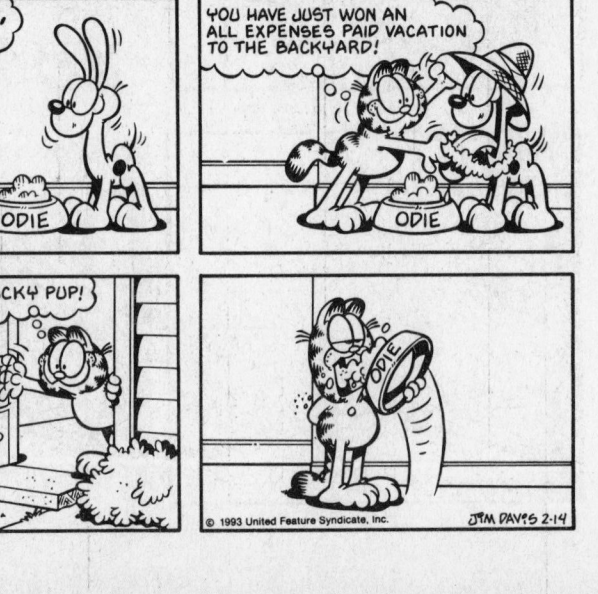

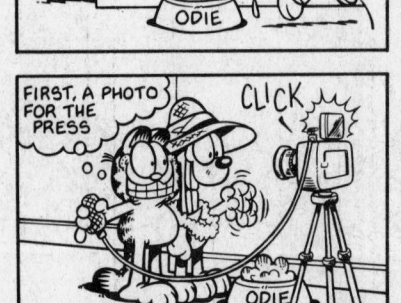

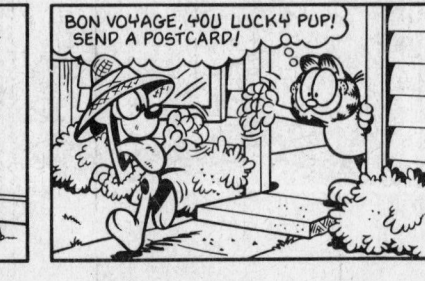

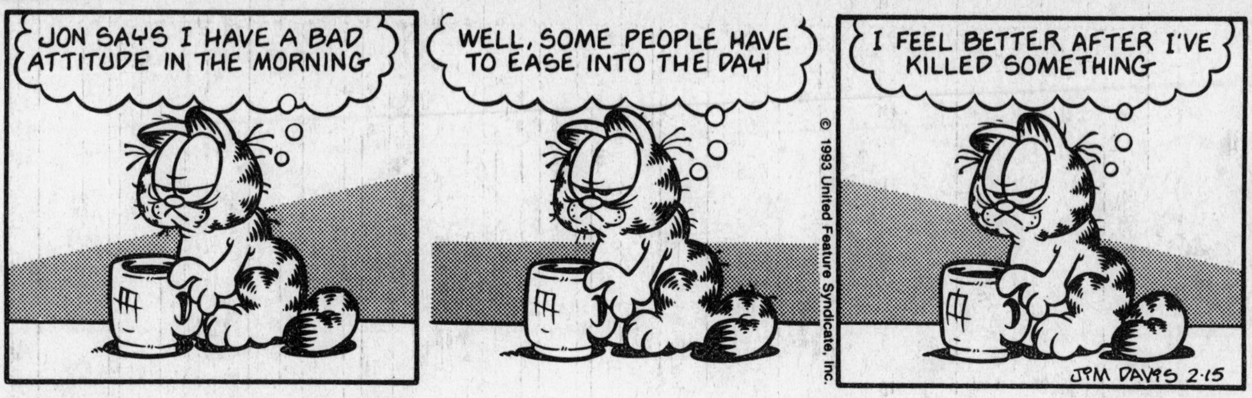
JON SAYS I HAVE A BAD ATTITUDE IN THE MORNING
WELL, SOME PEOPLE HAVE TO EASE INTO THE DAY
I FEEL BETTER AFTER I'VE KILLED SOMETHING
© 1993 United Feature Syndicate, Inc.
JIM DAVIS 2·15

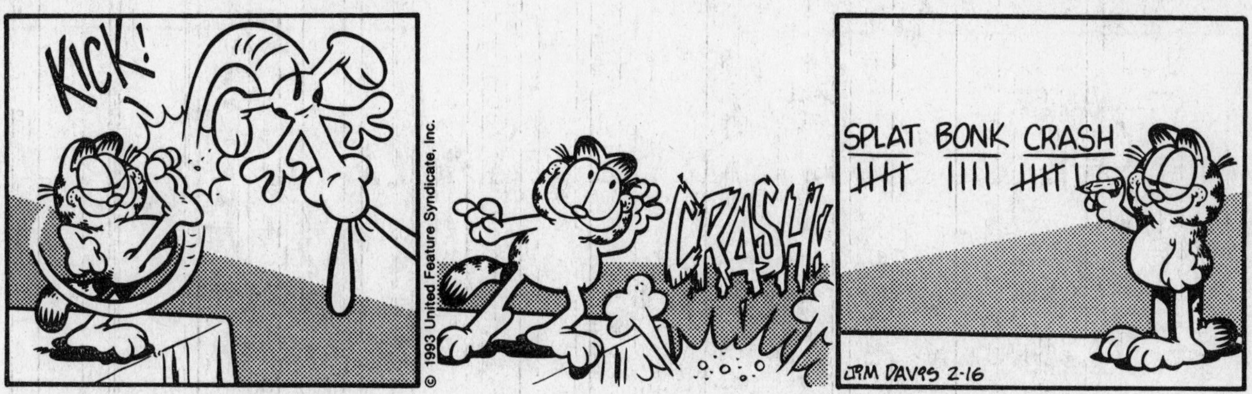
KICK!
CRASH!
SPLAT
BONK
CRASH
© 1993 United Feature Syndicate, Inc.
JIM DAVIS 2-16

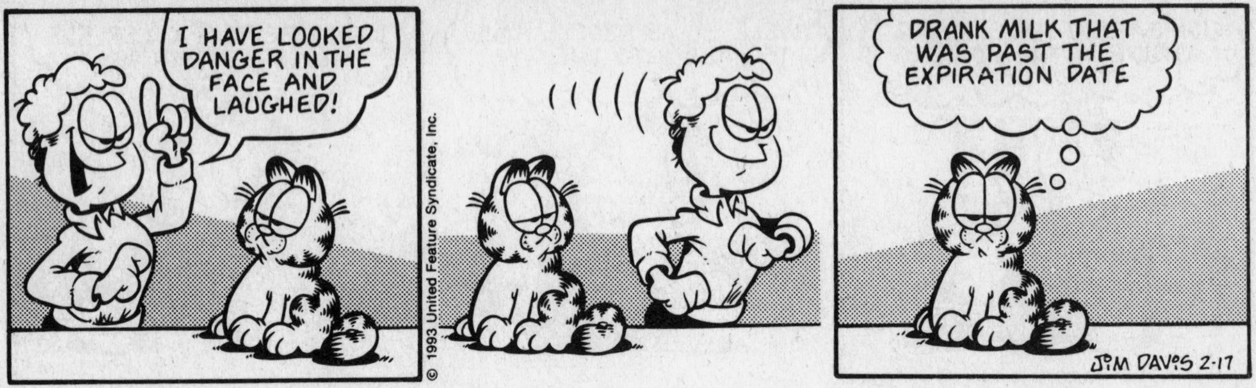
I HAVE LOOKED DANGER IN THE FACE AND LAUGHED!
DRANK MILK THAT WAS PAST THE EXPIRATION DATE
JIM DAVIS 2-17
© 1993 United Feature Syndicate, Inc.

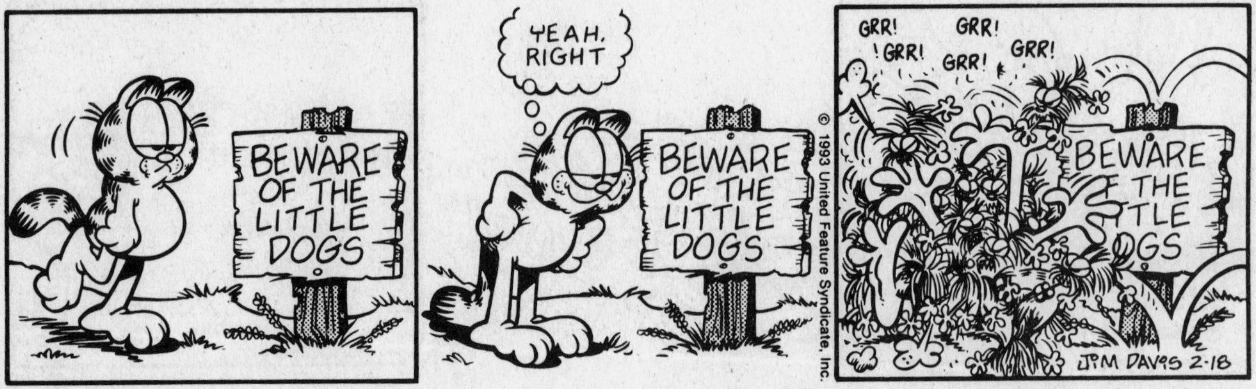
BEWARE OF THE LITTLE DOGS
YEAH, RIGHT
BEWARE OF THE LITTLE DOGS
GRR! GRR! GRR! GRR! GRR! GRR!
JIM DAVIS 2-18
© 1993 United Feature Syndicate, Inc.

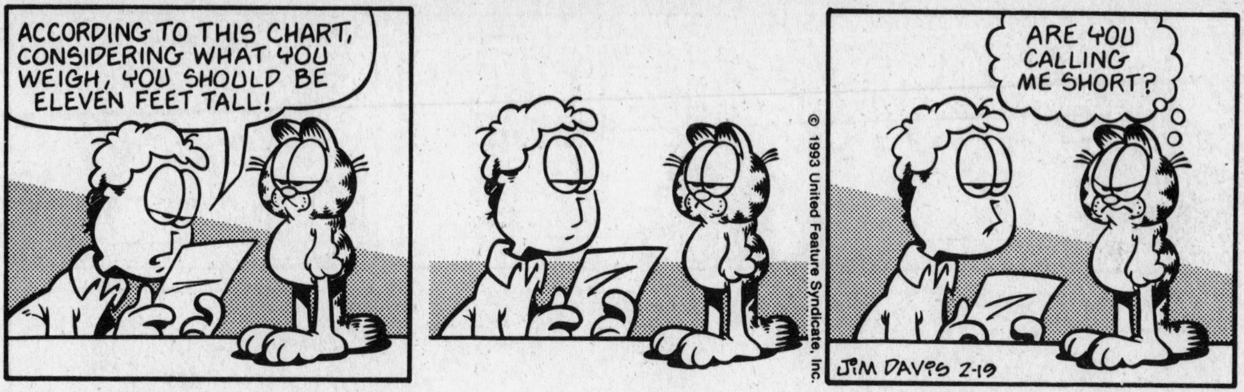
ACCORDING TO THIS CHART, CONSIDERING WHAT YOU WEIGH, YOU SHOULD BE ELEVEN FEET TALL!
ARE YOU CALLING ME SHORT?
JIM DAVIS 2-19
© 1993 United Feature Syndicate, Inc.

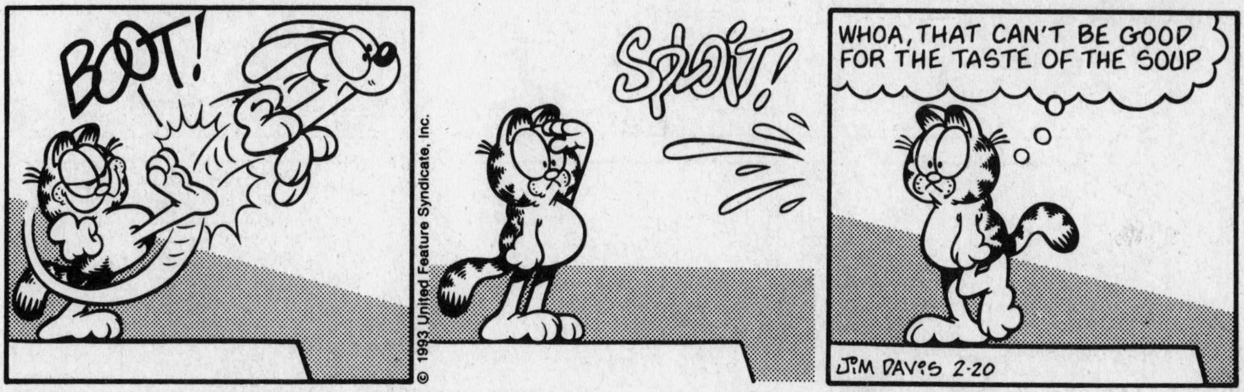
BOOT!
SPLOIT!
WHOA, THAT CAN'T BE GOOD FOR THE TASTE OF THE SOUP
JIM DAVIS 2-20
© 1993 United Feature Syndicate, Inc.

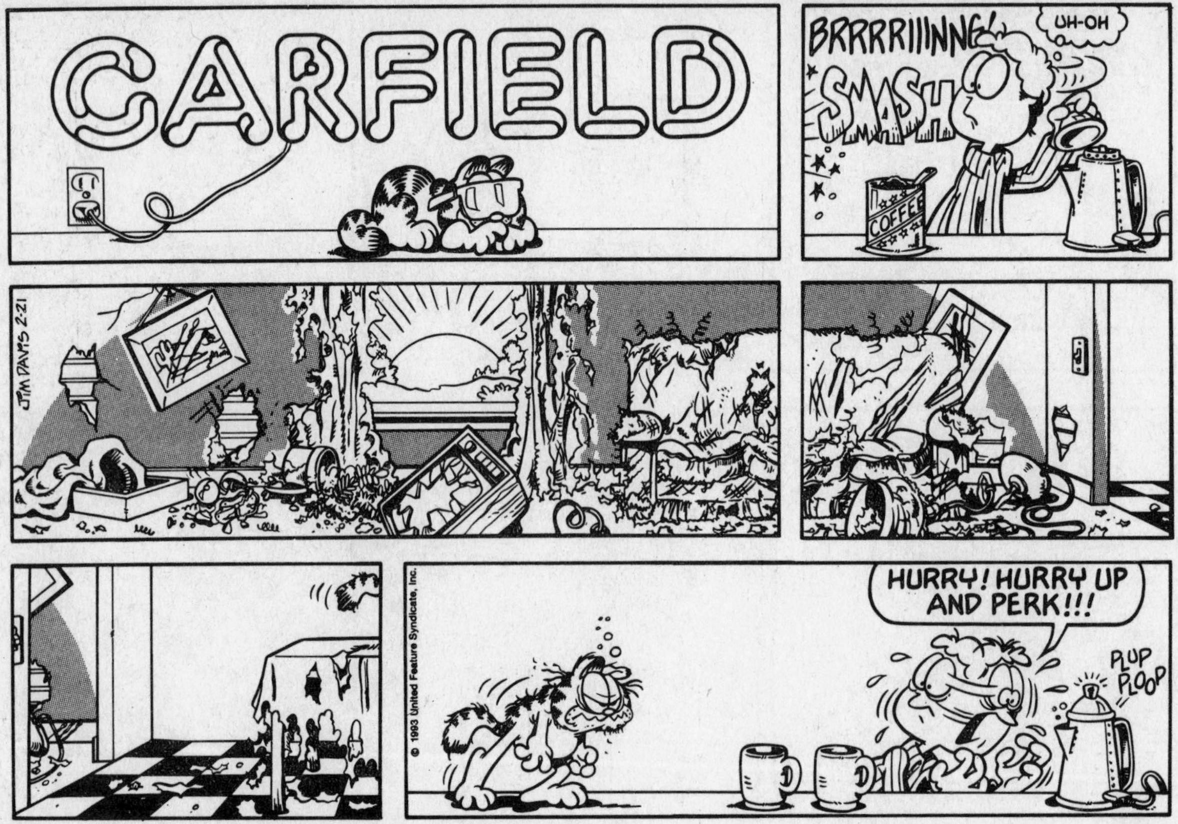
GARFIELD
BRRRRIIINNG!
UH-OH
SMASH
COFFEE
JIM DAVIS 2-21
© 1993 United Feature Syndicate, Inc.
HURRY! HURRY UP AND PERK!!!
PLUP PLOOP

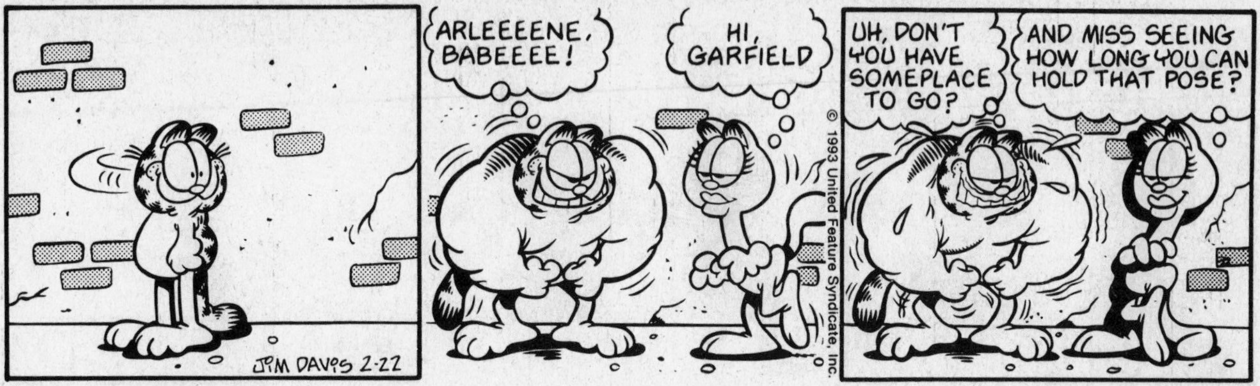
JIM DAVIS 2-22
ARLEEEENE, BABEEEEE!
HI, GARFIELD
© 1993 United Feature Syndicate, Inc.
UH, DON'T YOU HAVE SOMEPLACE TO GO?
AND MISS SEEING HOW LONG YOU CAN HOLD THAT POSE?

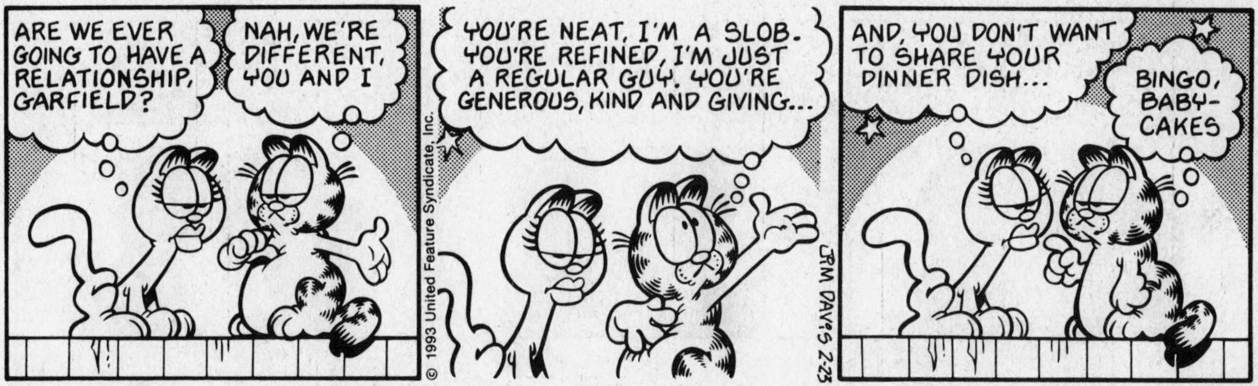
ARE WE EVER GOING TO HAVE A RELATIONSHIP, GARFIELD?
NAH, WE'RE DIFFERENT, YOU AND I
© 1993 United Feature Syndicate, Inc.
YOU'RE NEAT, I'M A SLOB. YOU'RE REFINED, I'M JUST A REGULAR GUY. YOU'RE GENEROUS, KIND AND GIVING...
JIM DAVIS 2-23
AND, YOU DON'T WANT TO SHARE YOUR DINNER DISH...
BINGO, BABY-CAKES

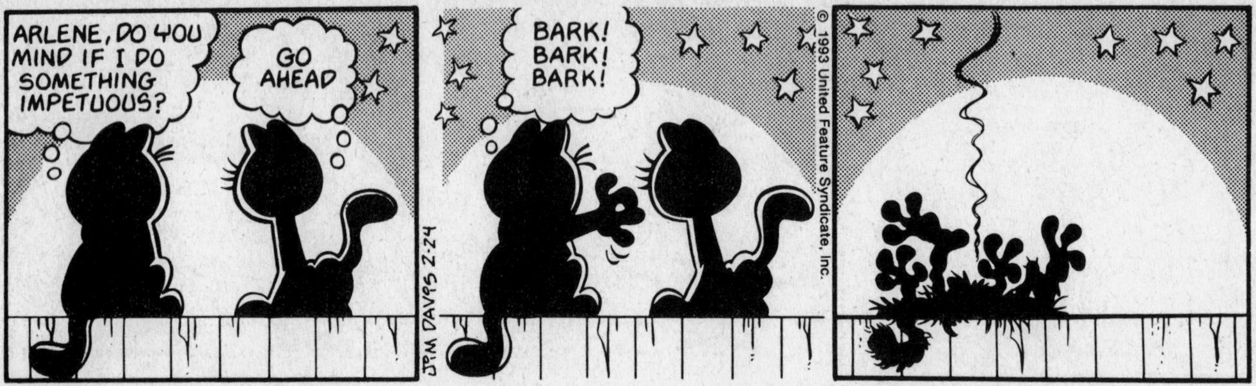
ARLENE, DO YOU MIND IF I DO SOMETHING IMPETUOUS?
GO AHEAD
BARK! BARK! BARK!
JPM DAVPS 2-24
© 1993 United Feature Syndicate, Inc.

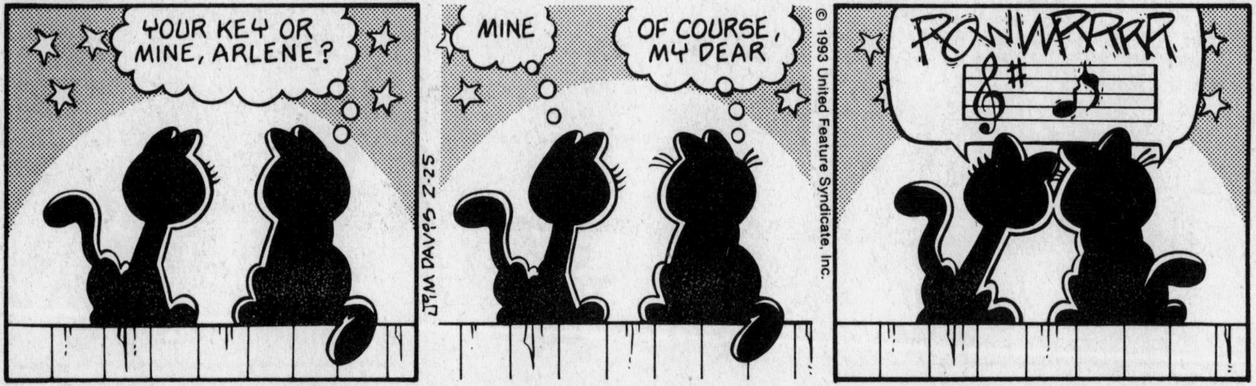
YOUR KEY OR MINE, ARLENE?
MINE
OF COURSE, MY DEAR
JPM DAVPS 2-25
© 1993 United Feature Syndicate, Inc.
ROWWRRRR

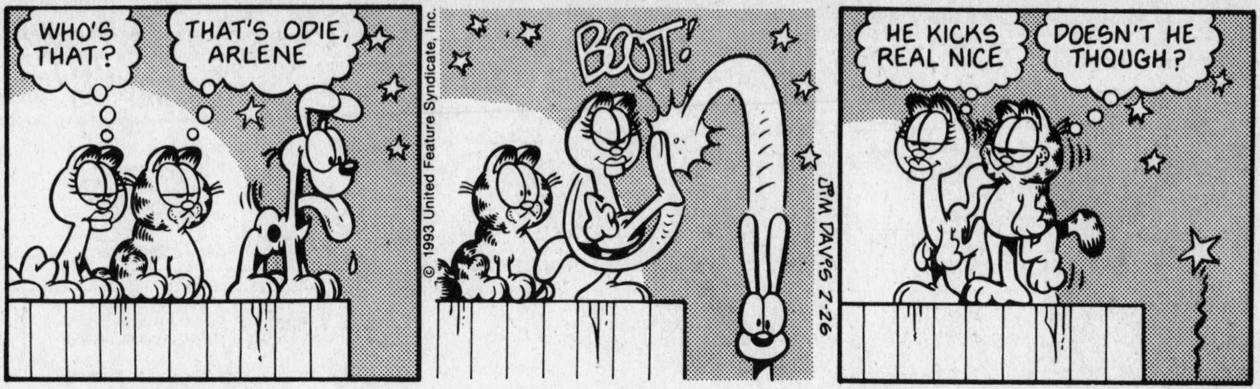
WHO'S THAT?
THAT'S ODIE, ARLENE
BOOT!
HE KICKS REAL NICE
DOESN'T HE THOUGH?
© 1993 United Feature Syndicate, Inc.
JIM DAVIS 2-26

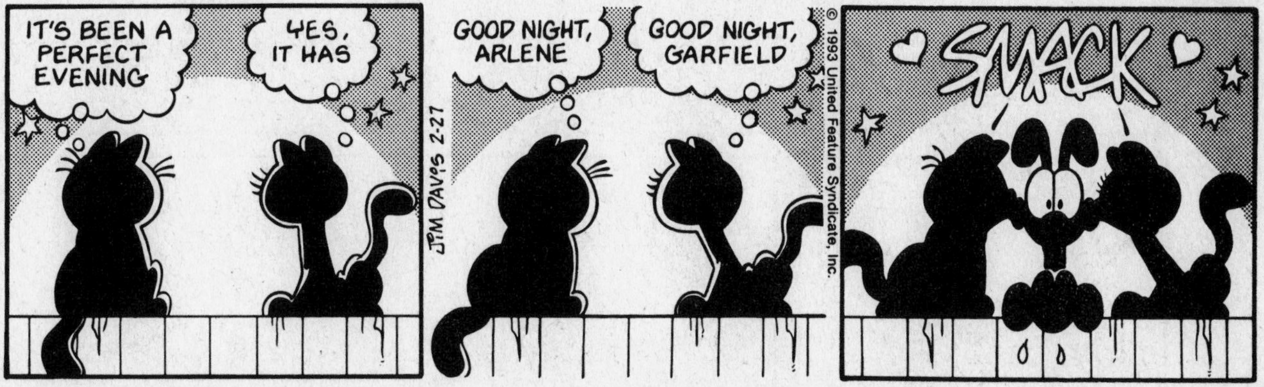
IT'S BEEN A PERFECT EVENING
YES, IT HAS
GOOD NIGHT, ARLENE
GOOD NIGHT, GARFIELD
SMACK
JIM DAVIS 2-27
© 1993 United Feature Syndicate, Inc.

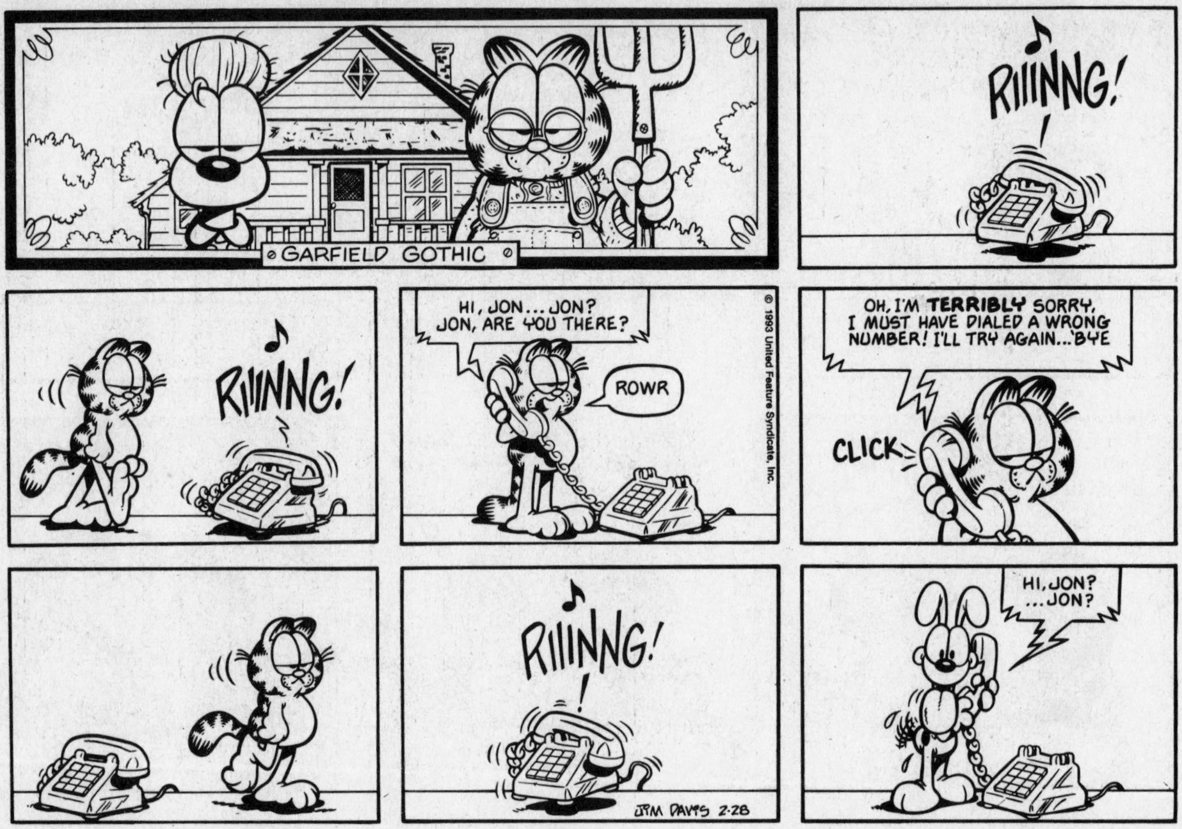
GARFIELD GOTHIC
RIIINNG!
RIIINNG!
HI, JON... JON? JON, ARE YOU THERE?
ROWR
OH, I'M TERRIBLY SORRY, I MUST HAVE DIALED A WRONG NUMBER! I'LL TRY AGAIN...'BYE
CLICK
RIIINNG!
JIM DAVIS 2-28
HI, JON? ...JON?
© 1993 United Feature Syndicate, Inc.

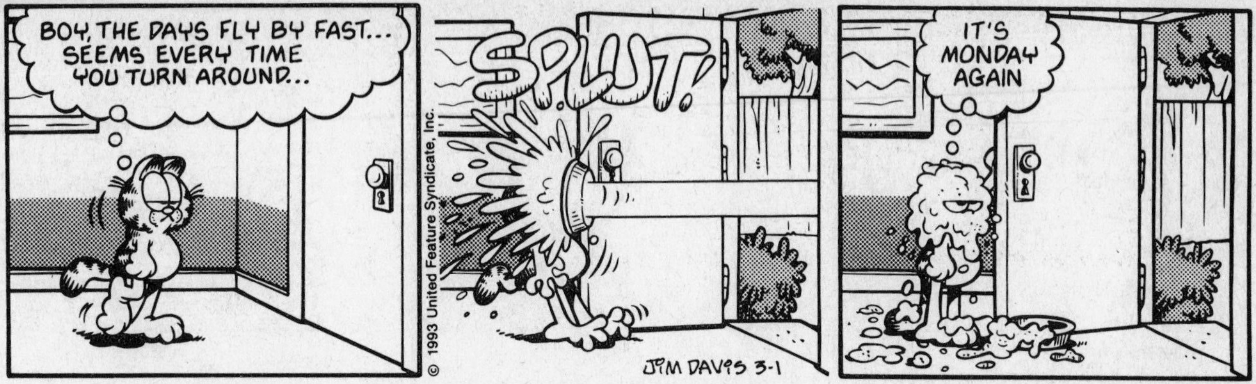
BOY, THE DAYS FLY BY FAST... SEEMS EVERY TIME YOU TURN AROUND...
SPLUT!
IT'S MONDAY AGAIN
JIM DAVIS 3-1
© 1993 United Feature Syndicate, Inc.

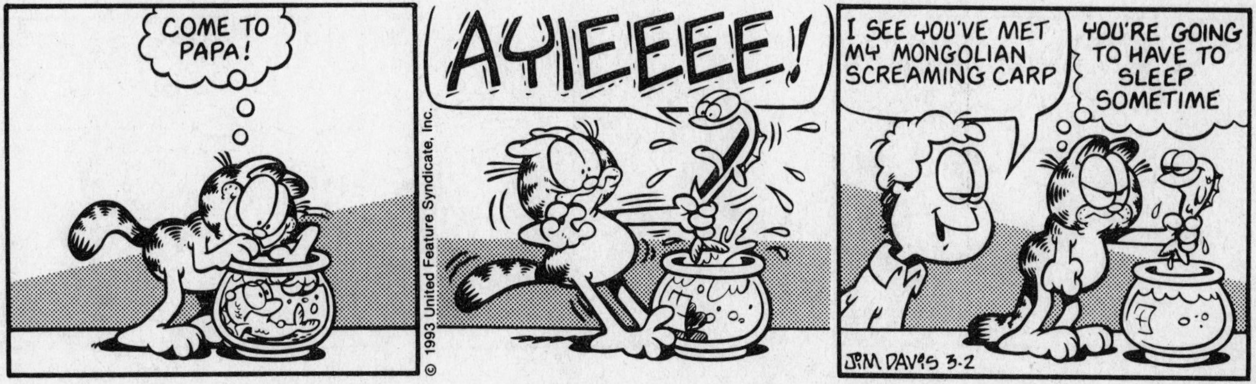
COME TO PAPA!
AYIEEEE!
I SEE YOU'VE MET MY MONGOLIAN SCREAMING CARP
YOU'RE GOING TO HAVE TO SLEEP SOMETIME
JIM DAVIS 3-2
© 1993 United Feature Syndicate, Inc.

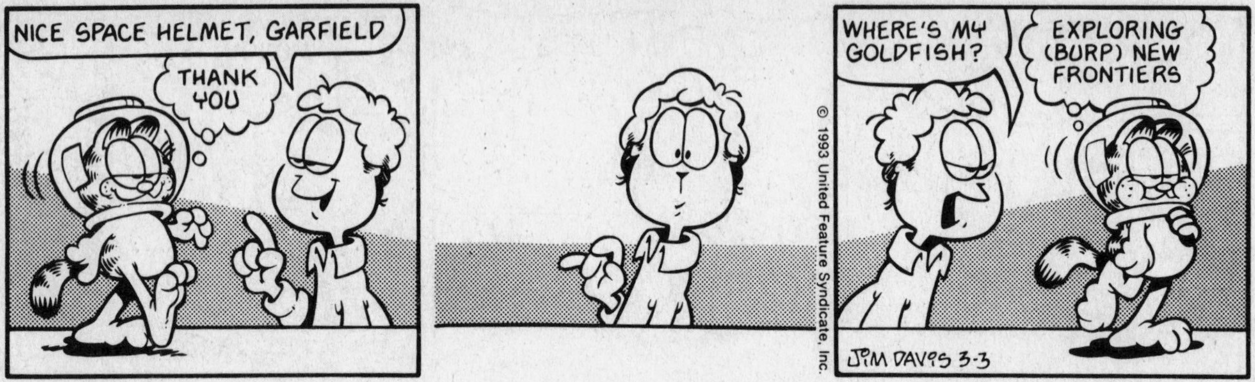
NICE SPACE HELMET, GARFIELD
THANK YOU
WHERE'S MY GOLDFISH?
EXPLORING (BURP) NEW FRONTIERS
JIM DAVIS 3-3
© 1993 United Feature Syndicate, Inc.

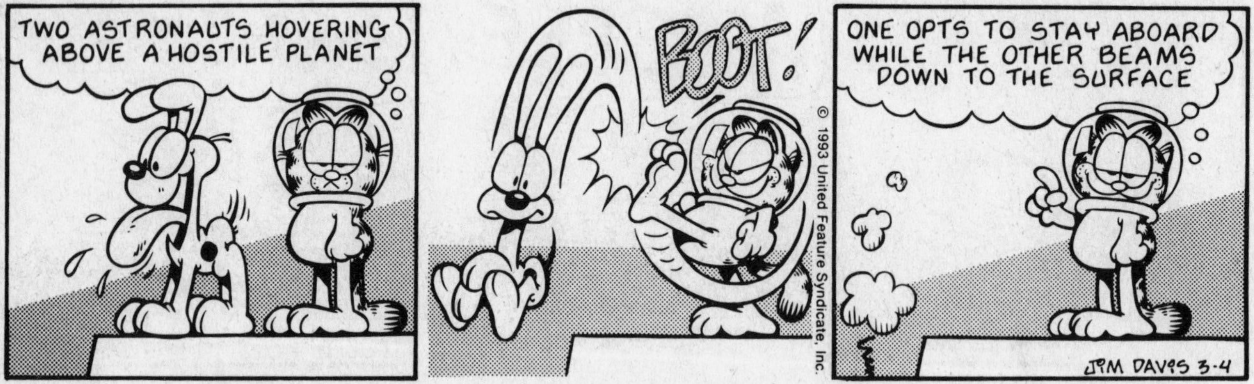
TWO ASTRONAUTS HOVERING ABOVE A HOSTILE PLANET
BOOT!
ONE OPTS TO STAY ABOARD WHILE THE OTHER BEAMS DOWN TO THE SURFACE
JIM DAVIS 3-4
© 1993 United Feature Syndicate, Inc.

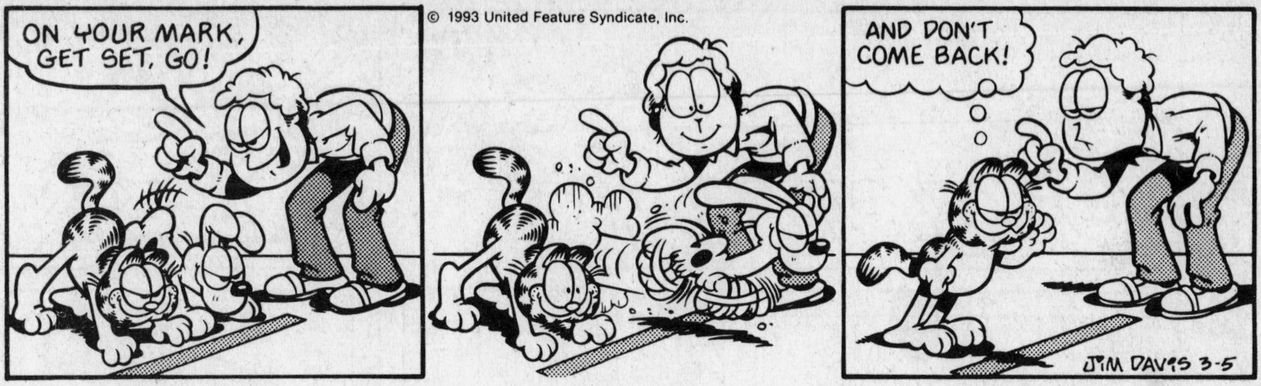
ON YOUR MARK, GET SET, GO!
© 1993 United Feature Syndicate, Inc.
AND DON'T COME BACK!
JIM DAVIS 3-5

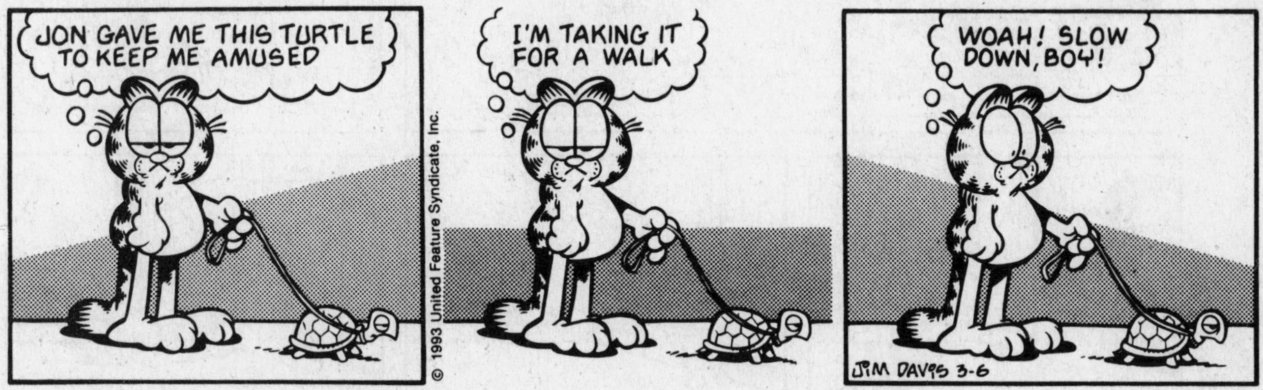
JON GAVE ME THIS TURTLE TO KEEP ME AMUSED
© 1993 United Feature Syndicate, Inc.
I'M TAKING IT FOR A WALK
WOAH! SLOW DOWN, BOY!
JIM DAVIS 3-6

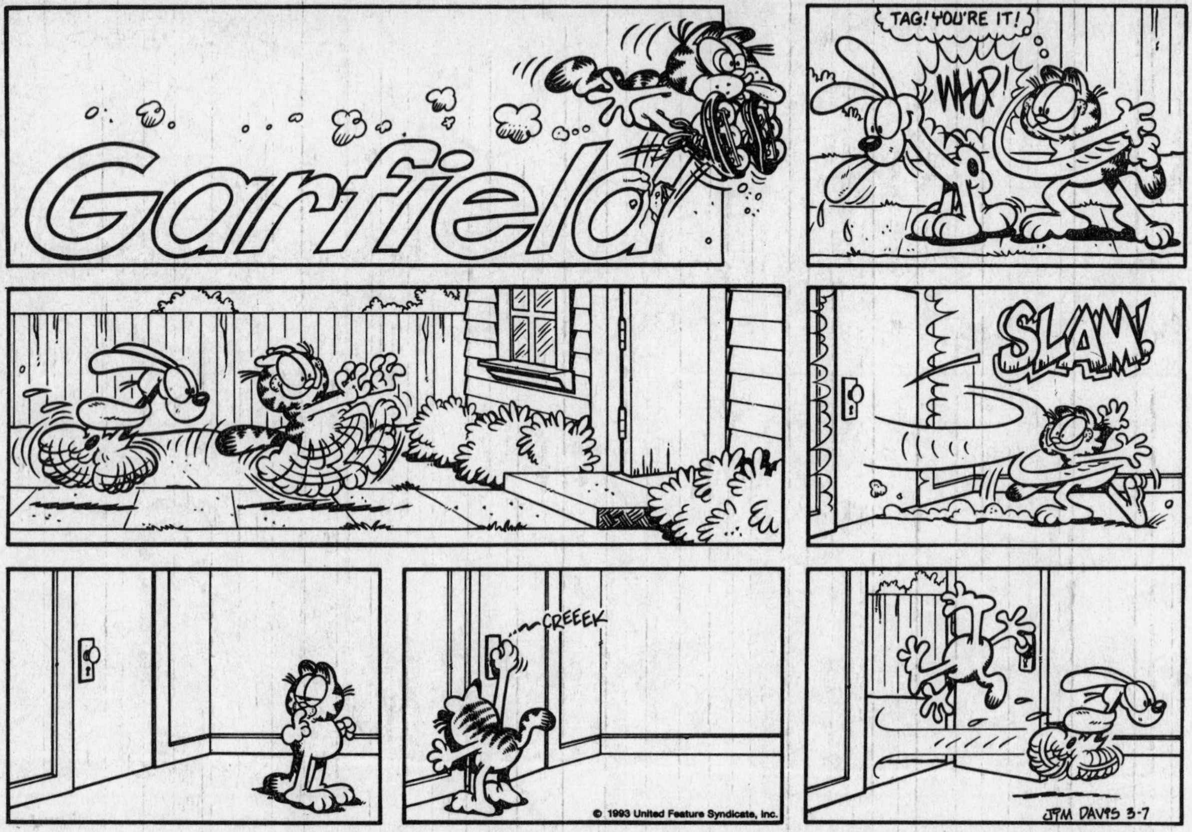
Garfield
TAG! YOU'RE IT!
WHAP!
SLAM!
CREEEK
© 1993 United Feature Syndicate, Inc.
JIM DAVIS 3-7

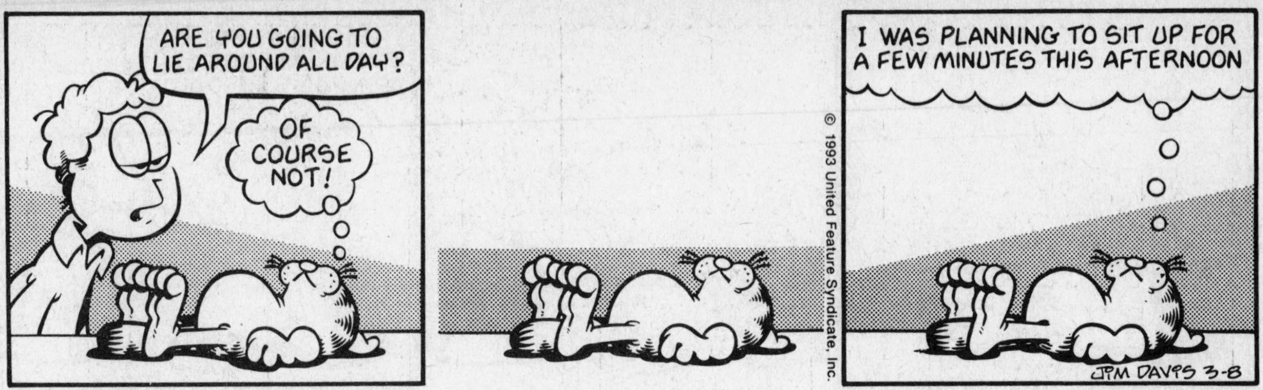
ARE YOU GOING TO LIE AROUND ALL DAY?
OF COURSE NOT!
I WAS PLANNING TO SIT UP FOR A FEW MINUTES THIS AFTERNOON
JIM DAVIS 3-8

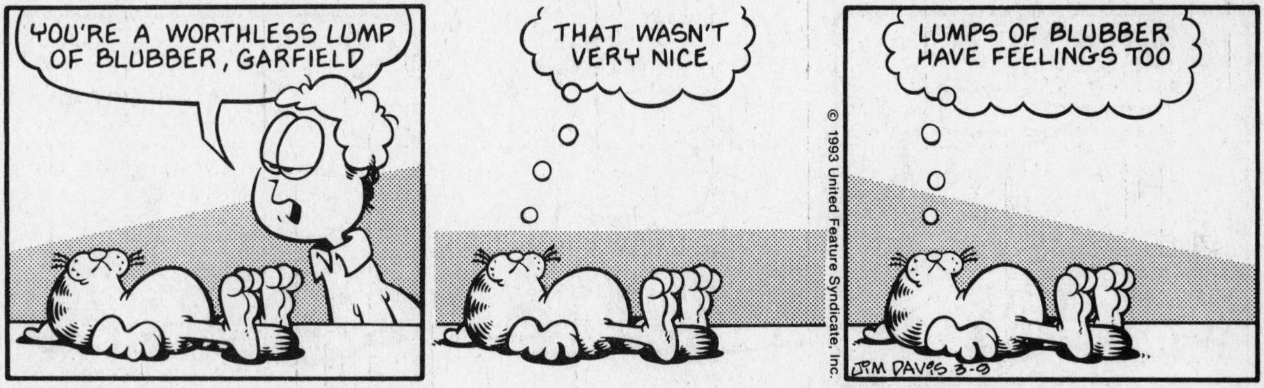
YOU'RE A WORTHLESS LUMP OF BLUBBER, GARFIELD
THAT WASN'T VERY NICE
LUMPS OF BLUBBER HAVE FEELINGS TOO
JIM DAVIS 3-9

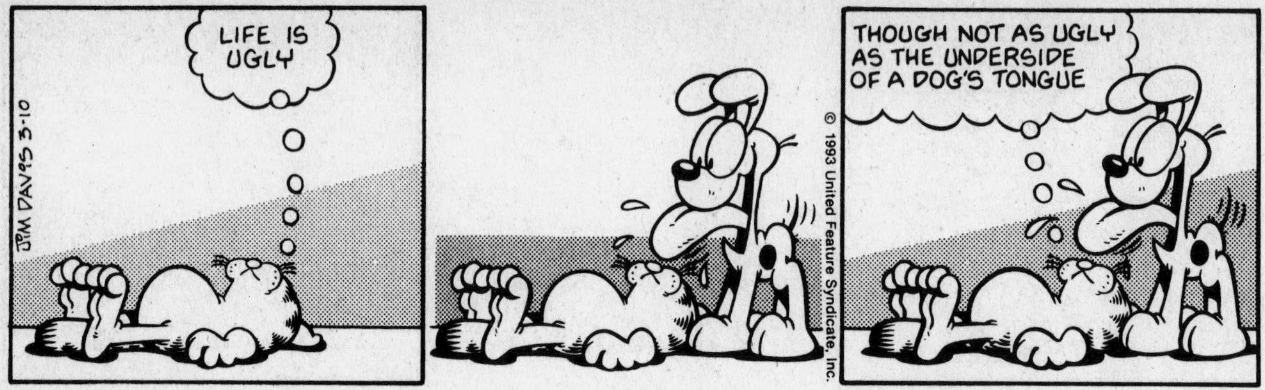
LIFE IS UGLY
JIM DAVIS 3-10
THOUGH NOT AS UGLY AS THE UNDERSIDE OF A DOG'S TONGUE
© 1993 United Feature Syndicate, Inc.

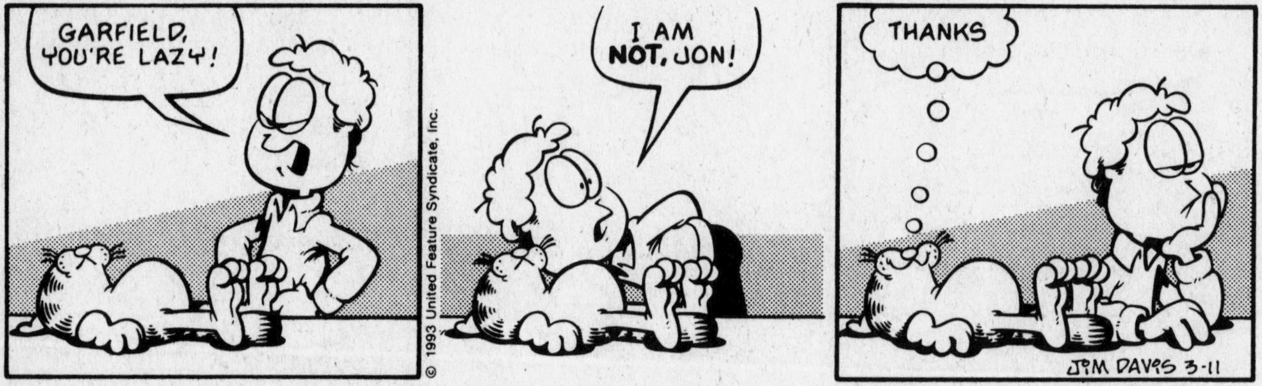
GARFIELD, YOU'RE LAZY!
© 1993 United Feature Syndicate, Inc.
I AM **NOT**, JON!
THANKS
JIM DAVIS 3-11

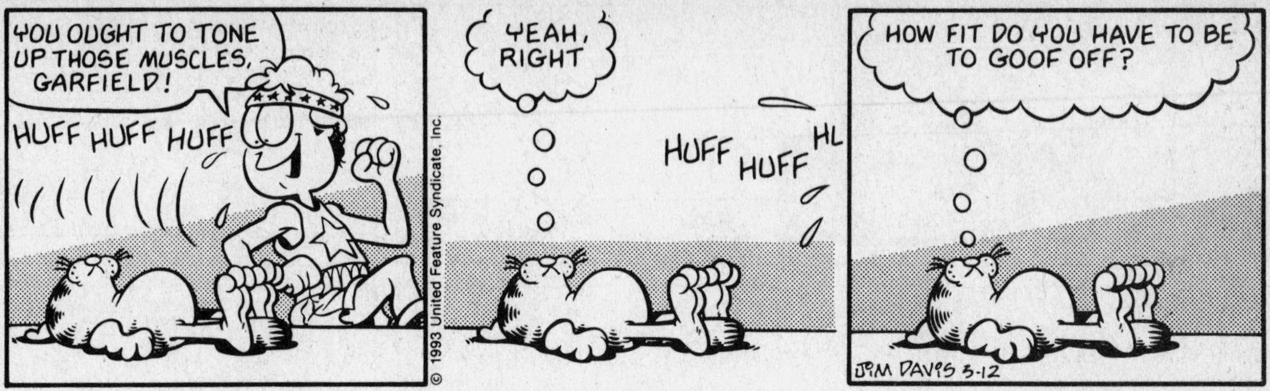
YOU OUGHT TO TONE UP THOSE MUSCLES, GARFIELD!
HUFF HUFF HUFF
YEAH, RIGHT
HUFF HUFF
HOW FIT DO YOU HAVE TO BE TO GOOF OFF?
JIM DAVIS 3-12
© 1993 United Feature Syndicate, Inc.

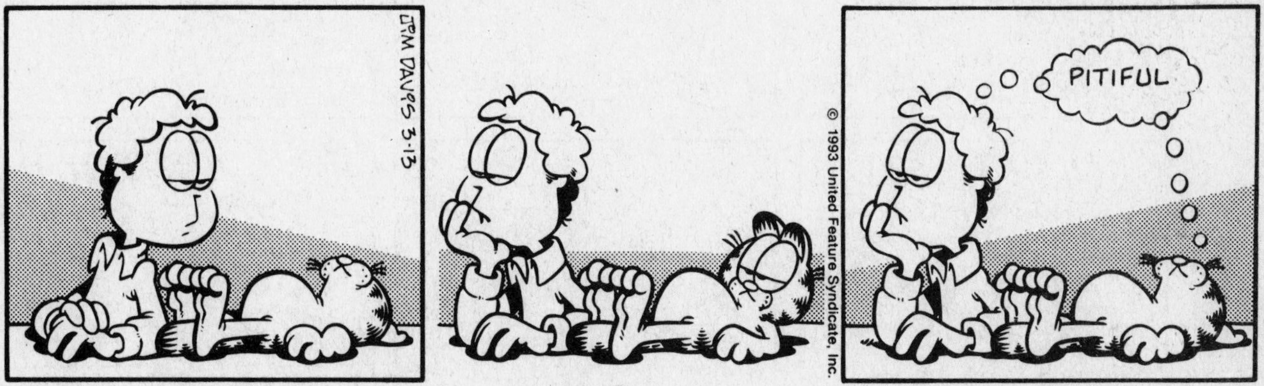
JIM DAVIS 3-13
PITIFUL
© 1993 United Feature Syndicate, Inc.

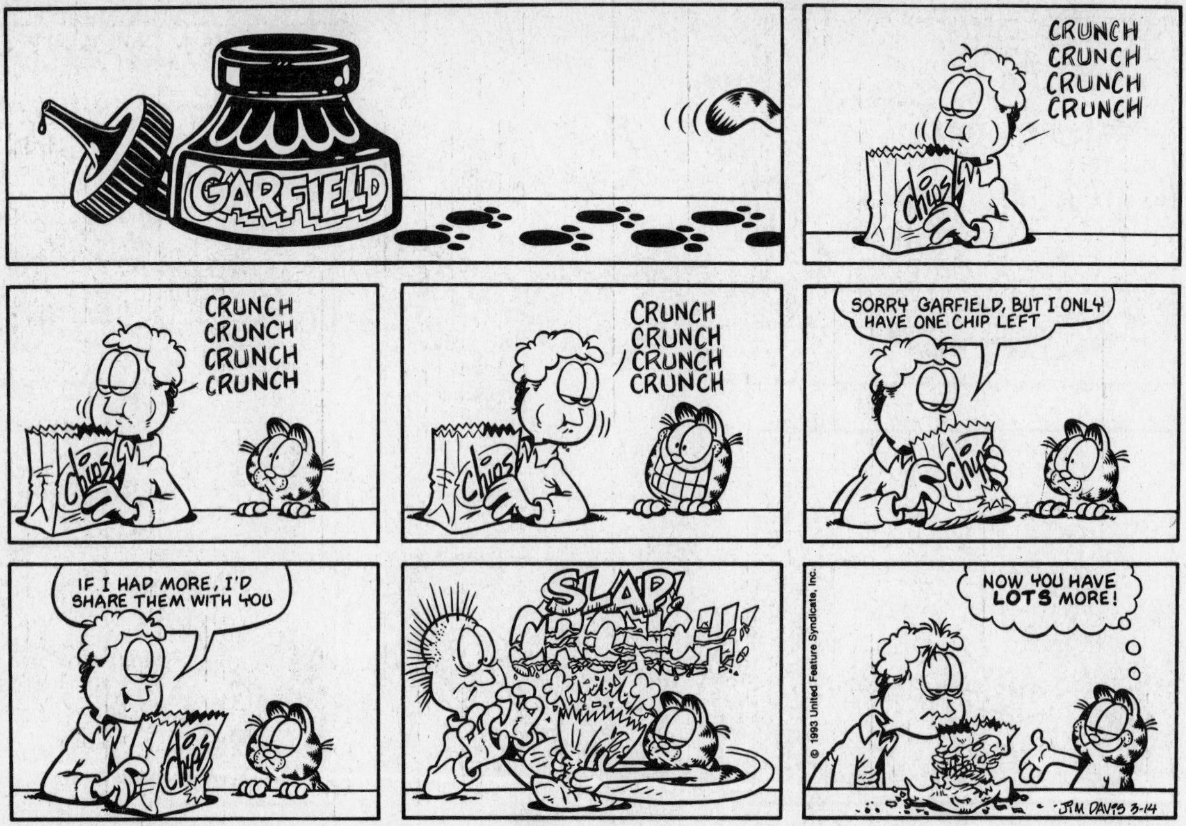
GARFIELD
CRUNCH CRUNCH CRUNCH CRUNCH
CRUNCH CRUNCH CRUNCH CRUNCH
CRUNCH CRUNCH CRUNCH CRUNCH
SORRY GARFIELD, BUT I ONLY HAVE ONE CHIP LEFT
IF I HAD MORE, I'D SHARE THEM WITH YOU
SLAP! CRUNCH!
NOW YOU HAVE LOTS MORE!
JIM DAVIS 3-14
© 1993 United Feature Syndicate, Inc.

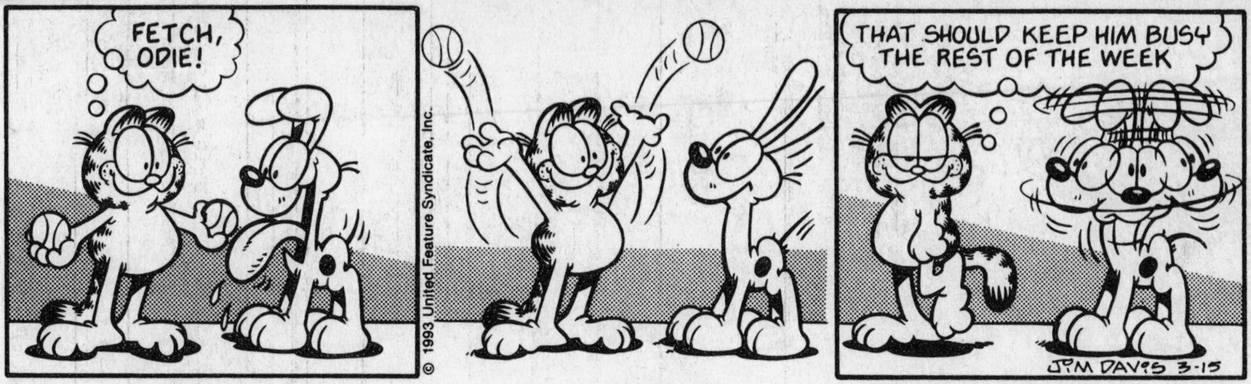
FETCH, ODIE!
THAT SHOULD KEEP HIM BUSY THE REST OF THE WEEK
JIM DAVIS 3-15

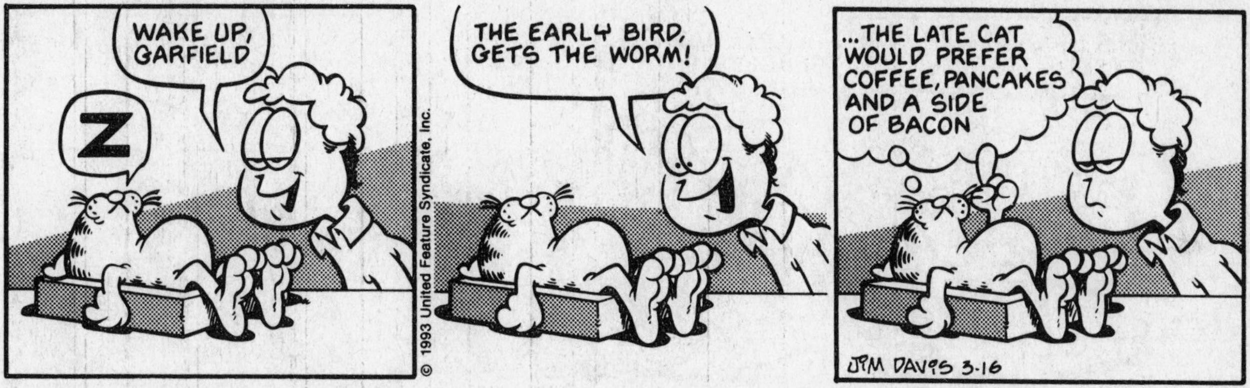
Z
WAKE UP, GARFIELD
THE EARLY BIRD GETS THE WORM!
...THE LATE CAT WOULD PREFER COFFEE, PANCAKES AND A SIDE OF BACON
JIM DAVIS 3-16

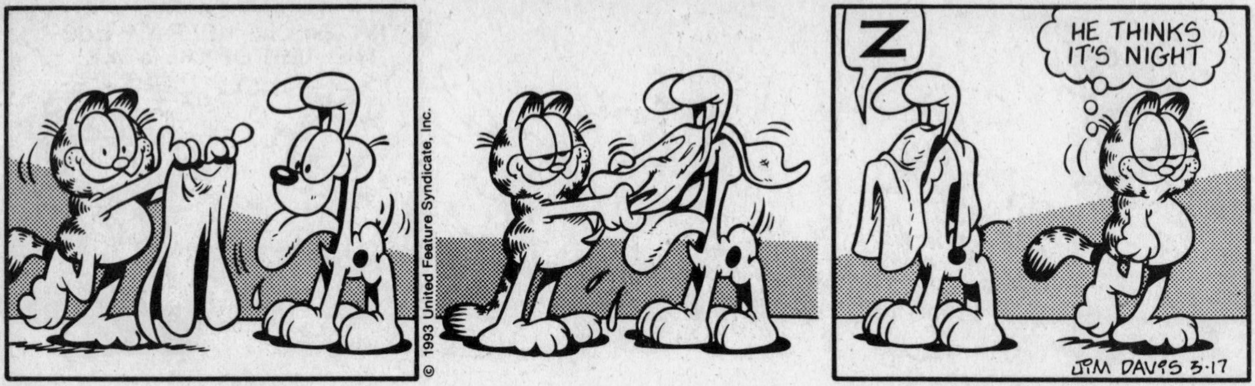
Z
HE THINKS IT'S NIGHT
JIM DAVIS 3-17

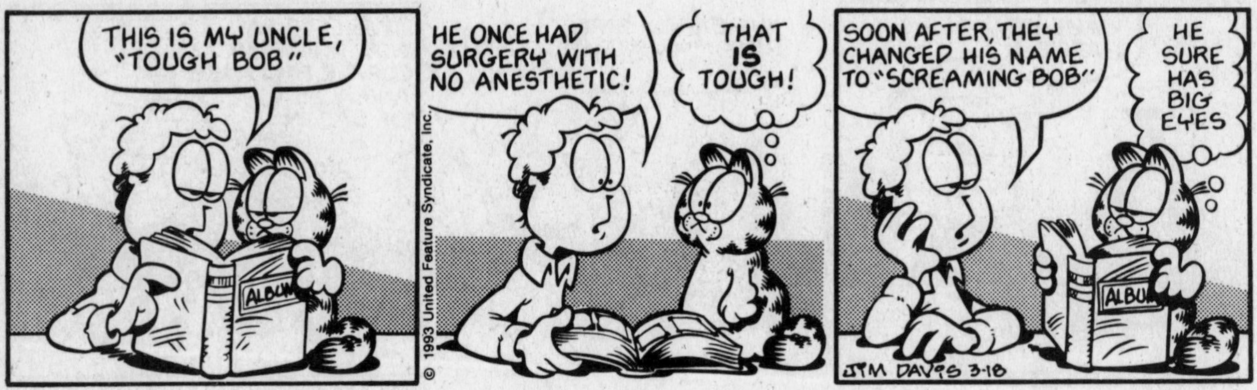
THIS IS MY UNCLE, "TOUGH BOB"
HE ONCE HAD SURGERY WITH NO ANESTHETIC!
THAT IS TOUGH!
SOON AFTER, THEY CHANGED HIS NAME TO "SCREAMING BOB"
HE SURE HAS BIG EYES
ALBUM
JIM DAVIS 3-18

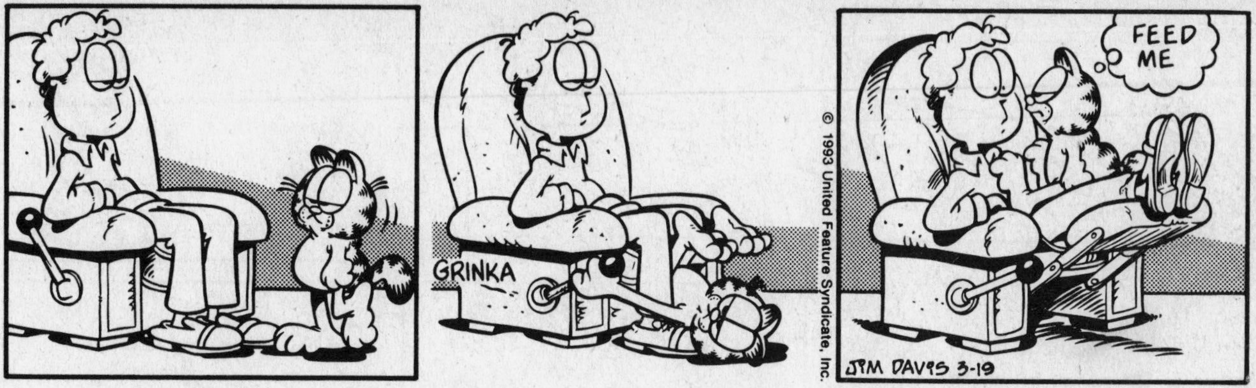
GRINKA
FEED ME
© 1993 United Feature Syndicate, Inc.
JIM DAVIS 3-19

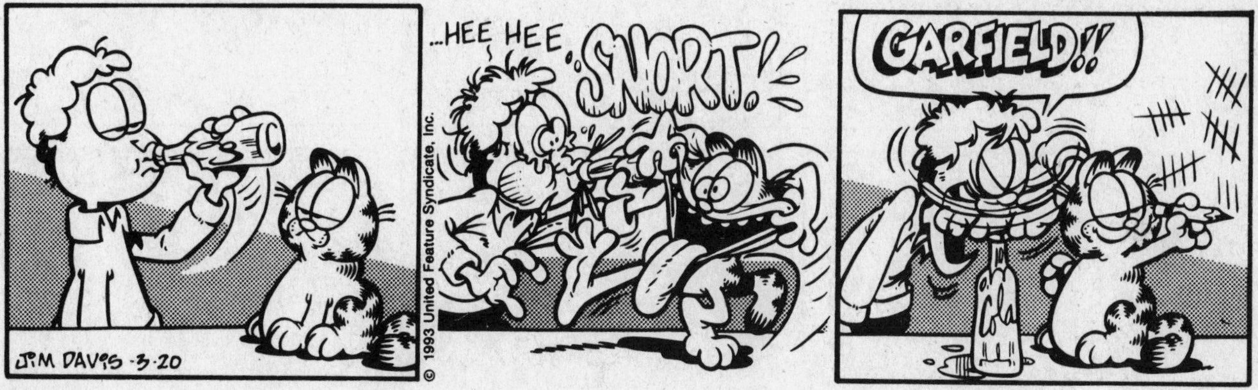
JIM DAVIS 3-20
© 1993 United Feature Syndicate, Inc.
...HEE HEE
SNORT!
GARFIELD!!

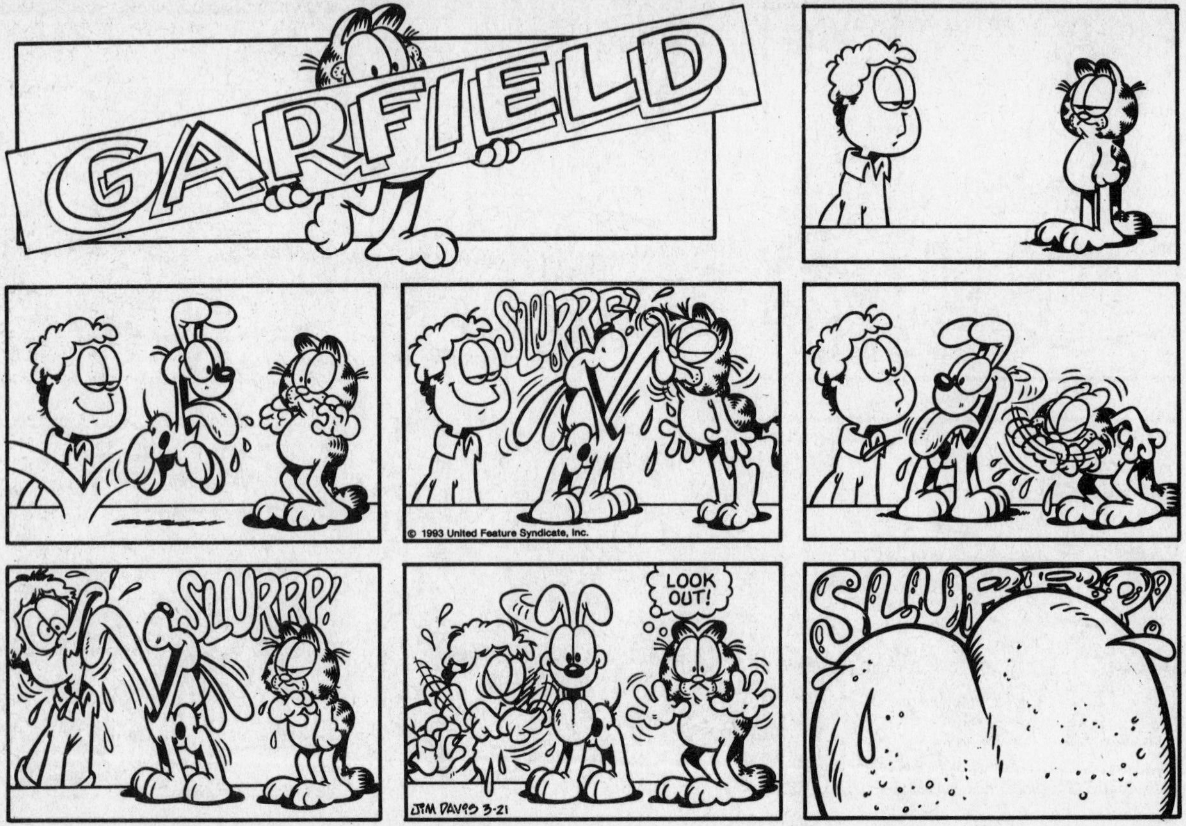
GARFIELD
SLURRP!
© 1993 United Feature Syndicate, Inc.
SLURRP!
LOOK OUT!
JIM DAVIS 3-21
SLURP!

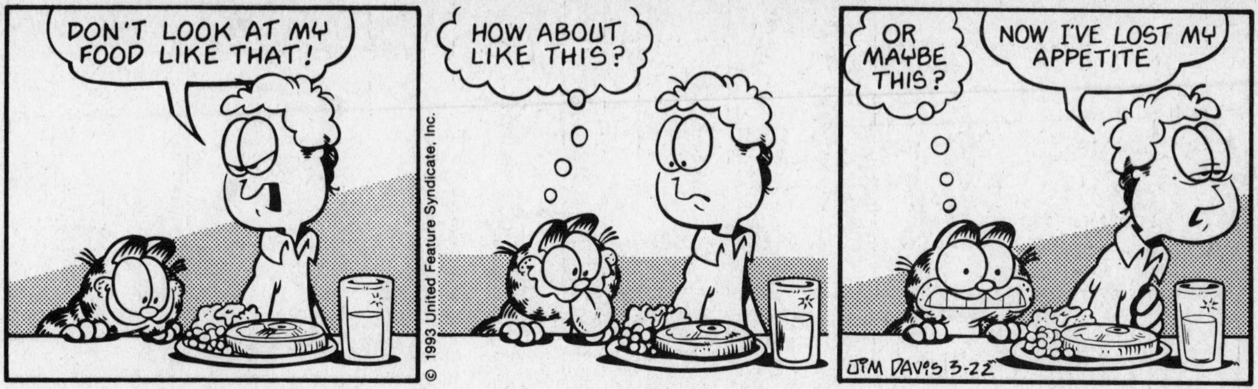
DON'T LOOK AT MY FOOD LIKE THAT!
HOW ABOUT LIKE THIS?
OR MAYBE THIS?
NOW I'VE LOST MY APPETITE
© 1993 United Feature Syndicate, Inc.
JIM DAVIS 3-22

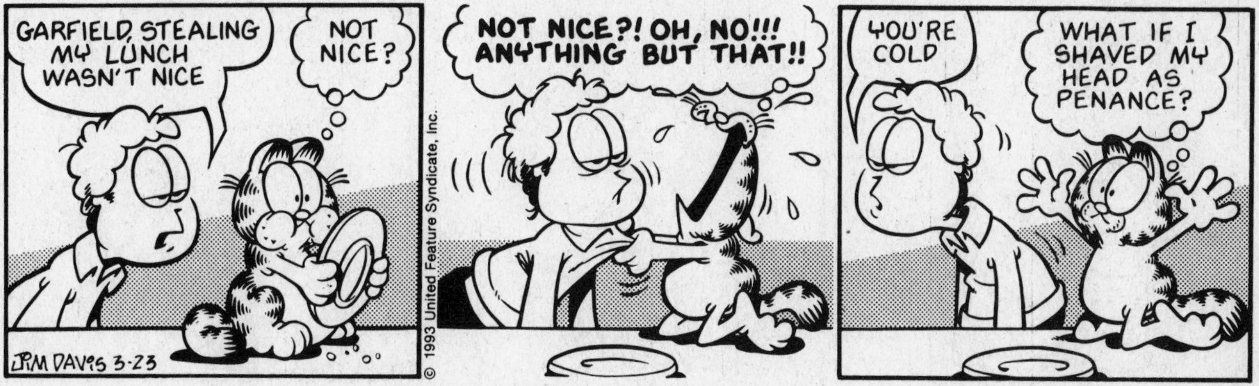
GARFIELD, STEALING MY LUNCH WASN'T NICE
NOT NICE?
NOT NICE?! OH, NO!!! ANYTHING BUT THAT!!
YOU'RE COLD
WHAT IF I SHAVED MY HEAD AS PENANCE?
© 1993 United Feature Syndicate, Inc.
JIM DAVIS 3-23

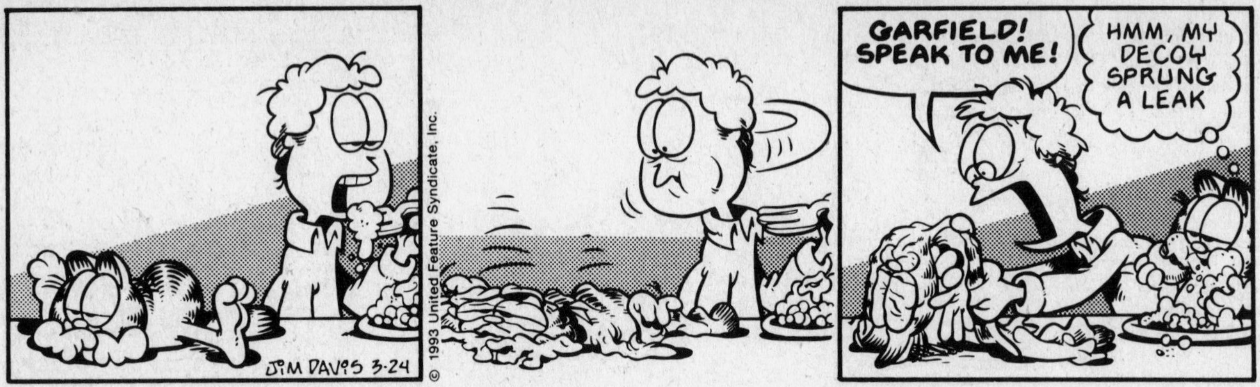
JIM DAVIS 3-24
© 1993 United Feature Syndicate, Inc.
GARFIELD! SPEAK TO ME!
HMM, MY DECOY SPRUNG A LEAK

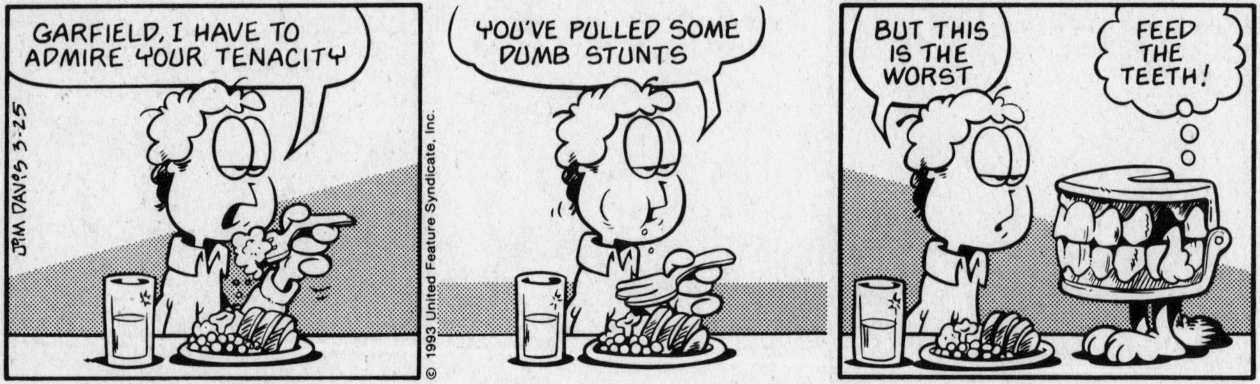
GARFIELD, I HAVE TO ADMIRE YOUR TENACITY
JIM DAVIS 3-25
© 1993 United Feature Syndicate, Inc.
YOU'VE PULLED SOME DUMB STUNTS
BUT THIS IS THE WORST
FEED THE TEETH!

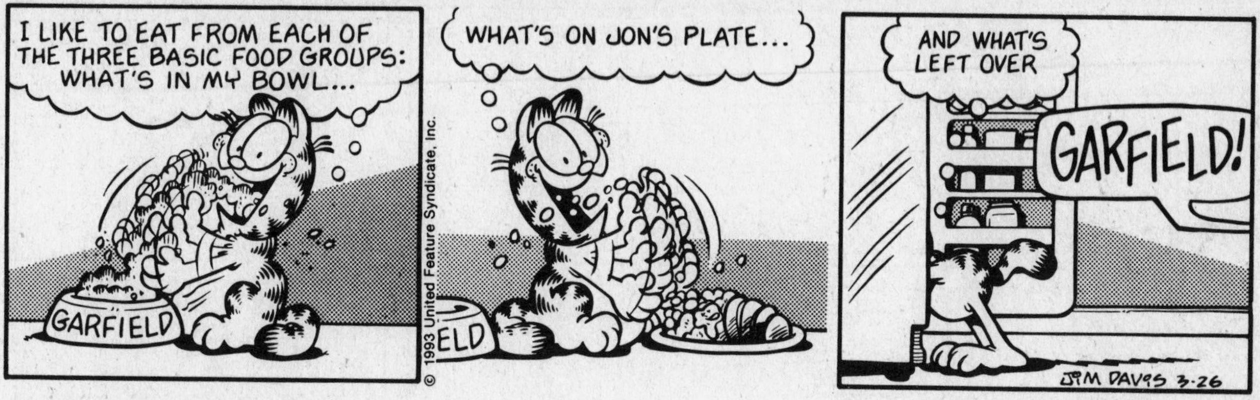
I LIKE TO EAT FROM EACH OF THE THREE BASIC FOOD GROUPS: WHAT'S IN MY BOWL...
GARFIELD
© 1993 United Feature Syndicate, Inc.
WHAT'S ON JON'S PLATE...
ELD
AND WHAT'S LEFT OVER
GARFIELD!
JIM DAVIS 3-26

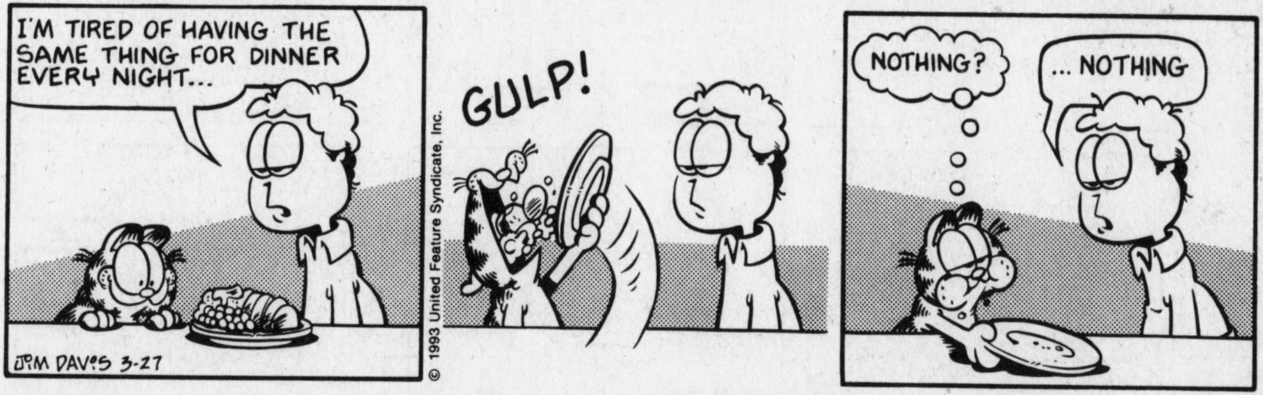
I'M TIRED OF HAVING THE SAME THING FOR DINNER EVERY NIGHT...
JIM DAVIS 3-27
© 1993 United Feature Syndicate, Inc.
GULP!
NOTHING?
... NOTHING

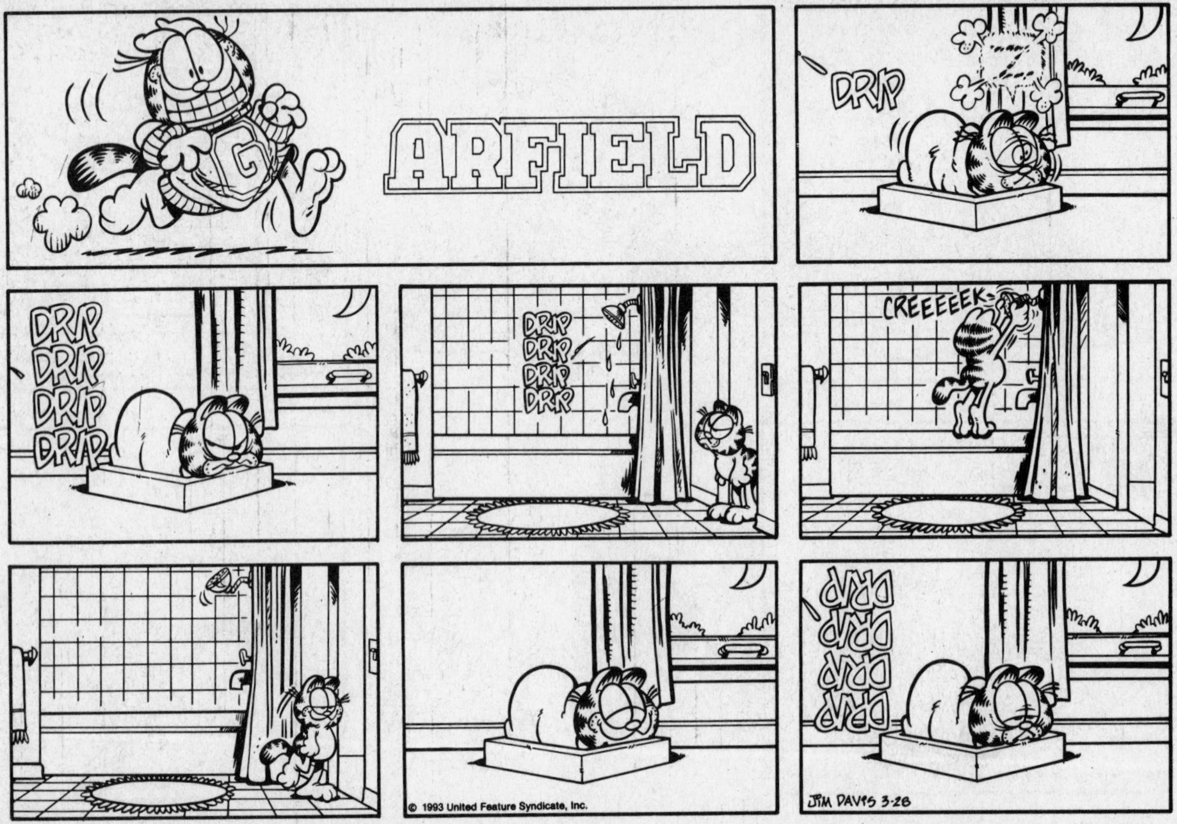
ARFIELD
DRIP
DRIP
DRIP
DRIP
DRIP
DRIP
DRIP
DRIP
DRIP
CREEEEEK
© 1993 United Feature Syndicate, Inc.
DRIP
DRIP
DRIP
DRIP
JIM DAVIS 3-28

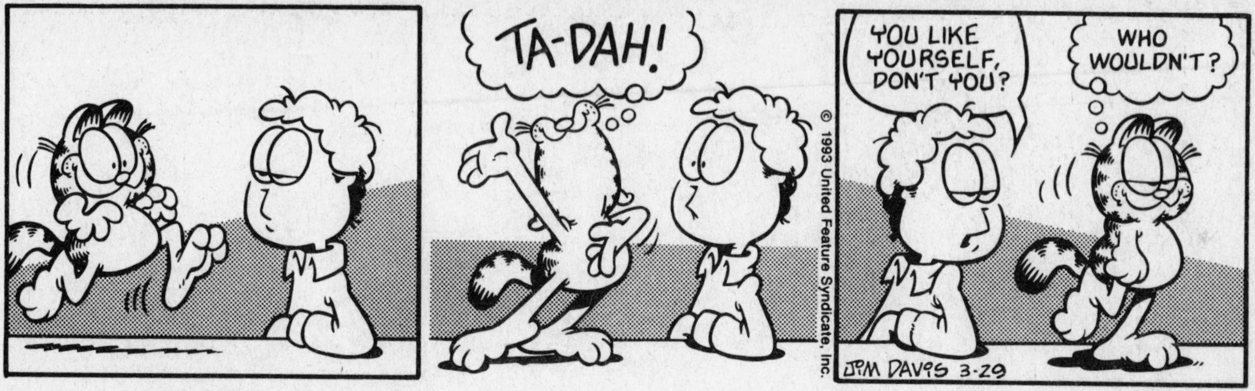
TA-DAH!
© 1993 United Feature Syndicate, Inc.
YOU LIKE YOURSELF, DON'T YOU?
WHO WOULDN'T?
JIM DAVIS 3-29

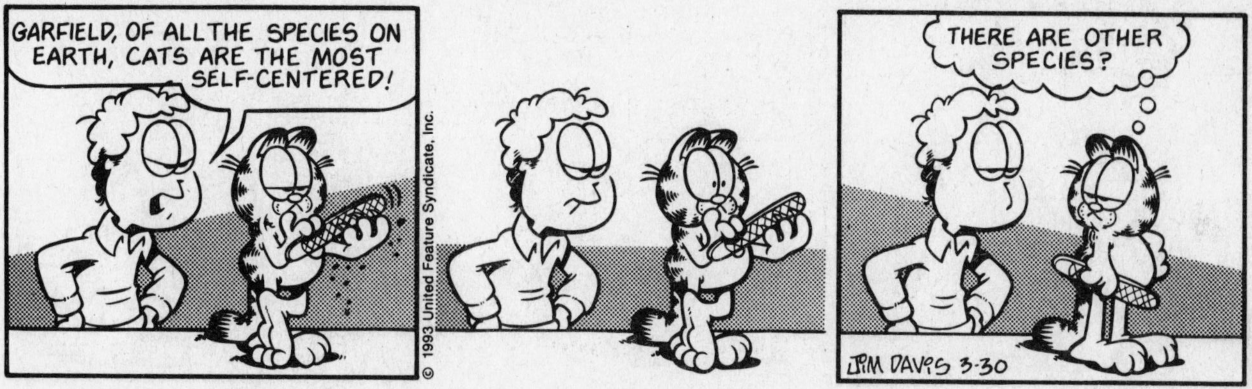
GARFIELD, OF ALL THE SPECIES ON EARTH, CATS ARE THE MOST SELF-CENTERED!
© 1993 United Feature Syndicate, Inc.
THERE ARE OTHER SPECIES?
JIM DAVIS 3-30

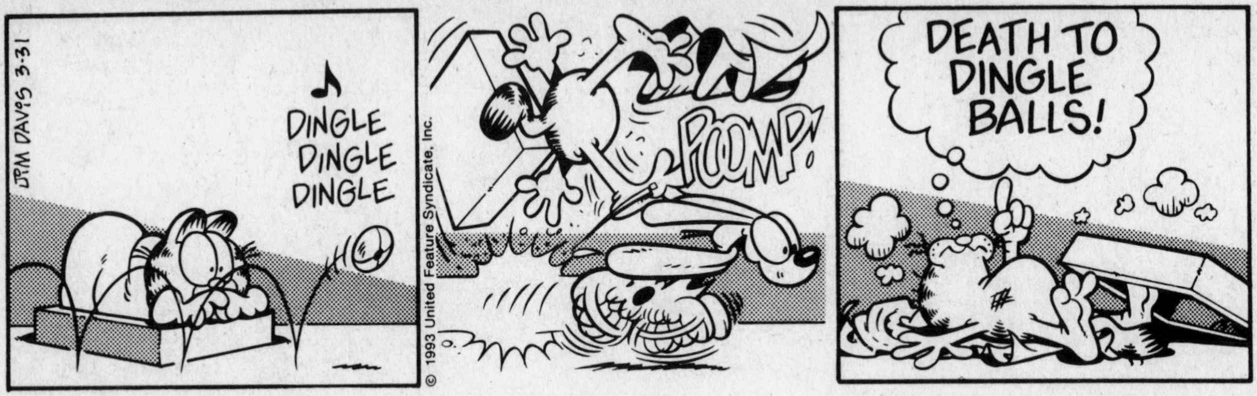
JIM DAVIS 3-31
DINGLE
DINGLE
DINGLE
POOMP!
DEATH TO DINGLE BALLS!
© 1993 United Feature Syndicate, Inc.

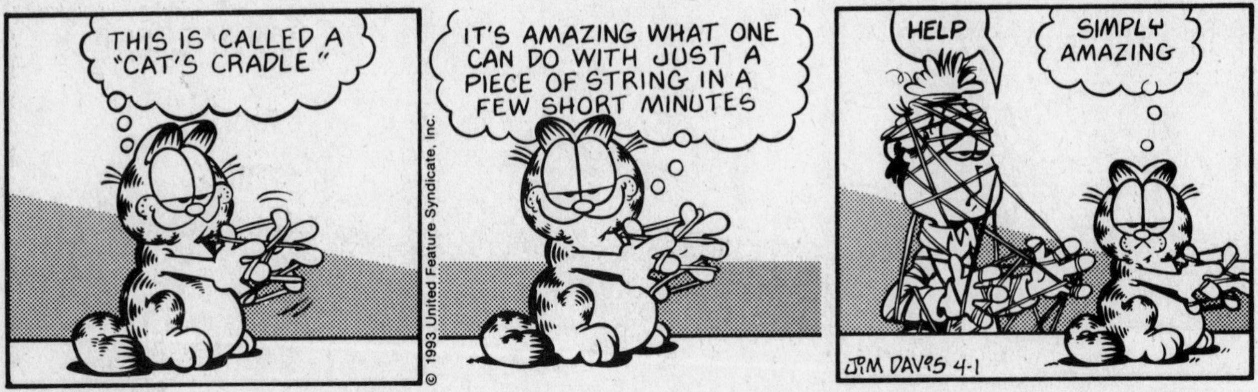
THIS IS CALLED A "CAT'S CRADLE"
IT'S AMAZING WHAT ONE CAN DO WITH JUST A PIECE OF STRING IN A FEW SHORT MINUTES
HELP
SIMPLY AMAZING
JIM DAVIS 4-1
© 1993 United Feature Syndicate, Inc.

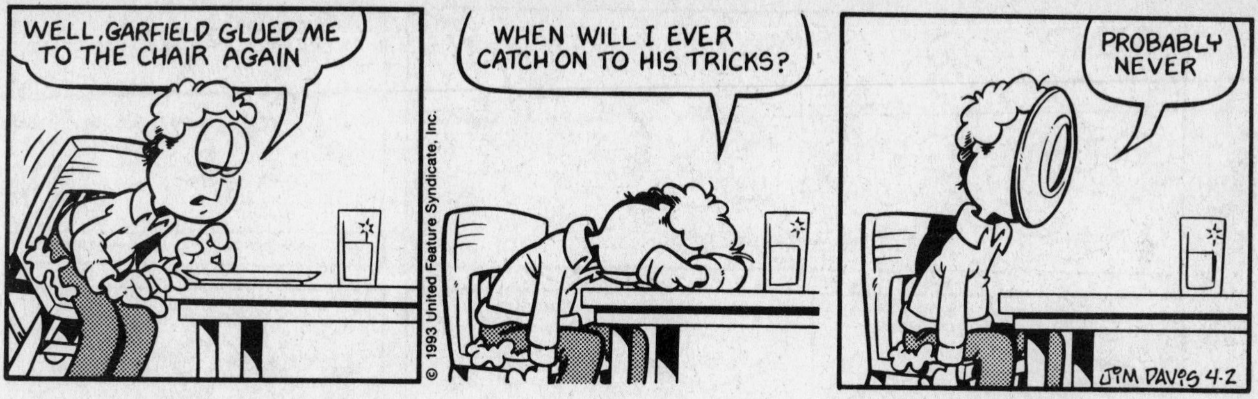
WELL, GARFIELD GLUED ME TO THE CHAIR AGAIN
WHEN WILL I EVER CATCH ON TO HIS TRICKS?
PROBABLY NEVER
© 1993 United Feature Syndicate, Inc.
JIM DAVIS 4-2

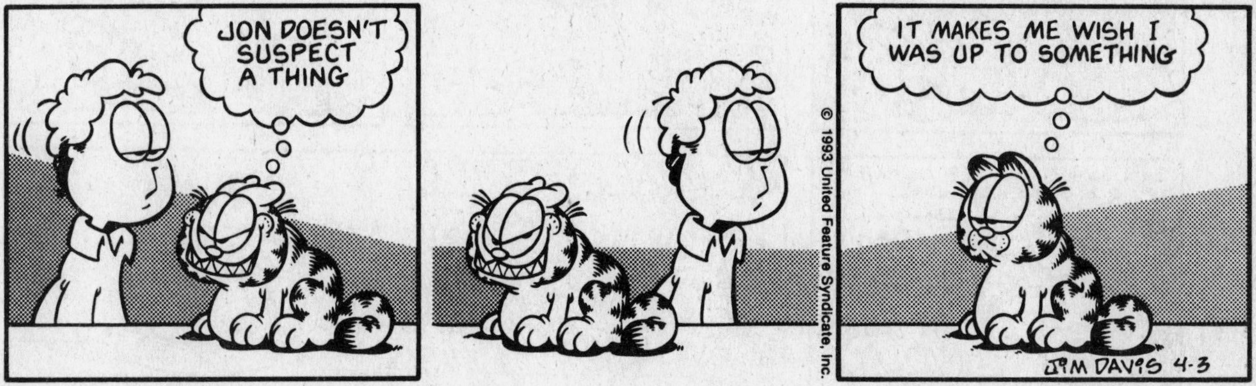
JON DOESN'T SUSPECT A THING
IT MAKES ME WISH I WAS UP TO SOMETHING
© 1993 United Feature Syndicate, Inc.
JIM DAVIS 4-3

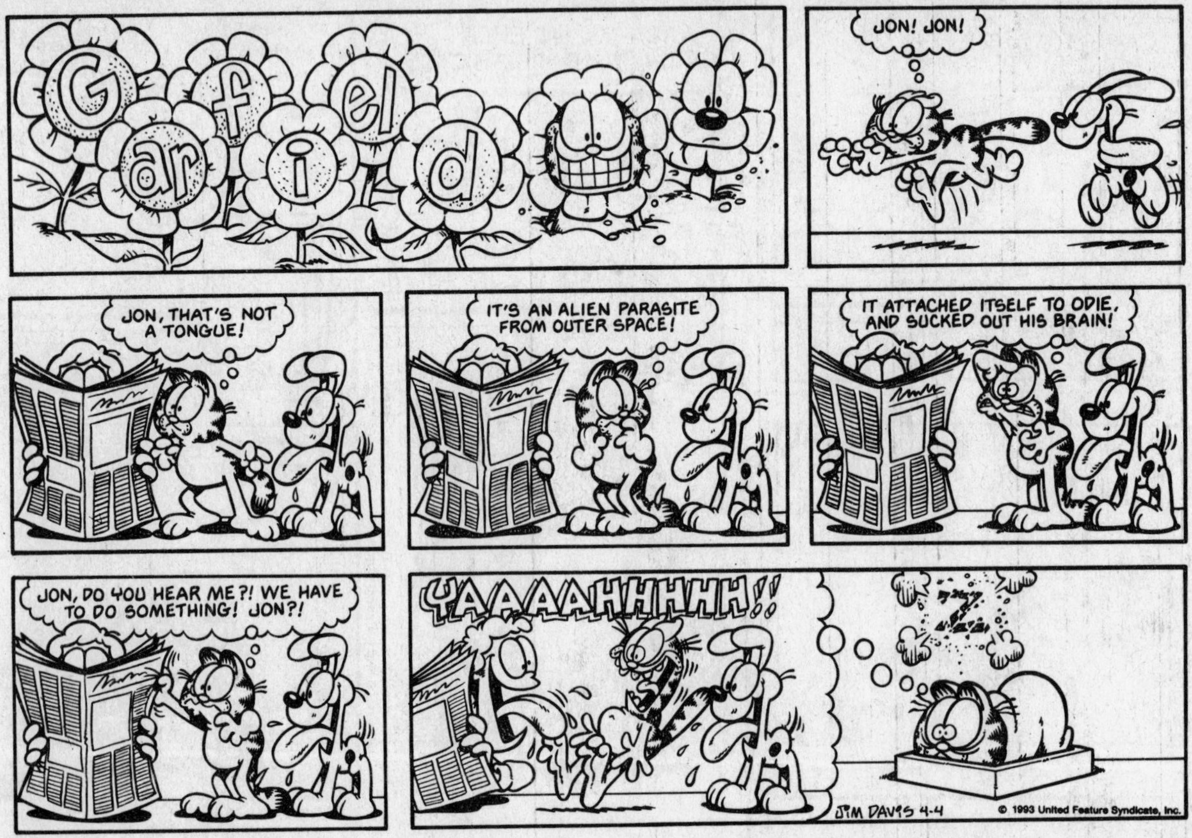
Garfield
JON! JON!
JON, THAT'S NOT A TONGUE!
IT'S AN ALIEN PARASITE FROM OUTER SPACE!
IT ATTACHED ITSELF TO ODIE, AND SUCKED OUT HIS BRAIN!
JON, DO YOU HEAR ME?! WE HAVE TO DO SOMETHING! JON?!
YAAAAHHHHH!!
JIM DAVIS 4-4
© 1993 United Feature Syndicate, Inc.

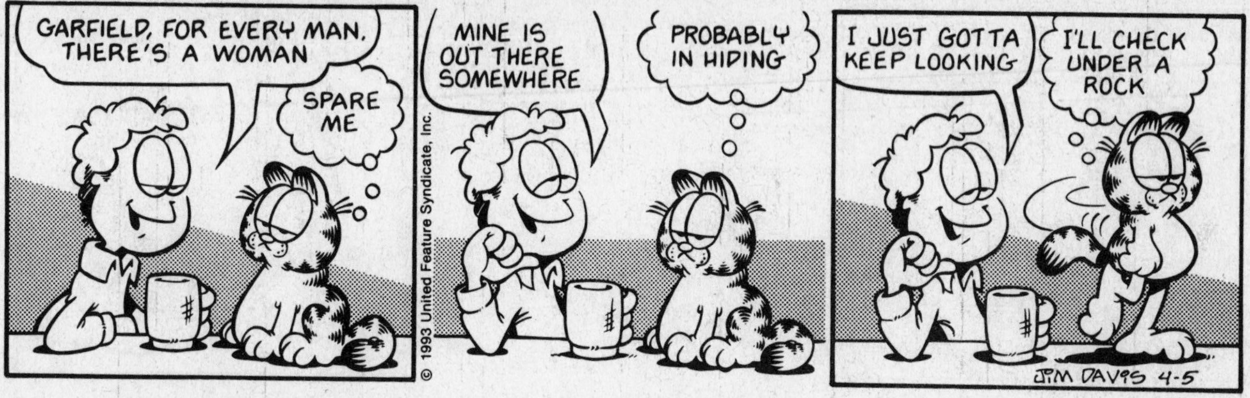
GARFIELD, FOR EVERY MAN, THERE'S A WOMAN
SPARE ME
MINE IS OUT THERE SOMEWHERE
PROBABLY IN HIDING
I JUST GOTTA KEEP LOOKING
I'LL CHECK UNDER A ROCK
© 1993 United Feature Syndicate, Inc.
JIM DAVIS 4-5

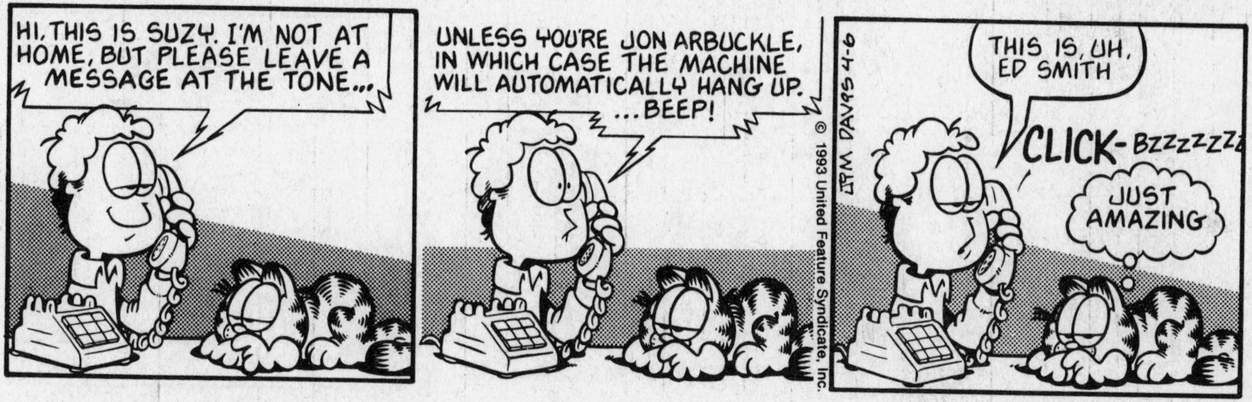
HI, THIS IS SUZY. I'M NOT AT HOME, BUT PLEASE LEAVE A MESSAGE AT THE TONE...
UNLESS YOU'RE JON ARBUCKLE, IN WHICH CASE THE MACHINE WILL AUTOMATICALLY HANG UP. ...BEEP!
THIS IS, UH, ED SMITH
CLICK-BZZZZZZ
JUST AMAZING
© 1993 United Feature Syndicate, Inc.
JIM DAVIS 4-6

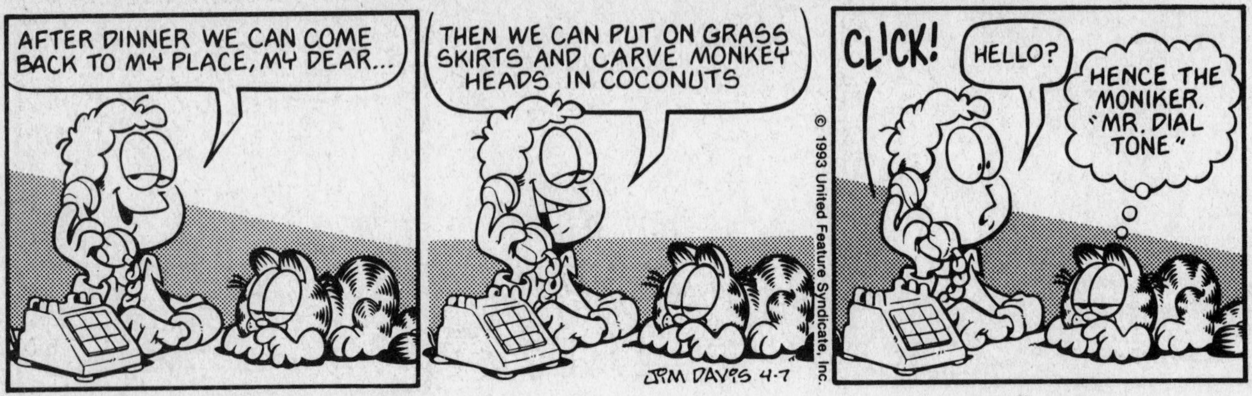
AFTER DINNER WE CAN COME BACK TO MY PLACE, MY DEAR...
THEN WE CAN PUT ON GRASS SKIRTS AND CARVE MONKEY HEADS IN COCONUTS
CLICK!
HELLO?
HENCE THE MONIKER, "MR. DIAL TONE"
JIM DAVIS 4-7
© 1993 United Feature Syndicate, Inc.

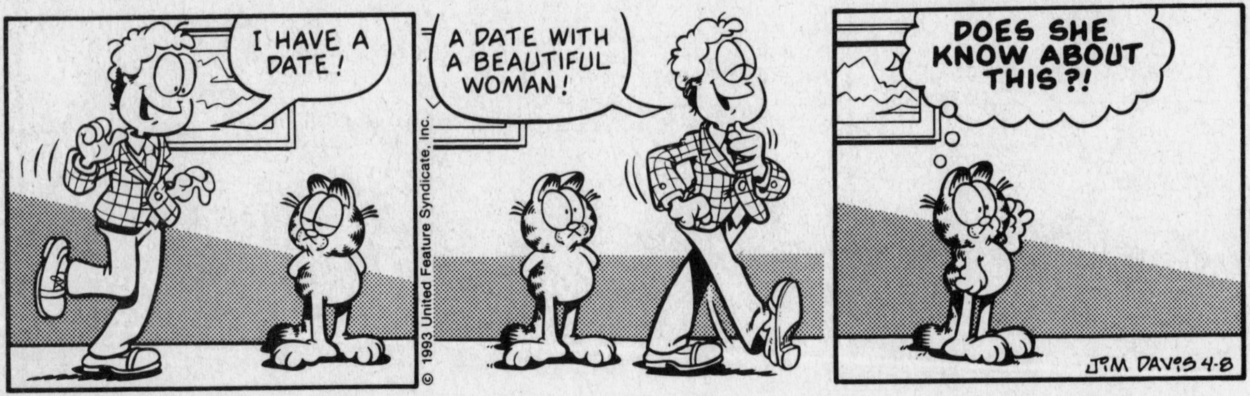
I HAVE A DATE!
A DATE WITH A BEAUTIFUL WOMAN!
DOES SHE KNOW ABOUT THIS?!
JIM DAVIS 4-8
© 1993 United Feature Syndicate, Inc.

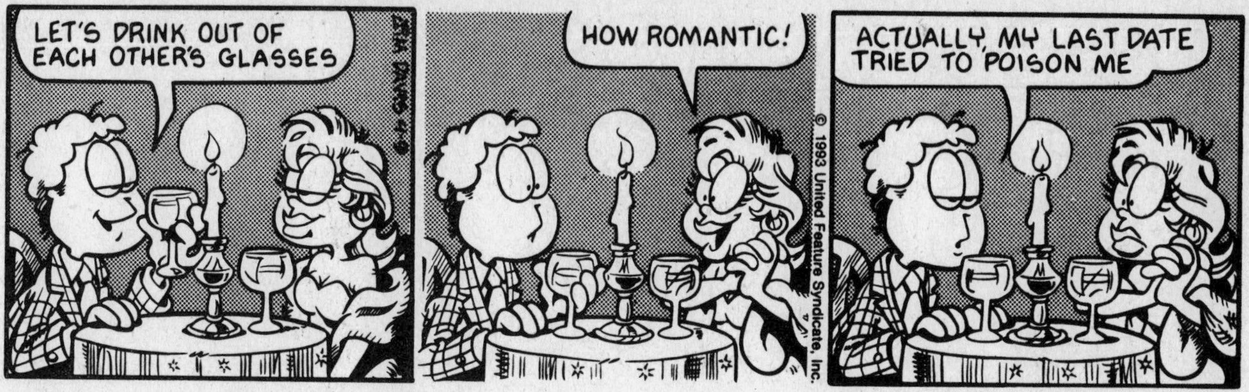
LET'S DRINK OUT OF EACH OTHER'S GLASSES
JIM DAVIS 4-9
HOW ROMANTIC!
© 1993 United Feature Syndicate, Inc.
ACTUALLY, MY LAST DATE TRIED TO POISON ME

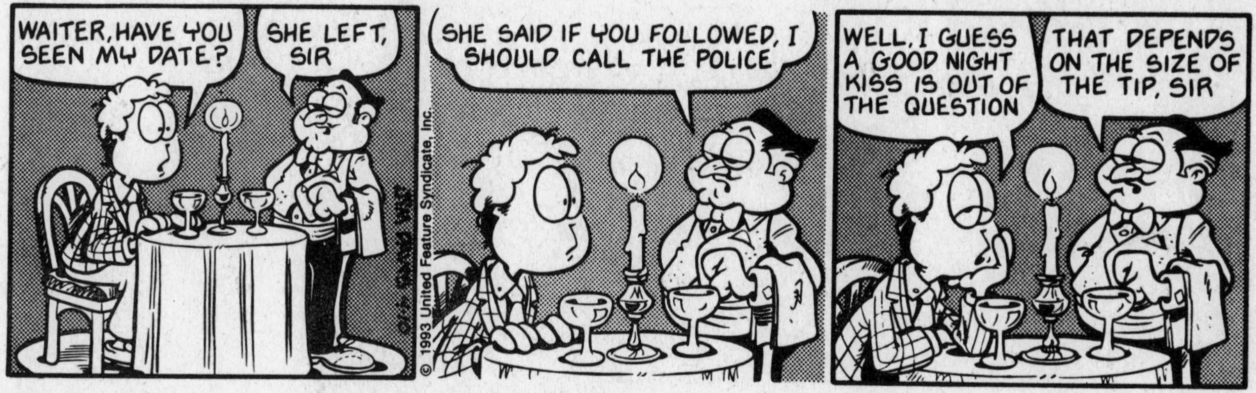
WAITER, HAVE YOU SEEN MY DATE?
SHE LEFT, SIR
JIM DAVIS 4-10
© 1993 United Feature Syndicate, Inc.
SHE SAID IF YOU FOLLOWED, I SHOULD CALL THE POLICE
WELL, I GUESS A GOOD NIGHT KISS IS OUT OF THE QUESTION
THAT DEPENDS ON THE SIZE OF THE TIP, SIR

Garfield pulls his weight

By: Jim Davis

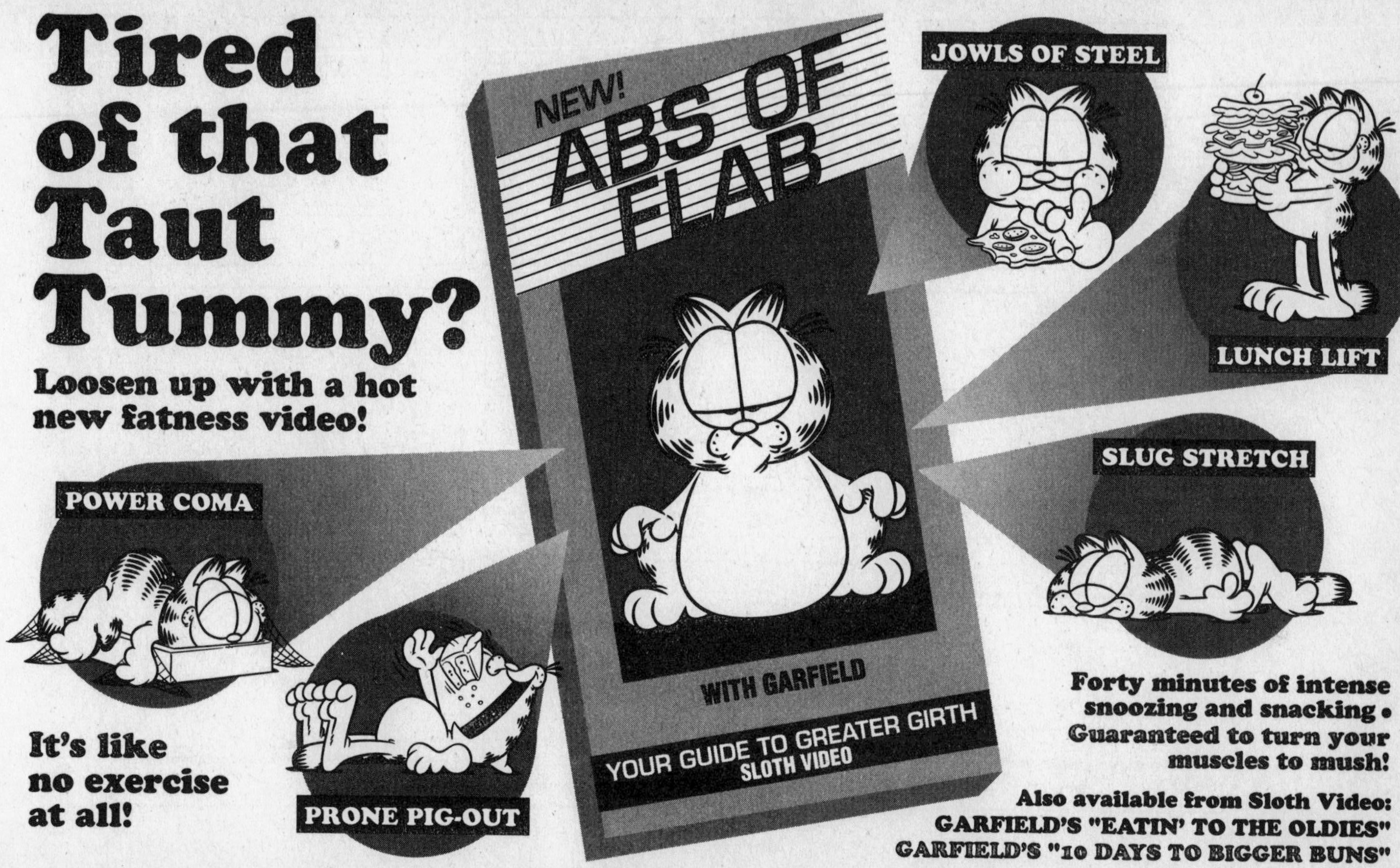
Tired of that Taut Tummy?
Loosen up with a hot new fatness video!
NEW!
ABS OF FLAB
WITH GARFIELD
YOUR GUIDE TO GREATER GIRTH
SLOTH VIDEO
JOWLS OF STEEL
LUNCH LIFT
SLUG STRETCH
POWER COMA
PRONE PIG-OUT
It's like no exercise at all!
Forty minutes of intense snoozing and snacking • Guaranteed to turn your muscles to mush!
Also available from Sloth Video:
GARFIELD'S "EATIN' TO THE OLDIES"
GARFIELD'S "10 DAYS TO BIGGER BUNS"

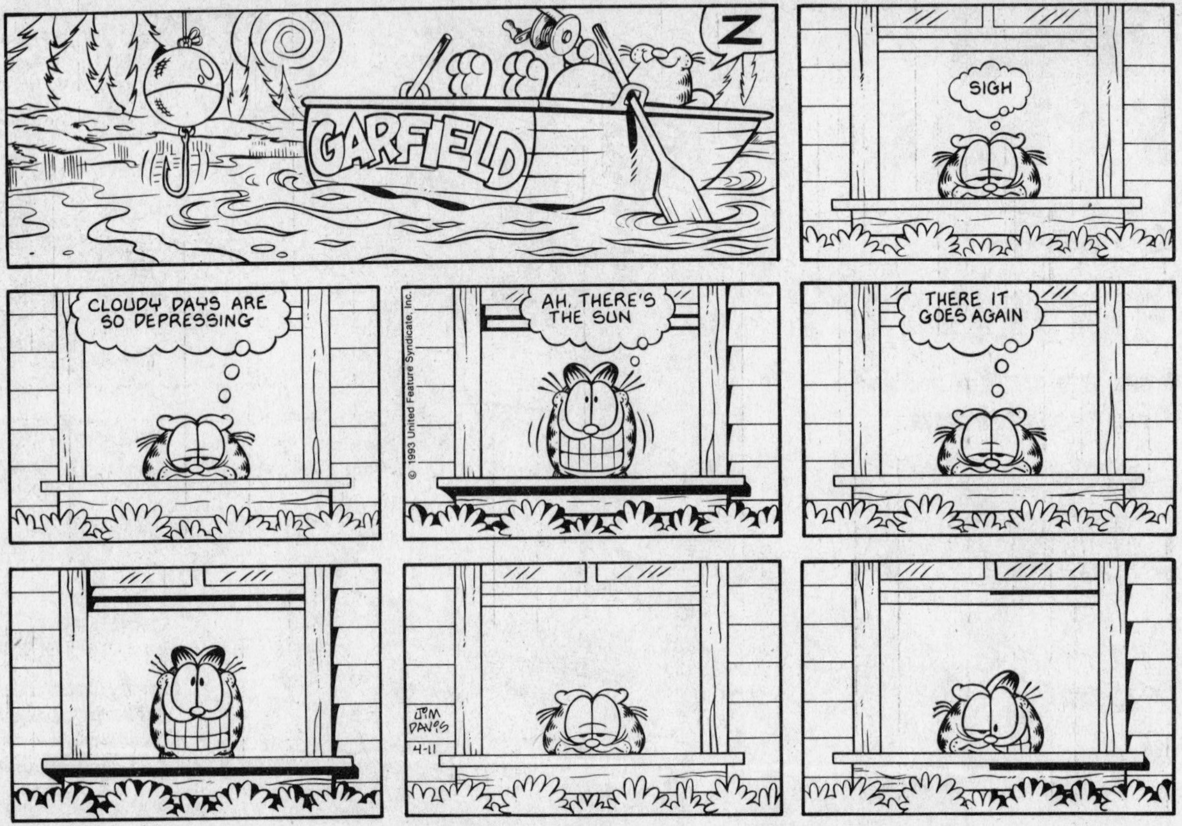

GARFIELD
Z
SIGH
CLOUDY DAYS ARE SO DEPRESSING
AH, THERE'S THE SUN
THERE IT GOES AGAIN
JIM DAVIS 4-11
© 1993 United Feature Syndicate, Inc.

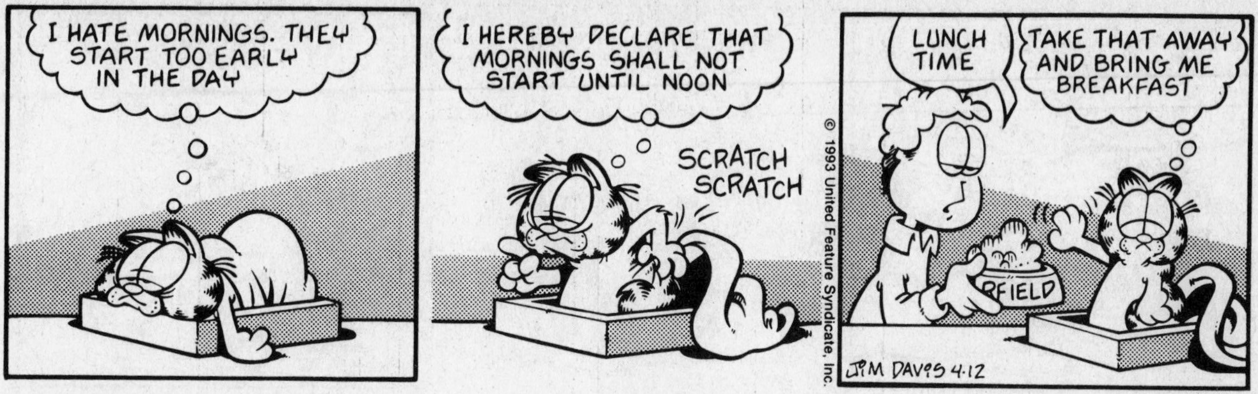
I HATE MORNINGS. THEY START TOO EARLY IN THE DAY
I HEREBY DECLARE THAT MORNINGS SHALL NOT START UNTIL NOON
SCRATCH SCRATCH
LUNCH TIME
TAKE THAT AWAY AND BRING ME BREAKFAST
RFIELD
JIM DAVIS 4-12
© 1993 United Feature Syndicate, Inc.

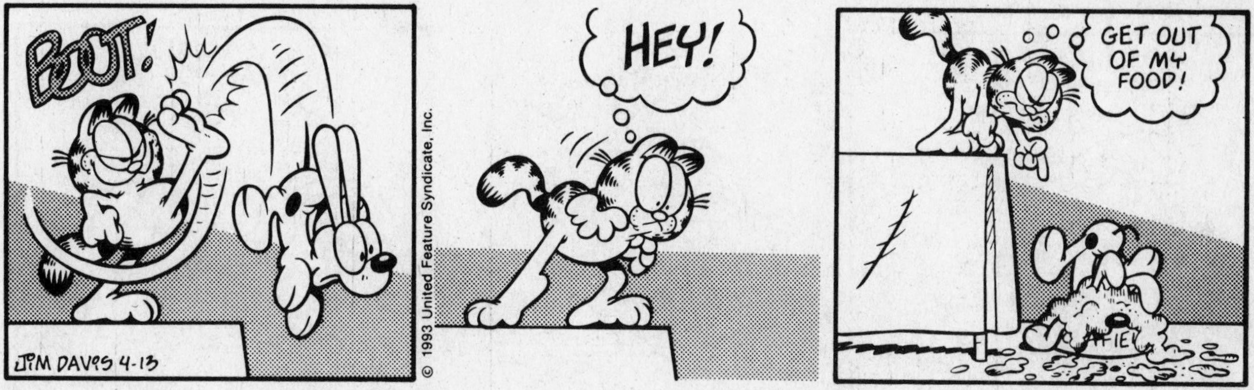
BOOT!
HEY!
GET OUT OF MY FOOD!
JIM DAVIS 4-13
© 1993 United Feature Syndicate, Inc.

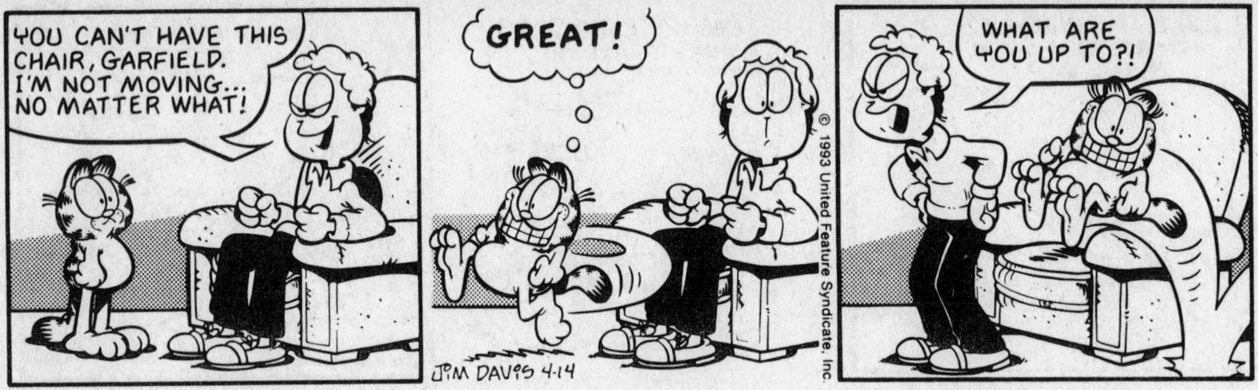
YOU CAN'T HAVE THIS CHAIR, GARFIELD. I'M NOT MOVING... NO MATTER WHAT!
GREAT!
WHAT ARE YOU UP TO?!
JIM DAVIS 4-14
© 1993 United Feature Syndicate, Inc.

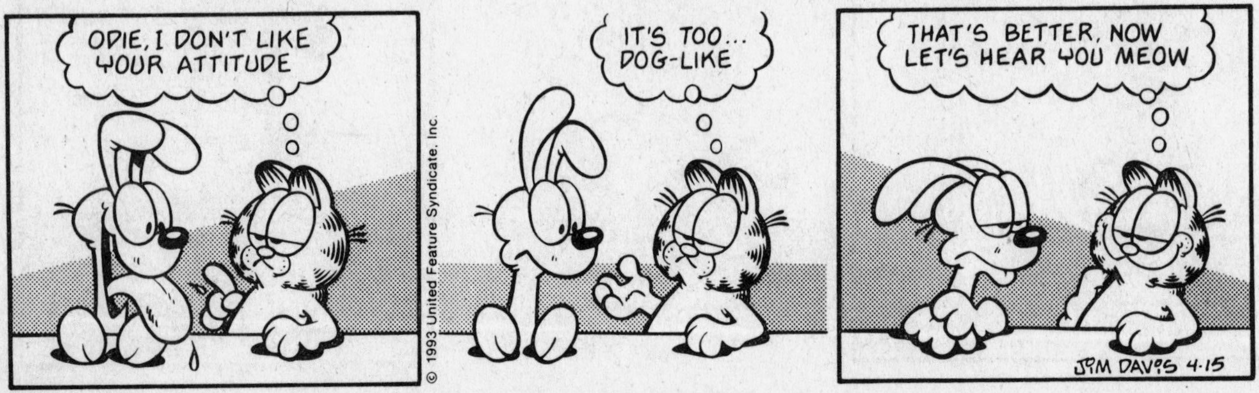
ODIE, I DON'T LIKE YOUR ATTITUDE
IT'S TOO... DOG-LIKE
THAT'S BETTER, NOW LET'S HEAR YOU MEOW
JIM DAVIS 4-15
© 1993 United Feature Syndicate, Inc.

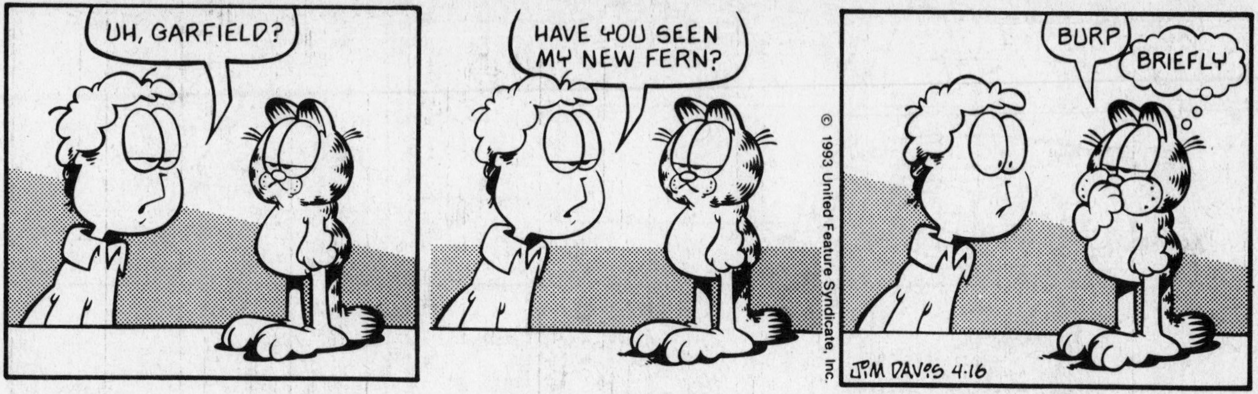
UH, GARFIELD?
HAVE YOU SEEN MY NEW FERN?
© 1993 United Feature Syndicate, Inc.
BURP
BRIEFLY
JIM DAVIS 4·16

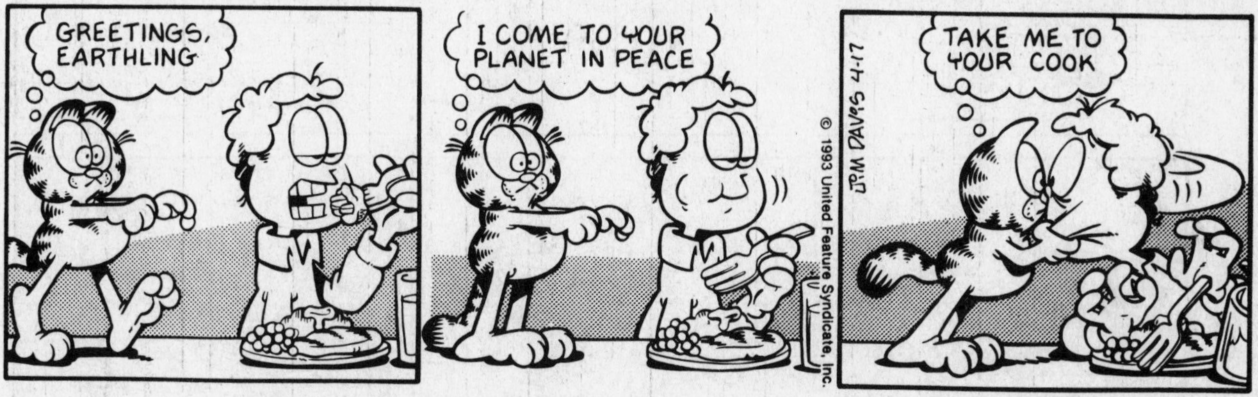
GREETINGS, EARTHLING
I COME TO YOUR PLANET IN PEACE
JIM DAVIS 4·17
© 1993 United Feature Syndicate, Inc.
TAKE ME TO YOUR COOK

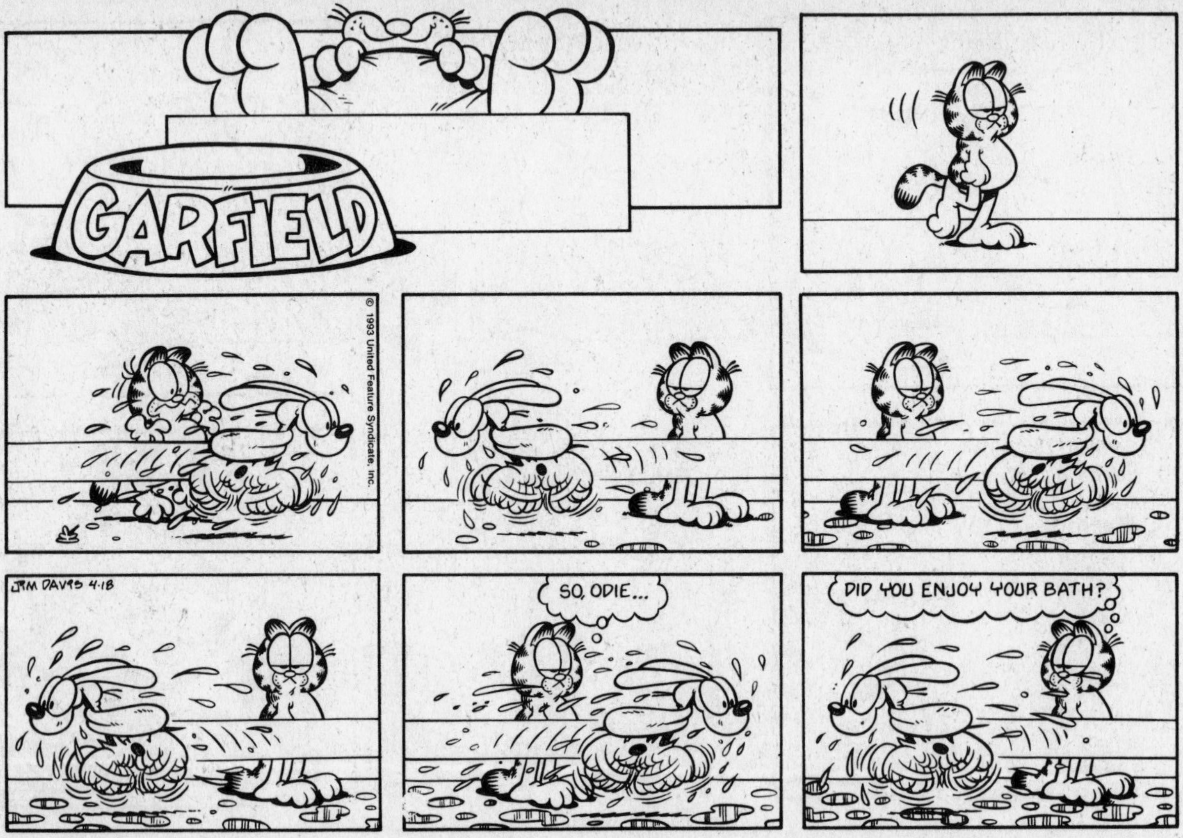
GARFIELD
© 1993 United Feature Syndicate, Inc.
JIM DAVIS 4·18
SO, ODIE...
DID YOU ENJOY YOUR BATH?

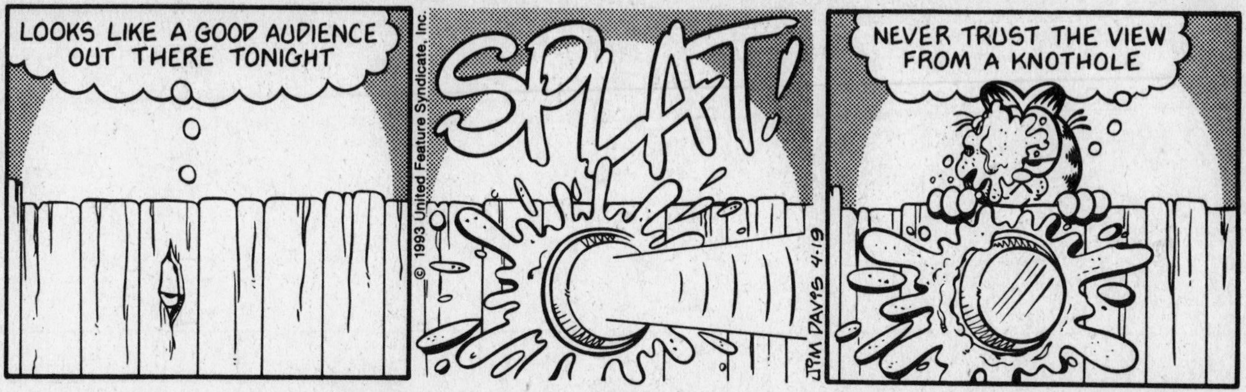
LOOKS LIKE A GOOD AUDIENCE OUT THERE TONIGHT
SPLAT!
© 1993 United Feature Syndicate, Inc.
JIM DAVIS 4-19
NEVER TRUST THE VIEW FROM A KNOTHOLE

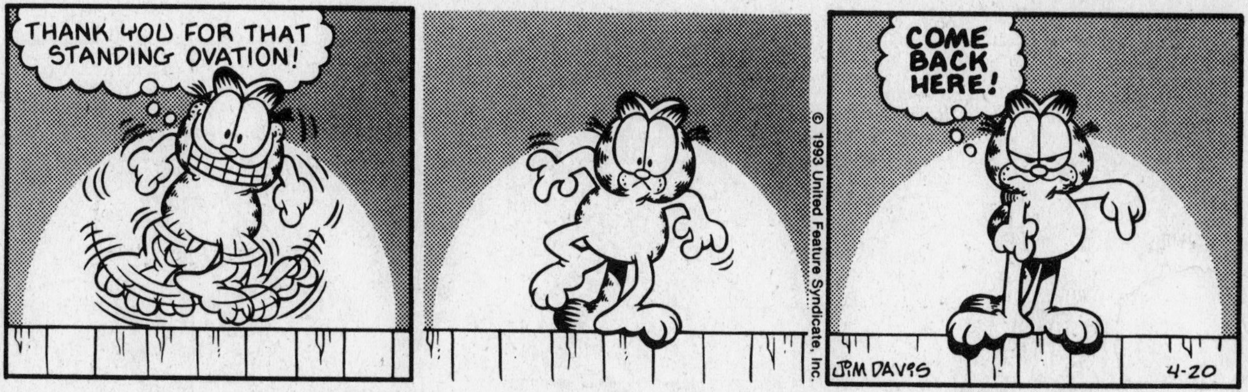
THANK YOU FOR THAT STANDING OVATION!
© 1993 United Feature Syndicate, Inc.
COME BACK HERE!
JIM DAVIS
4-20

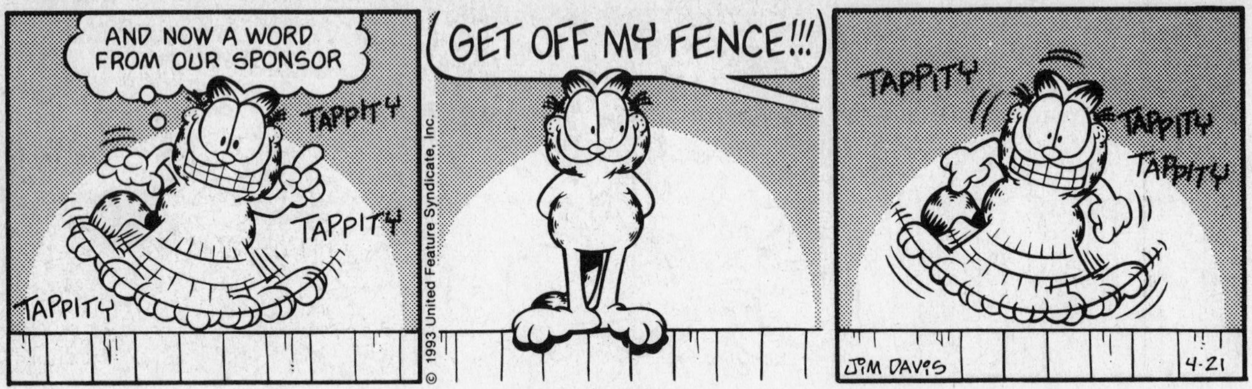
AND NOW A WORD FROM OUR SPONSOR
TAPPITY
TAPPITY
TAPPITY
© 1993 United Feature Syndicate, Inc.
GET OFF MY FENCE!!!
TAPPITY
TAPPITY
TAPPITY
JIM DAVIS
4-21

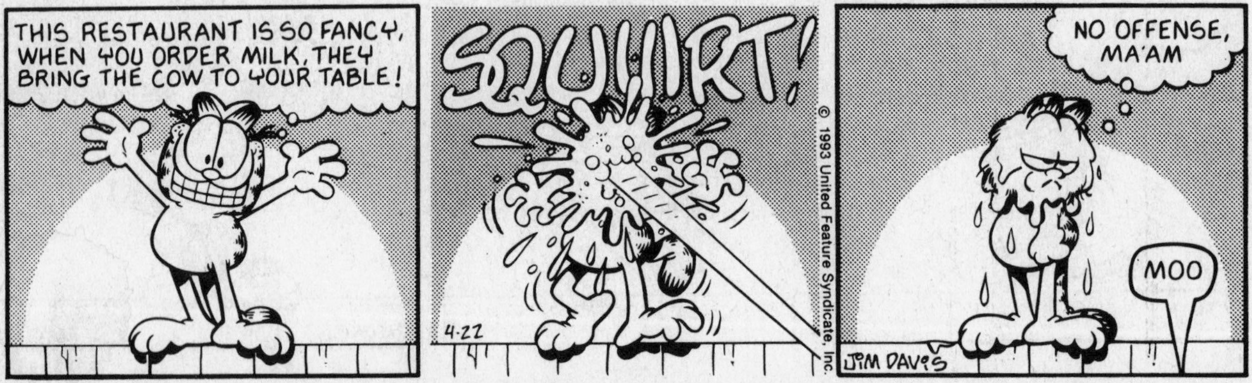
THIS RESTAURANT IS SO FANCY, WHEN YOU ORDER MILK, THEY BRING THE COW TO YOUR TABLE!
SQUIIRT!
4-22
© 1993 United Feature Syndicate, Inc.
NO OFFENSE, MA'AM
MOO
JIM DAVIS

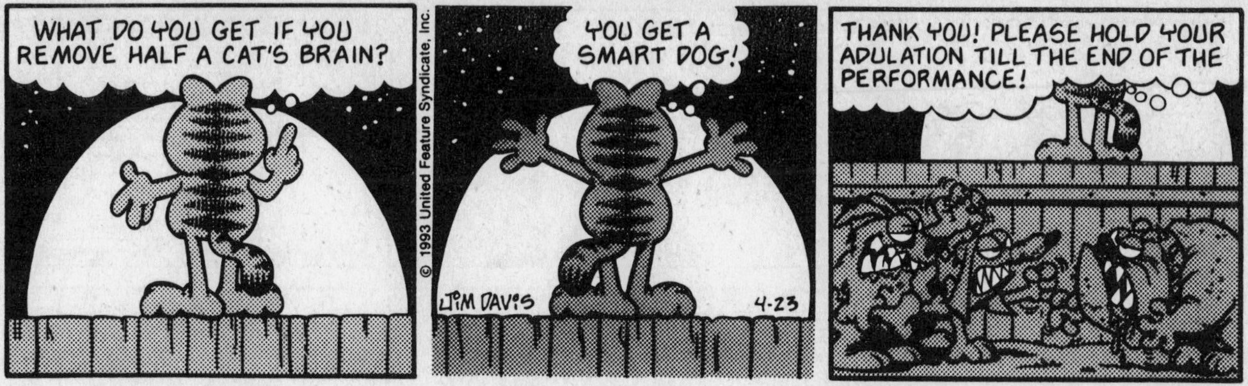
WHAT DO YOU GET IF YOU REMOVE HALF A CAT'S BRAIN?
© 1993 United Feature Syndicate, Inc.
YOU GET A SMART DOG!
JIM DAVIS
4-23
THANK YOU! PLEASE HOLD YOUR ADULATION TILL THE END OF THE PERFORMANCE!

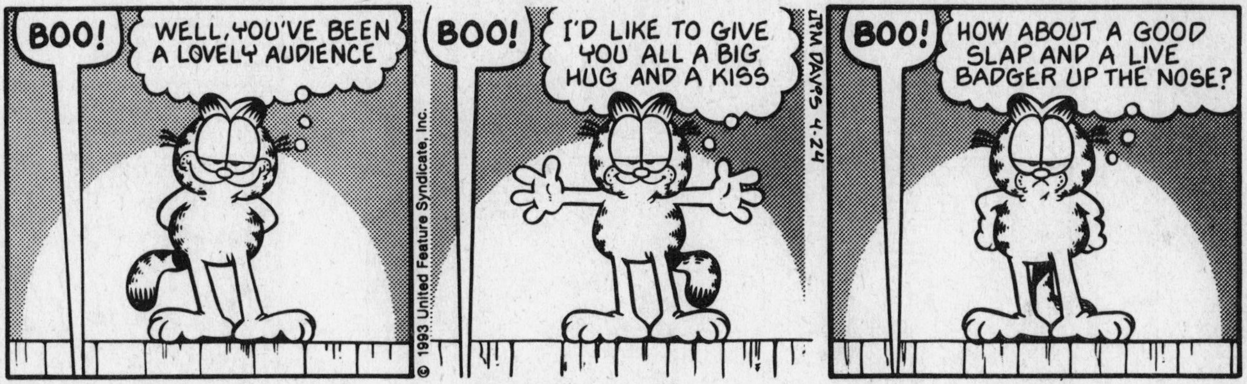
BOO!
WELL, YOU'VE BEEN A LOVELY AUDIENCE
© 1993 United Feature Syndicate, Inc.
BOO!
I'D LIKE TO GIVE YOU ALL A BIG HUG AND A KISS
JIM DAVIS 4-24
BOO!
HOW ABOUT A GOOD SLAP AND A LIVE BADGER UP THE NOSE?

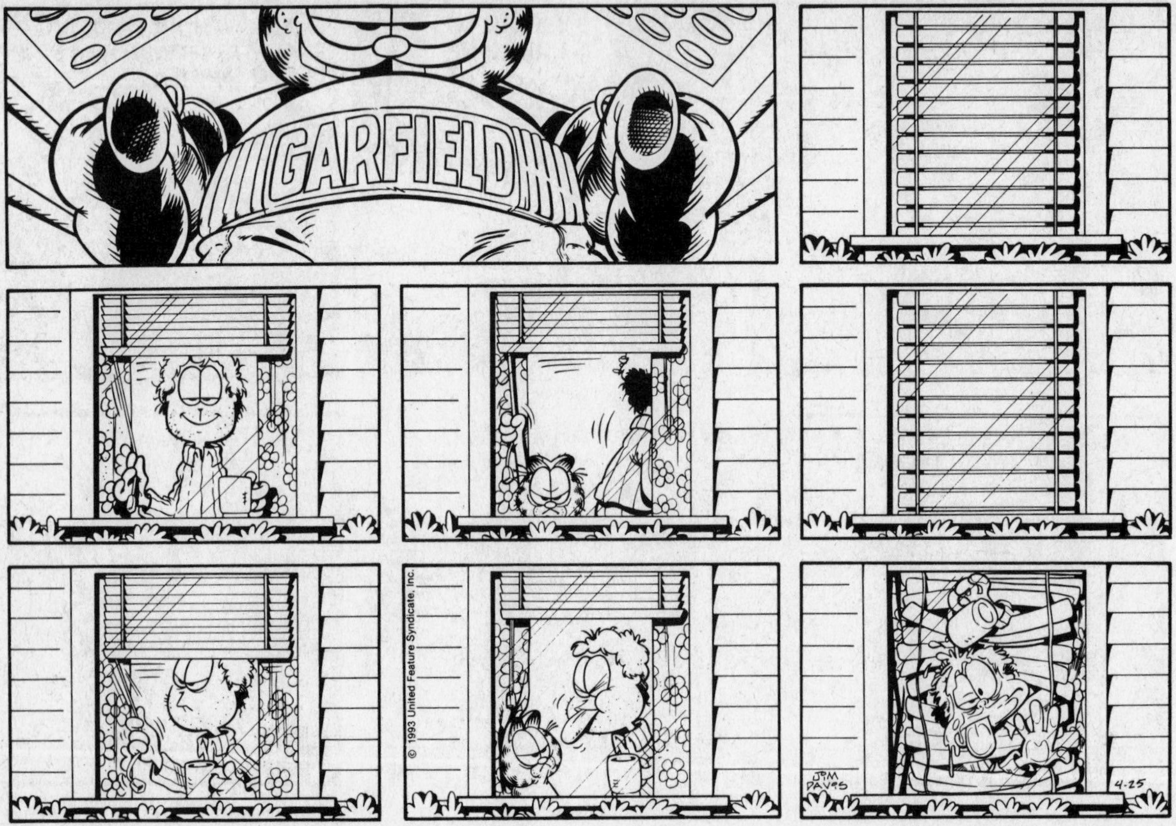
GARFIELD
© 1993 United Feature Syndicate, Inc.
JIM DAVIS
4-25

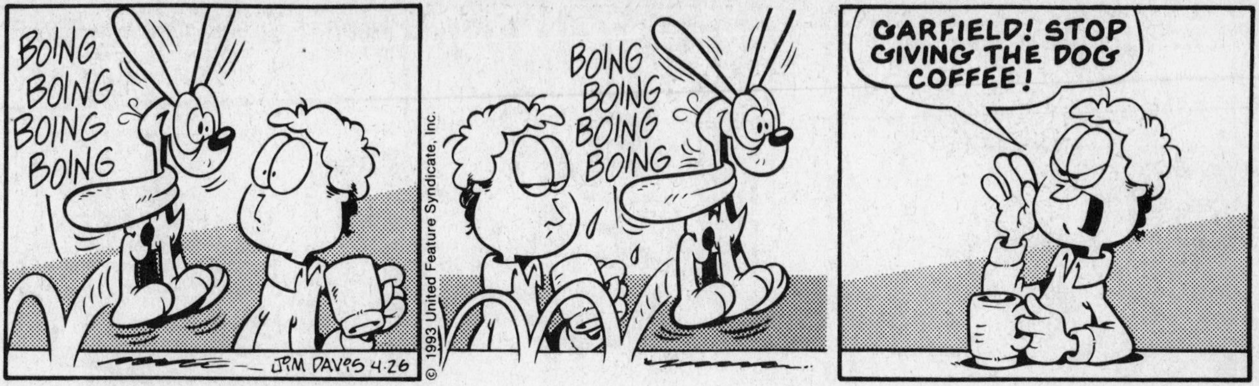
BOING BOING BOING BOING BOING
JIM DAVIS 4·26
© 1993 United Feature Syndicate, Inc.
BOING BOING BOING BOING BOING
GARFIELD! STOP GIVING THE DOG COFFEE!

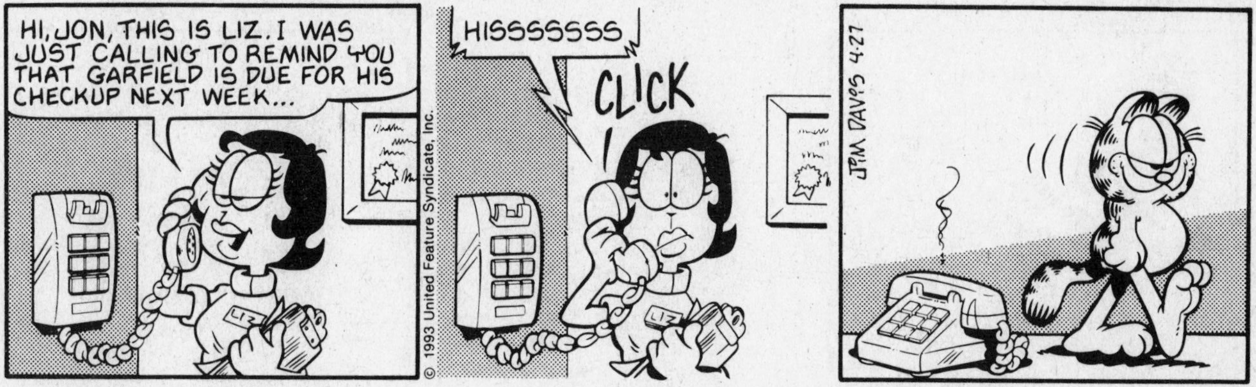
HI, JON, THIS IS LIZ. I WAS JUST CALLING TO REMIND YOU THAT GARFIELD IS DUE FOR HIS CHECKUP NEXT WEEK...
LIZ
© 1993 United Feature Syndicate, Inc.
HISSSSSSS
CLICK
LIZ
JIM DAVIS 4·27

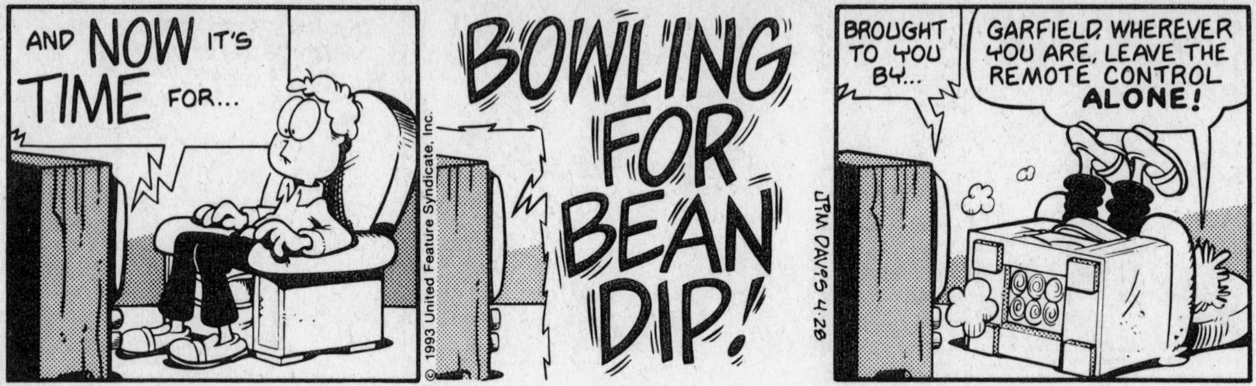
AND NOW IT'S TIME FOR...
BOWLING FOR BEAN DIP!
BROUGHT TO YOU BY...
GARFIELD, WHEREVER YOU ARE, LEAVE THE REMOTE CONTROL ALONE!
© 1993 United Feature Syndicate, Inc.
JIM DAVIS 4·28

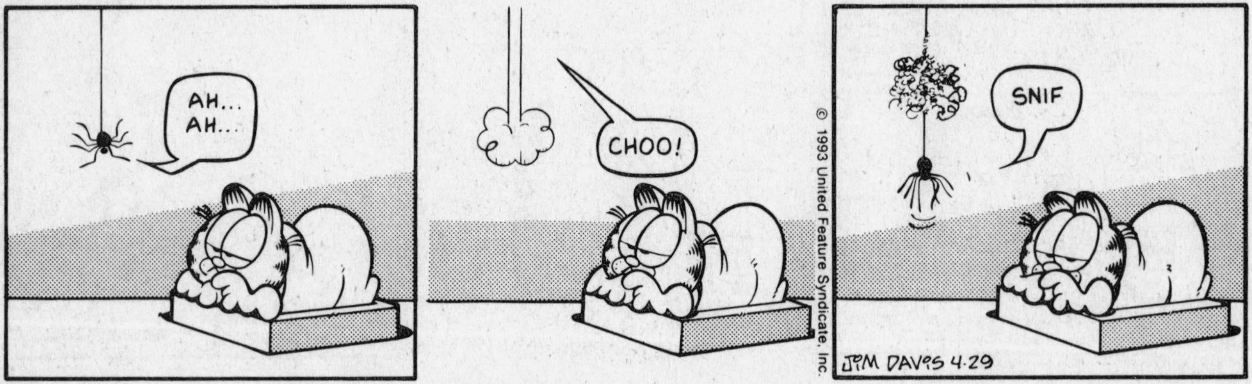
AH... AH...
CHOO!
SNIF
© 1993 United Feature Syndicate, Inc.
JIM DAVIS 4·29

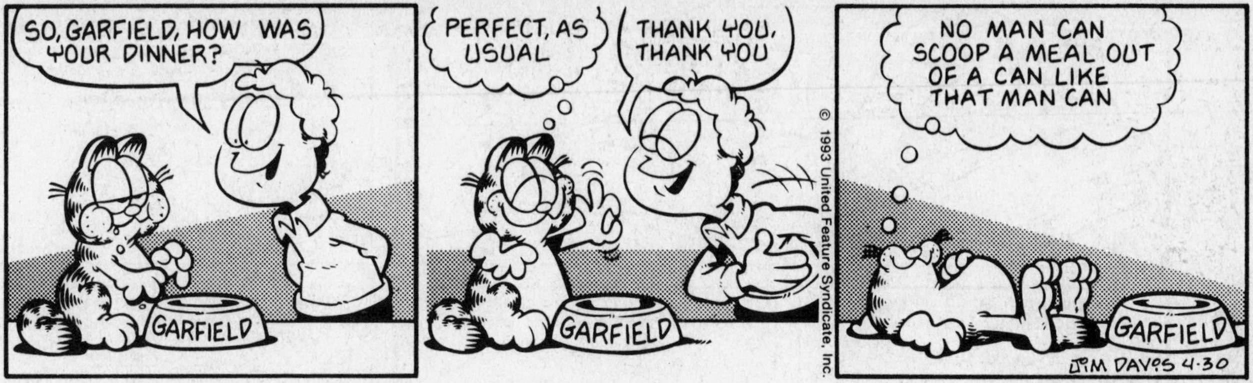
SO, GARFIELD, HOW WAS YOUR DINNER?
GARFIELD
PERFECT, AS USUAL
THANK YOU, THANK YOU
GARFIELD
© 1993 United Feature Syndicate, Inc.
NO MAN CAN SCOOP A MEAL OUT OF A CAN LIKE THAT MAN CAN
GARFIELD
JIM DAVIS 4-30

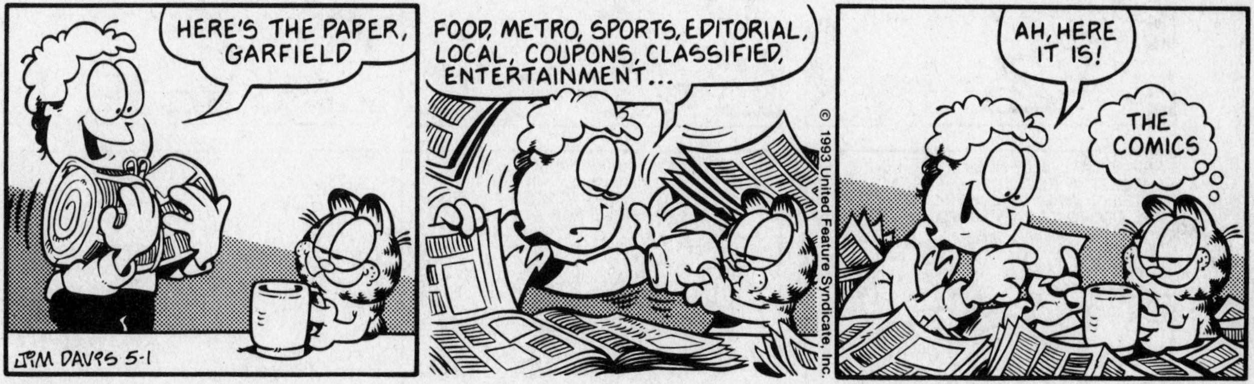
HERE'S THE PAPER, GARFIELD
JIM DAVIS 5-1
FOOD, METRO, SPORTS, EDITORIAL, LOCAL, COUPONS, CLASSIFIED, ENTERTAINMENT...
© 1993 United Feature Syndicate, Inc.
AH, HERE IT IS!
THE COMICS

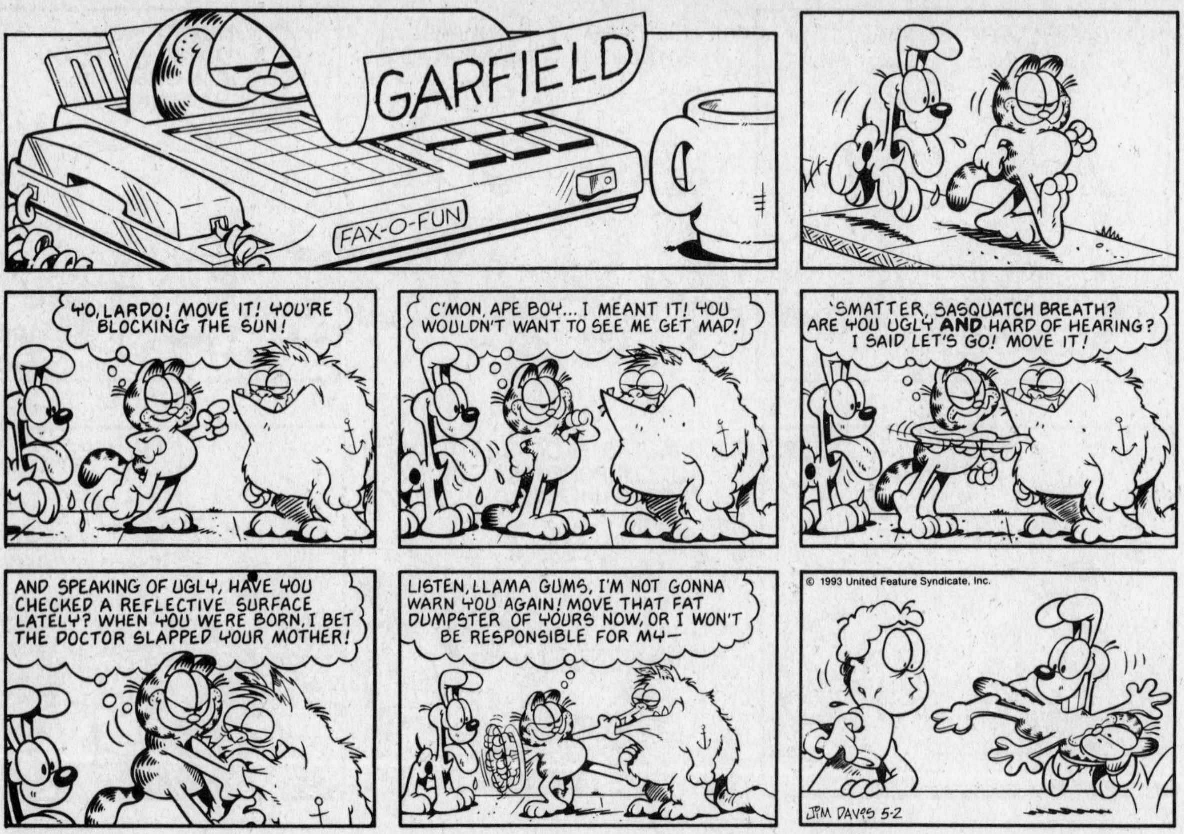
GARFIELD
FAX-O-FUN
YO, LARDO! MOVE IT! YOU'RE BLOCKING THE SUN!
C'MON, APE BOY... I MEANT IT! YOU WOULDN'T WANT TO SEE ME GET MAD!
'SMATTER, SASQUATCH BREATH? ARE YOU UGLY **AND** HARD OF HEARING? I SAID LET'S GO! MOVE IT!
AND SPEAKING OF UGLY, HAVE YOU CHECKED A REFLECTIVE SURFACE LATELY? WHEN YOU WERE BORN, I BET THE DOCTOR SLAPPED YOUR MOTHER!
LISTEN, LLAMA GUMS, I'M NOT GONNA WARN YOU AGAIN! MOVE THAT FAT DUMPSTER OF YOURS NOW, OR I WON'T BE RESPONSIBLE FOR MY—
© 1993 United Feature Syndicate, Inc.
JPM DAVIS 5-2

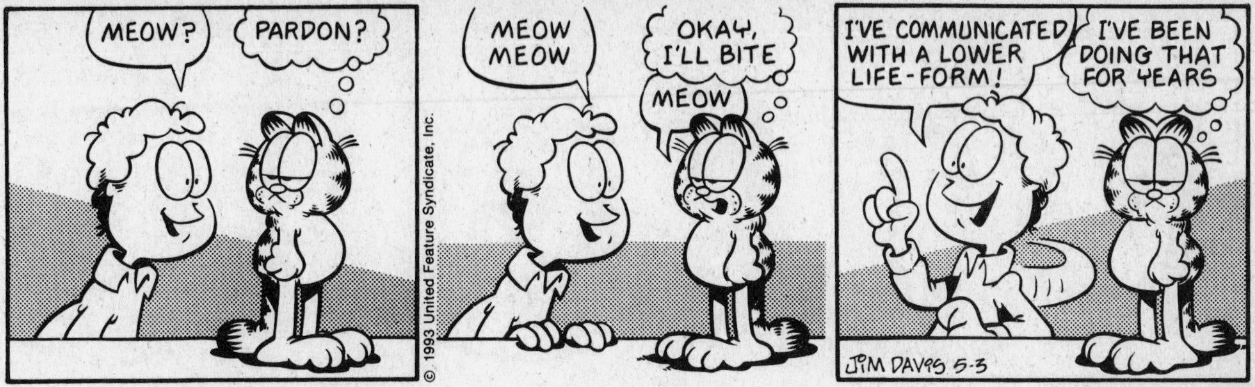
MEOW?
PARDON?
© 1993 United Feature Syndicate, Inc.
MEOW MEOW
OKAY, I'LL BITE
MEOW
I'VE COMMUNICATED WITH A LOWER LIFE-FORM!
I'VE BEEN DOING THAT FOR YEARS
JIM DAVIS 5-3

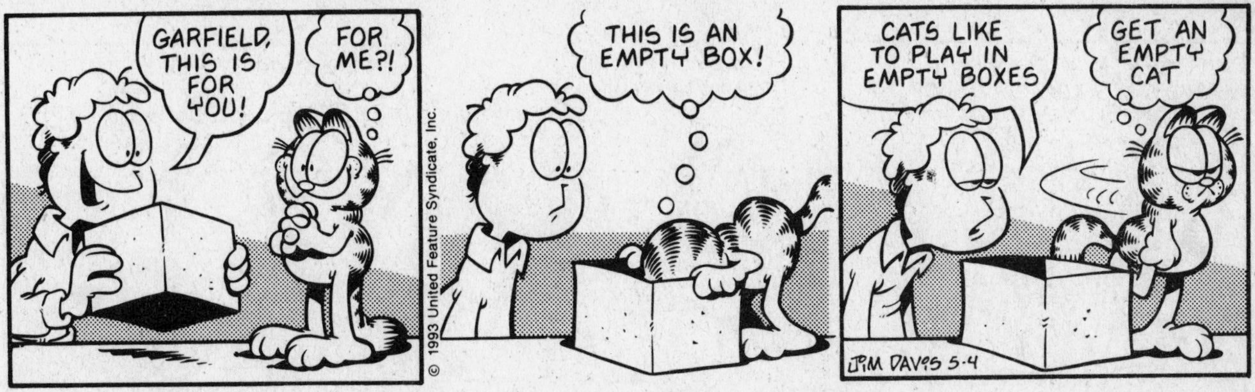
GARFIELD, THIS IS FOR YOU!
FOR ME?!
© 1993 United Feature Syndicate, Inc.
THIS IS AN EMPTY BOX!
CATS LIKE TO PLAY IN EMPTY BOXES
GET AN EMPTY CAT
JIM DAVIS 5-4

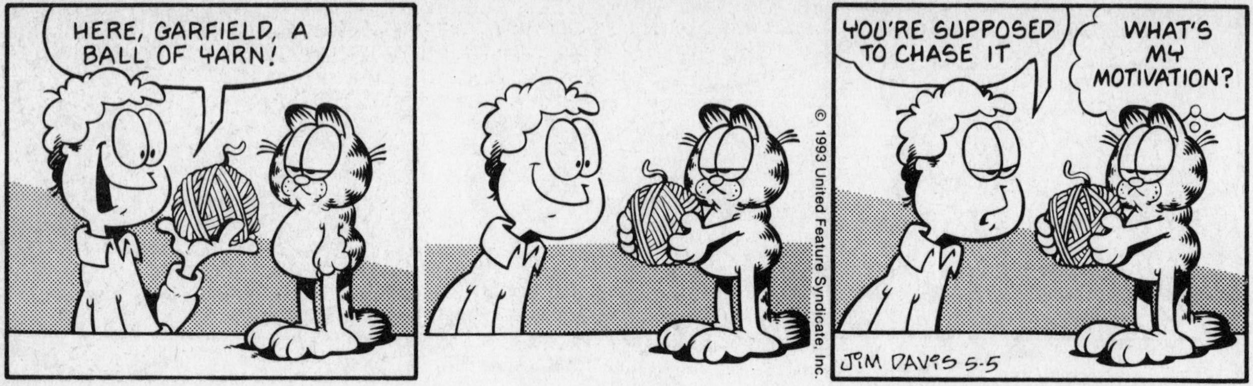
HERE, GARFIELD, A BALL OF YARN!
YOU'RE SUPPOSED TO CHASE IT
WHAT'S MY MOTIVATION?
JIM DAVIS 5-5
© 1993 United Feature Syndicate, Inc.

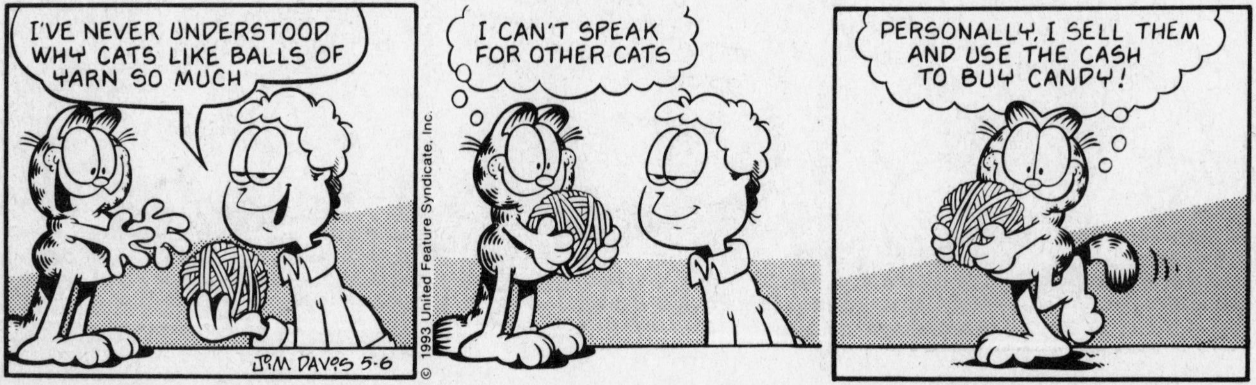
I'VE NEVER UNDERSTOOD WHY CATS LIKE BALLS OF YARN SO MUCH
JIM DAVIS 5-6
© 1993 United Feature Syndicate, Inc.
I CAN'T SPEAK FOR OTHER CATS
PERSONALLY, I SELL THEM AND USE THE CASH TO BUY CANDY!

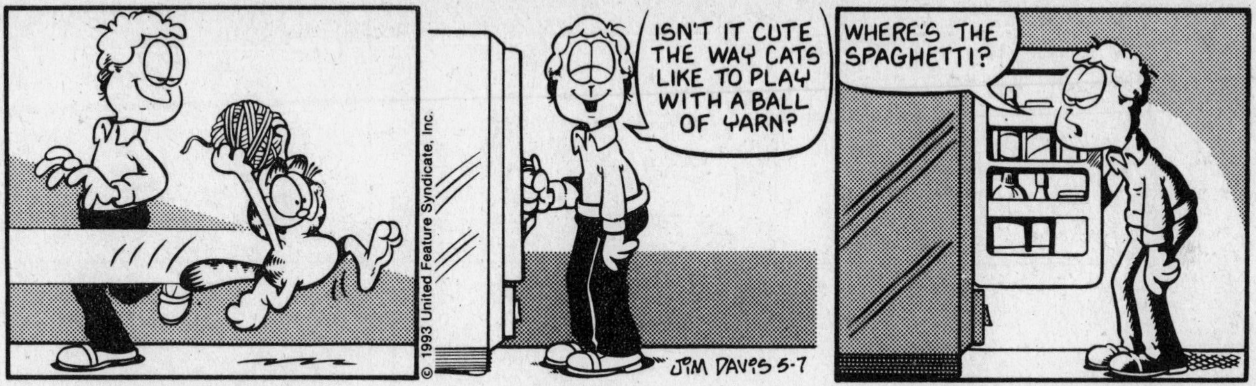
© 1993 United Feature Syndicate, Inc.
ISN'T IT CUTE THE WAY CATS LIKE TO PLAY WITH A BALL OF YARN?
JIM DAVIS 5-7
WHERE'S THE SPAGHETTI?

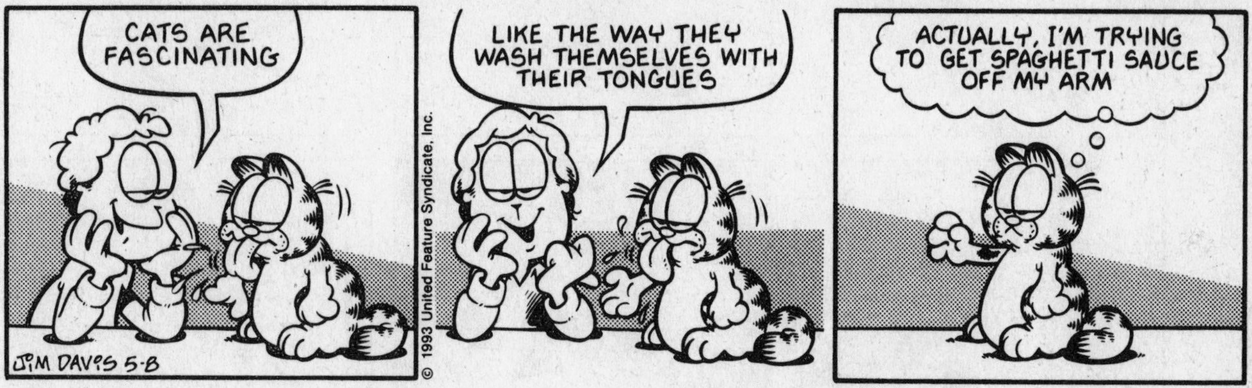
CATS ARE FASCINATING
JIM DAVIS 5-8
© 1993 United Feature Syndicate, Inc.
LIKE THE WAY THEY WASH THEMSELVES WITH THEIR TONGUES
ACTUALLY, I'M TRYING TO GET SPAGHETTI SAUCE OFF MY ARM

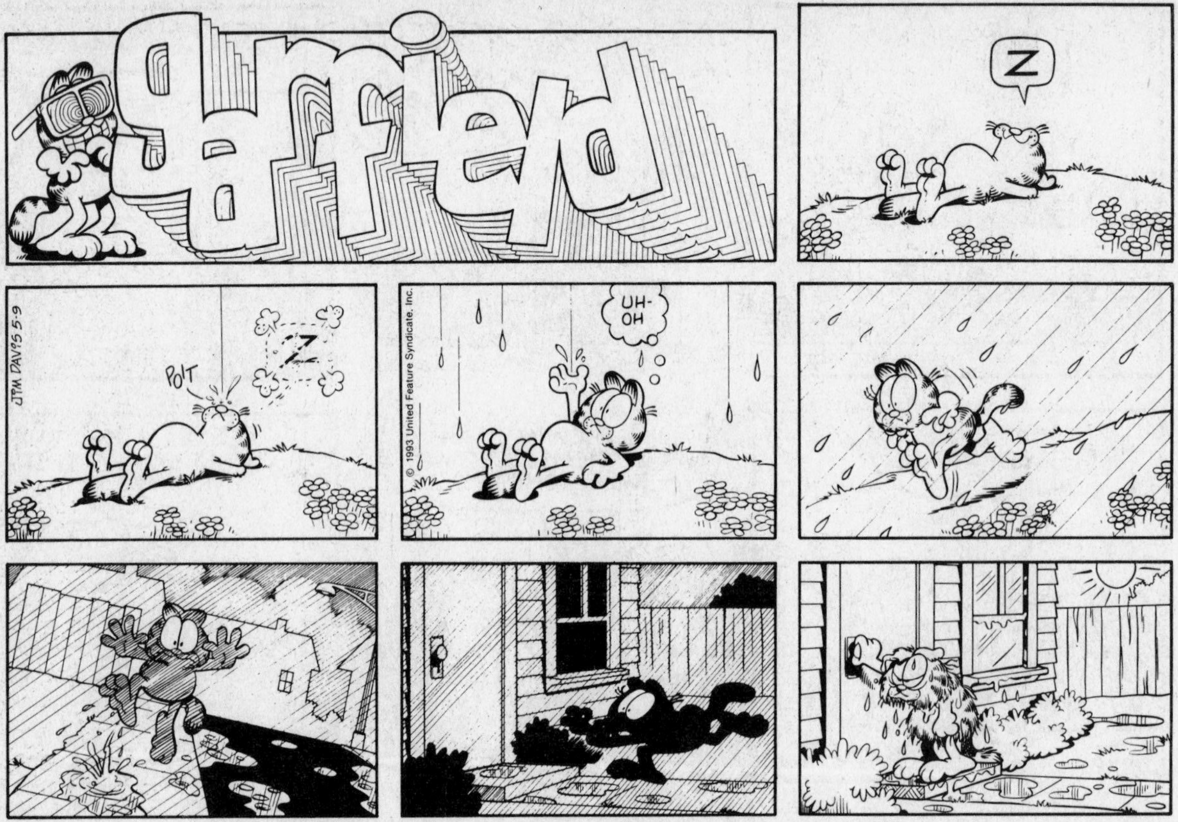
Garfield
Z
JPM DAVIS 5-9
POIT
Z
© 1993 United Feature Syndicate, Inc.
UH-OH

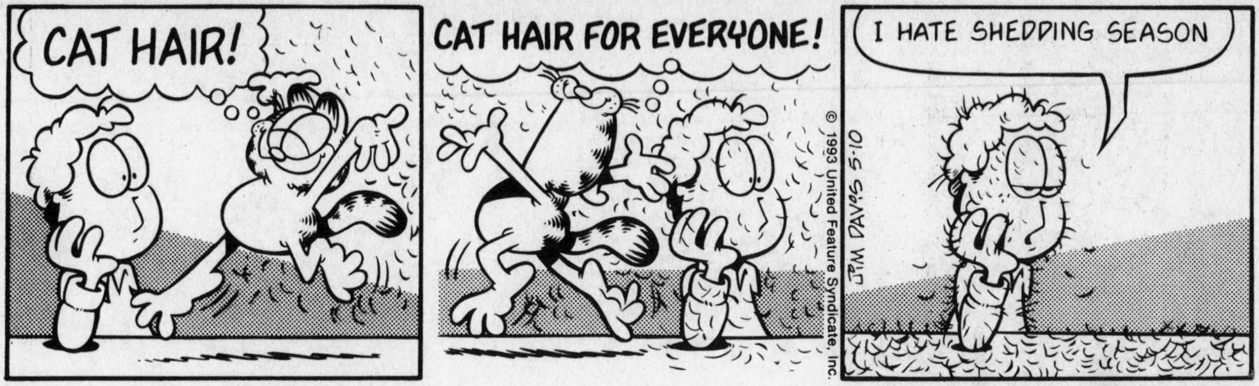
CAT HAIR!
CAT HAIR FOR EVERYONE!
I HATE SHEDDING SEASON
JIM DAVIS 5-10
© 1993 United Feature Syndicate, Inc.

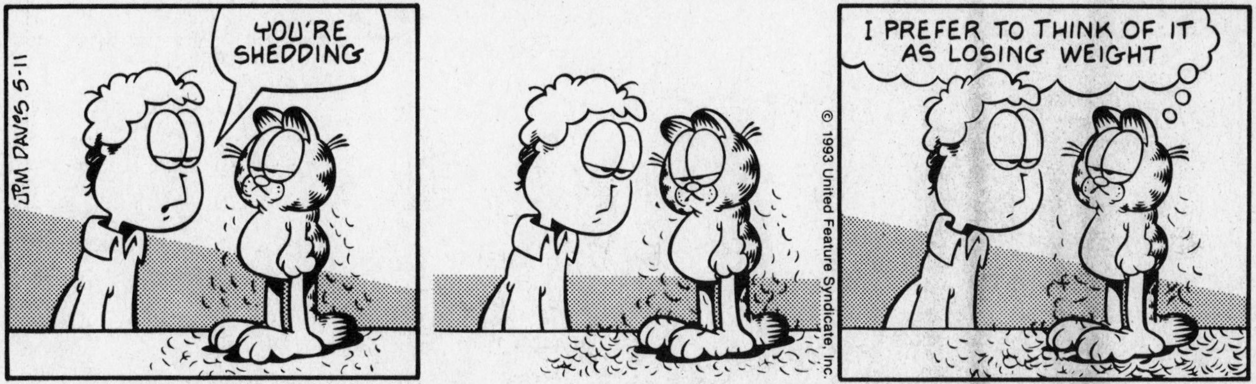
JIM DAVIS 5-11
YOU'RE SHEDDING
I PREFER TO THINK OF IT AS LOSING WEIGHT
© 1993 United Feature Syndicate, Inc.

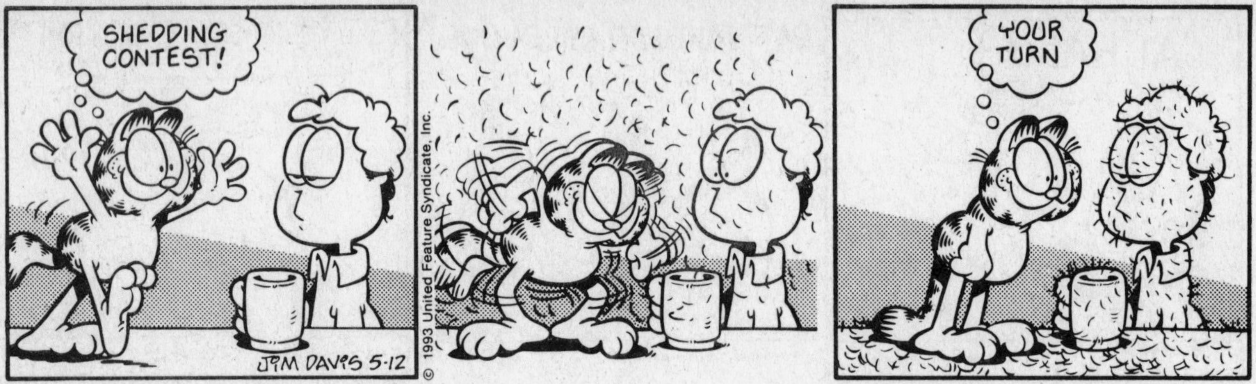
SHEDDING CONTEST!
JIM DAVIS 5-12
© 1993 United Feature Syndicate, Inc.
YOUR TURN

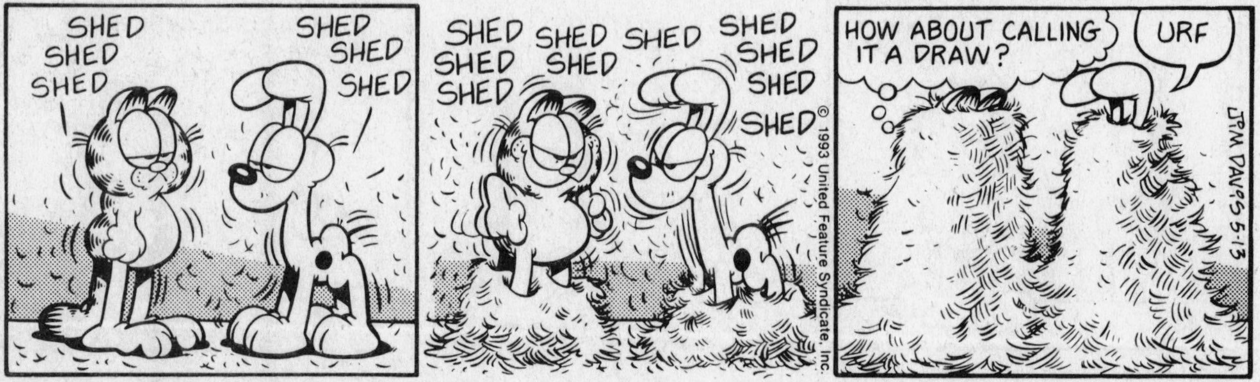
SHED SHED SHED
SHED SHED SHED
SHED SHED SHED
SHED SHED
SHED
SHED SHED SHED SHED
© 1993 United Feature Syndicate, Inc.
HOW ABOUT CALLING IT A DRAW?
URF
JIM DAVIS 5-13

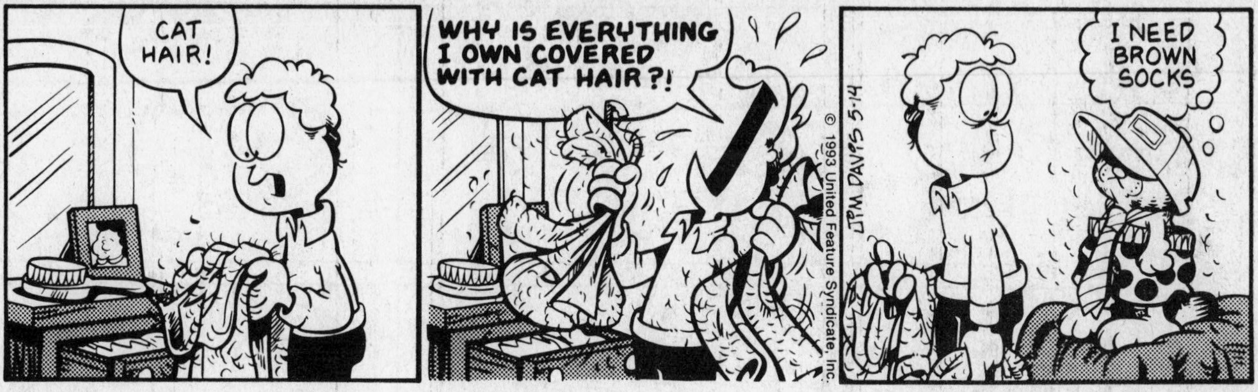
CAT HAIR!
WHY IS EVERYTHING I OWN COVERED WITH CAT HAIR?!
© 1993 United Feature Syndicate, Inc.
JIM DAVIS 5-14
I NEED BROWN SOCKS

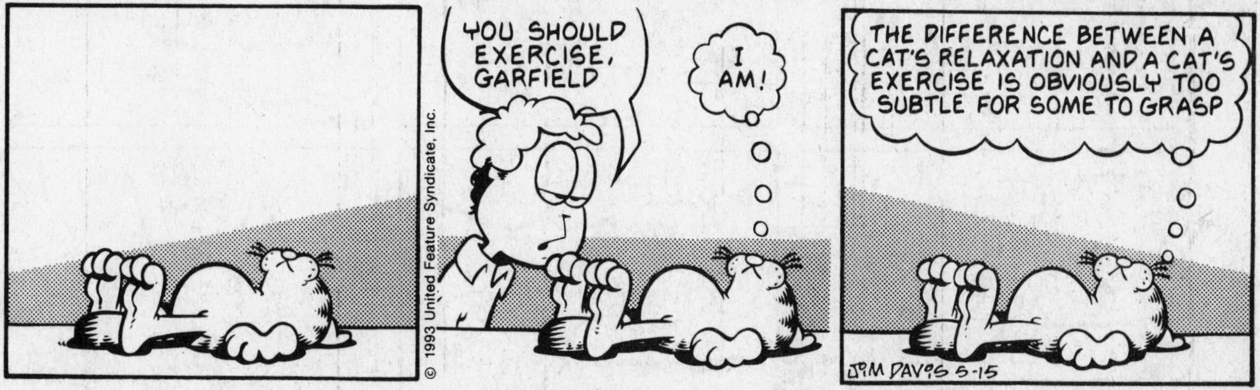
© 1993 United Feature Syndicate, Inc.
YOU SHOULD EXERCISE, GARFIELD
I AM!
THE DIFFERENCE BETWEEN A CAT'S RELAXATION AND A CAT'S EXERCISE IS OBVIOUSLY TOO SUBTLE FOR SOME TO GRASP
JIM DAVIS 5-15

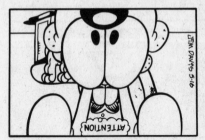

GARFIELD
© 1993 United Feature Syndicate, Inc.
SIGH
DOESN'T IT BUG YOU WHEN DOGS GET IN FRONT OF YOU JUST BECAUSE THEY WANT YOUR
JPM DAVPS 5-16
ATTENTION

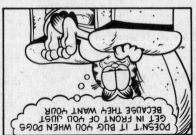

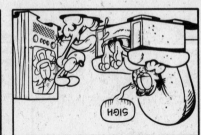

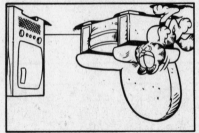

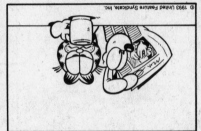

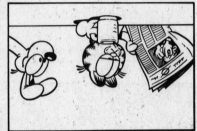

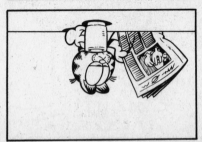

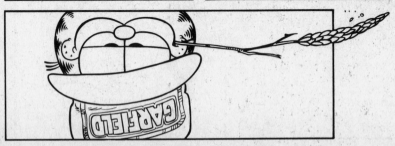

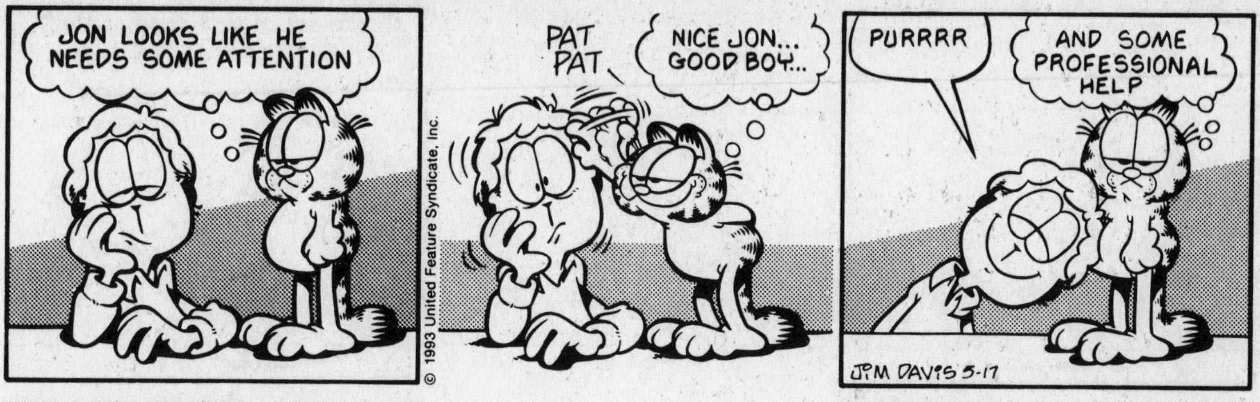
JON LOOKS LIKE HE NEEDS SOME ATTENTION
PAT PAT
NICE JON... GOOD BOY...
PURRRR
AND SOME PROFESSIONAL HELP
JIM DAVIS 5-17
© 1993 United Feature Syndicate, Inc.

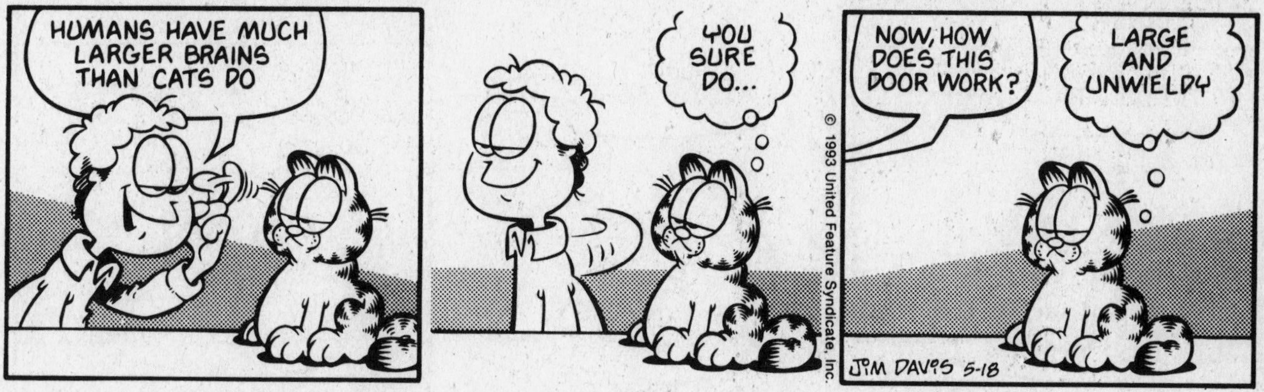
HUMANS HAVE MUCH LARGER BRAINS THAN CATS DO
YOU SURE DO...
NOW, HOW DOES THIS DOOR WORK?
LARGE AND UNWIELDY
JIM DAVIS 5-18
© 1993 United Feature Syndicate, Inc.

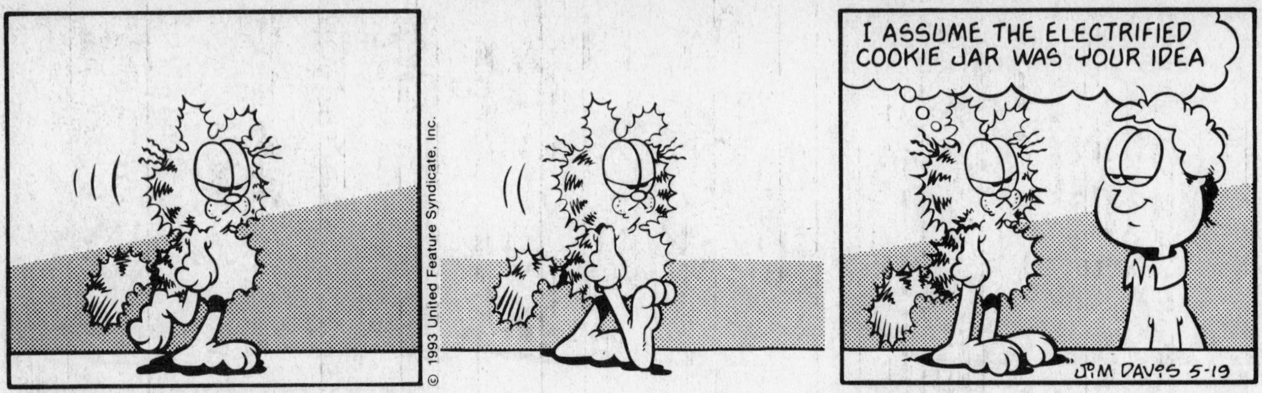
I ASSUME THE ELECTRIFIED COOKIE JAR WAS YOUR IDEA
JIM DAVIS 5-19

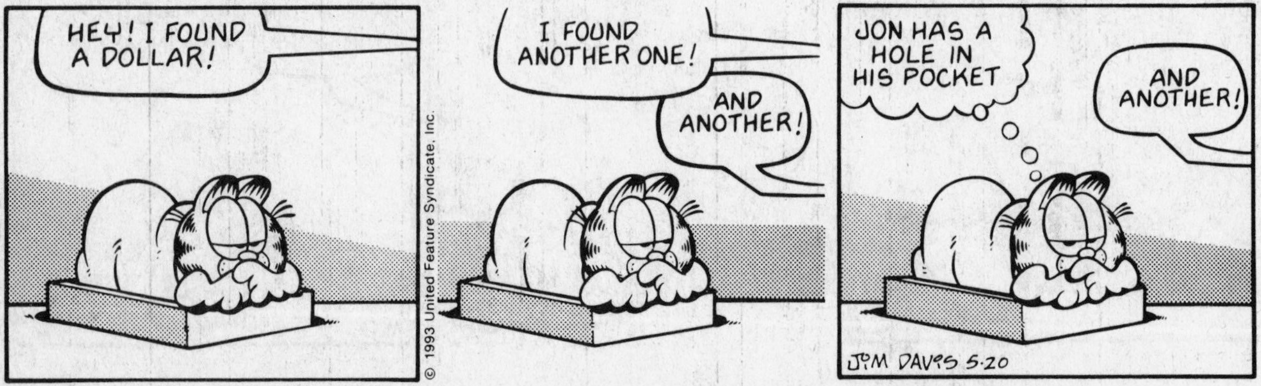
HEY! I FOUND A DOLLAR!
I FOUND ANOTHER ONE!
AND ANOTHER!
JON HAS A HOLE IN HIS POCKET
AND ANOTHER!
JIM DAVIS 5-20

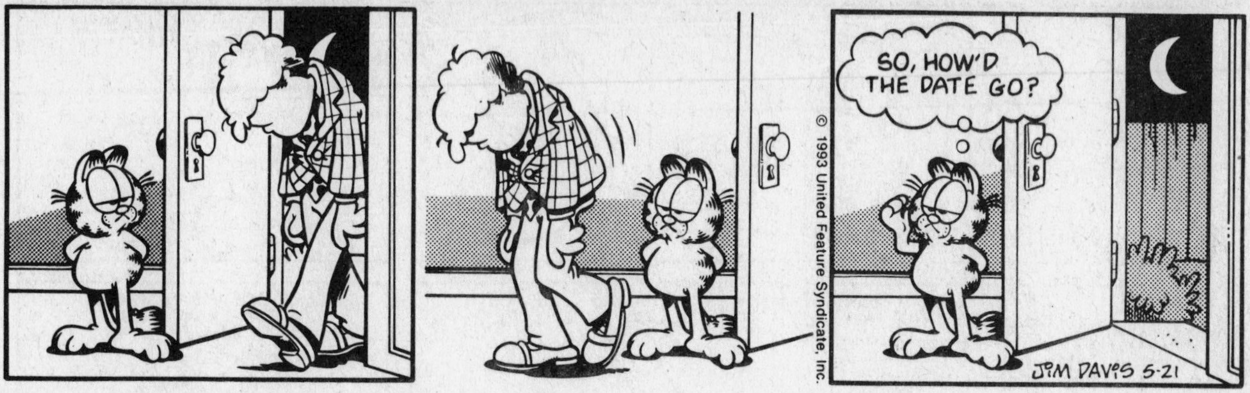
© 1993 United Feature Syndicate, Inc.
SO, HOW'D THE DATE GO?
JIM DAVIS 5-21

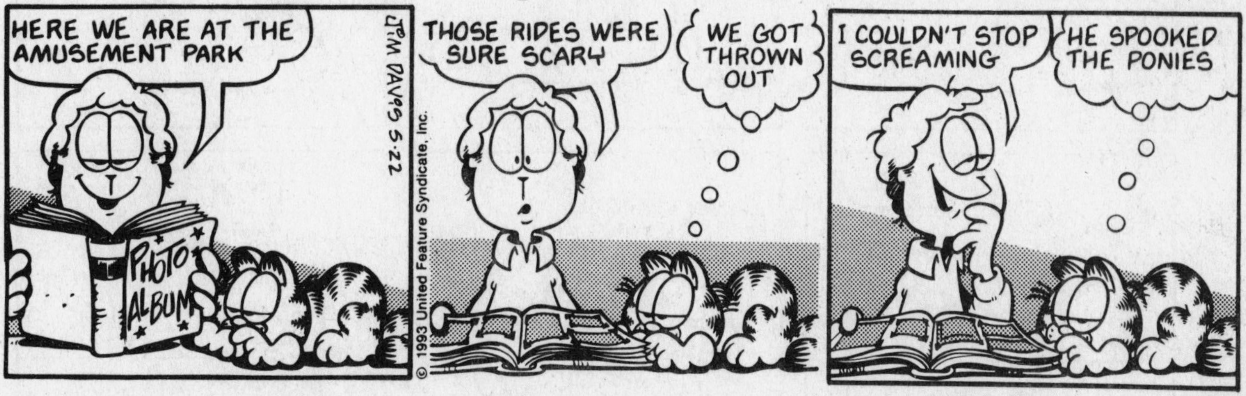
HERE WE ARE AT THE AMUSEMENT PARK
PHOTO ALBUM
JIM DAVIS 5-22
© 1993 United Feature Syndicate, Inc.
THOSE RIDES WERE SURE SCARY
WE GOT THROWN OUT
I COULDN'T STOP SCREAMING
HE SPOOKED THE PONIES

ME AND MY
BIG VOICE CHIP

JPM DAV95 5-23

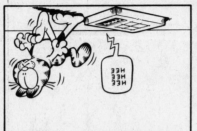

HEE
HEE
HEE

SIGH

WE COMPUTERS ARE INCAPABLE
OF LYING OR ANY HUMAN EMOTION.
YOU REALLY **ARE** THAT FAT

YOU MUST
BE LYING!

IMPOSSIBLE

© 1993 United Feature Syndicate, Inc.

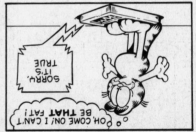

OH, COME ON! I CAN'T
BE **THAT** FAT!

SORRY.
IT'S
TRUE

WHAT?!

GARFIELD

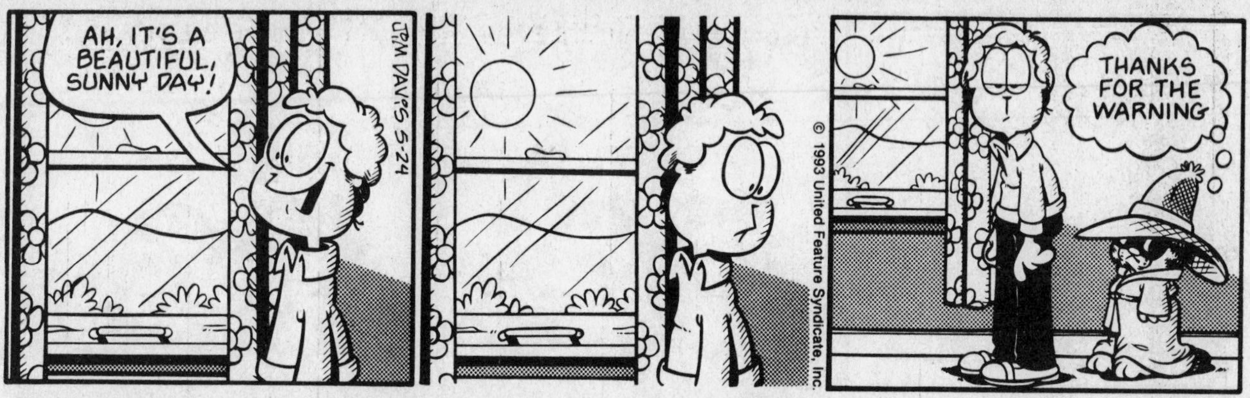
AH, IT'S A BEAUTIFUL, SUNNY DAY!
JIM DAVIS 5-24
© 1993 United Feature Syndicate, Inc.
THANKS FOR THE WARNING

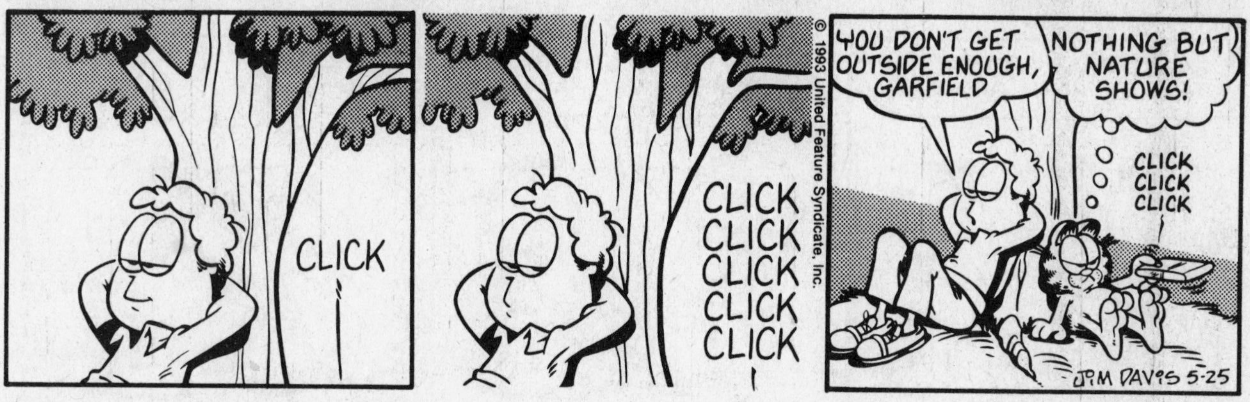
CLICK
CLICK CLICK CLICK CLICK CLICK
© 1993 United Feature Syndicate, Inc.
YOU DON'T GET OUTSIDE ENOUGH, GARFIELD
NOTHING BUT NATURE SHOWS!
CLICK CLICK CLICK
JIM DAVIS 5-25

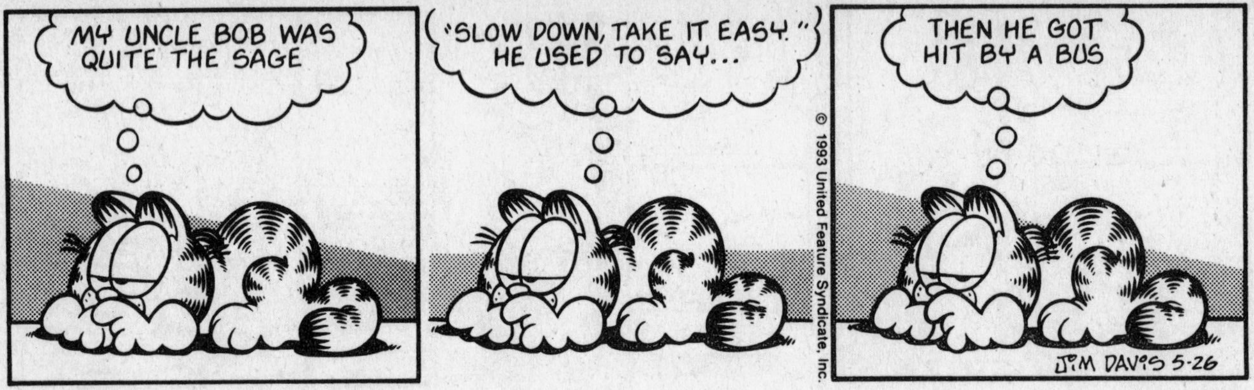
MY UNCLE BOB WAS QUITE THE SAGE
"SLOW DOWN, TAKE IT EASY." HE USED TO SAY...
THEN HE GOT HIT BY A BUS
JIM DAVIS 5-26
© 1993 United Feature Syndicate, Inc.

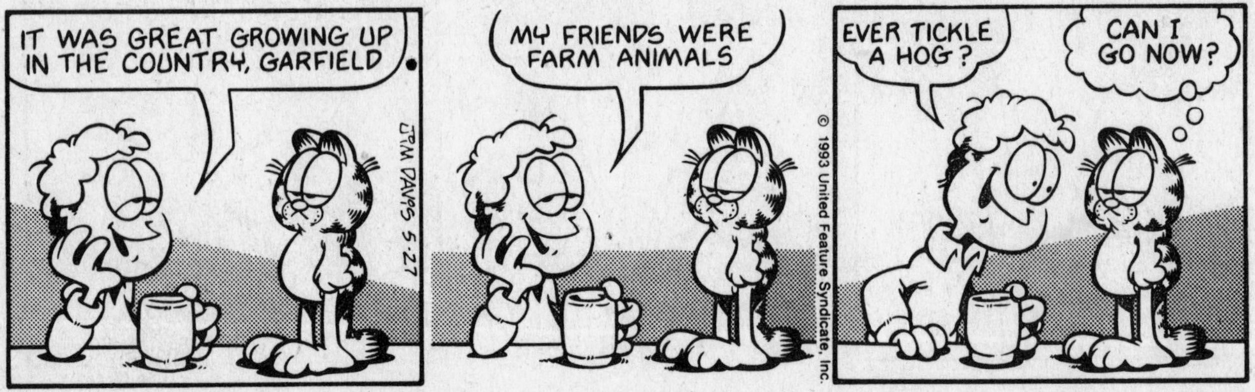
IT WAS GREAT GROWING UP IN THE COUNTRY, GARFIELD
JIM DAVIS 5-27
MY FRIENDS WERE FARM ANIMALS
EVER TICKLE A HOG?
CAN I GO NOW?
© 1993 United Feature Syndicate, Inc.

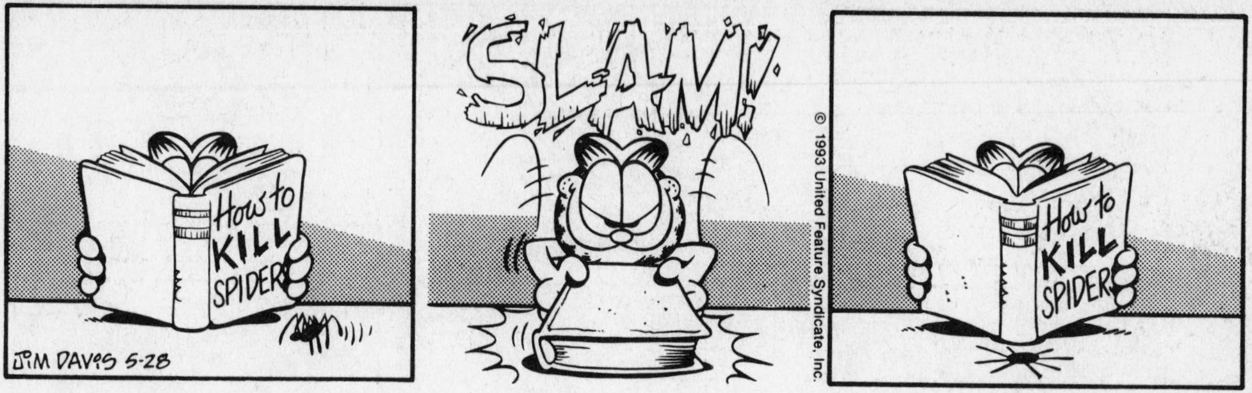
How to KILL SPIDERS
JIM DAVIS 5-28
SLAM!
© 1993 United Feature Syndicate, Inc.
How to KILL SPIDERS

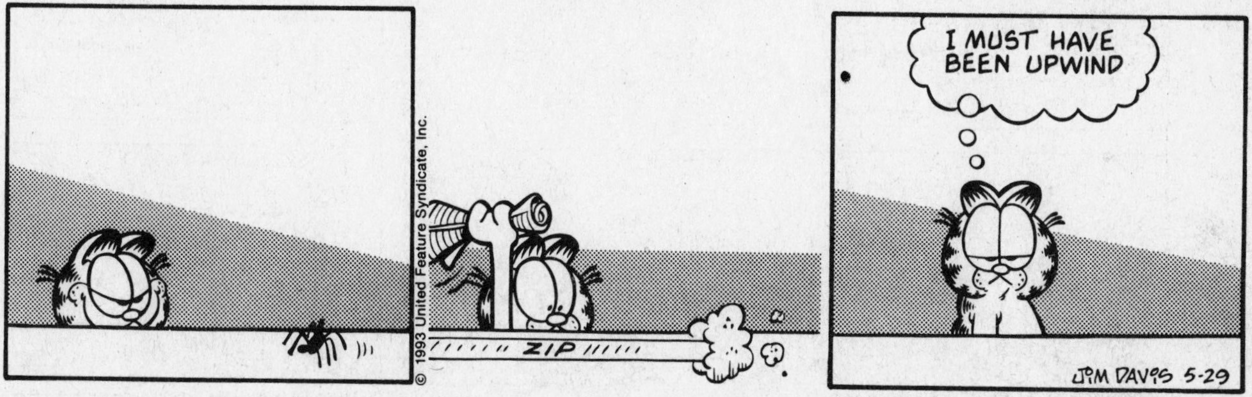
© 1993 United Feature Syndicate, Inc.
ZIP
I MUST HAVE BEEN UPWIND
JIM DAVIS 5-29

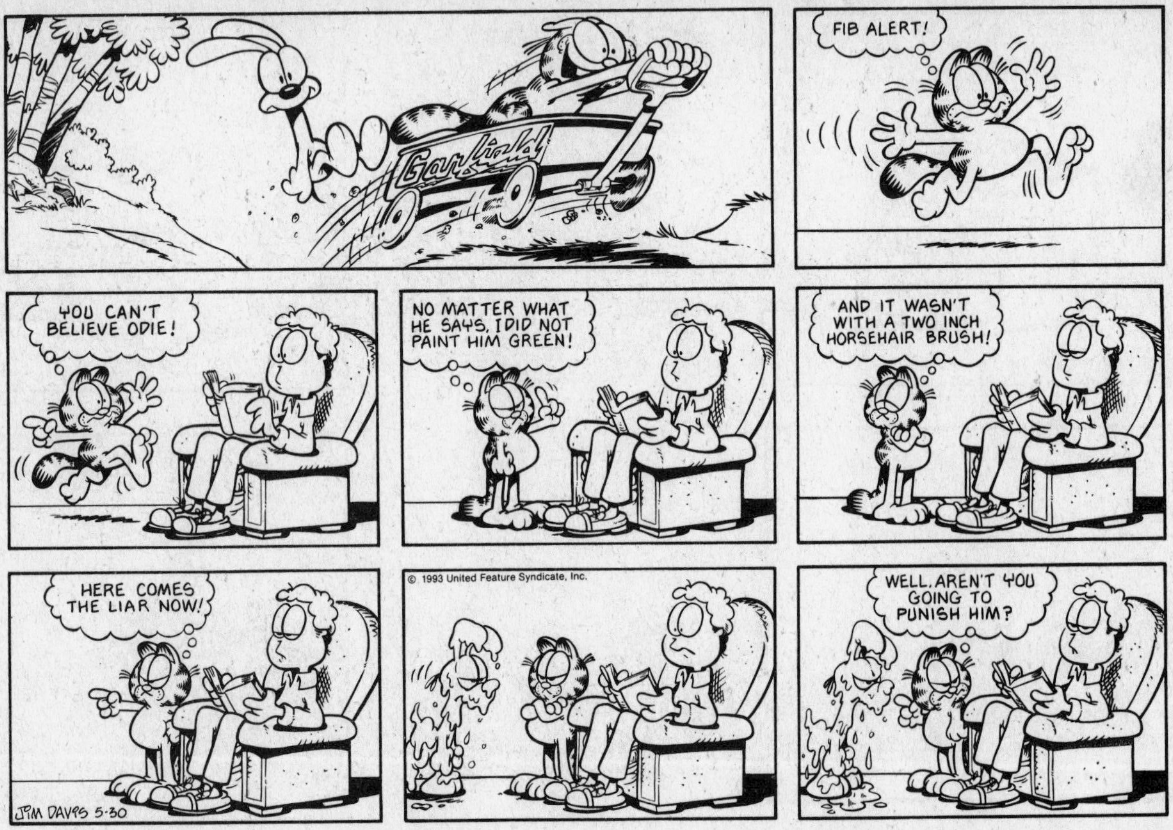
Garfield
FIB ALERT!
YOU CAN'T BELIEVE ODIE!
NO MATTER WHAT HE SAYS, I DID NOT PAINT HIM GREEN!
AND IT WASN'T WITH A TWO INCH HORSEHAIR BRUSH!
HERE COMES THE LIAR NOW!
WELL, AREN'T YOU GOING TO PUNISH HIM?
JIM DAVIS 5-30
© 1993 United Feature Syndicate, Inc.

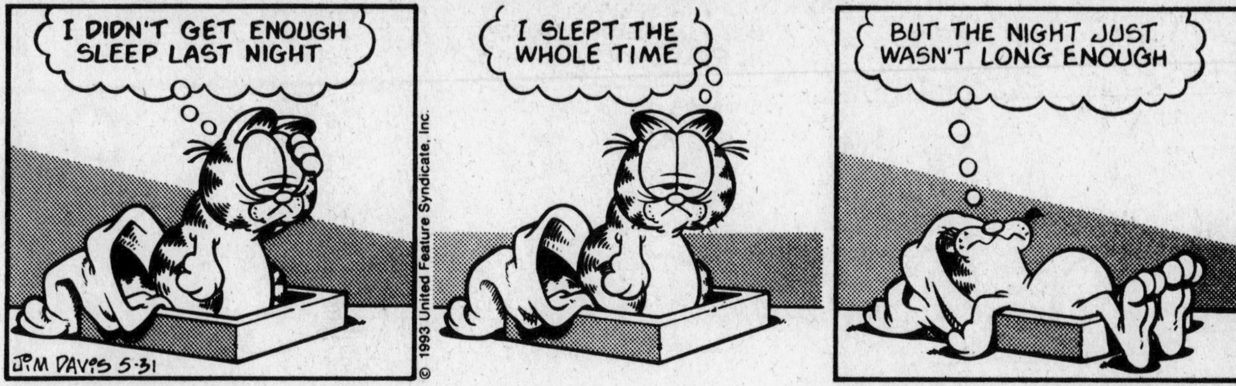
I DIDN'T GET ENOUGH SLEEP LAST NIGHT
I SLEPT THE WHOLE TIME
BUT THE NIGHT JUST WASN'T LONG ENOUGH
JIM DAVIS 5-31
© 1993 United Feature Syndicate, Inc.

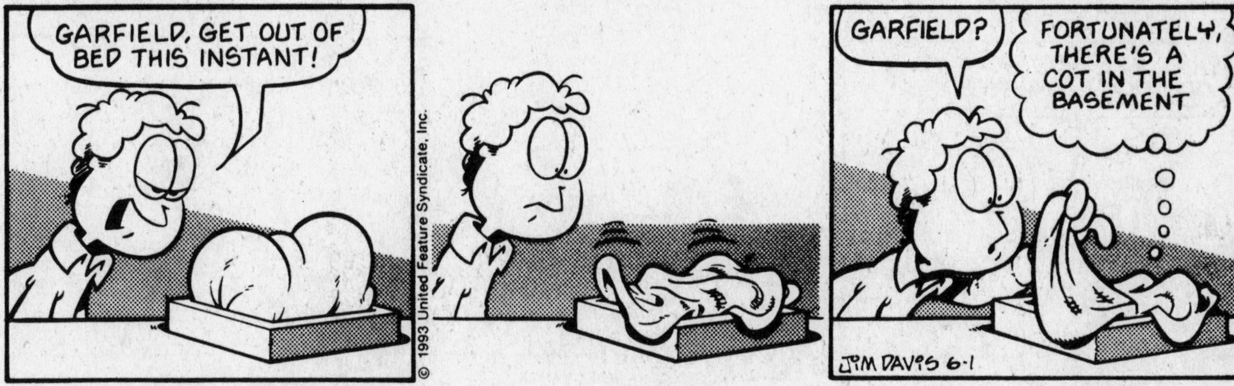
GARFIELD, GET OUT OF BED THIS INSTANT!
GARFIELD?
FORTUNATELY, THERE'S A COT IN THE BASEMENT
JIM DAVIS 6-1
© 1993 United Feature Syndicate, Inc.

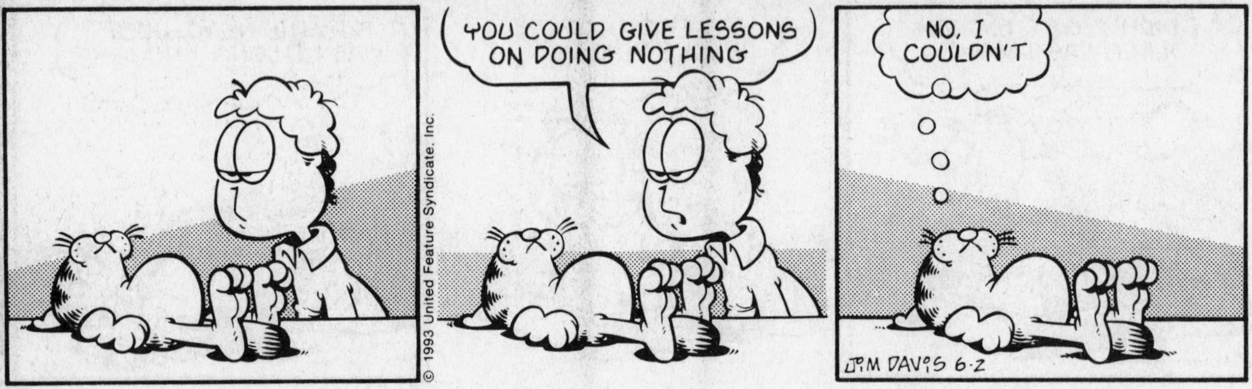
YOU COULD GIVE LESSONS ON DOING NOTHING
NO, I COULDN'T
JIM DAVIS 6-2
© 1993 United Feature Syndicate, Inc.

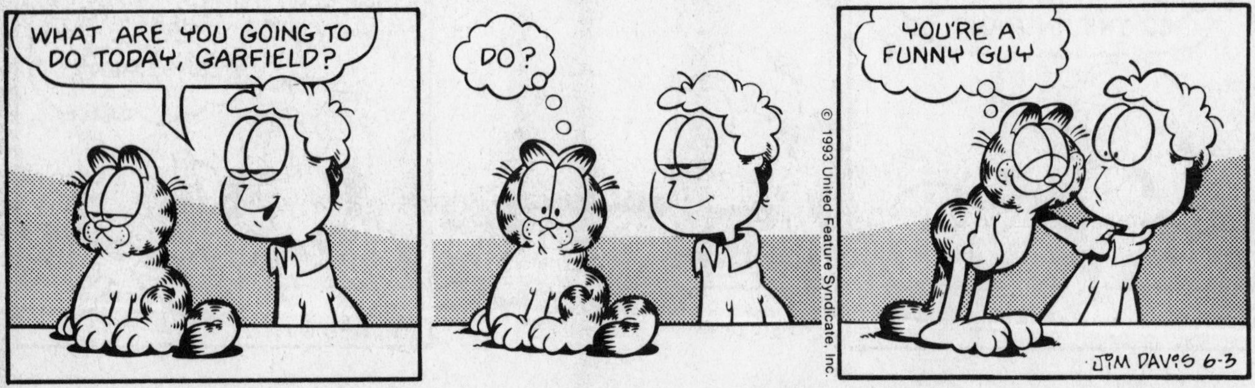
WHAT ARE YOU GOING TO DO TODAY, GARFIELD?
DO?
YOU'RE A FUNNY GUY
JIM DAVIS 6-3
© 1993 United Feature Syndicate, Inc.

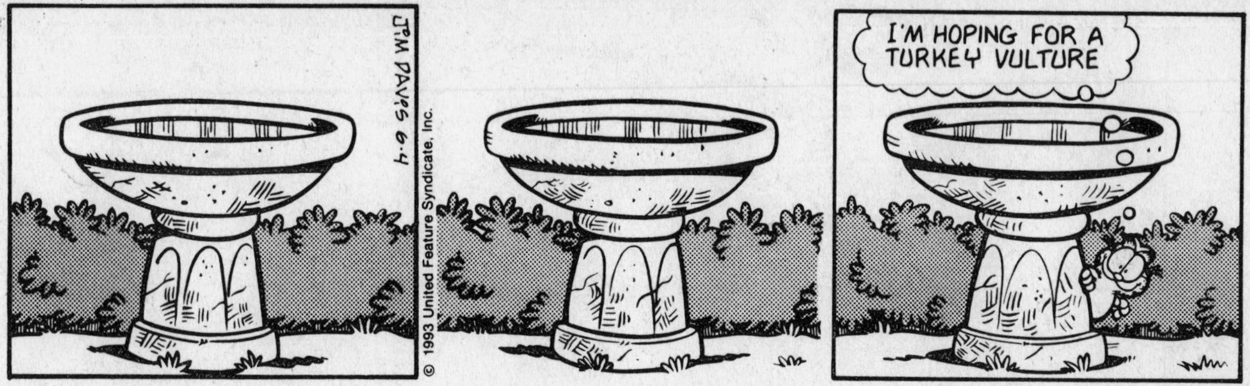
JIM DAVIS 6-4
© 1993 United Feature Syndicate, Inc.
I'M HOPING FOR A TURKEY VULTURE

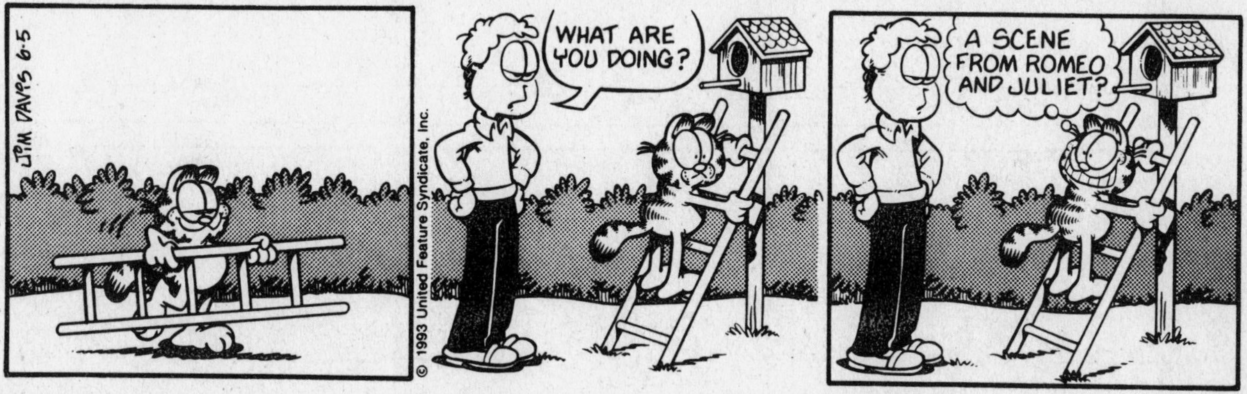
JIM DAVIS 6-5
© 1993 United Feature Syndicate, Inc.
WHAT ARE YOU DOING?
A SCENE FROM ROMEO AND JULIET?

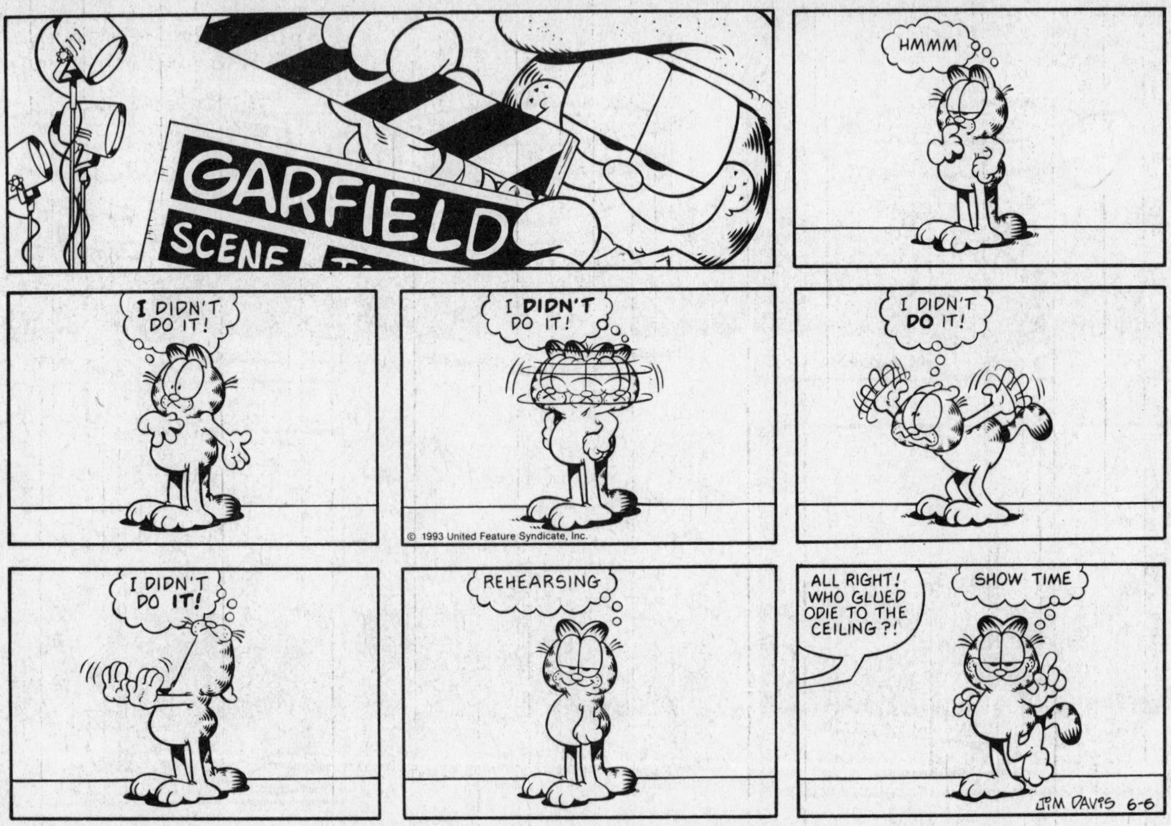
GARFIELD
SCENE
HMMM
I DIDN'T DO IT!
I DIDN'T DO IT!
I DIDN'T DO IT!
I DIDN'T DO IT!
REHEARSING
SHOW TIME
ALL RIGHT! WHO GLUED ODIE TO THE CEILING?!
JIM DAVIS 6-6

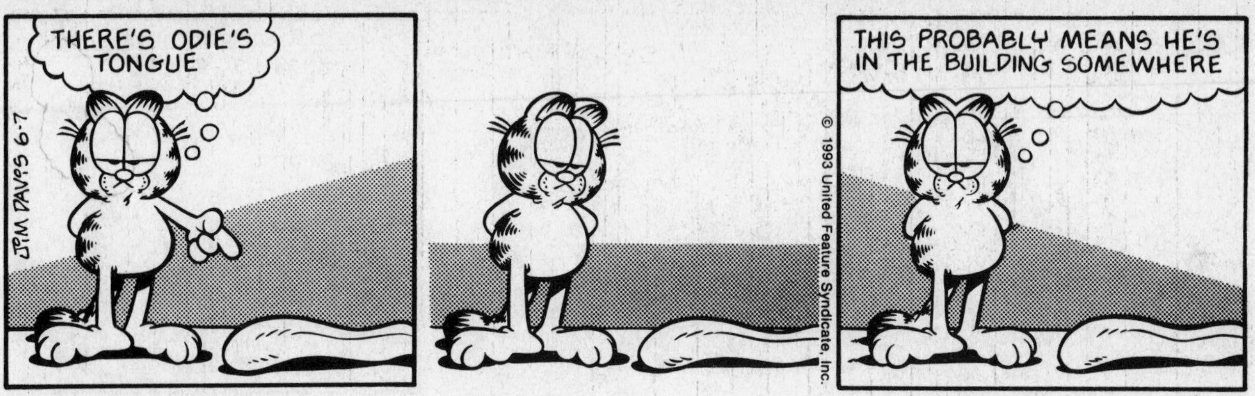
THERE'S ODIE'S TONGUE
THIS PROBABLY MEANS HE'S IN THE BUILDING SOMEWHERE
JIM DAVIS 6-7
© 1993 United Feature Syndicate, Inc.

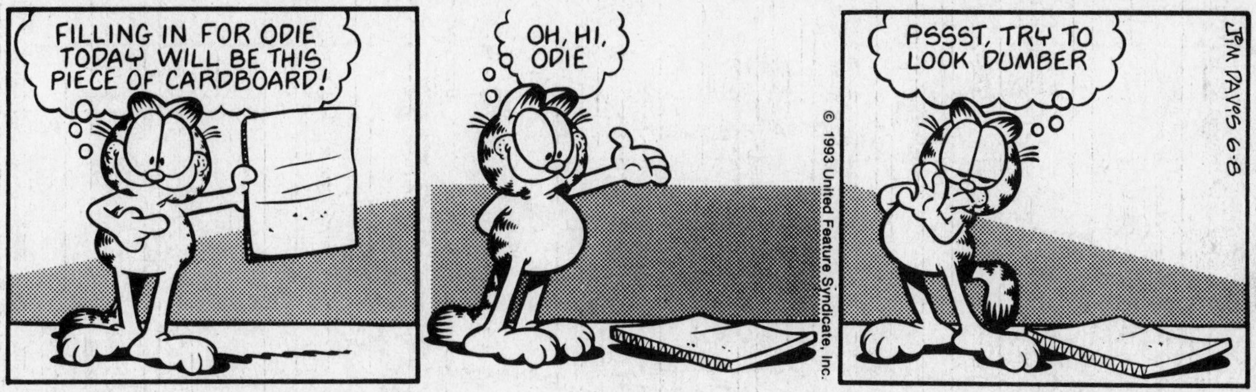
FILLING IN FOR ODIE TODAY WILL BE THIS PIECE OF CARDBOARD!
OH, HI, ODIE
PSSST, TRY TO LOOK DUMBER
JIM DAVIS 6-8
© 1993 United Feature Syndicate, Inc.

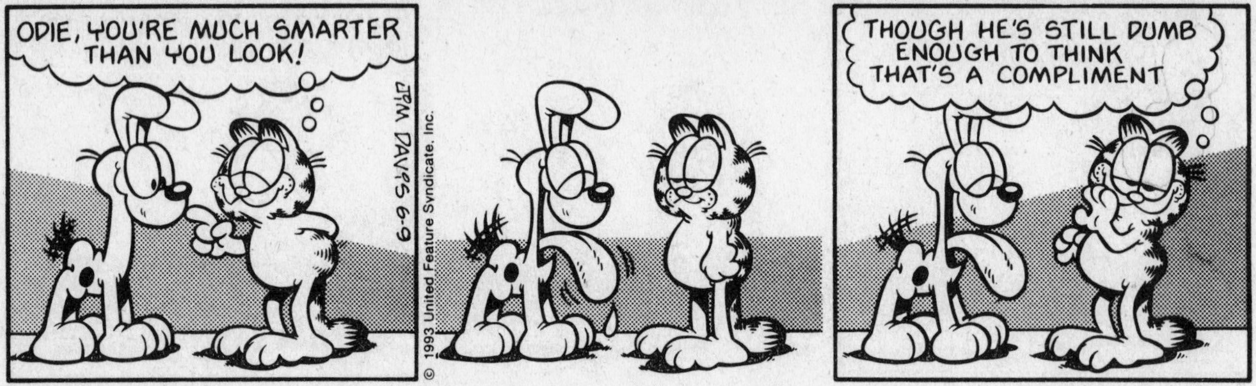
ODIE, YOU'RE MUCH SMARTER THAN YOU LOOK!
JIM DAVIS 6-9
© 1993 United Feature Syndicate, Inc.
THOUGH HE'S STILL DUMB ENOUGH TO THINK THAT'S A COMPLIMENT

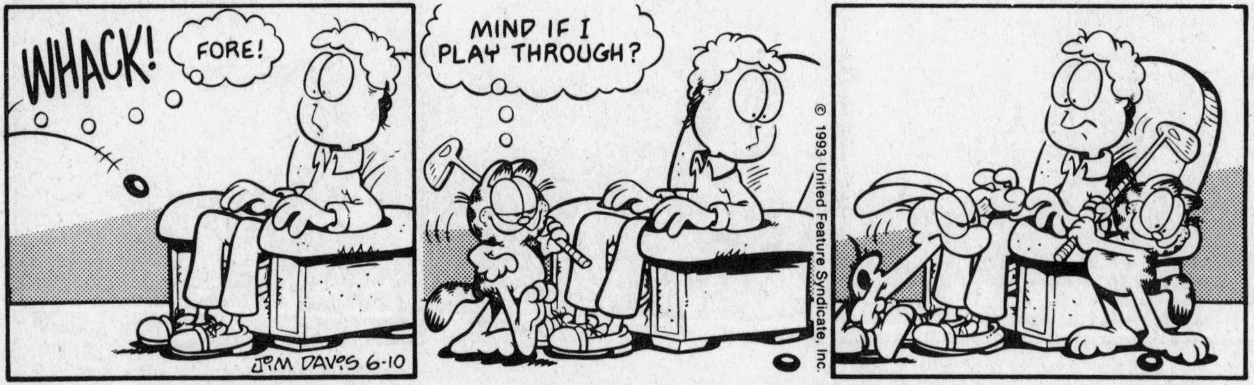
WHACK!
FORE!
JIM DAVIS 6-10
MIND IF I PLAY THROUGH?
© 1993 United Feature Syndicate, Inc.

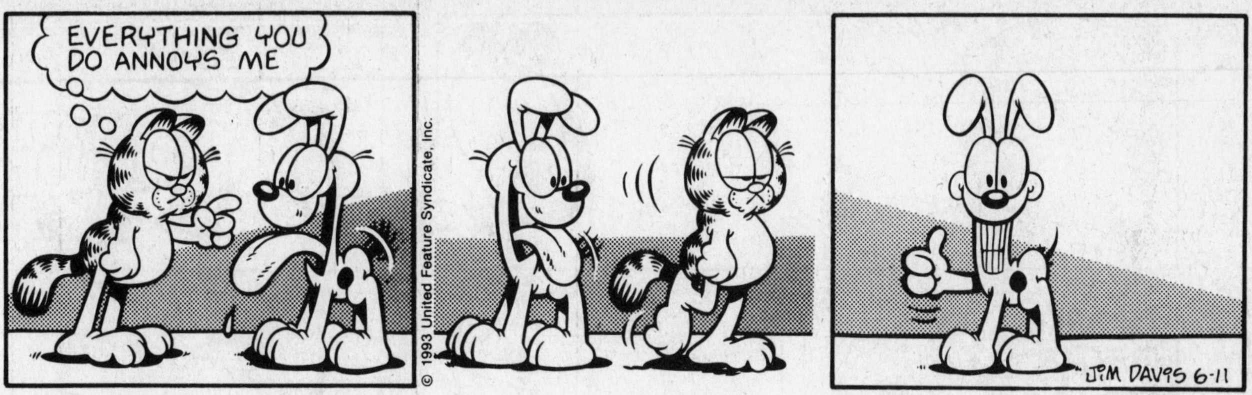
EVERYTHING YOU DO ANNOYS ME
© 1993 United Feature Syndicate, Inc.
JIM DAVIS 6-11

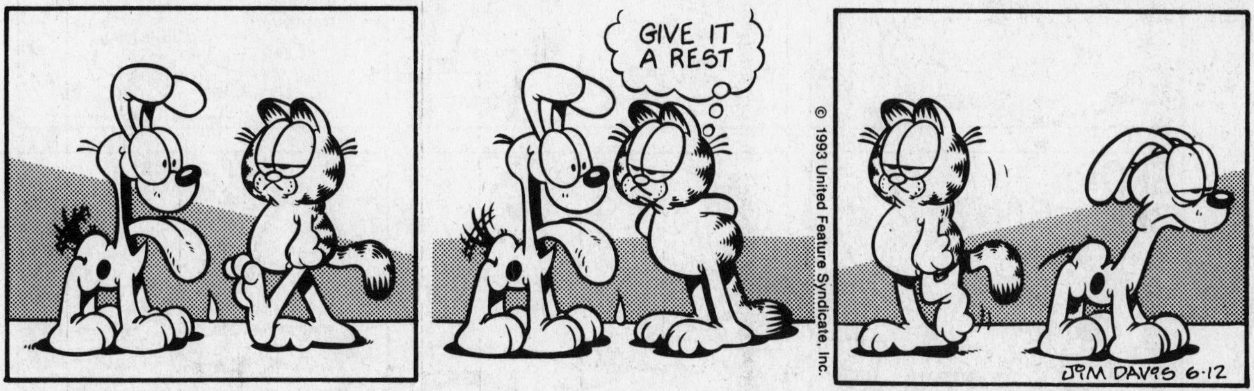
GIVE IT A REST
© 1993 United Feature Syndicate, Inc.
JIM DAVIS 6-12

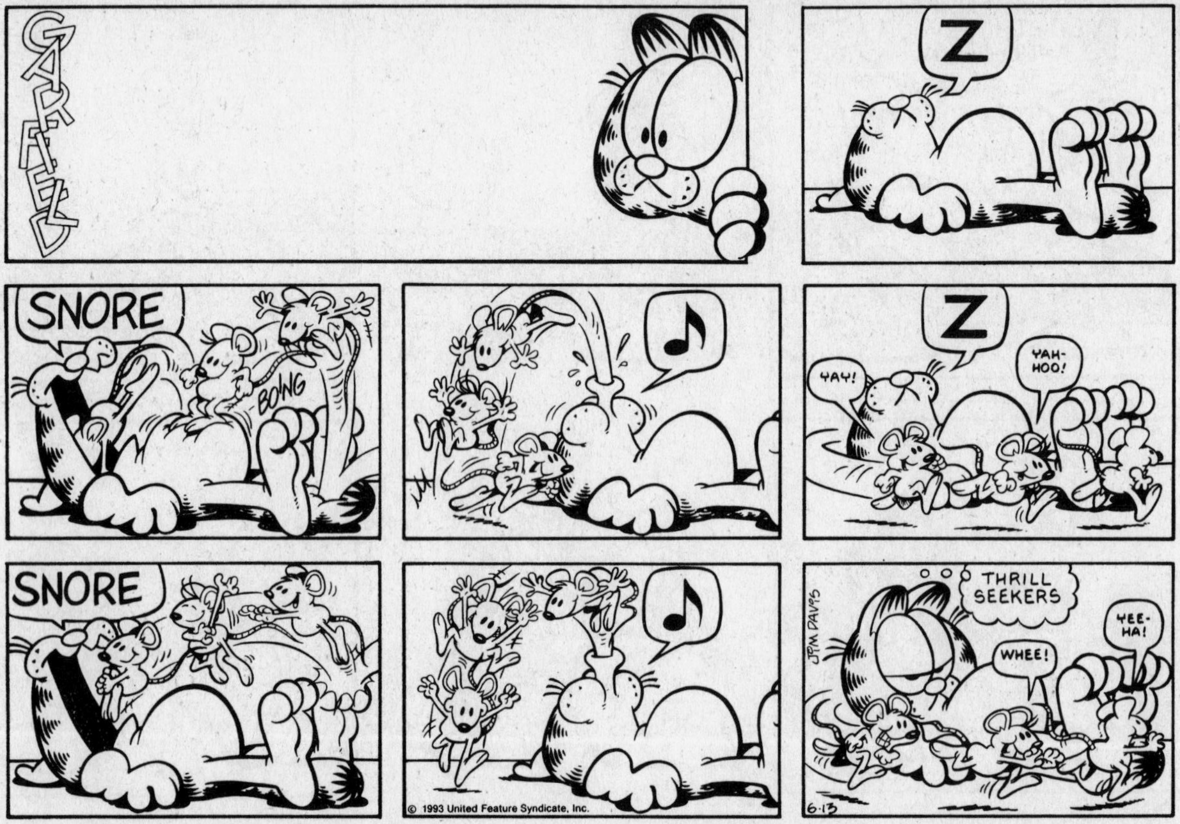
GARFIELD
Z
SNORE
BOING
♪
Z
YAY!
YAH-HOO!
SNORE
♪
THRILL SEEKERS
WHEE!
YEE-HA!
JPM DAVPS 6-13
© 1993 United Feature Syndicate, Inc.

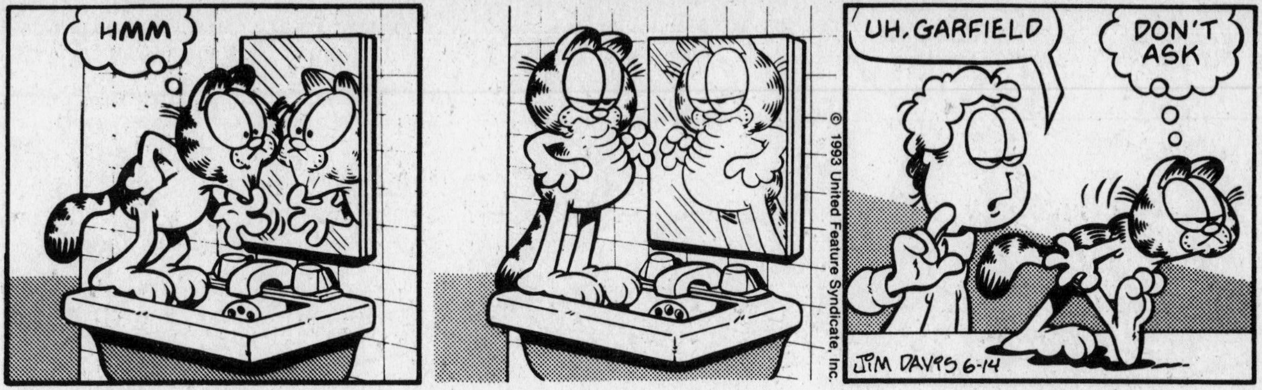
HMM
UH, GARFIELD
DON'T ASK
© 1993 United Feature Syndicate, Inc.
JIM DAVIS 6-14

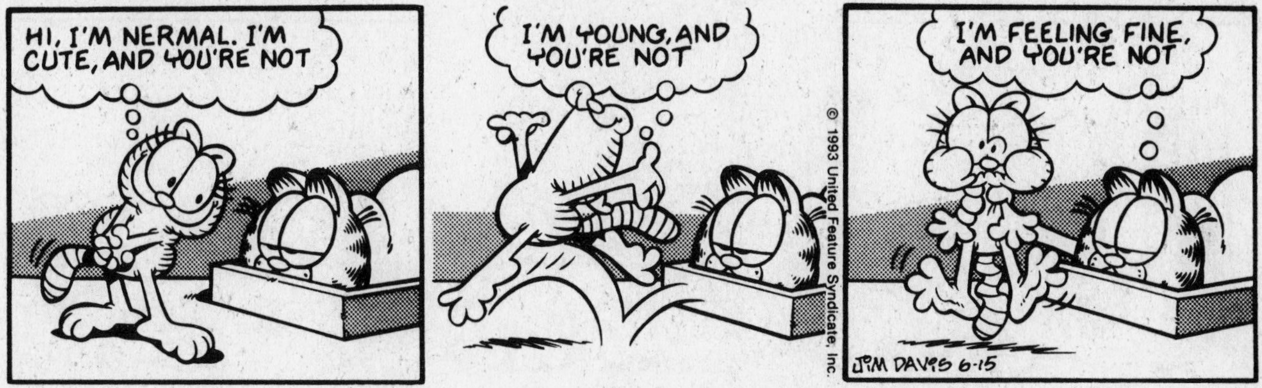
HI, I'M NERMAL. I'M CUTE, AND YOU'RE NOT
I'M YOUNG, AND YOU'RE NOT
I'M FEELING FINE, AND YOU'RE NOT
© 1993 United Feature Syndicate, Inc.
JIM DAVIS 6-15

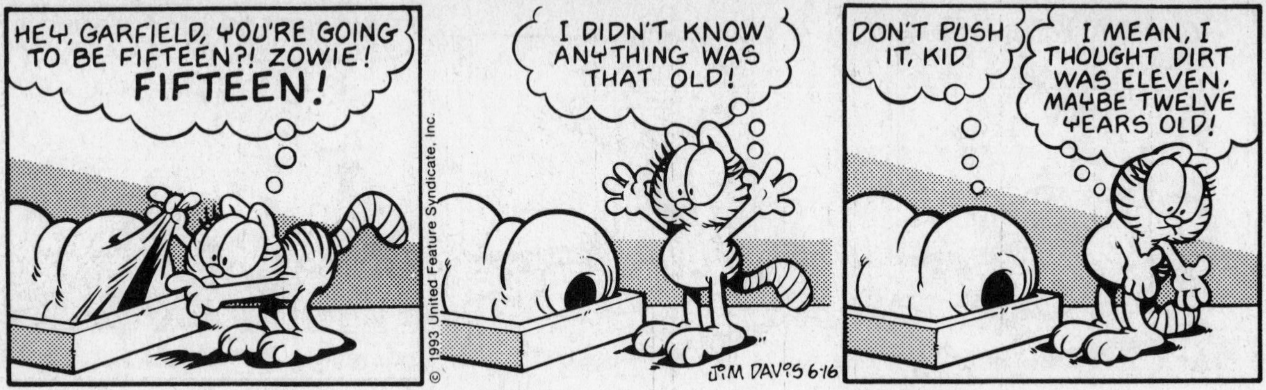
HEY, GARFIELD, YOU'RE GOING TO BE FIFTEEN?! ZOWIE! FIFTEEN!
© 1993 United Feature Syndicate, Inc.
I DIDN'T KNOW ANYTHING WAS THAT OLD!
JIM DAVIS 6-16
DON'T PUSH IT, KID
I MEAN, I THOUGHT DIRT WAS ELEVEN, MAYBE TWELVE YEARS OLD!

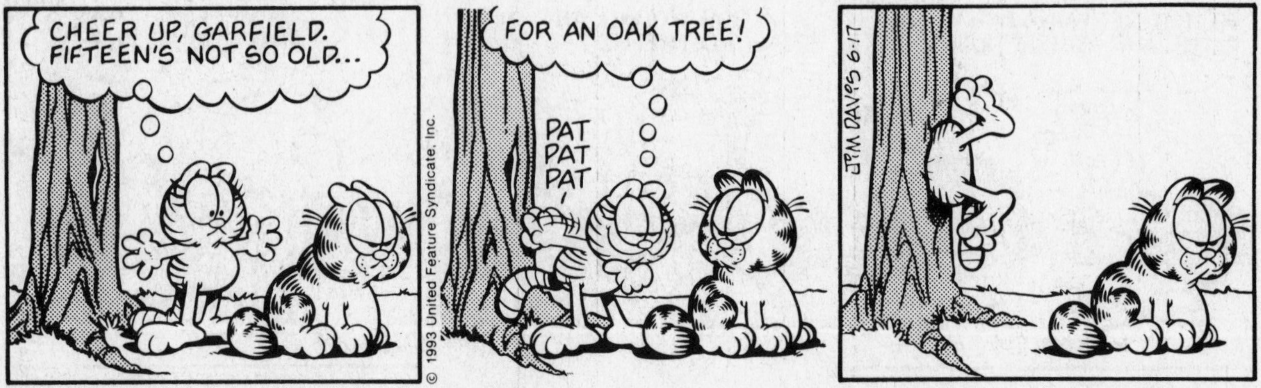
CHEER UP, GARFIELD. FIFTEEN'S NOT SO OLD...
© 1993 United Feature Syndicate, Inc.
FOR AN OAK TREE!
PAT PAT PAT
JIM DAVIS 6-17

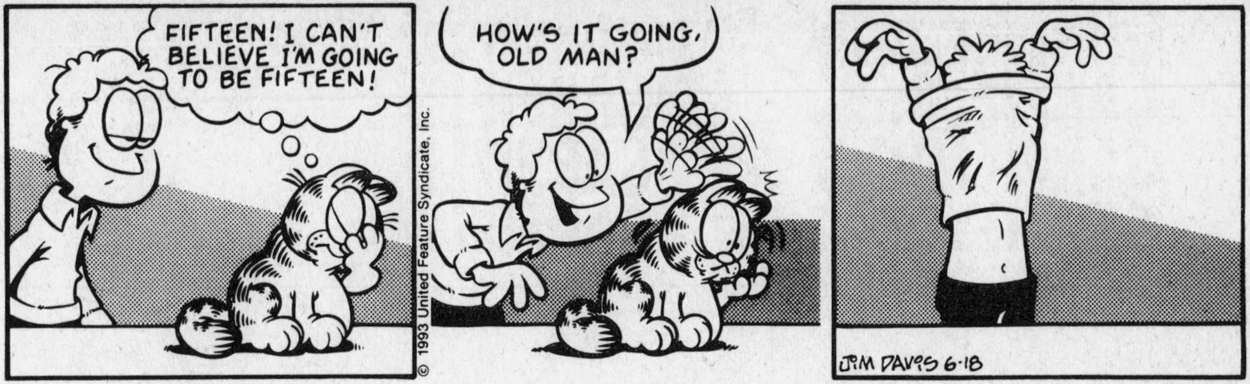
FIFTEEN! I CAN'T BELIEVE I'M GOING TO BE FIFTEEN!
HOW'S IT GOING, OLD MAN?
© 1993 United Feature Syndicate, Inc.
JIM DAVIS 6-18

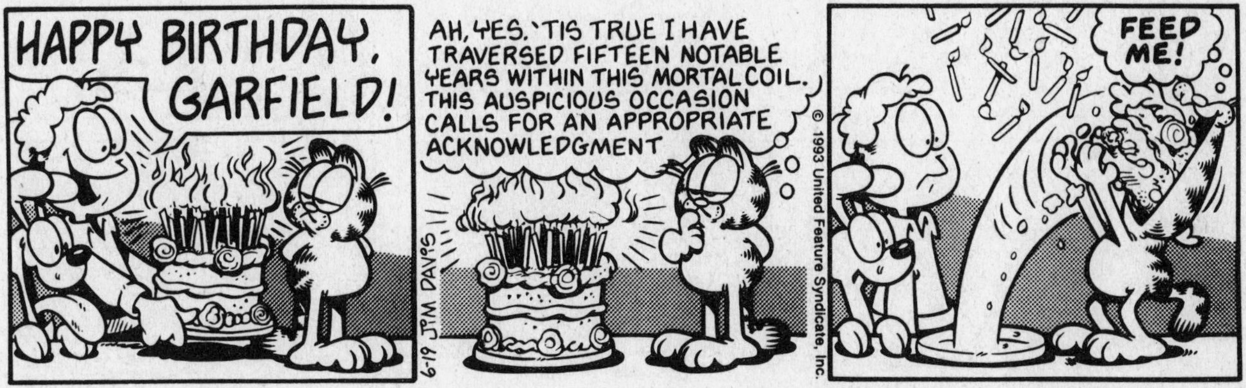
HAPPY BIRTHDAY, GARFIELD!
6-19 JIM DAVIS
AH, YES. 'TIS TRUE I HAVE TRAVERSED FIFTEEN NOTABLE YEARS WITHIN THIS MORTAL COIL. THIS AUSPICIOUS OCCASION CALLS FOR AN APPROPRIATE ACKNOWLEDGMENT
© 1993 United Feature Syndicate, Inc.
FEED ME!

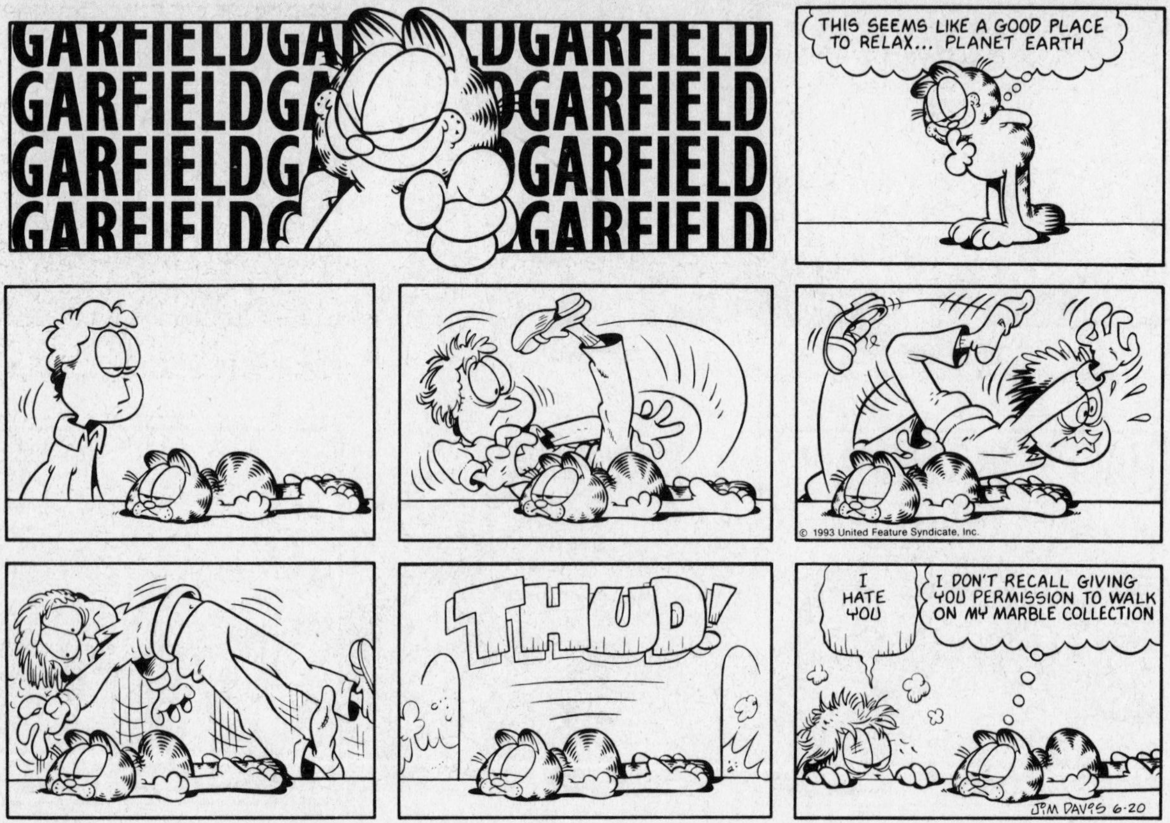
GARFIELD
THIS SEEMS LIKE A GOOD PLACE TO RELAX... PLANET EARTH
© 1993 United Feature Syndicate, Inc.
THUD!
I HATE YOU
I DON'T RECALL GIVING YOU PERMISSION TO WALK ON MY MARBLE COLLECTION
JIM DAVIS 6-20

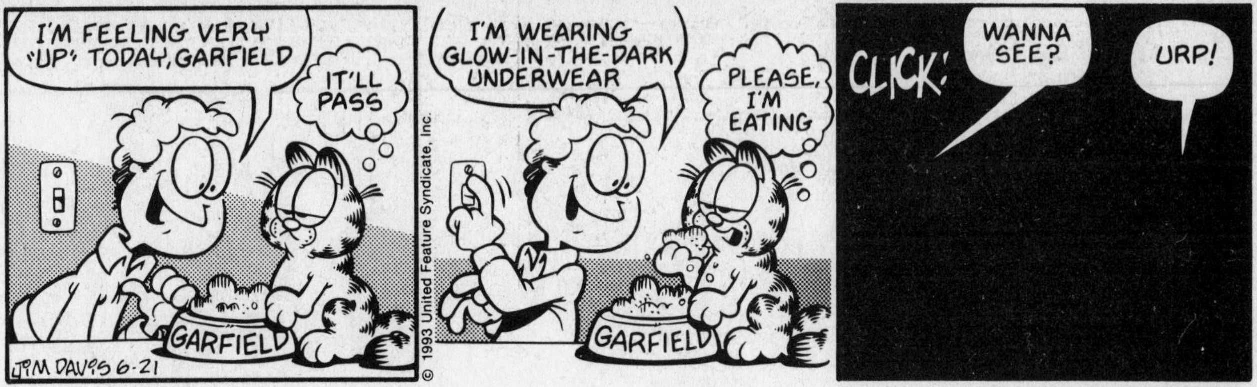
I'M FEELING VERY "UP" TODAY, GARFIELD
IT'LL PASS
GARFIELD
JIM DAVIS 6-21
© 1993 United Feature Syndicate, Inc.
I'M WEARING GLOW-IN-THE-DARK UNDERWEAR
PLEASE, I'M EATING
GARFIELD
CLICK!
WANNA SEE?
URP!

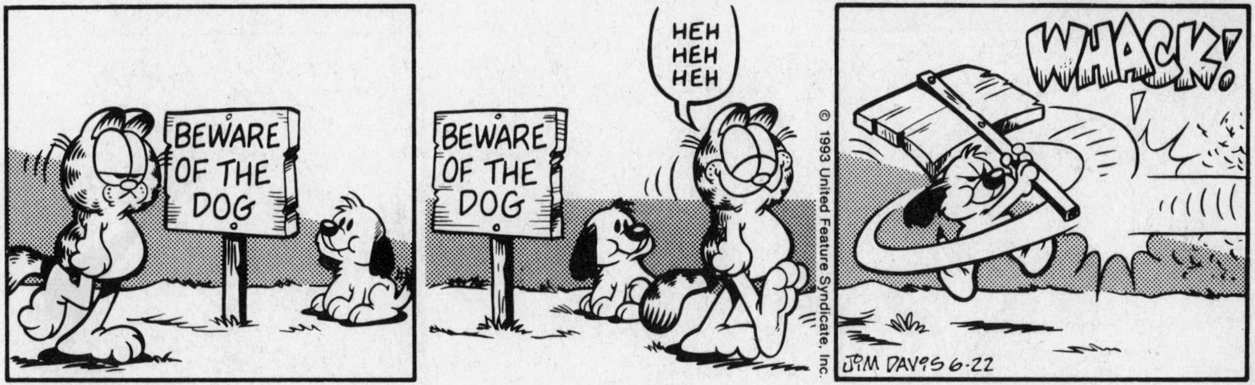
BEWARE OF THE DOG
BEWARE OF THE DOG
HEH HEH HEH
© 1993 United Feature Syndicate, Inc.
WHACK!
JIM DAVIS 6-22

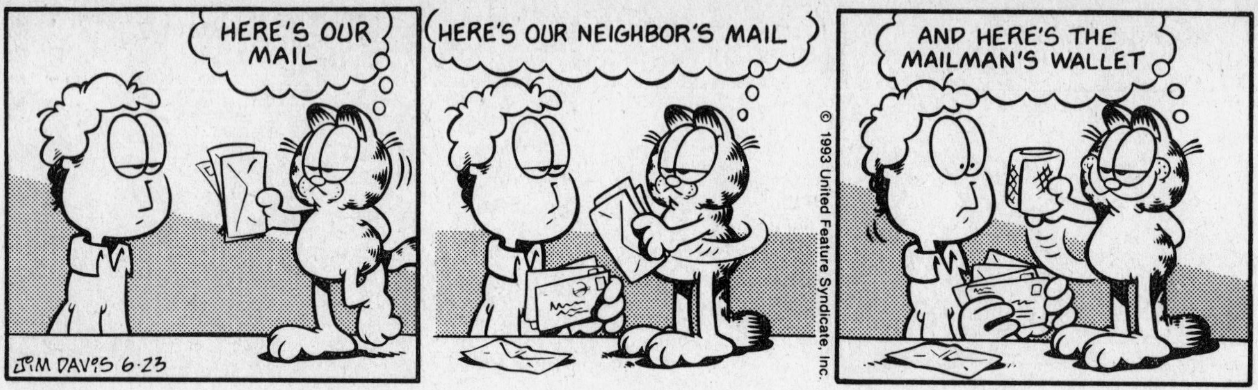
HERE'S OUR MAIL
HERE'S OUR NEIGHBOR'S MAIL
AND HERE'S THE MAILMAN'S WALLET
JIM DAVIS 6-23
© 1993 United Feature Syndicate, Inc.

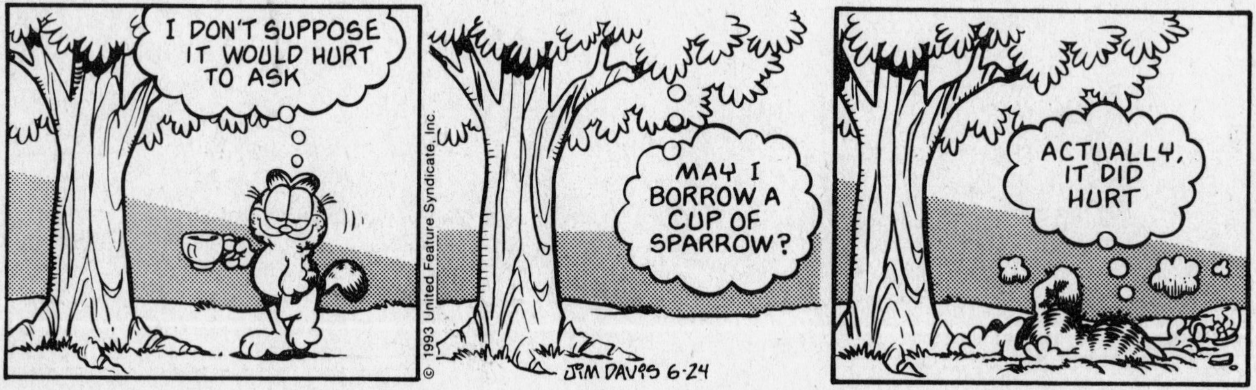
I DON'T SUPPOSE IT WOULD HURT TO ASK
MAY I BORROW A CUP OF SPARROW?
ACTUALLY, IT DID HURT
JIM DAVIS 6-24
© 1993 United Feature Syndicate, Inc.

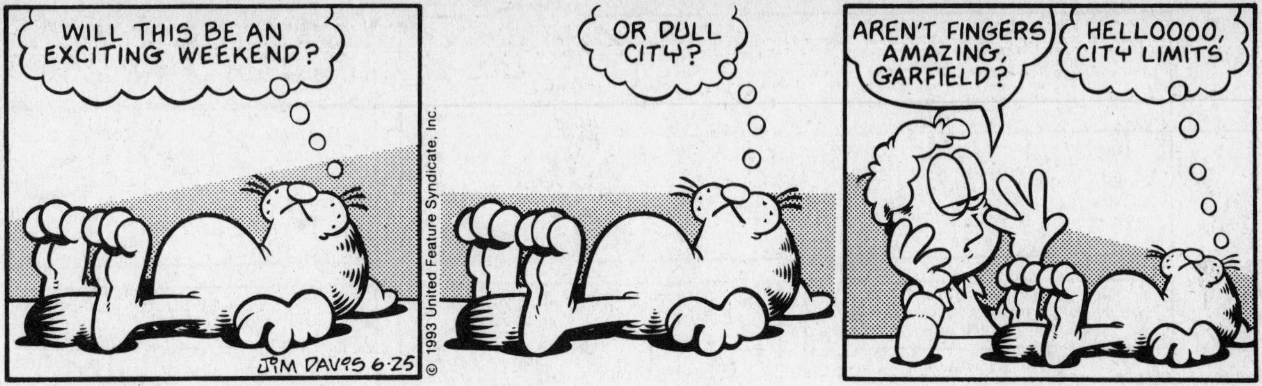
WILL THIS BE AN EXCITING WEEKEND?
JIM DAVIS 6-25
© 1993 United Feature Syndicate, Inc.
OR DULL CITY?
AREN'T FINGERS AMAZING, GARFIELD?
HELLOOOO, CITY LIMITS

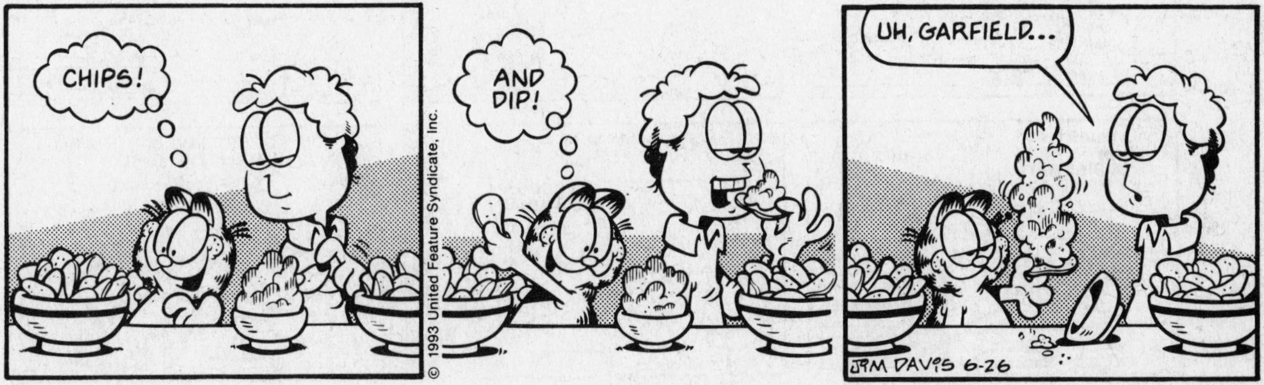
CHIPS!
© 1993 United Feature Syndicate, Inc.
AND DIP!
UH, GARFIELD...
JIM DAVIS 6-26

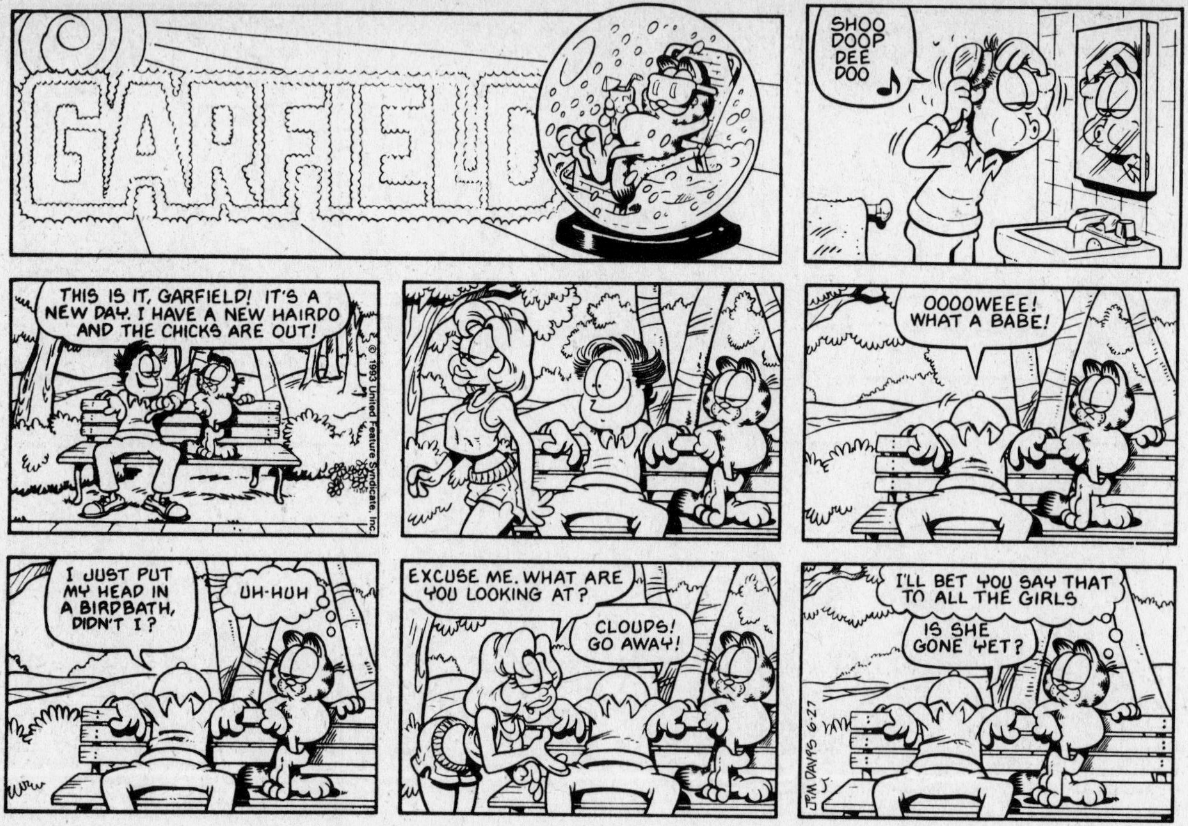
GARFIELD
SHOO DOOP DEE DOO
THIS IS IT, GARFIELD! IT'S A NEW DAY. I HAVE A NEW HAIRDO AND THE CHICKS ARE OUT!
© 1993 United Feature Syndicate, Inc.
OOOOWEEE! WHAT A BABE!
I JUST PUT MY HEAD IN A BIRDBATH, DIDN'T I?
UH-HUH
EXCUSE ME. WHAT ARE YOU LOOKING AT?
CLOUDS! GO AWAY!
I'LL BET YOU SAY THAT TO ALL THE GIRLS
IS SHE GONE YET?
JPM DAVPS 6-27

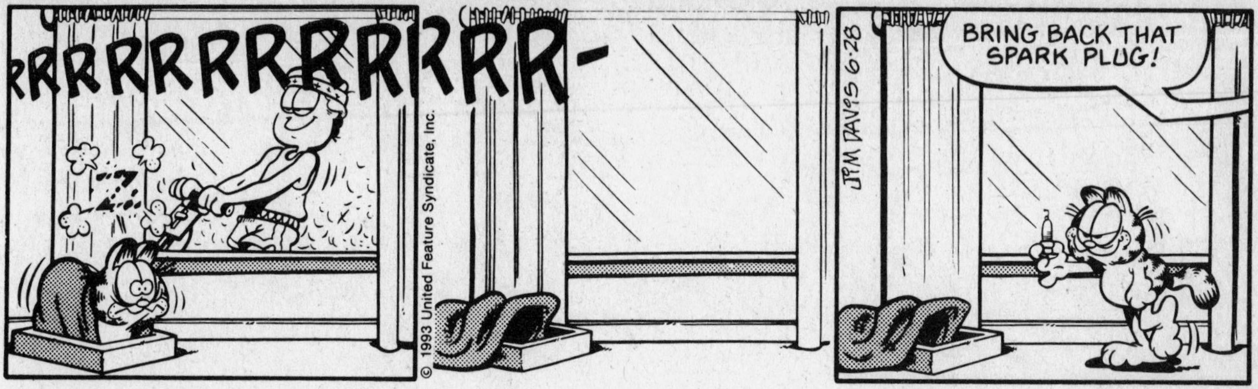
RRRRRRRRRRRRR-
© 1993 United Feature Syndicate, Inc.
JIM DAVIS 6-28
BRING BACK THAT SPARK PLUG!

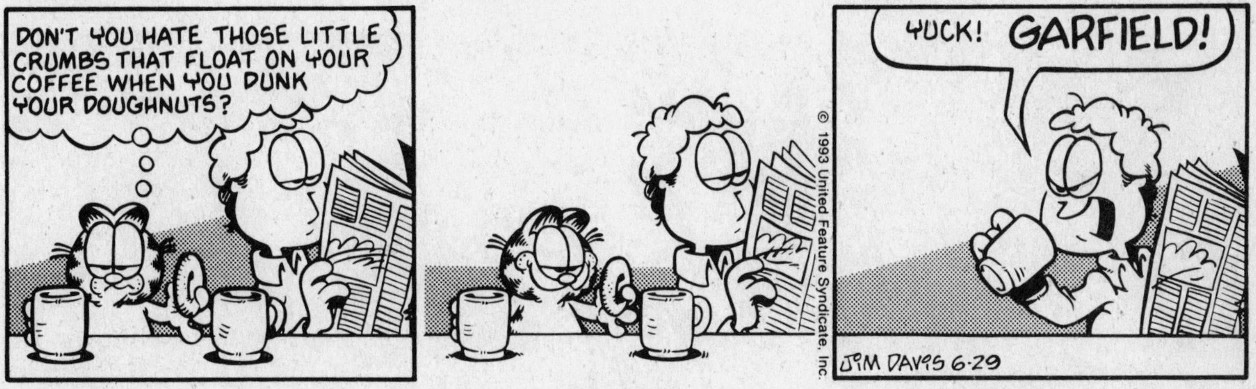
DON'T YOU HATE THOSE LITTLE CRUMBS THAT FLOAT ON YOUR COFFEE WHEN YOU DUNK YOUR DOUGHNUTS?
© 1993 United Feature Syndicate, Inc.
YUCK! GARFIELD!
JIM DAVIS 6-29

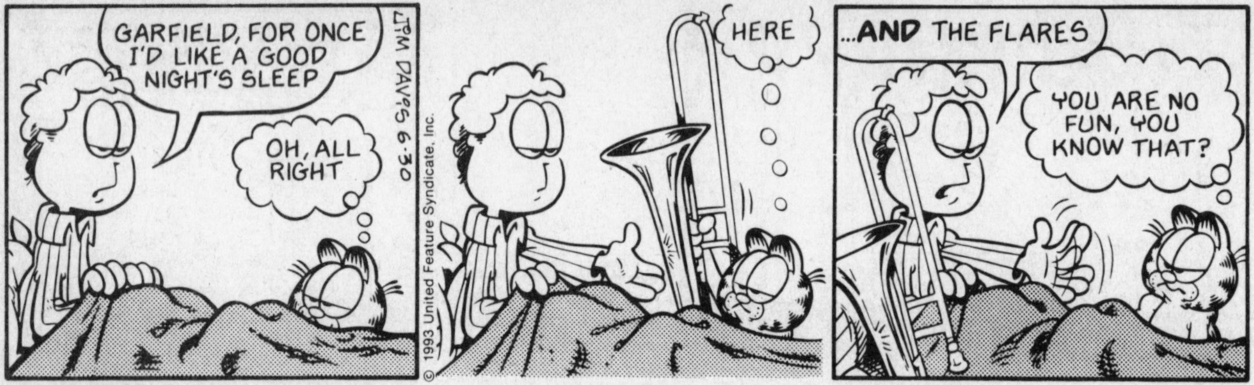
GARFIELD, FOR ONCE I'D LIKE A GOOD NIGHT'S SLEEP
OH, ALL RIGHT
JIM DAVIS 6-30
© 1993 United Feature Syndicate, Inc.
HERE
...AND THE FLARES
YOU ARE NO FUN, YOU KNOW THAT?

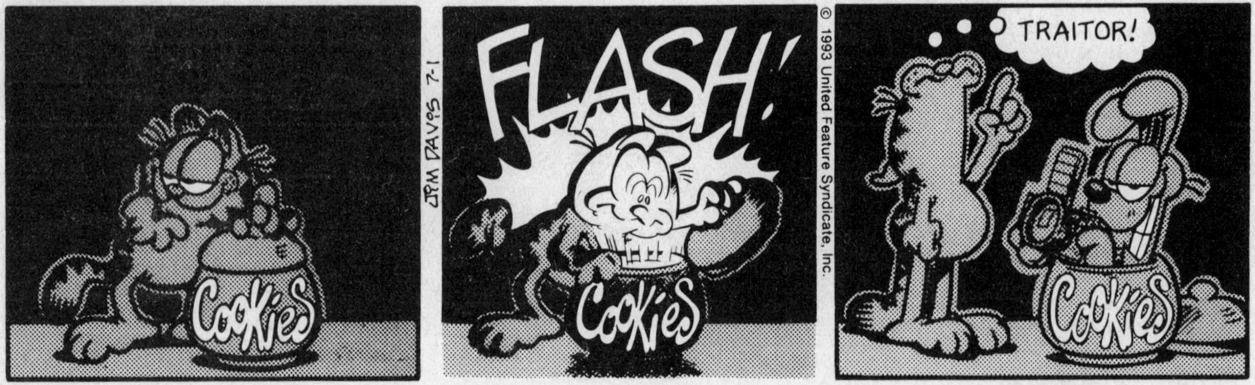
COOKIES
JIM DAVIS 7-1
FLASH!
COOKIES
© 1993 United Feature Syndicate, Inc.
TRAITOR!
COOKIES

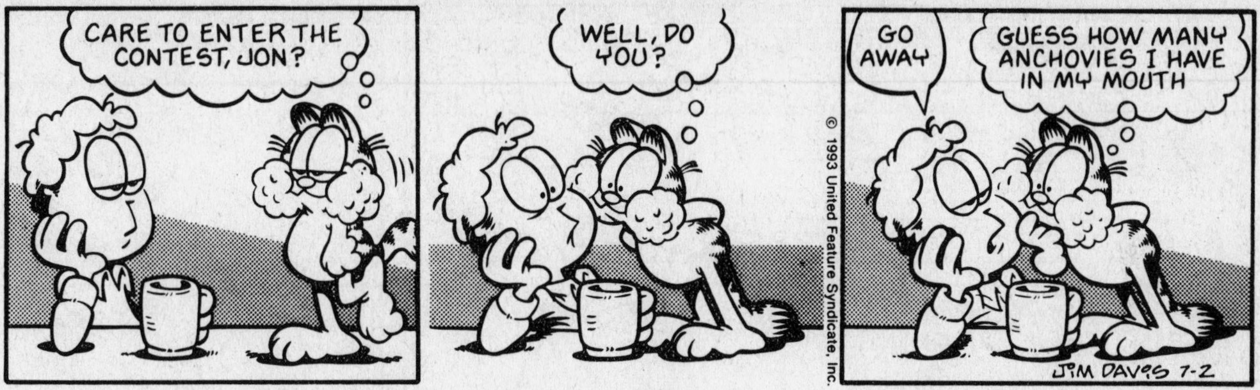
CARE TO ENTER THE CONTEST, JON?
WELL, DO YOU?
GO AWAY
GUESS HOW MANY ANCHOVIES I HAVE IN MY MOUTH
© 1993 United Feature Syndicate, Inc.
JIM DAVIS 7-2

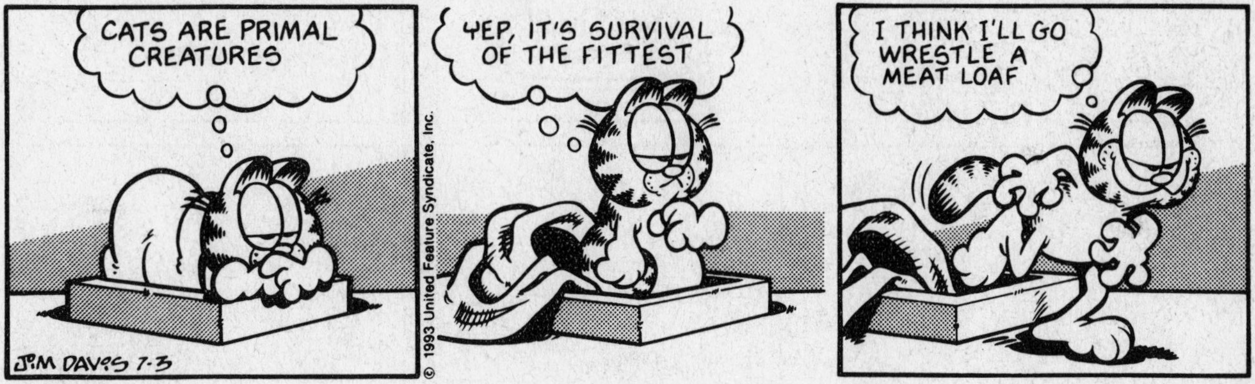
CATS ARE PRIMAL CREATURES
JIM DAVIS 7-3
© 1993 United Feature Syndicate, Inc.
YEP, IT'S SURVIVAL OF THE FITTEST
I THINK I'LL GO WRESTLE A MEAT LOAF

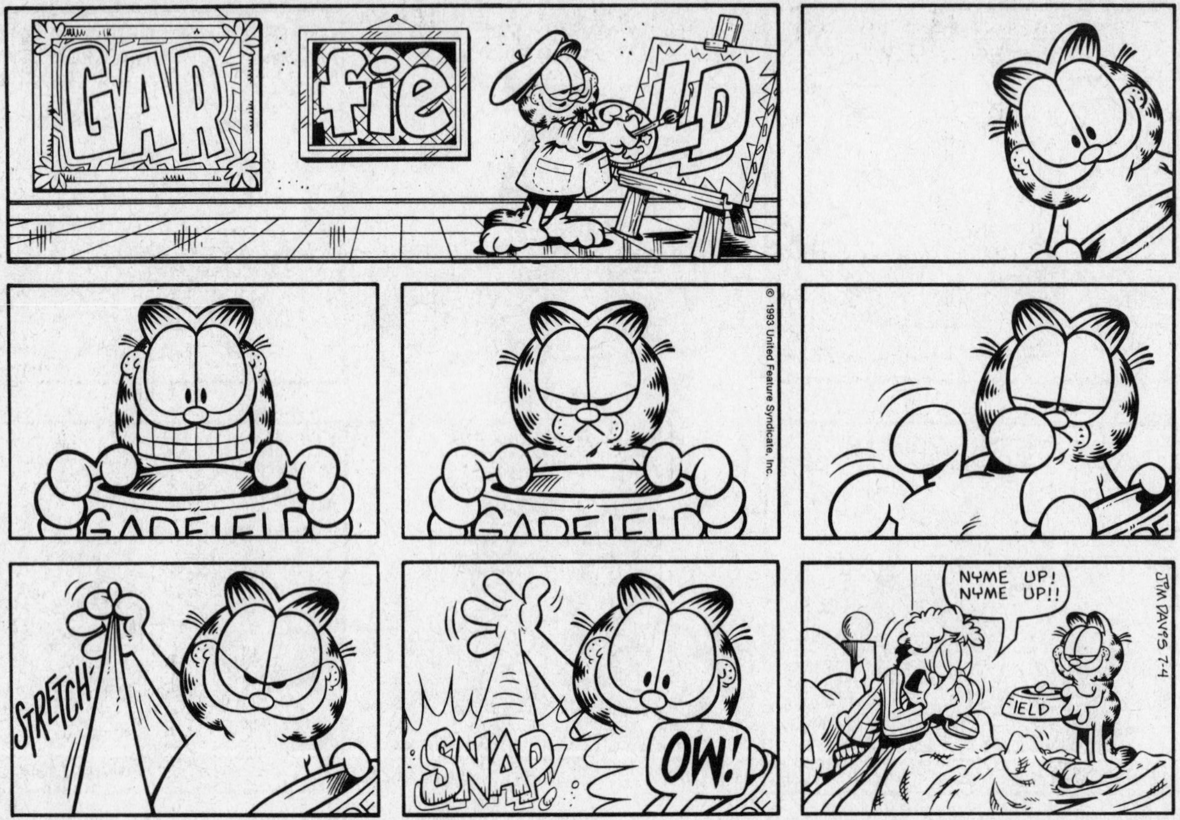

GAR
fie
LD
GAREIELD
GAREIELD
STRETCH
SNAP
OW!
NYME UP!
NYME UP!!
FIELD
JIM DAVIS 7-4
© 1993 United Feature Syndicate, Inc.

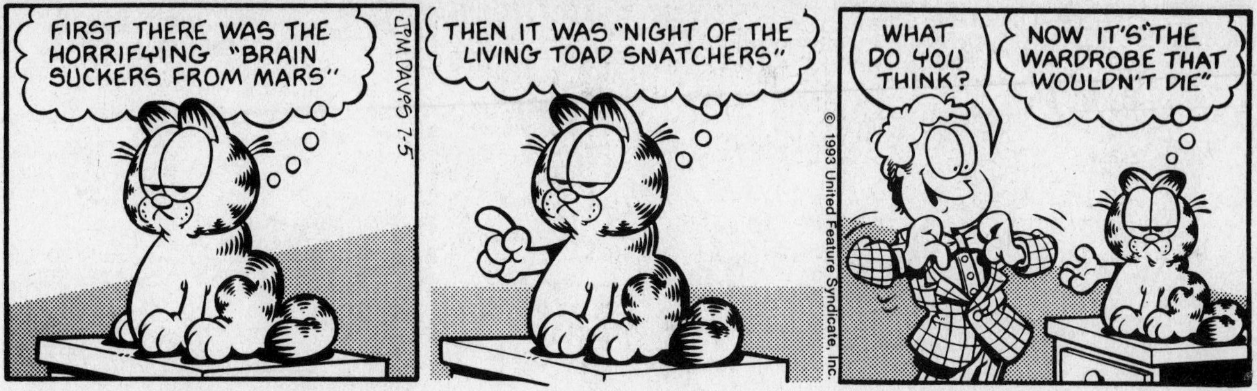
FIRST THERE WAS THE HORRIFYING "BRAIN SUCKERS FROM MARS"
JIM DAVIS 7-5
THEN IT WAS "NIGHT OF THE LIVING TOAD SNATCHERS"
© 1993 United Feature Syndicate, Inc.
WHAT DO YOU THINK?
NOW IT'S "THE WARDROBE THAT WOULDN'T DIE"

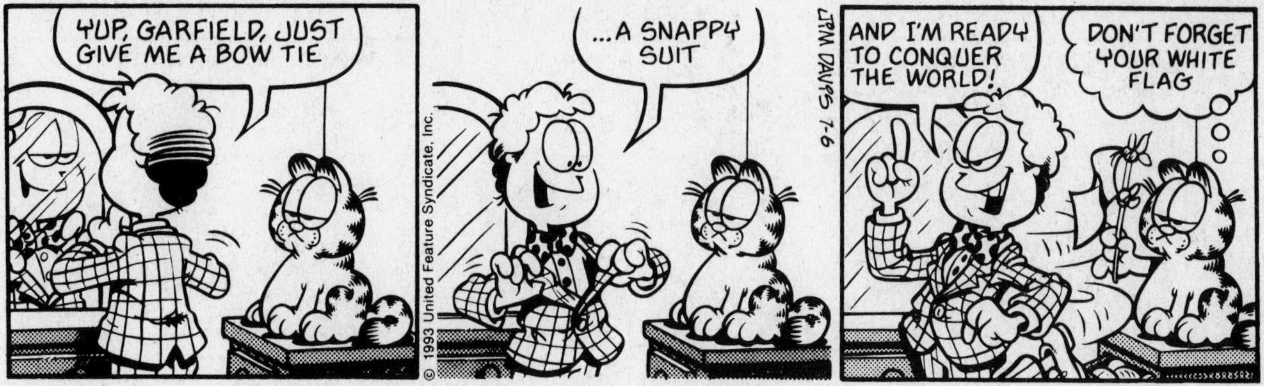
YUP, GARFIELD, JUST GIVE ME A BOW TIE
© 1993 United Feature Syndicate, Inc.
...A SNAPPY SUIT
JIM DAVIS 7-6
AND I'M READY TO CONQUER THE WORLD!
DON'T FORGET YOUR WHITE FLAG

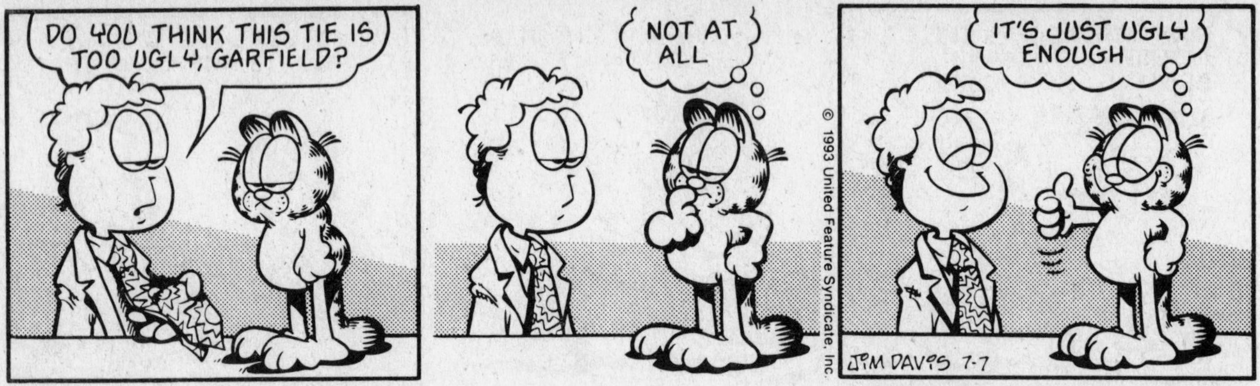
DO YOU THINK THIS TIE IS TOO UGLY, GARFIELD?
NOT AT ALL
IT'S JUST UGLY ENOUGH
JIM DAVIS 7-7
© 1993 United Feature Syndicate, Inc.

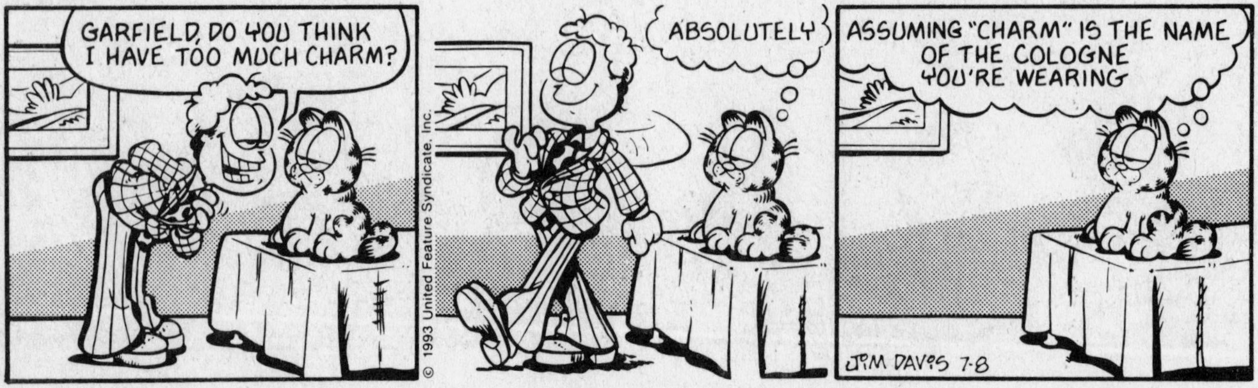
GARFIELD, DO YOU THINK I HAVE TOO MUCH CHARM?
ABSOLUTELY
ASSUMING "CHARM" IS THE NAME OF THE COLOGNE YOU'RE WEARING
JIM DAVIS 7-8
© 1993 United Feature Syndicate, Inc.

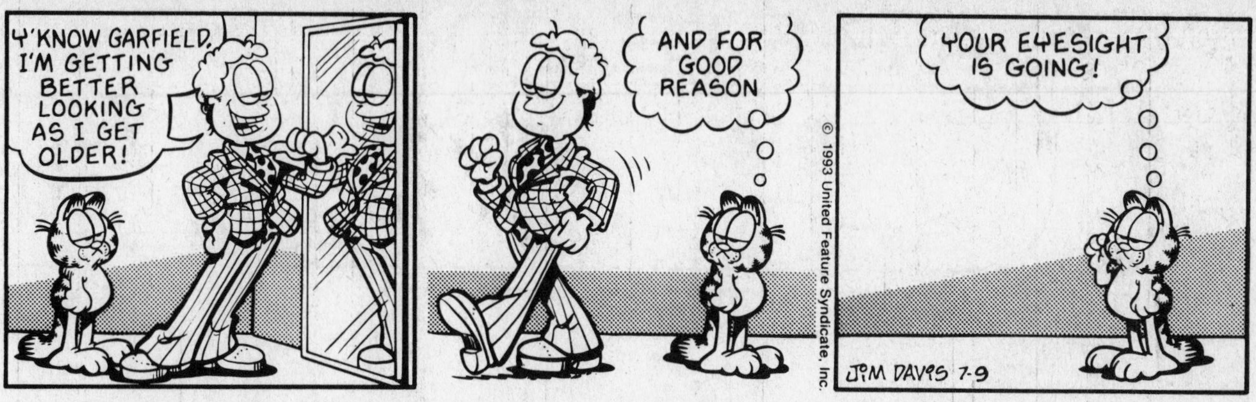
Y'KNOW GARFIELD, I'M GETTING BETTER LOOKING AS I GET OLDER!
AND FOR GOOD REASON
YOUR EYESIGHT IS GOING!
© 1993 United Feature Syndicate, Inc.
JIM DAVIS 7-9

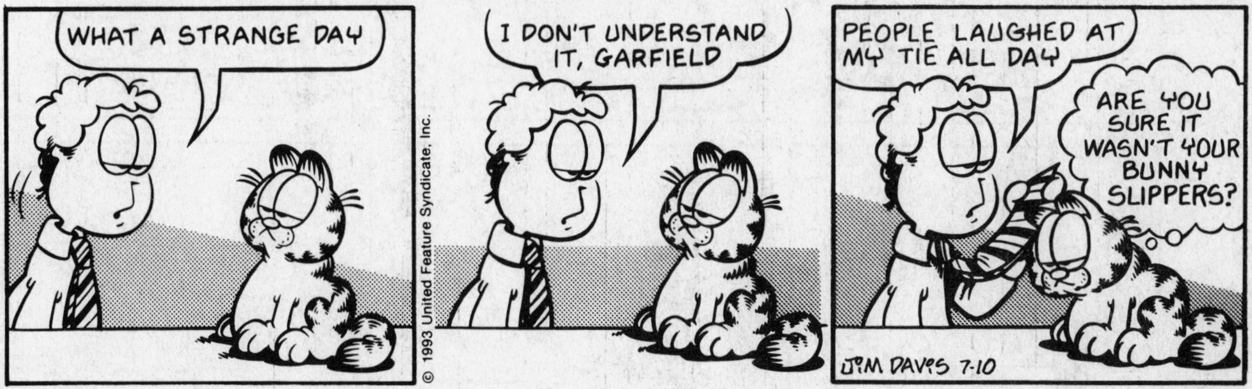
WHAT A STRANGE DAY
© 1993 United Feature Syndicate, Inc.
I DON'T UNDERSTAND IT, GARFIELD
PEOPLE LAUGHED AT MY TIE ALL DAY
ARE YOU SURE IT WASN'T YOUR BUNNY SLIPPERS?
JIM DAVIS 7-10

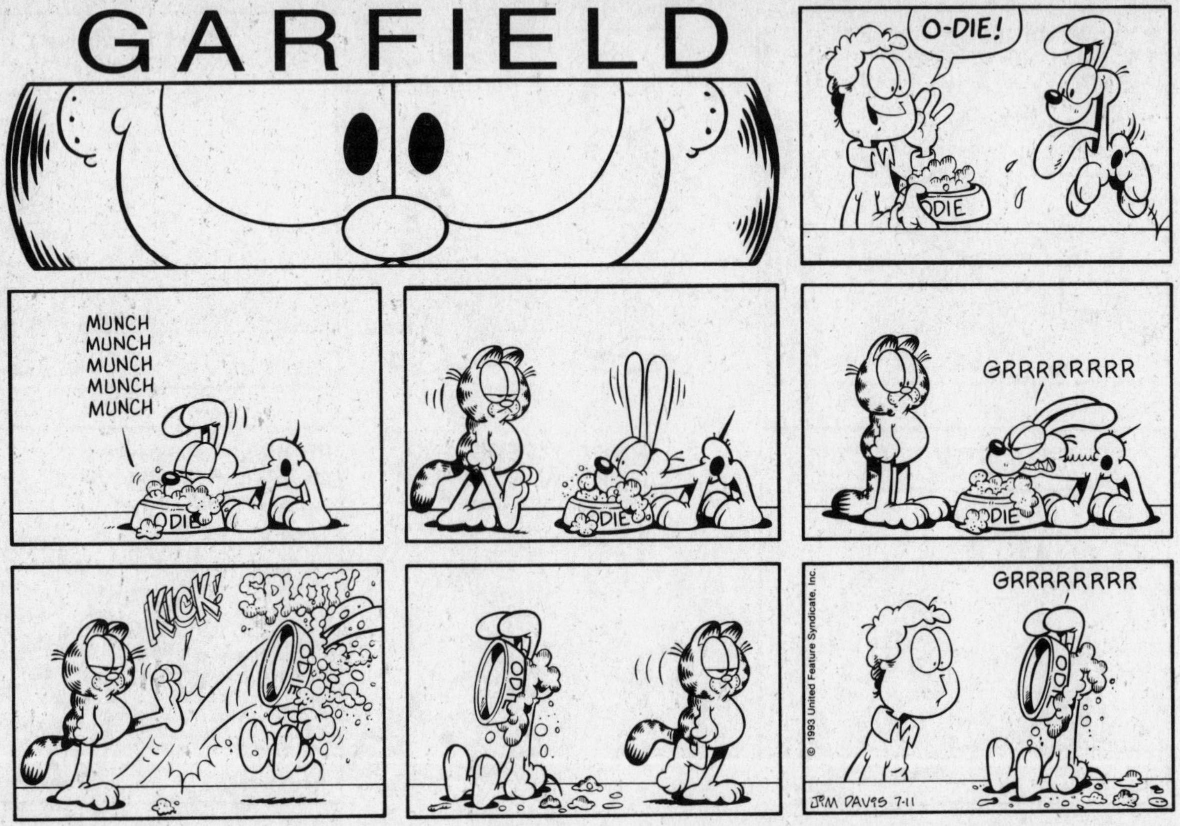
GARFIELD
O-DIE!
ODIE
MUNCH MUNCH MUNCH MUNCH MUNCH
GRRRRRRRR
KICK!
SPLOTT!
GRRRRRRRR
JIM DAVIS 7-11
© 1993 United Feature Syndicate, Inc.

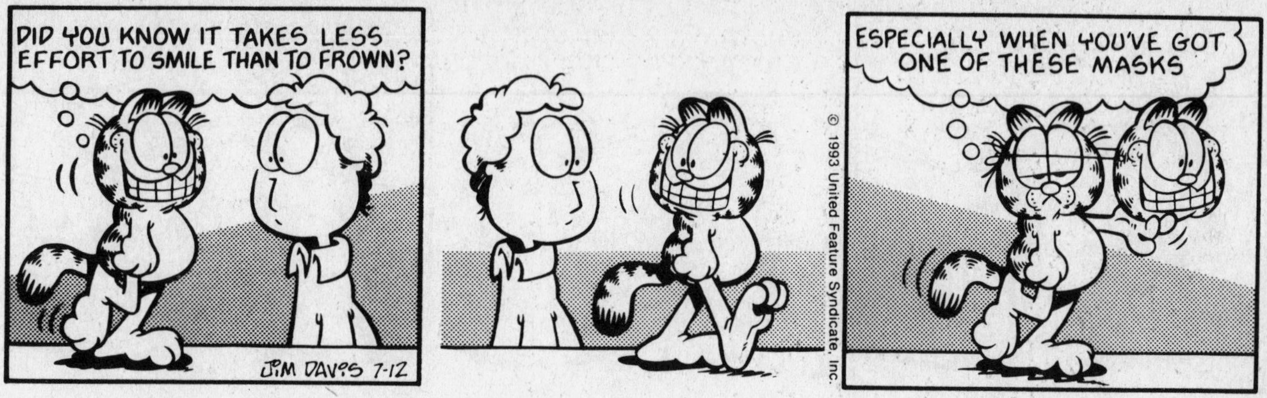
DID YOU KNOW IT TAKES LESS EFFORT TO SMILE THAN TO FROWN?
JIM DAVIS 7-12
© 1993 United Feature Syndicate, Inc.
ESPECIALLY WHEN YOU'VE GOT ONE OF THESE MASKS

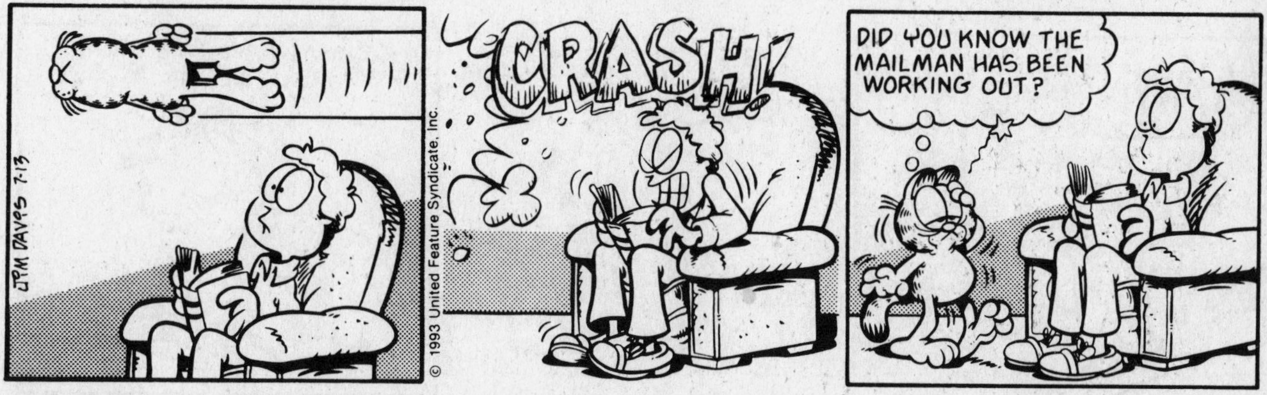
JIM DAVIS 7-13
© 1993 United Feature Syndicate, Inc.
CRASH!
DID YOU KNOW THE MAILMAN HAS BEEN WORKING OUT?

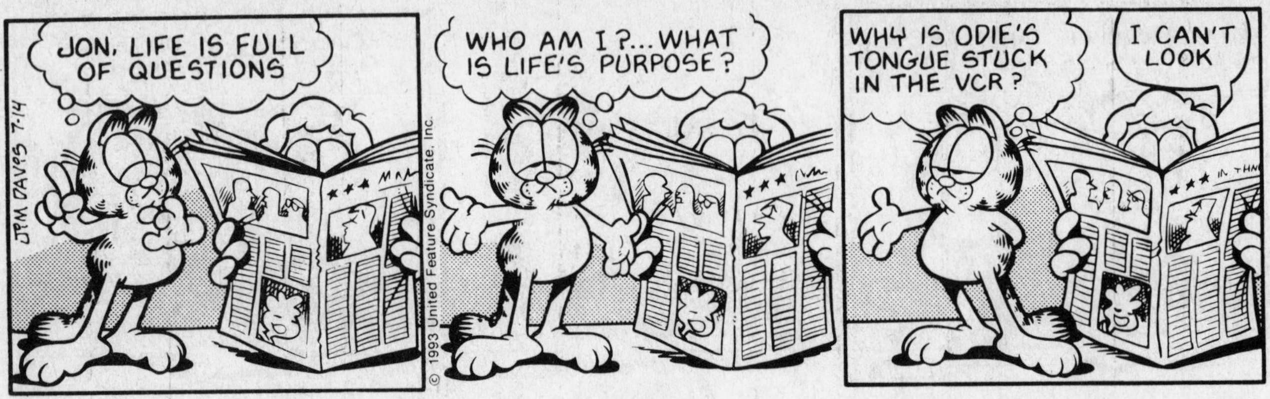
JON, LIFE IS FULL OF QUESTIONS
JIM DAVIS 7-14
WHO AM I?... WHAT IS LIFE'S PURPOSE?
WHY IS ODIE'S TONGUE STUCK IN THE VCR?
I CAN'T LOOK

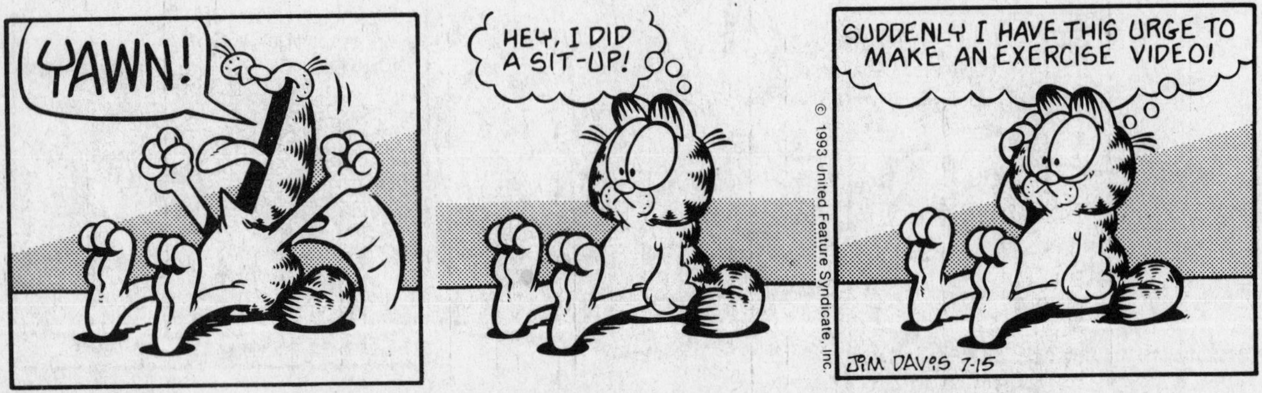
YAWN!
HEY, I DID A SIT-UP!
SUDDENLY I HAVE THIS URGE TO MAKE AN EXERCISE VIDEO!
JIM DAVIS 7-15

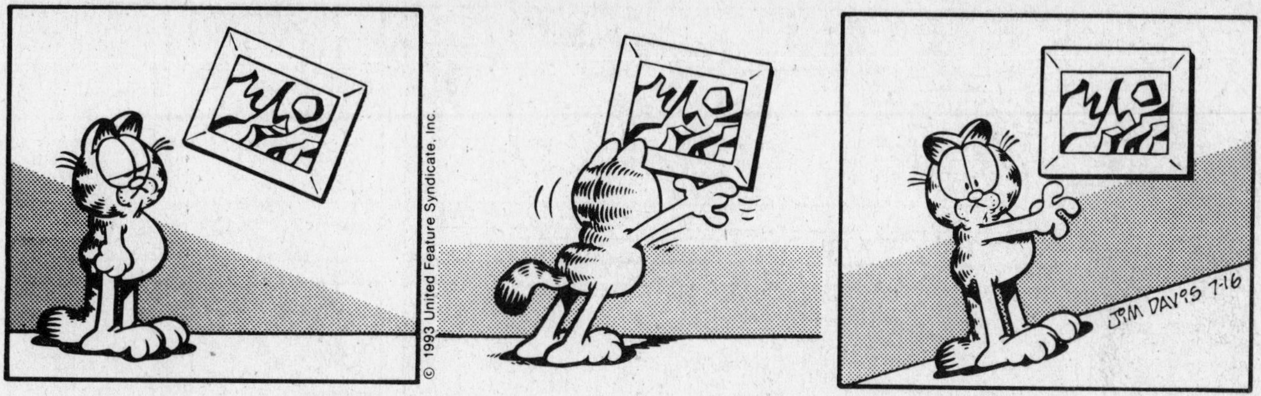
JIM DAVIS 7-16

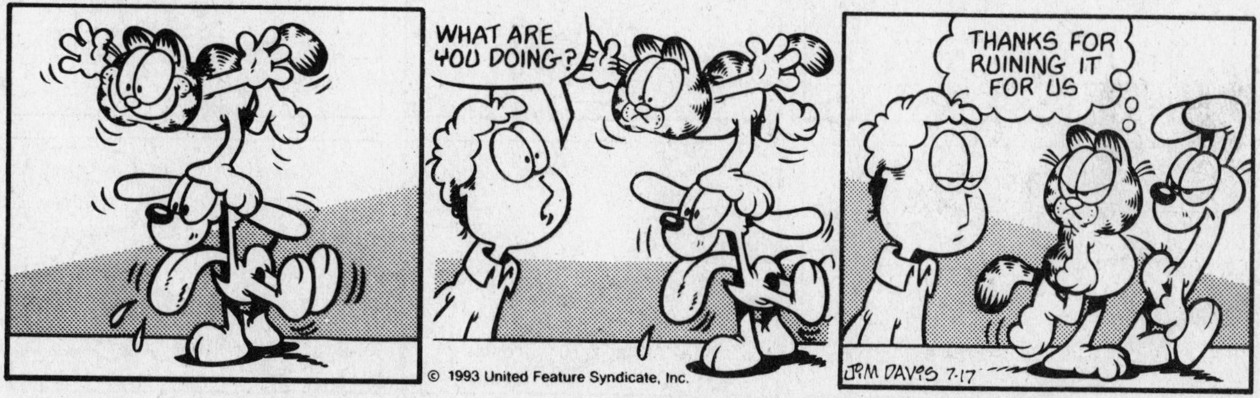
WHAT ARE YOU DOING?
THANKS FOR RUINING IT FOR US
JIM DAVIS 7-17

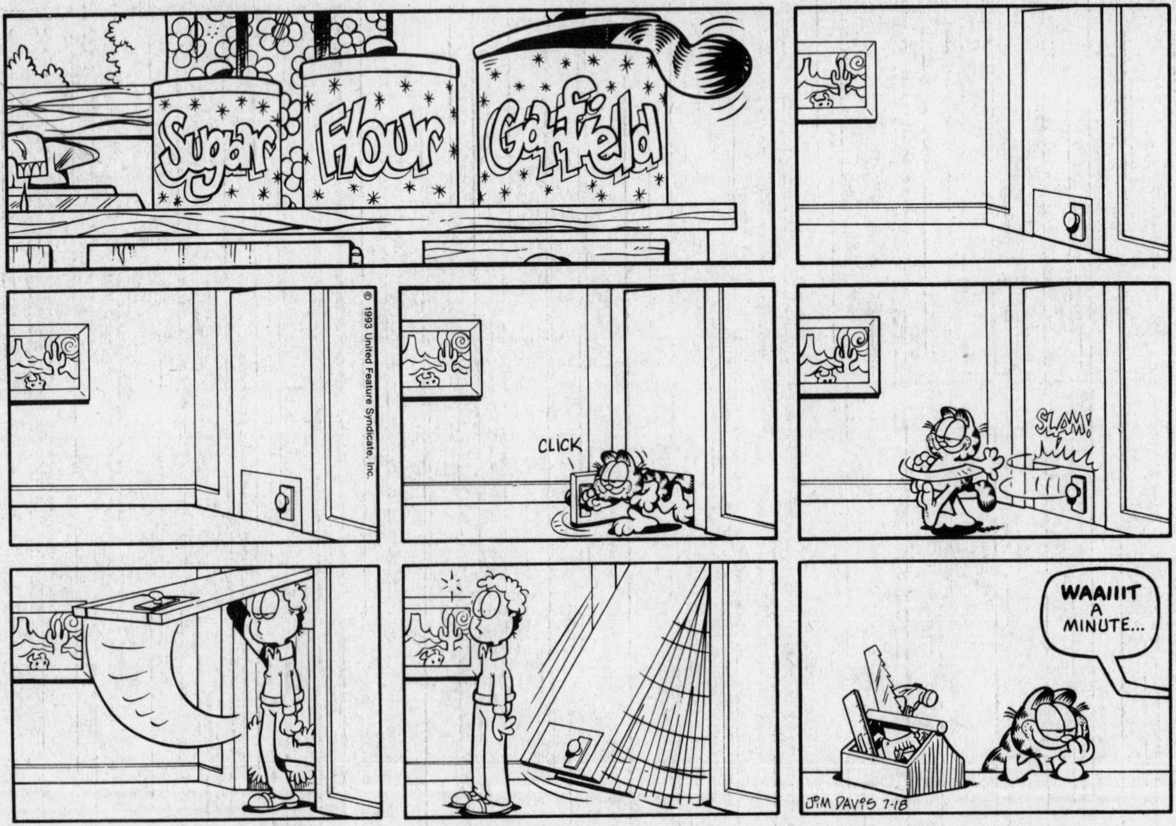
Sugar
Flour
Garfield
CLICK
SLAM!
WAAIIIT A MINUTE...
JIM DAVIS 7-18

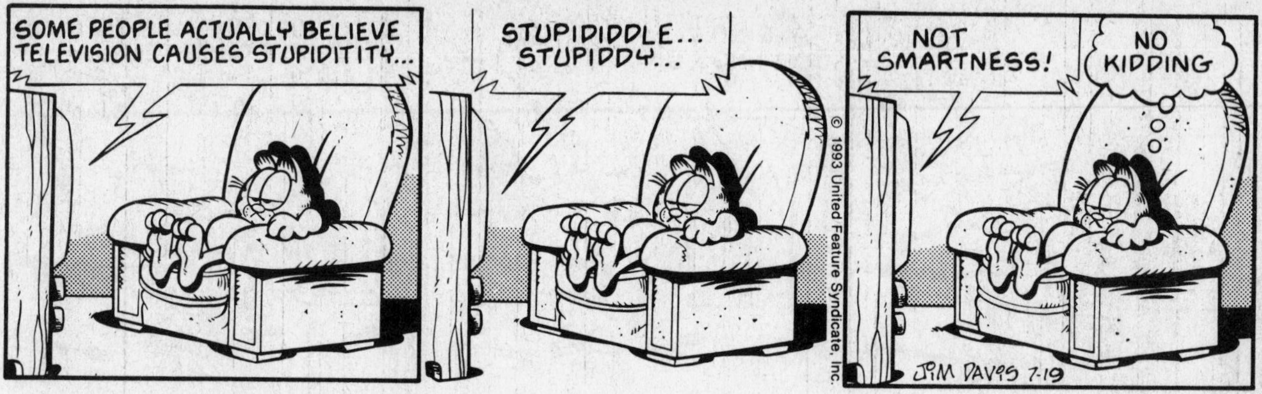
SOME PEOPLE ACTUALLY BELIEVE TELEVISION CAUSES STUPIDITITY...
STUPIDIDDLE... STUPIDDY...
NOT SMARTNESS!
NO KIDDING
© 1993 United Feature Syndicate, Inc.
JIM DAVIS 7-19

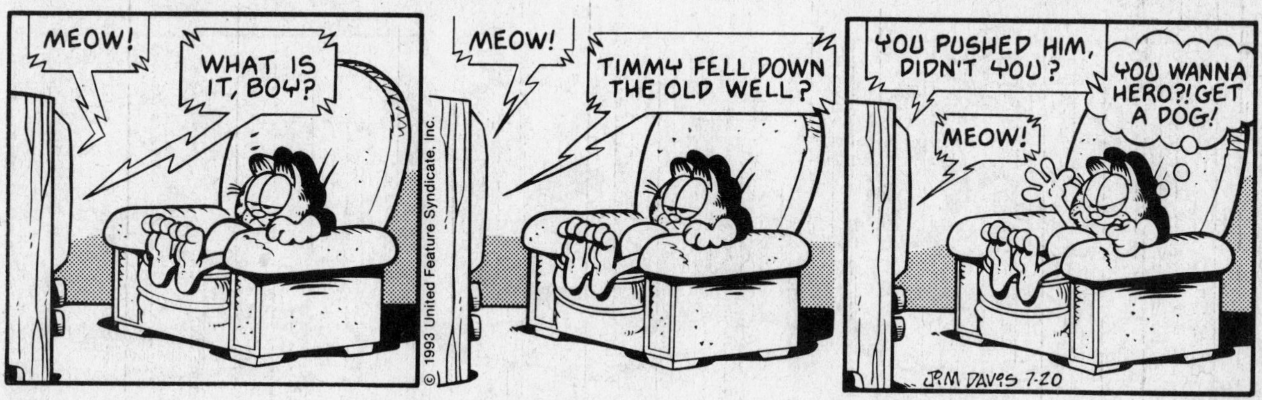
MEOW!
WHAT IS IT, BOY?
MEOW!
TIMMY FELL DOWN THE OLD WELL?
YOU PUSHED HIM, DIDN'T YOU?
MEOW!
YOU WANNA HERO?! GET A DOG!
© 1993 United Feature Syndicate, Inc.
JIM DAVIS 7-20

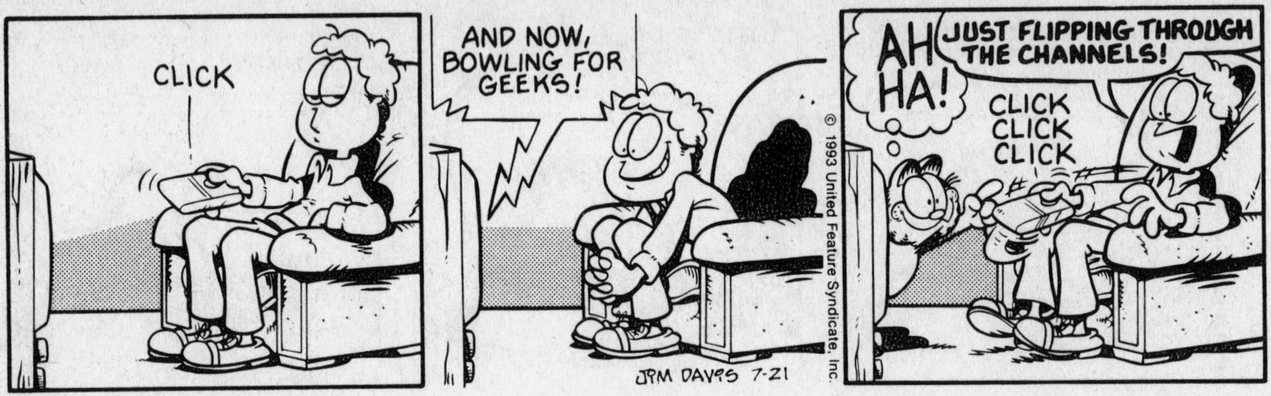
CLICK
AND NOW, BOWLING FOR GEEKS!
JUST FLIPPING THROUGH THE CHANNELS!
AH HA!
CLICK CLICK CLICK
JIM DAVIS 7-21
© 1993 United Feature Syndicate, Inc.

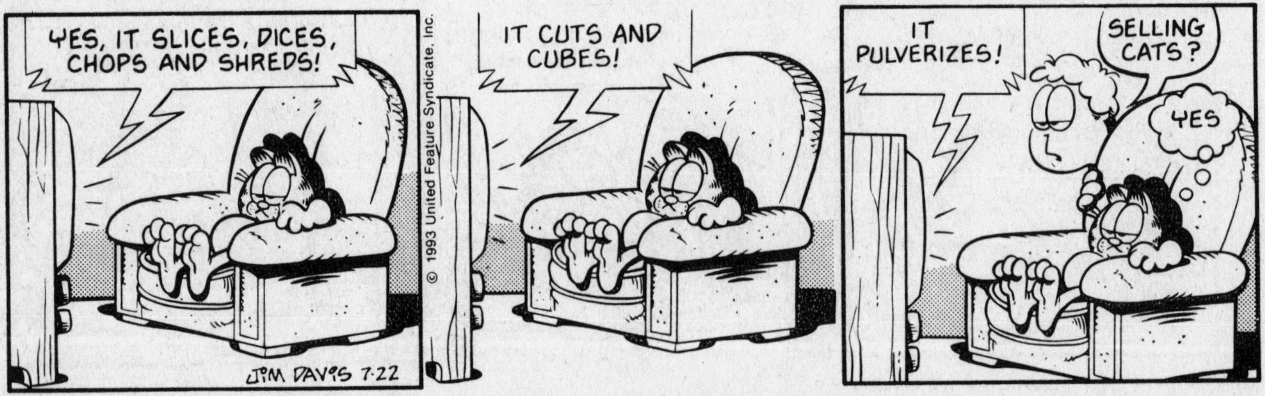
YES, IT SLICES, DICES, CHOPS AND SHREDS!
IT CUTS AND CUBES!
IT PULVERIZES!
SELLING CATS?
YES
JIM DAVIS 7-22
© 1993 United Feature Syndicate, Inc.

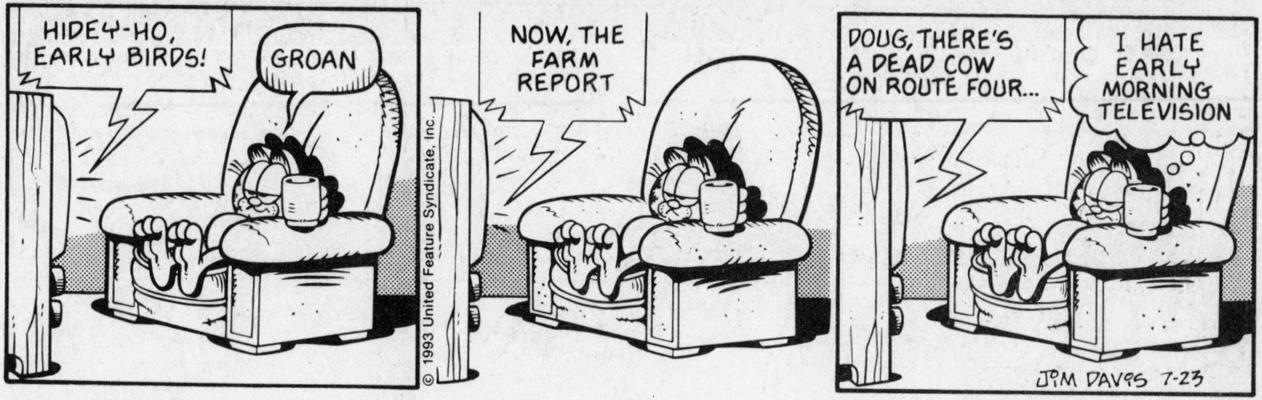
HIDEY-HO, EARLY BIRDS!
GROAN
NOW, THE FARM REPORT
DOUG, THERE'S A DEAD COW ON ROUTE FOUR...
I HATE EARLY MORNING TELEVISION
© 1993 United Feature Syndicate, Inc.
JIM DAVIS 7-23

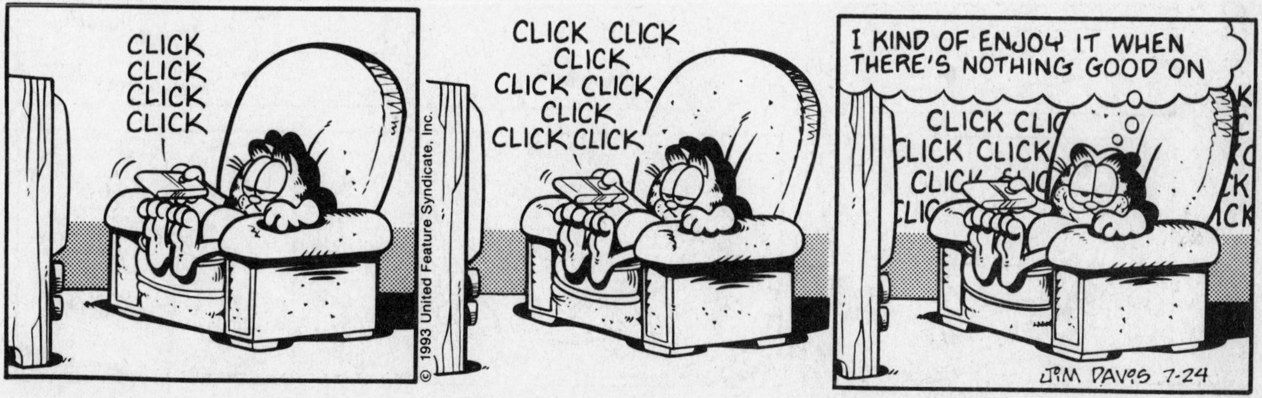
CLICK CLICK CLICK CLICK
CLICK CLICK CLICK CLICK CLICK CLICK CLICK CLICK
I KIND OF ENJOY IT WHEN THERE'S NOTHING GOOD ON
© 1993 United Feature Syndicate, Inc.
JIM DAVIS 7-24

GARFIELD
SIGH
RATS!
© 1993 United Feature Syndicate, Inc.
I JUST CAN'T GET COMFORTABLE
JIM DAVIS 7-25
Z

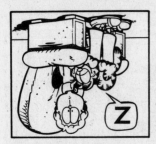

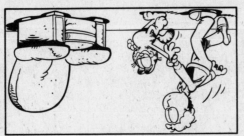

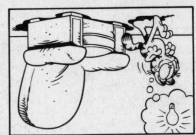

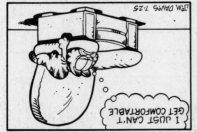

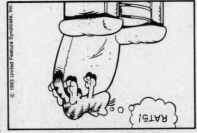

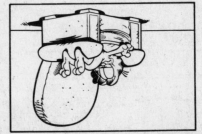

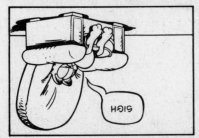

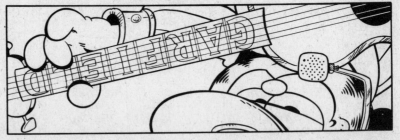

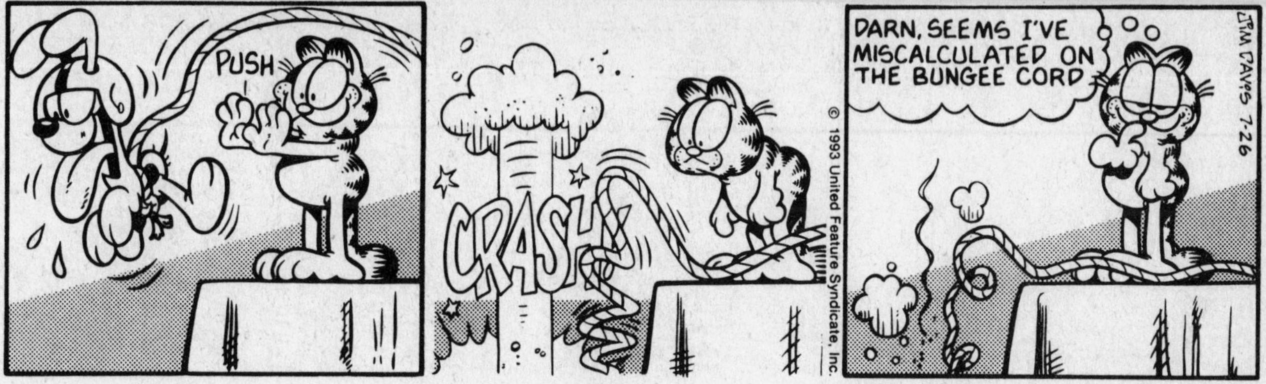
PUSH
CRASH
© 1993 United Feature Syndicate, Inc.
DARN, SEEMS I'VE MISCALCULATED ON THE BUNGEE CORD
JIM DAVIS 7-26

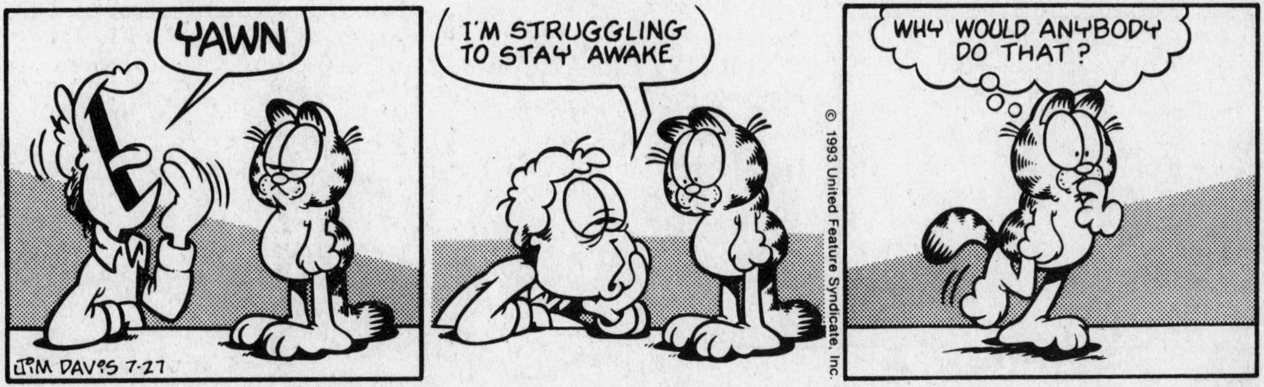
YAWN
JIM DAVIS 7-27
I'M STRUGGLING TO STAY AWAKE
© 1993 United Feature Syndicate, Inc.
WHY WOULD ANYBODY DO THAT?

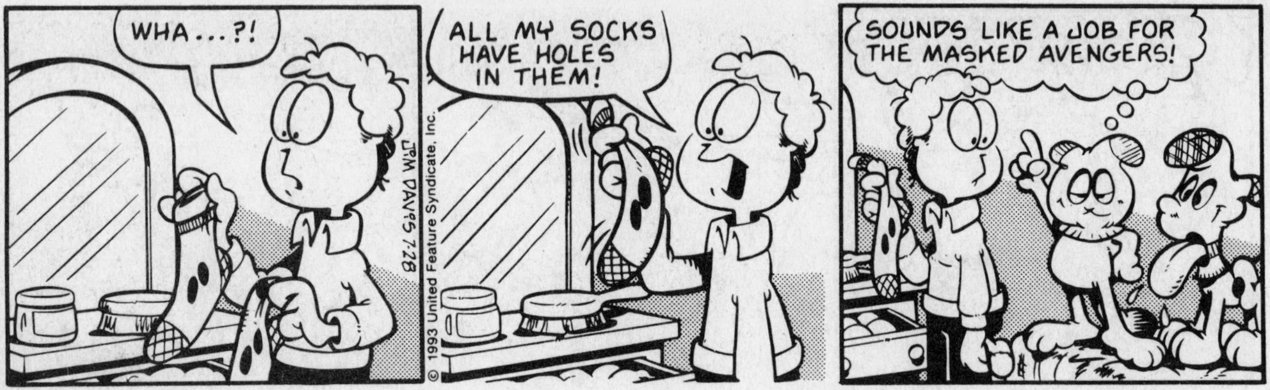
WHA...?!
ALL MY SOCKS HAVE HOLES IN THEM!
SOUNDS LIKE A JOB FOR THE MASKED AVENGERS!
JIM DAVIS 7-28
© 1993 United Feature Syndicate, Inc.

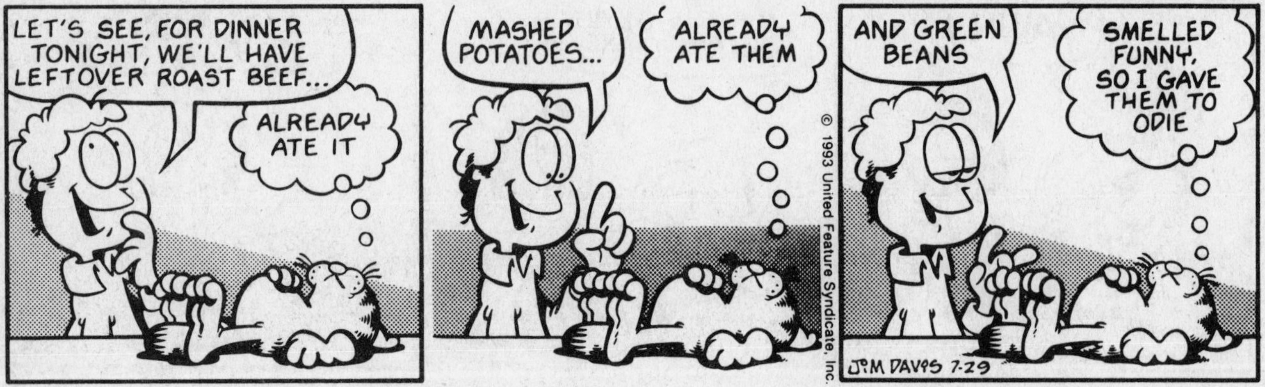
LET'S SEE, FOR DINNER TONIGHT, WE'LL HAVE LEFTOVER ROAST BEEF...
ALREADY ATE IT
MASHED POTATOES...
ALREADY ATE THEM
AND GREEN BEANS
SMELLED FUNNY, SO I GAVE THEM TO ODIE
JIM DAVIS 7-29
© 1993 United Feature Syndicate, Inc.

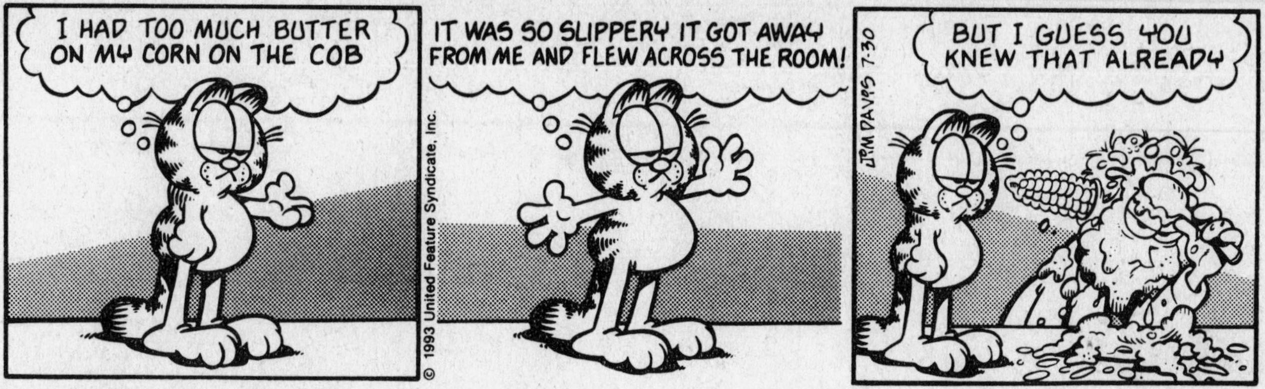
I HAD TOO MUCH BUTTER ON MY CORN ON THE COB
IT WAS SO SLIPPERY IT GOT AWAY FROM ME AND FLEW ACROSS THE ROOM!
© 1993 United Feature Syndicate, Inc.
JIM DAVIS 7-30
BUT I GUESS YOU KNEW THAT ALREADY

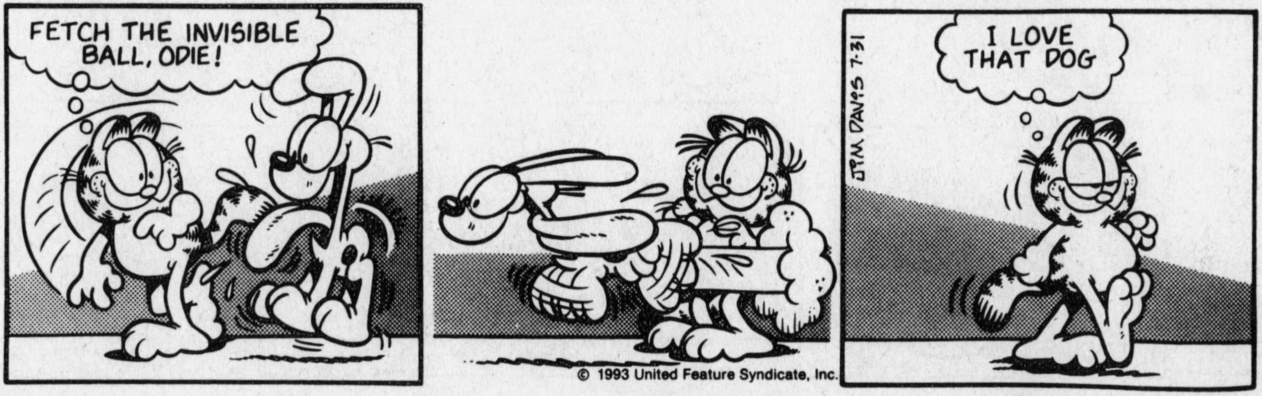
FETCH THE INVISIBLE BALL, ODIE!
© 1993 United Feature Syndicate, Inc.
JIM DAVIS 7-31
I LOVE THAT DOG

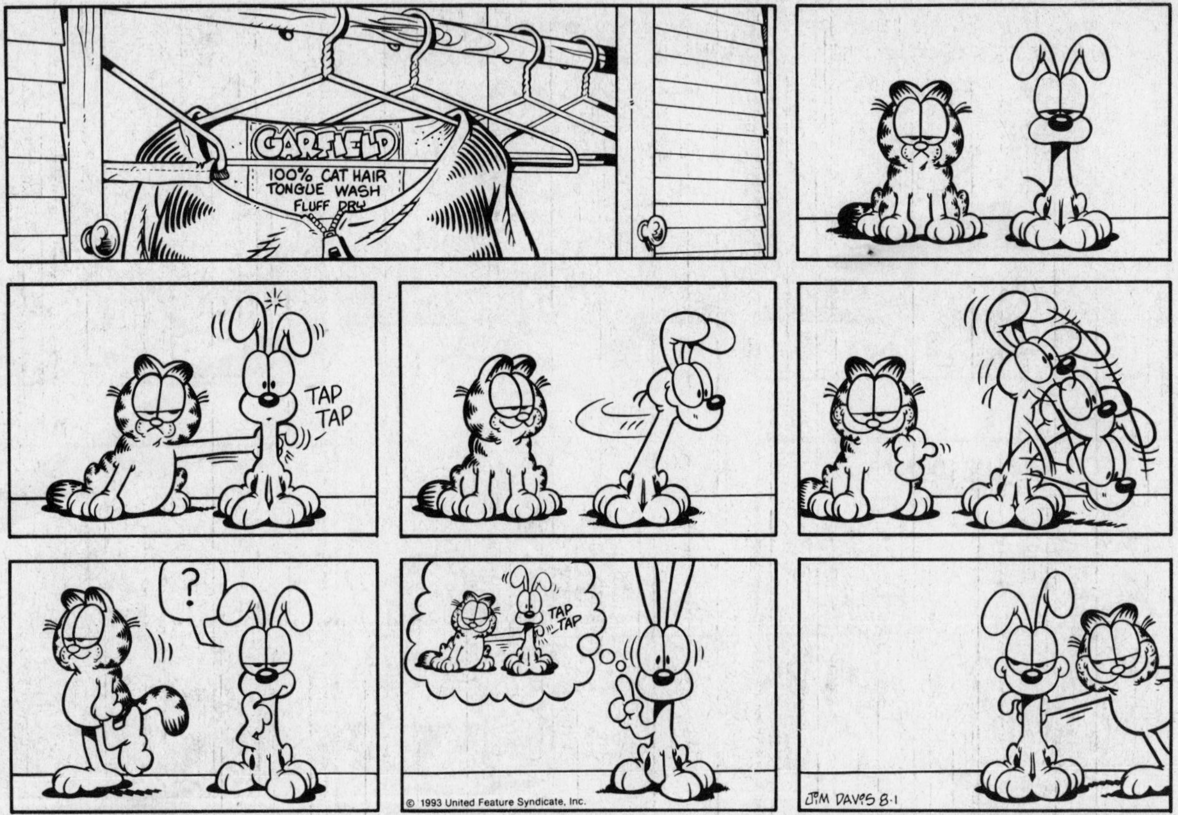
GARFIELD
100% CAT HAIR
TONGUE WASH
FLUFF DRY
TAP
TAP
?
TAP
TAP
© 1993 United Feature Syndicate, Inc.
JIM DAVIS 8-1

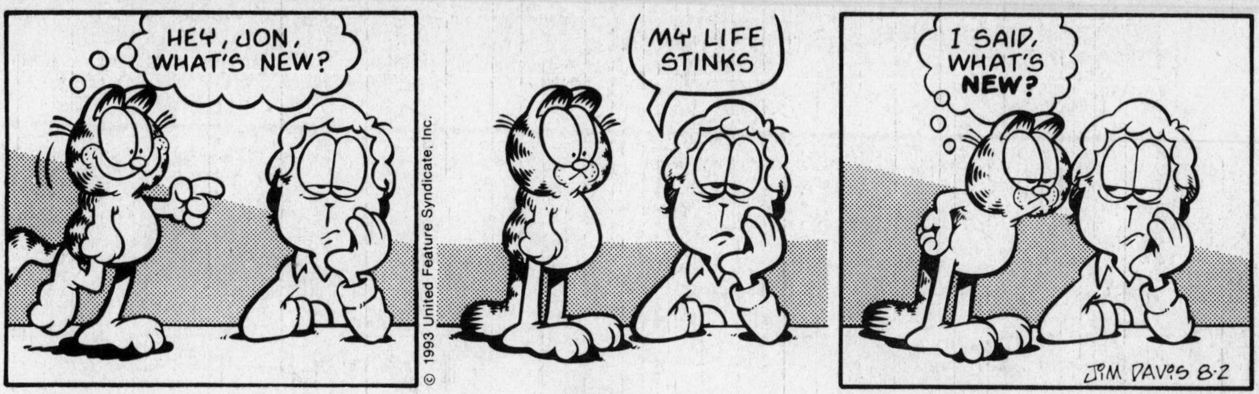
HEY, JON, WHAT'S NEW?
MY LIFE STINKS
I SAID, WHAT'S **NEW?**
JIM DAVIS 8-2

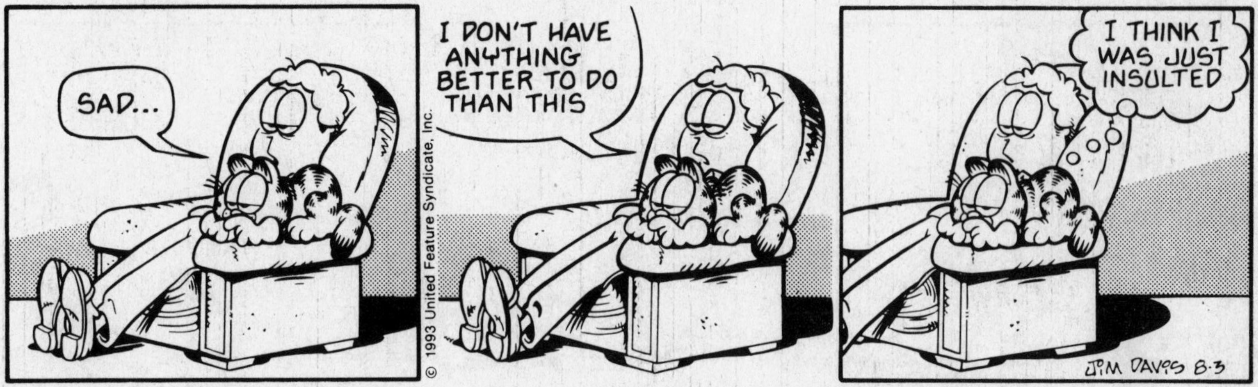
SAD...
I DON'T HAVE ANYTHING BETTER TO DO THAN THIS
I THINK I WAS JUST INSULTED
JIM DAVIS 8-3

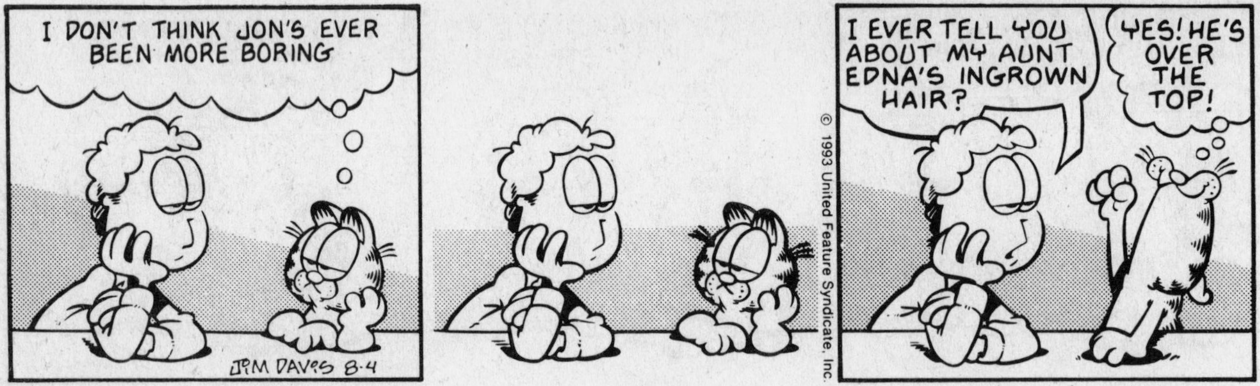
I DON'T THINK JON'S EVER BEEN MORE BORING
I EVER TELL YOU ABOUT MY AUNT EDNA'S INGROWN HAIR?
YES! HE'S OVER THE TOP!
JIM DAVIS 8-4

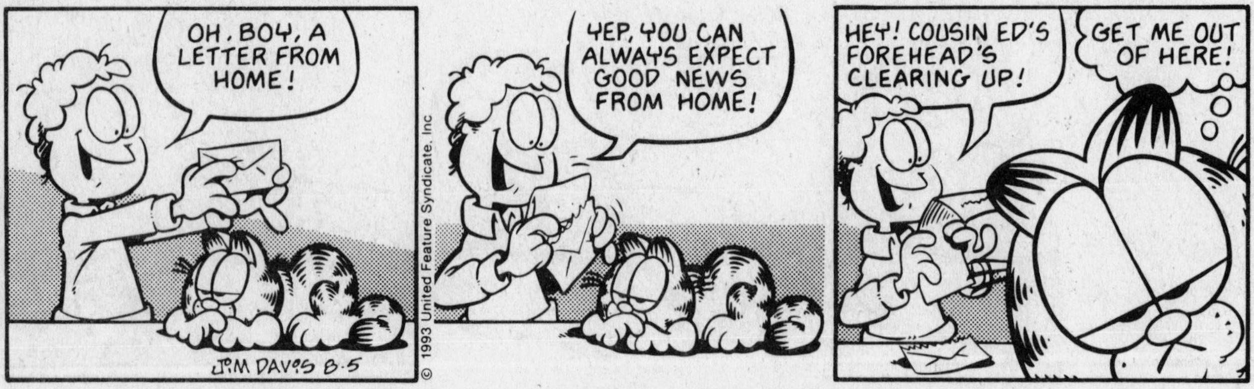
OH, BOY, A LETTER FROM HOME!
YEP, YOU CAN ALWAYS EXPECT GOOD NEWS FROM HOME!
HEY! COUSIN ED'S FOREHEAD'S CLEARING UP!
GET ME OUT OF HERE!
JIM DAVIS 8-5

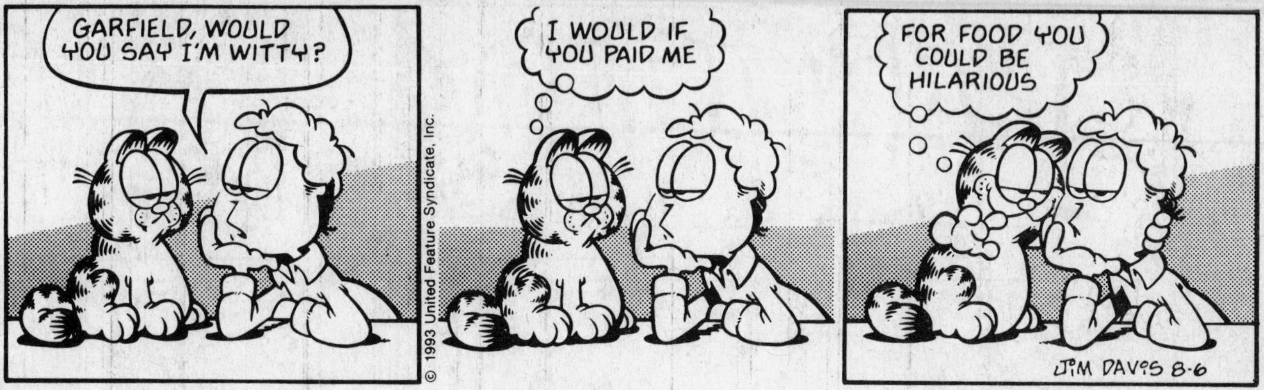
GARFIELD, WOULD YOU SAY I'M WITTY?
I WOULD IF YOU PAID ME
FOR FOOD YOU COULD BE HILARIOUS
© 1993 United Feature Syndicate, Inc.
JIM DAVIS 8-6

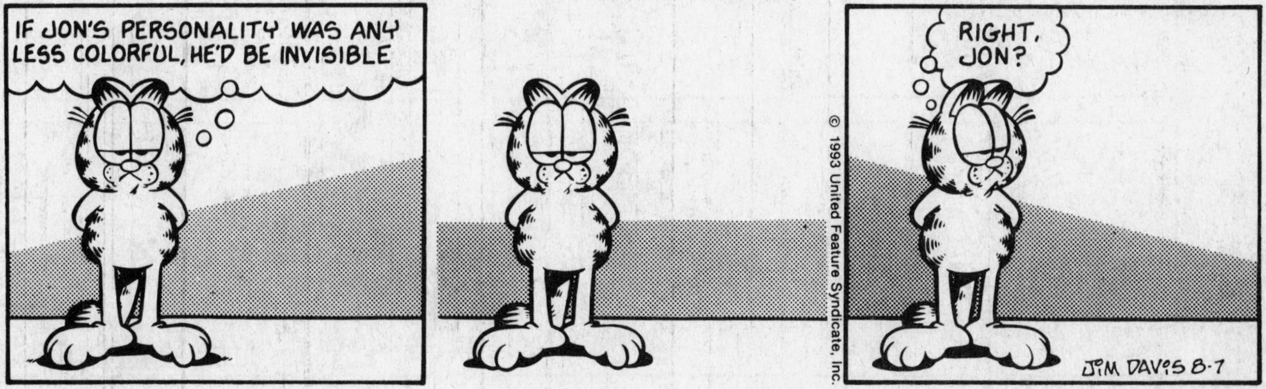
IF JON'S PERSONALITY WAS ANY LESS COLORFUL, HE'D BE INVISIBLE
RIGHT, JON?
© 1993 United Feature Syndicate, Inc.
JIM DAVIS 8-7

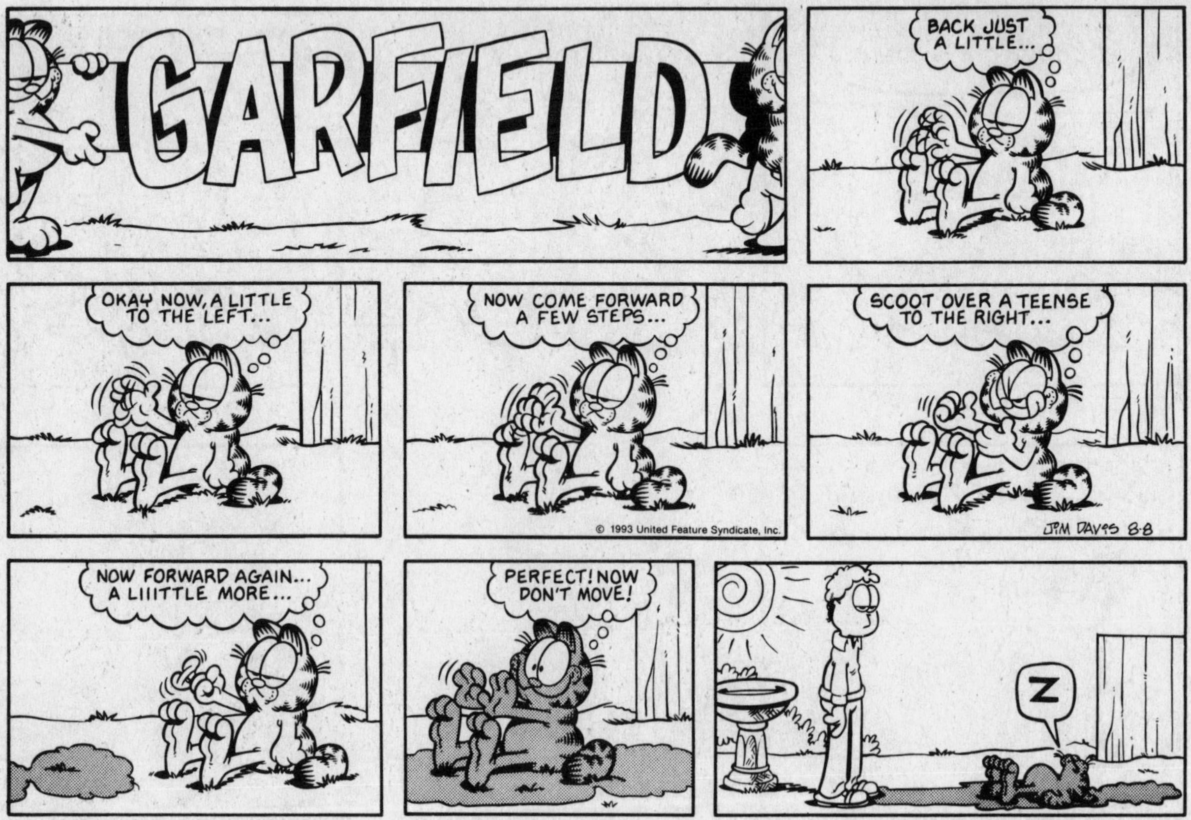
GARFIELD
BACK JUST A LITTLE...
OKAY NOW, A LITTLE TO THE LEFT...
NOW COME FORWARD A FEW STEPS...
© 1993 United Feature Syndicate, Inc.
SCOOT OVER A TEENSE TO THE RIGHT...
JIM DAVIS 8-8
NOW FORWARD AGAIN... A LIIITTLE MORE...
PERFECT! NOW DON'T MOVE!
Z

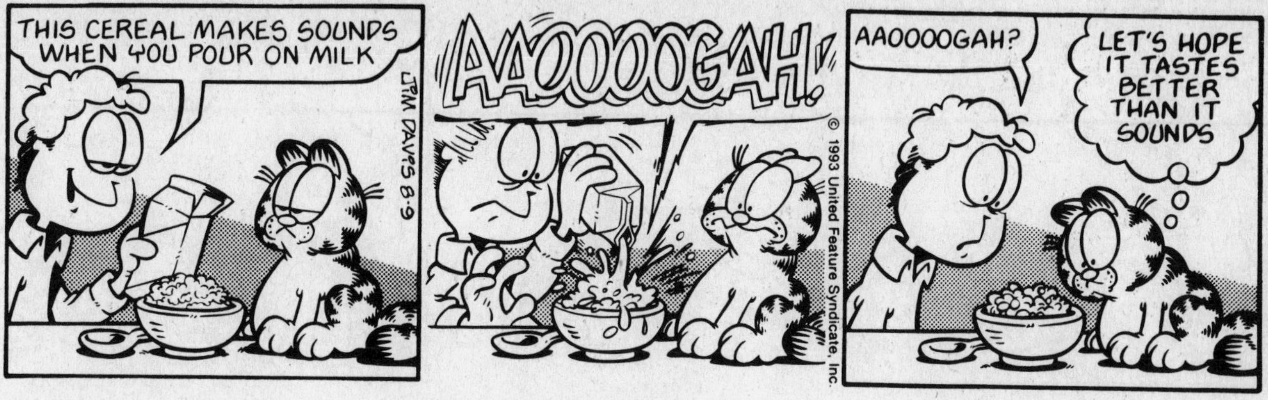
THIS CEREAL MAKES SOUNDS WHEN YOU POUR ON MILK
JIM DAVIS 8-9
AAOOOOOGAH!
© 1993 United Feature Syndicate, Inc.
AAOOOOGAH?
LET'S HOPE IT TASTES BETTER THAN IT SOUNDS

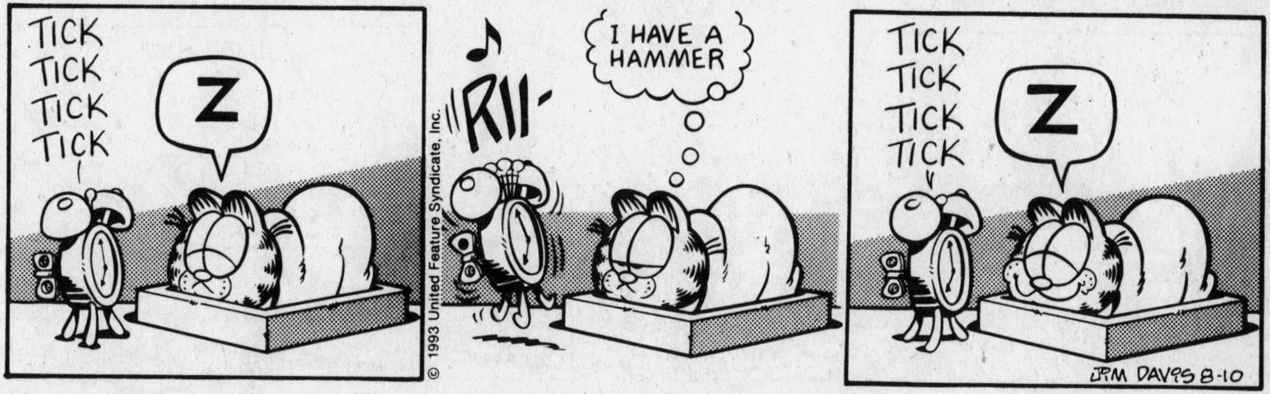
TICK TICK TICK TICK
Z
© 1993 United Feature Syndicate, Inc.
RII-
I HAVE A HAMMER
TICK TICK TICK TICK
Z
JIM DAVIS 8-10

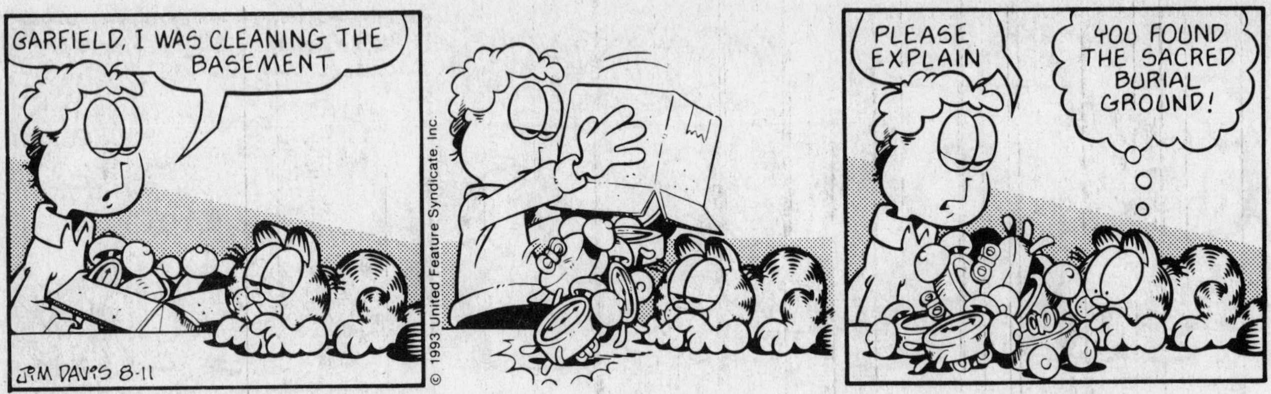
GARFIELD, I WAS CLEANING THE BASEMENT
JIM DAVIS 8-11
© 1993 United Feature Syndicate, Inc.
PLEASE EXPLAIN
YOU FOUND THE SACRED BURIAL GROUND!

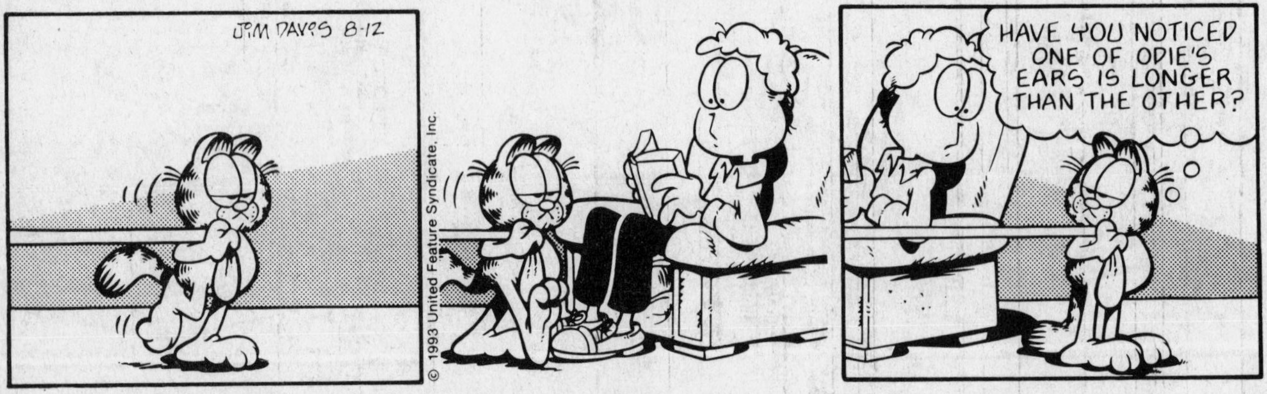
JIM DAVIS 8-12
© 1993 United Feature Syndicate, Inc.
HAVE YOU NOTICED ONE OF ODIE'S EARS IS LONGER THAN THE OTHER?

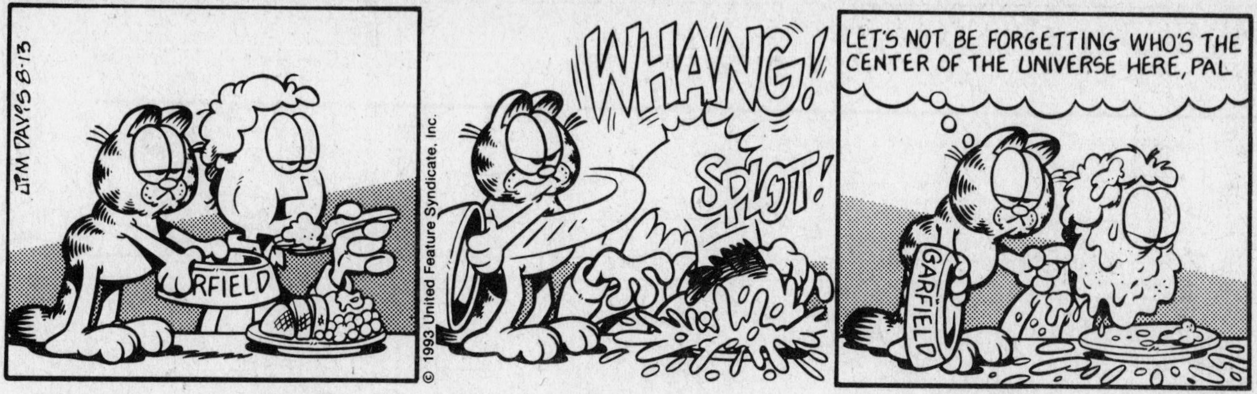
JIM DAVIS 8-13
RFIELD
© 1993 United Feature Syndicate, Inc.
WHANG!
SPLOT!
LET'S NOT BE FORGETTING WHO'S THE CENTER OF THE UNIVERSE HERE, PAL
GARFIELD

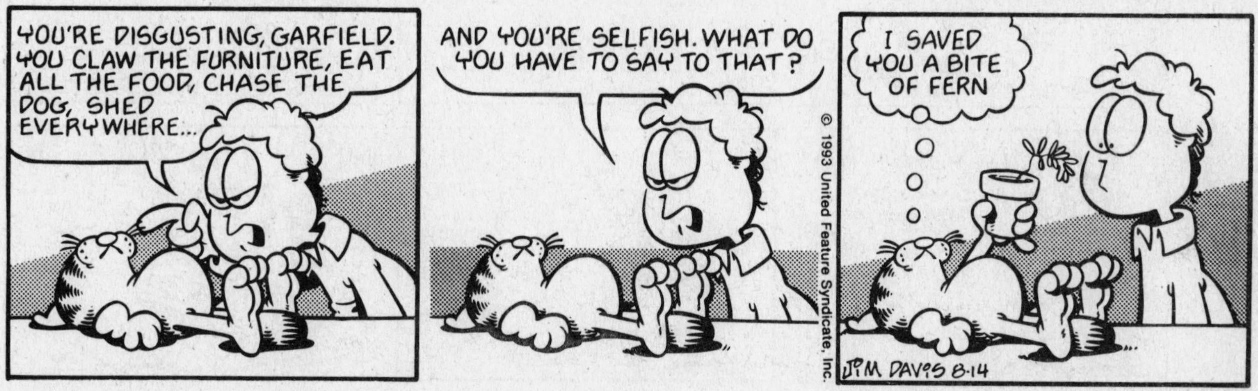
YOU'RE DISGUSTING, GARFIELD. YOU CLAW THE FURNITURE, EAT ALL THE FOOD, CHASE THE DOG, SHED EVERYWHERE...
AND YOU'RE SELFISH. WHAT DO YOU HAVE TO SAY TO THAT?
© 1993 United Feature Syndicate, Inc.
I SAVED YOU A BITE OF FERN
JIM DAVIS 8-14

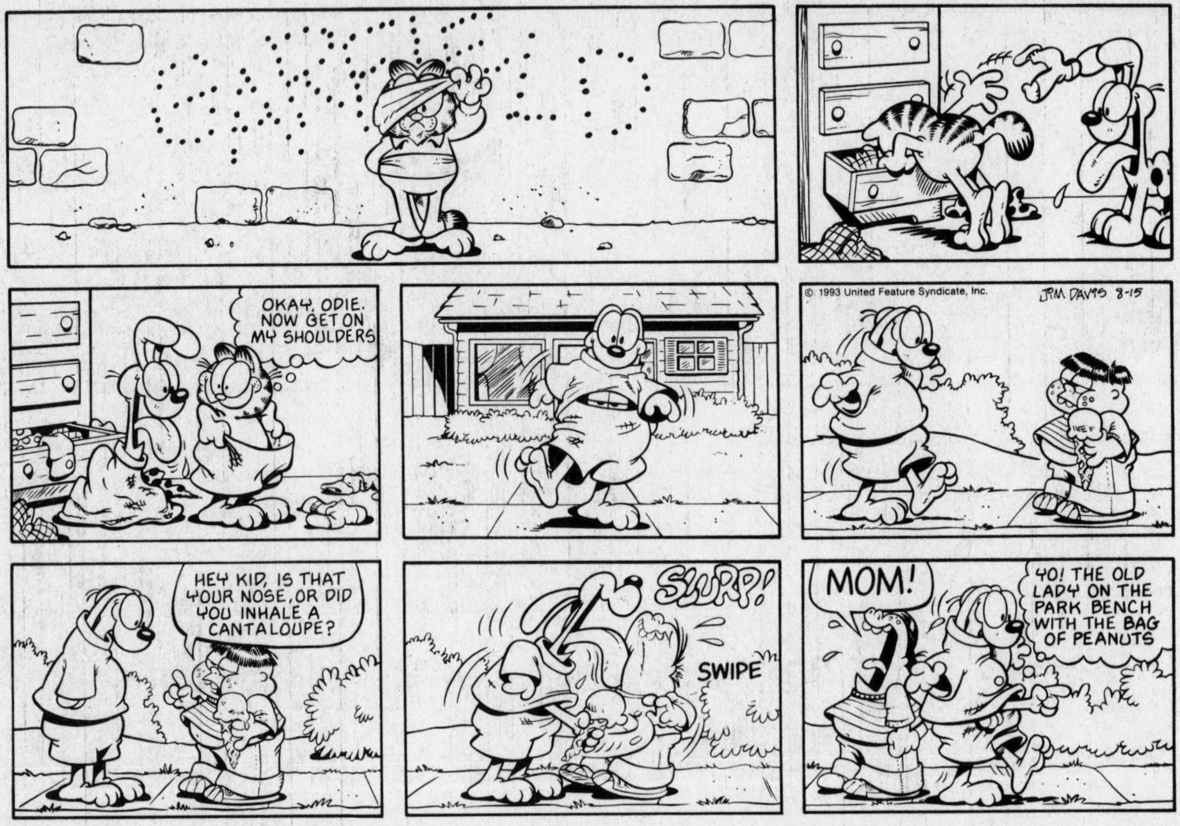
GARFIELD
OKAY, ODIE. NOW GET ON MY SHOULDERS
© 1993 United Feature Syndicate, Inc.
JPM DAV95 8-15
HEY KID, IS THAT YOUR NOSE, OR DID YOU INHALE A CANTALOUPE?
SLURP!
SWIPE
MOM!
YO! THE OLD LADY ON THE PARK BENCH WITH THE BAG OF PEANUTS

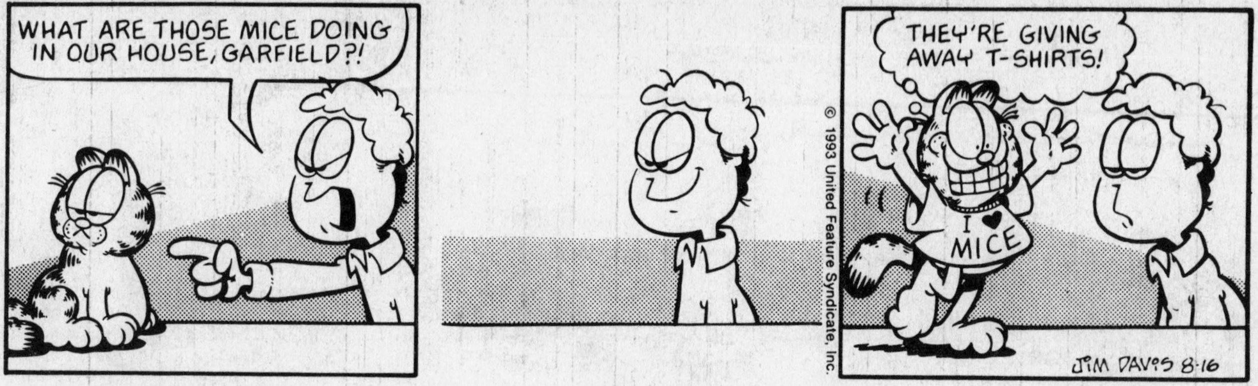
WHAT ARE THOSE MICE DOING IN OUR HOUSE, GARFIELD?!
THEY'RE GIVING AWAY T-SHIRTS!
I ♥ MICE
© 1993 United Feature Syndicate, Inc.
JIM DAVIS 8·16

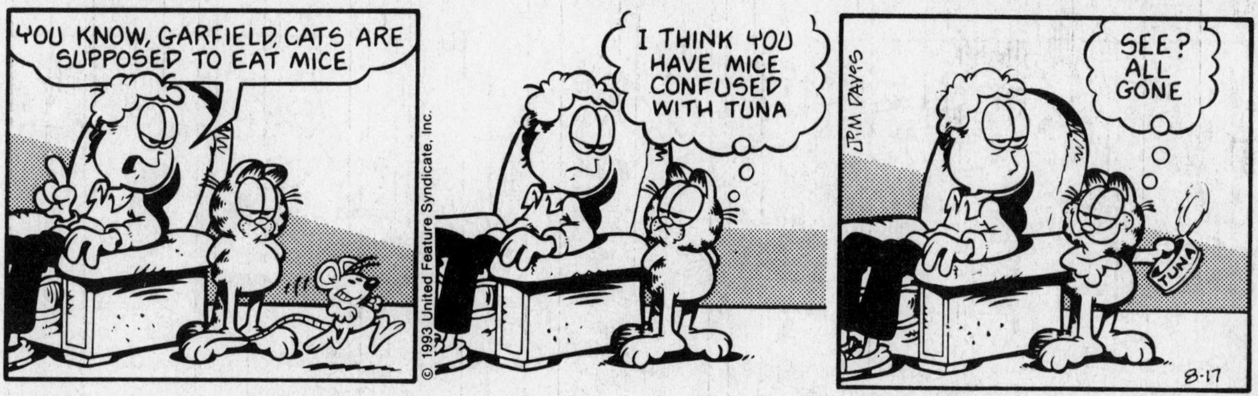
YOU KNOW, GARFIELD, CATS ARE SUPPOSED TO EAT MICE
© 1993 United Feature Syndicate, Inc.
I THINK YOU HAVE MICE CONFUSED WITH TUNA
JIM DAVIS
SEE? ALL GONE
TUNA
8·17

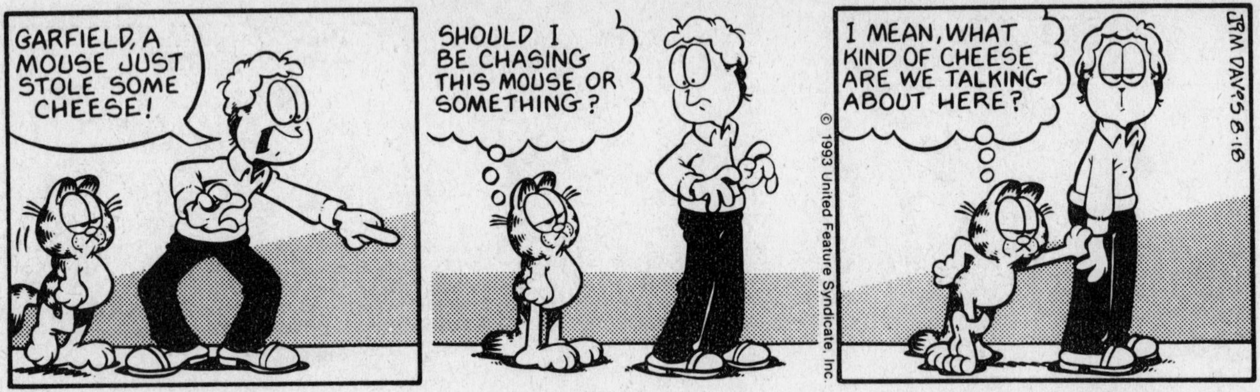
GARFIELD, A MOUSE JUST STOLE SOME CHEESE!
SHOULD I BE CHASING THIS MOUSE OR SOMETHING?
I MEAN, WHAT KIND OF CHEESE ARE WE TALKING ABOUT HERE?
JIM DAVIS 8-18
© 1993 United Feature Syndicate, Inc.

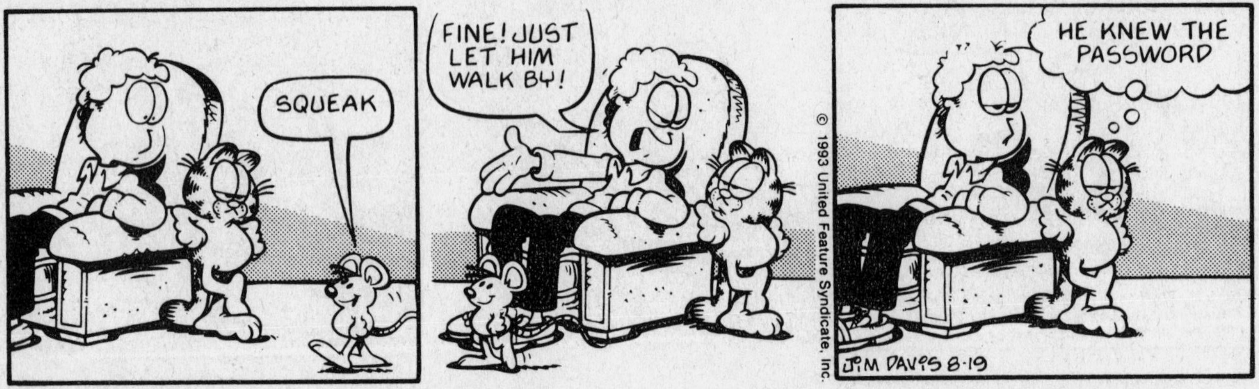
SQUEAK
FINE! JUST LET HIM WALK BY!
HE KNEW THE PASSWORD
JIM DAVIS 8-19
© 1993 United Feature Syndicate, Inc.

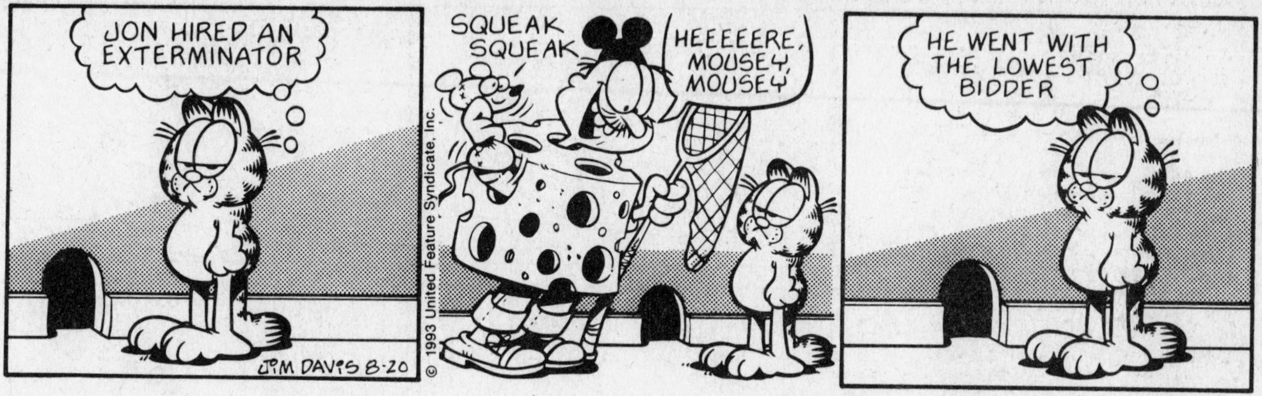
JON HIRED AN EXTERMINATOR
JIM DAVIS 8-20
SQUEAK SQUEAK
HEEEEERE, MOUSEY, MOUSEY
© 1993 United Feature Syndicate, Inc.
HE WENT WITH THE LOWEST BIDDER

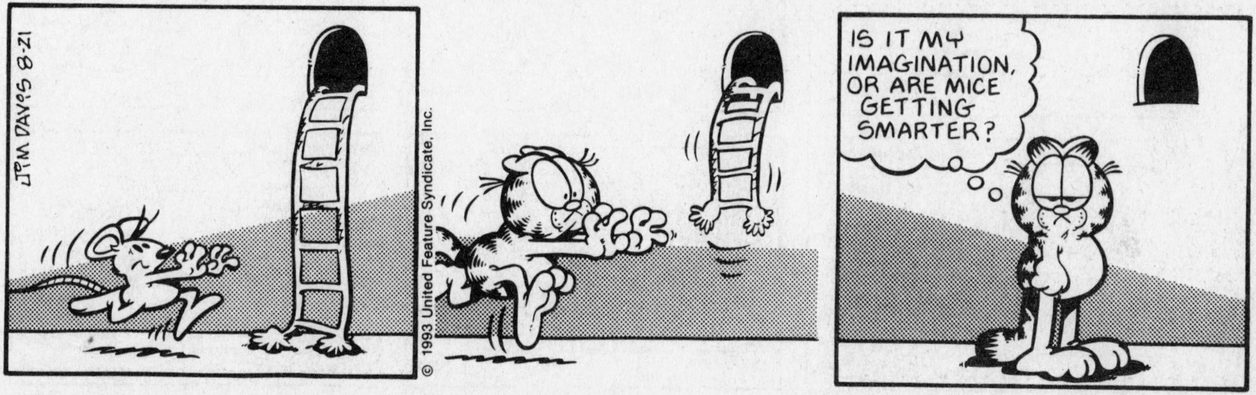
JIM DAVIS 8-21
© 1993 United Feature Syndicate, Inc.
IS IT MY IMAGINATION, OR ARE MICE GETTING SMARTER?

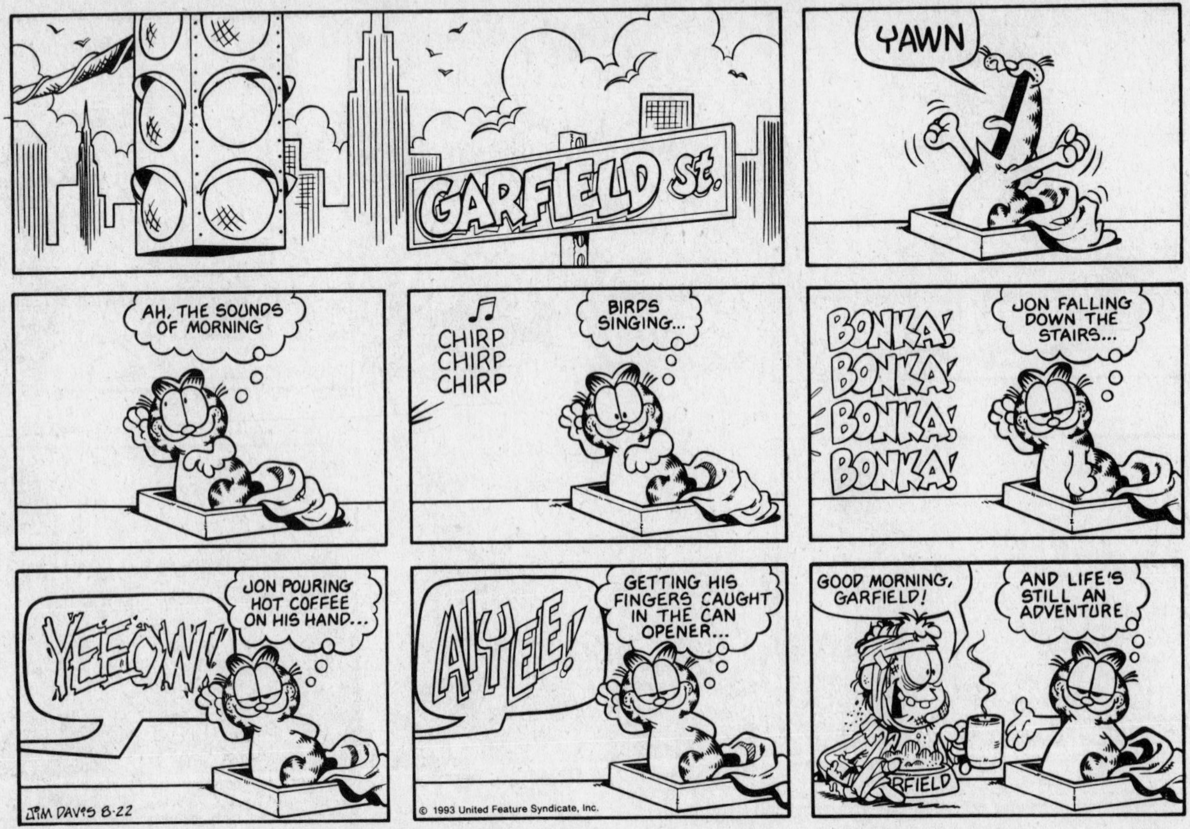
GARFIELD St.
YAWN
AH, THE SOUNDS OF MORNING
CHIRP CHIRP CHIRP
BIRDS SINGING...
BONKA! BONKA! BONKA! BONKA!
JON FALLING DOWN THE STAIRS...
YEEOW!
JON POURING HOT COFFEE ON HIS HAND...
AIYEE!
GETTING HIS FINGERS CAUGHT IN THE CAN OPENER...
GOOD MORNING, GARFIELD!
AND LIFE'S STILL AN ADVENTURE
JIM DAVIS 8-22
© 1993 United Feature Syndicate, Inc.

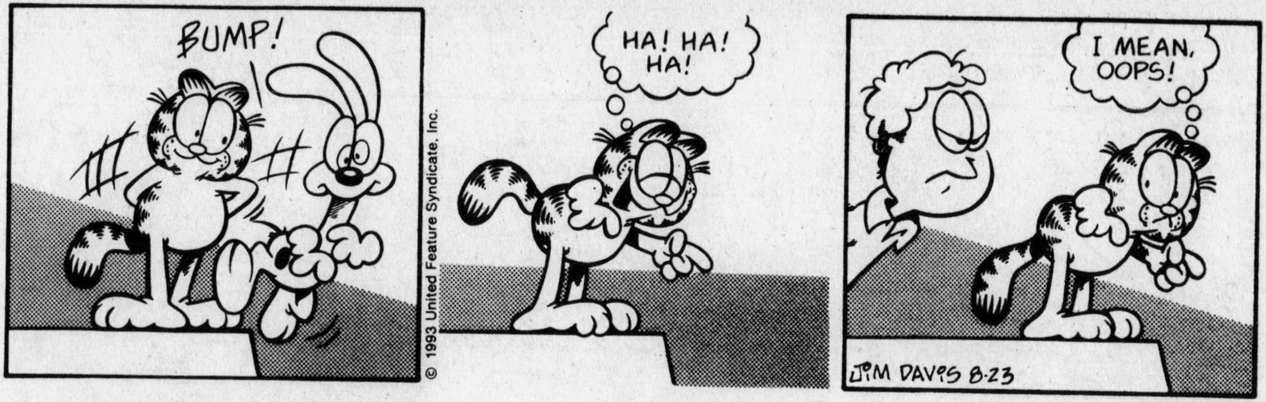
BUMP!
HA! HA! HA!
I MEAN, OOPS!
© 1993 United Feature Syndicate, Inc.
JIM DAVIS 8-23

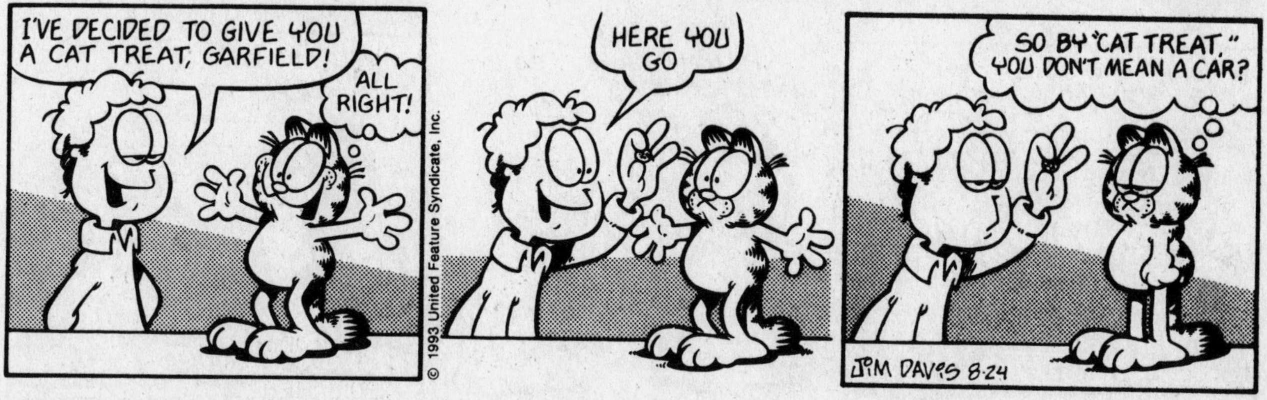
I'VE DECIDED TO GIVE YOU A CAT TREAT, GARFIELD!
ALL RIGHT!
HERE YOU GO
SO BY "CAT TREAT," YOU DON'T MEAN A CAR?
© 1993 United Feature Syndicate, Inc.
JIM DAVIS 8-24

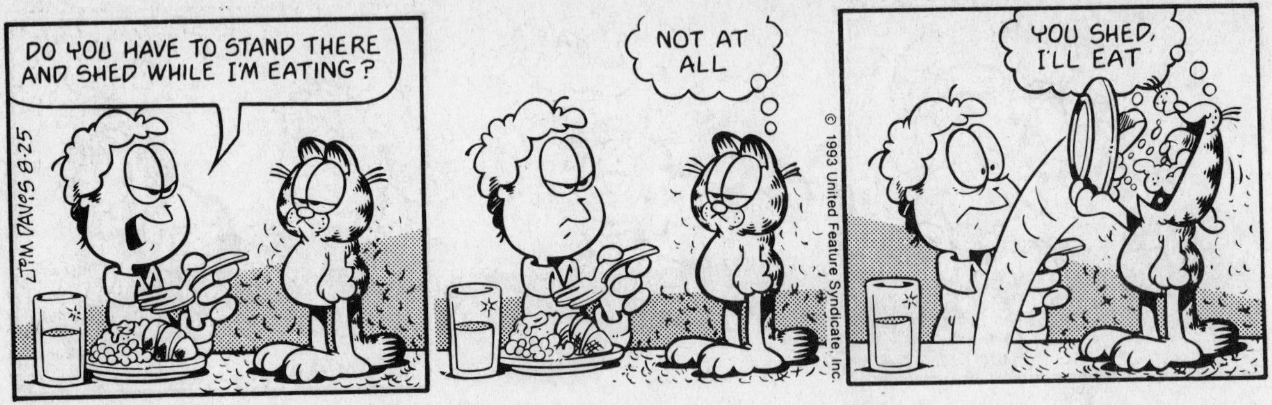
DO YOU HAVE TO STAND THERE AND SHED WHILE I'M EATING?
JIM DAVIS 8·25
NOT AT ALL
YOU SHED, I'LL EAT
© 1993 United Feature Syndicate, Inc.

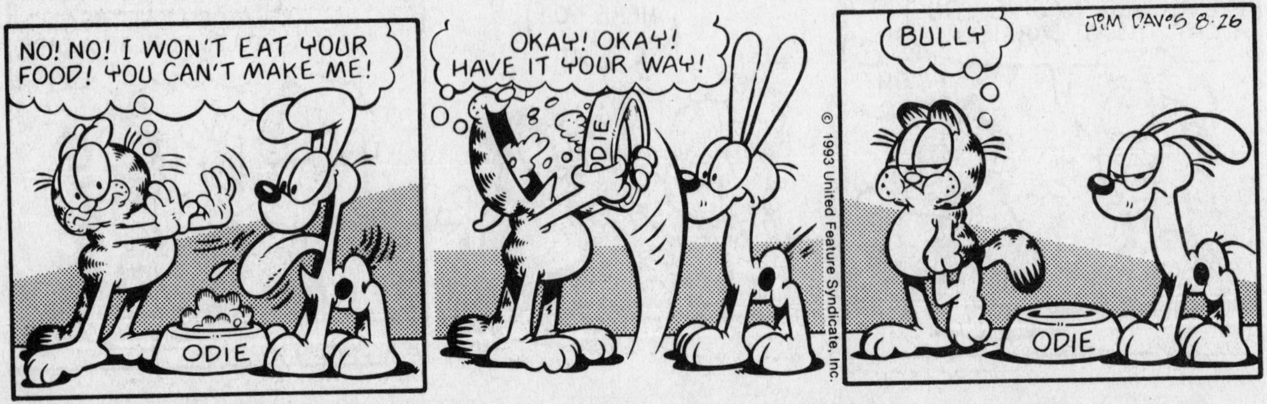
NO! NO! I WON'T EAT YOUR FOOD! YOU CAN'T MAKE ME!
ODIE
OKAY! OKAY! HAVE IT YOUR WAY!
ODIE
BULLY
JIM DAVIS 8·26
ODIE
© 1993 United Feature Syndicate, Inc.

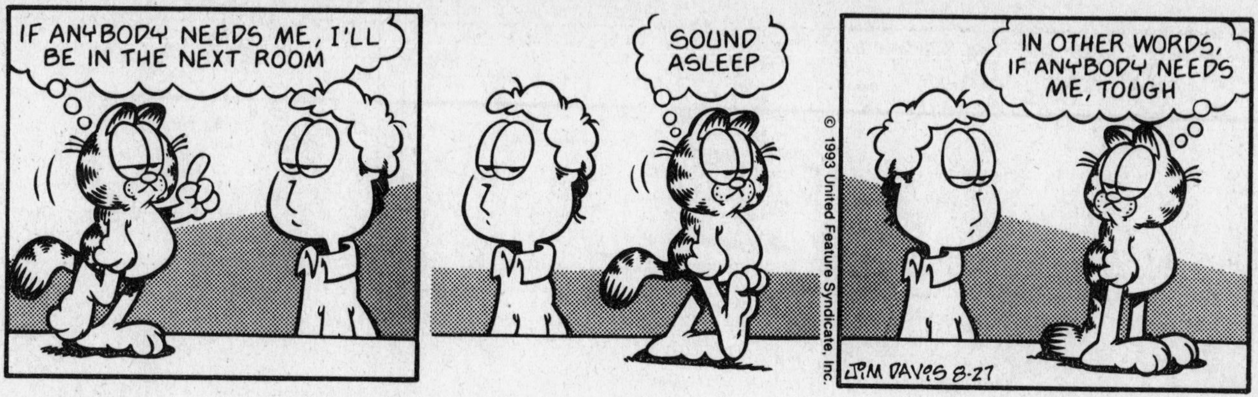
IF ANYBODY NEEDS ME, I'LL BE IN THE NEXT ROOM
SOUND ASLEEP
IN OTHER WORDS, IF ANYBODY NEEDS ME, TOUGH
JIM DAVIS 8-27
© 1993 United Feature Syndicate, Inc.

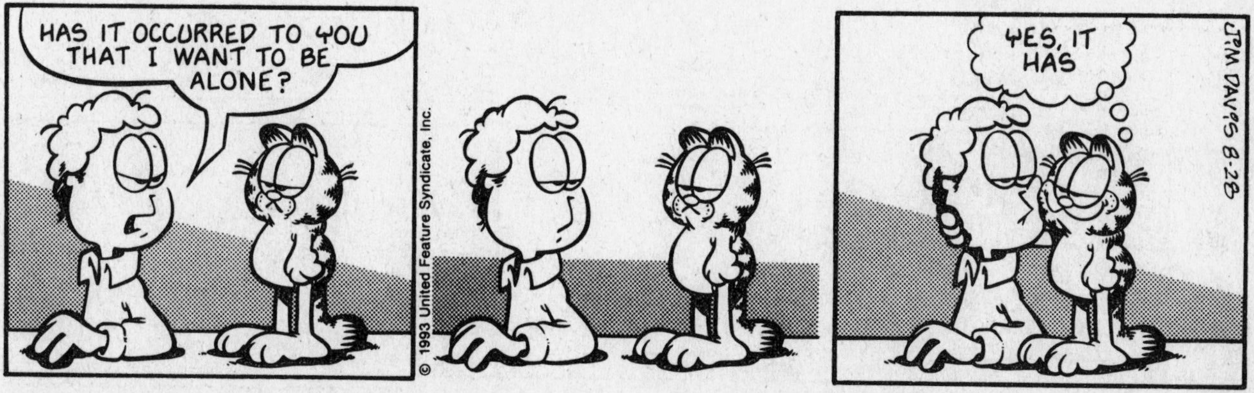
HAS IT OCCURRED TO YOU THAT I WANT TO BE ALONE?
YES, IT HAS
JIM DAVIS 8-28
© 1993 United Feature Syndicate, Inc.

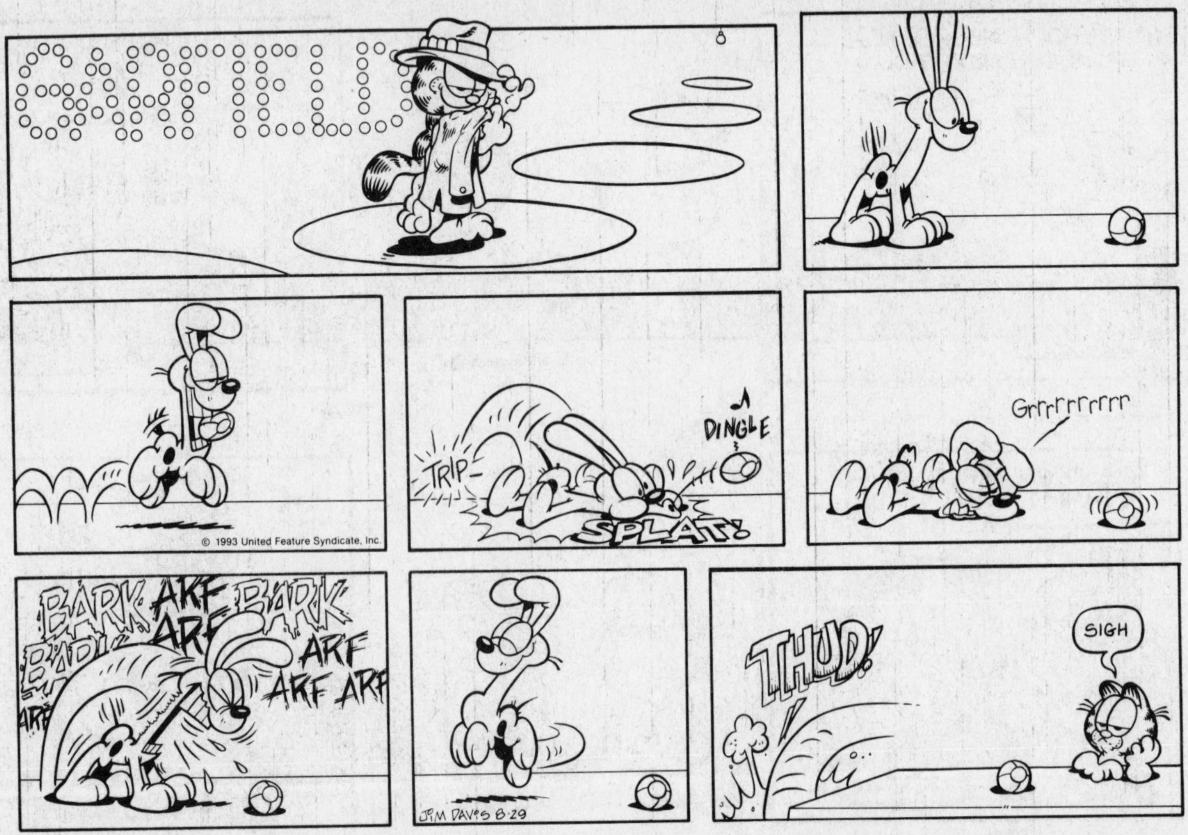
GARFIELD
TRIP
DINGLE
SPLAT!
Grrrrrrrrr
BARK ARF BARK
ARF
ARF
ARF ARF
JIM DAVIS 8-29
THUD!
SIGH

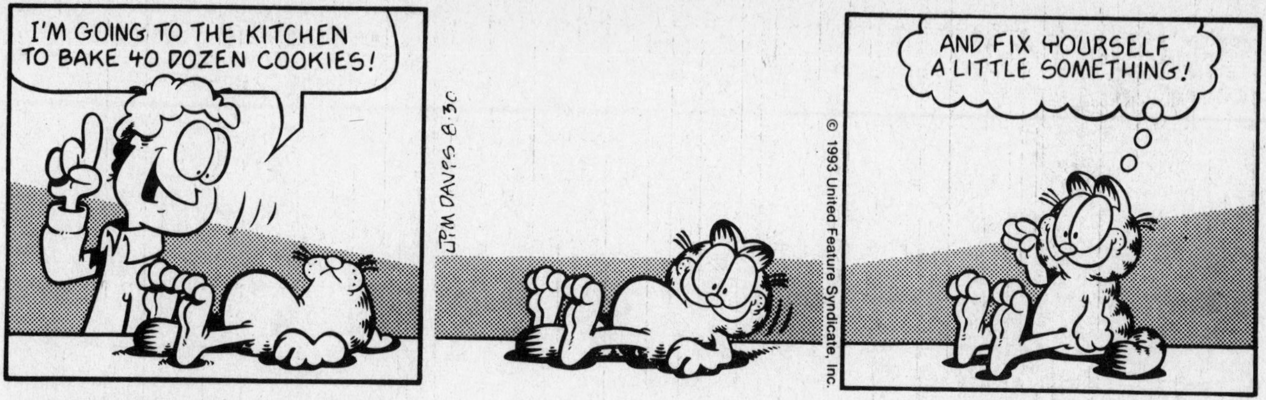
I'M GOING TO THE KITCHEN TO BAKE 40 DOZEN COOKIES!
JIM DAVIS 8-30
AND FIX YOURSELF A LITTLE SOMETHING!
© 1993 United Feature Syndicate, Inc.

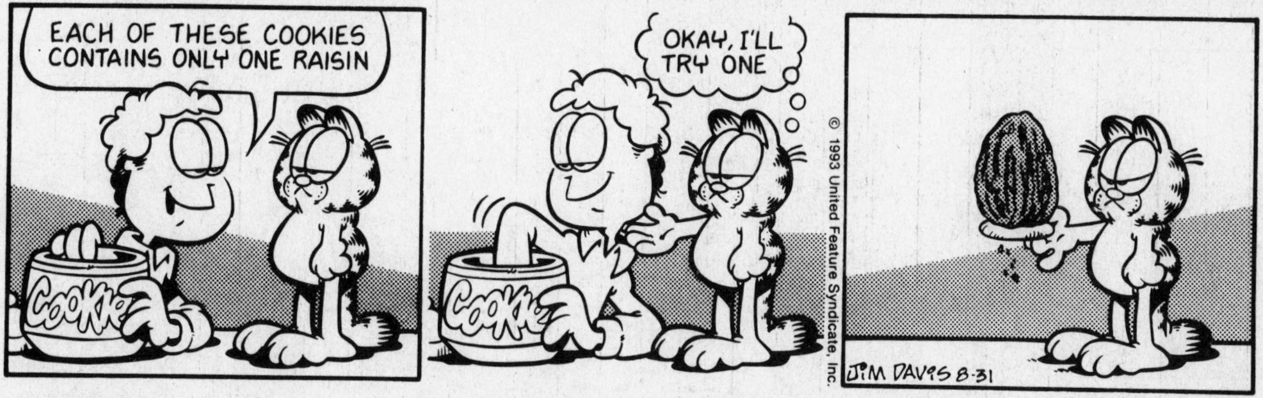
EACH OF THESE COOKIES CONTAINS ONLY ONE RAISIN
COOKIES
OKAY, I'LL TRY ONE
COOKIES
© 1993 United Feature Syndicate, Inc.
JIM DAVIS 8-31

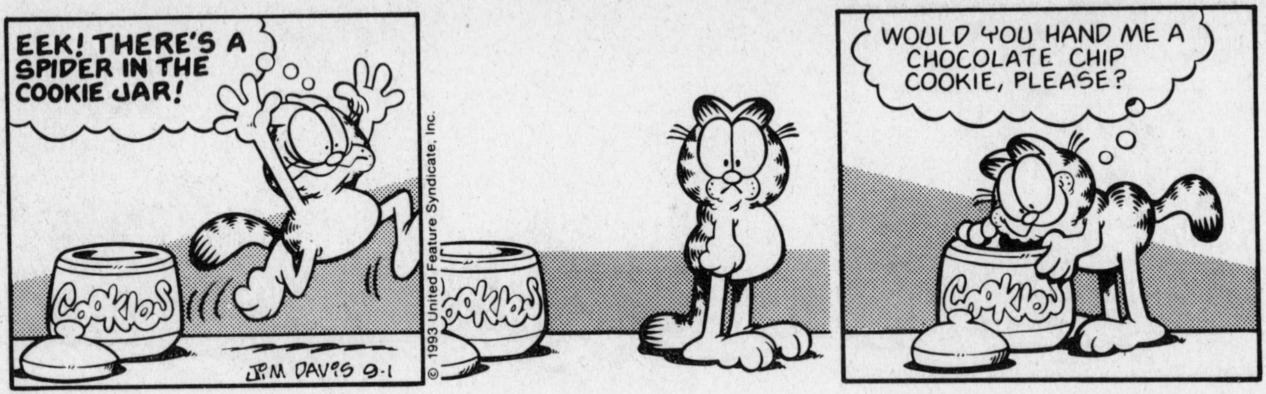
EEK! THERE'S A SPIDER IN THE COOKIE JAR!
COOKIES
JIM DAVIS 9-1
© 1993 United Feature Syndicate, Inc.
COOKIES
WOULD YOU HAND ME A CHOCOLATE CHIP COOKIE, PLEASE?
COOKIES

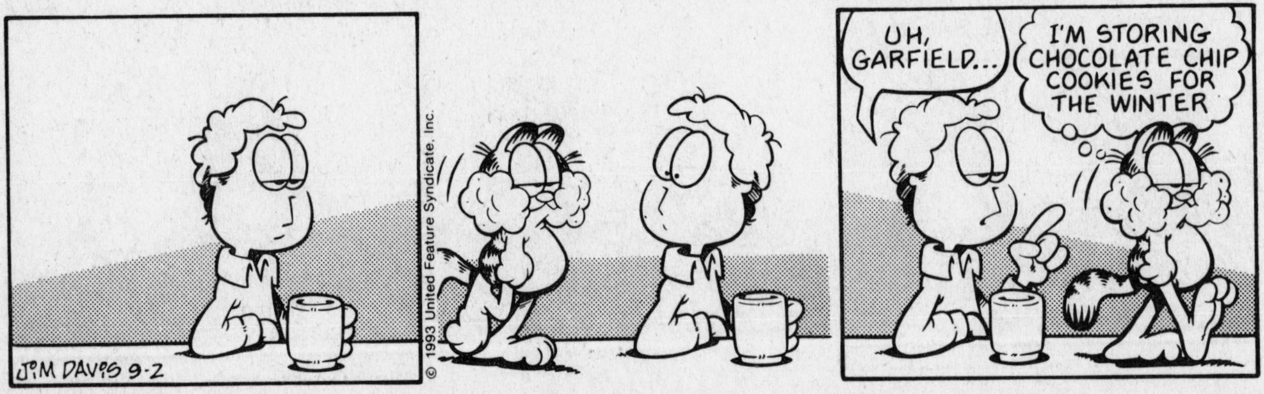
JIM DAVIS 9-2
© 1993 United Feature Syndicate, Inc.
UH, GARFIELD...
I'M STORING CHOCOLATE CHIP COOKIES FOR THE WINTER

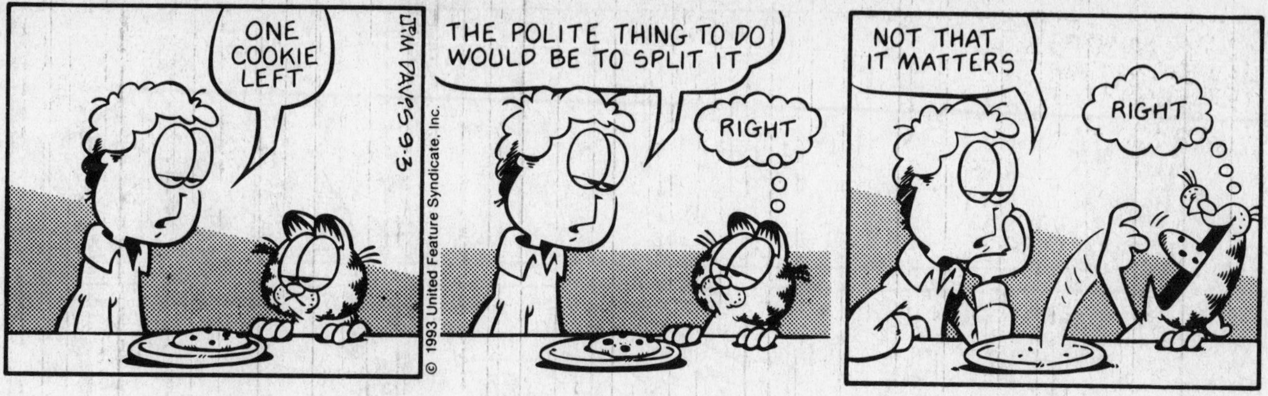
ONE COOKIE LEFT
JIM DAVIS 9-3
© 1993 United Feature Syndicate, Inc.
THE POLITE THING TO DO WOULD BE TO SPLIT IT
RIGHT
NOT THAT IT MATTERS
RIGHT

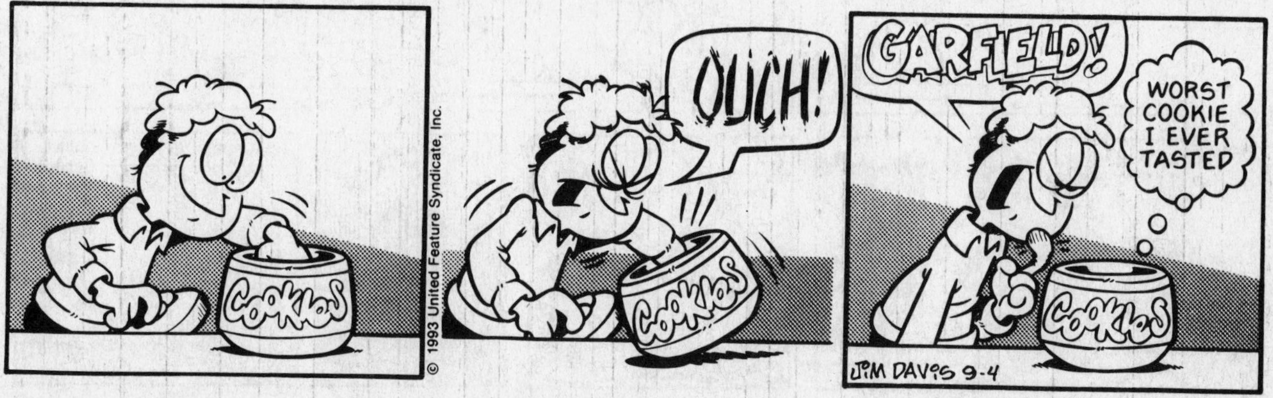
© 1993 United Feature Syndicate, Inc.
COOKIES
OUCH!
COOKIES
GARFIELD!
WORST COOKIE I EVER TASTED
COOKIES
JIM DAVIS 9-4

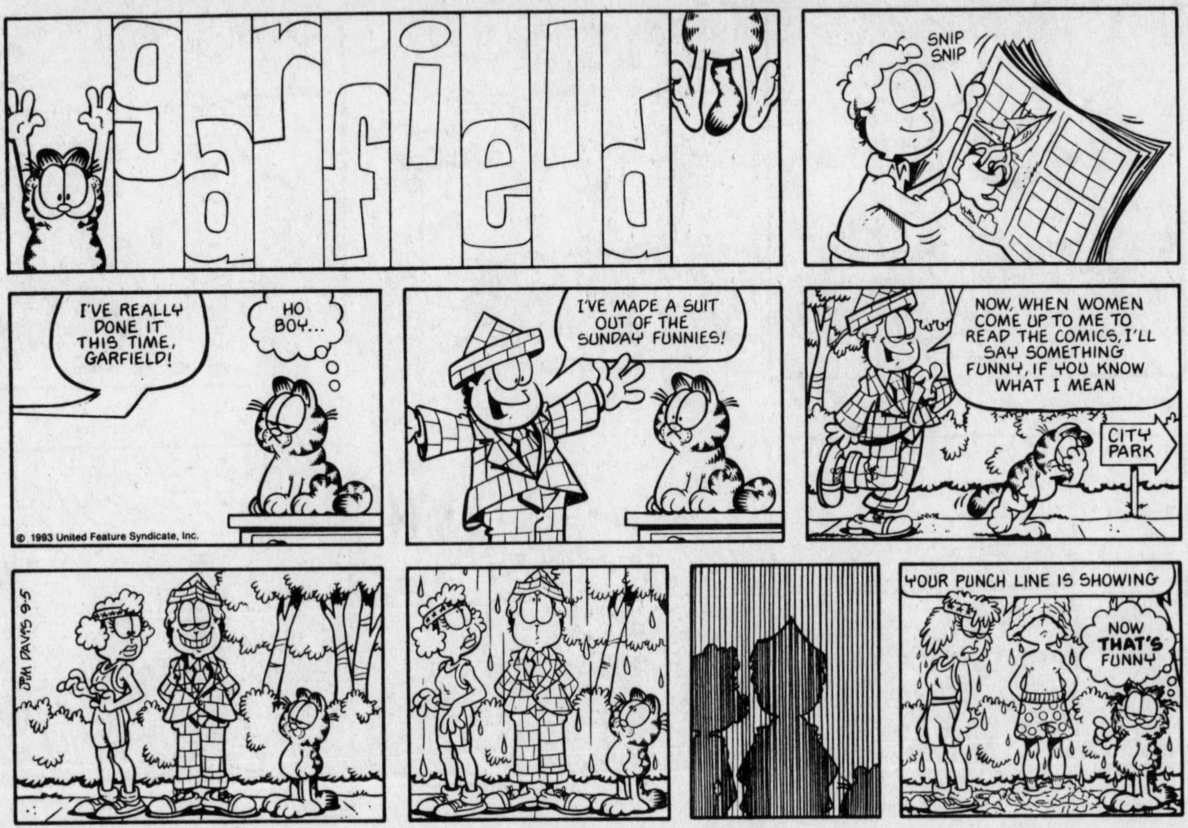
garfield
SNIP SNIP
I'VE REALLY DONE IT THIS TIME, GARFIELD!
HO BOY...
I'VE MADE A SUIT OUT OF THE SUNDAY FUNNIES!
NOW, WHEN WOMEN COME UP TO ME TO READ THE COMICS, I'LL SAY SOMETHING FUNNY, IF YOU KNOW WHAT I MEAN
CITY PARK
JPM DAVPS 9-5
YOUR PUNCH LINE IS SHOWING
NOW THAT'S FUNNY

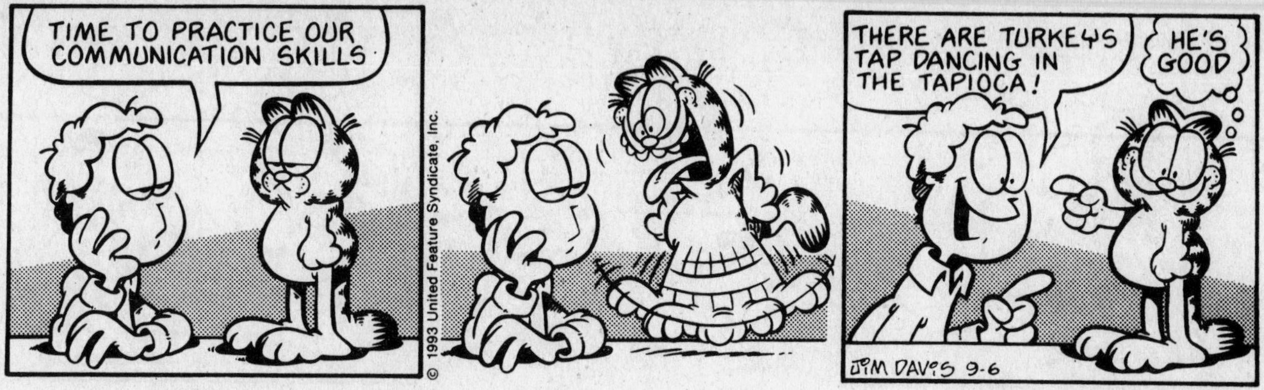
TIME TO PRACTICE OUR COMMUNICATION SKILLS
© 1993 United Feature Syndicate, Inc.
THERE ARE TURKEYS TAP DANCING IN THE TAPIOCA!
HE'S GOOD
JIM DAVIS 9-6

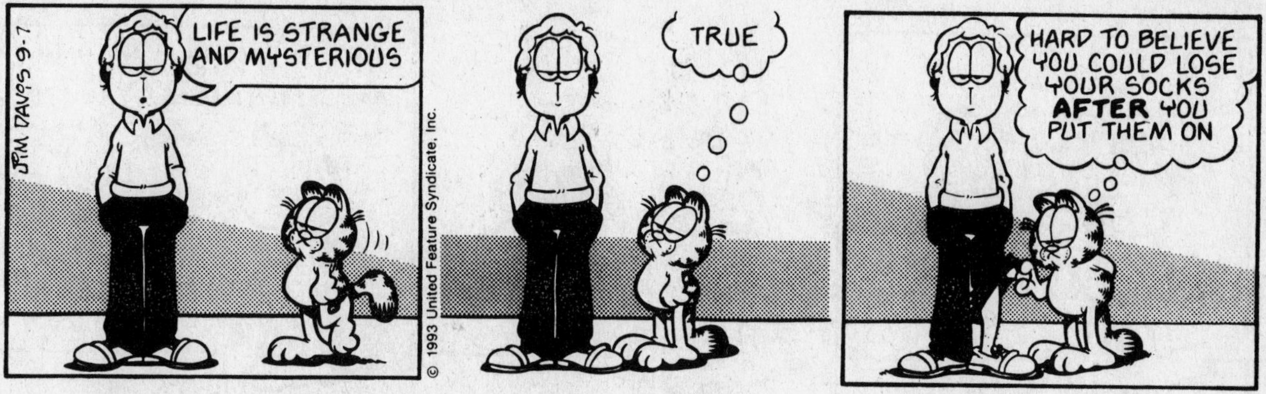
JIM DAVIS 9-7
LIFE IS STRANGE AND MYSTERIOUS
© 1993 United Feature Syndicate, Inc.
TRUE
HARD TO BELIEVE YOU COULD LOSE YOUR SOCKS **AFTER** YOU PUT THEM ON

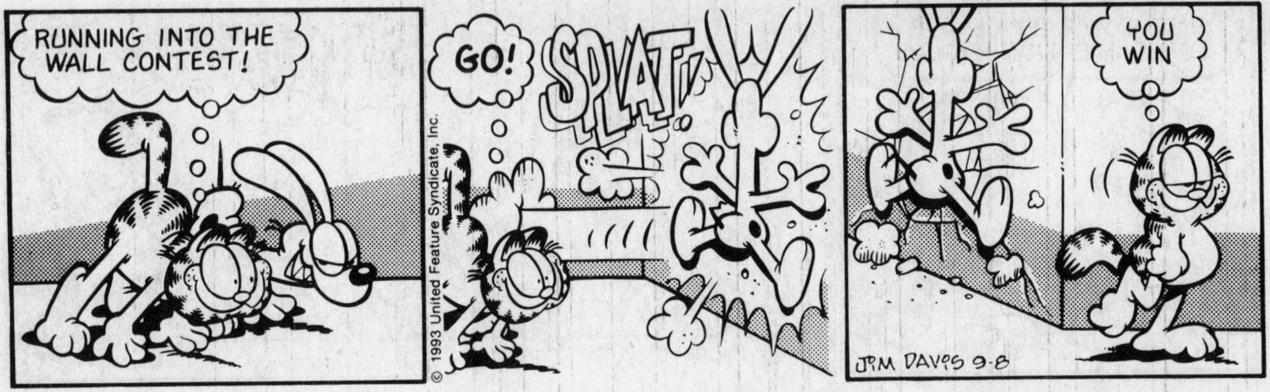
RUNNING INTO THE WALL CONTEST!
© 1993 United Feature Syndicate, Inc.
GO!
SPLAT!
YOU WIN
JIM DAVIS 9-8

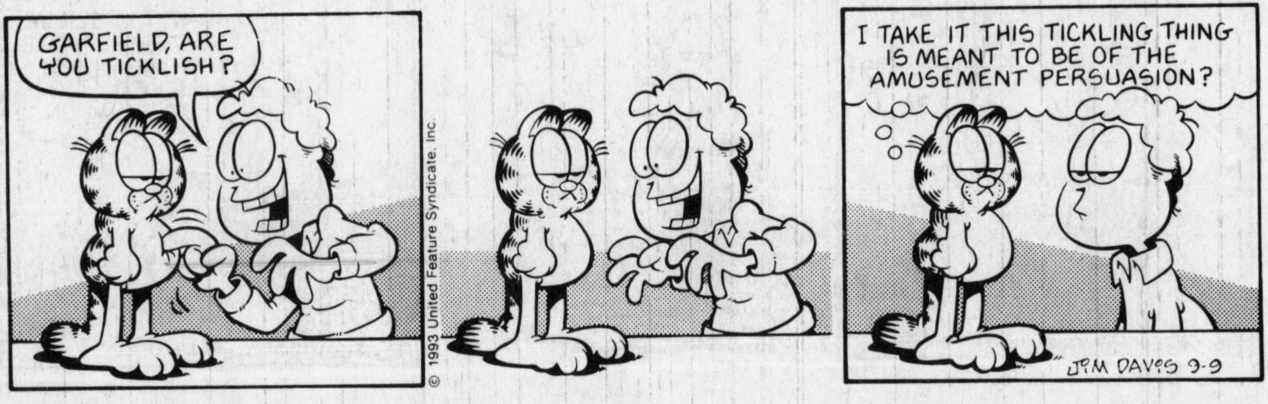
GARFIELD, ARE YOU TICKLISH?
© 1993 United Feature Syndicate, Inc.
I TAKE IT THIS TICKLING THING IS MEANT TO BE OF THE AMUSEMENT PERSUASION?
JIM DAVIS 9-9

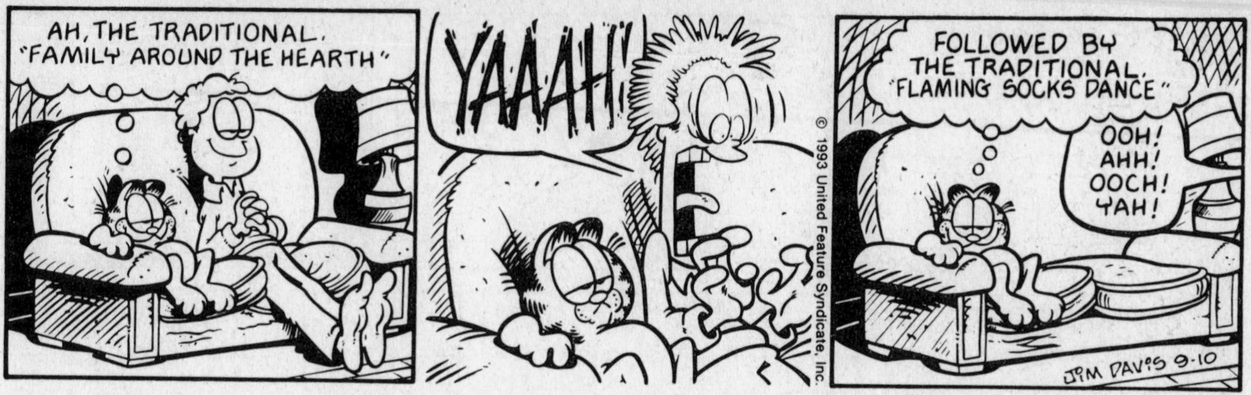
AH, THE TRADITIONAL "FAMILY AROUND THE HEARTH"
YAAAH!
© 1993 United Feature Syndicate, Inc.
FOLLOWED BY THE TRADITIONAL "FLAMING SOCKS DANCE"
OOH! AHH! OOCH! YAH!
JIM DAVIS 9-10

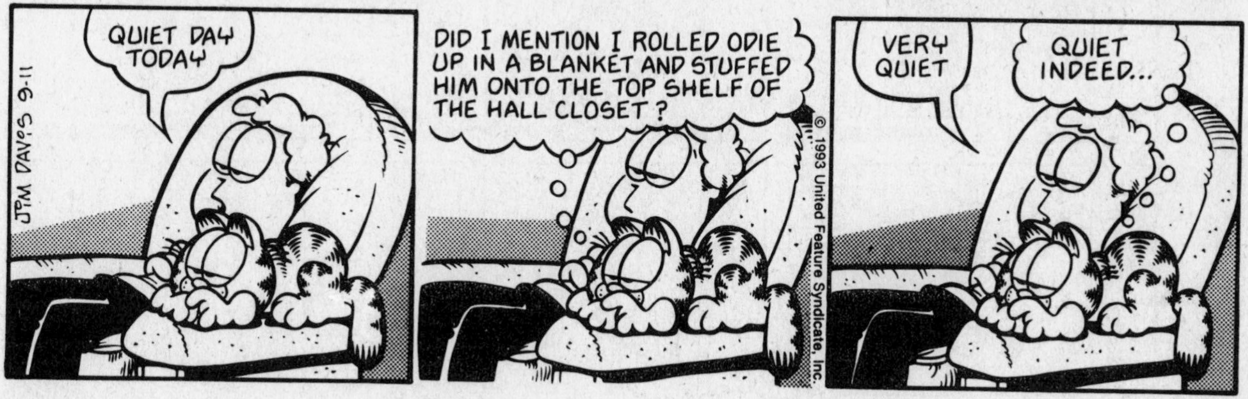
JIM DAVIS 9-11
QUIET DAY TODAY
DID I MENTION I ROLLED ODIE UP IN A BLANKET AND STUFFED HIM ONTO THE TOP SHELF OF THE HALL CLOSET ?
© 1993 United Feature Syndicate, Inc.
VERY QUIET
QUIET INDEED...

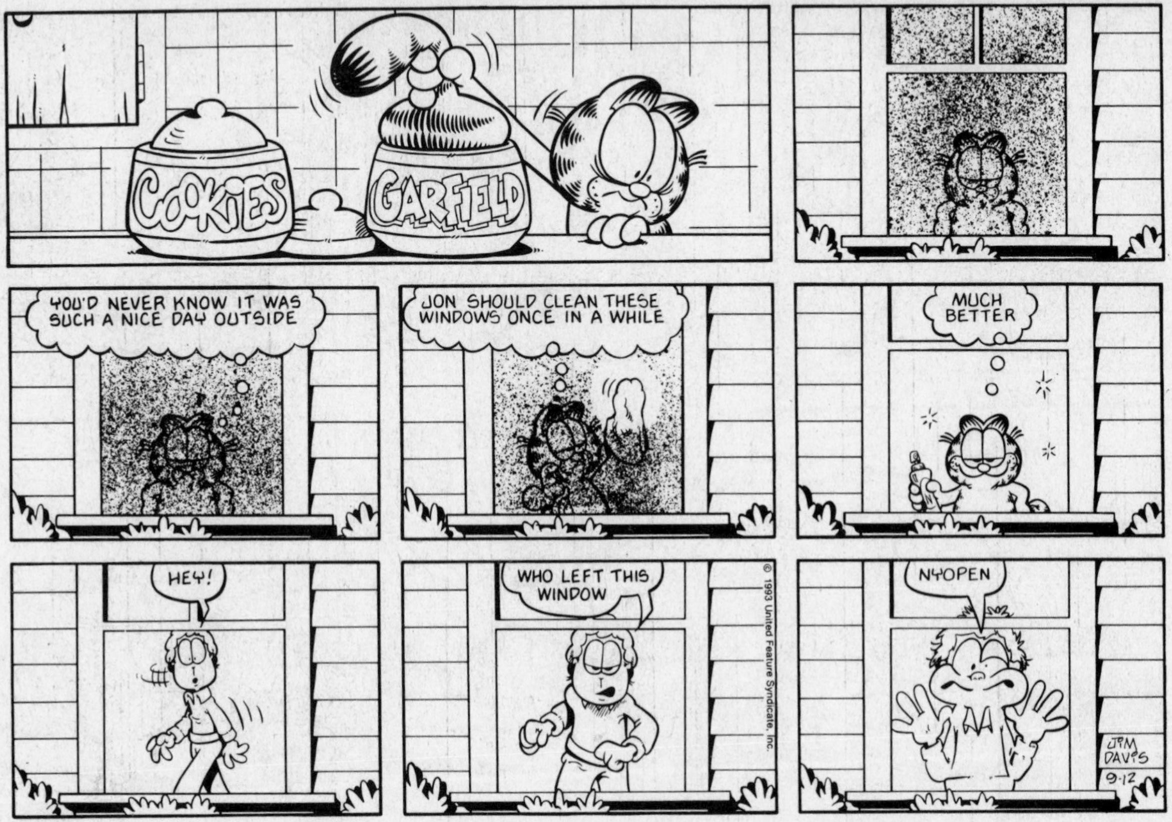
COOKIES
GARFIELD
YOU'D NEVER KNOW IT WAS SUCH A NICE DAY OUTSIDE
JON SHOULD CLEAN THESE WINDOWS ONCE IN A WHILE
MUCH BETTER
HEY!
WHO LEFT THIS WINDOW
NYOPEN
JIM DAVIS 9-12
© 1993 United Feature Syndicate, Inc.

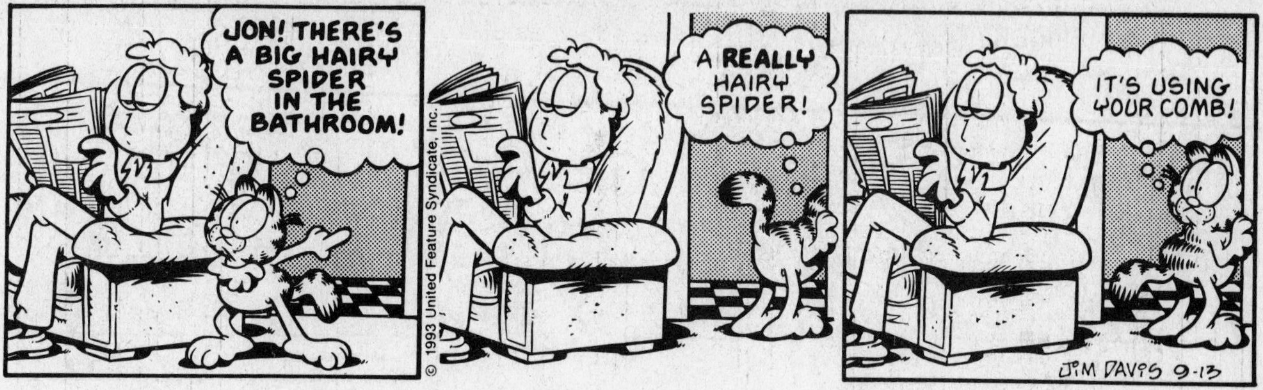
JON! THERE'S A BIG HAIRY SPIDER IN THE BATHROOM!
© 1993 United Feature Syndicate, Inc.
A **REALLY** HAIRY SPIDER!
IT'S USING YOUR COMB!
JIM DAVIS 9-13

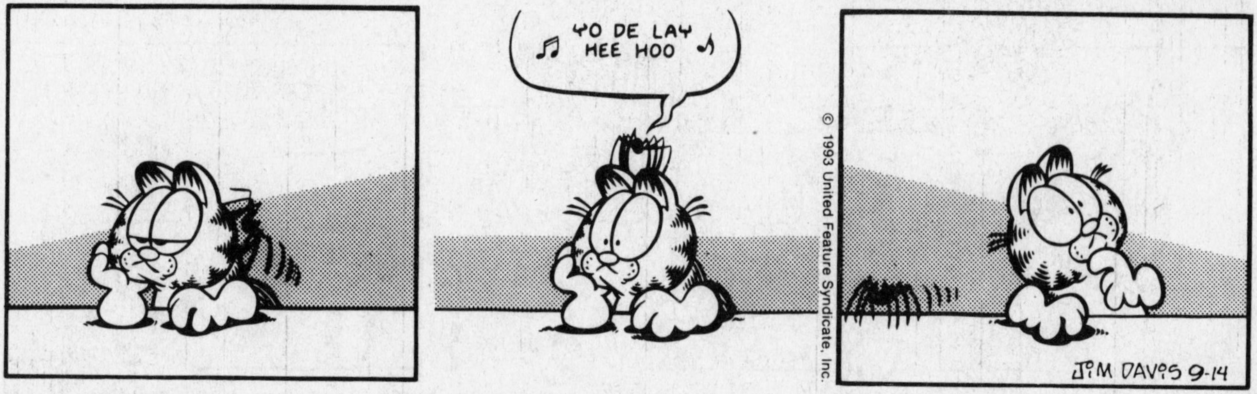
♫ YO DE LAY HEE HOO ♪
© 1993 United Feature Syndicate, Inc.
JIM DAVIS 9-14

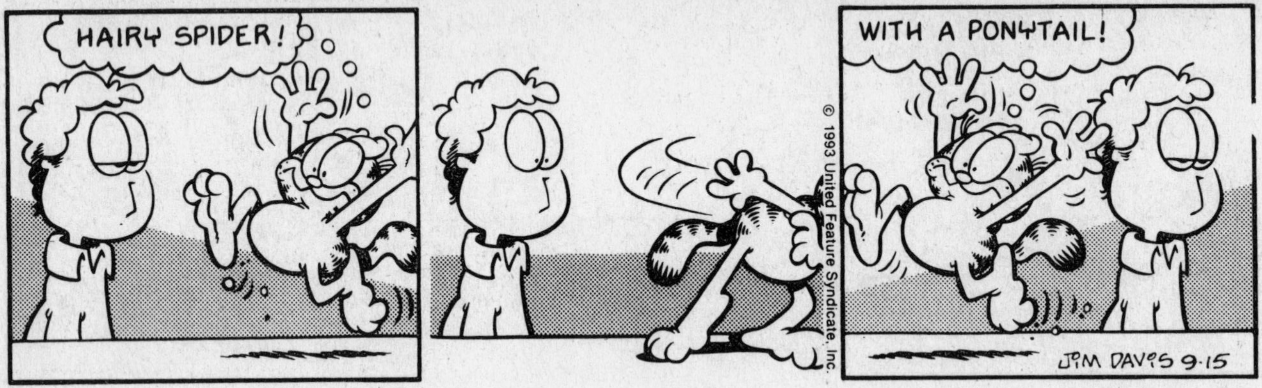
HAIRY SPIDER!
WITH A PONYTAIL!
© 1993 United Feature Syndicate, Inc.
JIM DAVIS 9-15

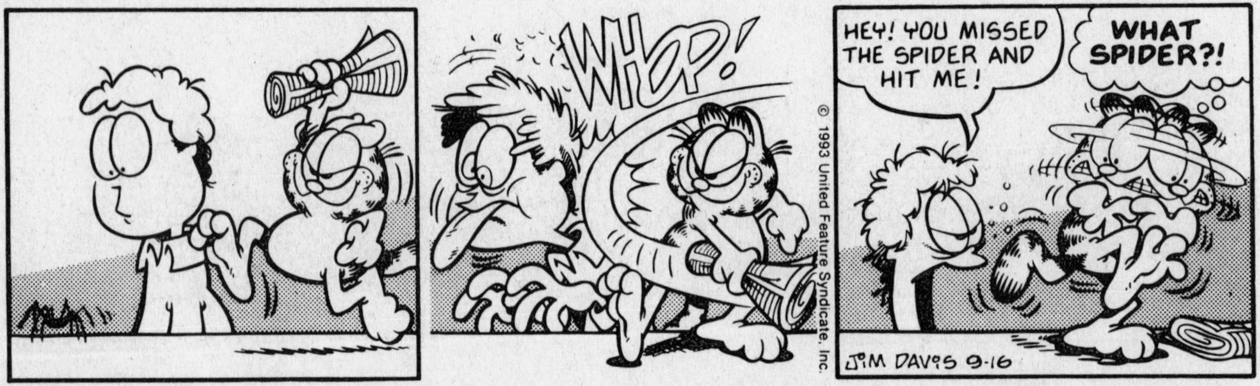
WHOP!
HEY! YOU MISSED THE SPIDER AND HIT ME!
WHAT SPIDER?!
© 1993 United Feature Syndicate, Inc.
JIM DAVIS 9-16

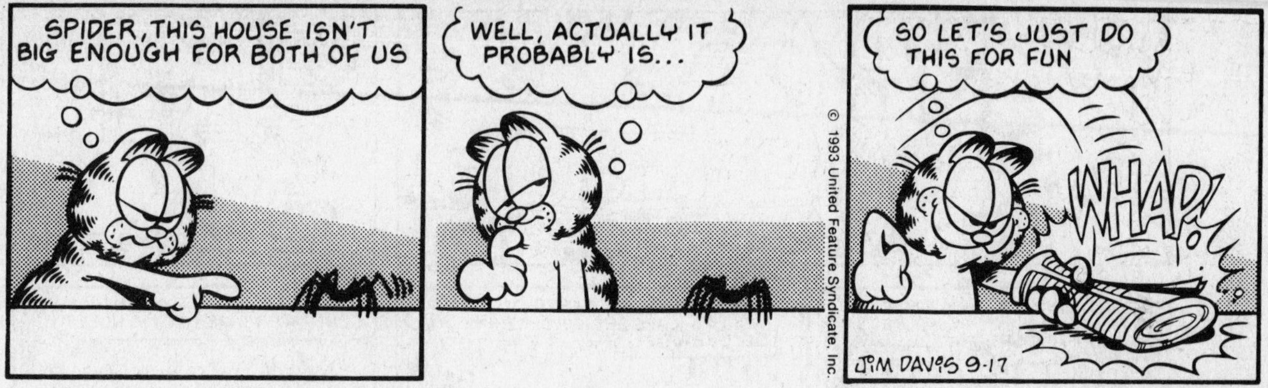
SPIDER, THIS HOUSE ISN'T BIG ENOUGH FOR BOTH OF US
WELL, ACTUALLY IT PROBABLY IS...
SO LET'S JUST DO THIS FOR FUN
WHAP!
JIM DAVIS 9-17

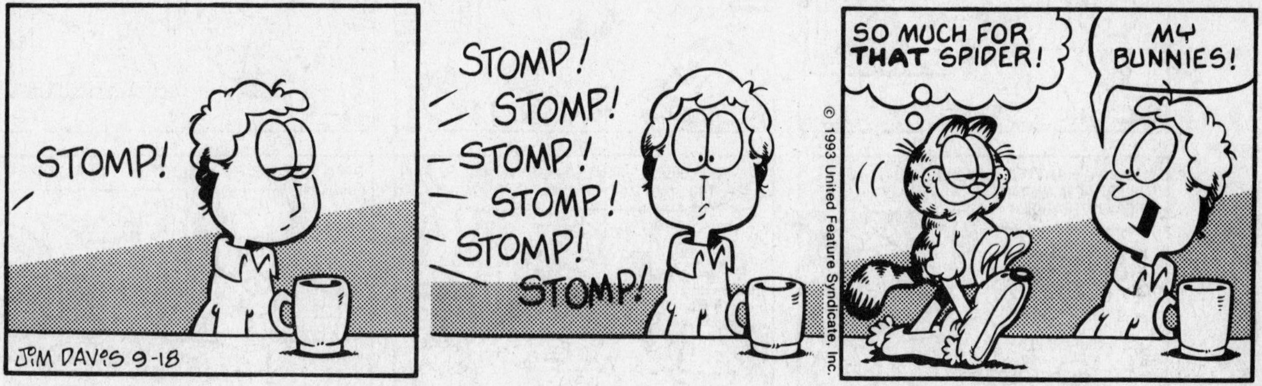
STOMP!
JIM DAVIS 9-18
STOMP!
STOMP!
STOMP!
STOMP!
STOMP!
STOMP!
SO MUCH FOR **THAT** SPIDER!
MY BUNNIES!

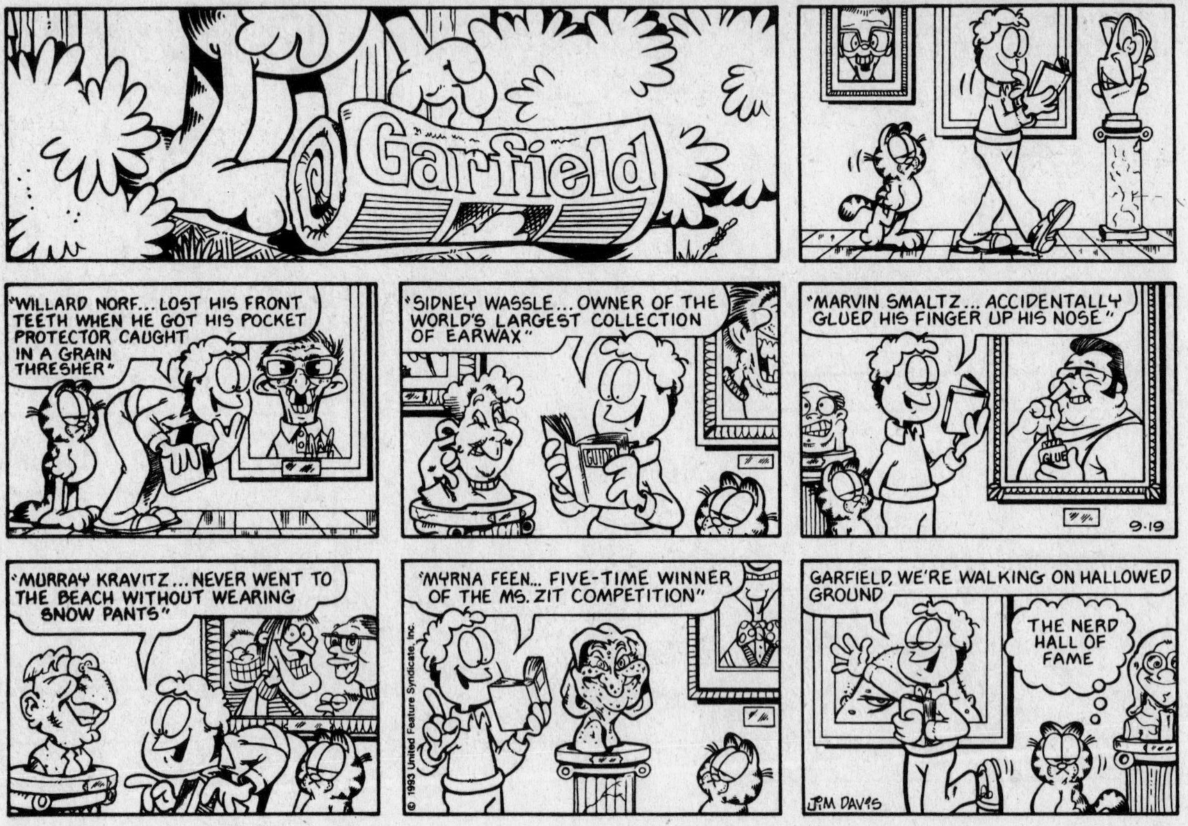
Garfield
"WILLARD NORF... LOST HIS FRONT TEETH WHEN HE GOT HIS POCKET PROTECTOR CAUGHT IN A GRAIN THRESHER"
"SIDNEY WASSLE... OWNER OF THE WORLD'S LARGEST COLLECTION OF EARWAX"
GUIDE
"MARVIN SMALTZ... ACCIDENTALLY GLUED HIS FINGER UP HIS NOSE"
GLUE
9·19
"MURRAY KRAVITZ... NEVER WENT TO THE BEACH WITHOUT WEARING SNOW PANTS"
"MYRNA FEEN... FIVE-TIME WINNER OF THE MS. ZIT COMPETITION"
© 1993 United Feature Syndicate, Inc.
GARFIELD, WE'RE WALKING ON HALLOWED GROUND
THE NERD HALL OF FAME
JIM DAVIS

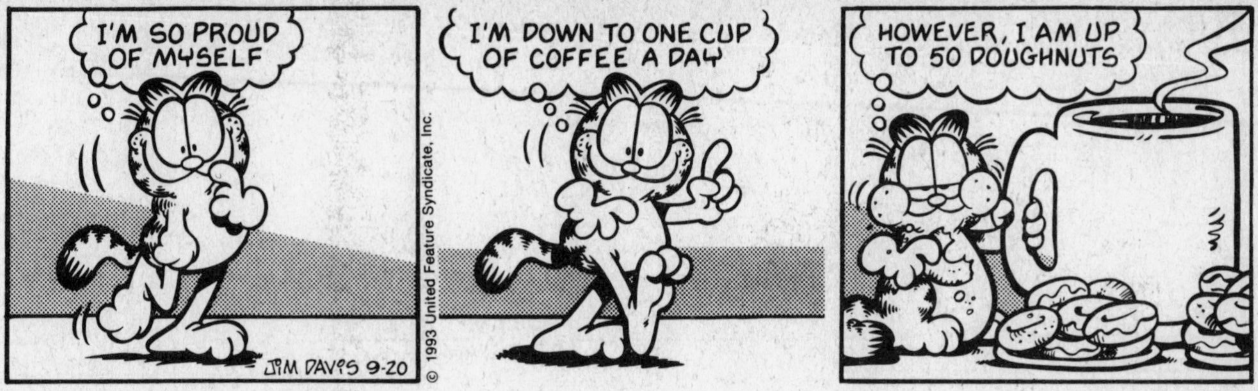
I'M SO PROUD OF MYSELF
JIM DAVIS 9-20
© 1993 United Feature Syndicate, Inc.
I'M DOWN TO ONE CUP OF COFFEE A DAY
HOWEVER, I AM UP TO 50 DOUGHNUTS

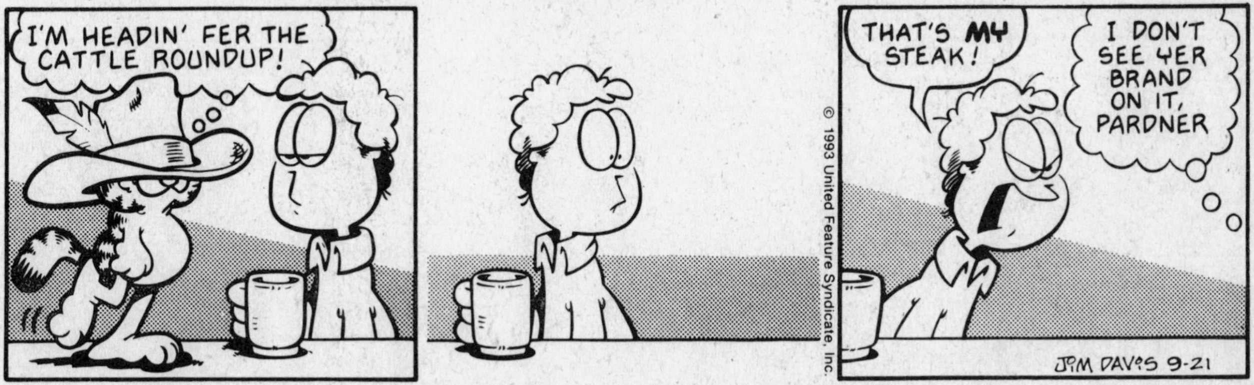
I'M HEADIN' FER THE CATTLE ROUNDUP!
© 1993 United Feature Syndicate, Inc.
THAT'S **MY** STEAK!
I DON'T SEE YER BRAND ON IT, PARDNER
JIM DAVIS 9-21

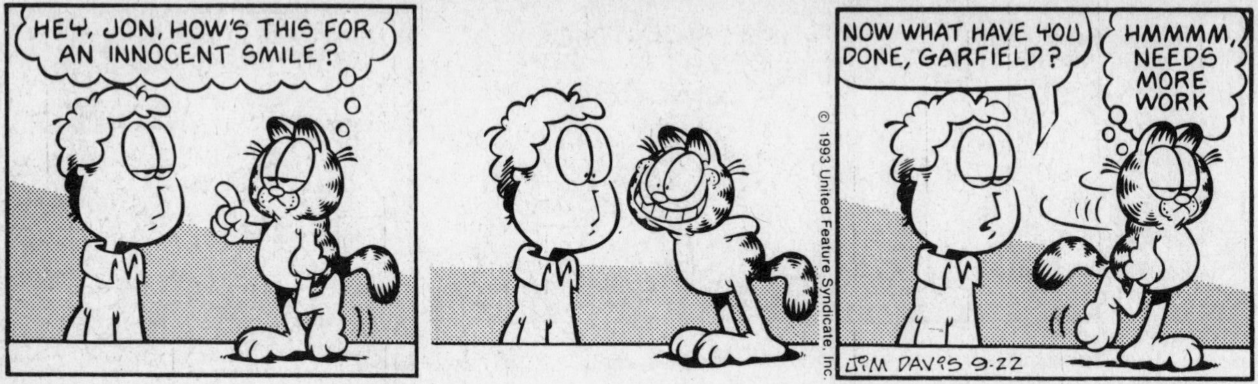
HEY, JON, HOW'S THIS FOR AN INNOCENT SMILE?
NOW WHAT HAVE YOU DONE, GARFIELD?
HMMMM, NEEDS MORE WORK
JIM DAVIS 9-22
© 1993 United Feature Syndicate, Inc.

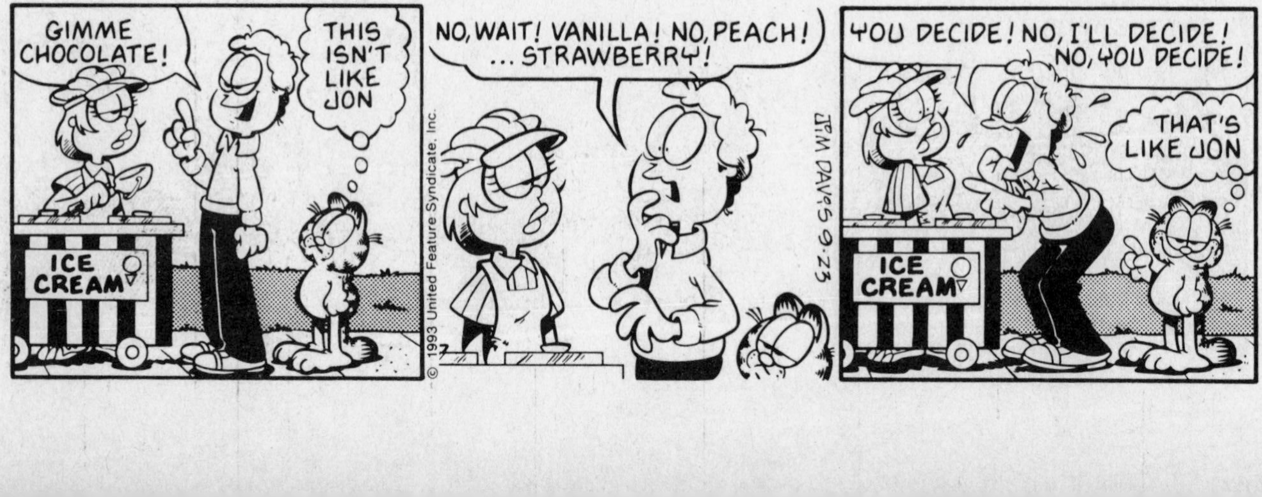
GIMME CHOCOLATE!
THIS ISN'T LIKE JON
ICE CREAM
© 1993 United Feature Syndicate, Inc.
NO, WAIT! VANILLA! NO, PEACH! ... STRAWBERRY!
JIM DAVIS 9-23
YOU DECIDE! NO, I'LL DECIDE! NO, YOU DECIDE!
THAT'S LIKE JON
ICE CREAM

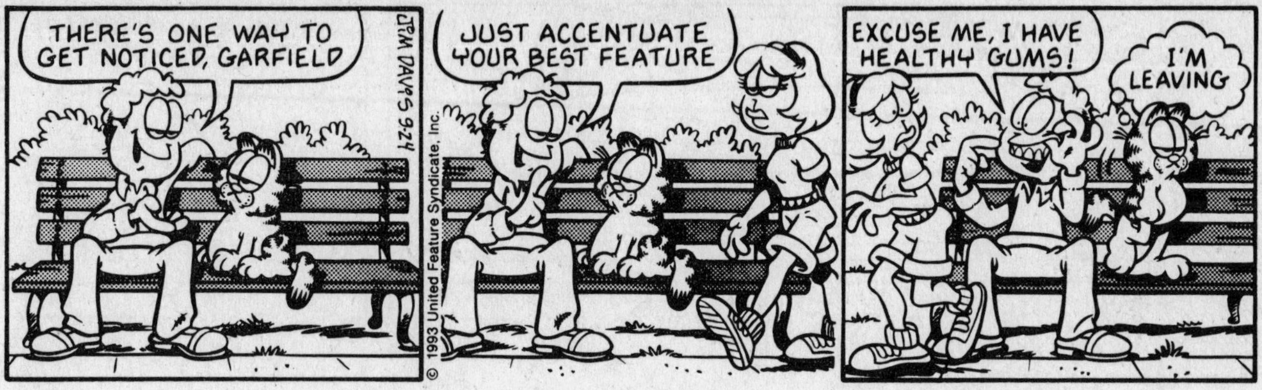
THERE'S ONE WAY TO GET NOTICED, GARFIELD
JIM DAVIS 9-24
© 1993 United Feature Syndicate, Inc.
JUST ACCENTUATE YOUR BEST FEATURE
EXCUSE ME, I HAVE HEALTHY GUMS!
I'M LEAVING

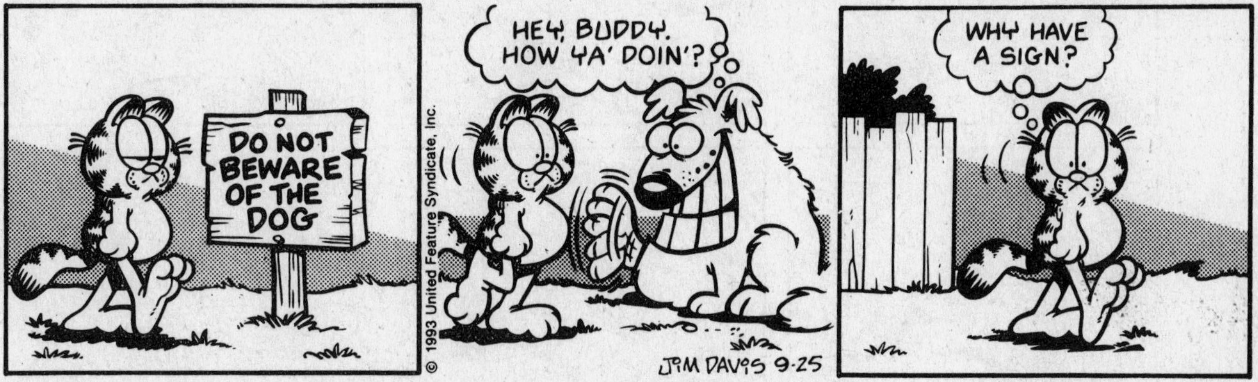
DO NOT BEWARE OF THE DOG
© 1993 United Feature Syndicate, Inc.
HEY, BUDDY. HOW YA' DOIN'?
JIM DAVIS 9-25
WHY HAVE A SIGN?

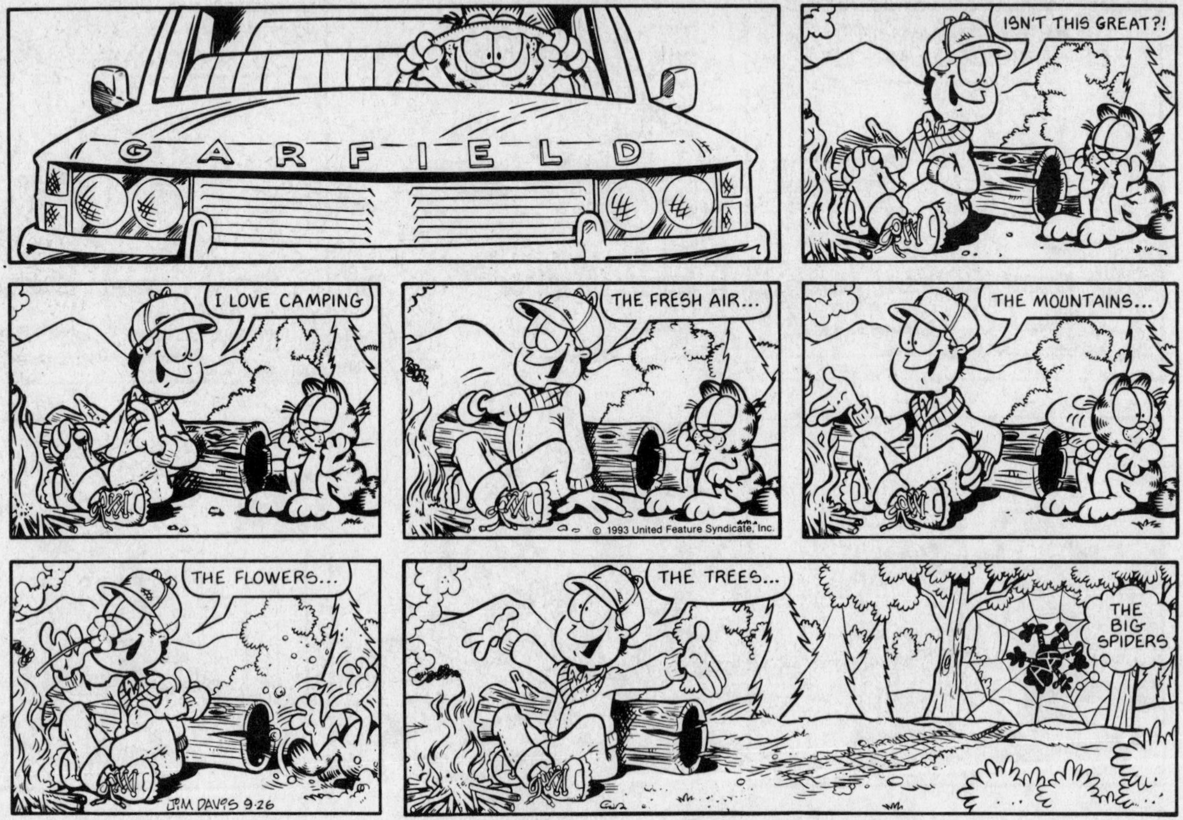
GARFIELD
ISN'T THIS GREAT?!
I LOVE CAMPING
THE FRESH AIR...
© 1993 United Feature Syndicate, Inc.
THE MOUNTAINS...
THE FLOWERS...
JIM DAVIS 9·26
THE TREES...
THE BIG SPIDERS

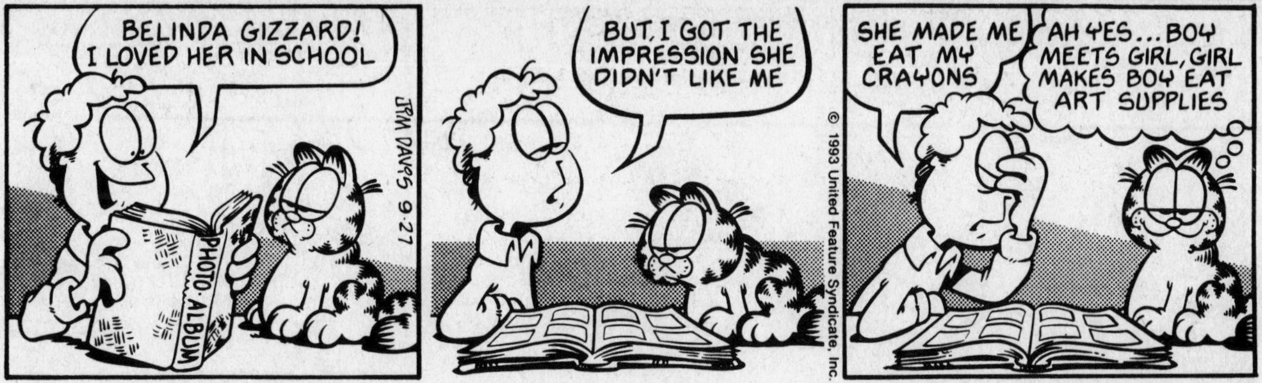
BELINDA GIZZARD! I LOVED HER IN SCHOOL
PHOTO ALBUM
JIM DAVIS 9-27
BUT, I GOT THE IMPRESSION SHE DIDN'T LIKE ME
© 1993 United Feature Syndicate, Inc.
SHE MADE ME EAT MY CRAYONS
AH YES... BOY MEETS GIRL, GIRL MAKES BOY EAT ART SUPPLIES

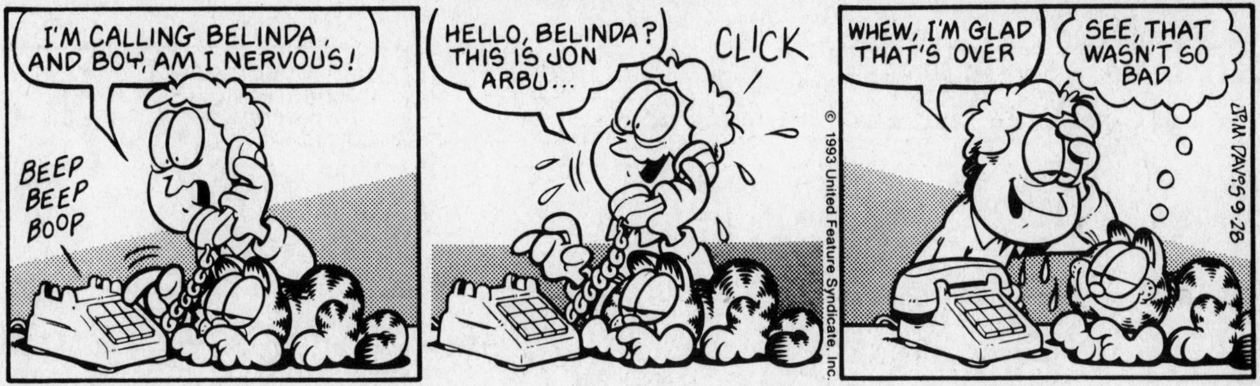
I'M CALLING BELINDA, AND BOY, AM I NERVOUS!
BEEP BEEP BOOP
HELLO, BELINDA? THIS IS JON ARBU...
CLICK
© 1993 United Feature Syndicate, Inc.
WHEW, I'M GLAD THAT'S OVER
SEE, THAT WASN'T SO BAD
JIM DAVIS 9-28

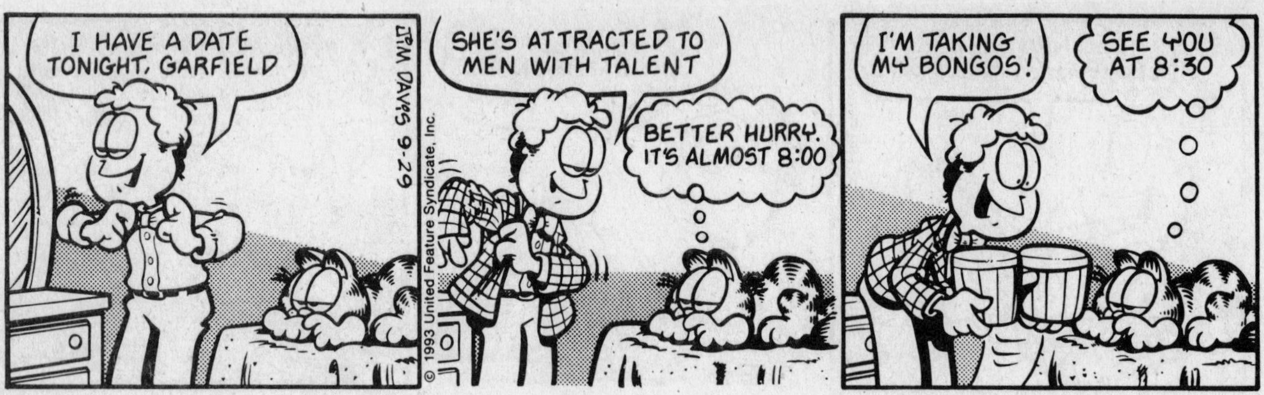
I HAVE A DATE TONIGHT, GARFIELD
JIM DAVIS 9-29
© 1993 United Feature Syndicate, Inc.
SHE'S ATTRACTED TO MEN WITH TALENT
BETTER HURRY. IT'S ALMOST 8:00
I'M TAKING MY BONGOS!
SEE YOU AT 8:30

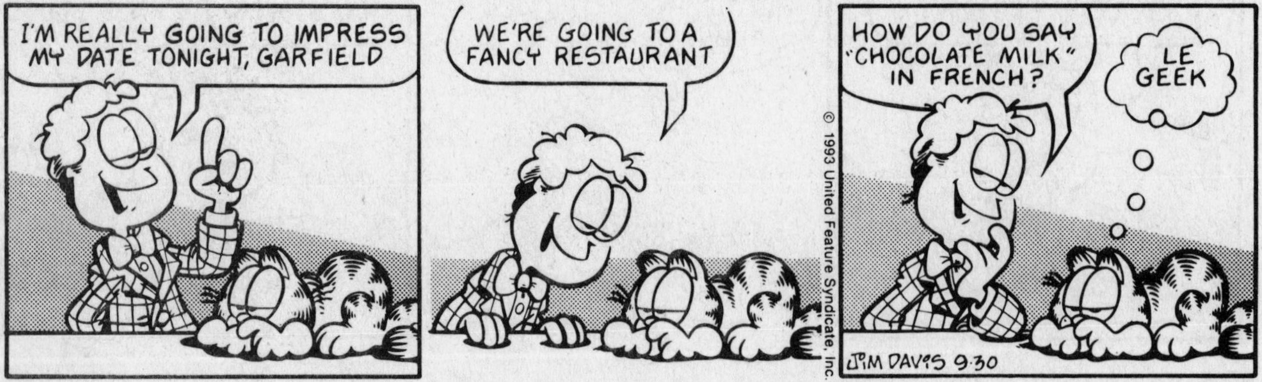
I'M REALLY GOING TO IMPRESS MY DATE TONIGHT, GARFIELD
WE'RE GOING TO A FANCY RESTAURANT
© 1993 United Feature Syndicate, Inc.
HOW DO YOU SAY "CHOCOLATE MILK" IN FRENCH?
LE GEEK
JIM DAVIS 9·30

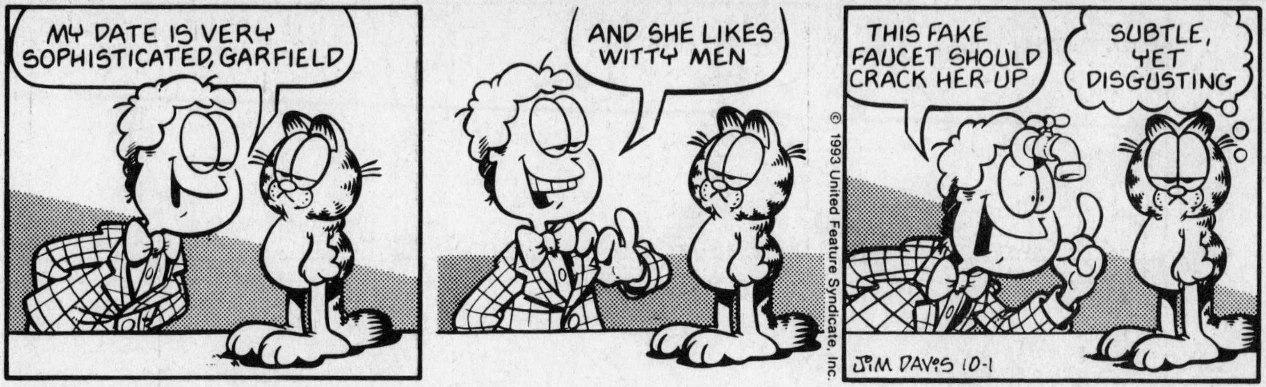
MY DATE IS VERY SOPHISTICATED, GARFIELD
AND SHE LIKES WITTY MEN
THIS FAKE FAUCET SHOULD CRACK HER UP
SUBTLE, YET DISGUSTING
JIM DAVIS 10-1
© 1993 United Feature Syndicate, Inc.

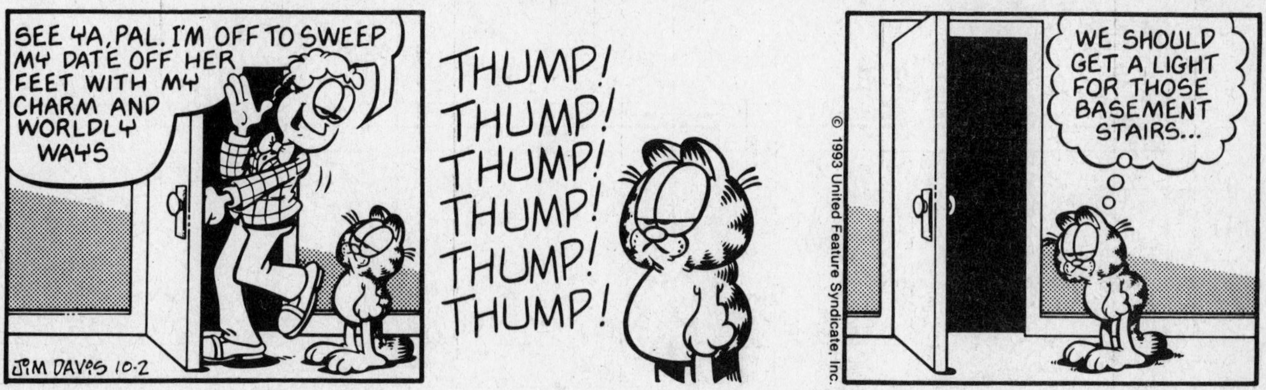
SEE YA, PAL. I'M OFF TO SWEEP MY DATE OFF HER FEET WITH MY CHARM AND WORLDLY WAYS
JIM DAVIS 10-2
THUMP! THUMP! THUMP! THUMP! THUMP! THUMP!
WE SHOULD GET A LIGHT FOR THOSE BASEMENT STAIRS...
© 1993 United Feature Syndicate, Inc.

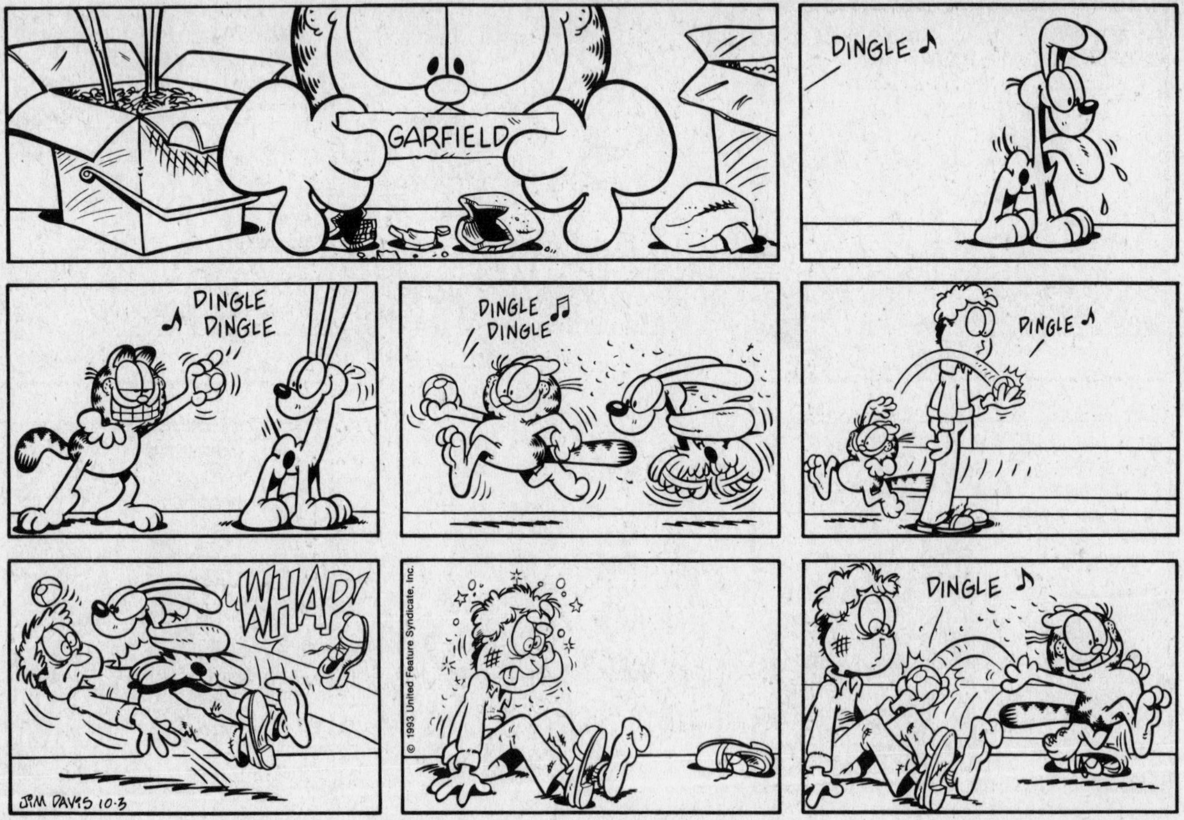
GARFIELD
DINGLE
DINGLE DINGLE
DINGLE DINGLE
DINGLE
WHAP!
JIM DAVIS 10-3
© 1993 United Feature Syndicate, Inc.
DINGLE

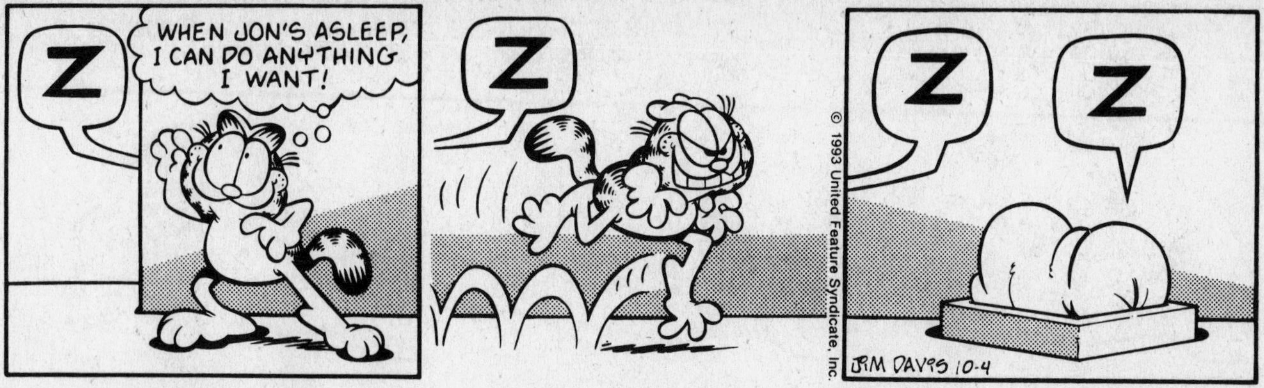
Z
WHEN JON'S ASLEEP, I CAN DO ANYTHING I WANT!
Z
Z
Z
© 1993 United Feature Syndicate, Inc.
JIM DAVIS 10-4

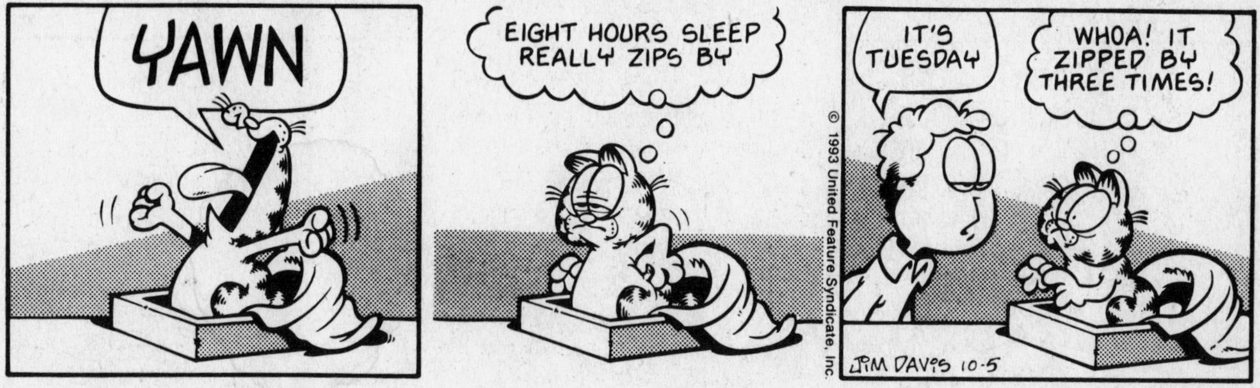
YAWN
EIGHT HOURS SLEEP REALLY ZIPS BY
IT'S TUESDAY
WHOA! IT ZIPPED BY THREE TIMES!
© 1993 United Feature Syndicate, Inc.
JIM DAVIS 10-5

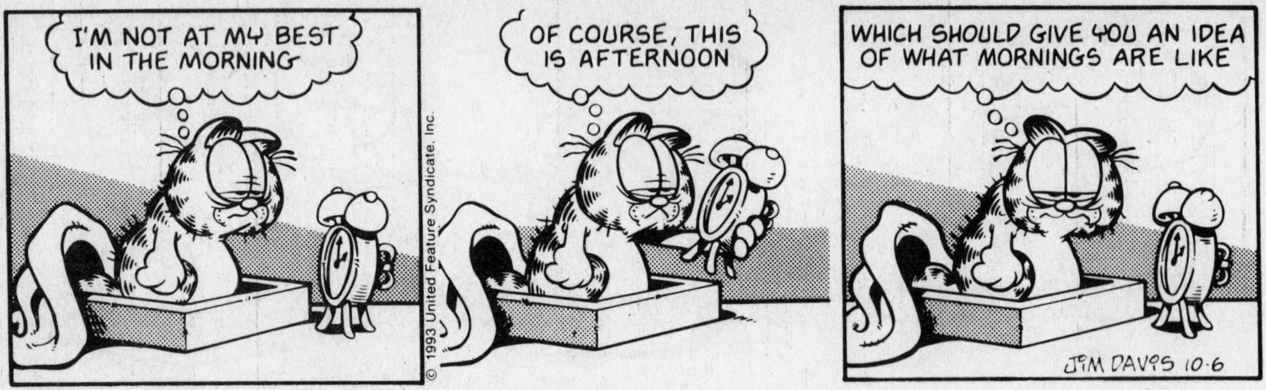
I'M NOT AT MY BEST IN THE MORNING
OF COURSE, THIS IS AFTERNOON
WHICH SHOULD GIVE YOU AN IDEA OF WHAT MORNINGS ARE LIKE
JIM DAVIS 10-6
© 1993 United Feature Syndicate, Inc.

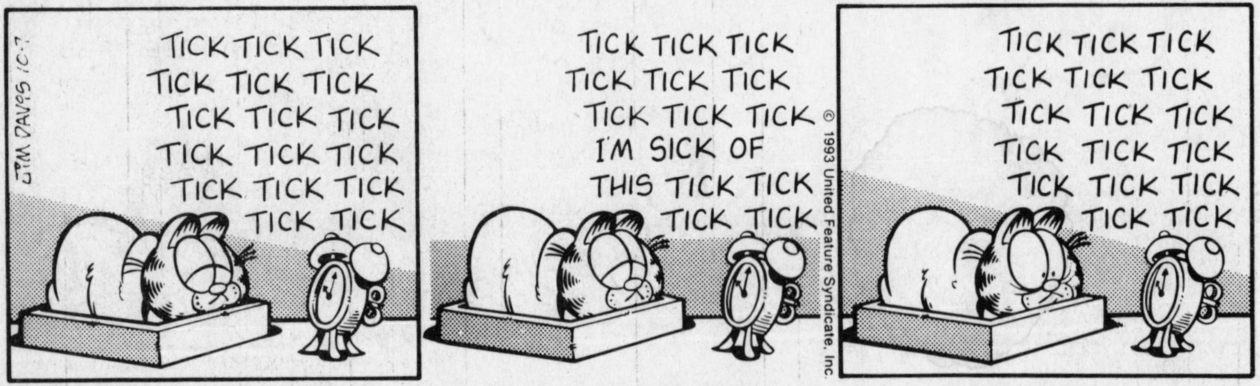
JIM DAVIS 10-7
TICK TICK TICK TICK TICK TICK TICK TICK TICK TICK TICK TICK TICK TICK TICK TICK TICK
TICK TICK TICK TICK TICK TICK TICK TICK TICK I'M SICK OF THIS TICK TICK TICK TICK
TICK TICK TICK TICK TICK TICK TICK TICK TICK TICK TICK TICK TICK TICK TICK TICK TICK
© 1993 United Feature Syndicate, Inc.

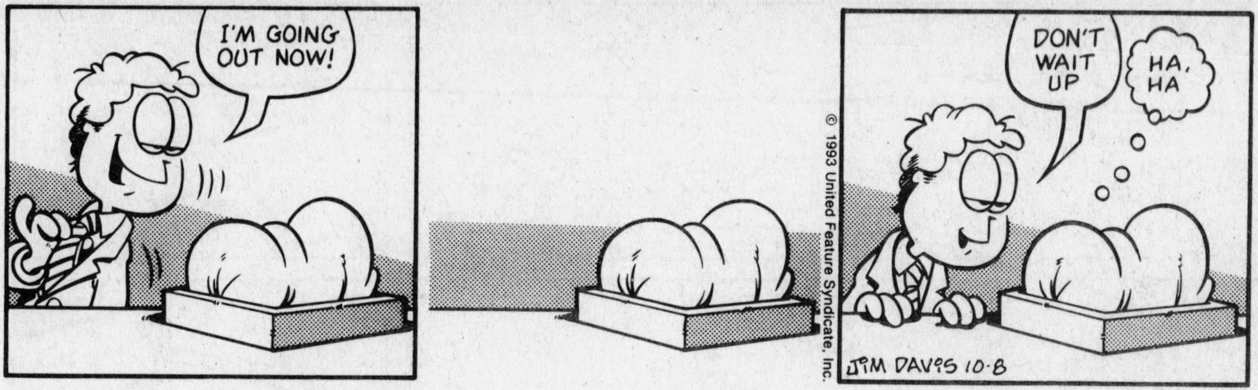
I'M GOING OUT NOW!
DON'T WAIT UP
HA, HA
JIM DAVIS 10-8

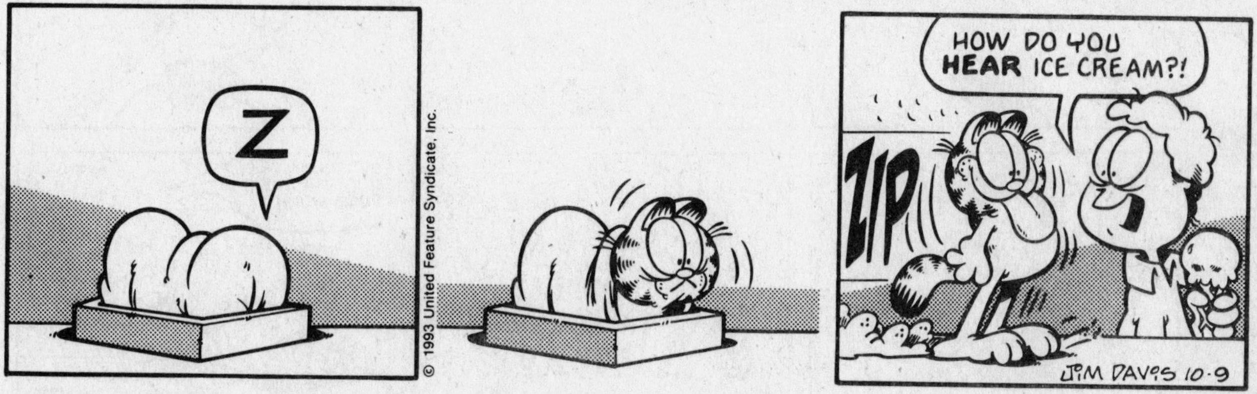
Z
ZIP
HOW DO YOU **HEAR** ICE CREAM?!
JIM DAVIS 10-9

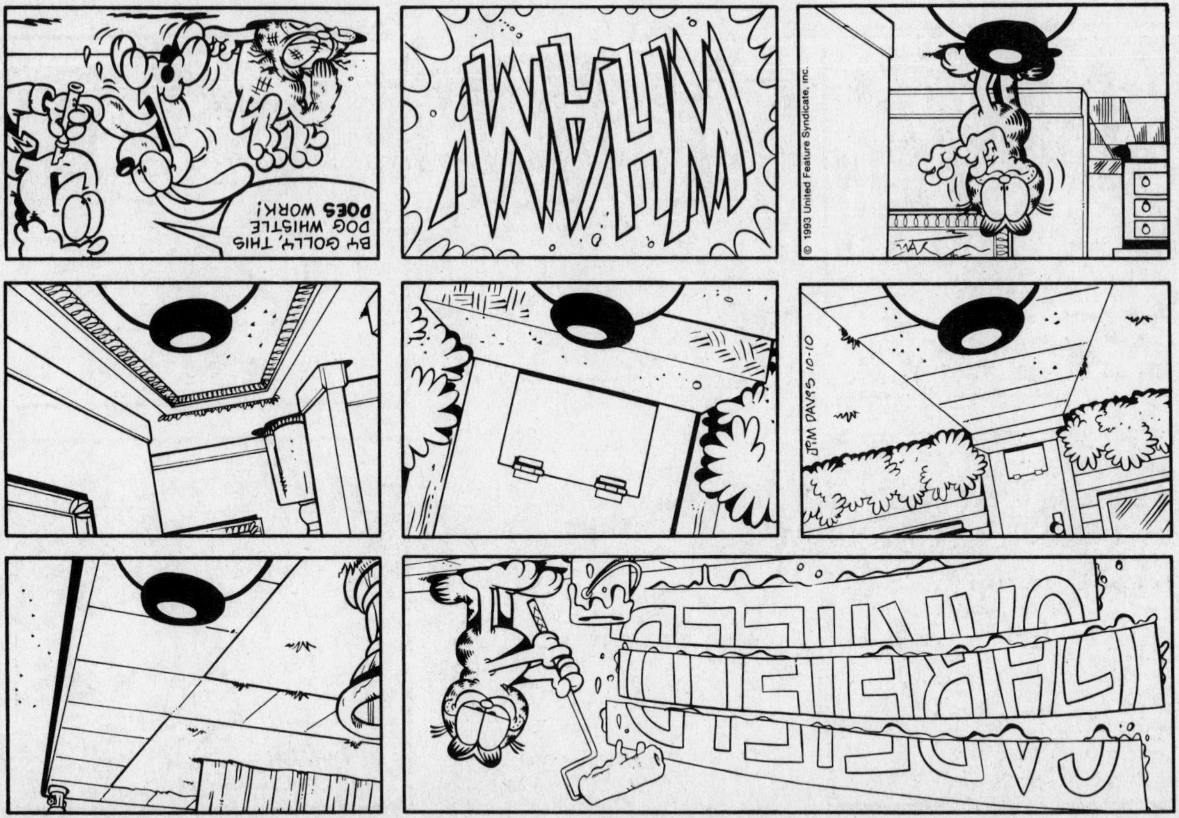
BY GOLLY, THIS DOG WHISTLE DOES WORK!
WHAM
© 1993 United Feature Syndicate, Inc.
JIM DAVIS 10-10
GARFIELD

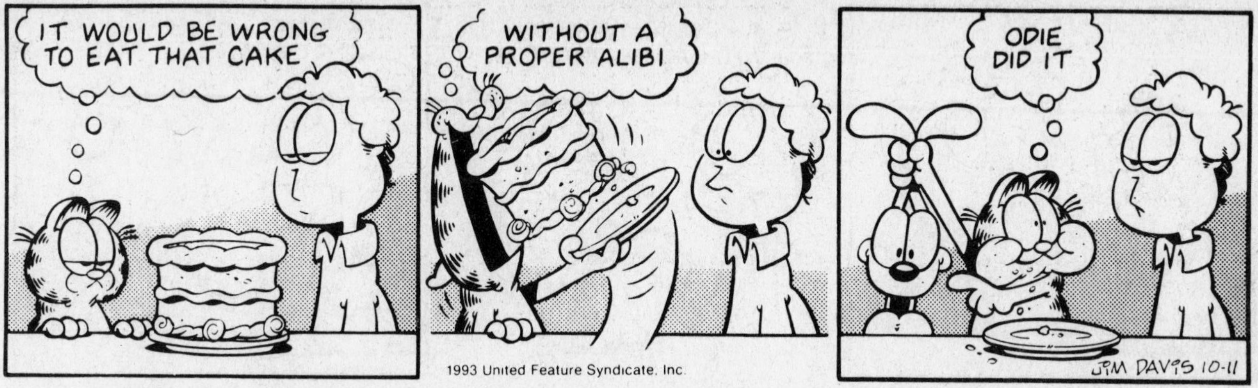
IT WOULD BE WRONG TO EAT THAT CAKE
WITHOUT A PROPER ALIBI
ODIE DID IT
1993 United Feature Syndicate, Inc.
JIM DAVIS 10-11

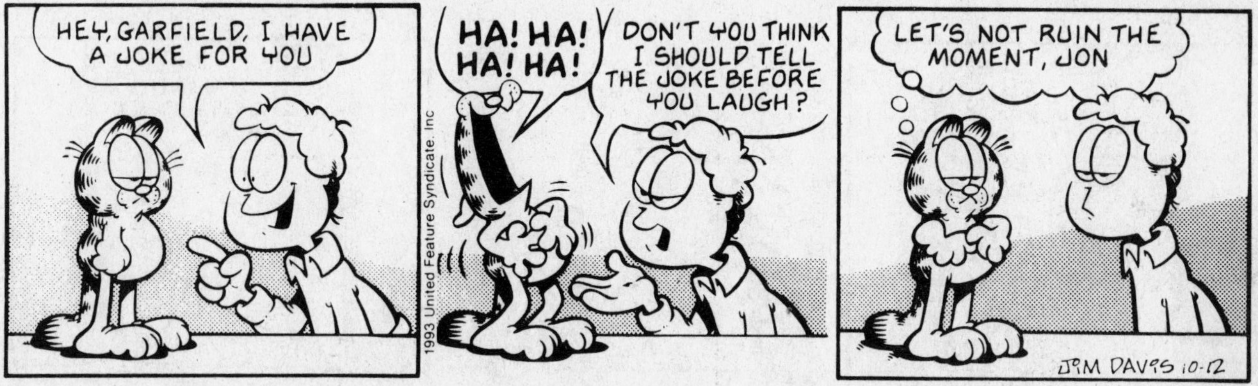
HEY, GARFIELD, I HAVE A JOKE FOR YOU
HA! HA! HA! HA!
DON'T YOU THINK I SHOULD TELL THE JOKE BEFORE YOU LAUGH?
LET'S NOT RUIN THE MOMENT, JON
1993 United Feature Syndicate, Inc
JIM DAVIS 10-12

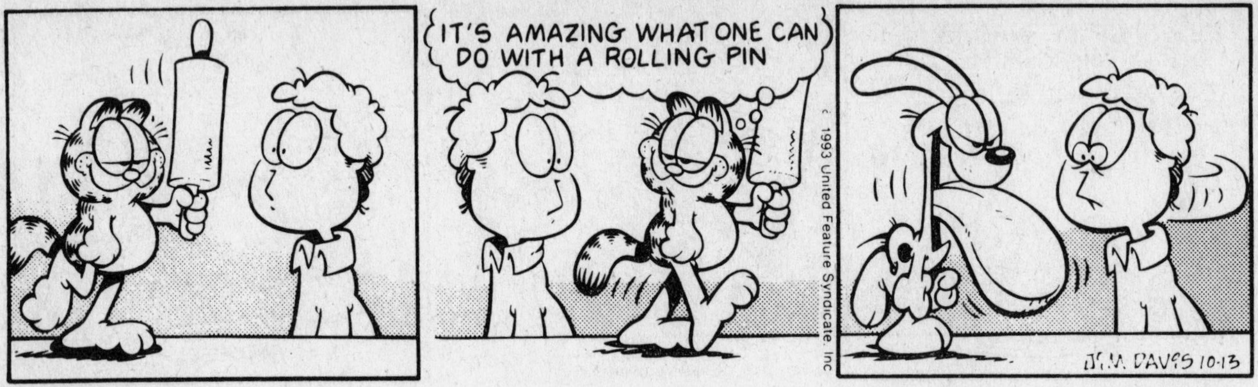
IT'S AMAZING WHAT ONE CAN DO WITH A ROLLING PIN
JIM DAVIS 10-13

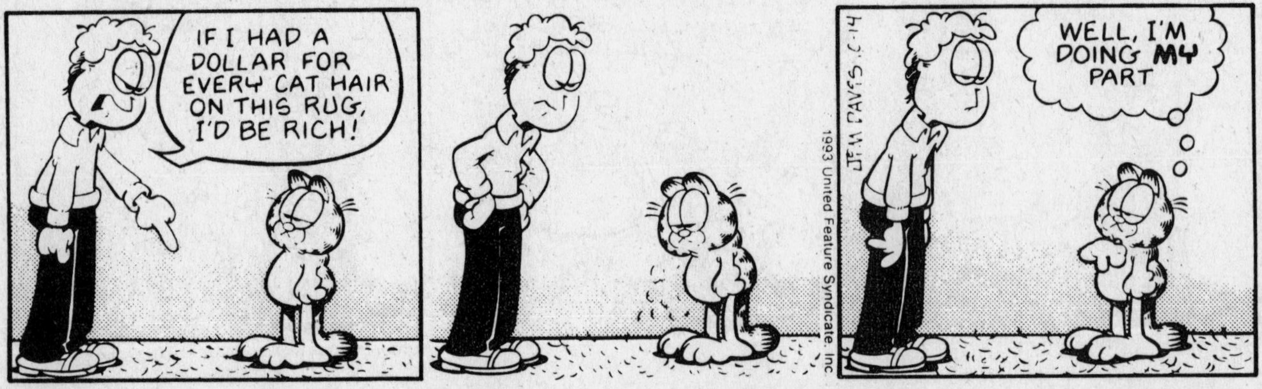
IF I HAD A DOLLAR FOR EVERY CAT HAIR ON THIS RUG, I'D BE RICH!
WELL, I'M DOING MY PART
JIM DAVIS 10-14

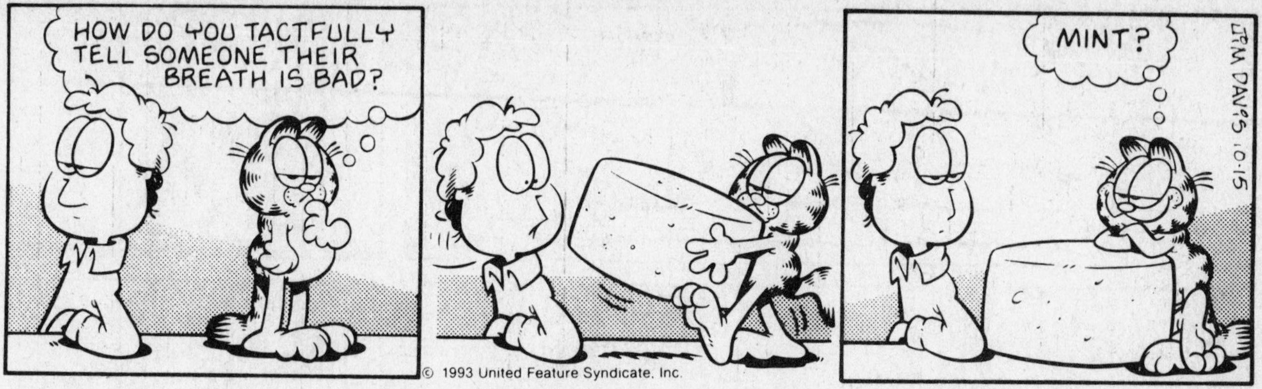
HOW DO YOU TACTFULLY TELL SOMEONE THEIR BREATH IS BAD?
© 1993 United Feature Syndicate, Inc.
MINT?
JIM DAVIS 10·15

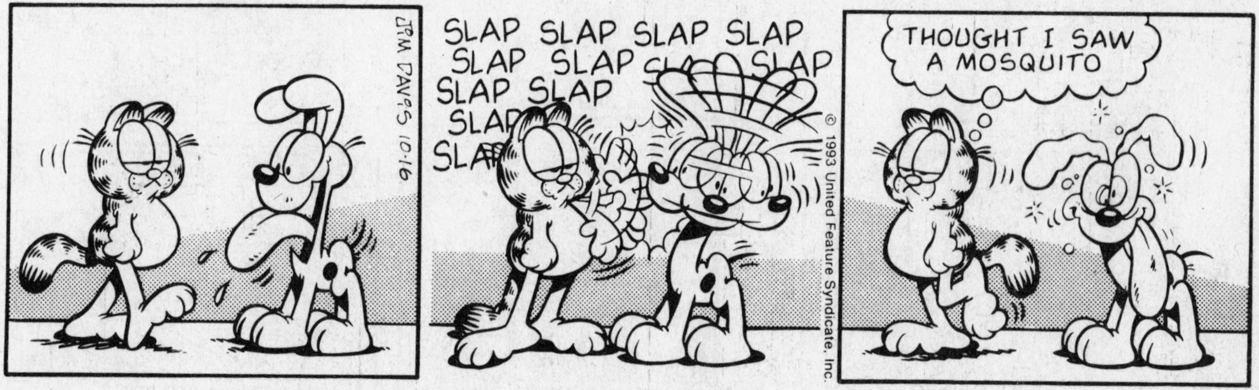
JIM DAVIS 10·16
SLAP SLAP SLAP SLAP
SLAP SLAP SLAP
SLAP SLAP
© 1993 United Feature Syndicate, Inc.
THOUGHT I SAW A MOSQUITO

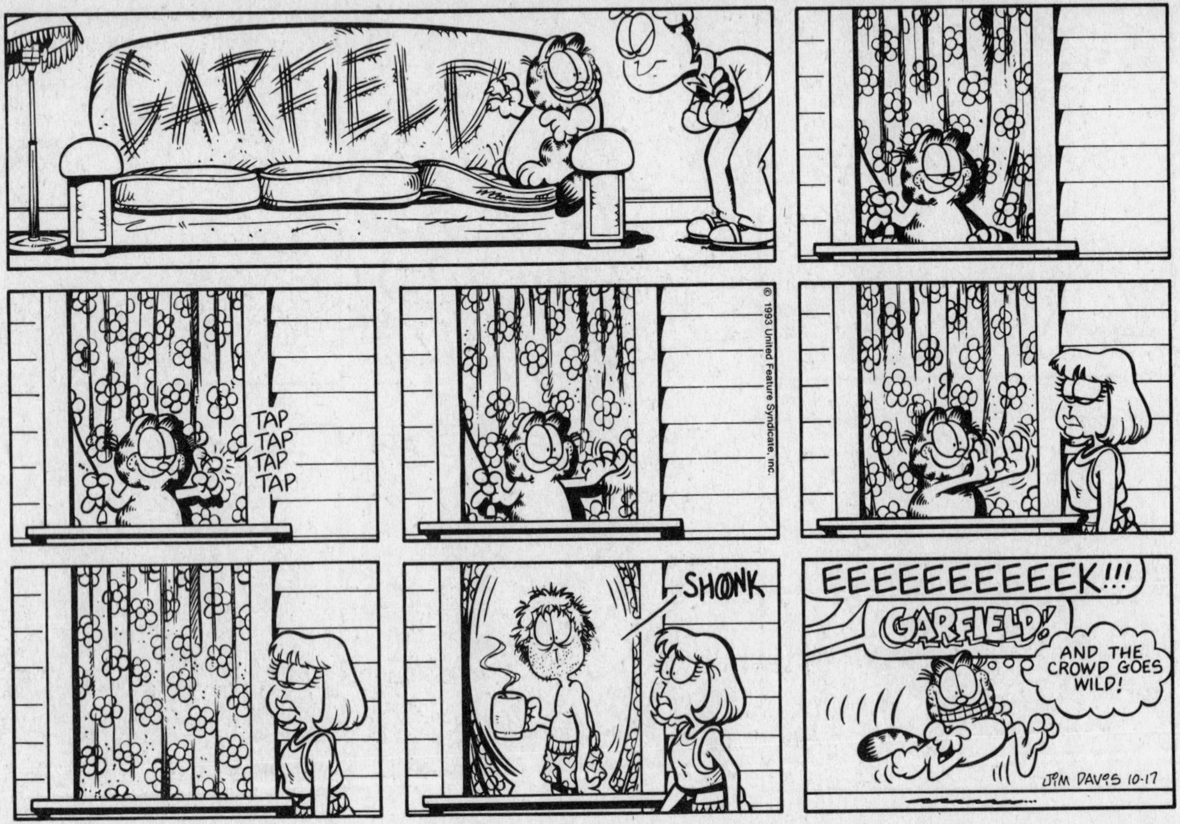
GARFIELD
TAP TAP TAP TAP
SHOONK
EEEEEEEEEEEK!!!
GARFIELD!
AND THE CROWD GOES WILD!
JIM DAVIS 10-17
© 1993 United Feature Syndicate, Inc.

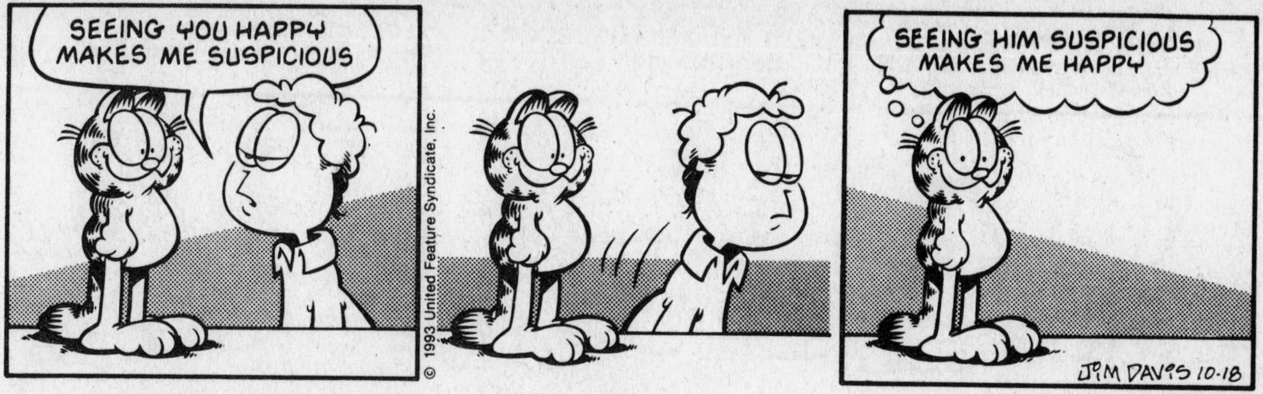
SEEING YOU HAPPY MAKES ME SUSPICIOUS
SEEING HIM SUSPICIOUS MAKES ME HAPPY
© 1993 United Feature Syndicate, Inc.
JIM DAVIS 10-18

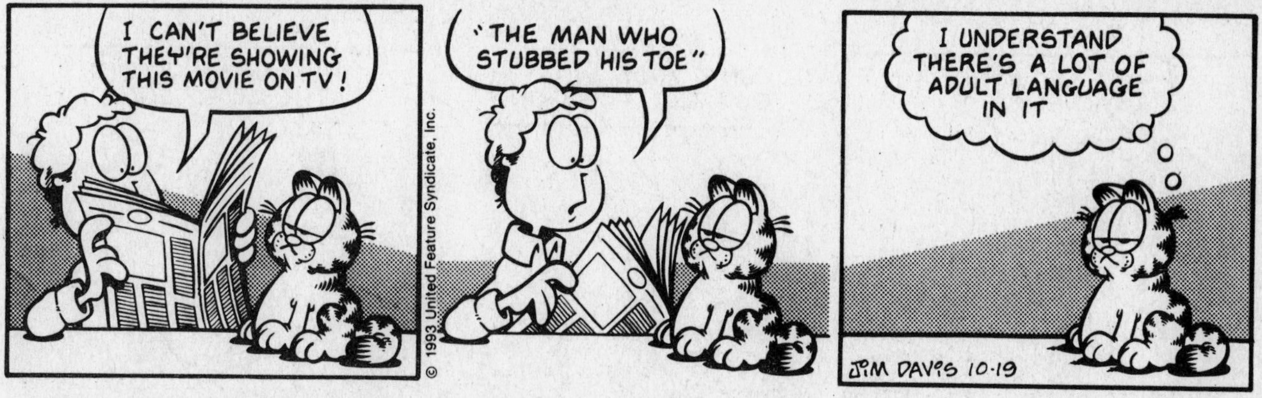
I CAN'T BELIEVE THEY'RE SHOWING THIS MOVIE ON TV!
"THE MAN WHO STUBBED HIS TOE"
I UNDERSTAND THERE'S A LOT OF ADULT LANGUAGE IN IT
© 1993 United Feature Syndicate, Inc.
JIM DAVIS 10-19

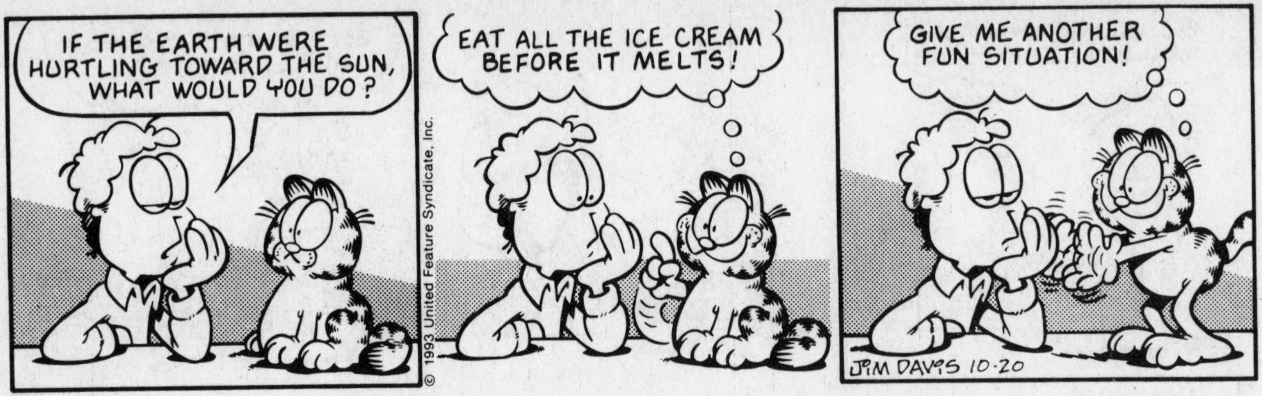
IF THE EARTH WERE HURTLING TOWARD THE SUN, WHAT WOULD YOU DO?
© 1993 United Feature Syndicate, Inc.
EAT ALL THE ICE CREAM BEFORE IT MELTS!
GIVE ME ANOTHER FUN SITUATION!
JIM DAVIS 10-20

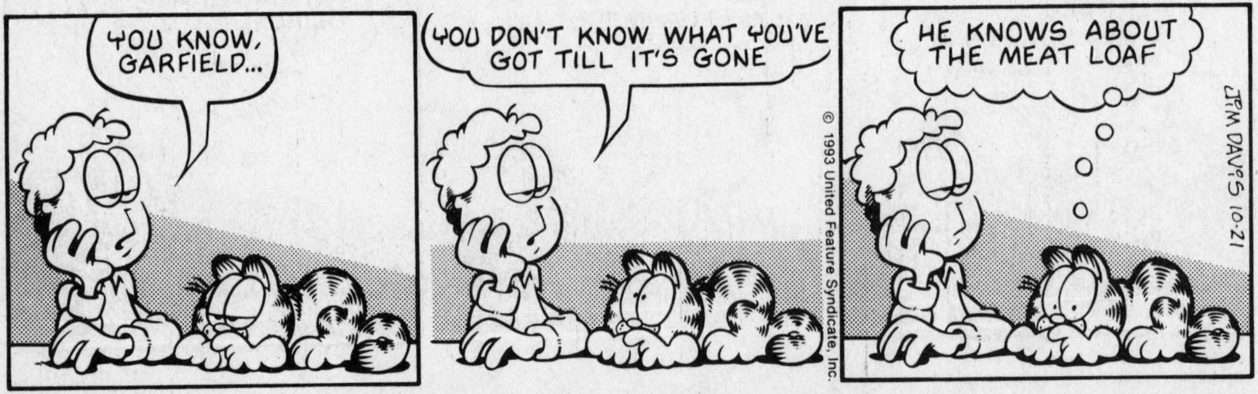
YOU KNOW, GARFIELD...
YOU DON'T KNOW WHAT YOU'VE GOT TILL IT'S GONE
© 1993 United Feature Syndicate, Inc.
HE KNOWS ABOUT THE MEAT LOAF
JIM DAVIS 10-21

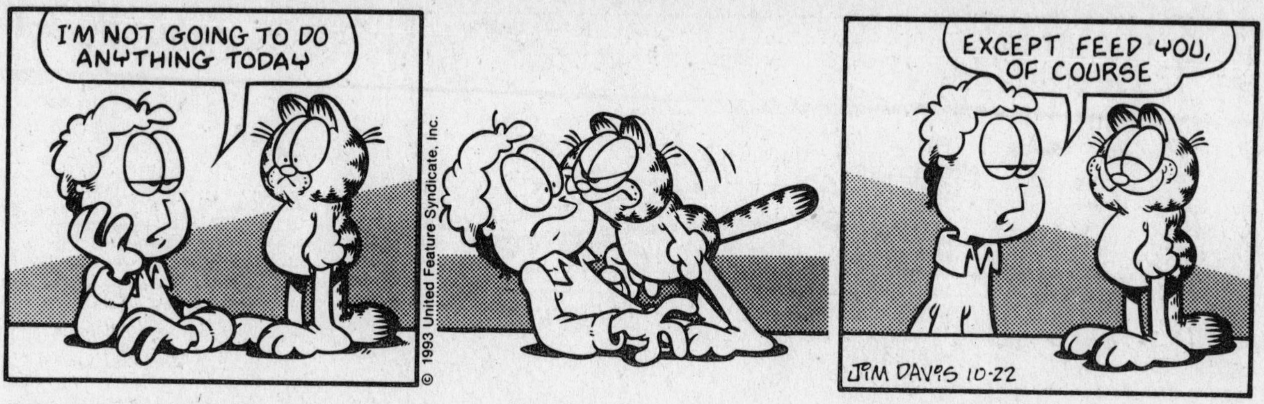
I'M NOT GOING TO DO ANYTHING TODAY
EXCEPT FEED YOU, OF COURSE
© 1993 United Feature Syndicate, Inc.
JIM DAVIS 10-22

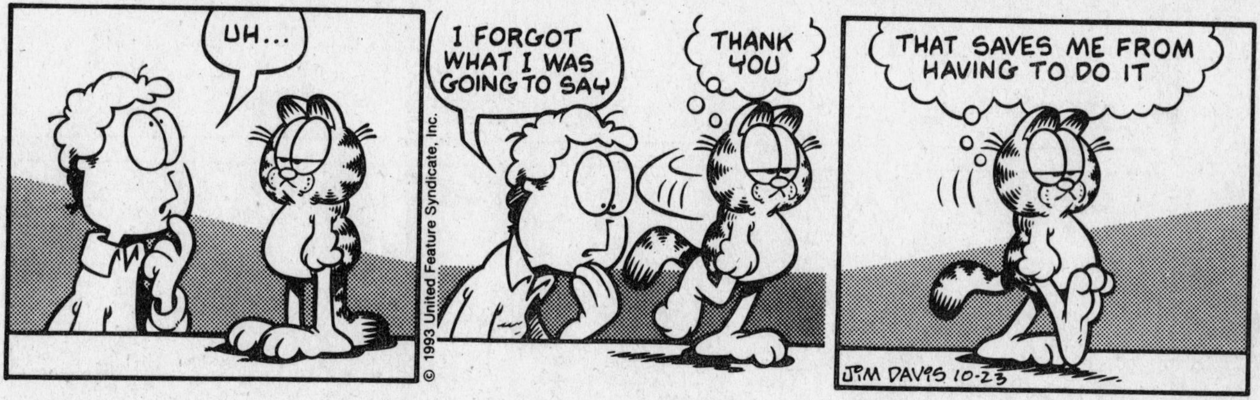
UH...
I FORGOT WHAT I WAS GOING TO SAY
THANK YOU
THAT SAVES ME FROM HAVING TO DO IT
© 1993 United Feature Syndicate, Inc.
JIM DAVIS 10-23

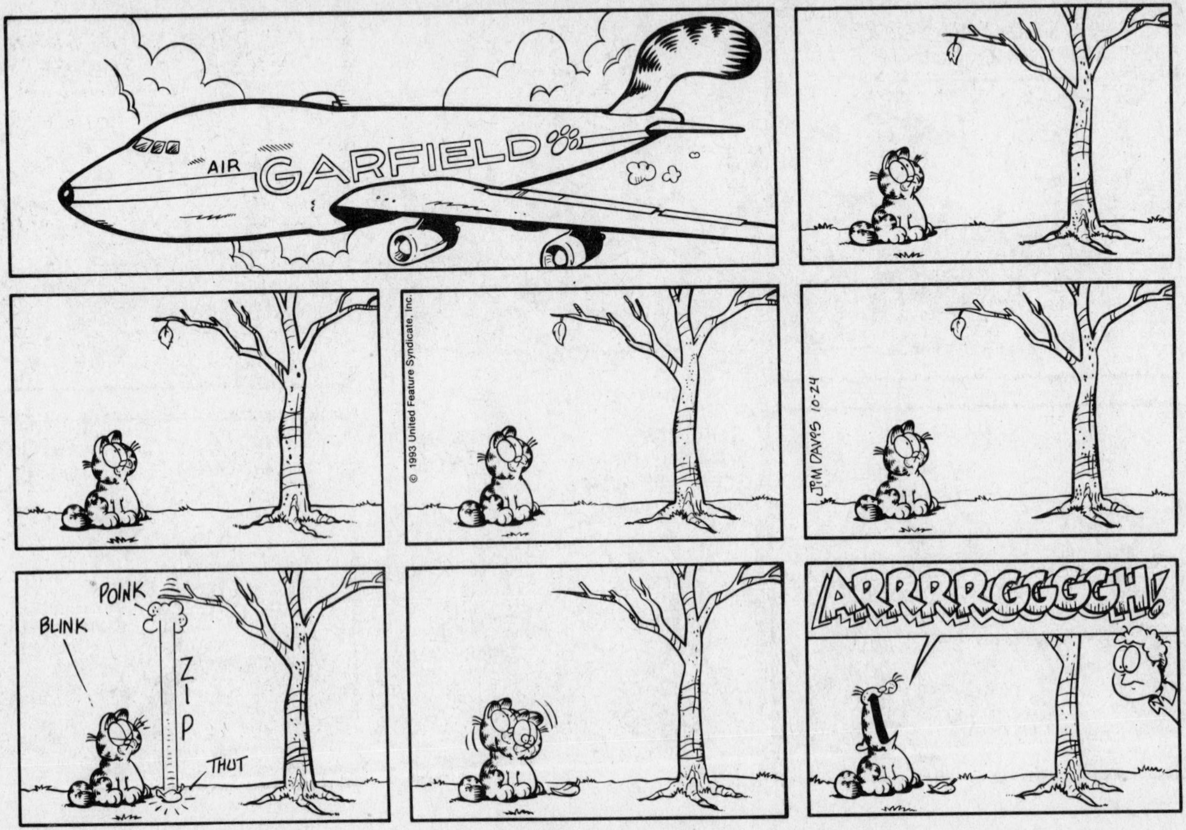

AIR GARFIELD
JIM DAVIS 10-24
© 1993 United Feature Syndicate, Inc.
BLINK
POINK
ZIP
THUT
ARRRRGGGGH!

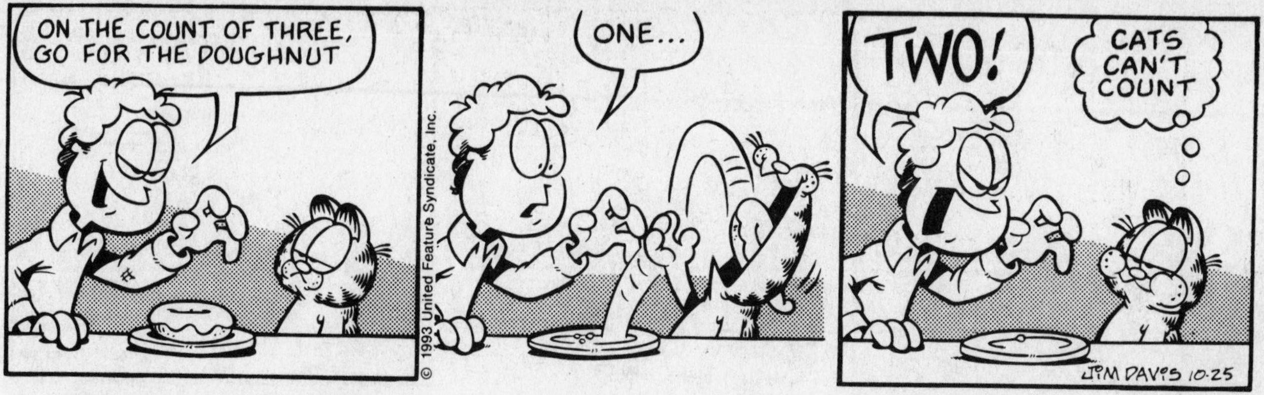
ON THE COUNT OF THREE, GO FOR THE DOUGHNUT
ONE...
TWO!
CATS CAN'T COUNT
© 1993 United Feature Syndicate, Inc.
JIM DAVIS 10-25

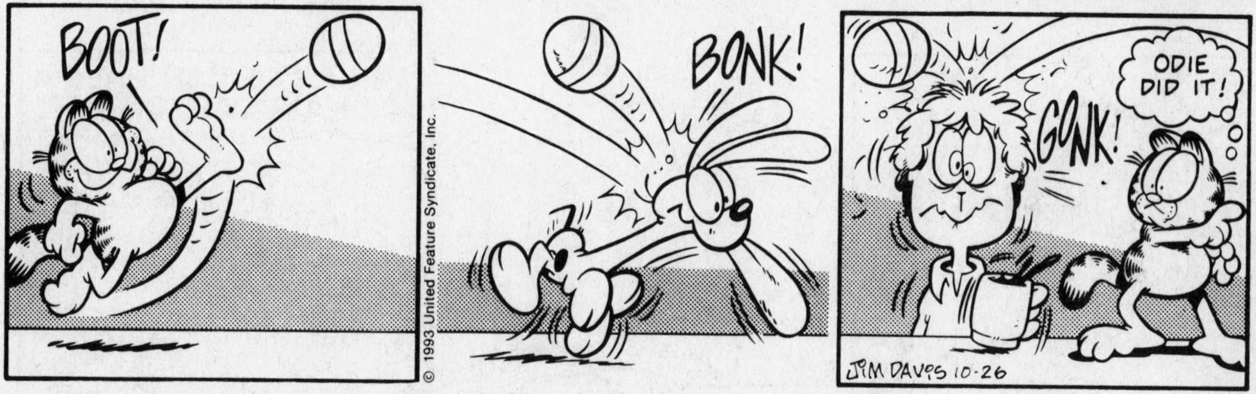
BOOT!
BONK!
GONK!
ODIE DID IT!
© 1993 United Feature Syndicate, Inc.
JIM DAVIS 10-26

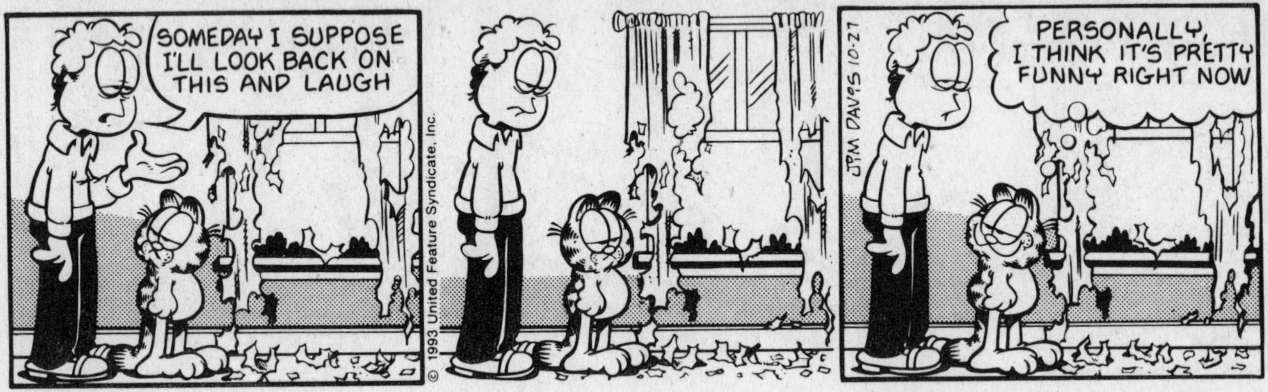
SOMEDAY I SUPPOSE I'LL LOOK BACK ON THIS AND LAUGH
© 1993 United Feature Syndicate, Inc.
JIM DAVIS 10-27
PERSONALLY, I THINK IT'S PRETTY FUNNY RIGHT NOW

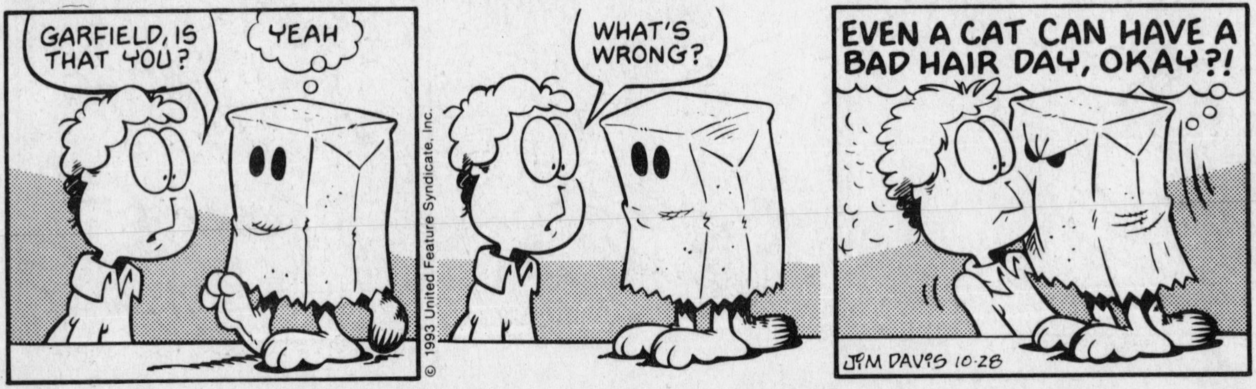
GARFIELD, IS THAT YOU?
YEAH
© 1993 United Feature Syndicate, Inc.
WHAT'S WRONG?
EVEN A CAT CAN HAVE A BAD HAIR DAY, OKAY?!
JIM DAVIS 10-28

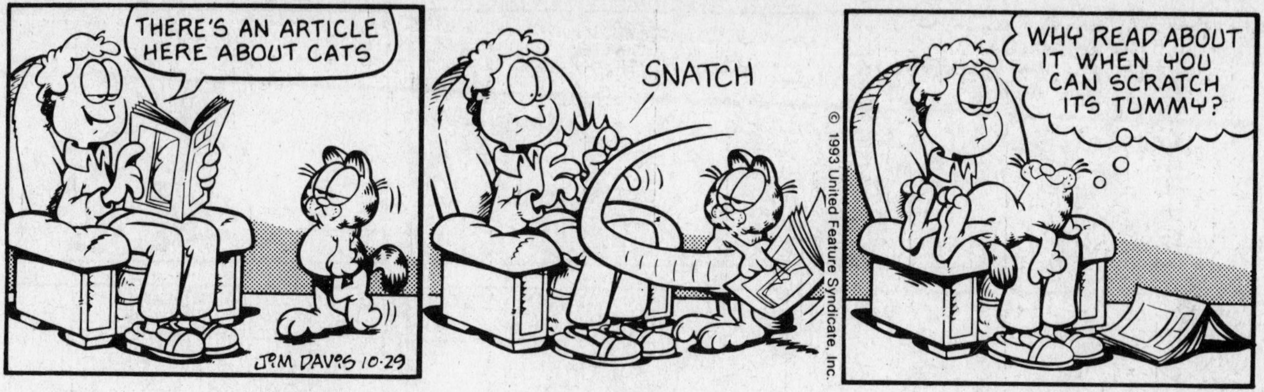
THERE'S AN ARTICLE HERE ABOUT CATS
JIM DAVIS 10-29
SNATCH
© 1993 United Feature Syndicate, Inc.
WHY READ ABOUT IT WHEN YOU CAN SCRATCH ITS TUMMY?

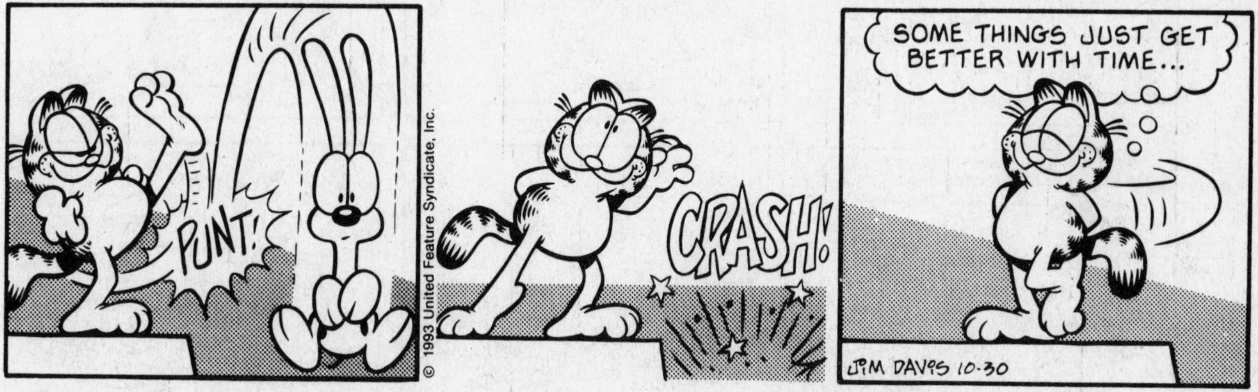
PUNT!
© 1993 United Feature Syndicate, Inc.
CRASH!
SOME THINGS JUST GET BETTER WITH TIME...
JIM DAVIS 10-30

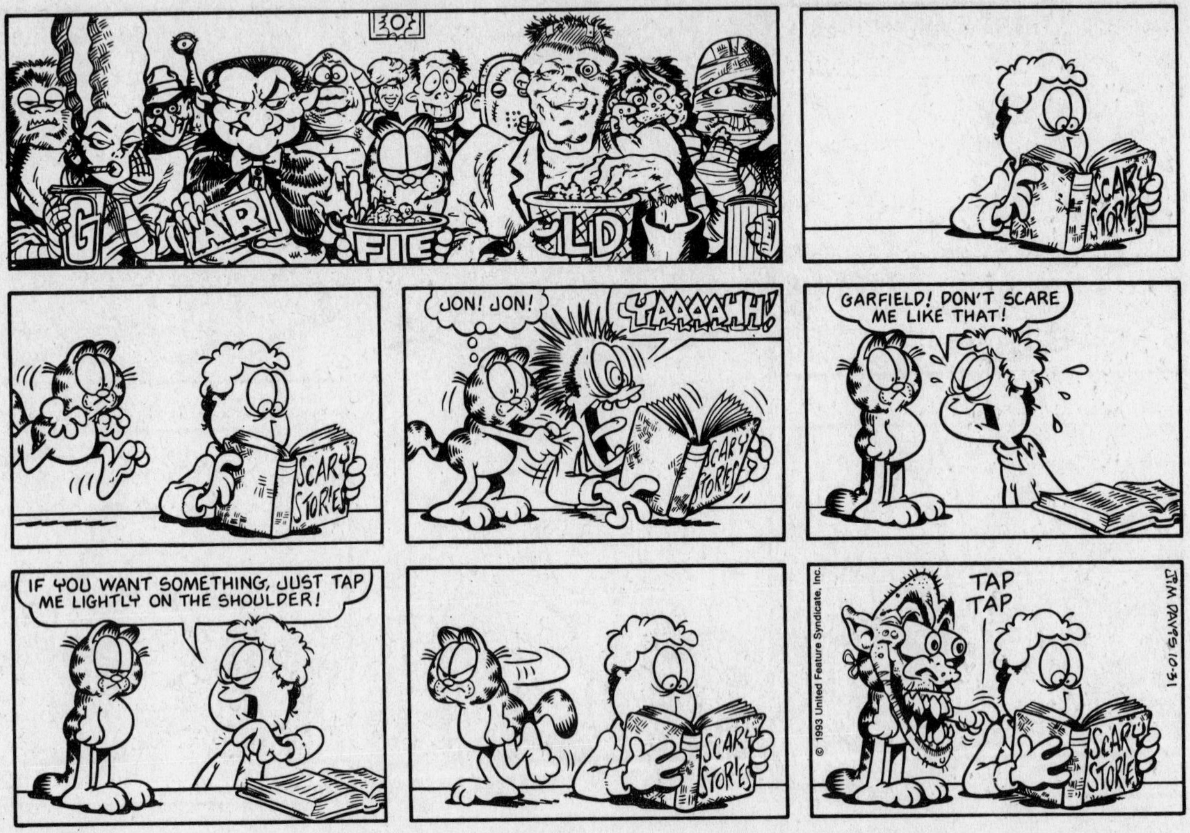
GARFIELD
SCARY STORIES
JON! JON!
YAAAAHH!
GARFIELD! DON'T SCARE ME LIKE THAT!
IF YOU WANT SOMETHING, JUST TAP ME LIGHTLY ON THE SHOULDER!
TAP TAP
© 1993 United Feature Syndicate, Inc.
JIM DAVIS 10-31

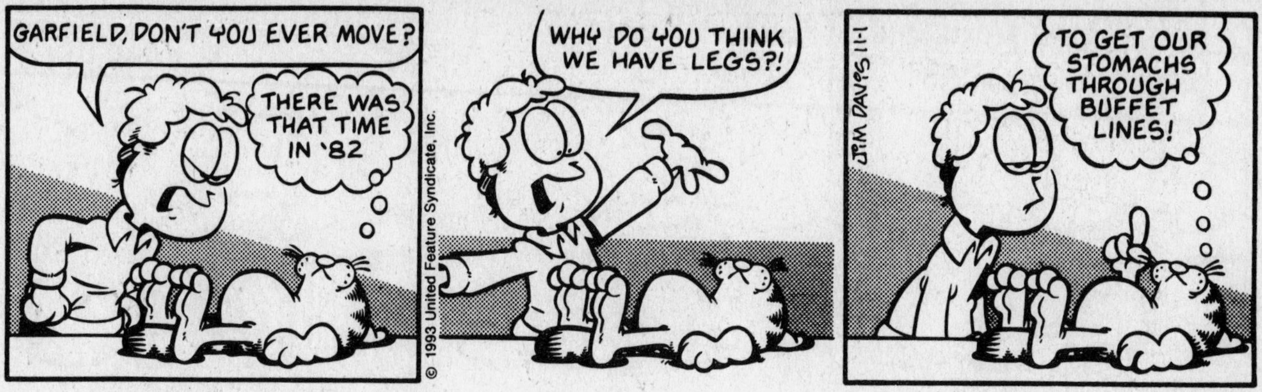
GARFIELD, DON'T YOU EVER MOVE?
THERE WAS THAT TIME IN '82
© 1993 United Feature Syndicate, Inc.
WHY DO YOU THINK WE HAVE LEGS?!
JIM DAVIS 11-1
TO GET OUR STOMACHS THROUGH BUFFET LINES!

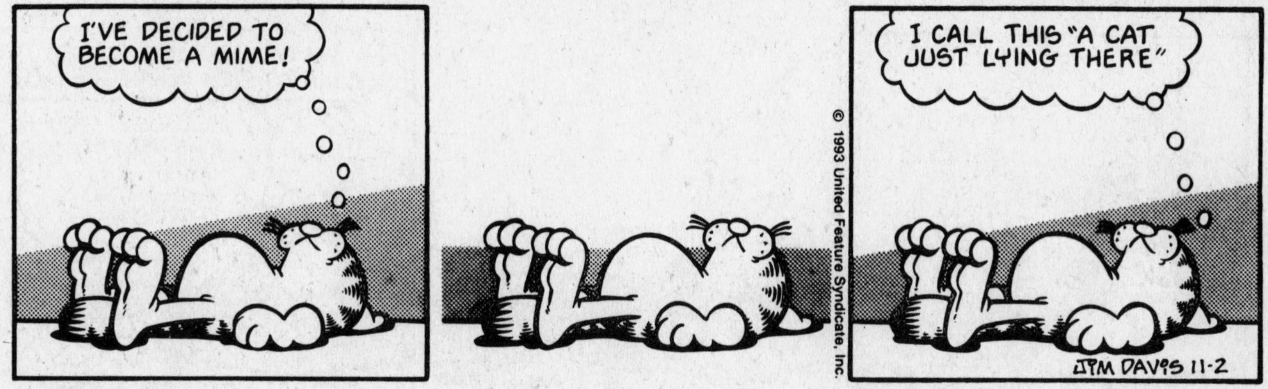
I'VE DECIDED TO BECOME A MIME!
© 1993 United Feature Syndicate, Inc.
I CALL THIS "A CAT JUST LYING THERE"
JIM DAVIS 11-2

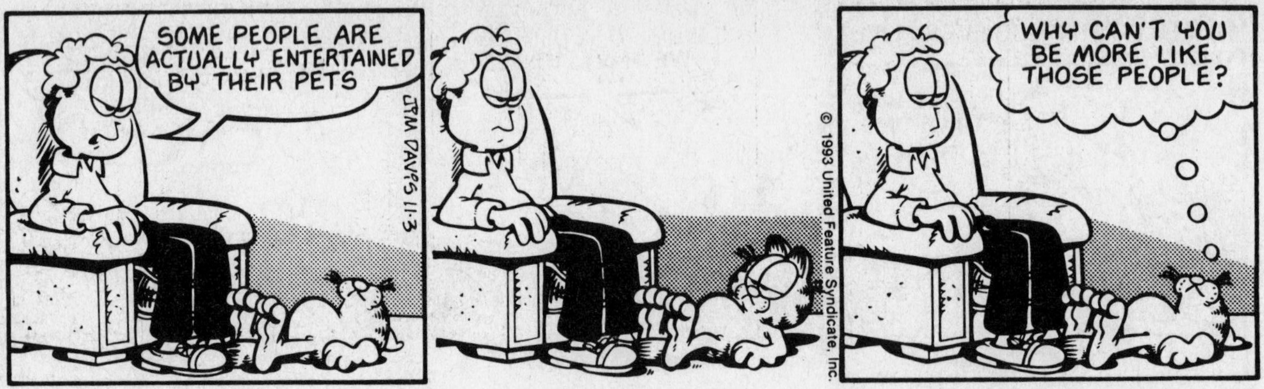

SOME PEOPLE ARE ACTUALLY ENTERTAINED BY THEIR PETS
JIM DAVIS 11-3
WHY CAN'T YOU BE MORE LIKE THOSE PEOPLE?
© 1993 United Feature Syndicate, Inc.

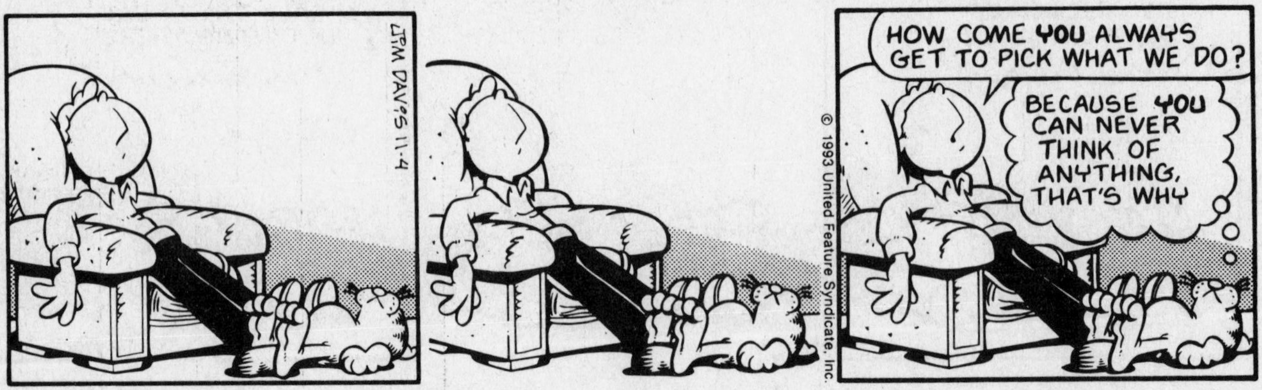

JIM DAVIS 11-4
HOW COME **YOU** ALWAYS GET TO PICK WHAT WE DO?
BECAUSE **YOU** CAN NEVER THINK OF ANYTHING, THAT'S WHY
© 1993 United Feature Syndicate, Inc.

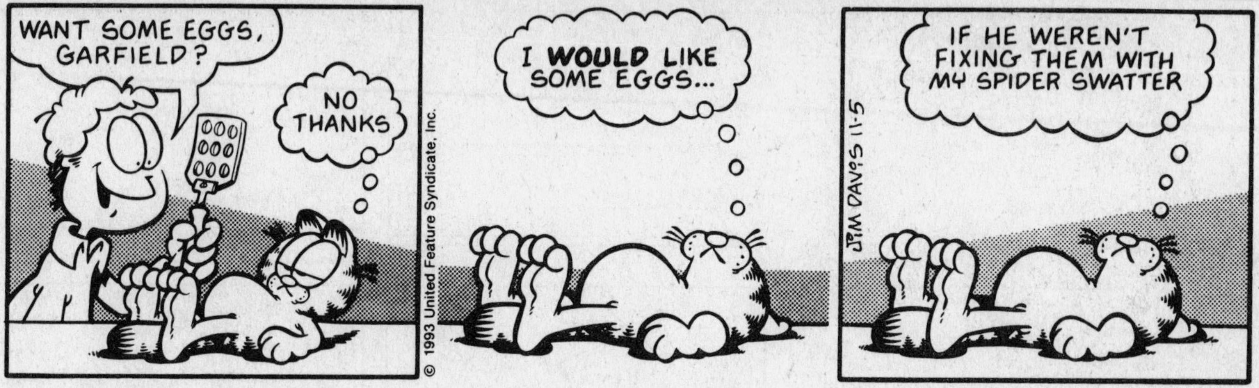
WANT SOME EGGS, GARFIELD?
NO THANKS
I **WOULD** LIKE SOME EGGS...
IF HE WEREN'T FIXING THEM WITH MY SPIDER SWATTER
JIM DAVIS 11-5
© 1993 United Feature Syndicate, Inc.

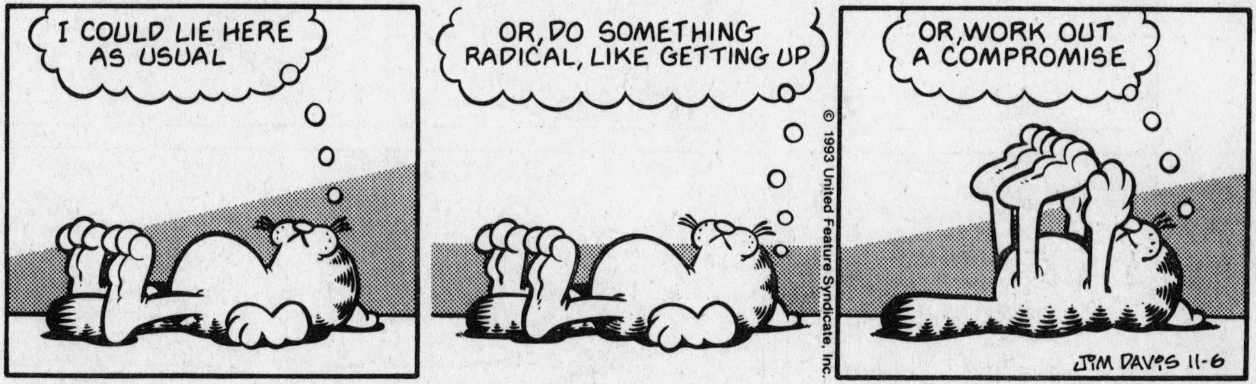
I COULD LIE HERE AS USUAL
OR, DO SOMETHING RADICAL, LIKE GETTING UP
OR, WORK OUT A COMPROMISE
JIM DAVIS 11-6
© 1993 United Feature Syndicate, Inc.

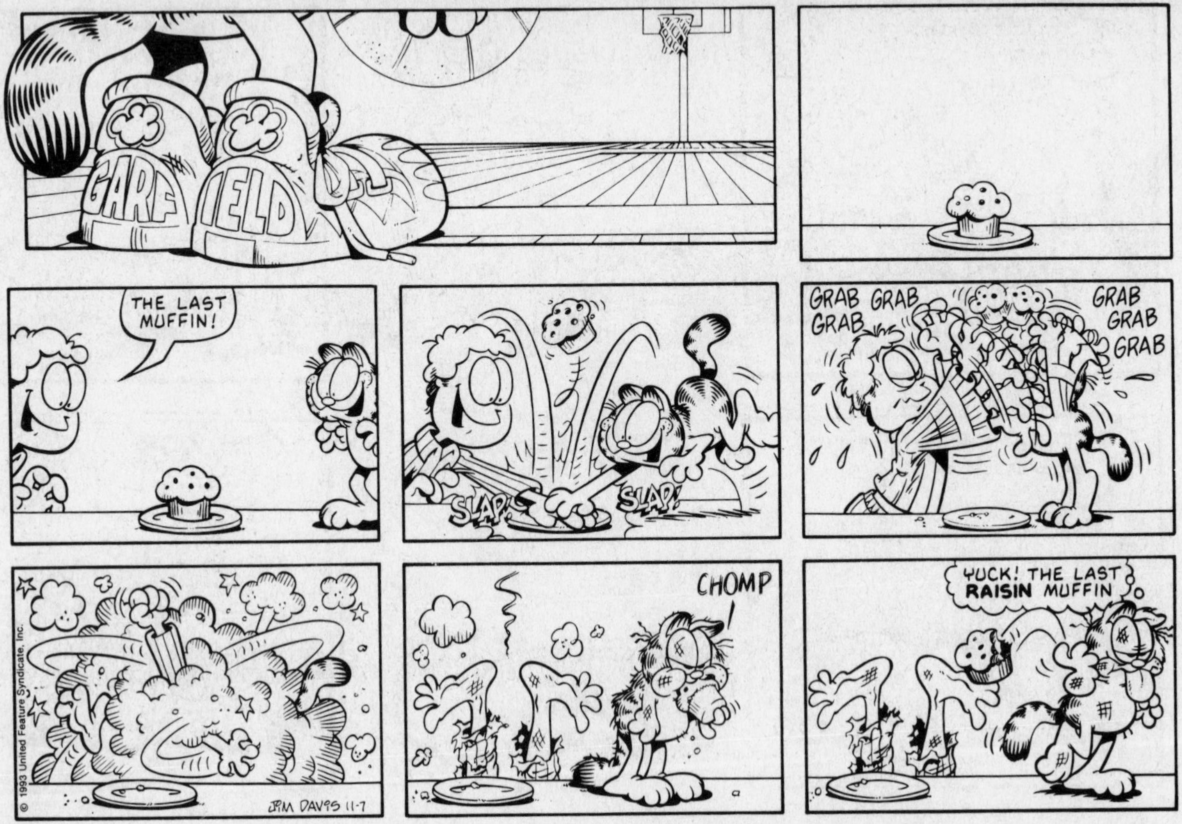
GARFIELD
THE LAST MUFFIN!
SLAP! SLAP!
GRAB GRAB GRAB
GRAB GRAB GRAB
© 1993 United Feature Syndicate, Inc.
JIM DAVIS 11-7
CHOMP
YUCK! THE LAST RAISIN MUFFIN

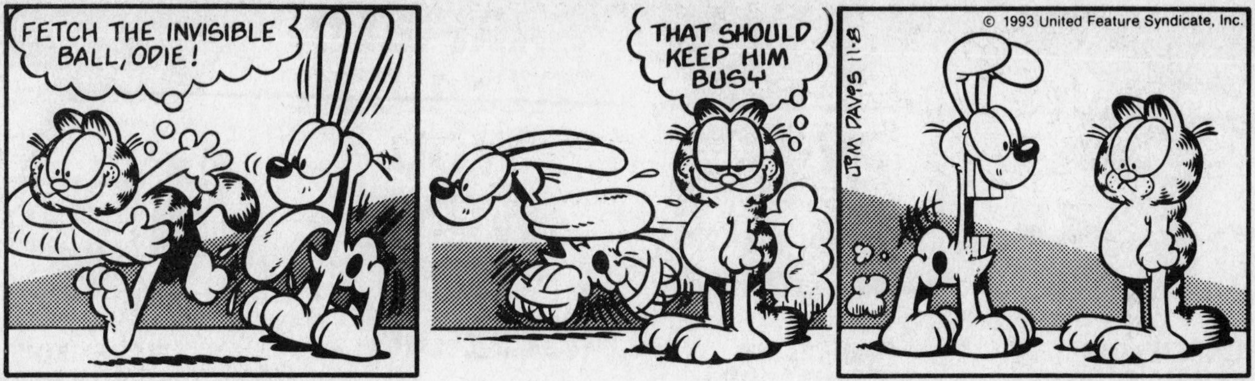
FETCH THE INVISIBLE BALL, ODIE!
THAT SHOULD KEEP HIM BUSY
JIM DAVIS 11-8
© 1993 United Feature Syndicate, Inc.

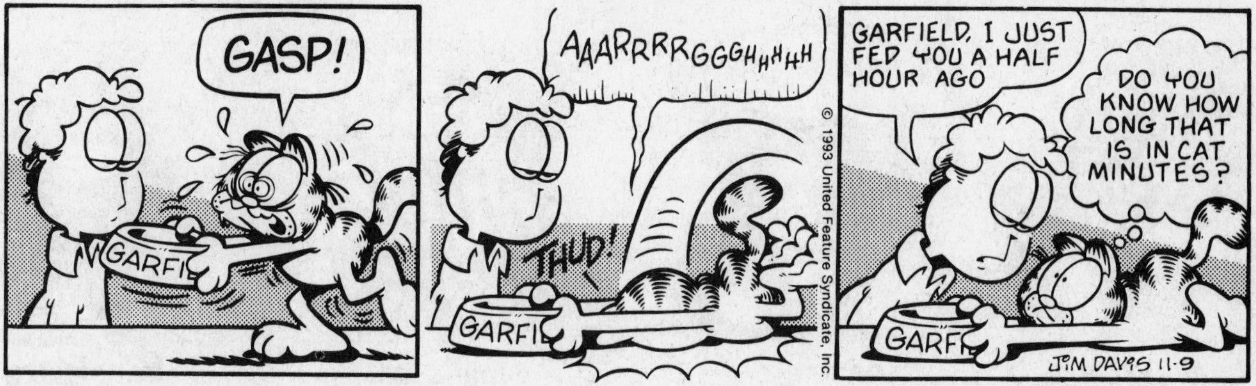
GASP!
GARFI
AAARRRRGGGHHHHH
THUD!
GARFI
© 1993 United Feature Syndicate, Inc.
GARFIELD, I JUST FED YOU A HALF HOUR AGO
DO YOU KNOW HOW LONG THAT IS IN CAT MINUTES?
GARFI
JIM DAVIS 11-9

GARFIELD PRODUCTS YOU WON'T BE SEEING...

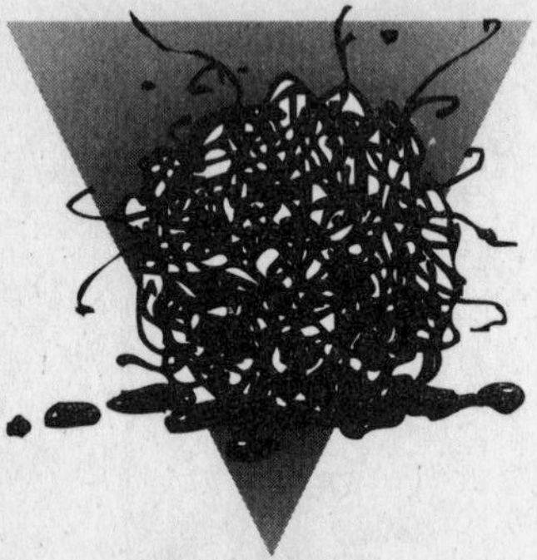

GARFIELD'S
"HAIRBALL O' FUN"

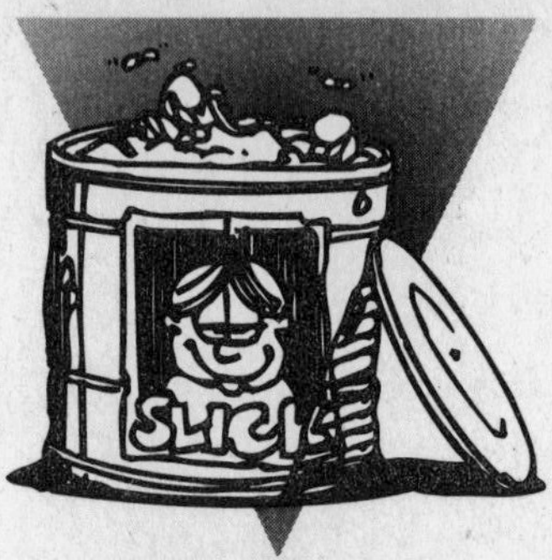
SLICK

GARFIELD'S
STYLING LARD

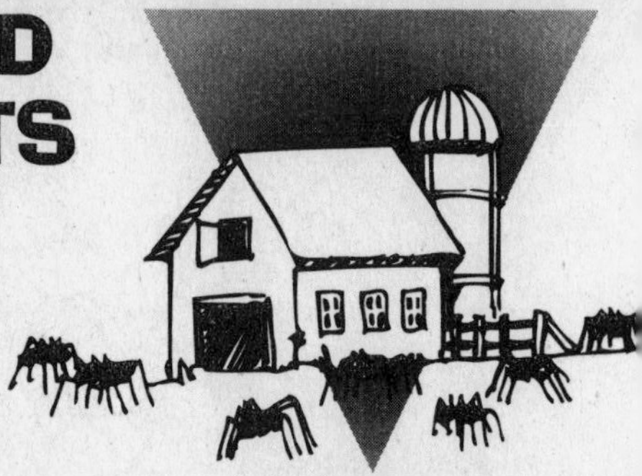

GARFIELD'S
TARANTULA FARM

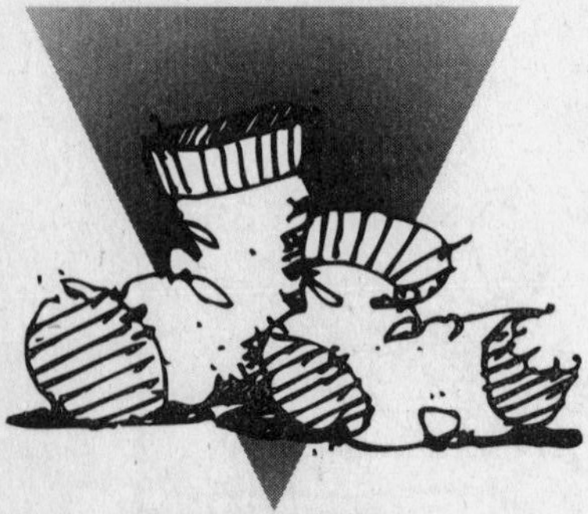

GARFIELD'S
EDIBLE SWEAT SOCKS

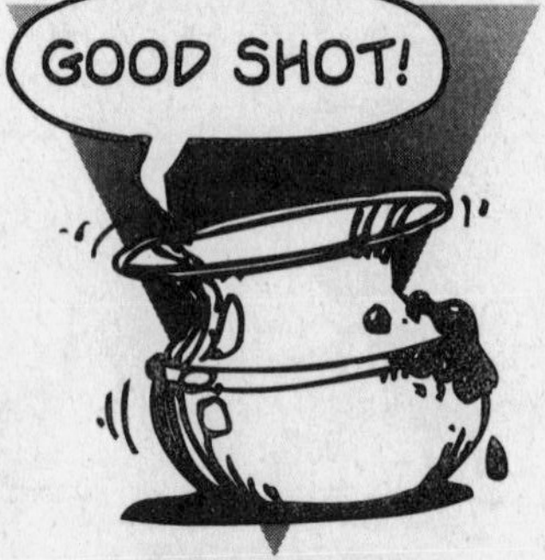
GOOD SHOT!

GARFIELD'S
TALKING SPITTOON

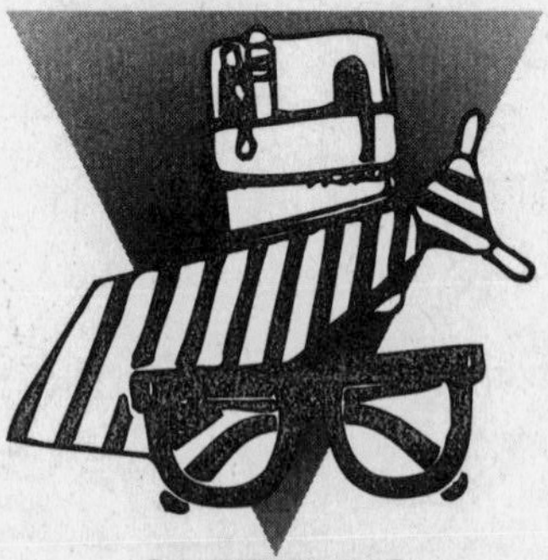

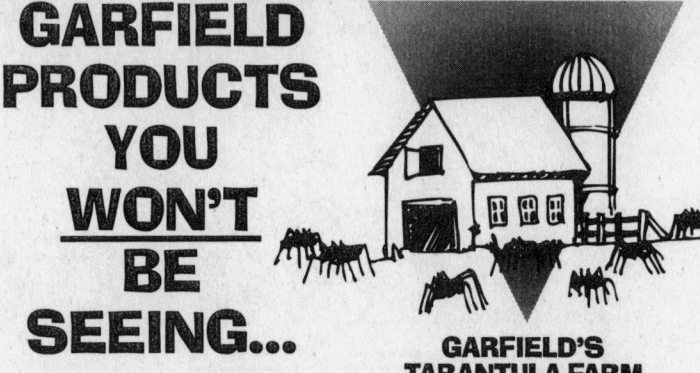

GARFIELD'S
"JR. ACCOUNTANT" KIT

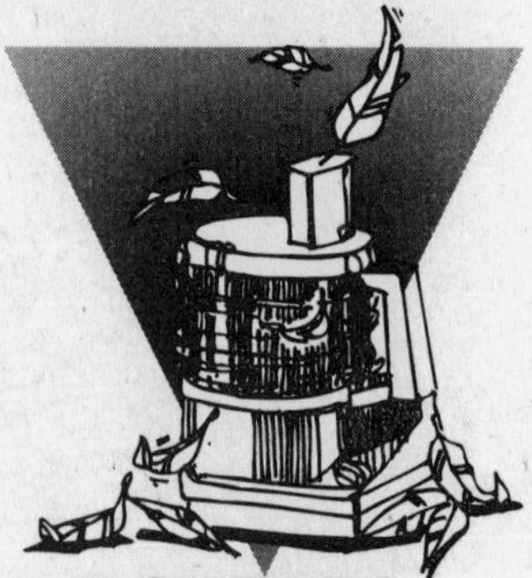

GARFIELD'S
BIRD PROCESSOR

Garfield
dishes
it out

BY: JIM DAVIS

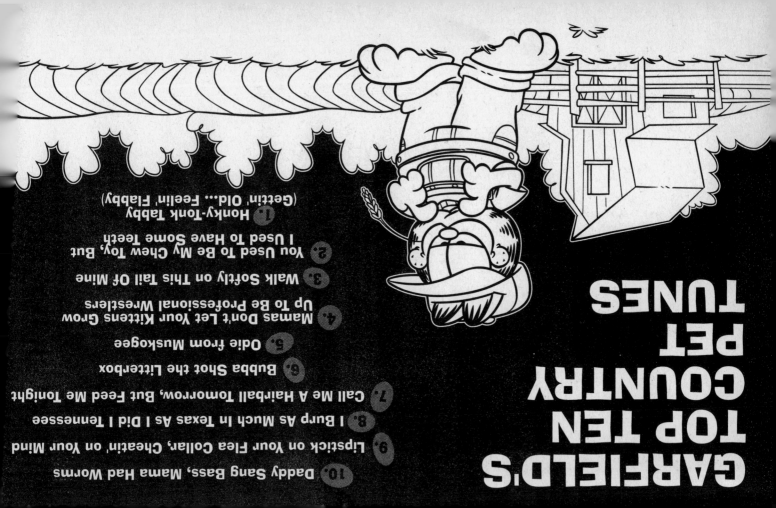

GARFIELD'S TOP TEN COUNTRY PET TUNES

1. Honky-Tonk Tabby (Gettin' Old... Feelin' Flabby)
2. You Used To Be My Chew Toy, But I Used To Have Some Teeth
3. Walk Softly on This Tail Of Mine
4. Mamas Don't Let Your Kittens Grow Up To Be Professional Wrestlers
5. Odie from Muskogee
6. Bubba Shot the Litterbox
7. Call Me A Hairball Tomorrow, But Feed Me Tonight
8. I Burp As Much In Texas As I Did I Tennessee
9. Lipstick on Your Flea Collar, Cheatin' on Your Mind
10. Daddy Sang Bass, Mama Had Worms

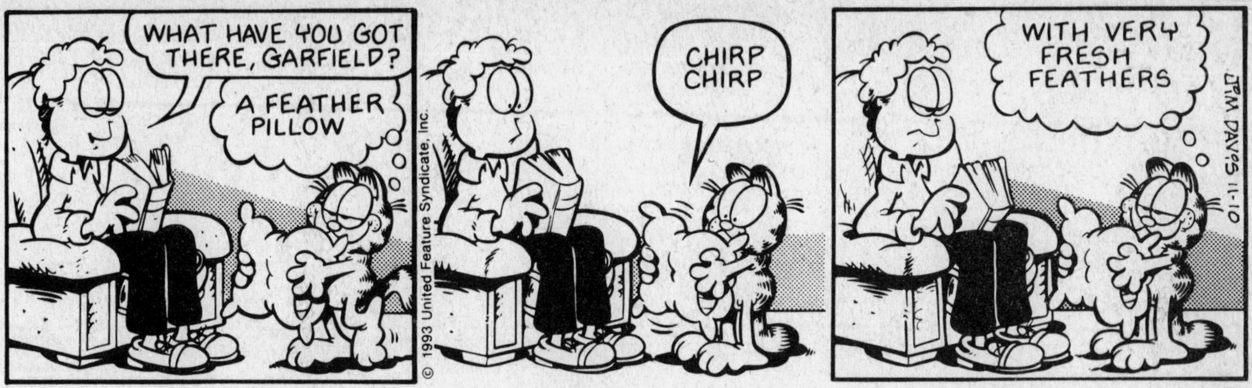
WHAT HAVE YOU GOT THERE, GARFIELD?
A FEATHER PILLOW
© 1993 United Feature Syndicate, Inc.
CHIRP CHIRP
WITH VERY FRESH FEATHERS
JIM DAVIS 11-10

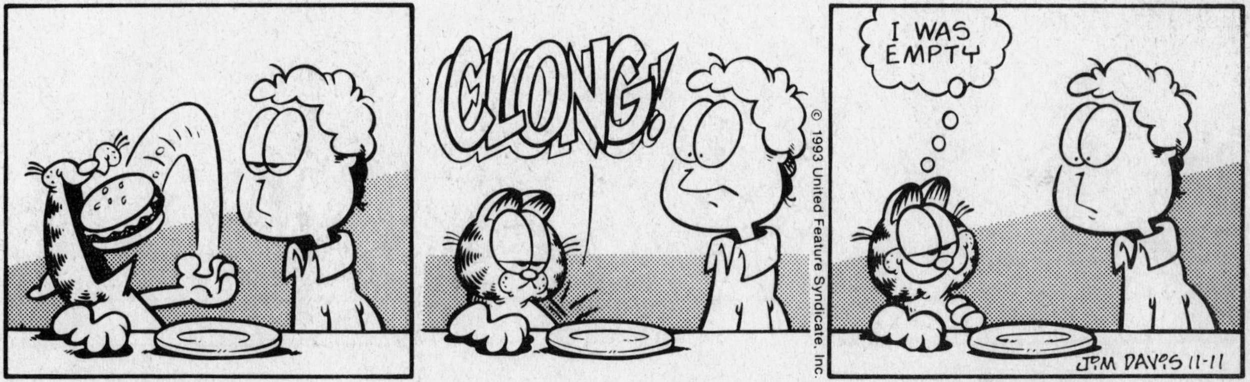
CLONG!
© 1993 United Feature Syndicate, Inc.
I WAS EMPTY
JIM DAVIS 11-11

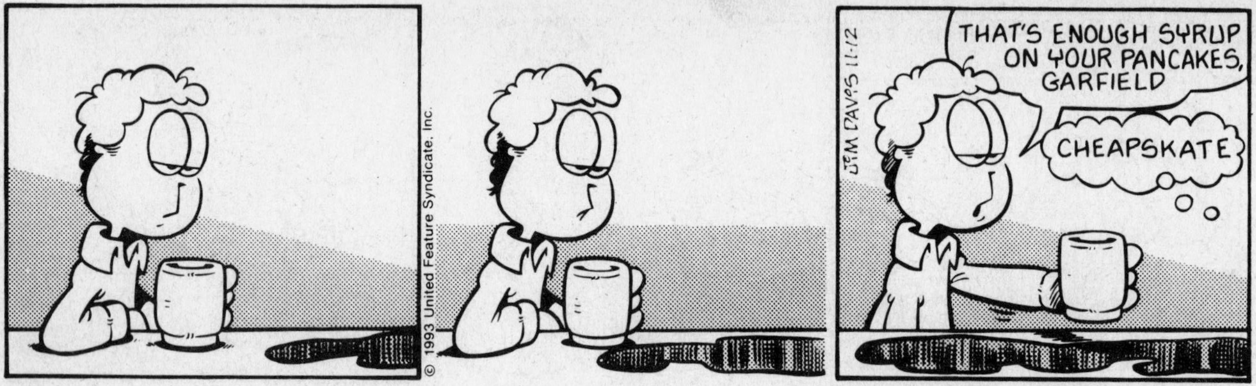
THAT'S ENOUGH SYRUP ON YOUR PANCAKES, GARFIELD
CHEAPSKATE
JIM DAVIS 11-12
© 1993 United Feature Syndicate, Inc.

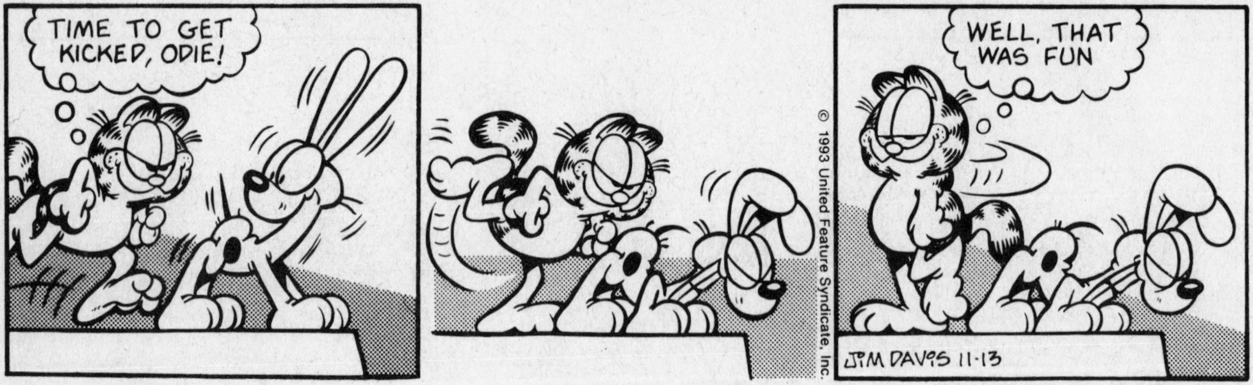
TIME TO GET KICKED, ODIE!
WELL, THAT WAS FUN
JIM DAVIS 11-13
© 1993 United Feature Syndicate, Inc.

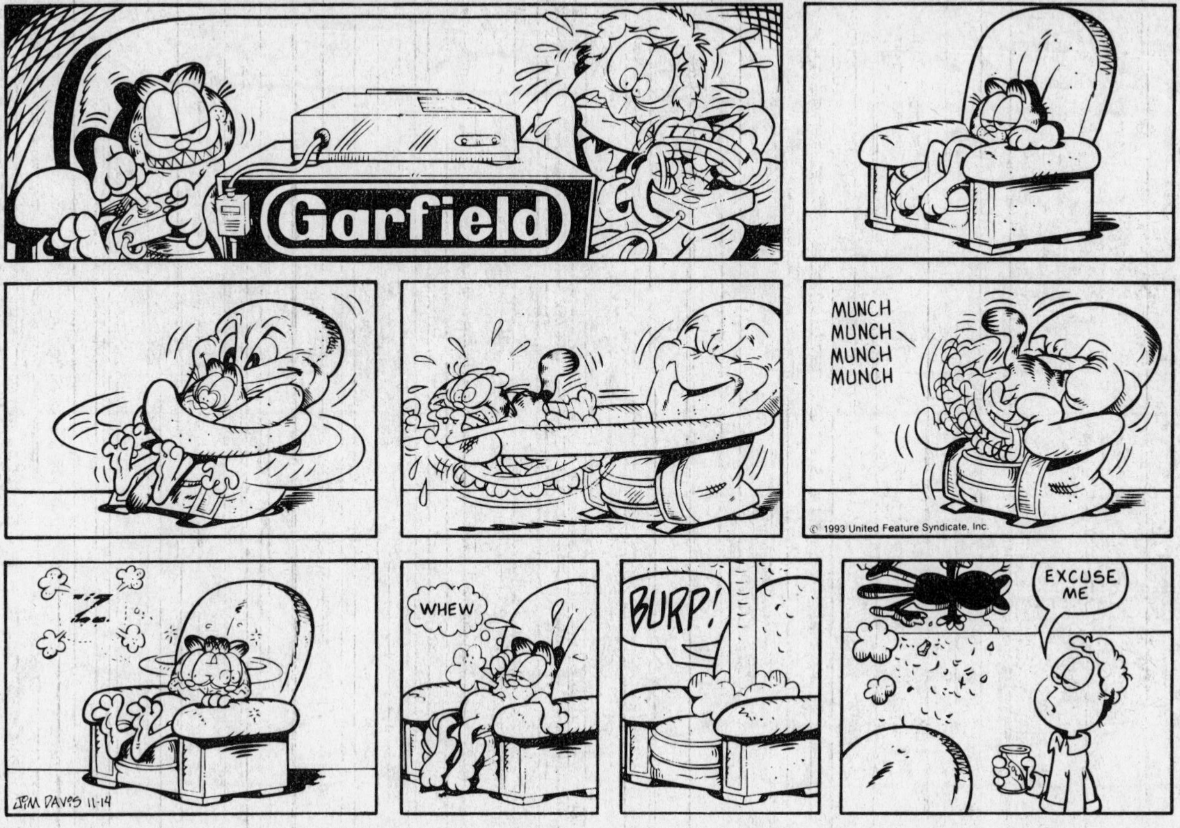
Garfield
MUNCH
MUNCH
MUNCH
MUNCH
© 1993 United Feature Syndicate, Inc.
JIM DAVIS 11-14
WHEW
BURP!
EXCUSE ME

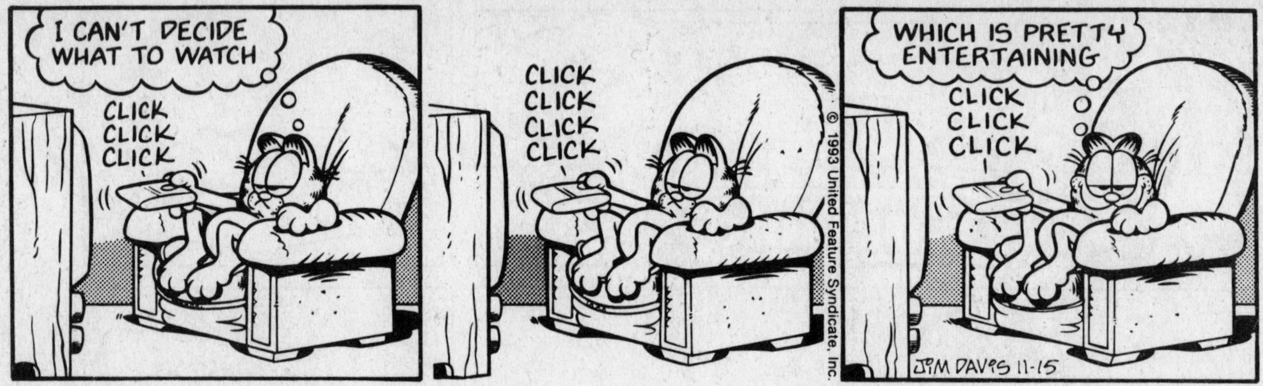

I CAN'T DECIDE WHAT TO WATCH
CLICK CLICK CLICK
CLICK CLICK CLICK CLICK
WHICH IS PRETTY ENTERTAINING
CLICK CLICK CLICK
JIM DAVIS 11-15
© 1993 United Feature Syndicate, Inc.

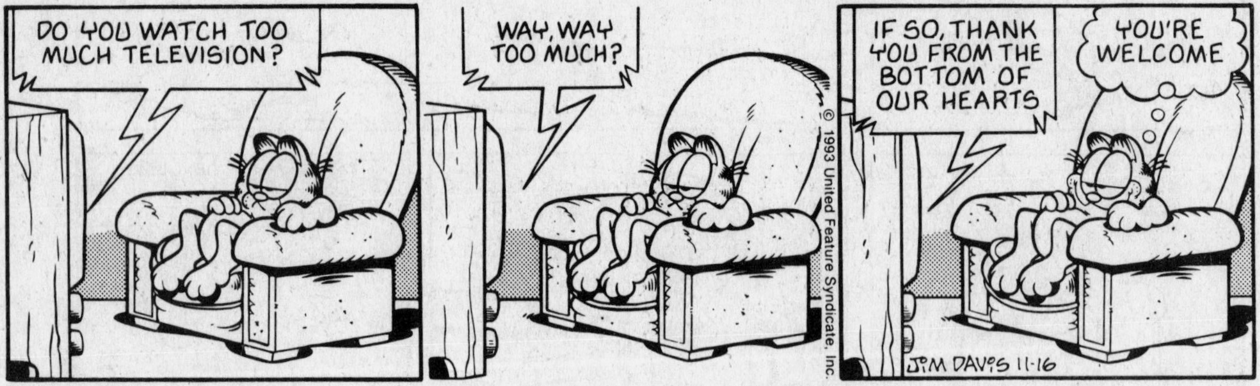

DO YOU WATCH TOO MUCH TELEVISION?
WAY, WAY TOO MUCH?
IF SO, THANK YOU FROM THE BOTTOM OF OUR HEARTS
YOU'RE WELCOME
JIM DAVIS 11-16
© 1993 United Feature Syndicate, Inc.

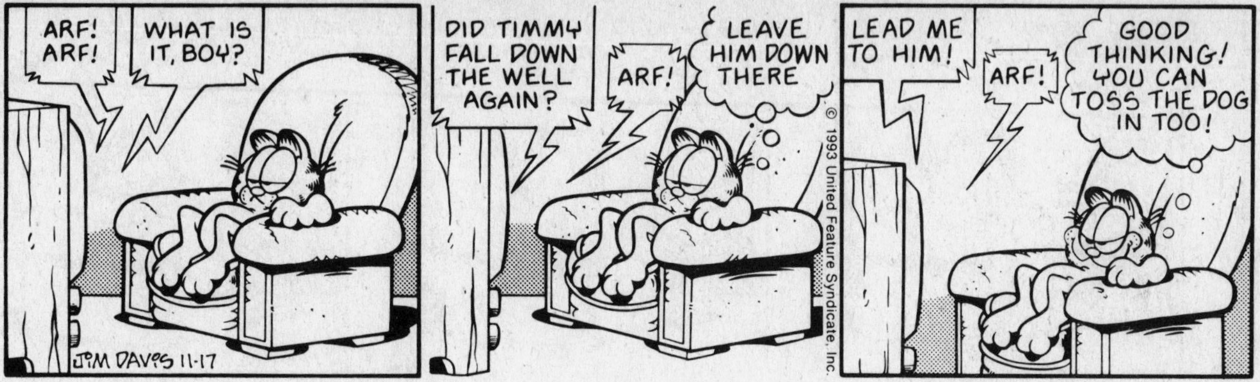
ARF! ARF!
WHAT IS IT, BOY?
JIM DAVIS 11-17
DID TIMMY FALL DOWN THE WELL AGAIN?
ARF!
LEAVE HIM DOWN THERE
© 1993 United Feature Syndicate, Inc.
LEAD ME TO HIM!
ARF!
GOOD THINKING! YOU CAN TOSS THE DOG IN TOO!

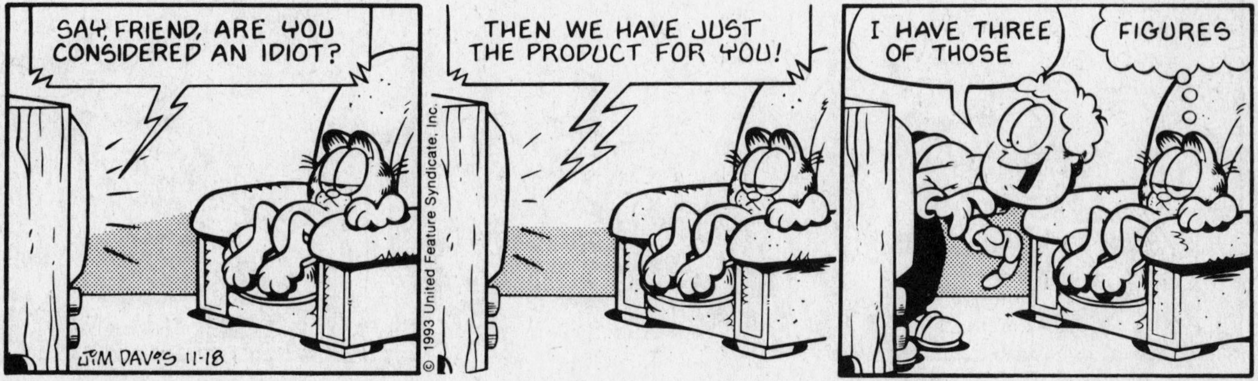
SAY, FRIEND, ARE YOU CONSIDERED AN IDIOT?
JIM DAVIS 11-18
© 1993 United Feature Syndicate, Inc.
THEN WE HAVE JUST THE PRODUCT FOR YOU!
I HAVE THREE OF THOSE
FIGURES

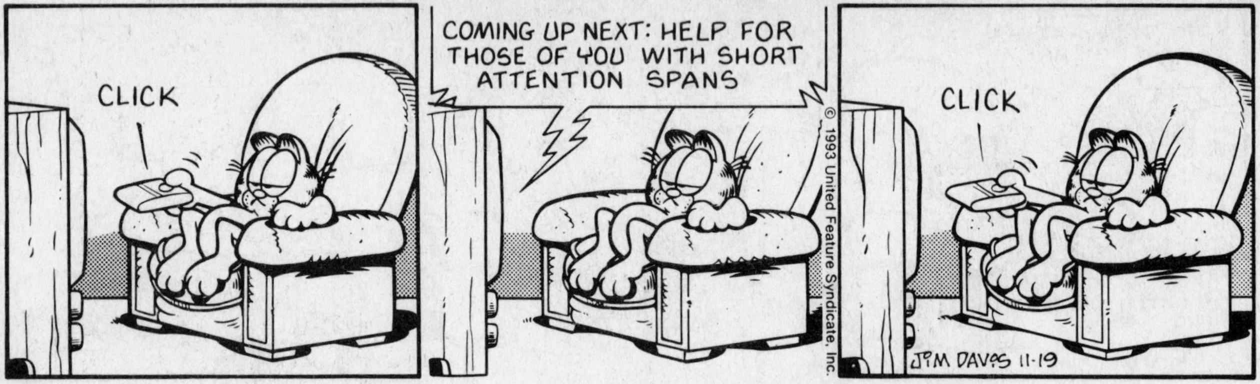
CLICK
COMING UP NEXT: HELP FOR THOSE OF YOU WITH SHORT ATTENTION SPANS
© 1993 United Feature Syndicate, Inc.
CLICK
JIM DAVIS 11-19

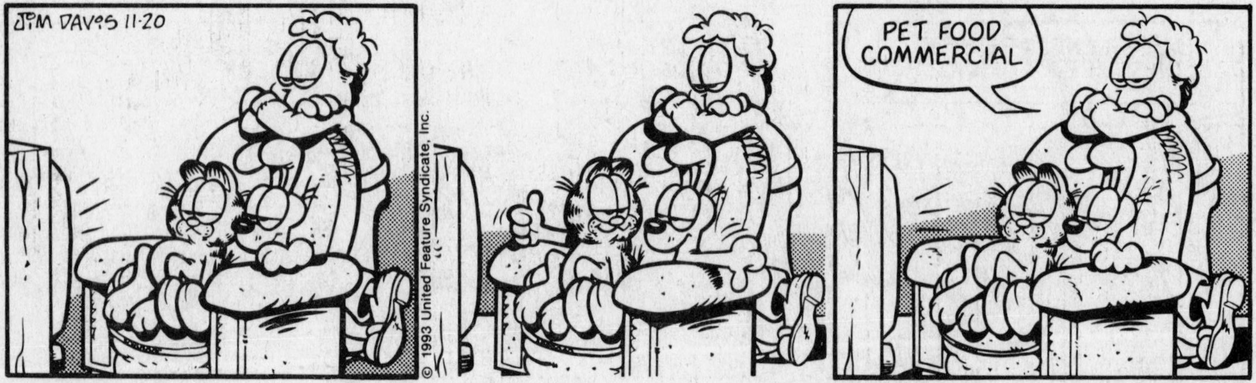
JIM DAVIS 11-20
© 1993 United Feature Syndicate, Inc.
PET FOOD COMMERCIAL

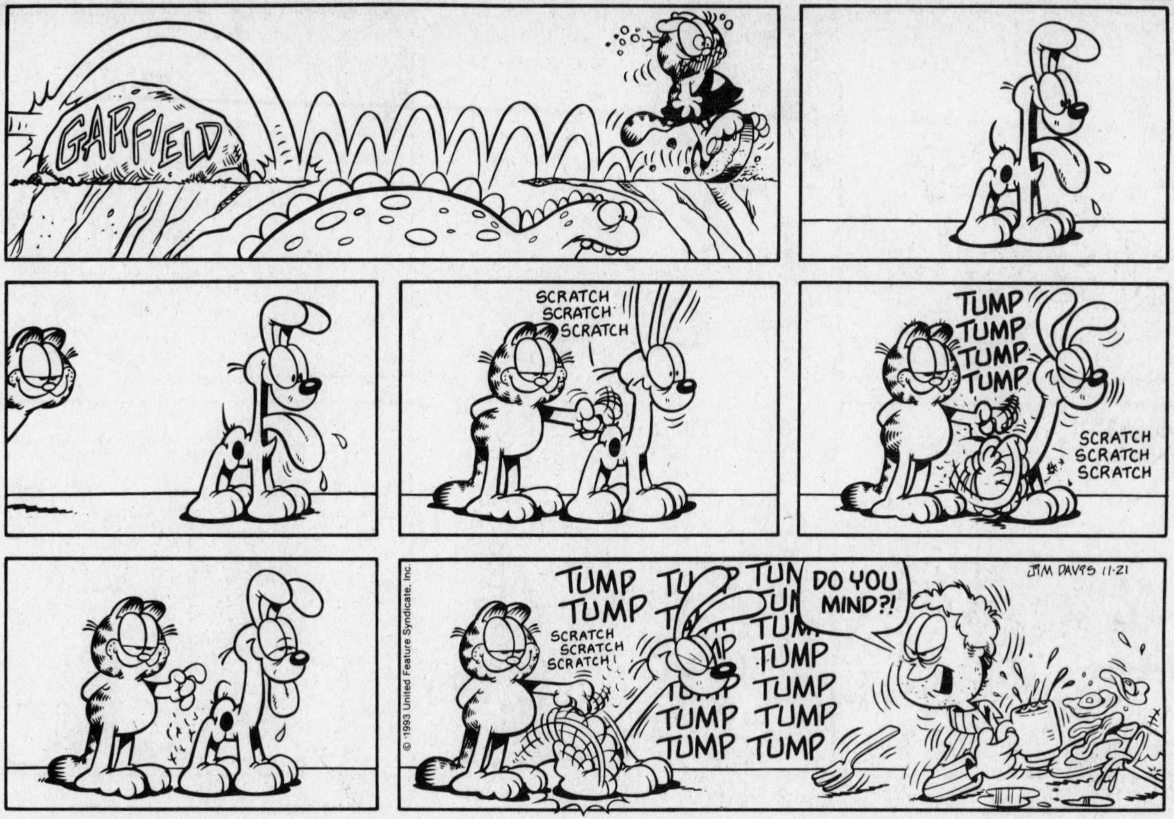
GARFIELD
SCRATCH
SCRATCH
SCRATCH
TUMP
TUMP
TUMP
TUMP
SCRATCH
SCRATCH
SCRATCH
© 1993 United Feature Syndicate, Inc.
TUMP
TUMP
SCRATCH
SCRATCH
SCRATCH
TUMP
TUMP
TUMP
TUMP
TUMP
TUMP
TUMP
DO YOU MIND?!
JIM DAVIS 11-21

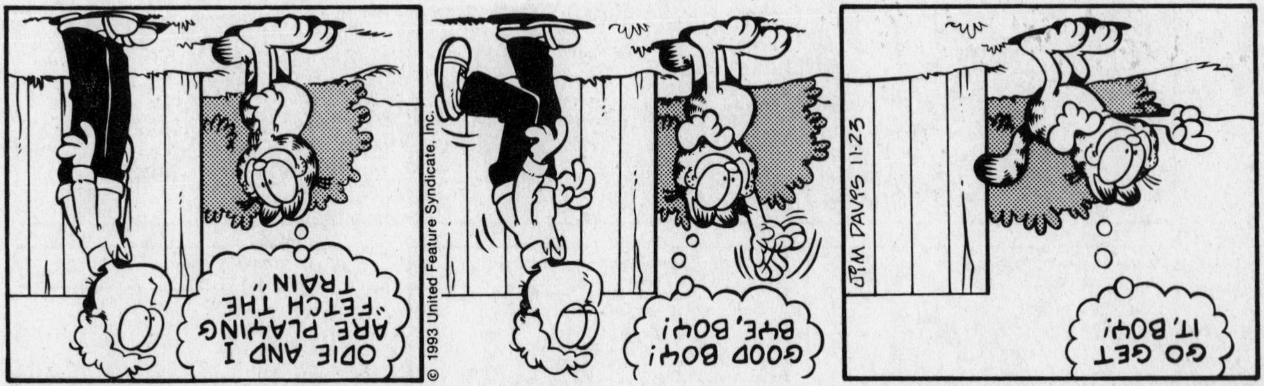
GO GET IT, BOY!
GOOD BOY! BYE, BOY!
ODIE AND I ARE PLAYING "FETCH THE TRAIN."
JIM DAVIS 11-23
© 1993 United Feature Syndicate, Inc.

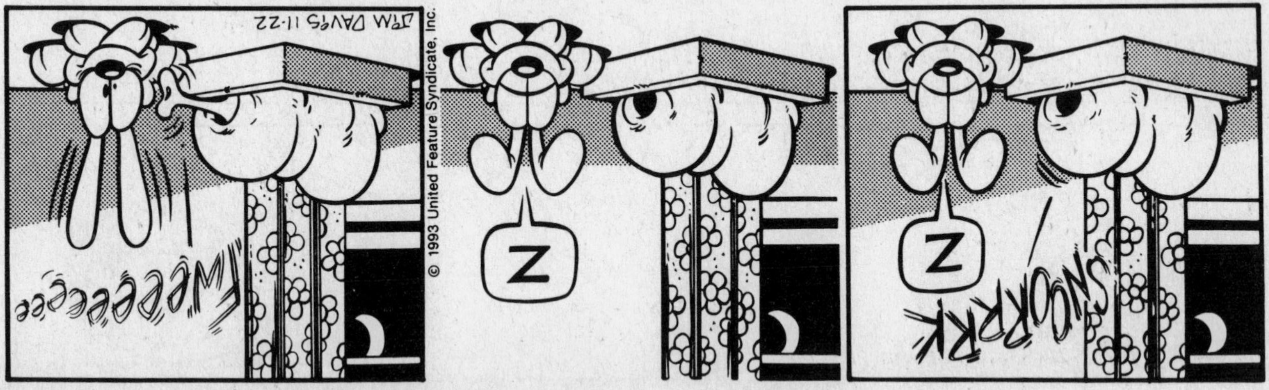
JIM DAVIS 11-22
FWeeeeeeeee
Z
Z
SNORRRK
© 1993 United Feature Syndicate, Inc.

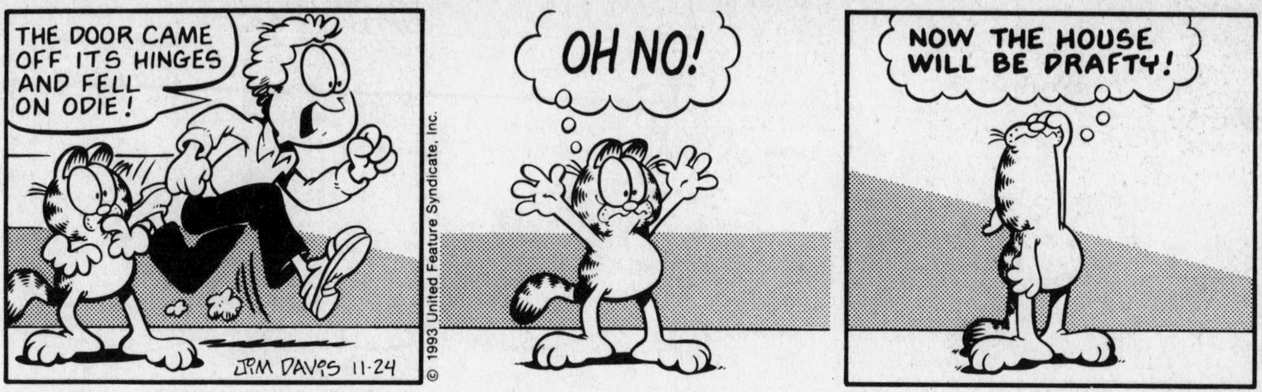
THE DOOR CAME OFF ITS HINGES AND FELL ON ODIE!
JIM DAVIS 11-24
© 1993 United Feature Syndicate, Inc.
OH NO!
NOW THE HOUSE WILL BE DRAFTY!

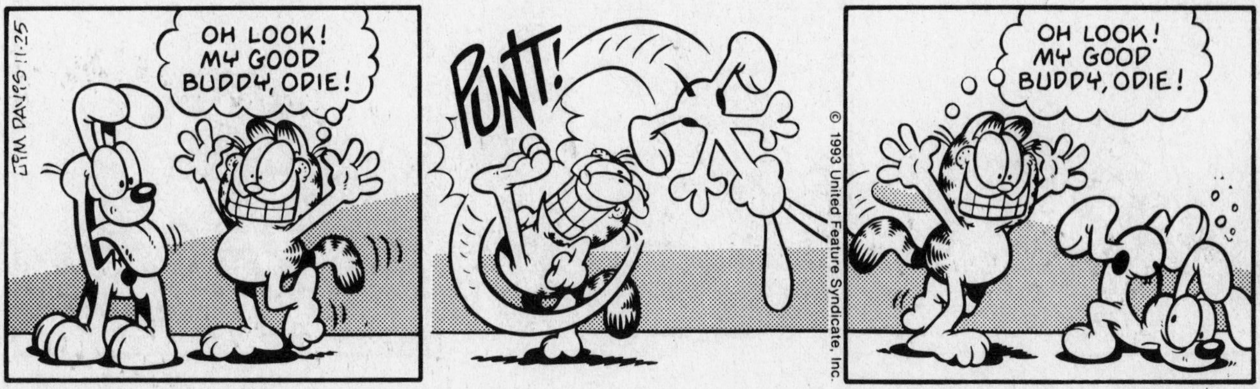
JIM DAVIS 11-25
OH LOOK! MY GOOD BUDDY, ODIE!
PUNT!
© 1993 United Feature Syndicate, Inc.
OH LOOK! MY GOOD BUDDY, ODIE!

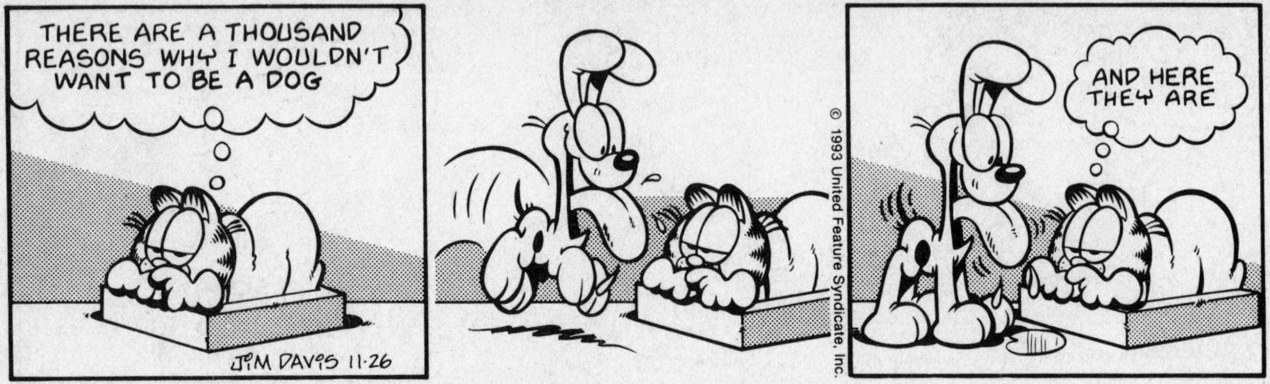
THERE ARE A THOUSAND REASONS WHY I WOULDN'T WANT TO BE A DOG
JIM DAVIS 11-26
AND HERE THEY ARE
© 1993 United Feature Syndicate, Inc.

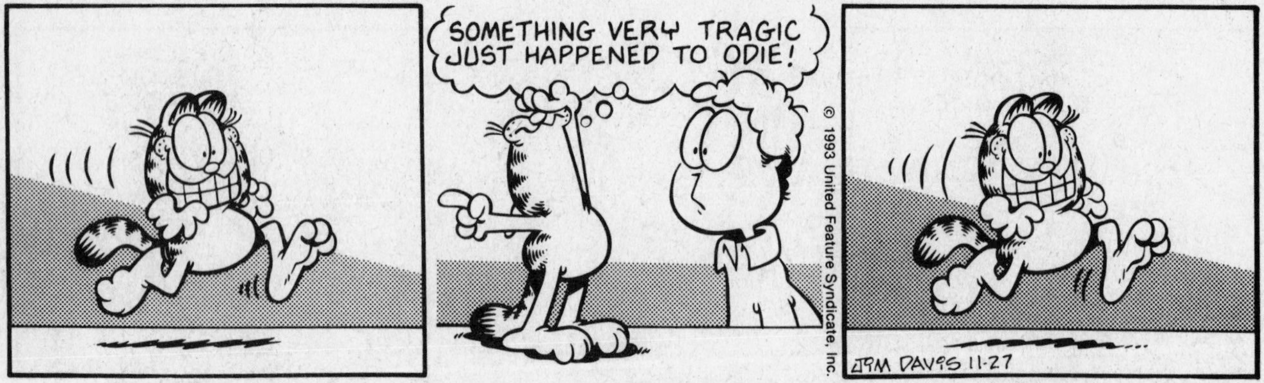
SOMETHING VERY TRAGIC JUST HAPPENED TO ODIE!
© 1993 United Feature Syndicate, Inc.
JIM DAVIS 11-27

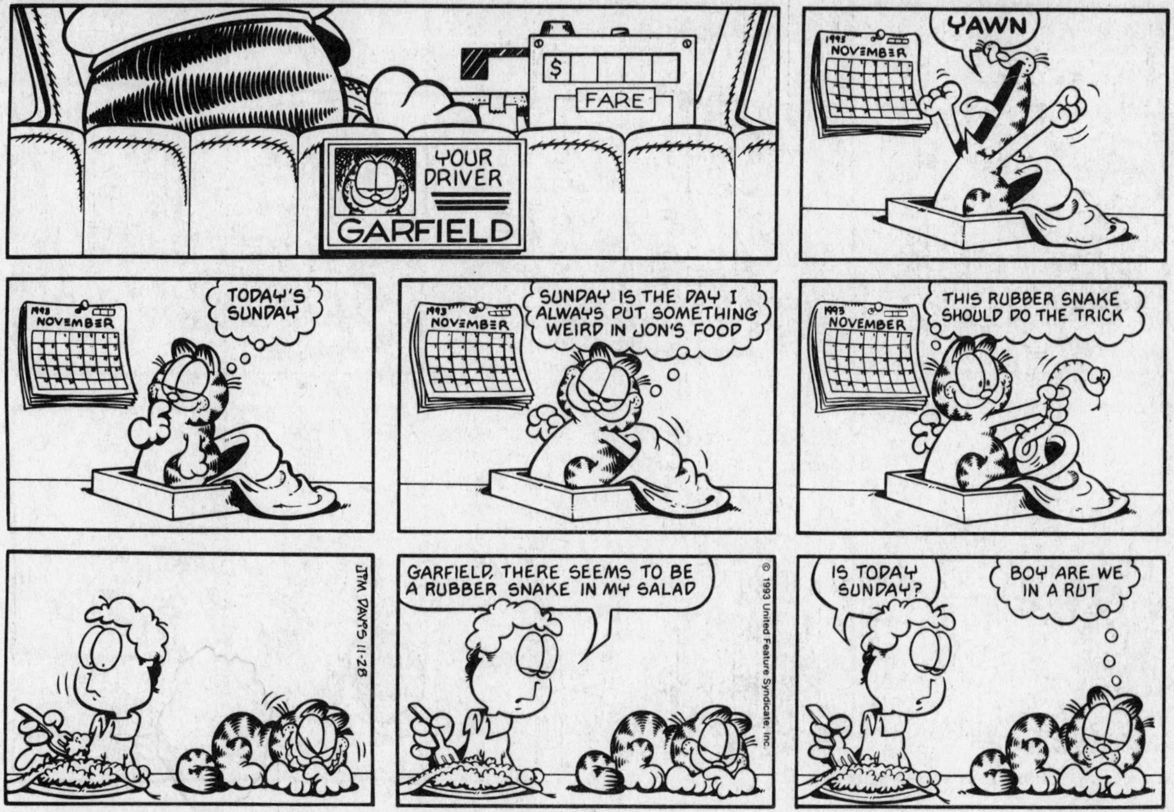
YOUR DRIVER
GARFIELD
$
FARE
YAWN
1993 NOVEMBER
TODAY'S SUNDAY
SUNDAY IS THE DAY I ALWAYS PUT SOMETHING WEIRD IN JON'S FOOD
THIS RUBBER SNAKE SHOULD DO THE TRICK
JIM DAVIS 11-28
GARFIELD, THERE SEEMS TO BE A RUBBER SNAKE IN MY SALAD
© 1993 United Feature Syndicate, Inc.
IS TODAY SUNDAY?
BOY ARE WE IN A RUT

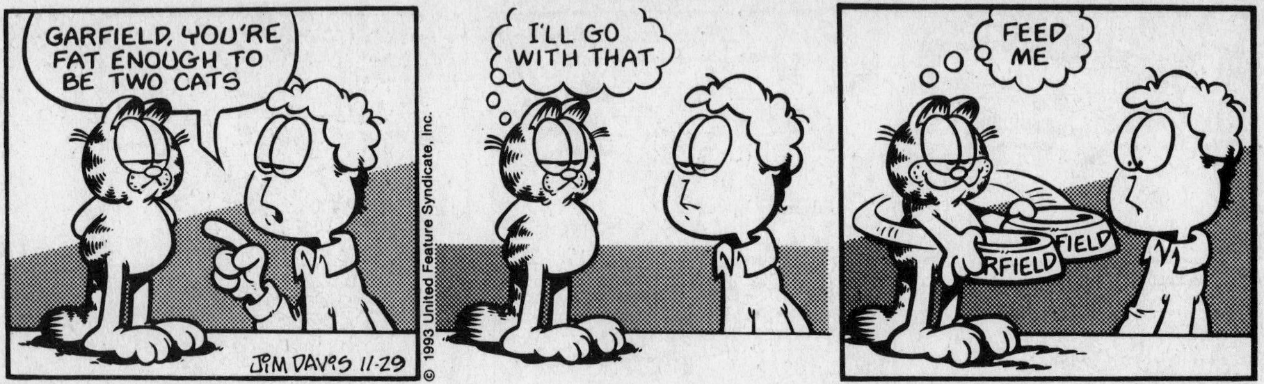
GARFIELD, YOU'RE FAT ENOUGH TO BE TWO CATS
I'LL GO WITH THAT
FEED ME
RFIELD
FIELD
JIM DAVIS 11-29
© 1993 United Feature Syndicate, Inc.

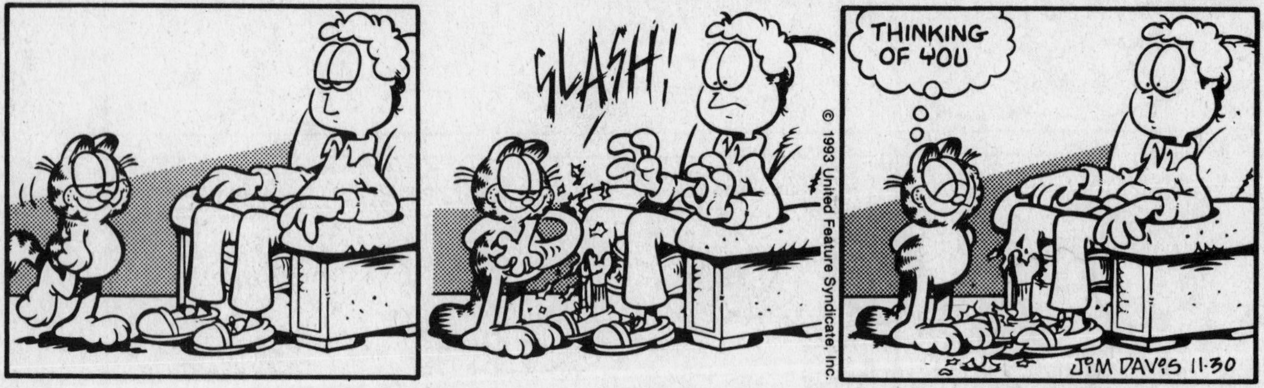
SLASH!
THINKING OF YOU
JIM DAVIS 11-30
© 1993 United Feature Syndicate, Inc.

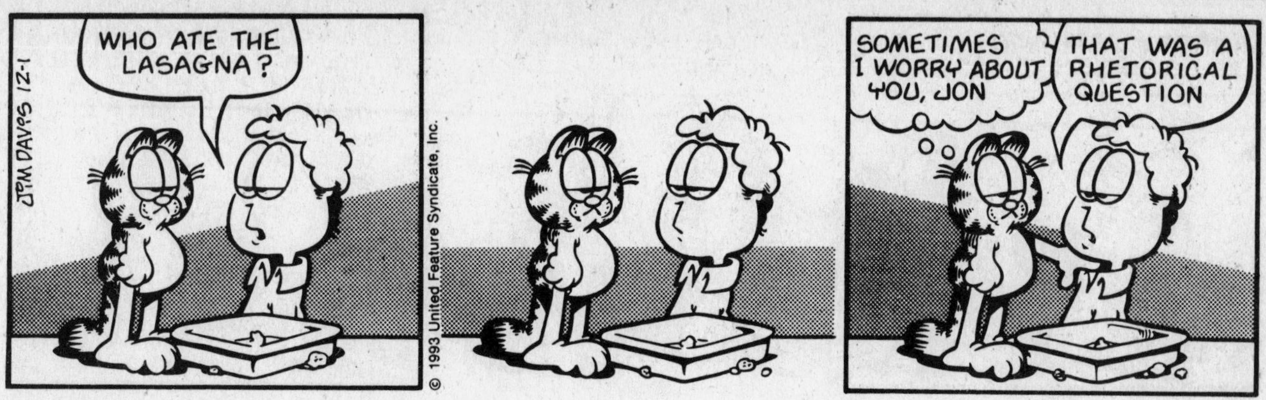
JIM DAVIS 12-1
WHO ATE THE LASAGNA?
© 1993 United Feature Syndicate, Inc.
SOMETIMES I WORRY ABOUT YOU, JON
THAT WAS A RHETORICAL QUESTION

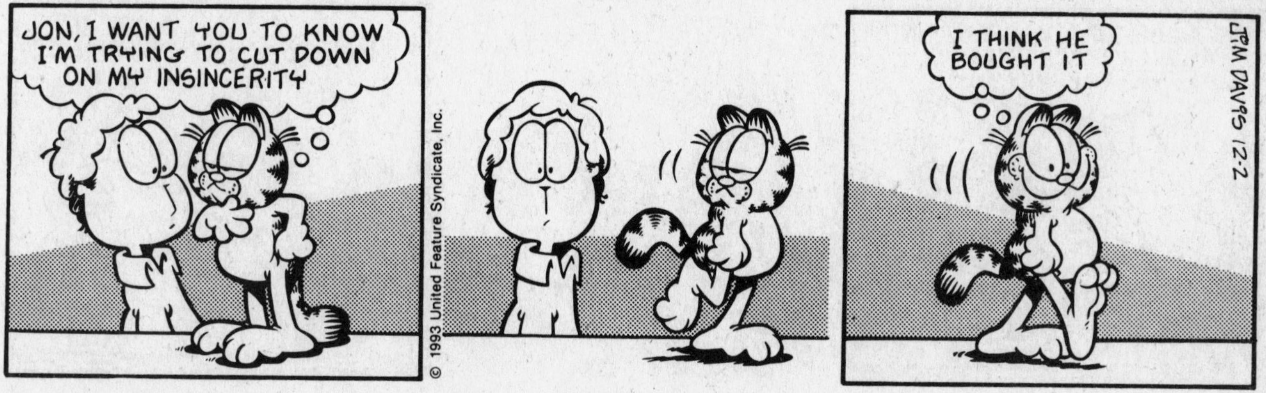
JON, I WANT YOU TO KNOW I'M TRYING TO CUT DOWN ON MY INSINCERITY
© 1993 United Feature Syndicate, Inc.
I THINK HE BOUGHT IT
JIM DAVIS 12-2

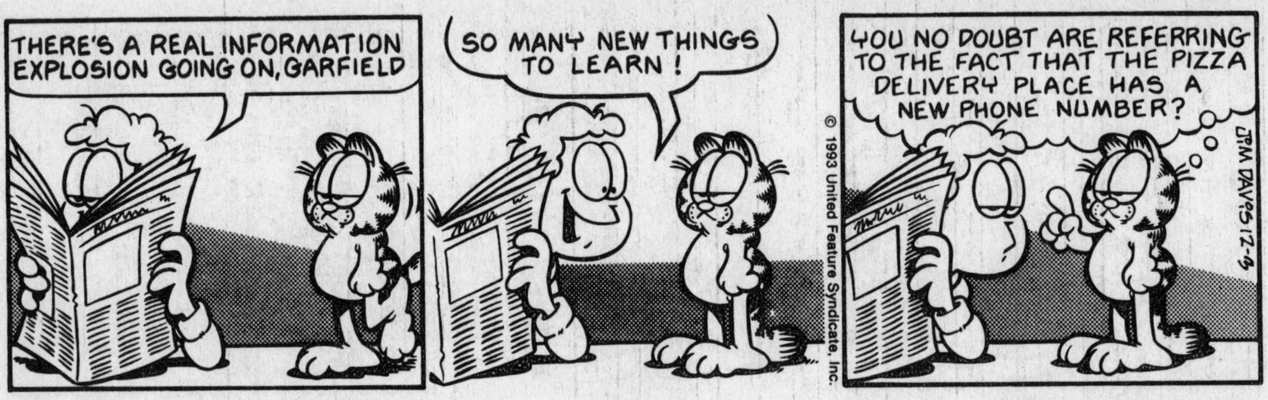
THERE'S A REAL INFORMATION EXPLOSION GOING ON, GARFIELD
SO MANY NEW THINGS TO LEARN!
YOU NO DOUBT ARE REFERRING TO THE FACT THAT THE PIZZA DELIVERY PLACE HAS A NEW PHONE NUMBER?
JIM DAVIS 12-3
© 1993 United Feature Syndicate, Inc.

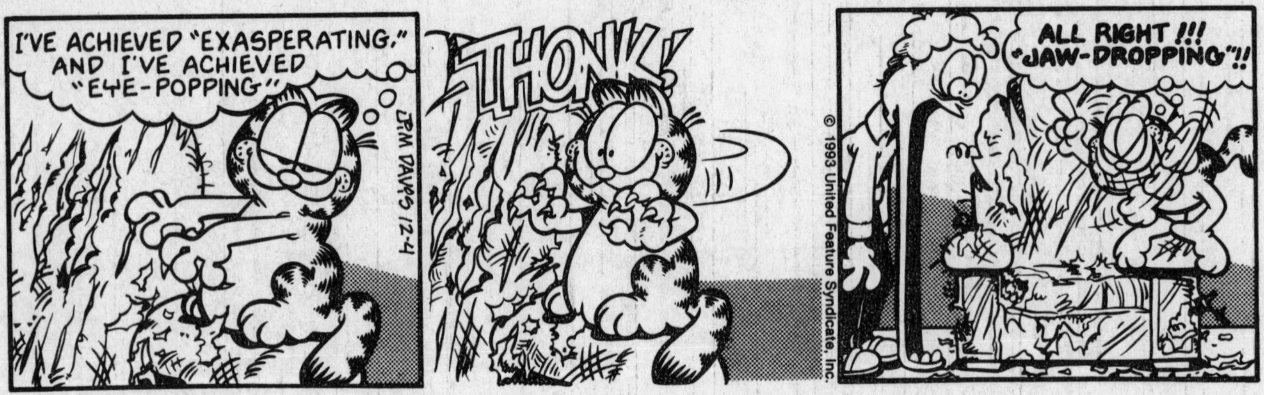
I'VE ACHIEVED "EXASPERATING," AND I'VE ACHIEVED "EYE-POPPING"
JIM DAVIS 12-4
THONK!
ALL RIGHT!!! "JAW-DROPPING"!!
© 1993 United Feature Syndicate, Inc.

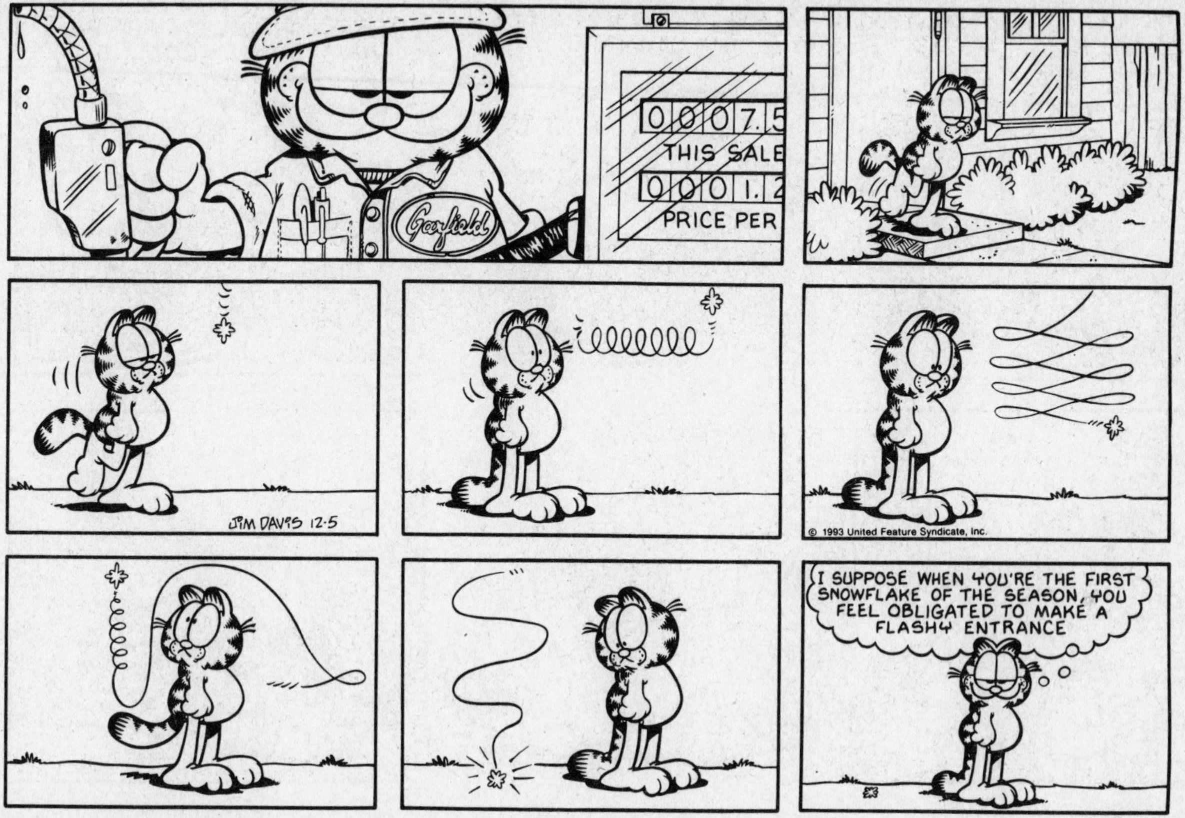
0007.5
THIS SALE
0001.2
PRICE PER
Garfield
JIM DAVIS 12-5
© 1993 United Feature Syndicate, Inc.
I SUPPOSE WHEN YOU'RE THE FIRST SNOWFLAKE OF THE SEASON, YOU FEEL OBLIGATED TO MAKE A FLASHY ENTRANCE

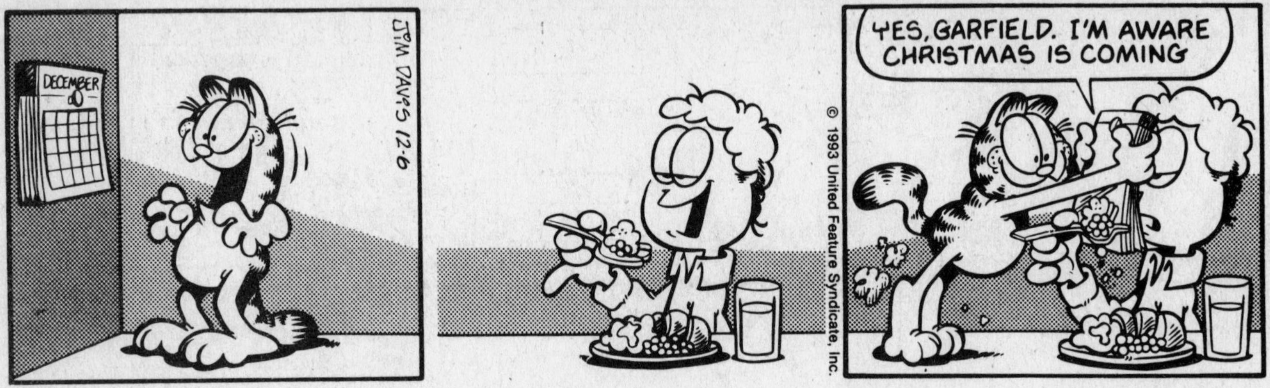
DECEMBER
6
JIM DAVIS 12-6
YES, GARFIELD. I'M AWARE CHRISTMAS IS COMING
© 1993 United Feature Syndicate, Inc.

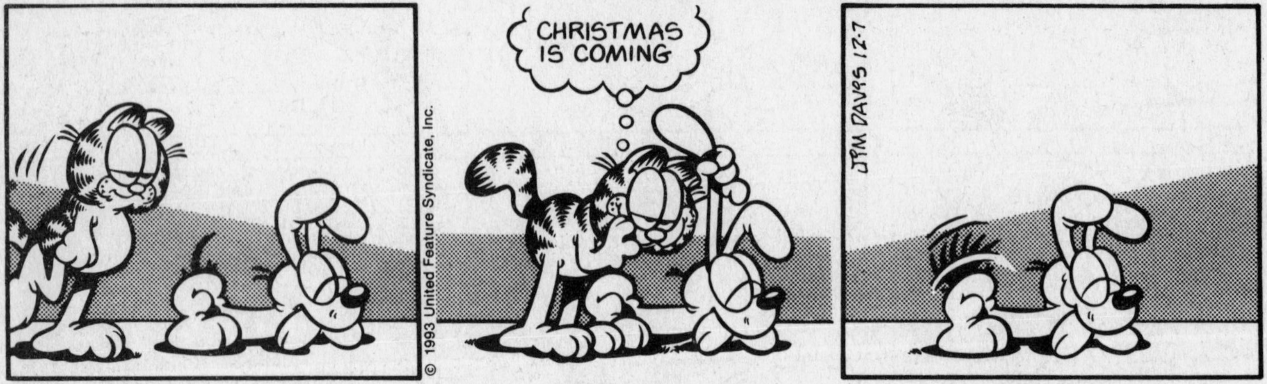
CHRISTMAS IS COMING
JIM DAVIS 12-7
© 1993 United Feature Syndicate, Inc.

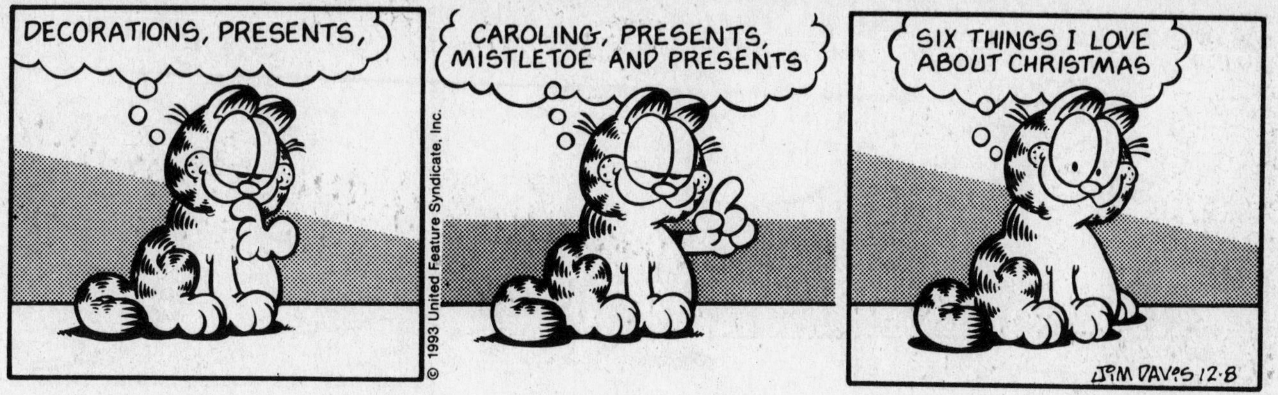
DECORATIONS, PRESENTS,
CAROLING, PRESENTS, MISTLETOE AND PRESENTS
SIX THINGS I LOVE ABOUT CHRISTMAS
© 1993 United Feature Syndicate, Inc.
JIM DAVIS 12·8

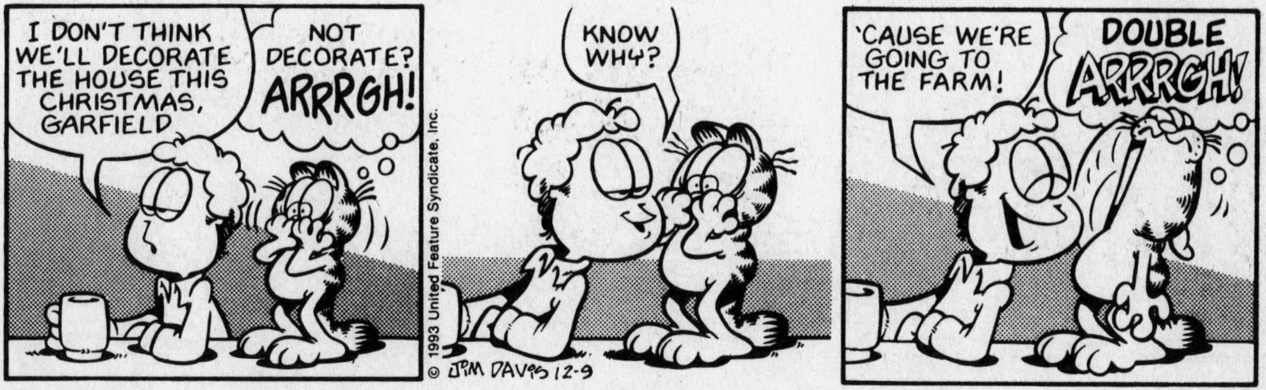
I DON'T THINK WE'LL DECORATE THE HOUSE THIS CHRISTMAS, GARFIELD
NOT DECORATE? ARRRGH!
KNOW WHY?
'CAUSE WE'RE GOING TO THE FARM!
DOUBLE ARRRGH!
© 1993 United Feature Syndicate, Inc.
JIM DAVIS 12-9

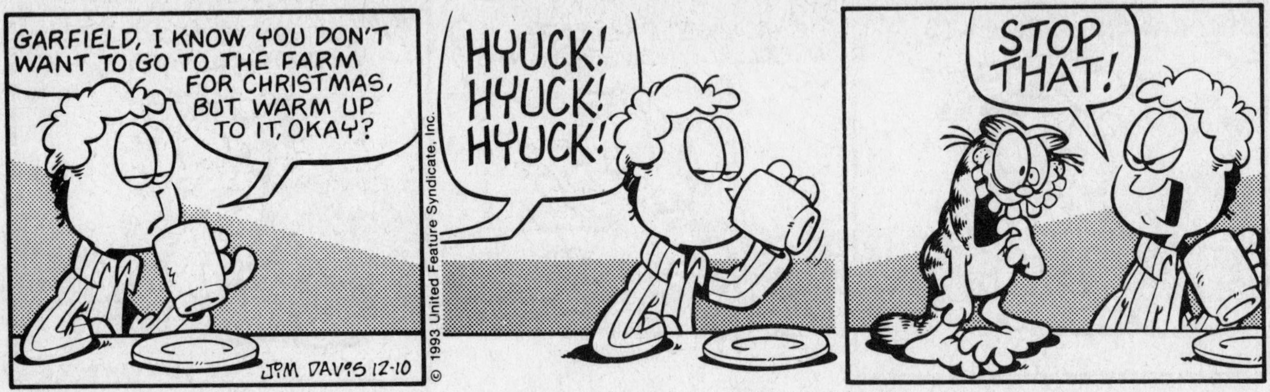
GARFIELD, I KNOW YOU DON'T WANT TO GO TO THE FARM FOR CHRISTMAS, BUT WARM UP TO IT, OKAY?
JIM DAVIS 12-10
HYUCK! HYUCK! HYUCK!
STOP THAT!

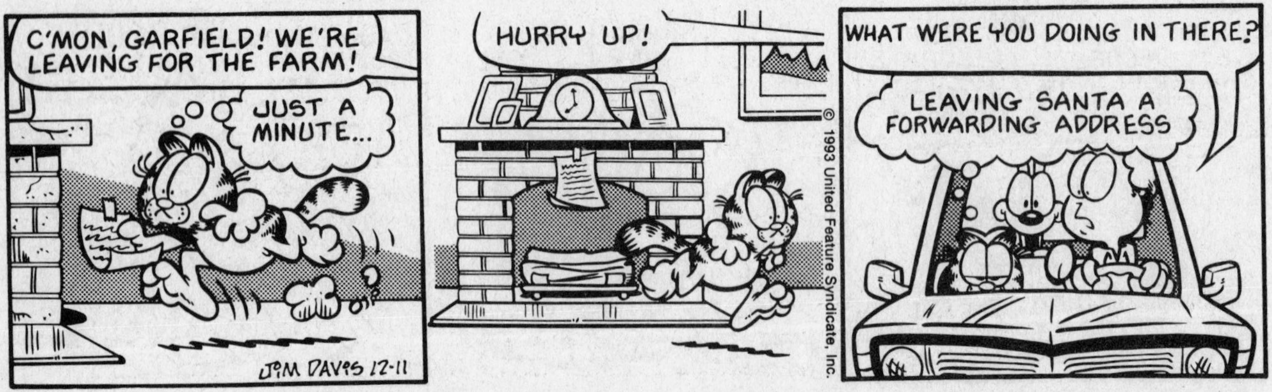
C'MON, GARFIELD! WE'RE LEAVING FOR THE FARM!
JUST A MINUTE...
JIM DAVIS 12-11
HURRY UP!
WHAT WERE YOU DOING IN THERE?
LEAVING SANTA A FORWARDING ADDRESS

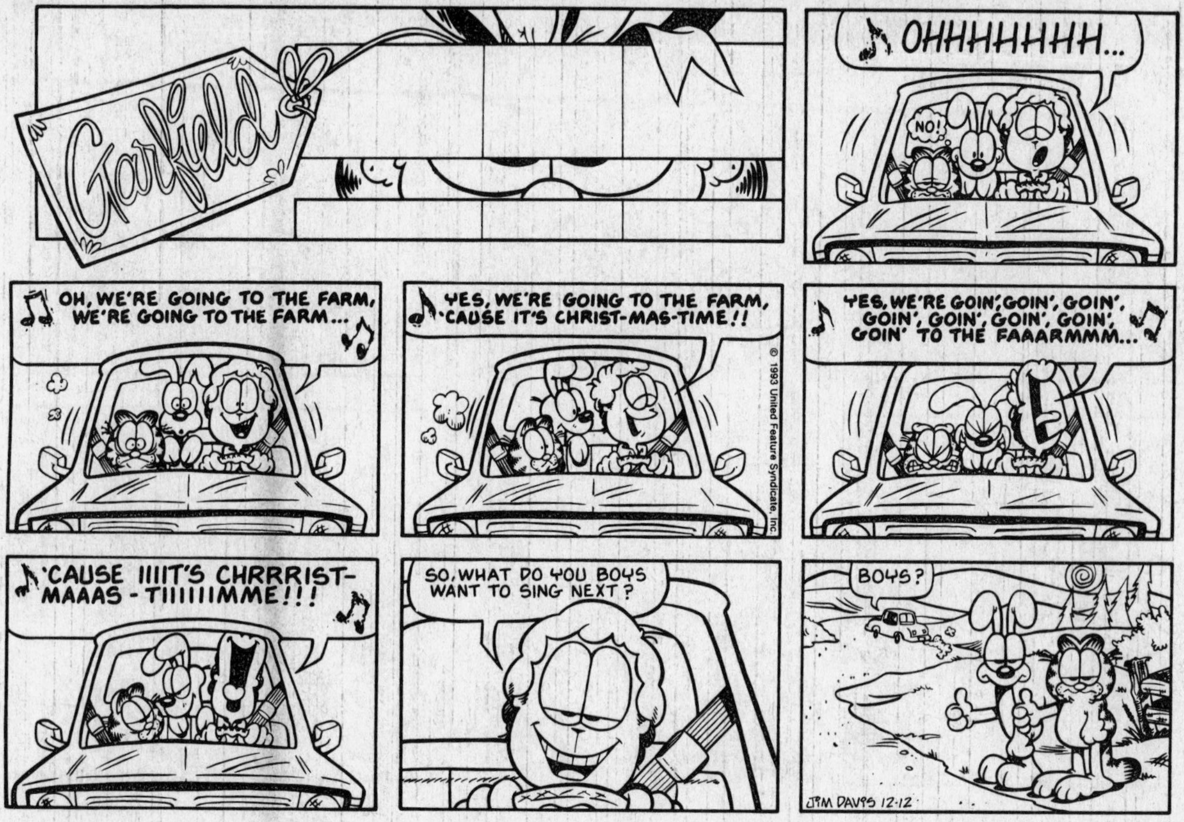
Garfield
NO!
OHHHHHHHH...
OH, WE'RE GOING TO THE FARM, WE'RE GOING TO THE FARM...
YES, WE'RE GOING TO THE FARM, 'CAUSE IT'S CHRIST-MAS-TIME!!
© 1993 United Feature Syndicate, Inc.
YES, WE'RE GOIN', GOIN', GOIN', GOIN', GOIN', GOIN', GOIN', GOIN' TO THE FAAARMMM...
'CAUSE IIIIT'S CHRRRIST-MAAAS - TIIIIIIMME!!!
SO, WHAT DO YOU BOYS WANT TO SING NEXT?
BOYS?
JIM DAVIS 12-12

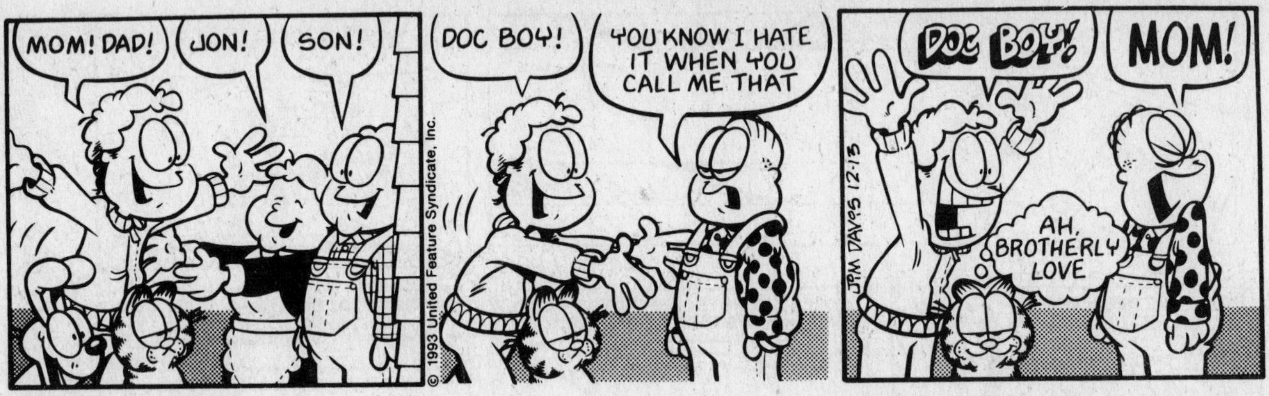
MOM! DAD!
JON!
SON!
DOC BOY!
YOU KNOW I HATE IT WHEN YOU CALL ME THAT
DOC BOY!
MOM!
AH, BROTHERLY LOVE
JPM DAVPS 12-13
© 1993 United Feature Syndicate, Inc.

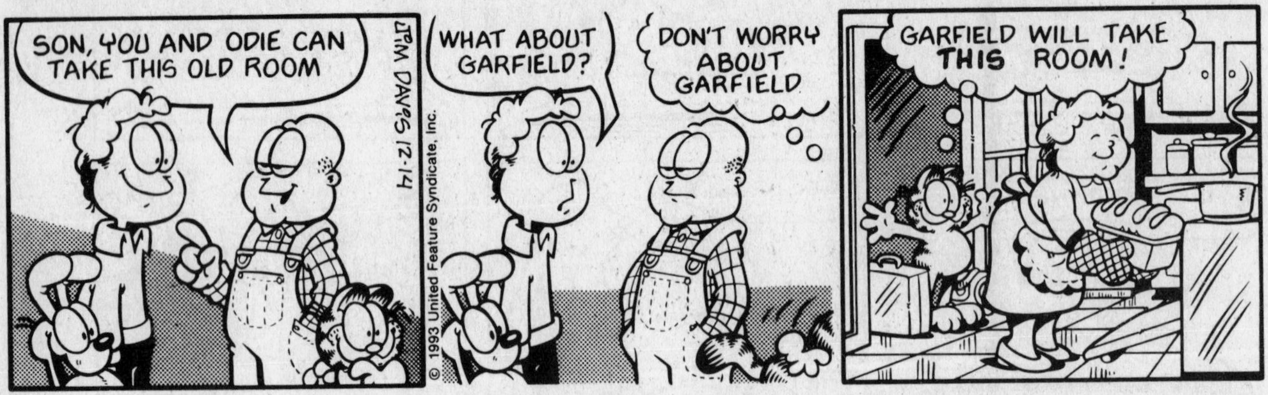
SON, YOU AND ODIE CAN TAKE THIS OLD ROOM
WHAT ABOUT GARFIELD?
DON'T WORRY ABOUT GARFIELD
GARFIELD WILL TAKE **THIS** ROOM!
JPM DAVPS 12-14
© 1993 United Feature Syndicate, Inc.

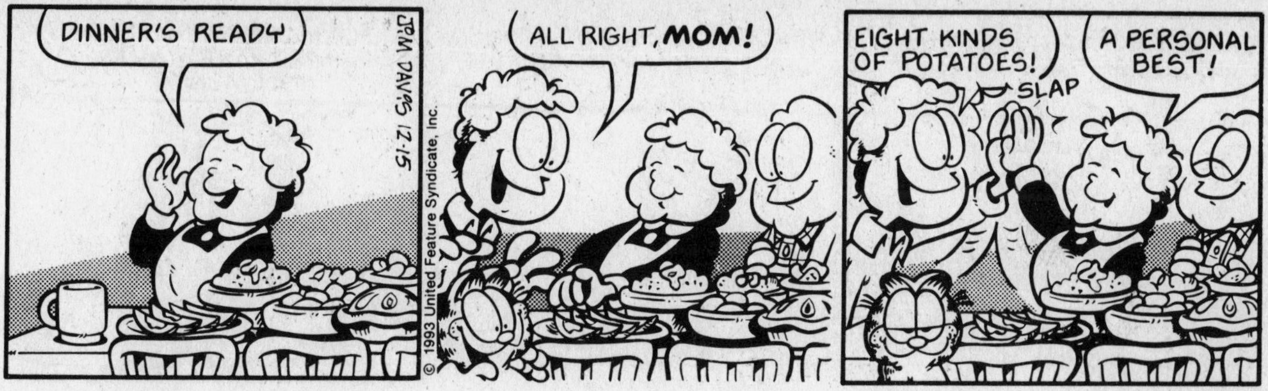
DINNER'S READY
JIM DAVIS 12-15
© 1993 United Feature Syndicate, Inc.
ALL RIGHT, **MOM!**
EIGHT KINDS OF POTATOES!
SLAP
A PERSONAL BEST!

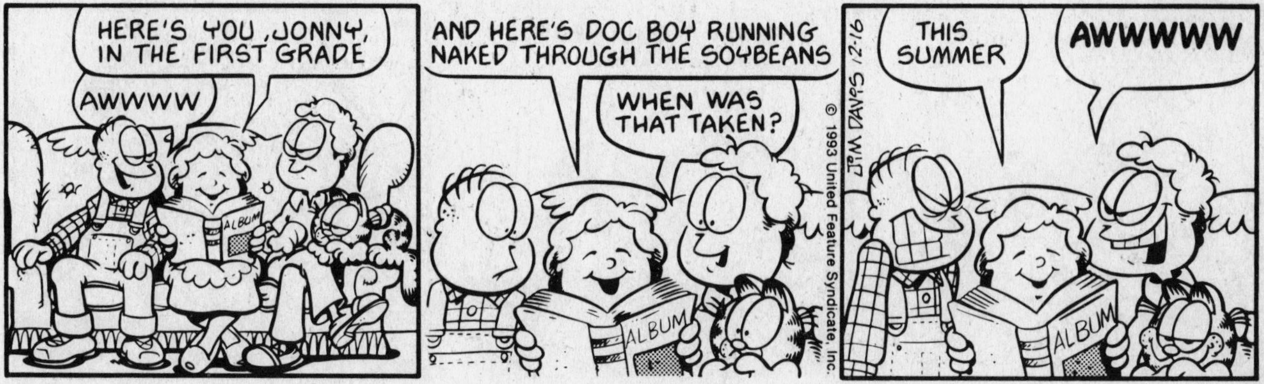
HERE'S YOU, JONNY, IN THE FIRST GRADE
AWWWW
ALBUM
AND HERE'S DOC BOY RUNNING NAKED THROUGH THE SOYBEANS
WHEN WAS THAT TAKEN?
ALBUM
© 1993 United Feature Syndicate, Inc.
JIM DAVIS 12-16
THIS SUMMER
AWWWWW
ALBUM

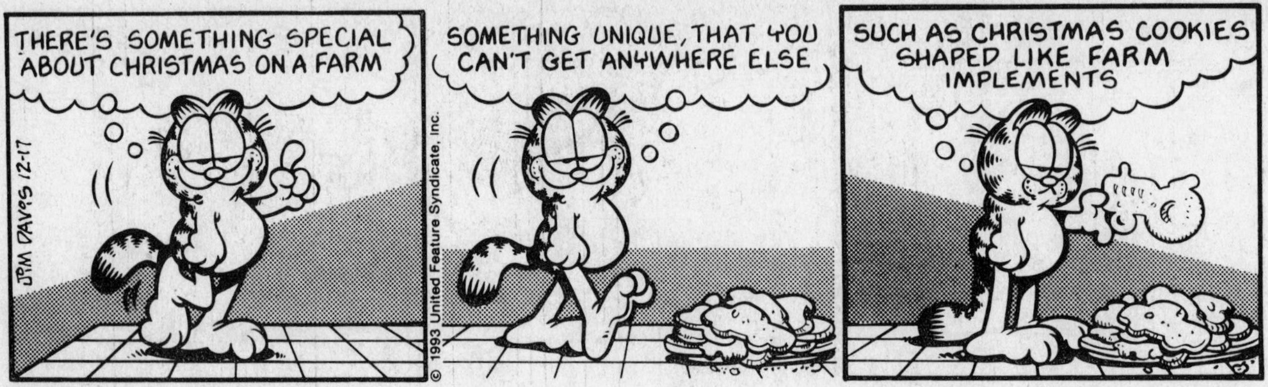
THERE'S SOMETHING SPECIAL ABOUT CHRISTMAS ON A FARM
SOMETHING UNIQUE, THAT YOU CAN'T GET ANYWHERE ELSE
SUCH AS CHRISTMAS COOKIES SHAPED LIKE FARM IMPLEMENTS
JIM DAVIS 12-17
© 1993 United Feature Syndicate, Inc.

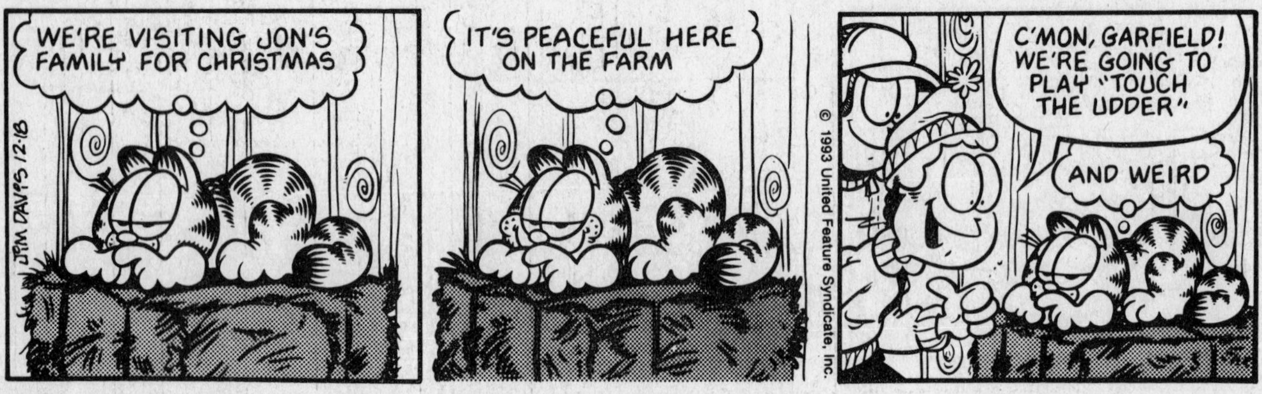
WE'RE VISITING JON'S FAMILY FOR CHRISTMAS
IT'S PEACEFUL HERE ON THE FARM
C'MON, GARFIELD! WE'RE GOING TO PLAY "TOUCH THE UDDER"
AND WEIRD
JIM DAVIS 12-18
© 1993 United Feature Syndicate, Inc.

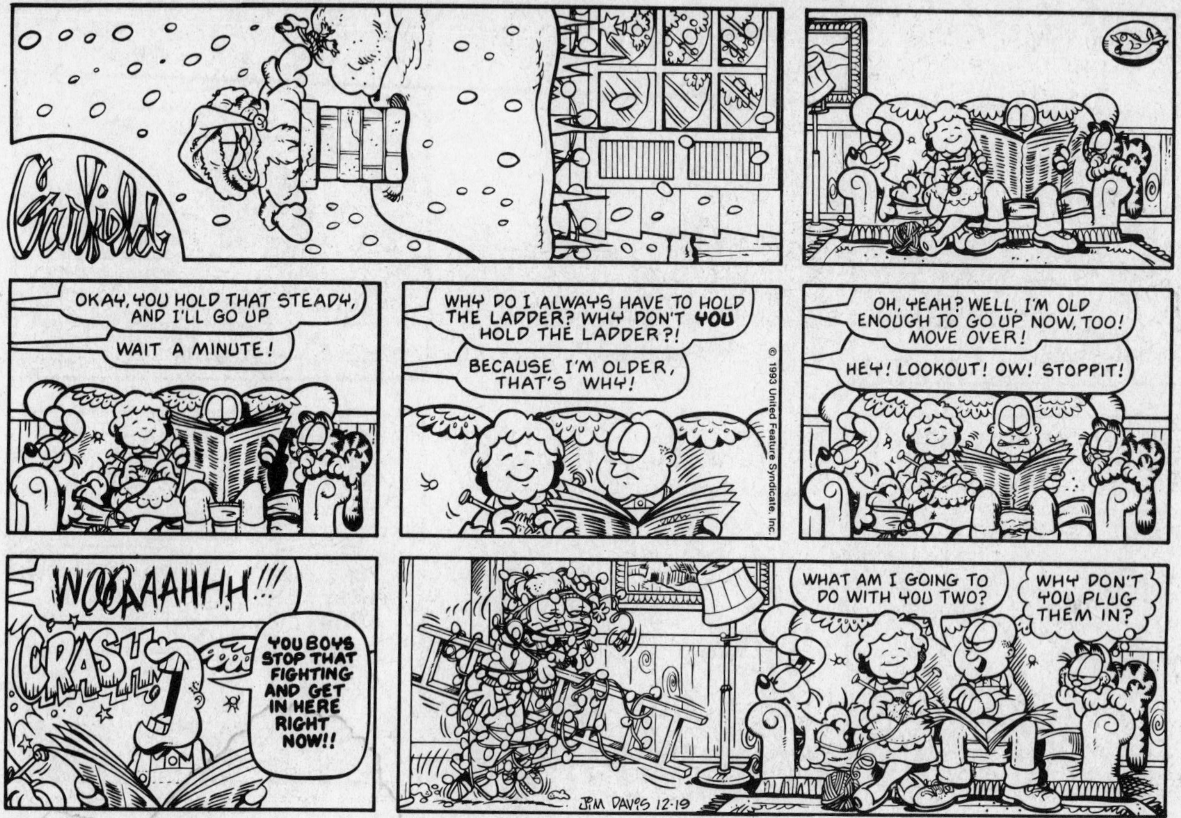

Garfield
OKAY, YOU HOLD THAT STEADY, AND I'LL GO UP
WAIT A MINUTE!
WHY DO I ALWAYS HAVE TO HOLD THE LADDER? WHY DON'T **YOU** HOLD THE LADDER?!
BECAUSE I'M OLDER, THAT'S WHY!
© 1993 United Feature Syndicate, Inc.
OH, YEAH? WELL, I'M OLD ENOUGH TO GO UP NOW, TOO! MOVE OVER!
HEY! LOOKOUT! OW! STOPPIT!
WOOAAAHHH!!!
CRASH
YOU BOYS STOP THAT FIGHTING AND GET IN HERE RIGHT NOW!!
WHAT AM I GOING TO DO WITH YOU TWO?
WHY DON'T YOU PLUG THEM IN?
JIM DAVIS 12-19

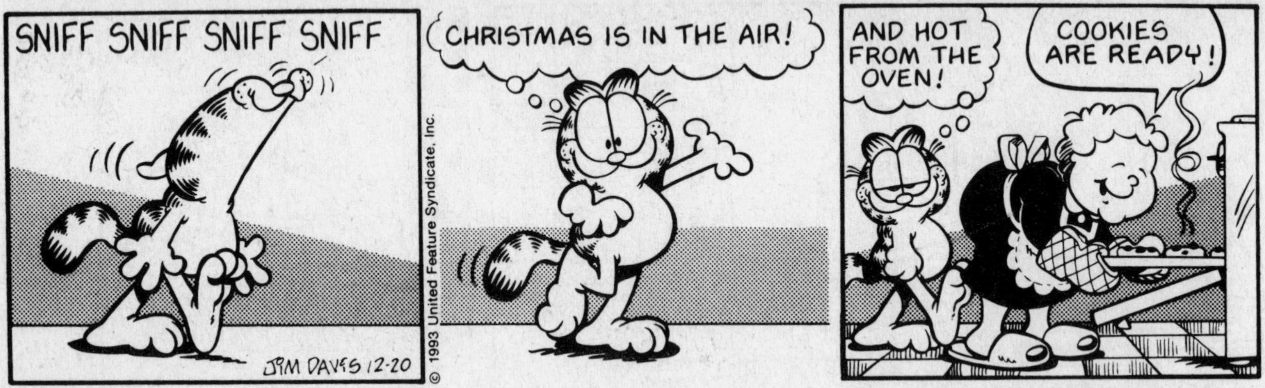
SNIFF SNIFF SNIFF SNIFF
JIM DAVIS 12-20
© 1993 United Feature Syndicate, Inc.
CHRISTMAS IS IN THE AIR!
AND HOT FROM THE OVEN!
COOKIES ARE READY!

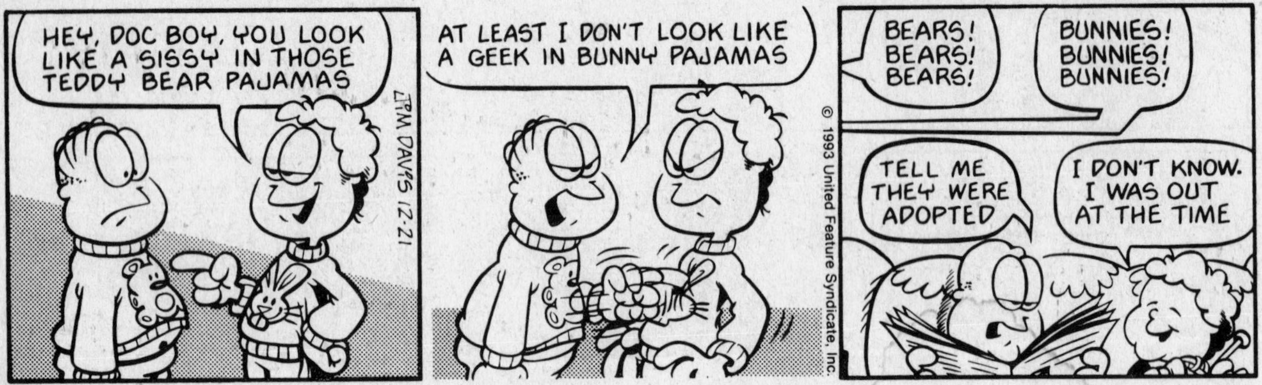
HEY, DOC BOY, YOU LOOK LIKE A SISSY IN THOSE TEDDY BEAR PAJAMAS
JIM DAVIS 12-21
AT LEAST I DON'T LOOK LIKE A GEEK IN BUNNY PAJAMAS
© 1993 United Feature Syndicate, Inc.
BEARS! BEARS! BEARS!
BUNNIES! BUNNIES! BUNNIES!
TELL ME THEY WERE ADOPTED
I DON'T KNOW. I WAS OUT AT THE TIME

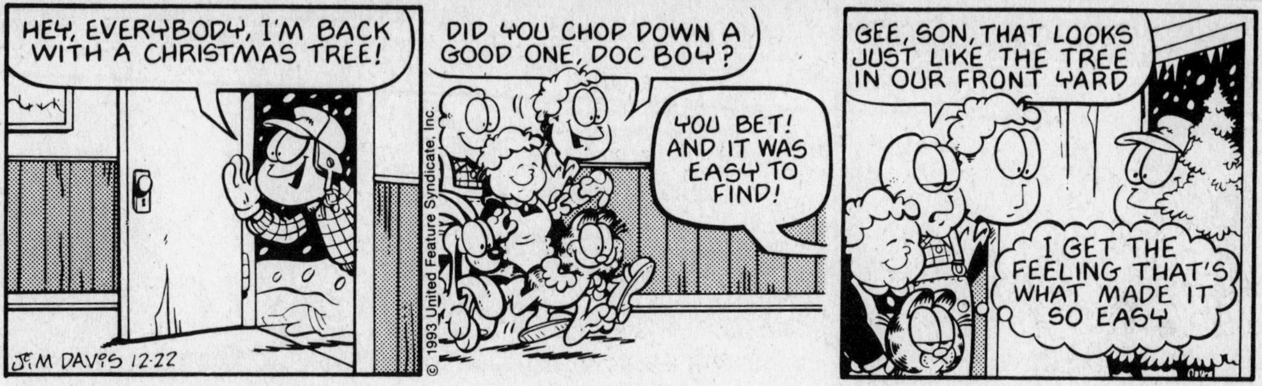
HEY, EVERYBODY, I'M BACK WITH A CHRISTMAS TREE!
JIM DAVIS 12-22
© 1993 United Feature Syndicate, Inc.
DID YOU CHOP DOWN A GOOD ONE, DOC BOY?
YOU BET! AND IT WAS EASY TO FIND!
GEE, SON, THAT LOOKS JUST LIKE THE TREE IN OUR FRONT YARD
I GET THE FEELING THAT'S WHAT MADE IT SO EASY

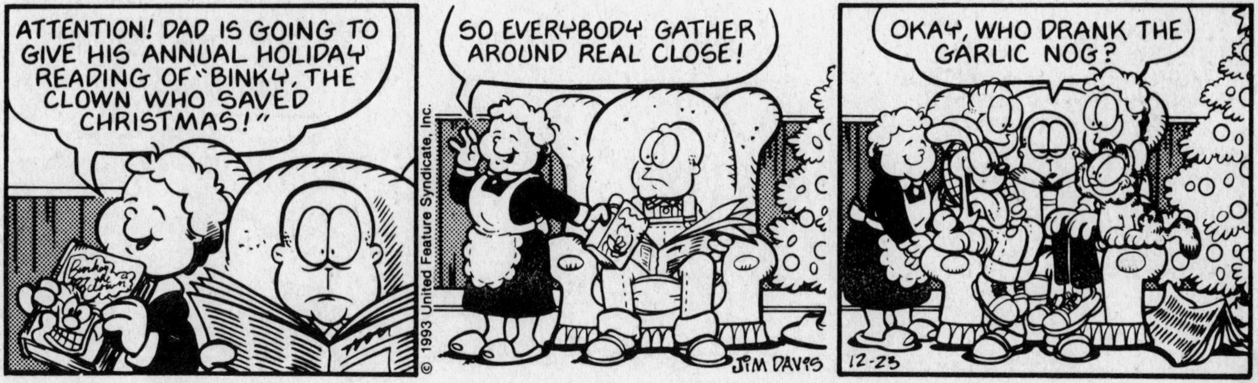
ATTENTION! DAD IS GOING TO GIVE HIS ANNUAL HOLIDAY READING OF "BINKY, THE CLOWN WHO SAVED CHRISTMAS!"
© 1993 United Feature Syndicate, Inc.
SO EVERYBODY GATHER AROUND REAL CLOSE!
JIM DAVIS
OKAY, WHO DRANK THE GARLIC NOG?
12-23

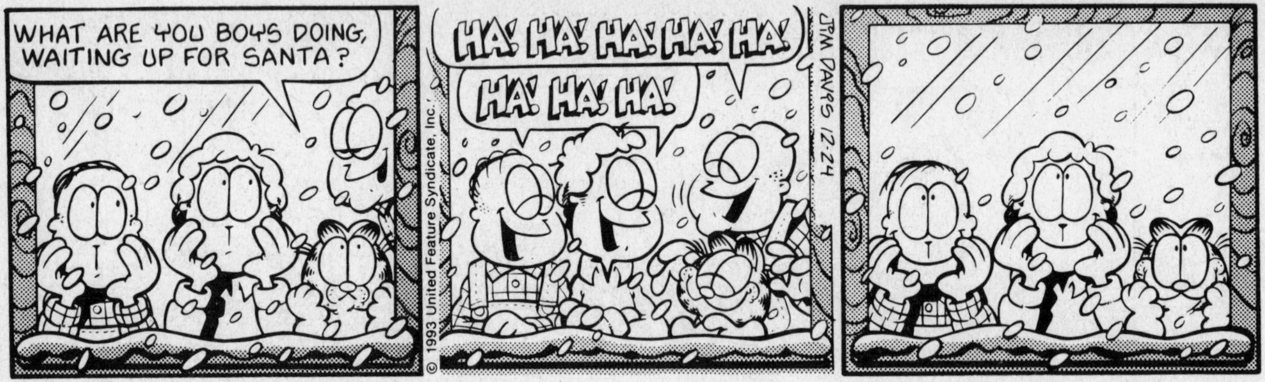
WHAT ARE YOU BOYS DOING, WAITING UP FOR SANTA?
HA! HA! HA! HA! HA!
HA! HA! HA!
© 1993 United Feature Syndicate, Inc.
JIM DAVIS 12-24

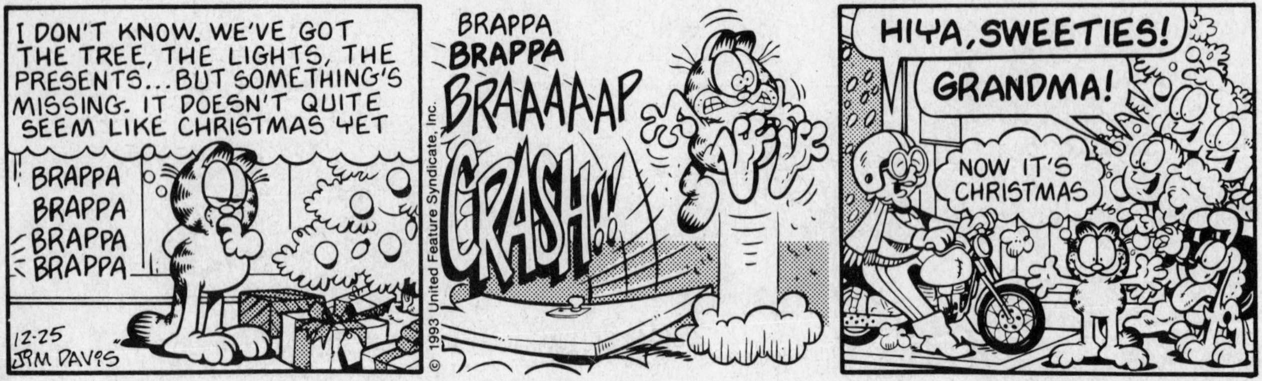
I DON'T KNOW. WE'VE GOT THE TREE, THE LIGHTS, THE PRESENTS... BUT SOMETHING'S MISSING. IT DOESN'T QUITE SEEM LIKE CHRISTMAS YET
BRAPPA BRAPPA BRAPPA BRAPPA
12-25 JIM DAVIS
BRAPPA BRAPPA BRAAAAAP
CRASH!!
© 1993 United Feature Syndicate, Inc.
HIYA, SWEETIES!
GRANDMA!
NOW IT'S CHRISTMAS

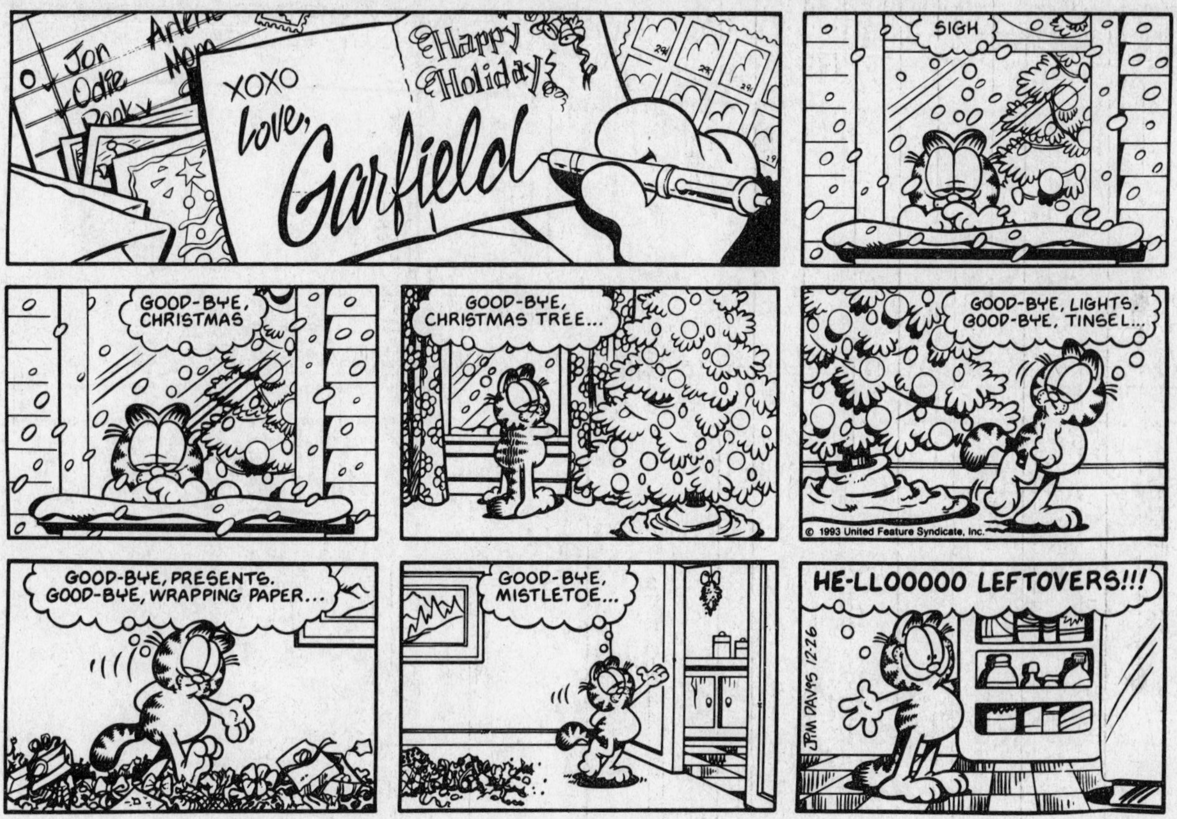
Jon
Odie
Pooky
Arlene
Mom
XOXO
Love,
Garfield
Happy Holidays
SIGH
GOOD-BYE, CHRISTMAS
GOOD-BYE, CHRISTMAS TREE...
GOOD-BYE, LIGHTS. GOOD-BYE, TINSEL...
© 1993 United Feature Syndicate, Inc.
GOOD-BYE, PRESENTS. GOOD-BYE, WRAPPING PAPER...
GOOD-BYE, MISTLETOE...
HE-LLOOOOO LEFTOVERS!!!
JPM DAVIS 12-26

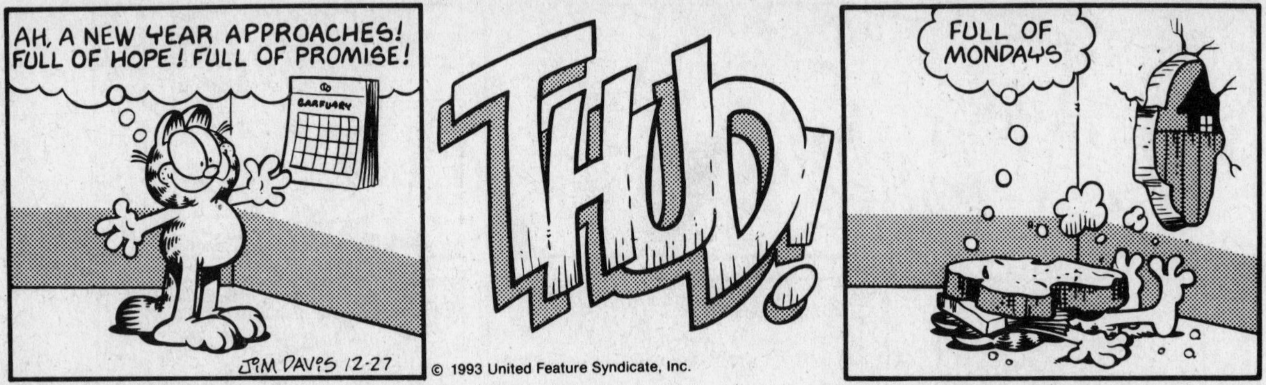
AH, A NEW YEAR APPROACHES! FULL OF HOPE! FULL OF PROMISE!
GARFUARY
THUD!
FULL OF MONDAYS
JIM DAVIS 12-27
© 1993 United Feature Syndicate, Inc.

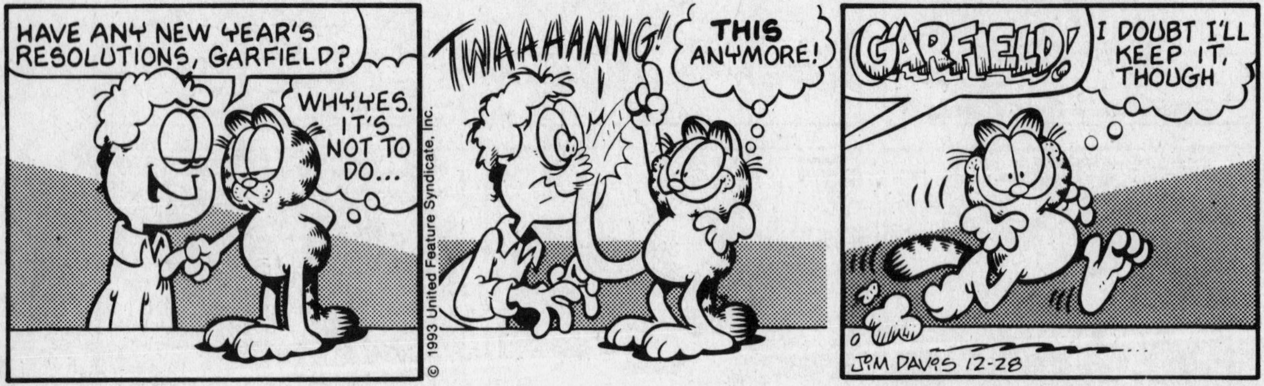
HAVE ANY NEW YEAR'S RESOLUTIONS, GARFIELD?
WHY, YES. IT'S NOT TO DO...
TWAAAANNG!
THIS ANYMORE!
GARFIELD!
I DOUBT I'LL KEEP IT, THOUGH
JIM DAVIS 12-28
© 1993 United Feature Syndicate, Inc.

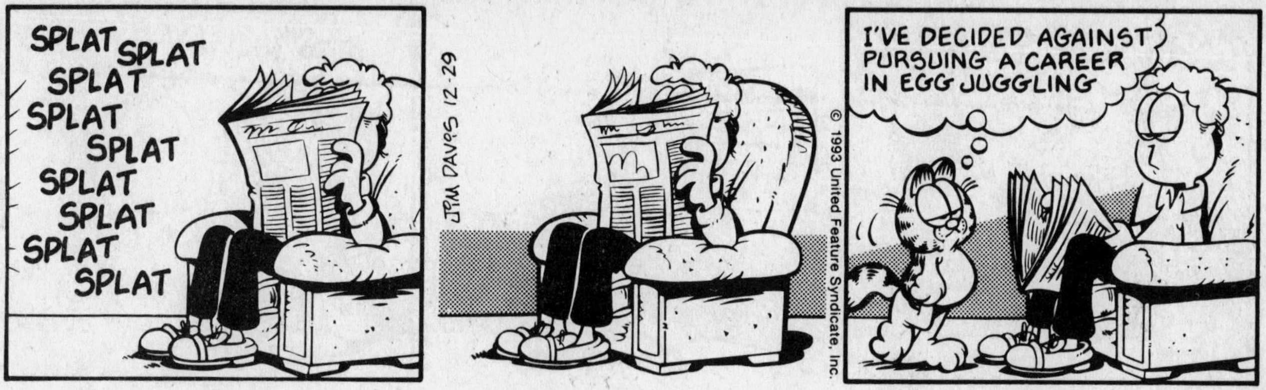
SPLAT SPLAT SPLAT SPLAT SPLAT SPLAT SPLAT SPLAT SPLAT
JIM DAVIS 12-29
I'VE DECIDED AGAINST PURSUING A CAREER IN EGG JUGGLING
© 1993 United Feature Syndicate, Inc.

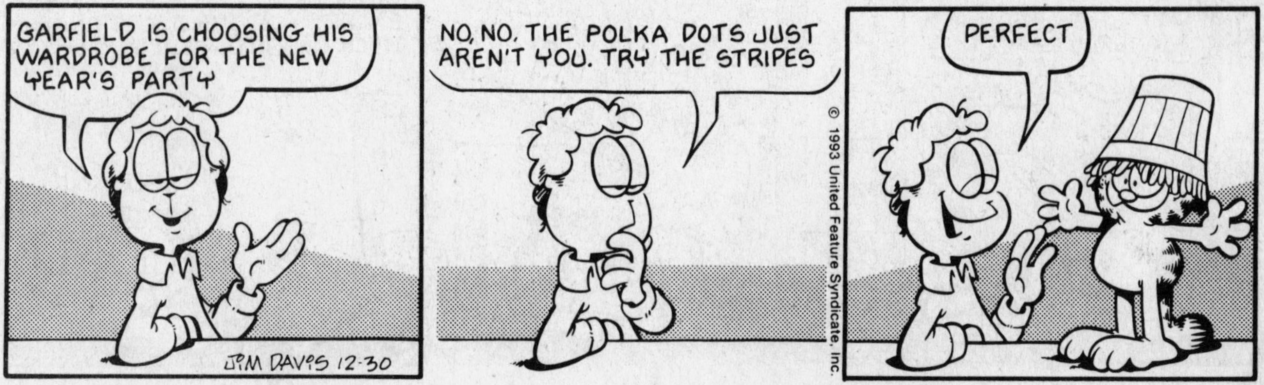
GARFIELD IS CHOOSING HIS WARDROBE FOR THE NEW YEAR'S PARTY
JIM DAVIS 12-30
NO, NO. THE POLKA DOTS JUST AREN'T YOU. TRY THE STRIPES
© 1993 United Feature Syndicate, Inc.
PERFECT

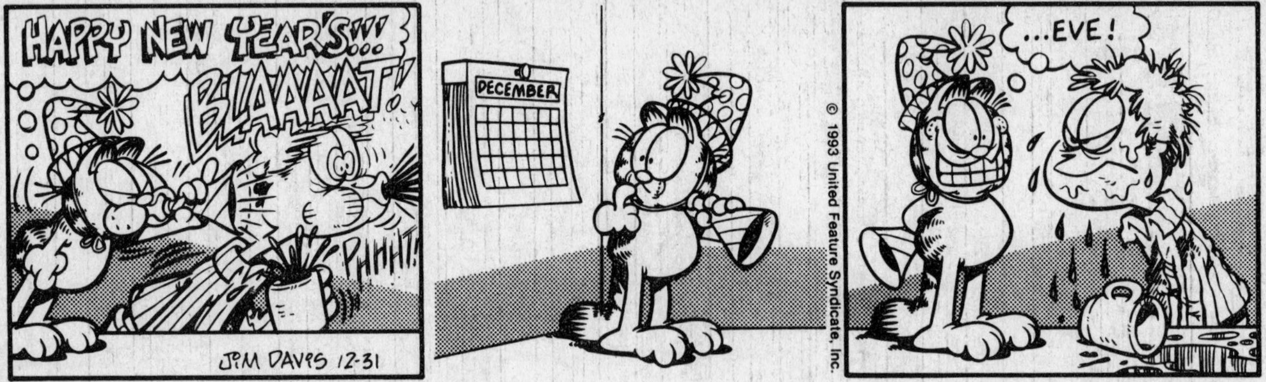
HAPPY NEW YEAR'S!!!...
BLAAAAT!
PHHHT!
JIM DAVIS 12-31
DECEMBER
...EVE!
© 1993 United Feature Syndicate, Inc.

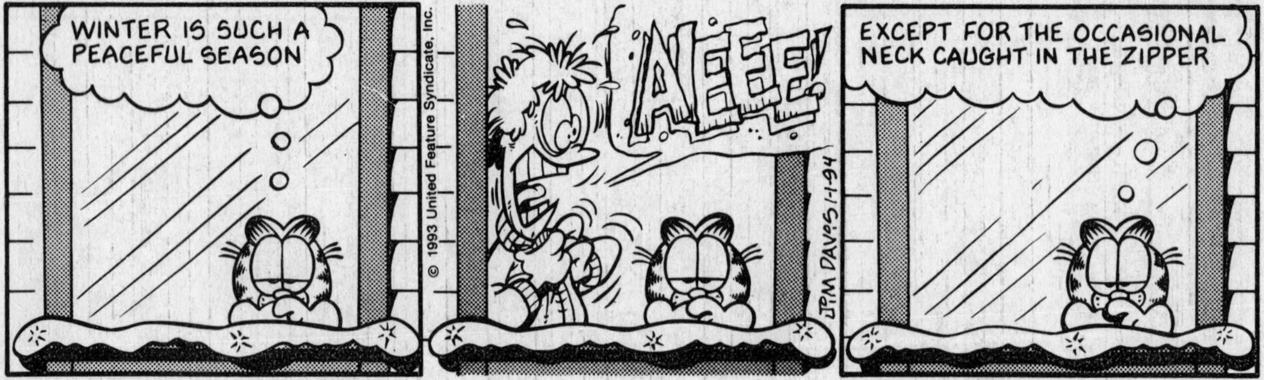
WINTER IS SUCH A
PEACEFUL SEASON
© 1993 United Feature Syndicate, Inc.
AEEEE!
JIM DAVIS 1-1-94
EXCEPT FOR THE OCCASIONAL
NECK CAUGHT IN THE ZIPPER

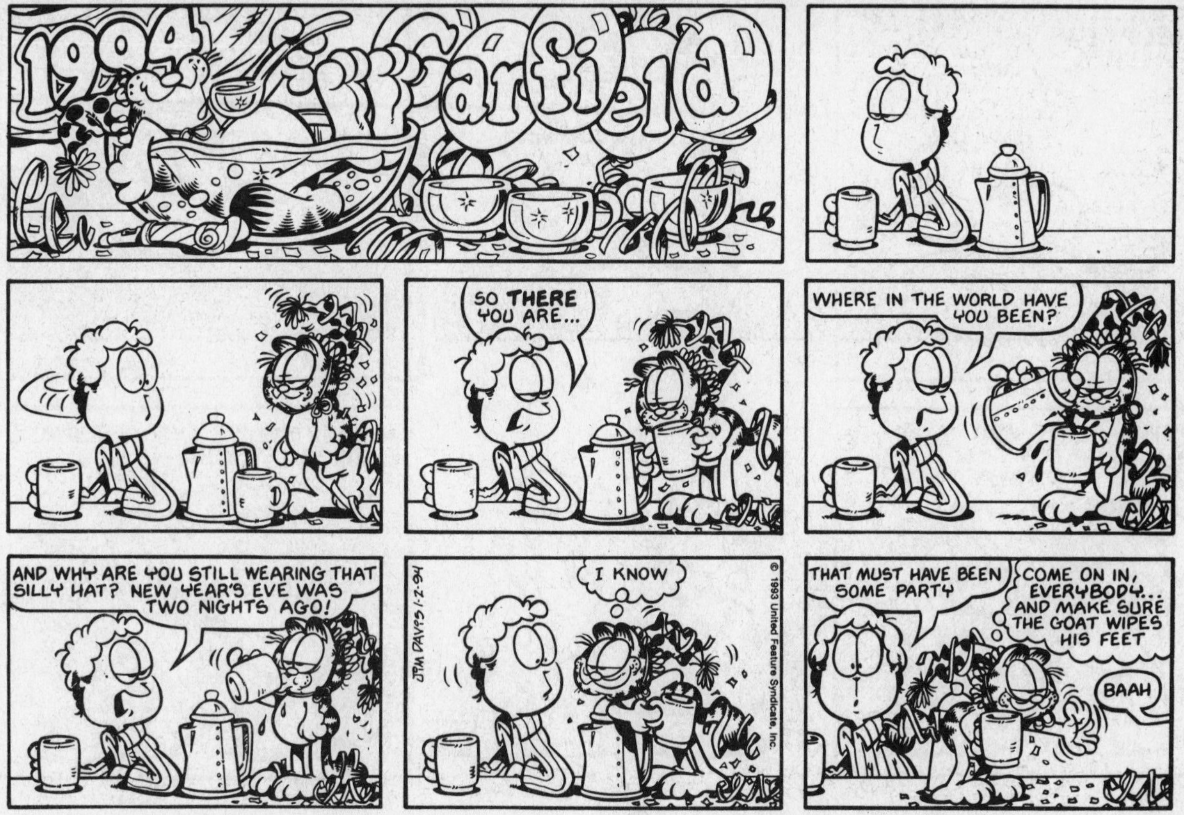
1994
Garfield
SO THERE YOU ARE...
WHERE IN THE WORLD HAVE YOU BEEN?
AND WHY ARE YOU STILL WEARING THAT SILLY HAT? NEW YEAR'S EVE WAS TWO NIGHTS AGO!
JPM DAVIS 1-2-94
I KNOW
© 1993 United Feature Syndicate, Inc.
THAT MUST HAVE BEEN SOME PARTY
COME ON IN, EVERYBODY... AND MAKE SURE THE GOAT WIPES HIS FEET
BAAH

HELP! I'M FALLING!
JUST KIDDING
IT'S AN OVERHEAD SHOT
JPM DAVPS 1-3-94
© 1993 United Feature Syndicate, Inc.

ODIE, HOW CAN YOU BE SO STUPID?
JPM DAVPS 1-4-94
© 1993 United Feature Syndicate, Inc.
WELL, IF YOU'VE GOT A PERMIT, I GUESS IT'S OKAY

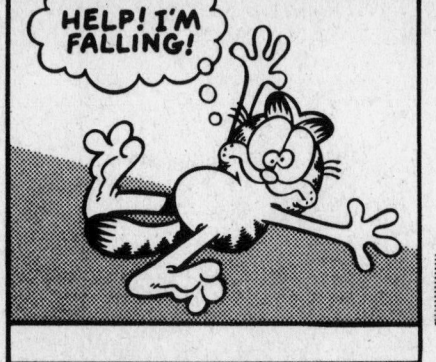

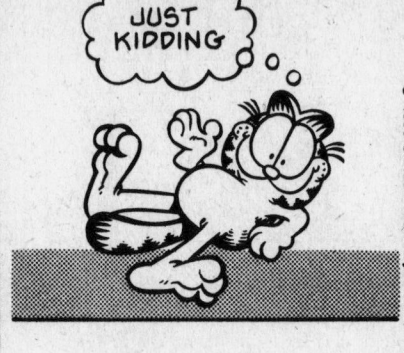

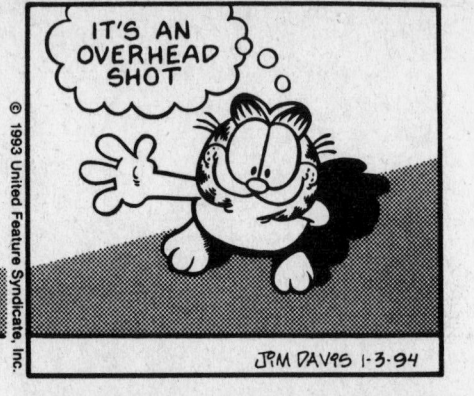

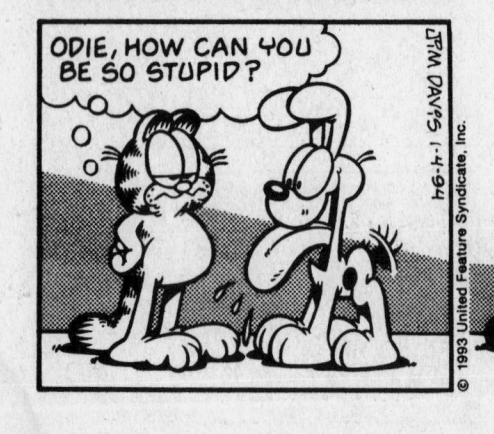

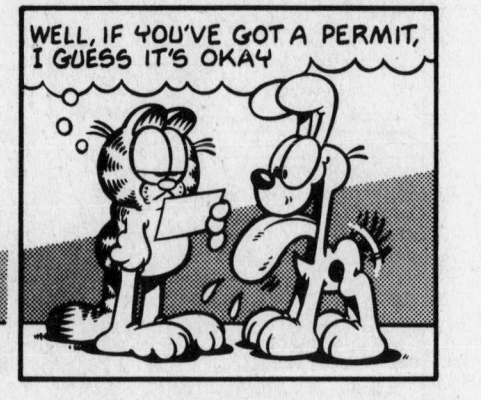

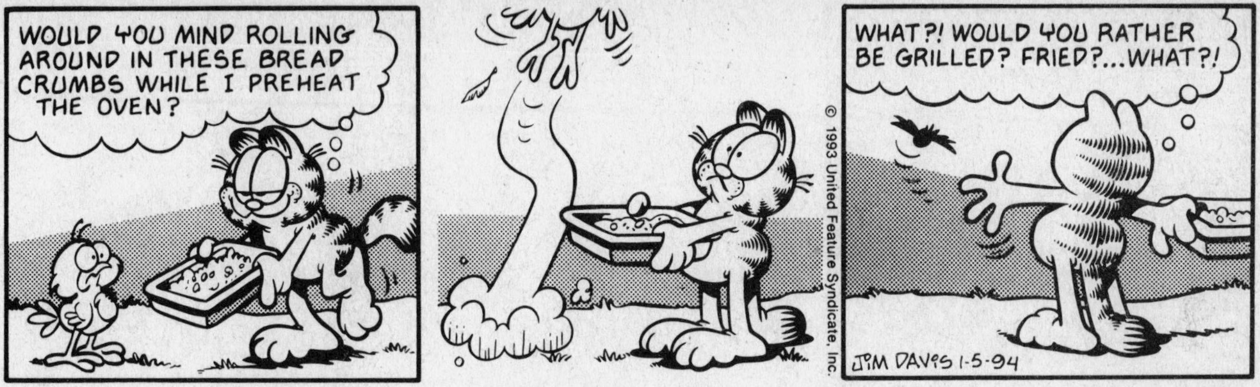
WOULD YOU MIND ROLLING AROUND IN THESE BREAD CRUMBS WHILE I PREHEAT THE OVEN?
WHAT?! WOULD YOU RATHER BE GRILLED? FRIED?...WHAT?!
© 1993 United Feature Syndicate, Inc.
JIM DAVIS 1-5-94

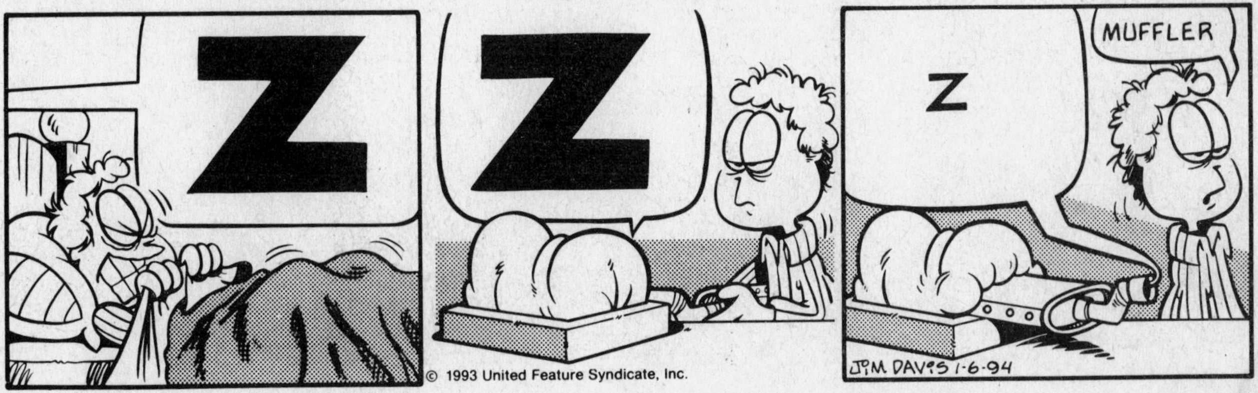
Z
Z
Z
MUFFLER
© 1993 United Feature Syndicate, Inc.
JIM DAVIS 1-6-94

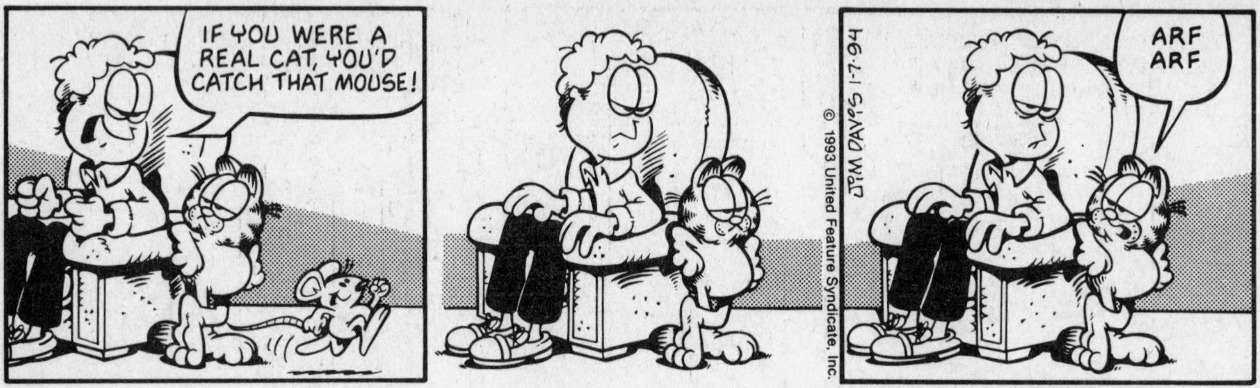
IF YOU WERE A REAL CAT, YOU'D CATCH THAT MOUSE!
ARF ARF
JIM DAVIS 1-7-94

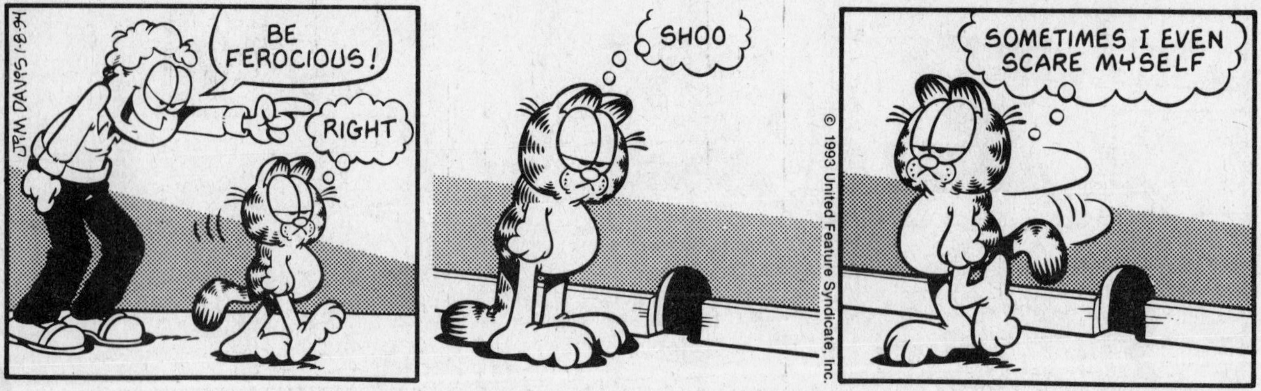
JIM DAVIS 1-8-94
BE FEROCIOUS!
RIGHT
SHOO
SOMETIMES I EVEN SCARE MYSELF

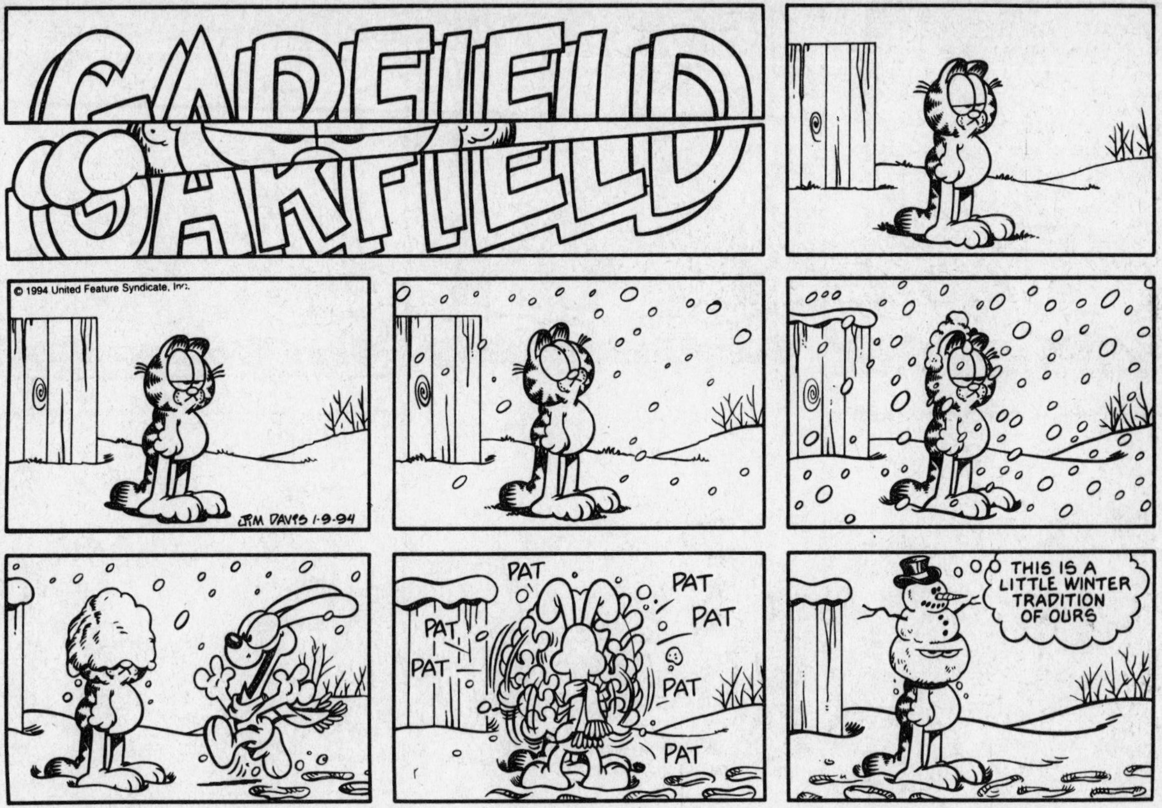
GARFIELD
© 1994 United Feature Syndicate, Inc.
JIM DAVIS 1-9-94
PAT
PAT
PAT
PAT
PAT
PAT
PAT
THIS IS A LITTLE WINTER TRADITION OF OURS

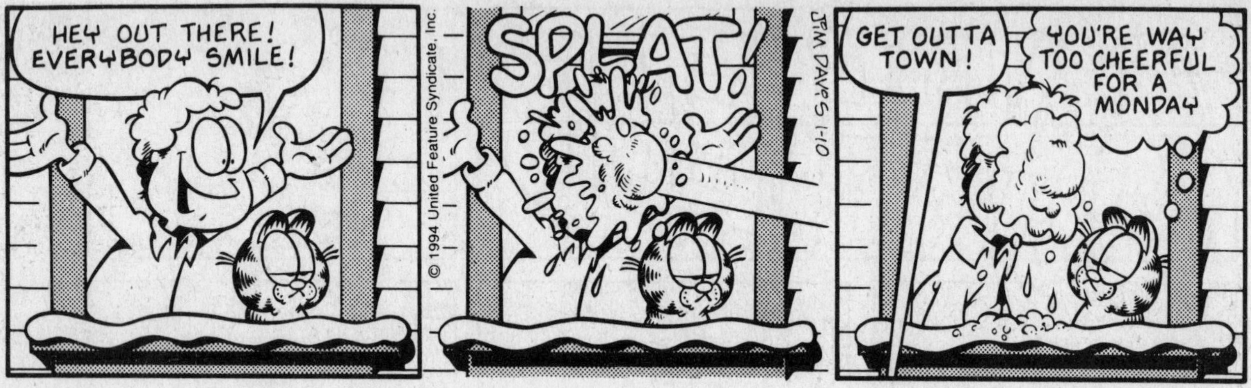

HEY OUT THERE! EVERYBODY SMILE!
© 1994 United Feature Syndicate, Inc.
SPLAT!
JIM DAVIS 1-10
GET OUTTA TOWN!
YOU'RE WAY TOO CHEERFUL FOR A MONDAY

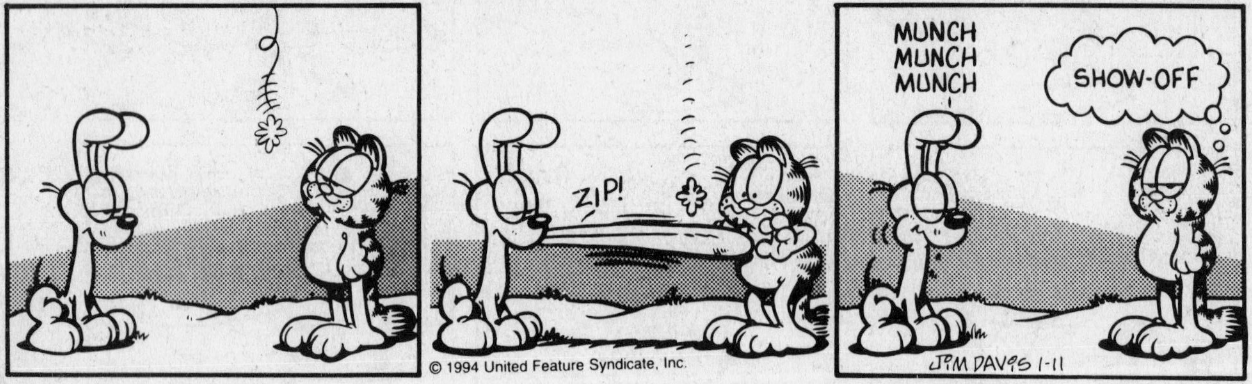

ZIP!
© 1994 United Feature Syndicate, Inc.
MUNCH MUNCH MUNCH
SHOW-OFF
JIM DAVIS 1-11

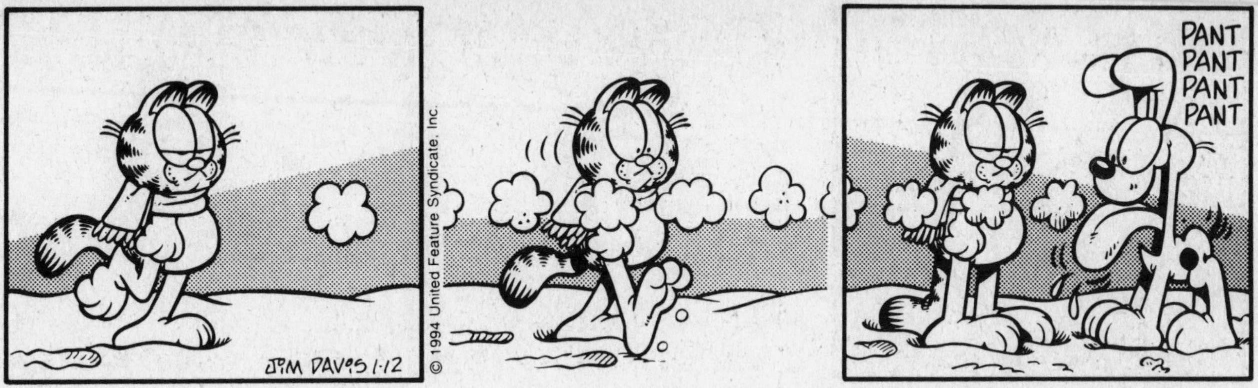
JIM DAVIS 1-12
© 1994 United Feature Syndicate, Inc.
PANT
PANT
PANT
PANT

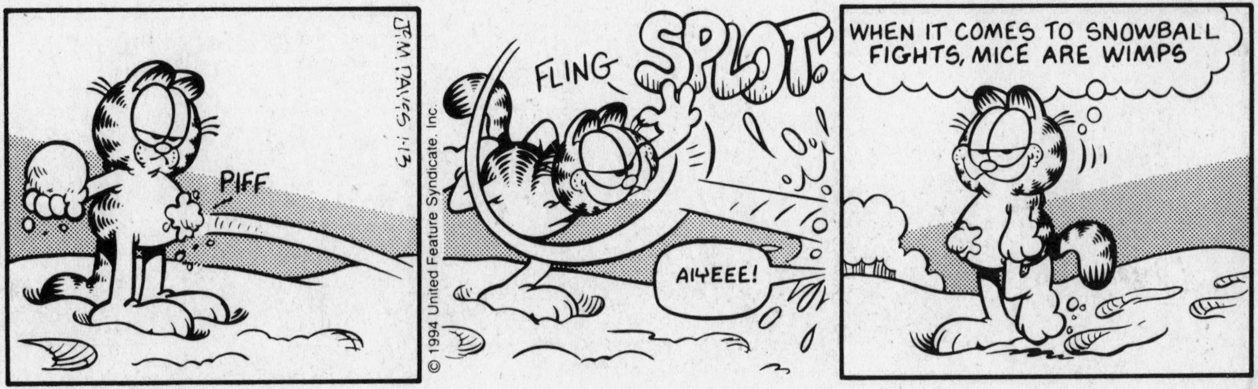
JIM DAVIS 1-13
PIFF
© 1994 United Feature Syndicate, Inc.
FLING
SPLOT!
AIYEEE!
WHEN IT COMES TO SNOWBALL FIGHTS, MICE ARE WIMPS

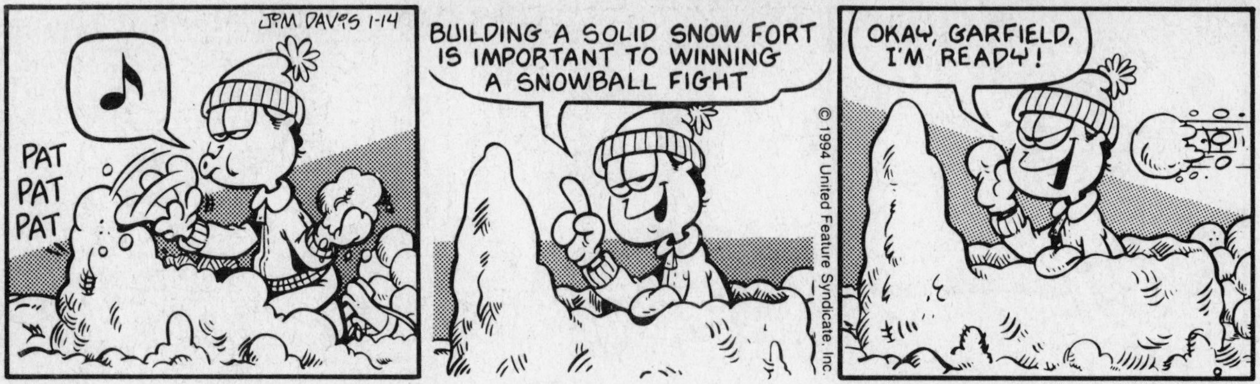
JIM DAVIS 1-14
♪
PAT
PAT
PAT
BUILDING A SOLID SNOW FORT IS IMPORTANT TO WINNING A SNOWBALL FIGHT
© 1994 United Feature Syndicate, Inc.
OKAY, GARFIELD, I'M READY!

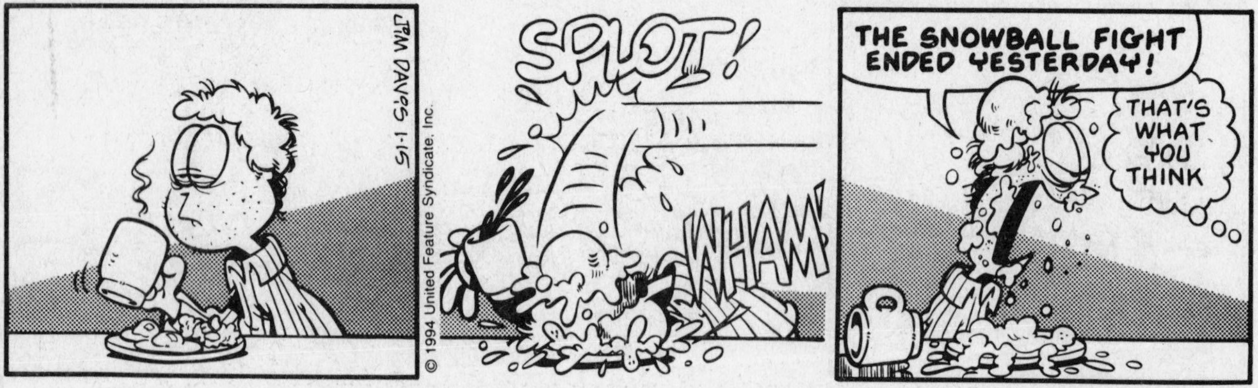
JIM DAVIS 1-15
© 1994 United Feature Syndicate, Inc.
SPLOT!
WHAM!
THE SNOWBALL FIGHT ENDED YESTERDAY!
THAT'S WHAT YOU THINK

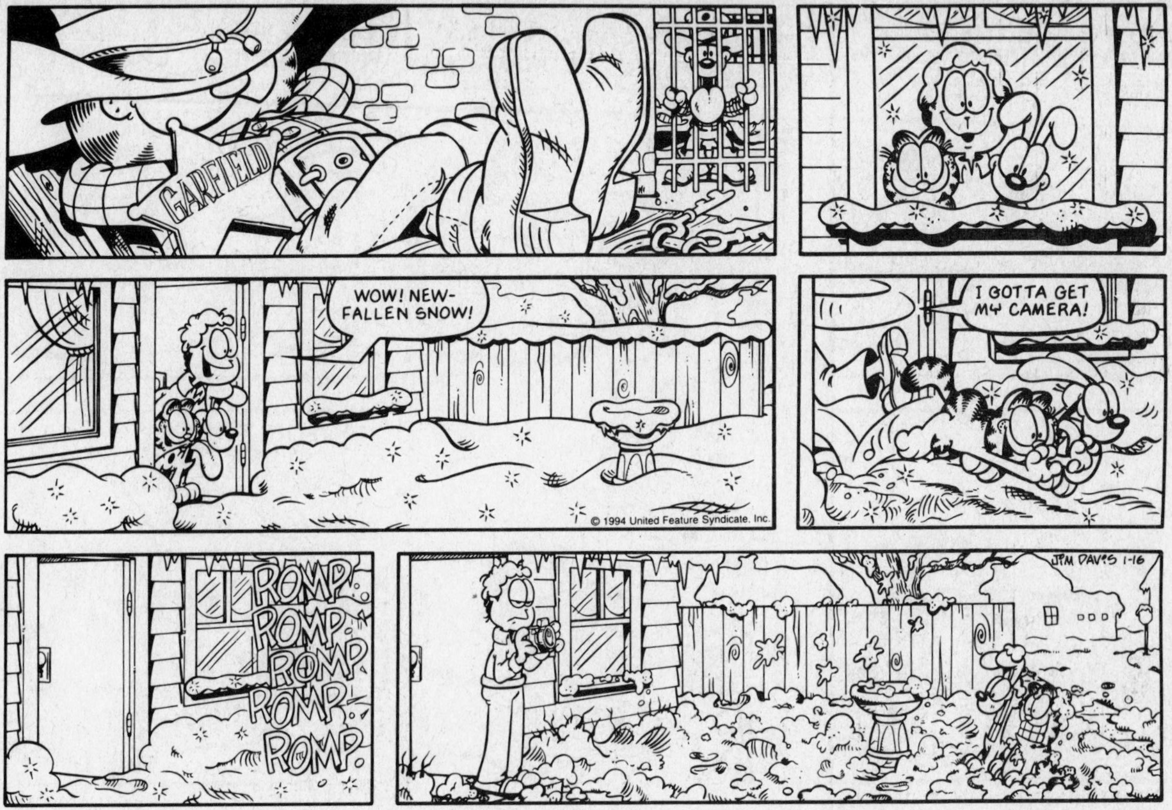
GARFIELD
WOW! NEW-FALLEN SNOW!
© 1994 United Feature Syndicate, Inc.
I GOTTA GET MY CAMERA!
ROMP ROMP ROMP ROMP ROMP
JIM DAVIS 1-16

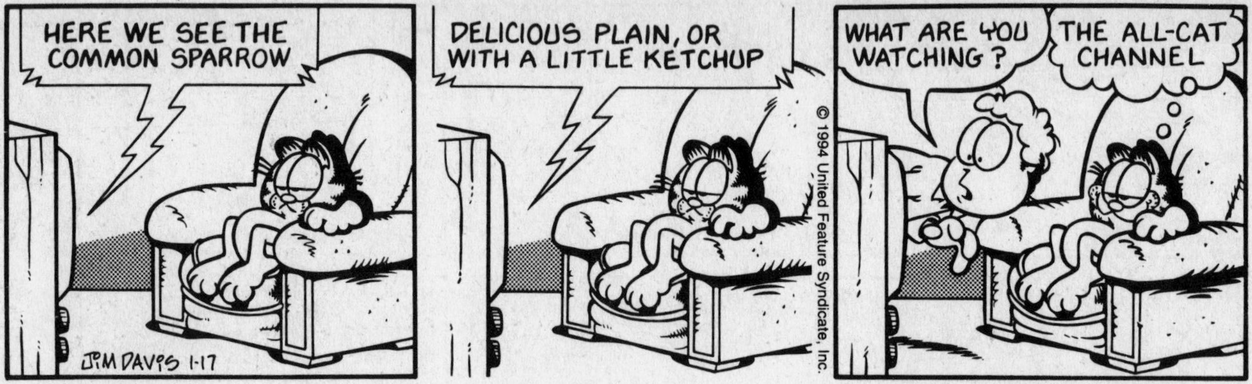
HERE WE SEE THE COMMON SPARROW
JIM DAVIS 1-17
DELICIOUS PLAIN, OR WITH A LITTLE KETCHUP
© 1994 United Feature Syndicate, Inc.
WHAT ARE YOU WATCHING ?
THE ALL-CAT CHANNEL

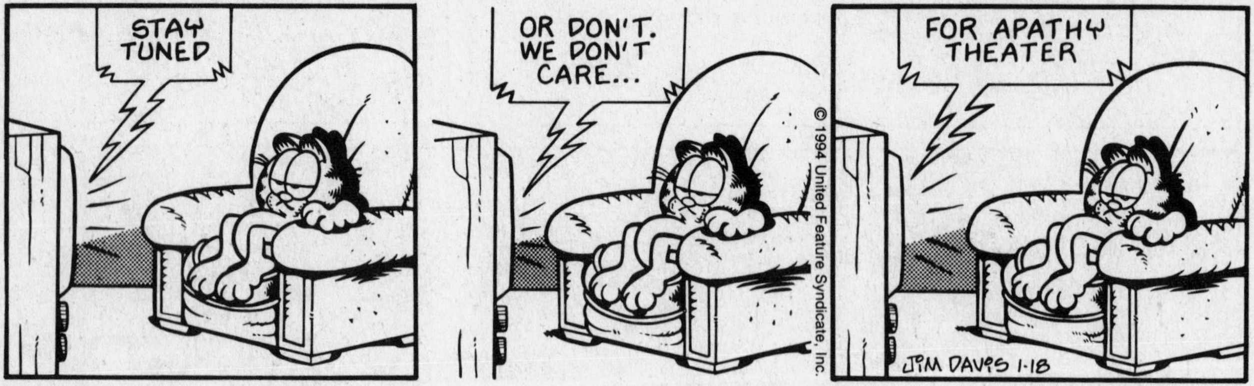
STAY TUNED
OR DON'T. WE DON'T CARE...
© 1994 United Feature Syndicate, Inc.
FOR APATHY THEATER
JIM DAVIS 1-18

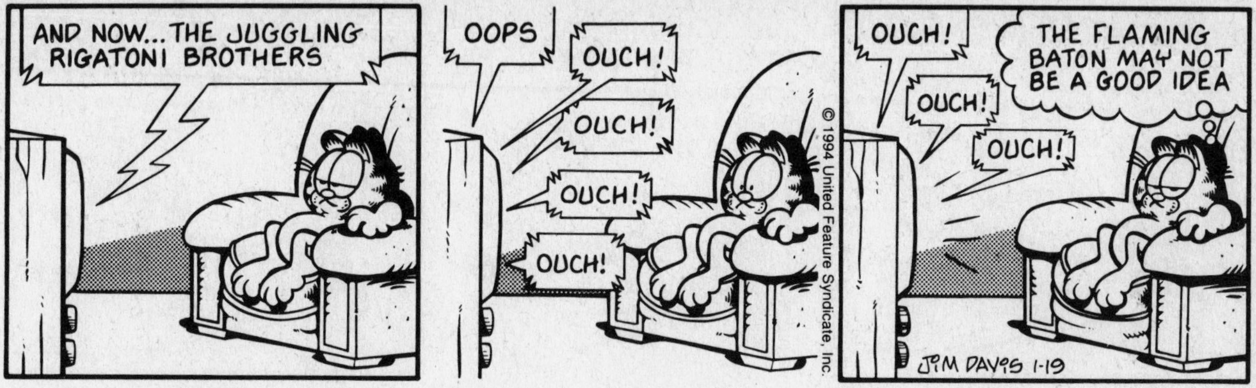
AND NOW... THE JUGGLING RIGATONI BROTHERS
OOPS
OUCH!
OUCH!
OUCH!
OUCH!
OUCH!
OUCH!
OUCH!
THE FLAMING BATON MAY NOT BE A GOOD IDEA
© 1994 United Feature Syndicate, Inc.
JIM DAVIS 1-19

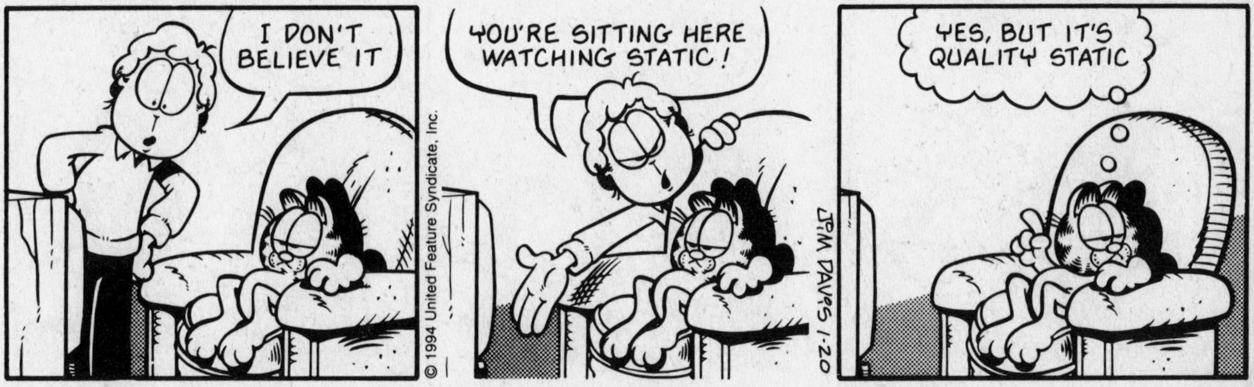
I DON'T BELIEVE IT
YOU'RE SITTING HERE WATCHING STATIC!
YES, BUT IT'S QUALITY STATIC
© 1994 United Feature Syndicate, Inc.
JIM DAVIS 1-20

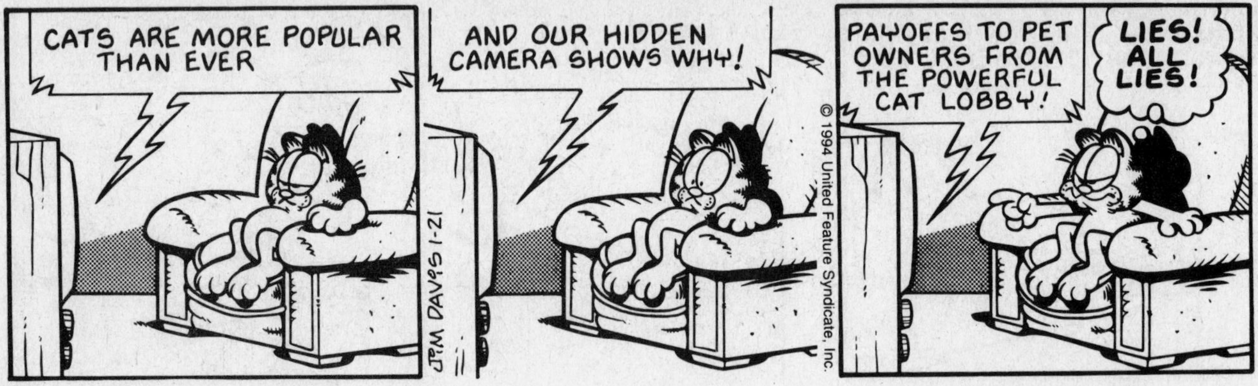
CATS ARE MORE POPULAR THAN EVER
AND OUR HIDDEN CAMERA SHOWS WHY!
PAYOFFS TO PET OWNERS FROM THE POWERFUL CAT LOBBY!
LIES! ALL LIES!
JPM DAVPS 1-21
© 1994 United Feature Syndicate, Inc.

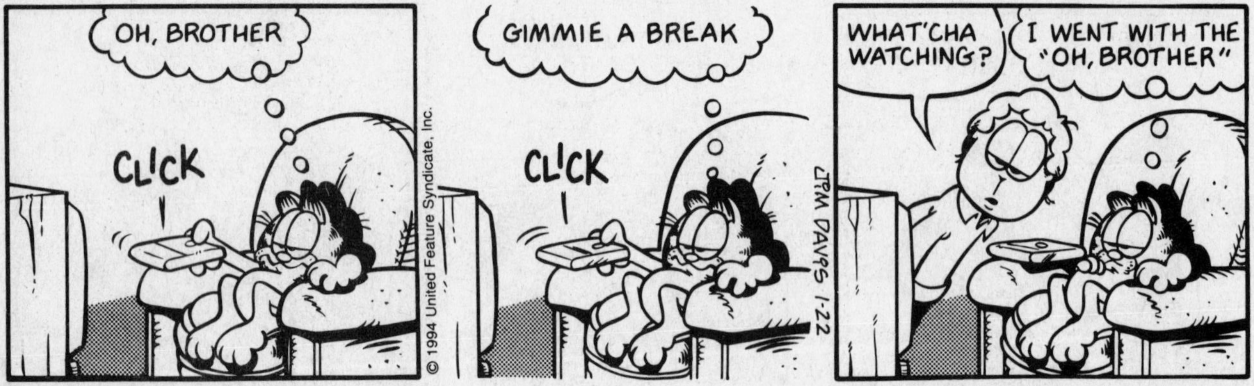
OH, BROTHER
CLICK
GIMMIE A BREAK
CLICK
WHAT'CHA WATCHING?
I WENT WITH THE "OH, BROTHER"
© 1994 United Feature Syndicate, Inc.
JPM DAVPS 1-22

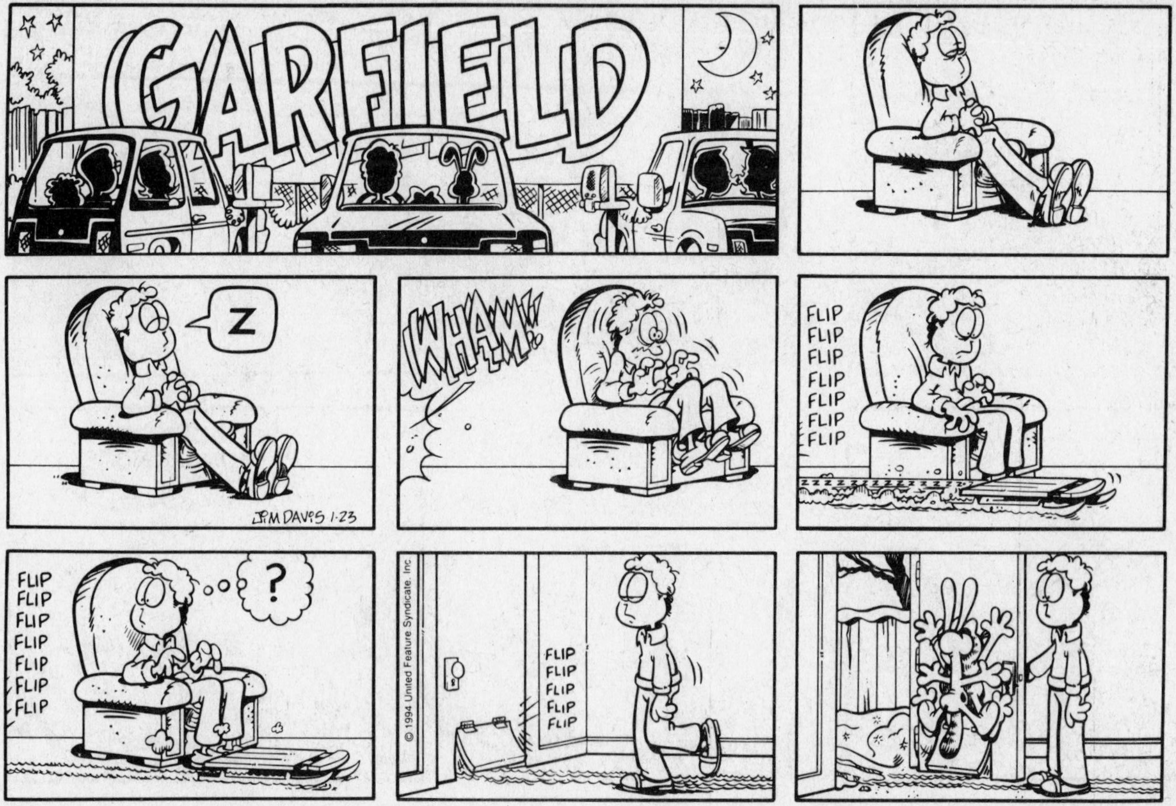
GARFIELD
Z
JIM DAVIS 1-23
WHAM!
FLIP
FLIP
FLIP
FLIP
FLIP
FLIP
FLIP
ZZZZZZZZZZZZZZ
FLIP
FLIP
FLIP
FLIP
FLIP
FLIP
FLIP
?
© 1994 United Feature Syndicate, Inc
FLIP
FLIP
FLIP
FLIP
FLIP

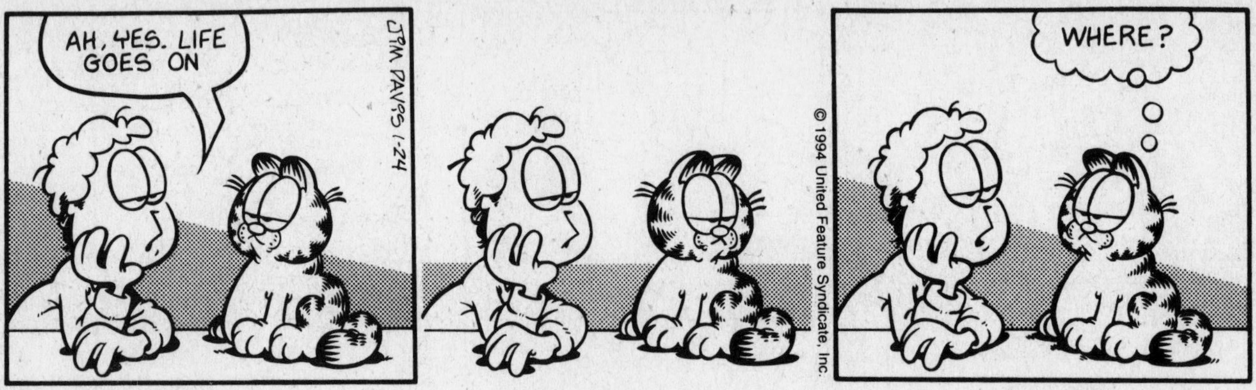
AH, YES. LIFE GOES ON
JIM DAVIS 1-24
WHERE?
© 1994 United Feature Syndicate, Inc.

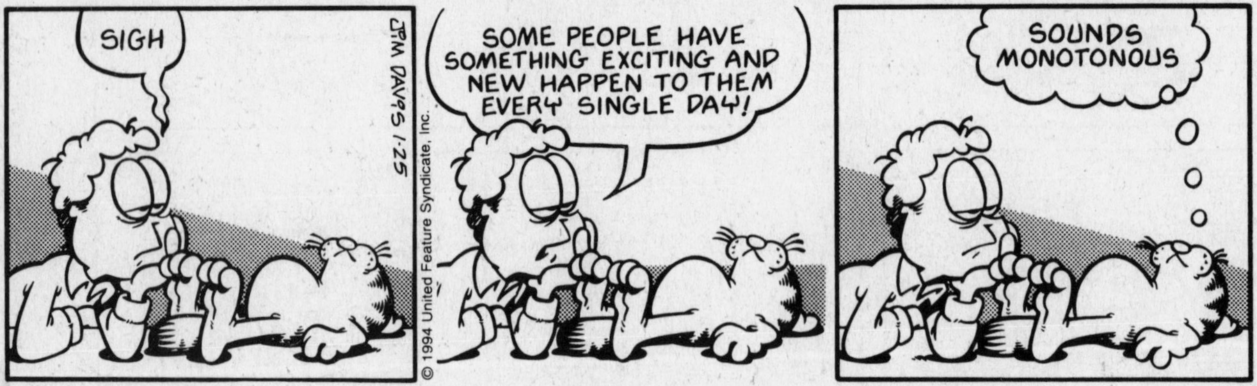
SIGH
JIM DAVIS 1-25
SOME PEOPLE HAVE SOMETHING EXCITING AND NEW HAPPEN TO THEM EVERY SINGLE DAY!
SOUNDS MONOTONOUS
© 1994 United Feature Syndicate, Inc.

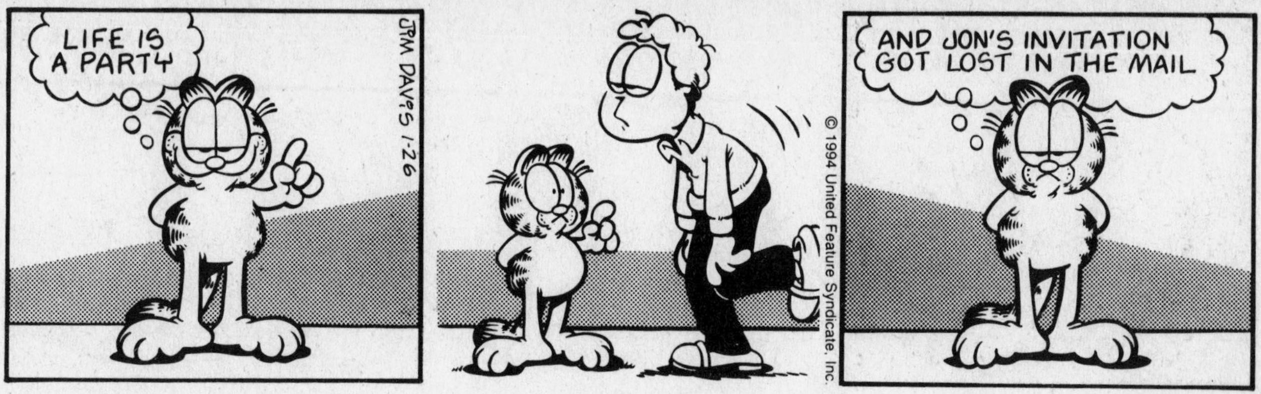
LIFE IS A PARTY
JIM DAVIS 1-26
© 1994 United Feature Syndicate, Inc.
AND JON'S INVITATION GOT LOST IN THE MAIL

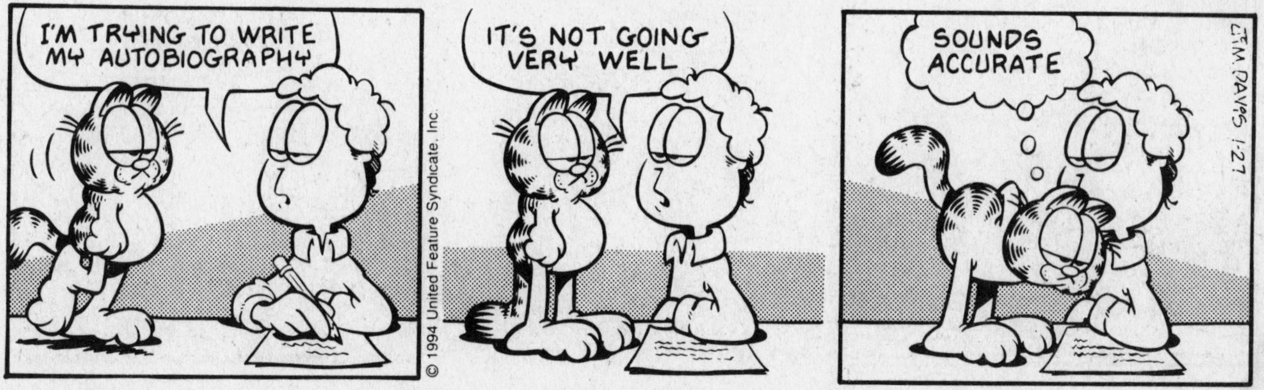
I'M TRYING TO WRITE MY AUTOBIOGRAPHY
© 1994 United Feature Syndicate, Inc.
IT'S NOT GOING VERY WELL
SOUNDS ACCURATE
JIM DAVIS 1-27

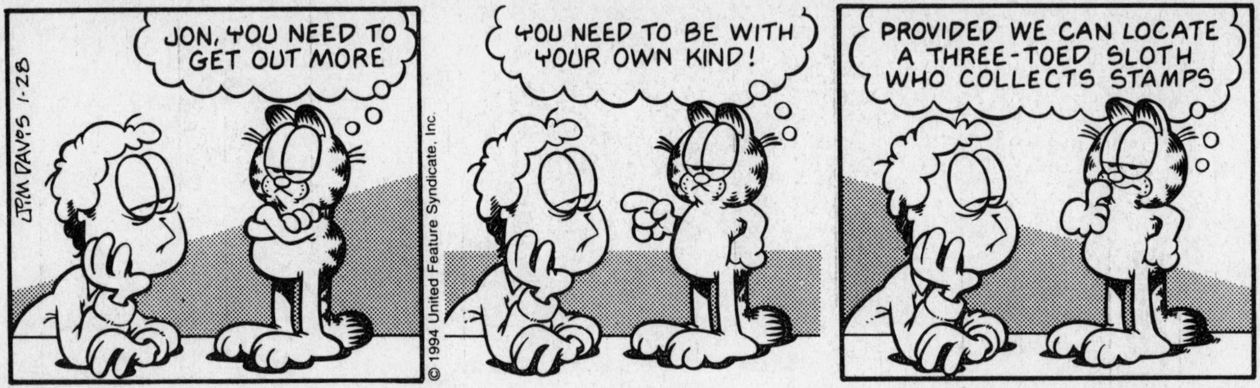
JIM DAVIS 1-28
JON, YOU NEED TO GET OUT MORE
© 1994 United Feature Syndicate, Inc.
YOU NEED TO BE WITH YOUR OWN KIND!
PROVIDED WE CAN LOCATE A THREE-TOED SLOTH WHO COLLECTS STAMPS

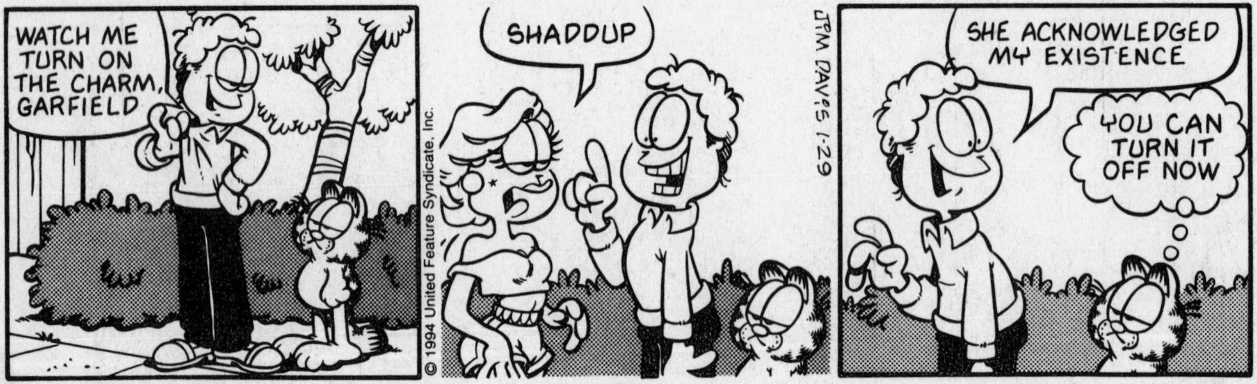
WATCH ME TURN ON THE CHARM, GARFIELD
© 1994 United Feature Syndicate, Inc.
SHADDUP
JIM DAVIS 1-29
SHE ACKNOWLEDGED MY EXISTENCE
YOU CAN TURN IT OFF NOW

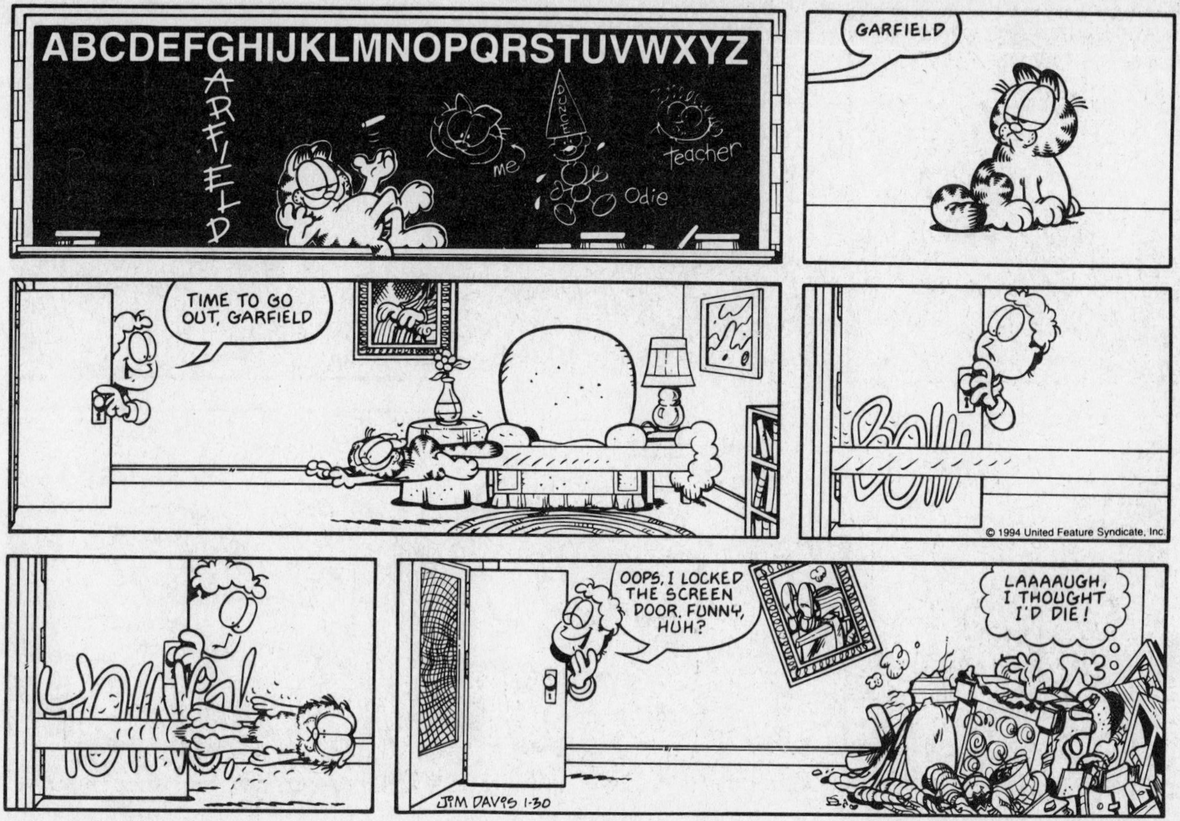
ABCDEFGHIJKLMNOPQRSTUVWXYZ
GARFIELD
me
DUNCE
Odie
teacher
GARFIELD
TIME TO GO OUT, GARFIELD
© 1994 United Feature Syndicate, Inc.
OOPS, I LOCKED THE SCREEN DOOR. FUNNY, HUH?
LAAAAUGH, I THOUGHT I'D DIE!
JIM DAVIS 1-30

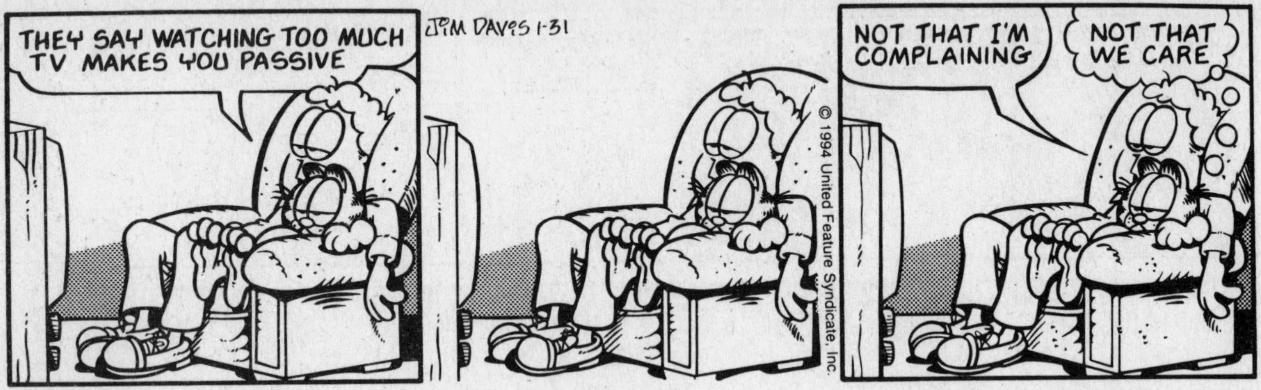
THEY SAY WATCHING TOO MUCH TV MAKES YOU PASSIVE
JIM DAVIS 1-31
NOT THAT I'M COMPLAINING
NOT THAT WE CARE
© 1994 United Feature Syndicate, Inc.

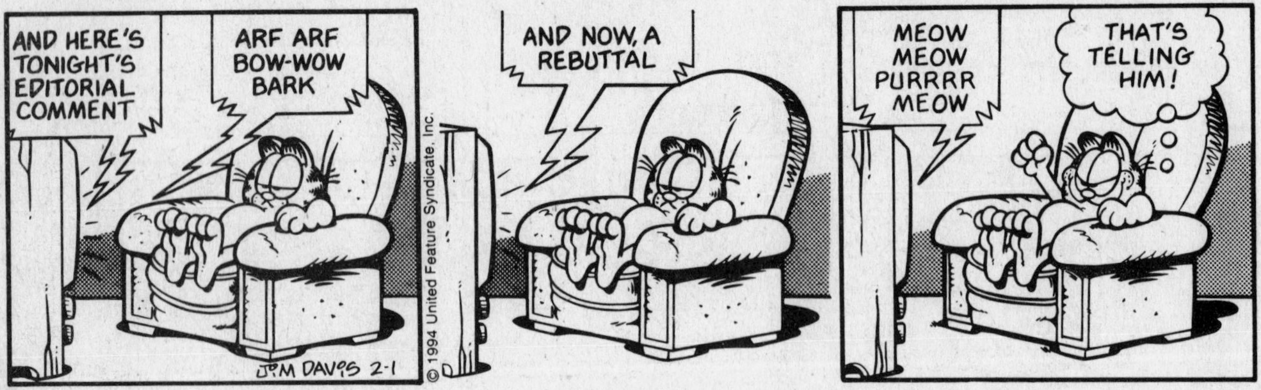
AND HERE'S TONIGHT'S EDITORIAL COMMENT
ARF ARF BOW-WOW BARK
JIM DAVIS 2-1
© 1994 United Feature Syndicate, Inc.
AND NOW, A REBUTTAL
MEOW MEOW PURRRR MEOW
THAT'S TELLING HIM!

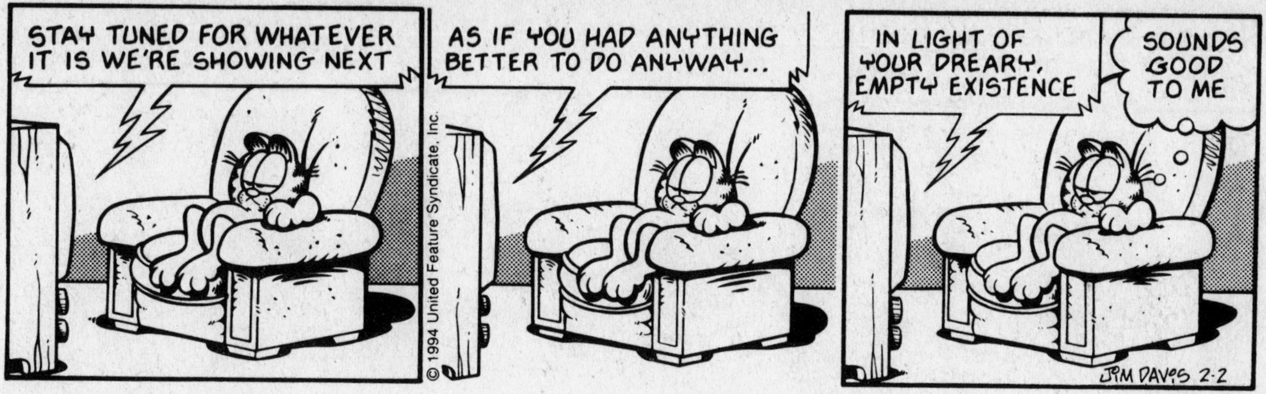
STAY TUNED FOR WHATEVER IT IS WE'RE SHOWING NEXT
© 1994 United Feature Syndicate, Inc.
AS IF YOU HAD ANYTHING BETTER TO DO ANYWAY...
IN LIGHT OF YOUR DREARY, EMPTY EXISTENCE
SOUNDS GOOD TO ME
JIM DAVIS 2-2

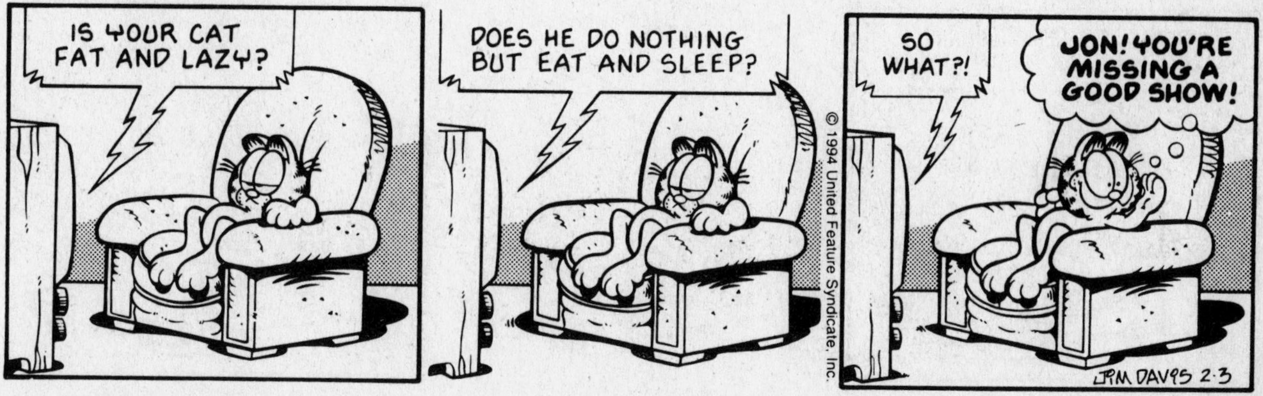
IS YOUR CAT FAT AND LAZY?
DOES HE DO NOTHING BUT EAT AND SLEEP?
© 1994 United Feature Syndicate, Inc.
SO WHAT?!
JON! YOU'RE MISSING A GOOD SHOW!
JIM DAVIS 2-3

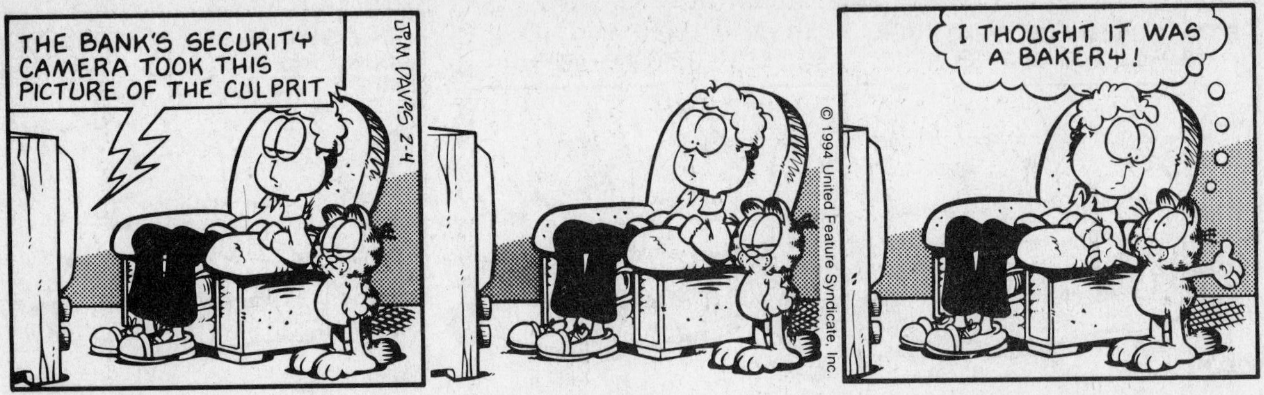
THE BANK'S SECURITY CAMERA TOOK THIS PICTURE OF THE CULPRIT
JIM DAVIS 2-4
I THOUGHT IT WAS A BAKERY!
© 1994 United Feature Syndicate, Inc.

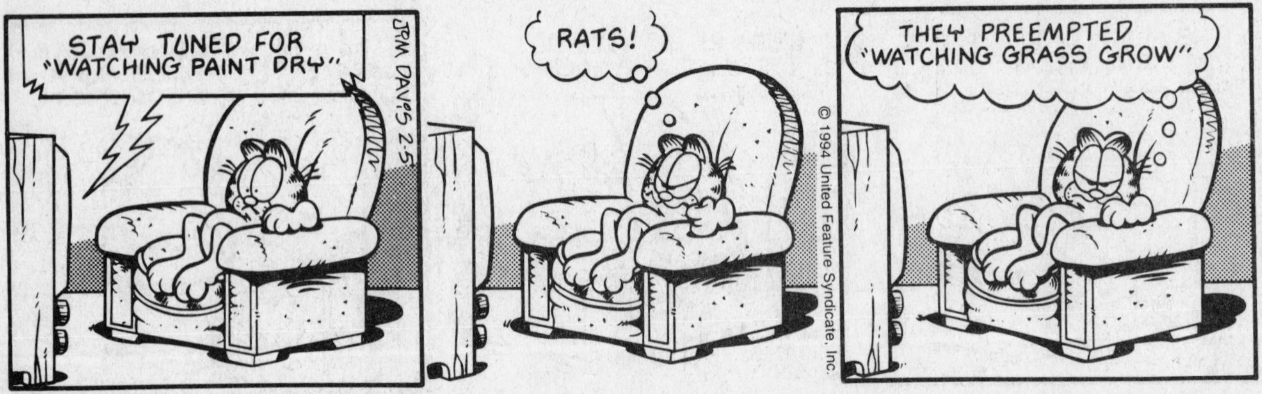
STAY TUNED FOR "WATCHING PAINT DRY"
JIM DAVIS 2-5
RATS!
THEY PREEMPTED "WATCHING GRASS GROW"
© 1994 United Feature Syndicate, Inc.

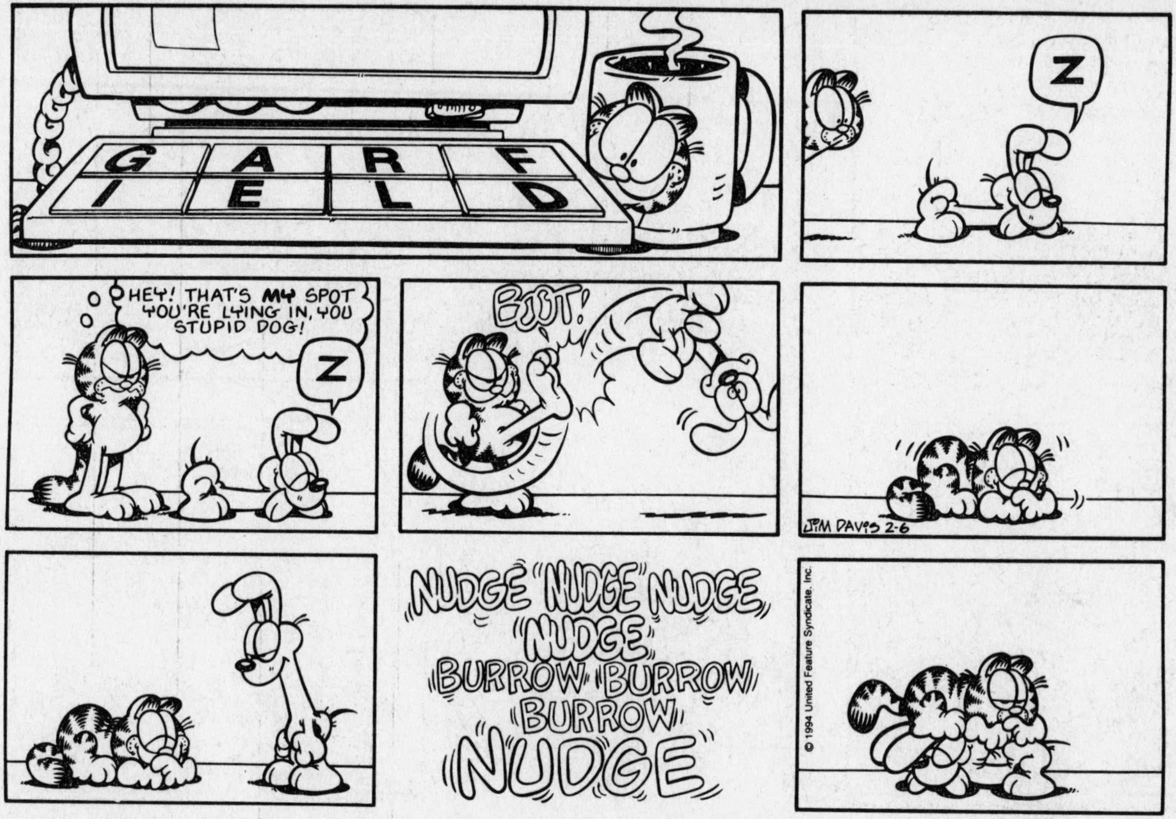

GARFIELD
Z
HEY! THAT'S MY SPOT YOU'RE LYING IN, YOU STUPID DOG!
Z
BOOT!
JIM DAVIS 2-6
NUDGE NUDGE NUDGE
NUDGE
BURROW BURROW
BURROW
NUDGE
© 1994 United Feature Syndicate, Inc.

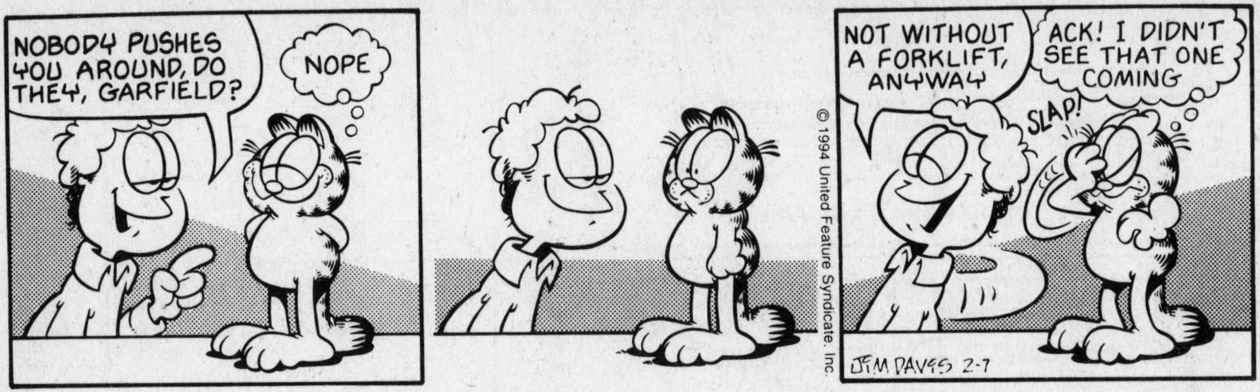
NOBODY PUSHES YOU AROUND, DO THEY, GARFIELD?
NOPE
NOT WITHOUT A FORKLIFT, ANYWAY
ACK! I DIDN'T SEE THAT ONE COMING
SLAP!
JIM DAVIS 2-7
© 1994 United Feature Syndicate, Inc.

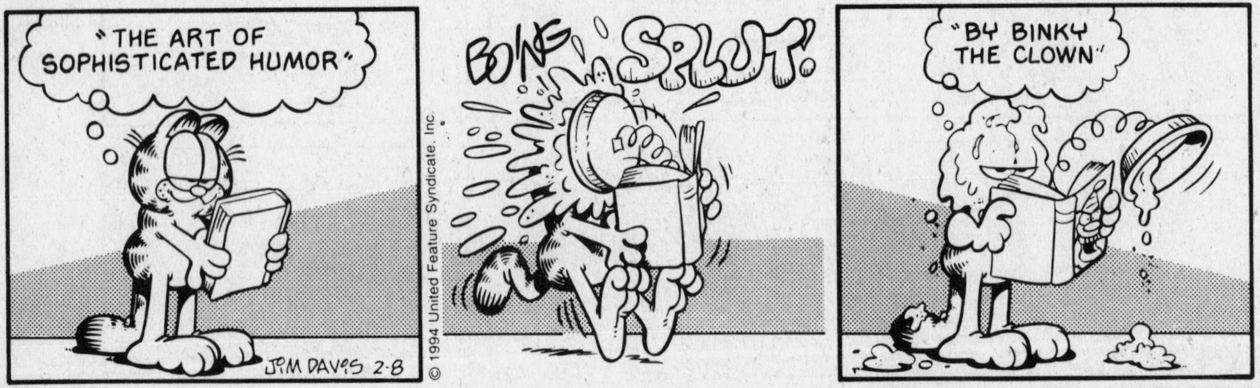
"THE ART OF SOPHISTICATED HUMOR"
JIM DAVIS 2-8
© 1994 United Feature Syndicate, Inc.
BOING
SPLUT!
"BY BINKY THE CLOWN"

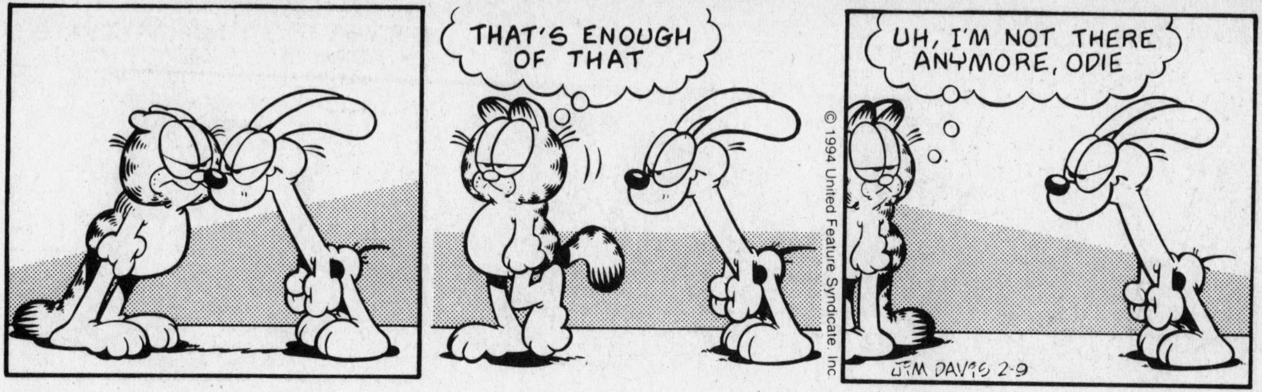
THAT'S ENOUGH OF THAT
UH, I'M NOT THERE ANYMORE, ODIE
JIM DAVIS 2-9

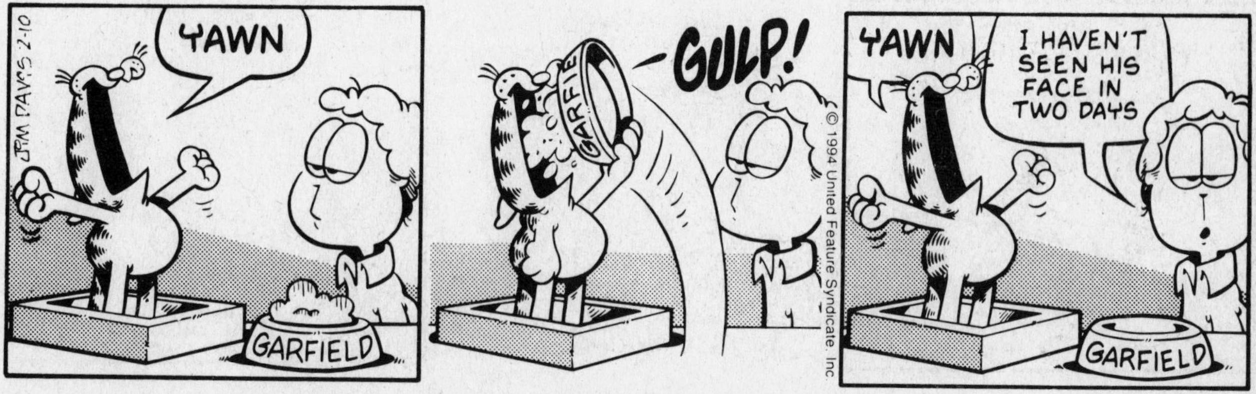
JIM DAVIS 2-10
YAWN
GARFIELD
GARFIE
-GULP!
YAWN
I HAVEN'T SEEN HIS FACE IN TWO DAYS
GARFIELD

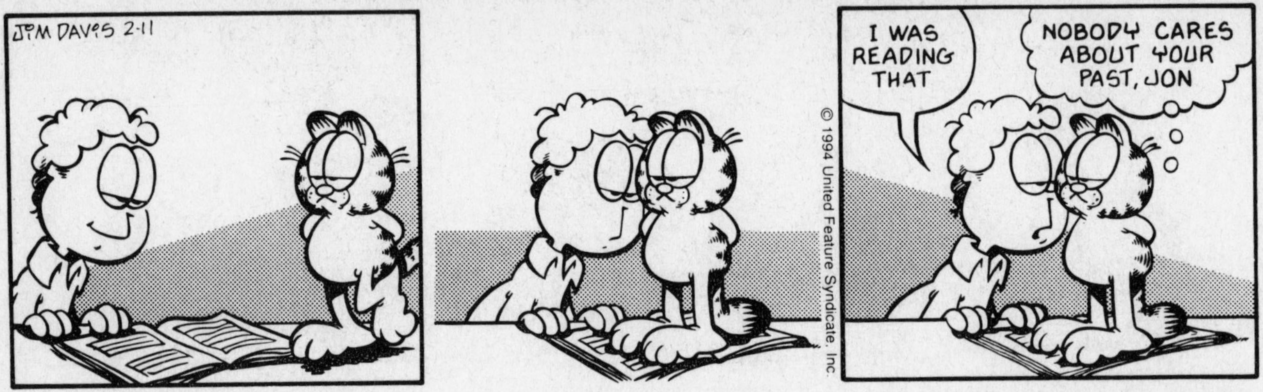
JIM DAVIS 2-11
I WAS READING THAT
NOBODY CARES ABOUT YOUR PAST, JON
© 1994 United Feature Syndicate, Inc.

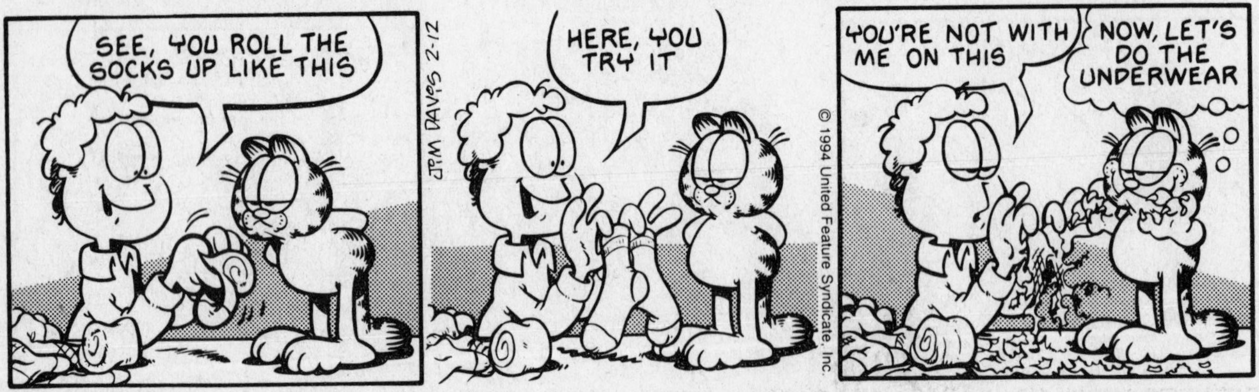
SEE, YOU ROLL THE SOCKS UP LIKE THIS
JIM DAVIS 2-12
HERE, YOU TRY IT
YOU'RE NOT WITH ME ON THIS
NOW, LET'S DO THE UNDERWEAR
© 1994 United Feature Syndicate, Inc.

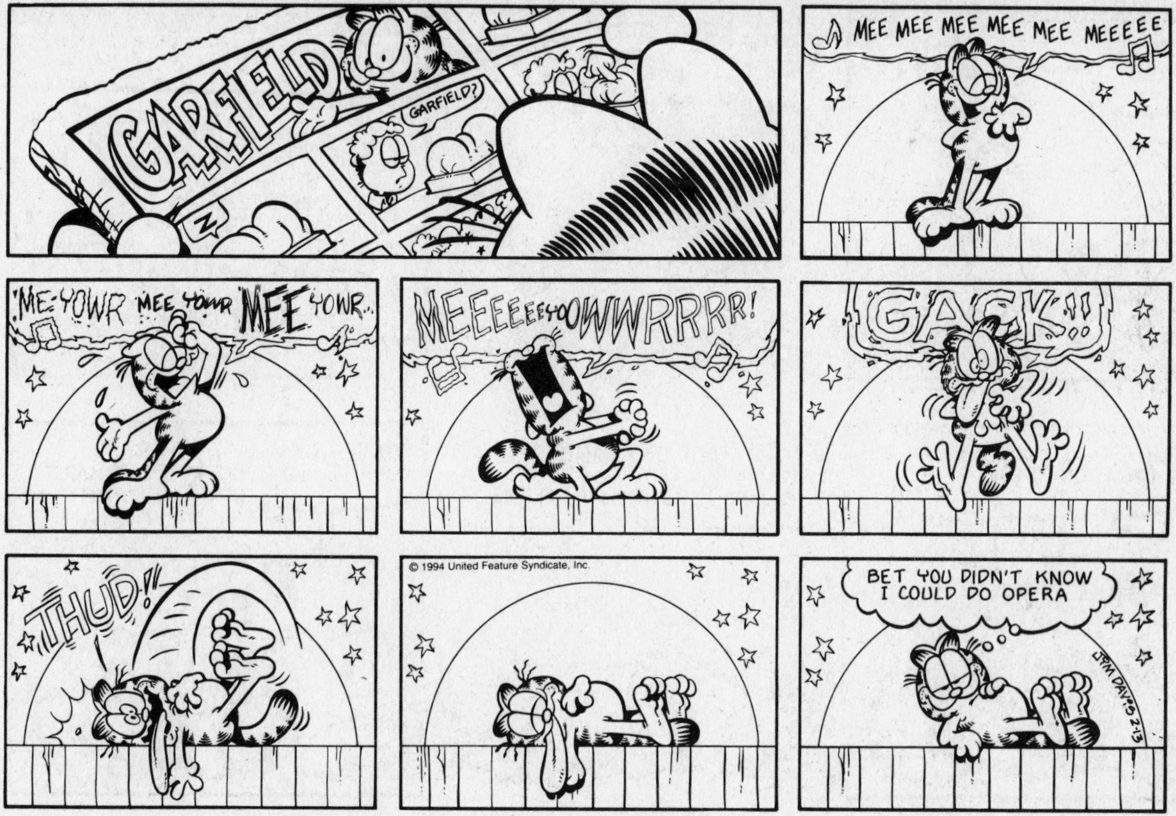
GARFIELD
GARFIELD?
Z
MEE MEE MEE MEE MEE MEEEEE
ME-YOWR MEE YOWR MEE YOWR...
MEEEEEEEYOOWWRRRRR!
GACK!!
THUD!!
© 1994 United Feature Syndicate, Inc.
BET YOU DIDN'T KNOW I COULD DO OPERA
JIM DAVIS 2-13

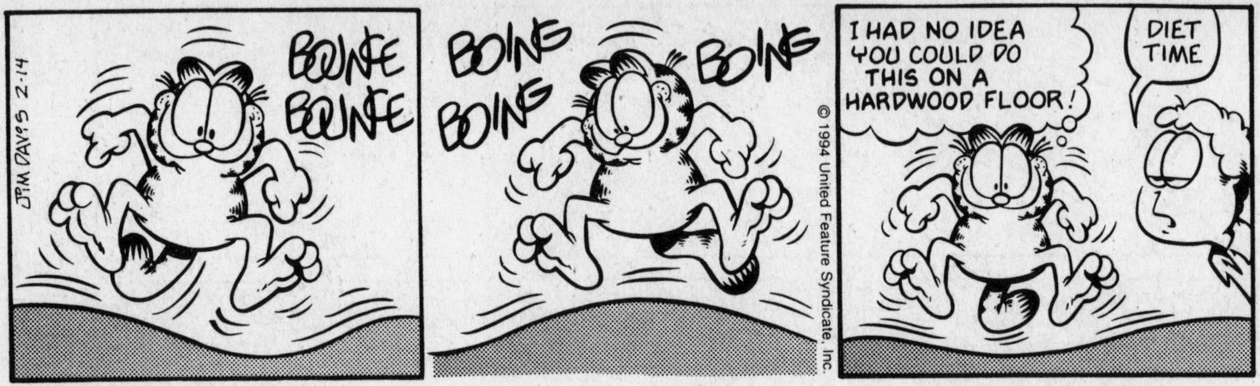
JIM DAVIS 2·14
BOUNCE
BOUNCE
BOING
BOING
BOING
I HAD NO IDEA YOU COULD DO THIS ON A HARDWOOD FLOOR!
DIET TIME
© 1994 United Feature Syndicate, Inc.

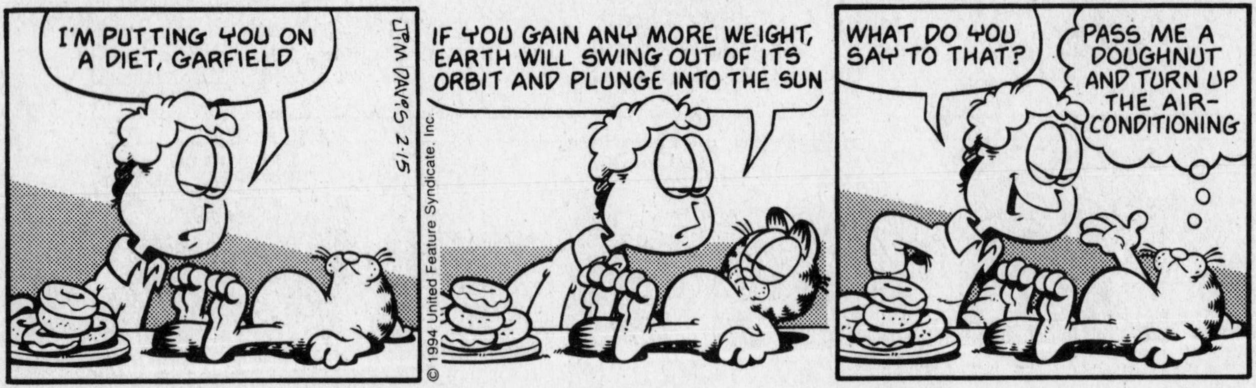
I'M PUTTING YOU ON A DIET, GARFIELD
JIM DAVIS 2·15
IF YOU GAIN ANY MORE WEIGHT, EARTH WILL SWING OUT OF ITS ORBIT AND PLUNGE INTO THE SUN
WHAT DO YOU SAY TO THAT?
PASS ME A DOUGHNUT AND TURN UP THE AIR-CONDITIONING
© 1994 United Feature Syndicate, Inc.

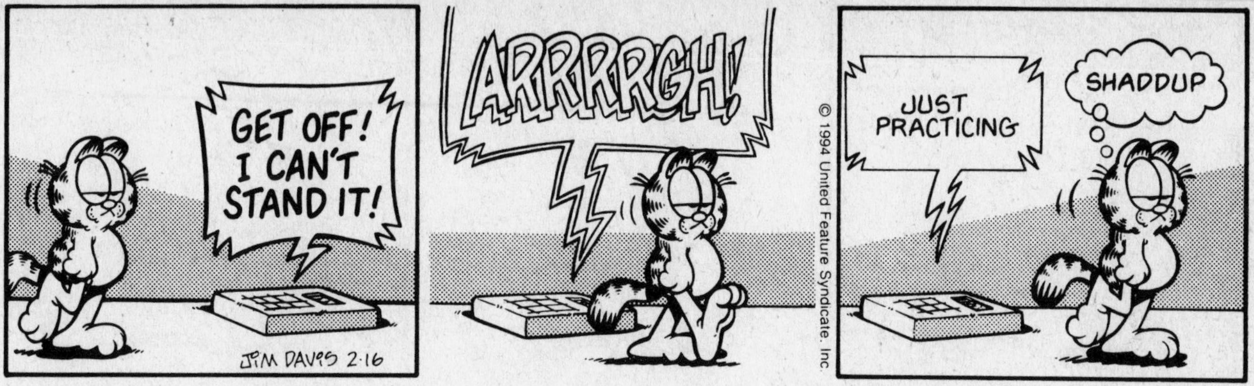
GET OFF! I CAN'T STAND IT!
JIM DAVIS 2·16
ARRRRGH!
© 1994 United Feature Syndicate, Inc.
JUST PRACTICING
SHADDUP

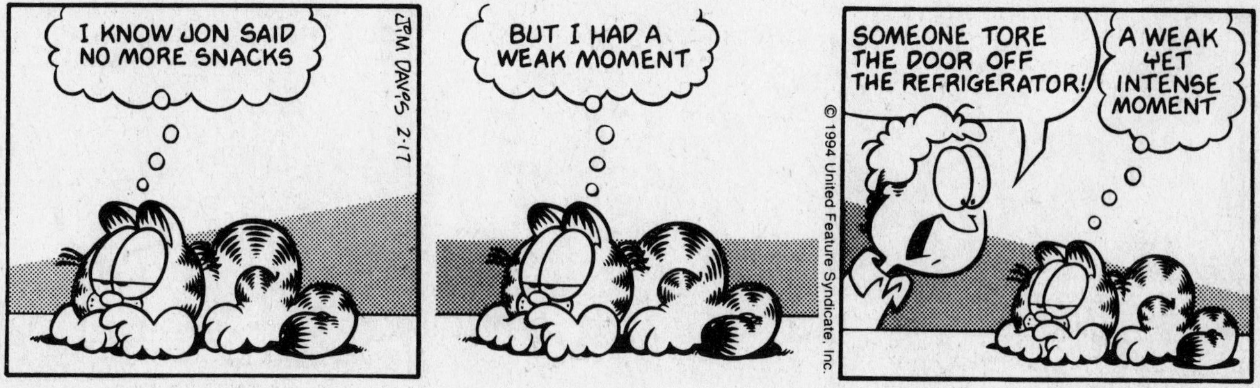
I KNOW JON SAID NO MORE SNACKS
JIM DAVIS 2·17
BUT I HAD A WEAK MOMENT
© 1994 United Feature Syndicate, Inc.
SOMEONE TORE THE DOOR OFF THE REFRIGERATOR!
A WEAK YET INTENSE MOMENT

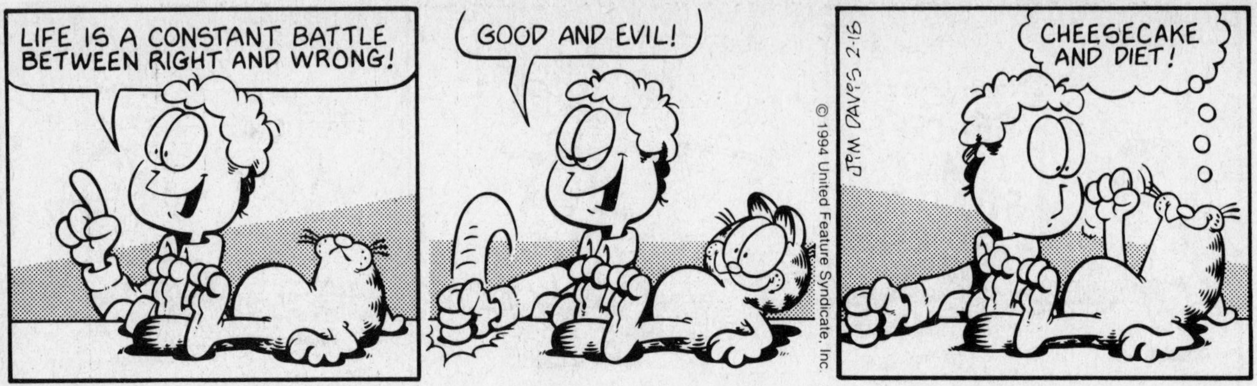
LIFE IS A CONSTANT BATTLE BETWEEN RIGHT AND WRONG!
GOOD AND EVIL!
CHEESECAKE AND DIET!
JIM DAVIS 2-18
© 1994 United Feature Syndicate, Inc.

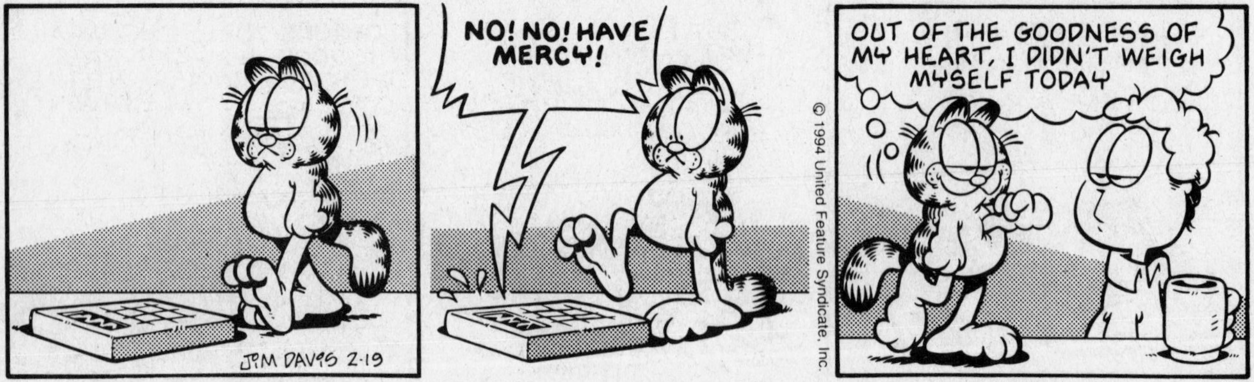
JIM DAVIS 2-19
NO! NO! HAVE MERCY!
OUT OF THE GOODNESS OF MY HEART, I DIDN'T WEIGH MYSELF TODAY
© 1994 United Feature Syndicate, Inc.

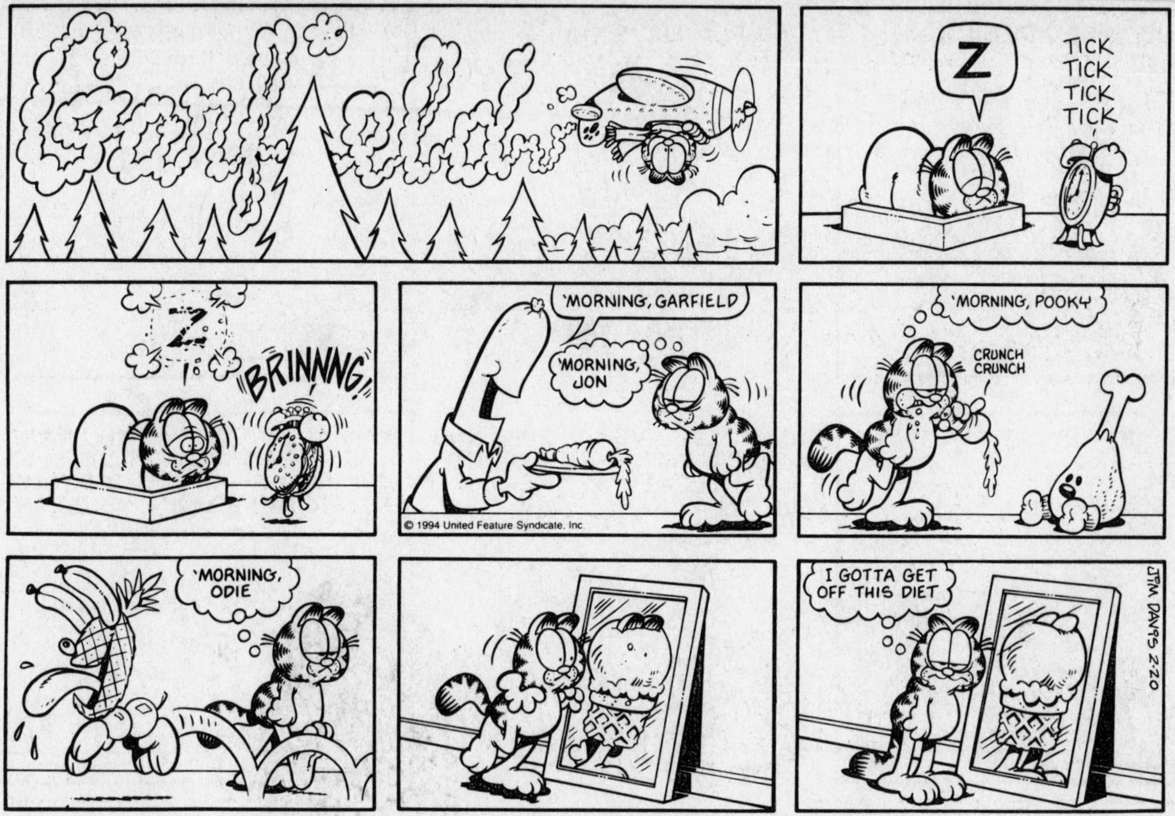
Garfield
Z
TICK
TICK
TICK
TICK
BRINNNG!
'MORNING, GARFIELD
'MORNING, JON
© 1994 United Feature Syndicate, Inc.
'MORNING, POOKY
CRUNCH
CRUNCH
'MORNING, ODIE
I GOTTA GET OFF THIS DIET
JIM DAVIS 2-20

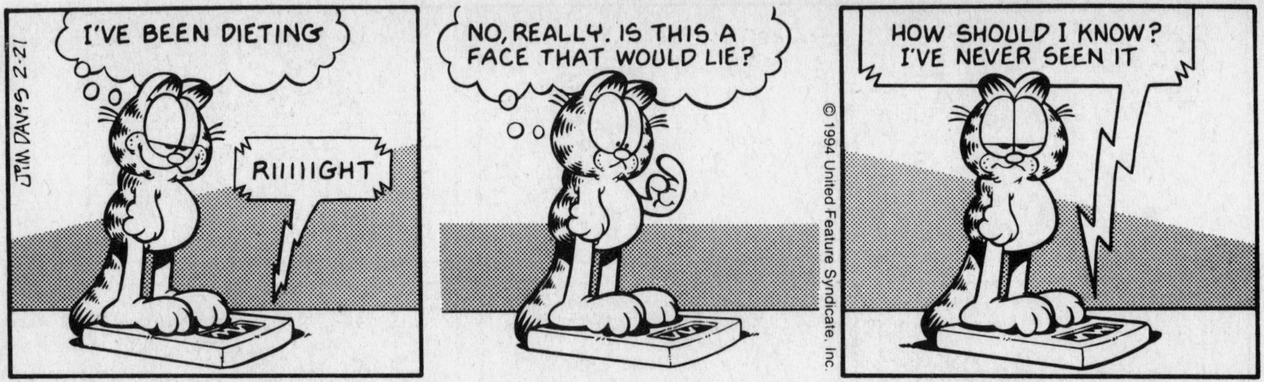
JIM DAVIS 2·21
I'VE BEEN DIETING
RIIIIIGHT
NO, REALLY. IS THIS A FACE THAT WOULD LIE?
HOW SHOULD I KNOW? I'VE NEVER SEEN IT
© 1994 United Feature Syndicate, Inc.

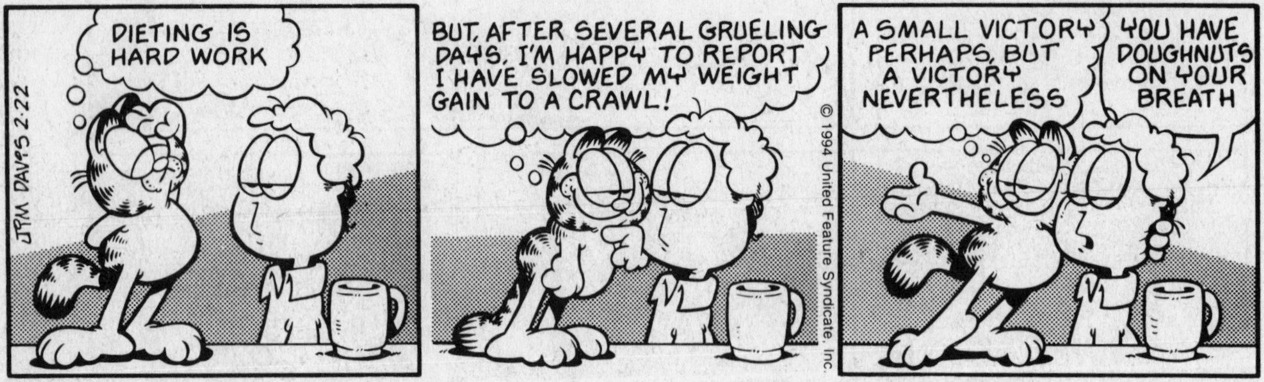
JIM DAVIS 2·22
DIETING IS HARD WORK
BUT, AFTER SEVERAL GRUELING DAYS, I'M HAPPY TO REPORT I HAVE SLOWED MY WEIGHT GAIN TO A CRAWL!
A SMALL VICTORY PERHAPS, BUT A VICTORY NEVERTHELESS
YOU HAVE DOUGHNUTS ON YOUR BREATH
© 1994 United Feature Syndicate, Inc.

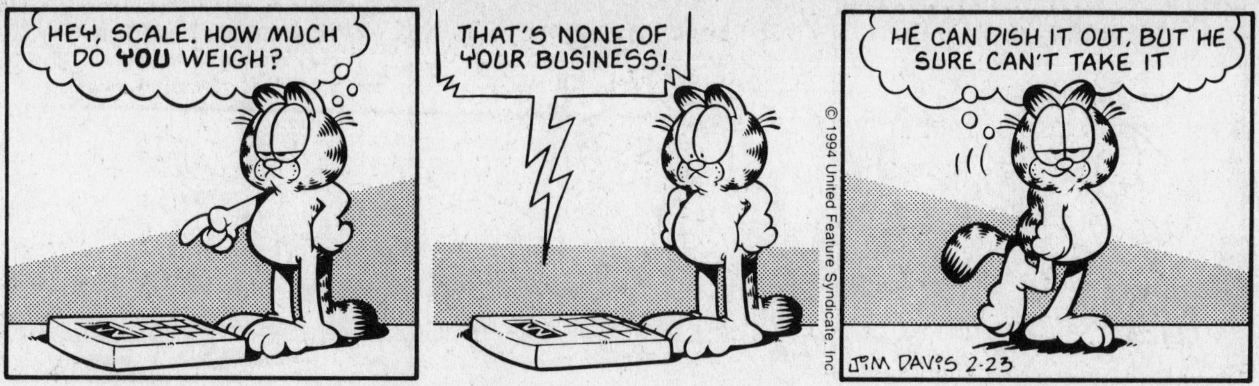
HEY, SCALE. HOW MUCH DO **YOU** WEIGH?
THAT'S NONE OF YOUR BUSINESS!
HE CAN DISH IT OUT, BUT HE SURE CAN'T TAKE IT
© 1994 United Feature Syndicate, Inc.
JIM DAVIS 2-23

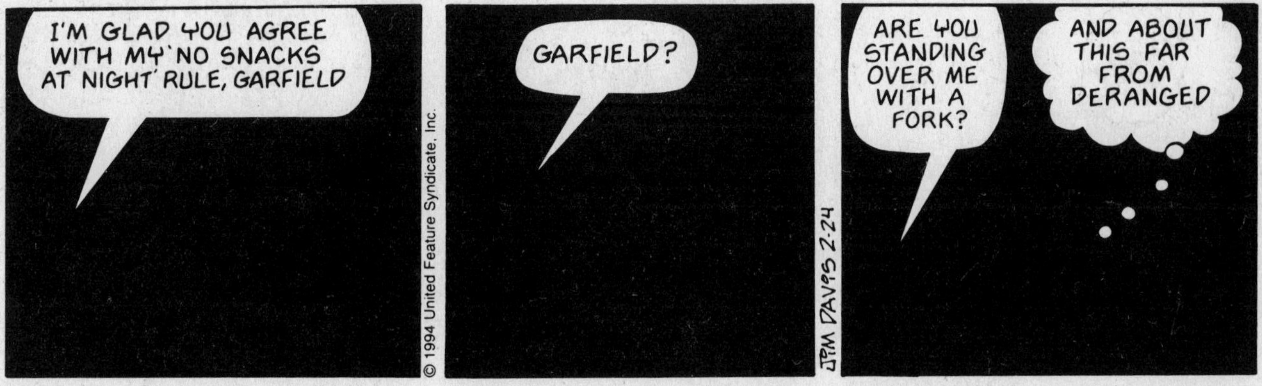
I'M GLAD YOU AGREE WITH MY 'NO SNACKS AT NIGHT' RULE, GARFIELD
© 1994 United Feature Syndicate, Inc.
GARFIELD?
JIM DAVIS 2-24
ARE YOU STANDING OVER ME WITH A FORK?
AND ABOUT THIS FAR FROM DERANGED

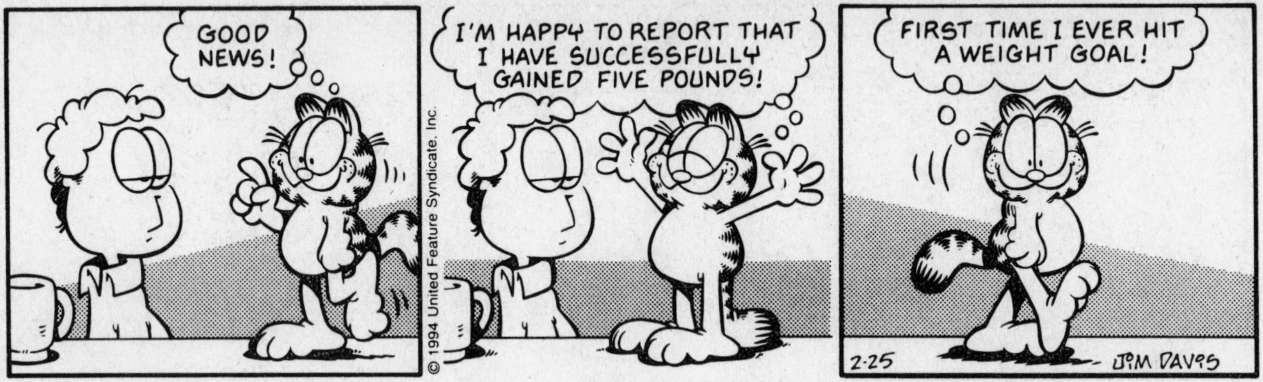
GOOD NEWS!
I'M HAPPY TO REPORT THAT I HAVE SUCCESSFULLY GAINED FIVE POUNDS!
FIRST TIME I EVER HIT A WEIGHT GOAL!
2-25
JIM DAVIS
© 1994 United Feature Syndicate, Inc.

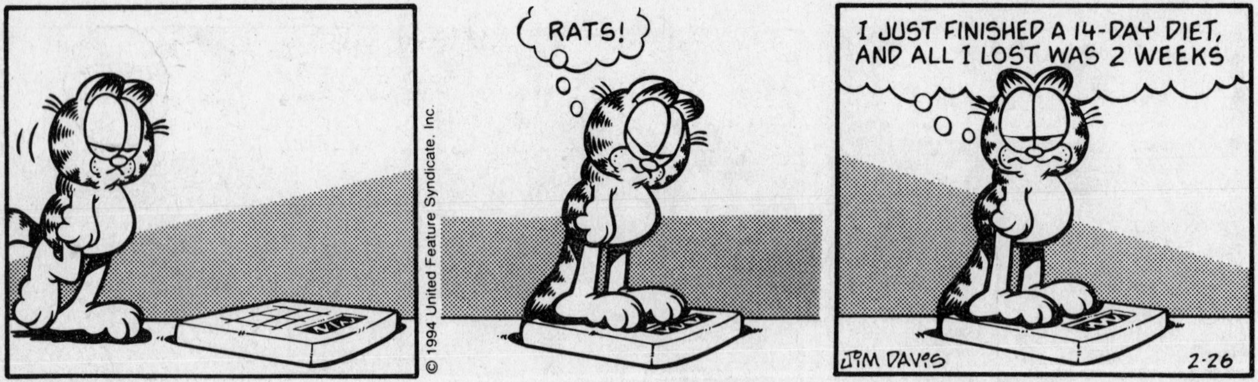
RATS!
I JUST FINISHED A 14-DAY DIET, AND ALL I LOST WAS 2 WEEKS
JIM DAVIS
2-26
© 1994 United Feature Syndicate, Inc.

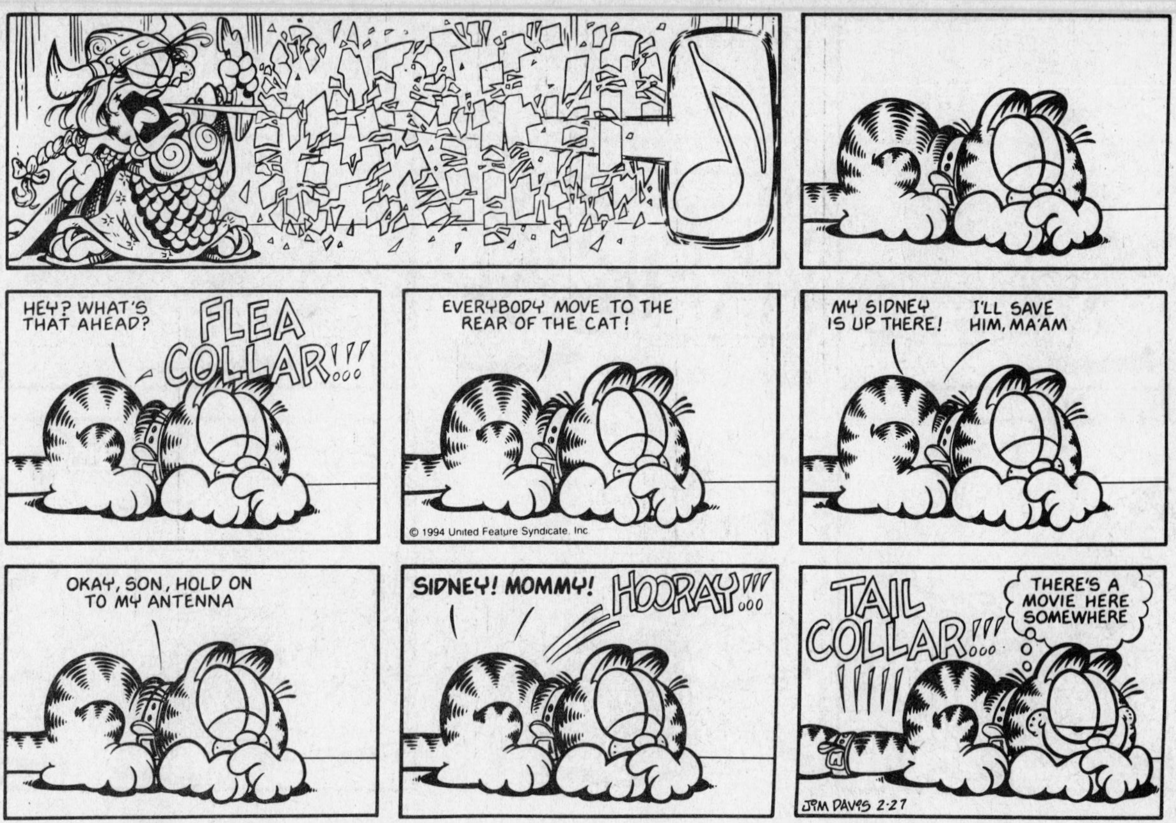
HEY? WHAT'S THAT AHEAD?
FLEA COLLAR!!!ooo
EVERYBODY MOVE TO THE REAR OF THE CAT!
© 1994 United Feature Syndicate, Inc.
MY SIDNEY IS UP THERE!
I'LL SAVE HIM, MA'AM
OKAY, SON, HOLD ON TO MY ANTENNA
SIDNEY! MOMMY!
HOORAY!!!ooo
TAIL COLLAR!!!ooo
THERE'S A MOVIE HERE SOMEWHERE
JIM DAVIS 2-27

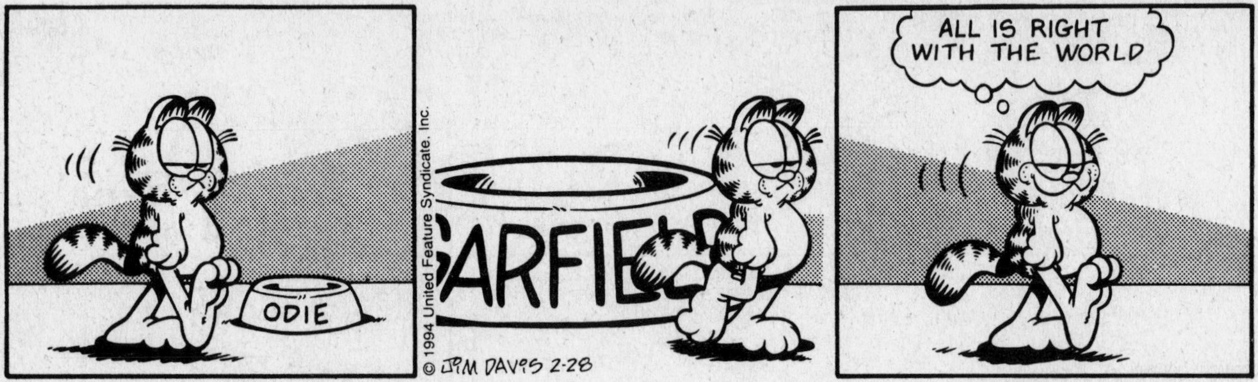
ODIE
GARFIELD
ALL IS RIGHT WITH THE WORLD
© 1994 United Feature Syndicate, Inc.
JIM DAVIS 2-28

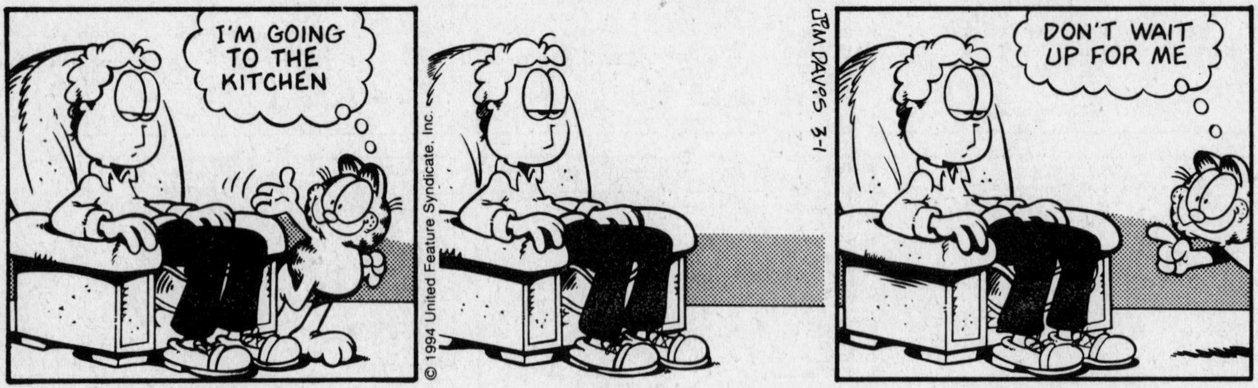
I'M GOING TO THE KITCHEN
DON'T WAIT UP FOR ME
© 1994 United Feature Syndicate, Inc.
JIM DAVIS 3-1

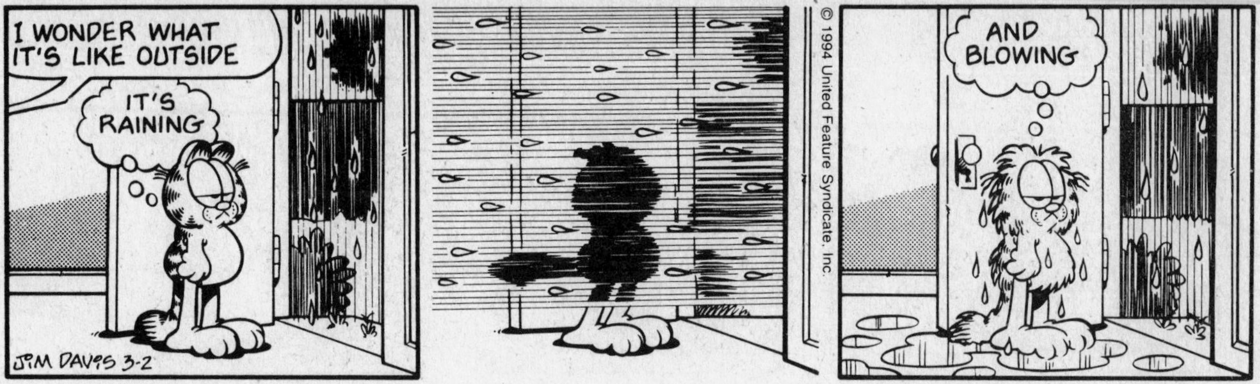
I WONDER WHAT IT'S LIKE OUTSIDE
IT'S RAINING
AND BLOWING
JIM DAVIS 3-2
© 1994 United Feature Syndicate, Inc.

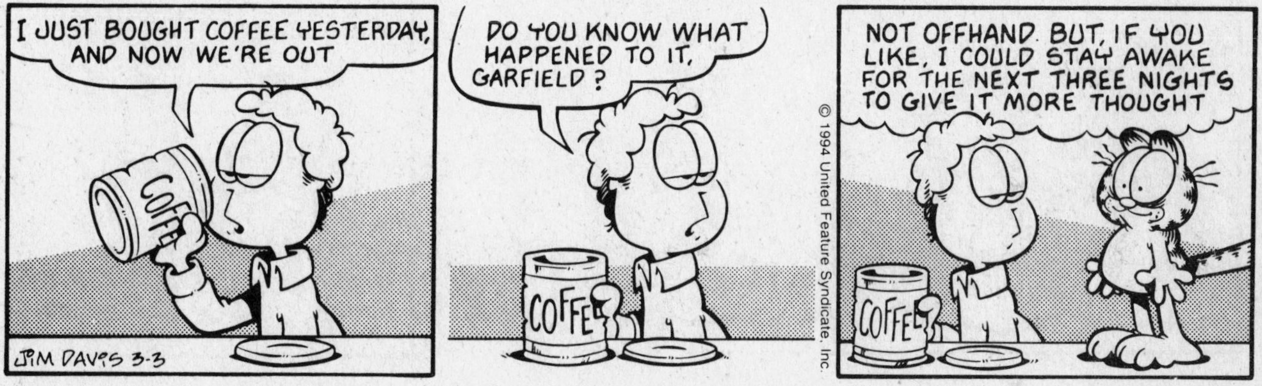
I JUST BOUGHT COFFEE YESTERDAY, AND NOW WE'RE OUT
COFFEE
DO YOU KNOW WHAT HAPPENED TO IT, GARFIELD?
COFFEE
NOT OFFHAND. BUT, IF YOU LIKE, I COULD STAY AWAKE FOR THE NEXT THREE NIGHTS TO GIVE IT MORE THOUGHT
COFFEE
JIM DAVIS 3-3
© 1994 United Feature Syndicate, Inc.

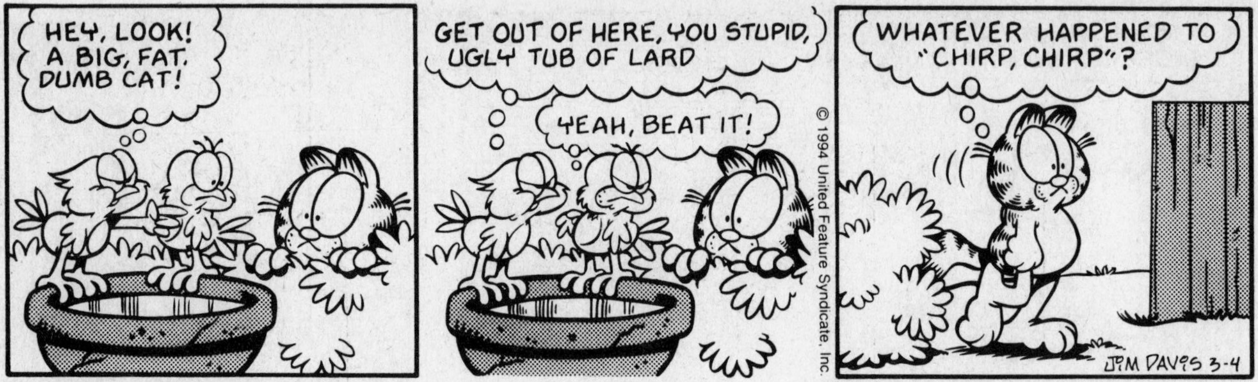
HEY, LOOK! A BIG, FAT, DUMB CAT!
GET OUT OF HERE, YOU STUPID, UGLY TUB OF LARD
YEAH, BEAT IT!
WHATEVER HAPPENED TO "CHIRP, CHIRP"?
JIM DAVIS 3-4
© 1994 United Feature Syndicate, Inc.

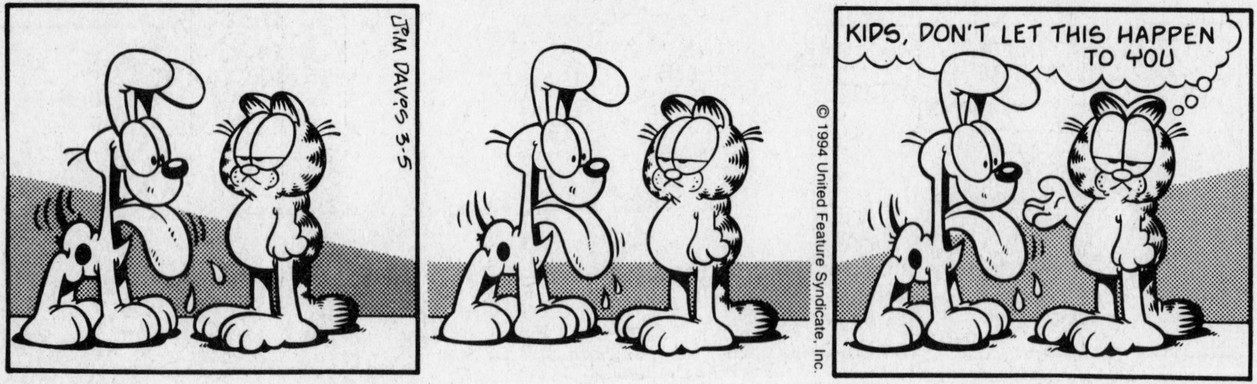
JIM DAVIS 3-5
KIDS, DON'T LET THIS HAPPEN TO YOU
© 1994 United Feature Syndicate, Inc.

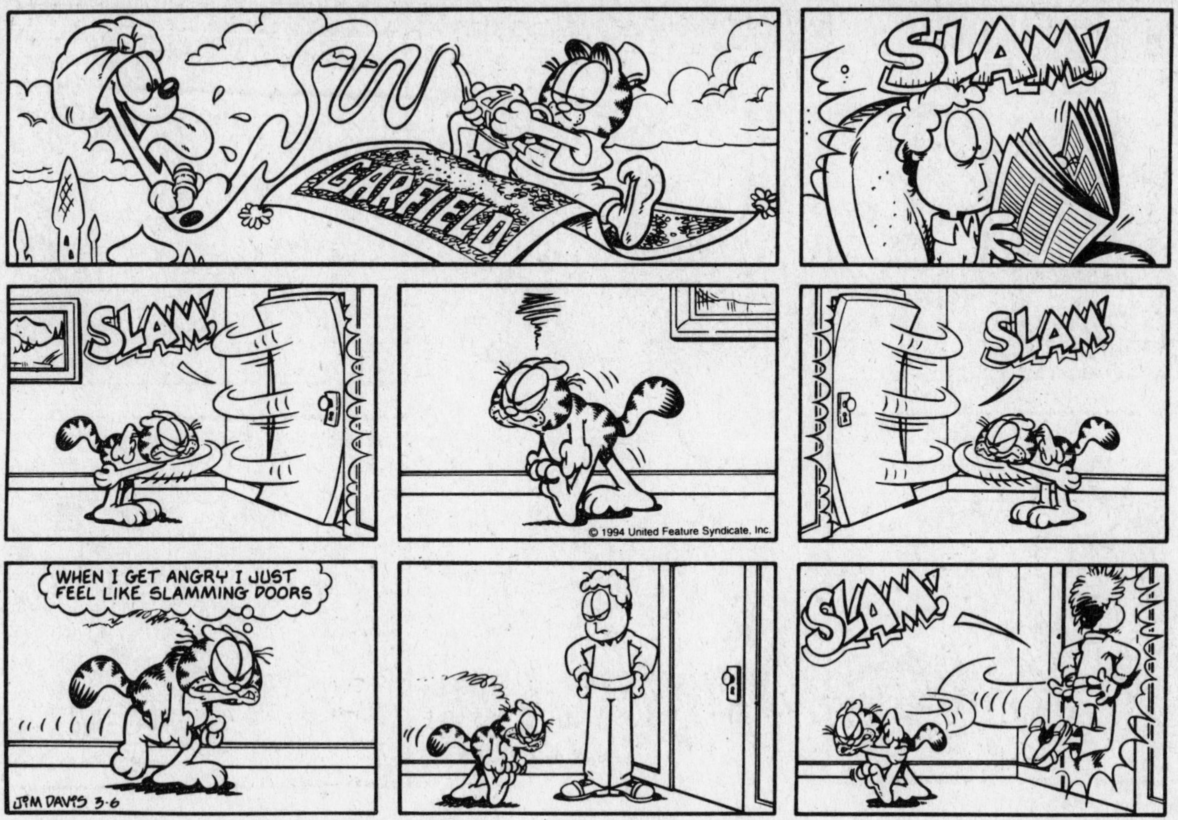
GARFIELD
SLAM!
SLAM!
© 1994 United Feature Syndicate, Inc.
SLAM!
WHEN I GET ANGRY I JUST FEEL LIKE SLAMMING DOORS
JIM DAVIS 3-6
SLAM!

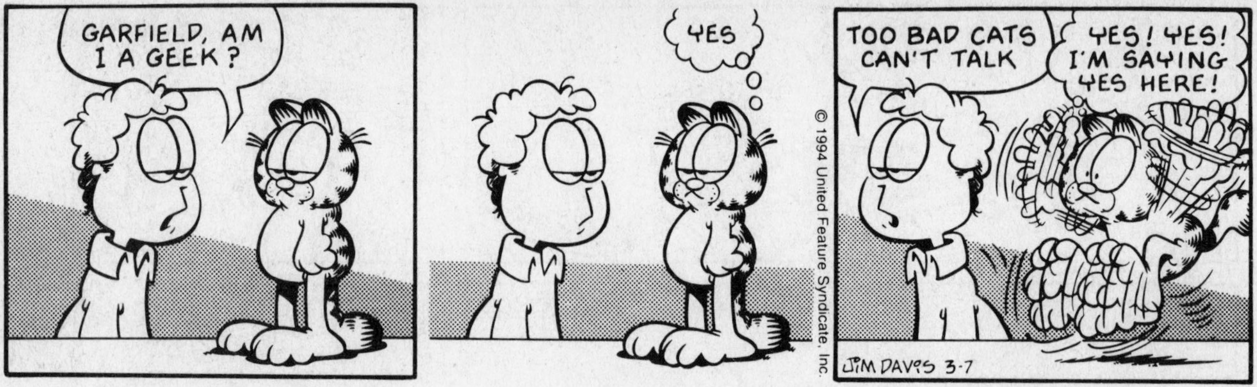
GARFIELD, AM I A GEEK?
YES
TOO BAD CATS CAN'T TALK
YES! YES! I'M SAYING YES HERE!
JIM DAVIS 3-7
© 1994 United Feature Syndicate, Inc.

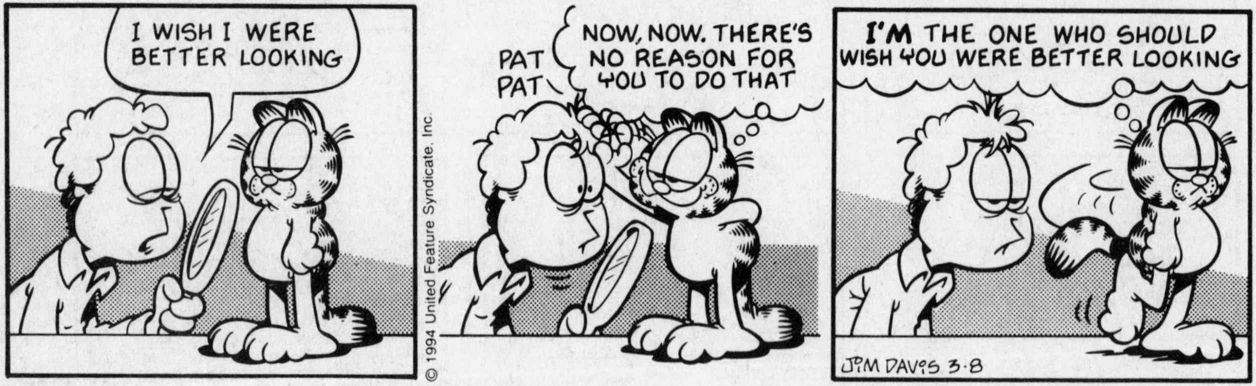
I WISH I WERE BETTER LOOKING
PAT PAT
NOW, NOW. THERE'S NO REASON FOR YOU TO DO THAT
I'M THE ONE WHO SHOULD WISH YOU WERE BETTER LOOKING
JIM DAVIS 3-8
© 1994 United Feature Syndicate, Inc.

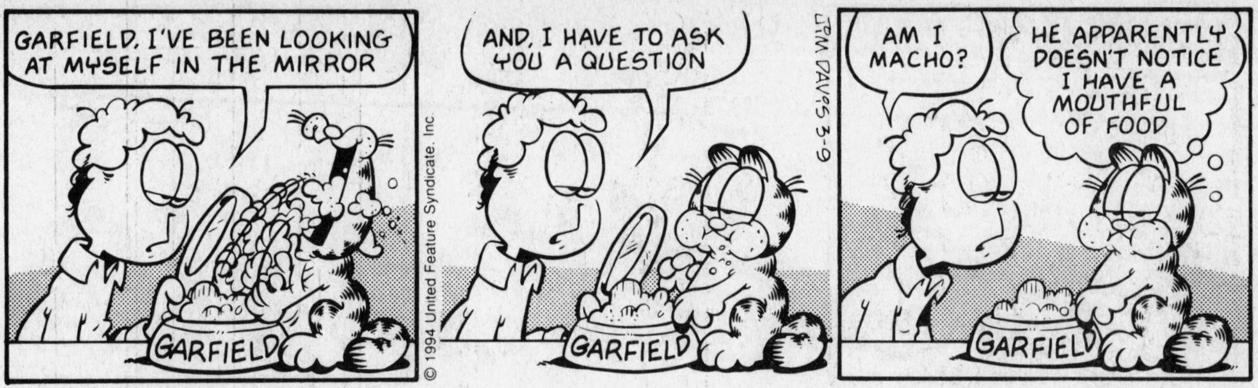
GARFIELD, I'VE BEEN LOOKING AT MYSELF IN THE MIRROR
GARFIELD
© 1994 United Feature Syndicate, Inc.
AND, I HAVE TO ASK YOU A QUESTION
GARFIELD
JIM DAVIS 3-9
AM I MACHO?
HE APPARENTLY DOESN'T NOTICE I HAVE A MOUTHFUL OF FOOD
GARFIELD

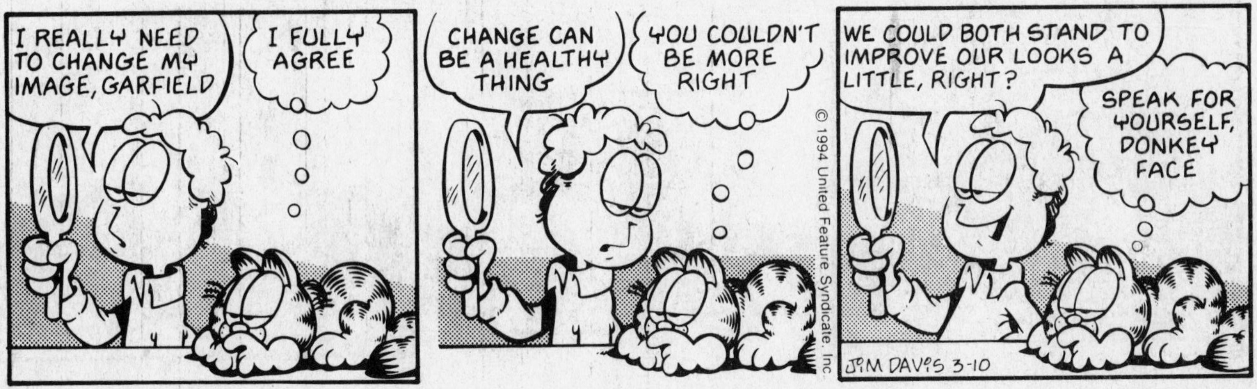
I REALLY NEED TO CHANGE MY IMAGE, GARFIELD
I FULLY AGREE
CHANGE CAN BE A HEALTHY THING
YOU COULDN'T BE MORE RIGHT
© 1994 United Feature Syndicate, Inc.
WE COULD BOTH STAND TO IMPROVE OUR LOOKS A LITTLE, RIGHT?
SPEAK FOR YOURSELF, DONKEY FACE
JIM DAVIS 3-10

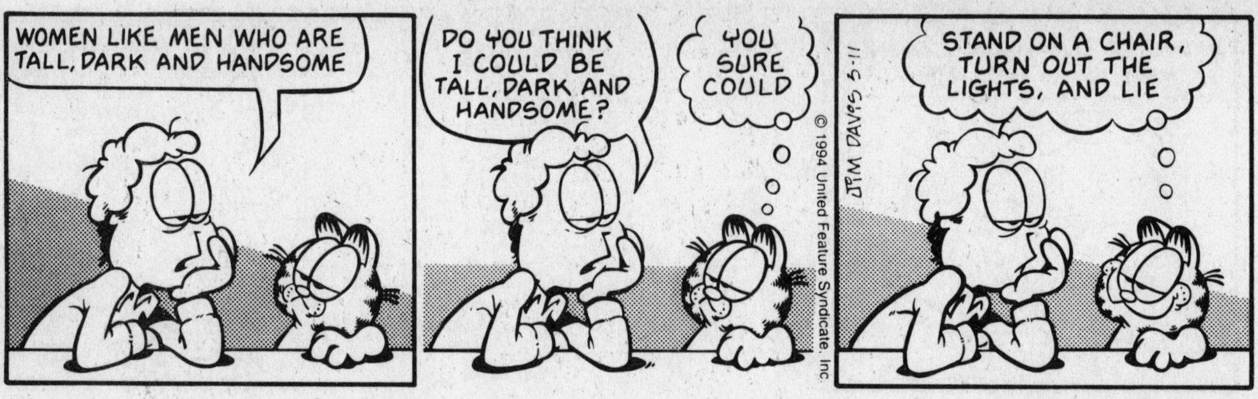
WOMEN LIKE MEN WHO ARE TALL, DARK AND HANDSOME
DO YOU THINK I COULD BE TALL, DARK AND HANDSOME?
YOU SURE COULD
STAND ON A CHAIR, TURN OUT THE LIGHTS, AND LIE
JIM DAVIS 3-11
© 1994 United Feature Syndicate, Inc.

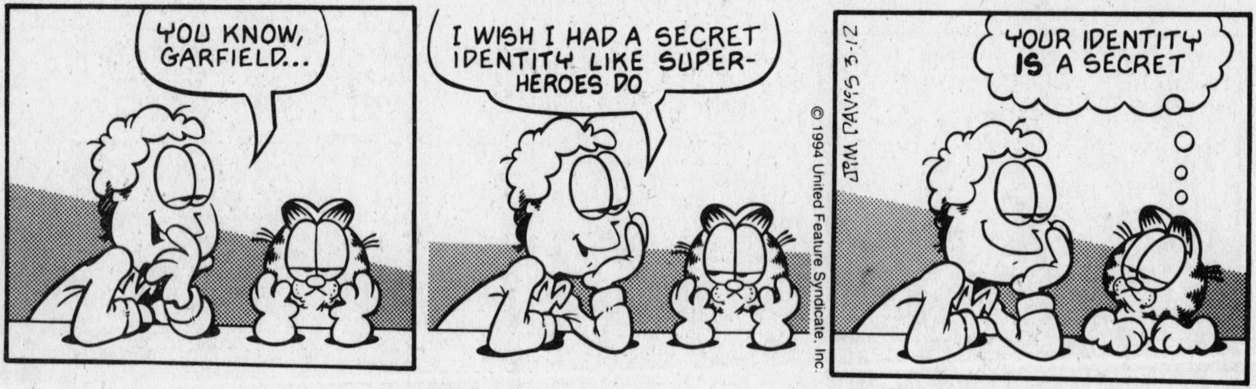
YOU KNOW, GARFIELD...
I WISH I HAD A SECRET IDENTITY LIKE SUPER-HEROES DO
YOUR IDENTITY IS A SECRET
JIM DAVIS 3-12
© 1994 United Feature Syndicate, Inc.

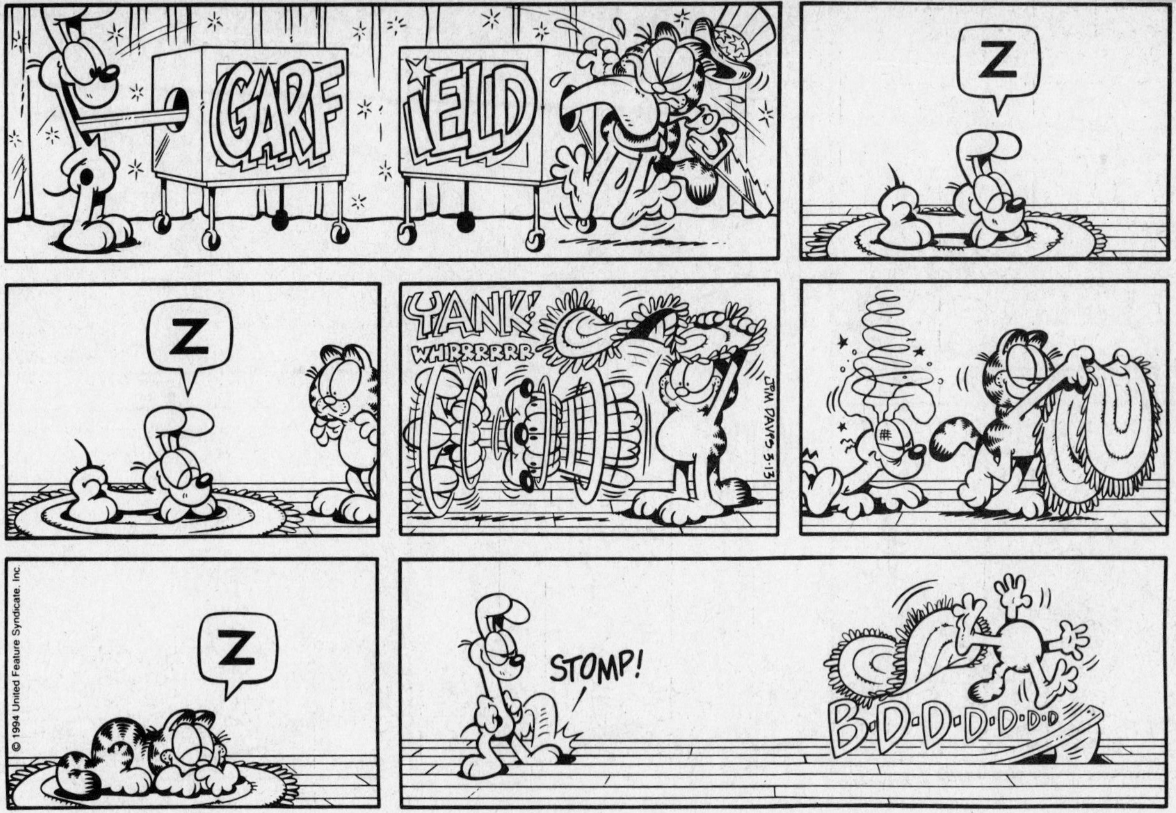
GARF
IELD
Z
Z
YANK!
WHIRRRRRR
JIM DAVIS 3-13
Z
© 1994 United Feature Syndicate, Inc.
STOMP!
B·D·D·D·D·D·D·D

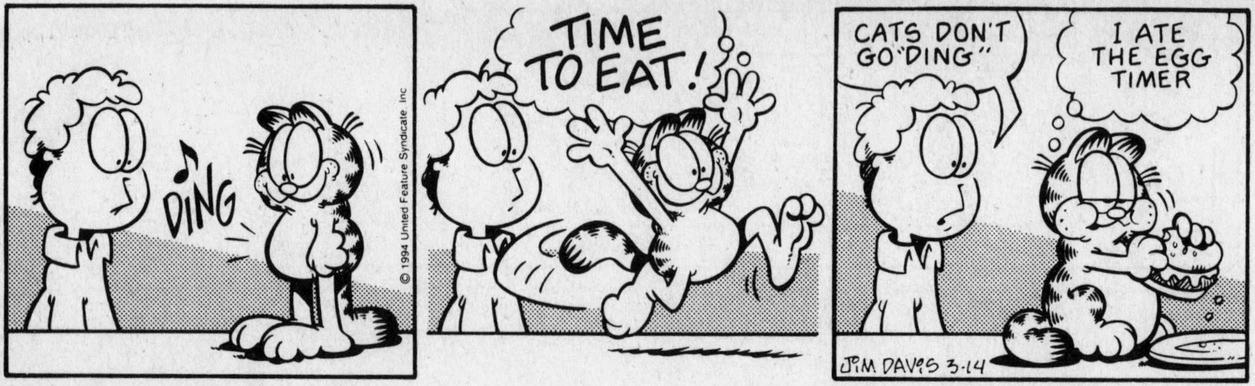
DING
TIME TO EAT!
CATS DON'T GO "DING"
I ATE THE EGG TIMER
JIM DAVIS 3-14
© 1994 United Feature Syndicate, Inc.

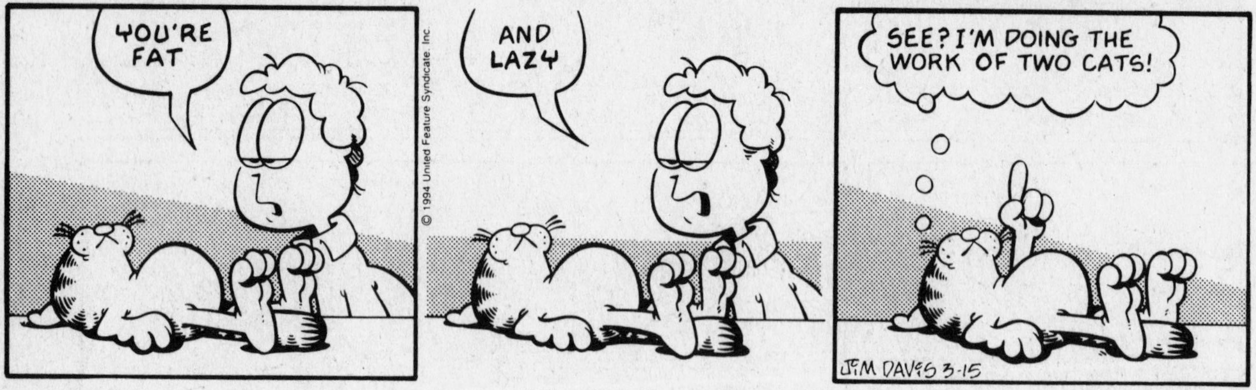
YOU'RE FAT
AND LAZY
SEE? I'M DOING THE WORK OF TWO CATS!
JIM DAVIS 3-15
© 1994 United Feature Syndicate, Inc.

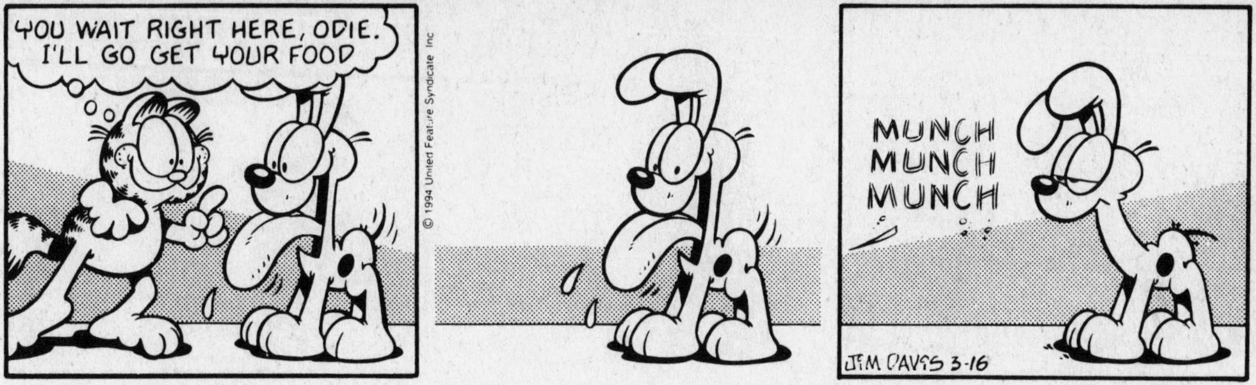
YOU WAIT RIGHT HERE, ODIE. I'LL GO GET YOUR FOOD
© 1994 United Feature Syndicate Inc
MUNCH
MUNCH
MUNCH
JIM DAVIS 3-16

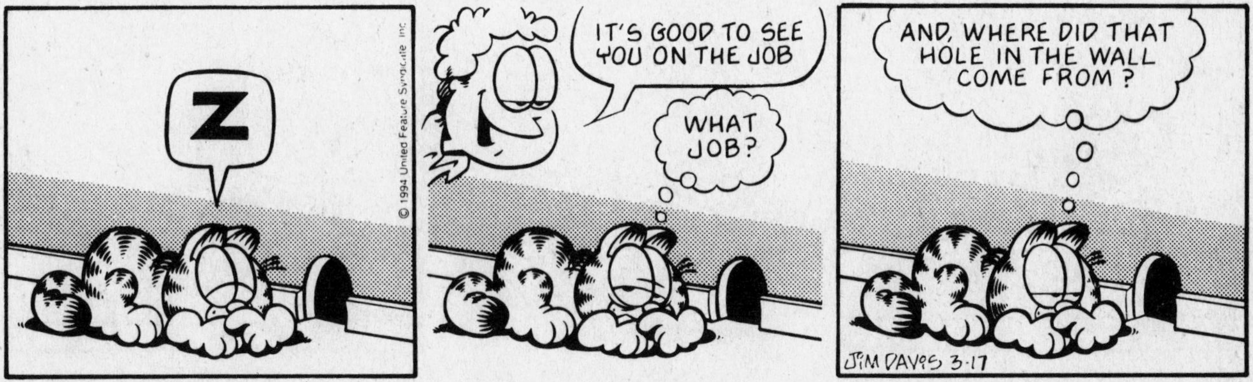
Z
© 1994 United Feature Syndicate Inc
IT'S GOOD TO SEE YOU ON THE JOB
WHAT JOB?
AND, WHERE DID THAT HOLE IN THE WALL COME FROM?
JIM DAVIS 3-17

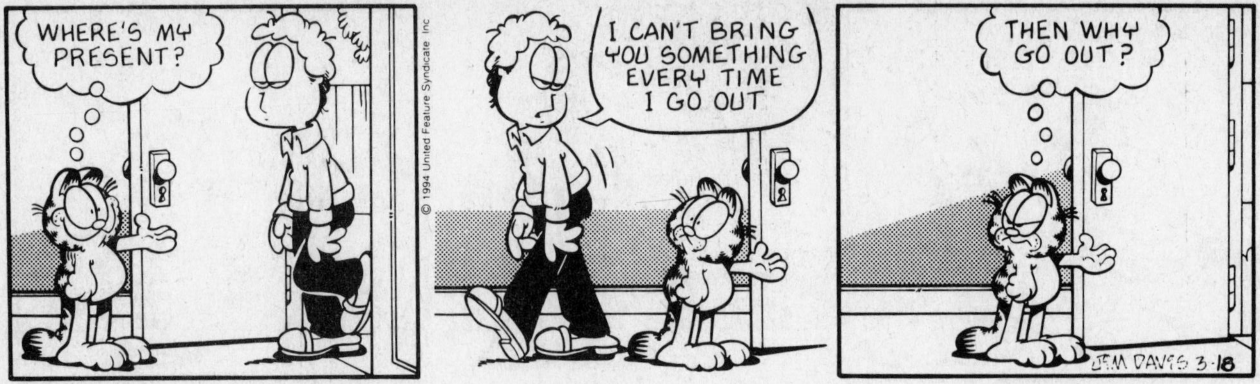
WHERE'S MY PRESENT?
© 1994 United Feature Syndicate, Inc
I CAN'T BRING YOU SOMETHING EVERY TIME I GO OUT
THEN WHY GO OUT?
JIM DAVIS 3-18

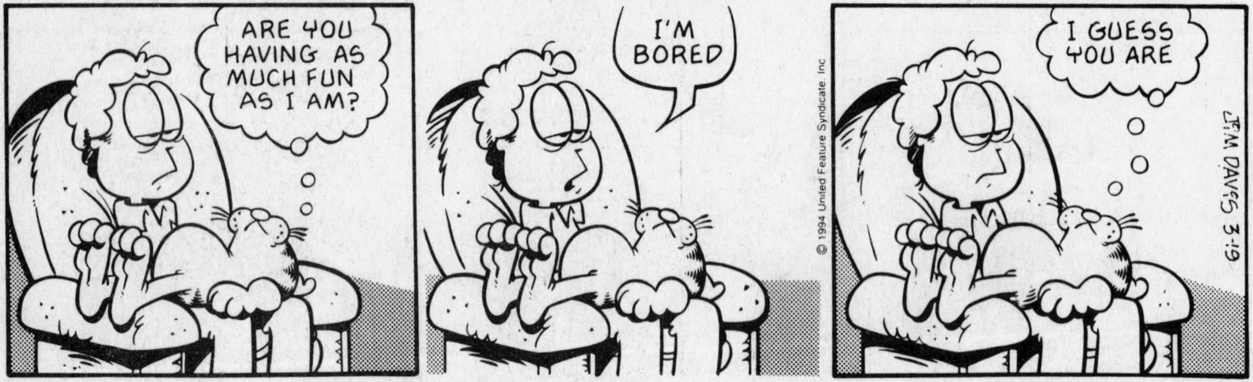
ARE YOU HAVING AS MUCH FUN AS I AM?
I'M BORED
© 1994 United Feature Syndicate, Inc
I GUESS YOU ARE
JIM DAVIS 3-19

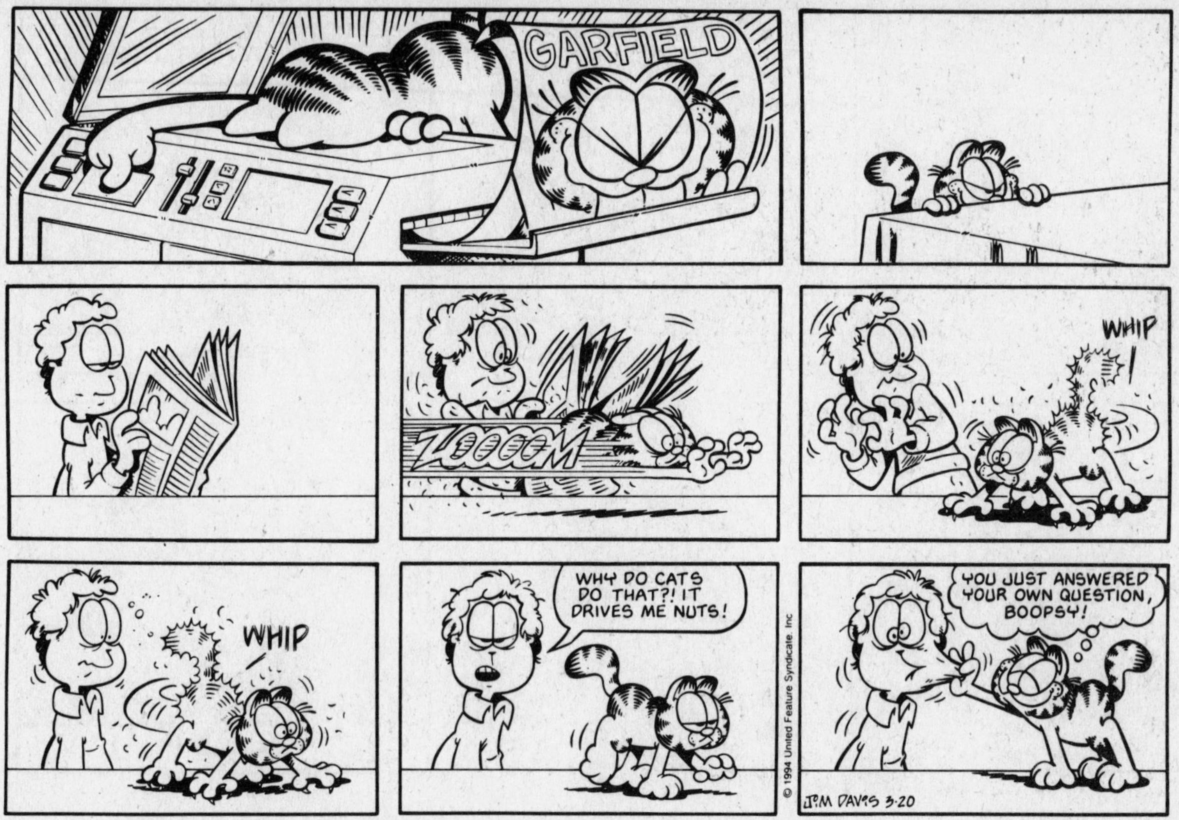
GARFIELD
ZOOOOM
WHIP!
WHIP
WHY DO CATS DO THAT?! IT DRIVES ME NUTS!
YOU JUST ANSWERED YOUR OWN QUESTION, BOOPSY!
© 1994 United Feature Syndicate, Inc
JIM DAVIS 3-20

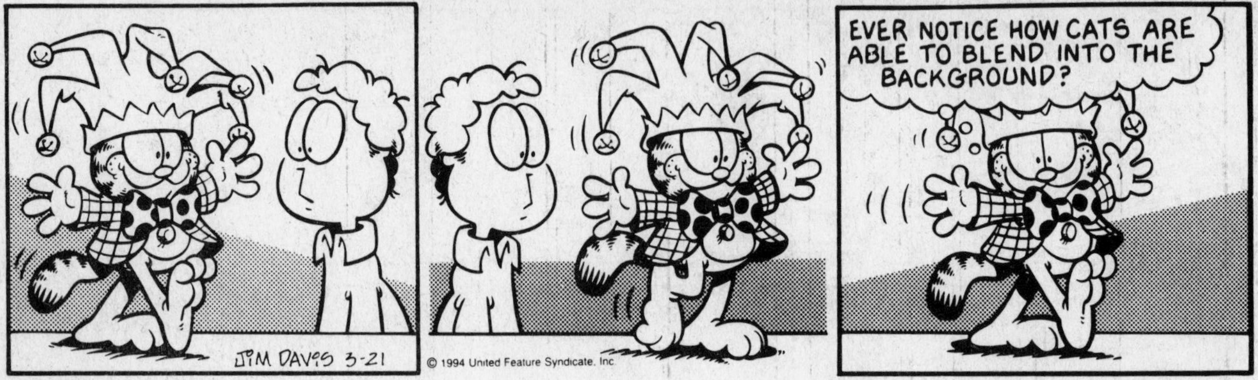
JIM DAVIS 3-21
© 1994 United Feature Syndicate, Inc
EVER NOTICE HOW CATS ARE ABLE TO BLEND INTO THE BACKGROUND?

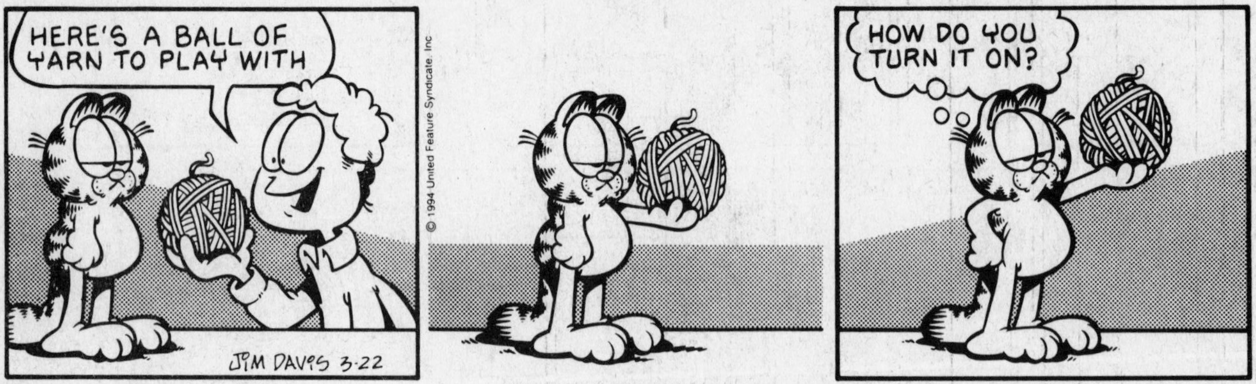
HERE'S A BALL OF YARN TO PLAY WITH
JIM DAVIS 3-22
© 1994 United Feature Syndicate, Inc
HOW DO YOU TURN IT ON?

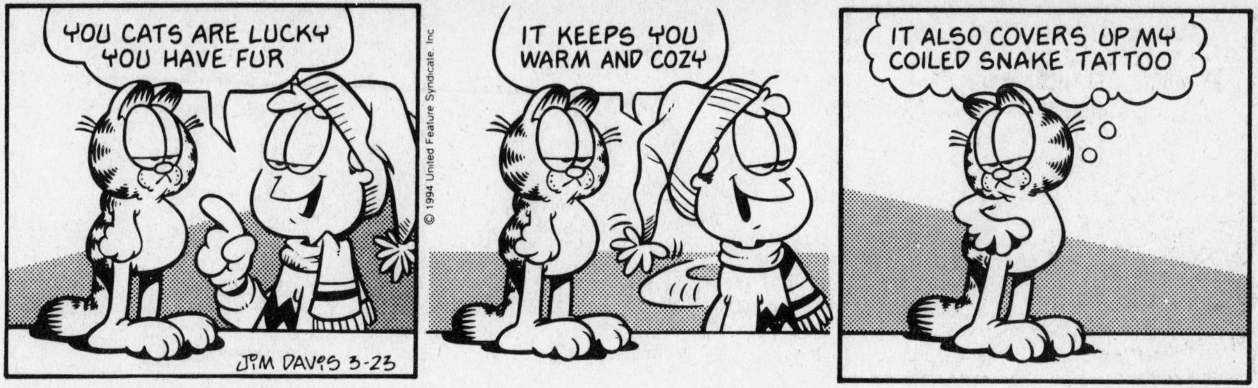
YOU CATS ARE LUCKY YOU HAVE FUR
IT KEEPS YOU WARM AND COZY
IT ALSO COVERS UP MY COILED SNAKE TATTOO
JIM DAVIS 3-23
© 1994 United Feature Syndicate, Inc

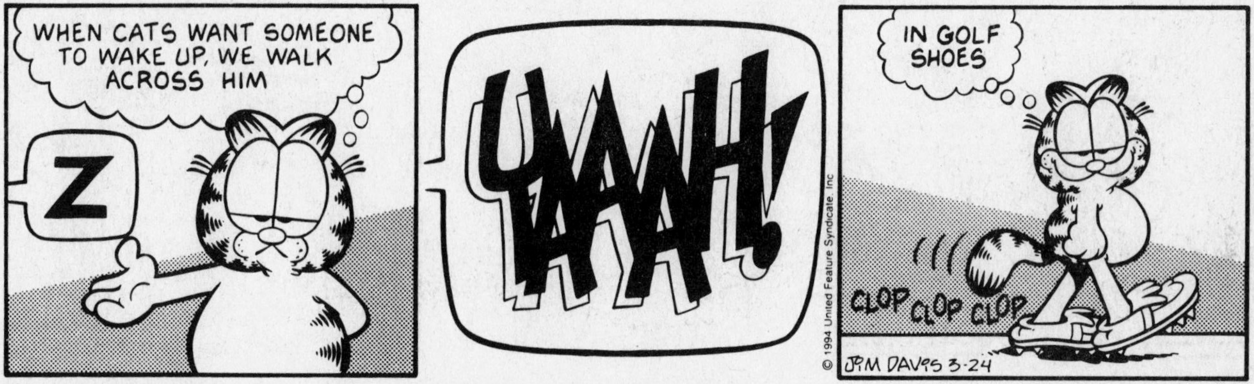
WHEN CATS WANT SOMEONE TO WAKE UP, WE WALK ACROSS HIM
Z
YAAAH!
IN GOLF SHOES
CLOP CLOP CLOP
JIM DAVIS 3-24
© 1994 United Feature Syndicate, Inc

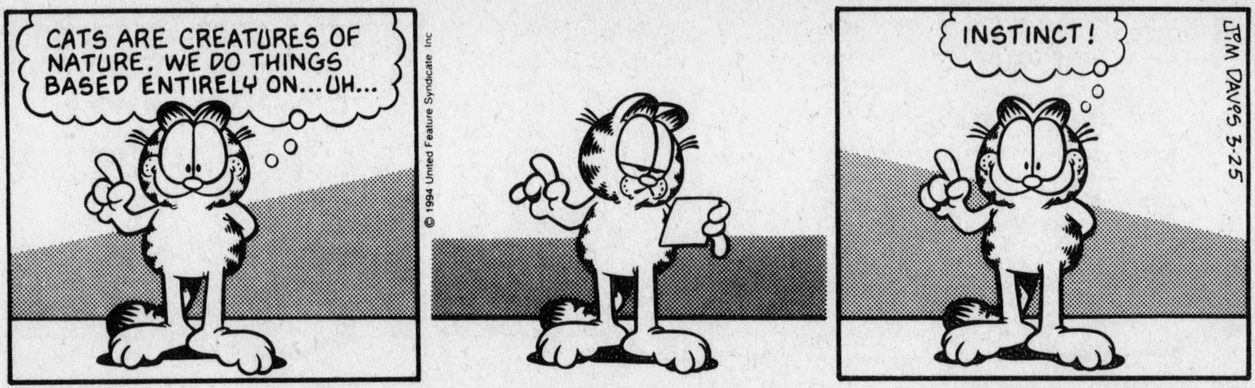
CATS ARE CREATURES OF NATURE. WE DO THINGS BASED ENTIRELY ON...UH...
INSTINCT!
JIM DAVIS 3-25
© 1994 United Feature Syndicate Inc

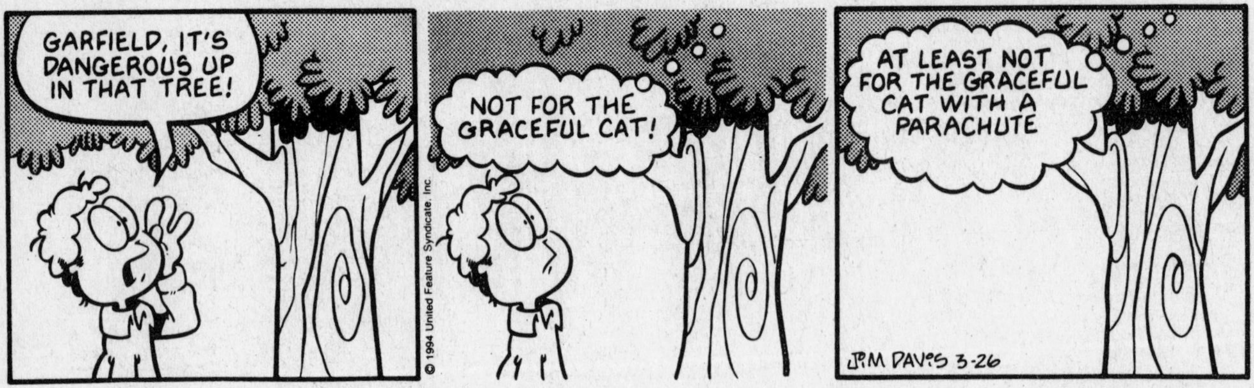
GARFIELD, IT'S DANGEROUS UP IN THAT TREE!
NOT FOR THE GRACEFUL CAT!
AT LEAST NOT FOR THE GRACEFUL CAT WITH A PARACHUTE
JIM DAVIS 3-26
© 1994 United Feature Syndicate, Inc.

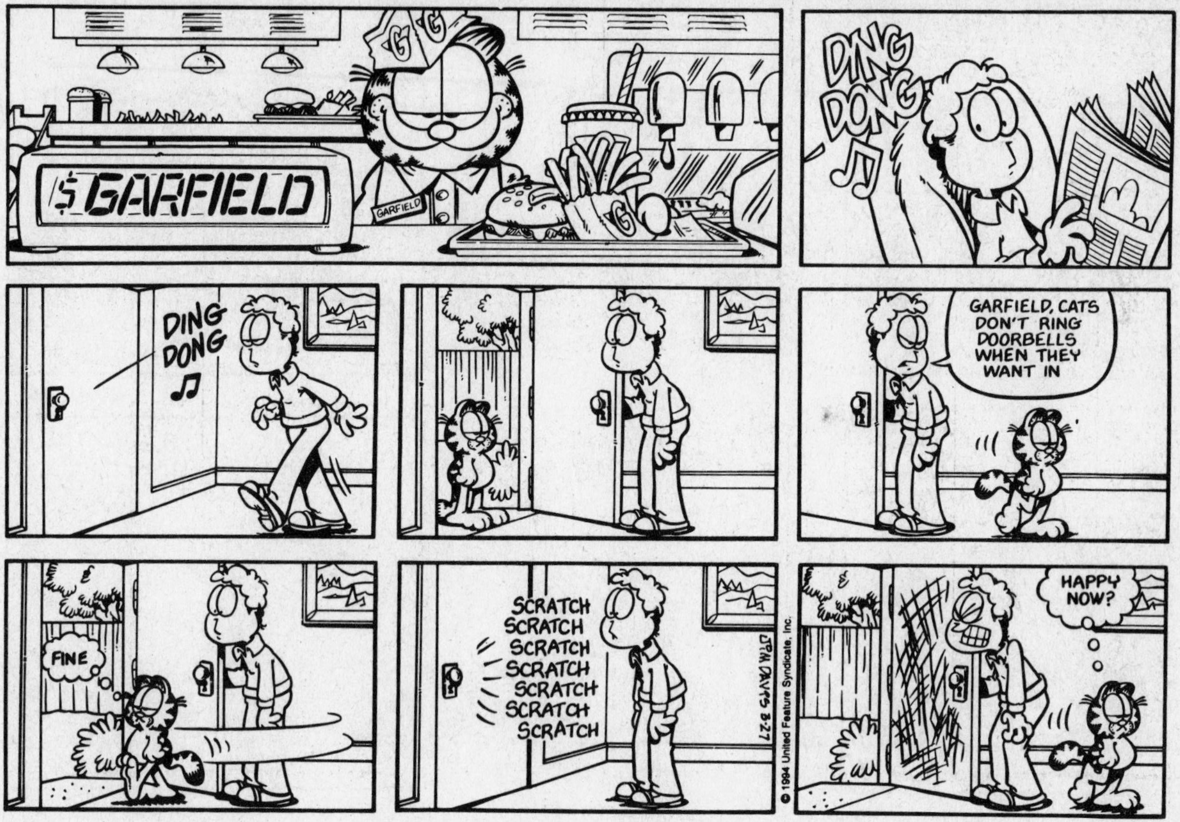
$GARFIELD
GARFIELD
DING DONG
DING DONG
GARFIELD, CATS DON'T RING DOORBELLS WHEN THEY WANT IN
FINE
SCRATCH
SCRATCH
SCRATCH
SCRATCH
SCRATCH
SCRATCH
SCRATCH
JIM DAVIS 3-27
© 1994 United Feature Syndicate, Inc.
HAPPY NOW?

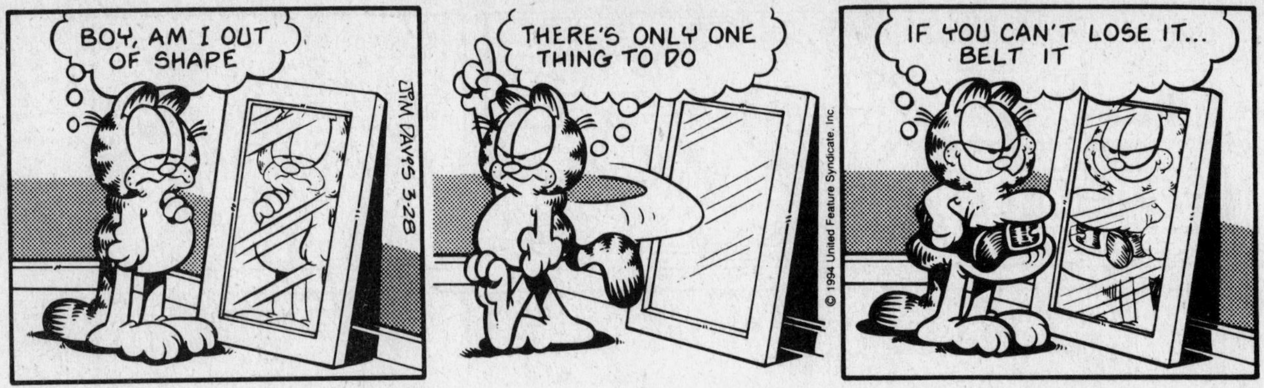
BOY, AM I OUT OF SHAPE
JIM DAVIS 3-28
THERE'S ONLY ONE THING TO DO
IF YOU CAN'T LOSE IT... BELT IT
© 1994 United Feature Syndicate, Inc.

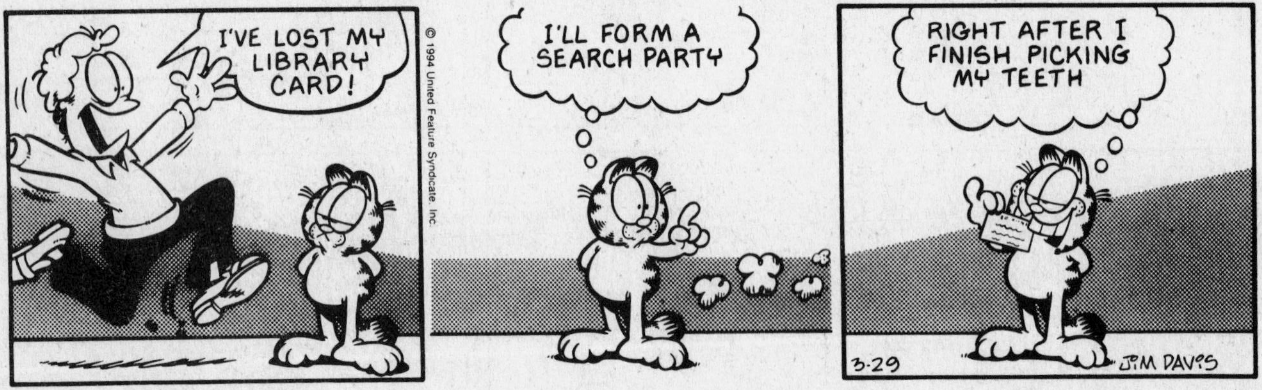
I'VE LOST MY LIBRARY CARD!
© 1994 United Feature Syndicate, Inc.
I'LL FORM A SEARCH PARTY
RIGHT AFTER I FINISH PICKING MY TEETH
3-29
JIM DAVIS

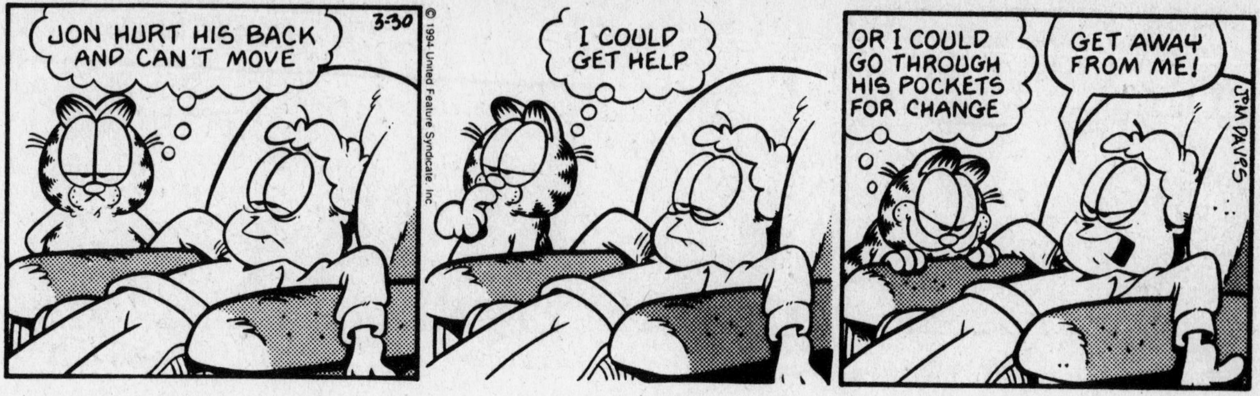
JON HURT HIS BACK AND CAN'T MOVE
3-30
© 1994 United Feature Syndicate, Inc.
I COULD GET HELP
OR I COULD GO THROUGH HIS POCKETS FOR CHANGE
GET AWAY FROM ME!
JIM DAVIS

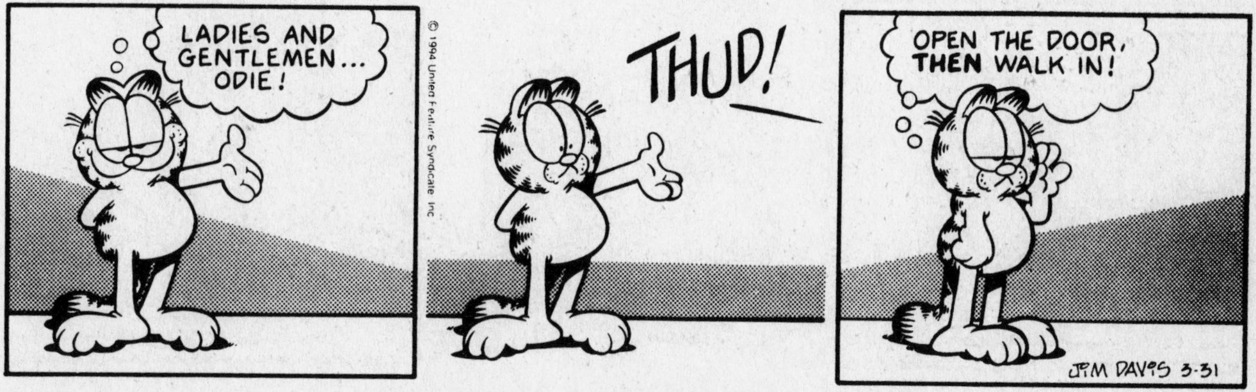
LADIES AND GENTLEMEN... ODIE!
© 1994 United Feature Syndicate, Inc.
THUD!
OPEN THE DOOR, **THEN** WALK IN!
JIM DAVIS 3-31

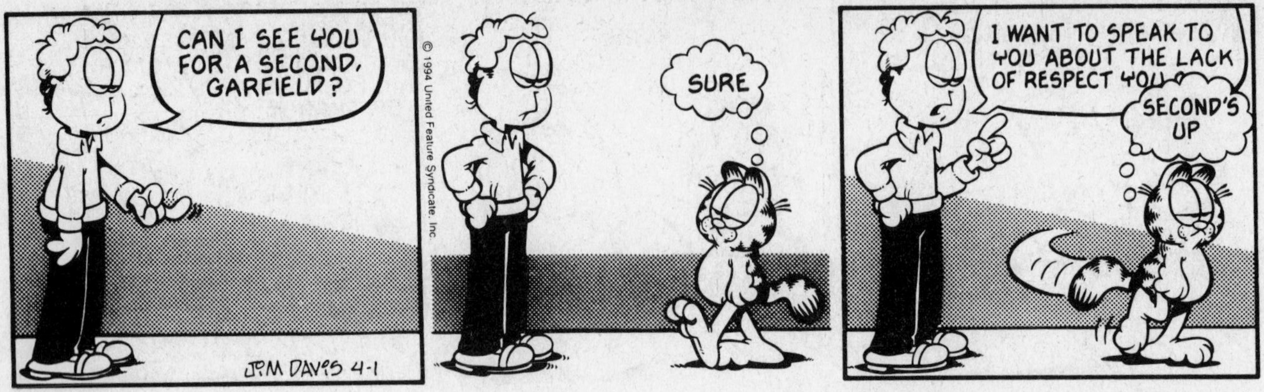
CAN I SEE YOU FOR A SECOND, GARFIELD?
SURE
I WANT TO SPEAK TO YOU ABOUT THE LACK OF RESPECT YOU
SECOND'S UP
JIM DAVIS 4-1
© 1994 United Feature Syndicate, Inc.

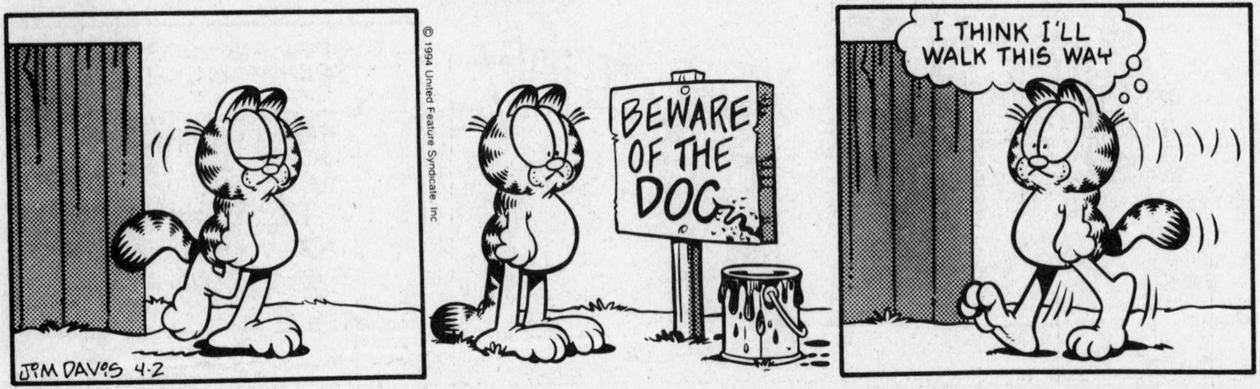
JIM DAVIS 4-2
© 1994 United Feature Syndicate, Inc.
BEWARE OF THE DOG
I THINK I'LL WALK THIS WAY

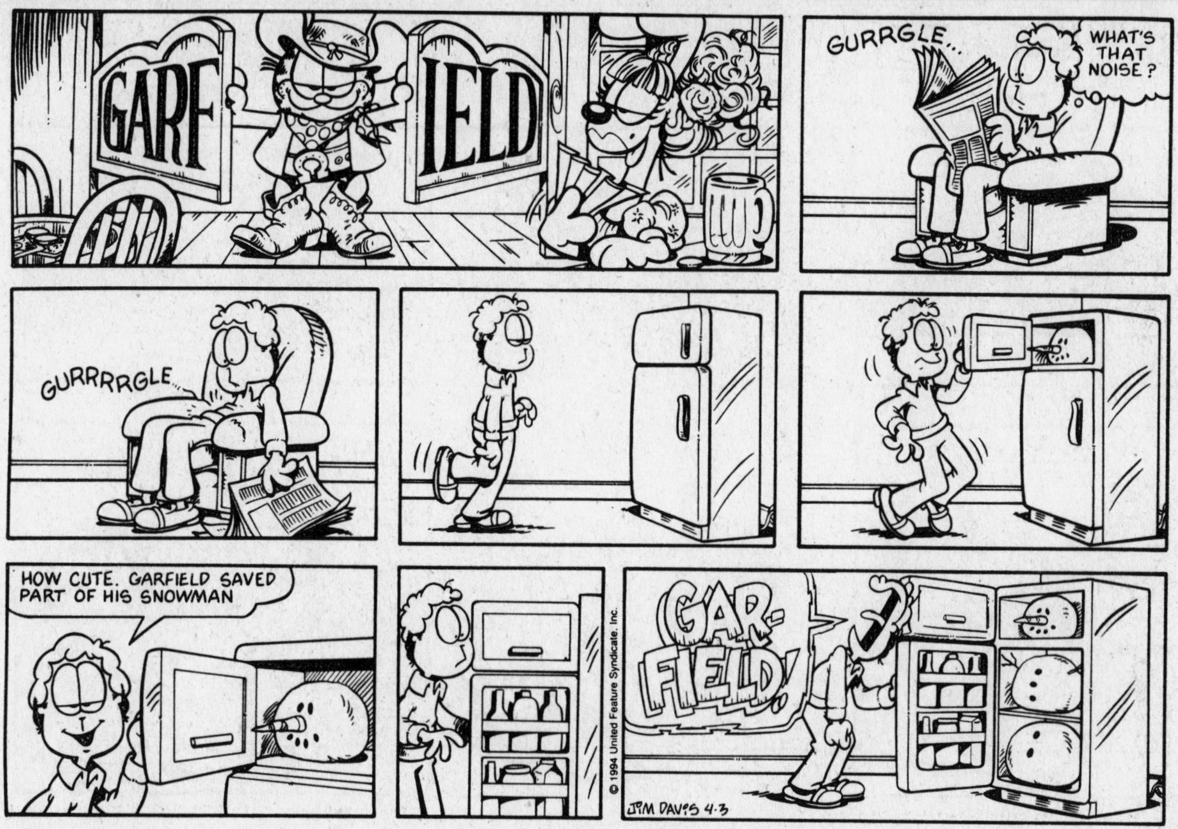
GARF IELD
GURRGLE...
WHAT'S THAT NOISE?
GURRRRGLE...
HOW CUTE. GARFIELD SAVED PART OF HIS SNOWMAN
GAR-FIELD!
© 1994 United Feature Syndicate, Inc.
JIM DAVIS 4-3

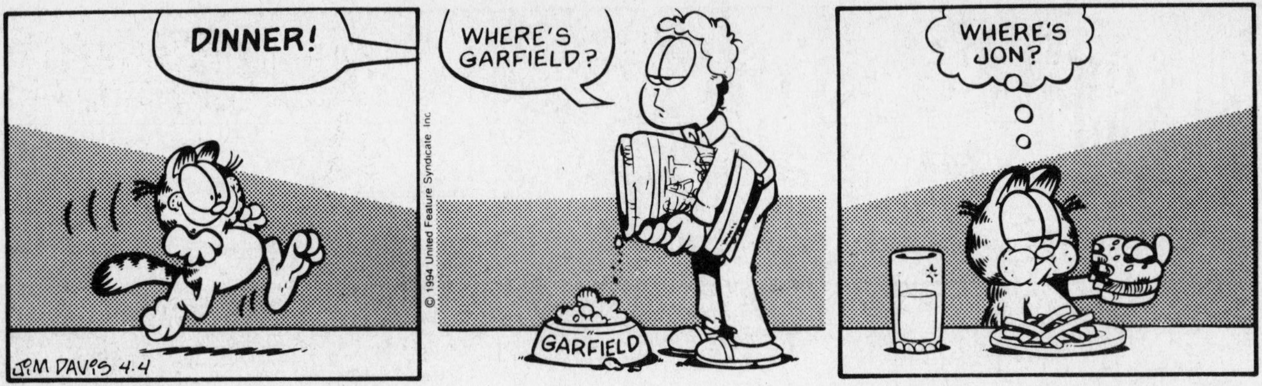
DINNER!
WHERE'S GARFIELD?
GARFIELD
WHERE'S JON?
JIM DAVIS 4-4
© 1994 United Feature Syndicate, Inc

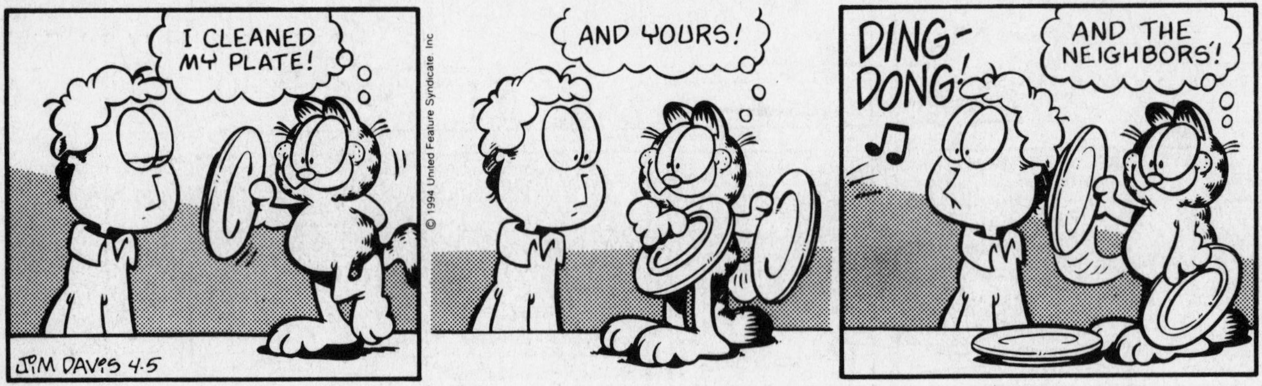
I CLEANED MY PLATE!
AND YOURS!
DING-DONG!
AND THE NEIGHBORS'!
JIM DAVIS 4-5
© 1994 United Feature Syndicate, Inc

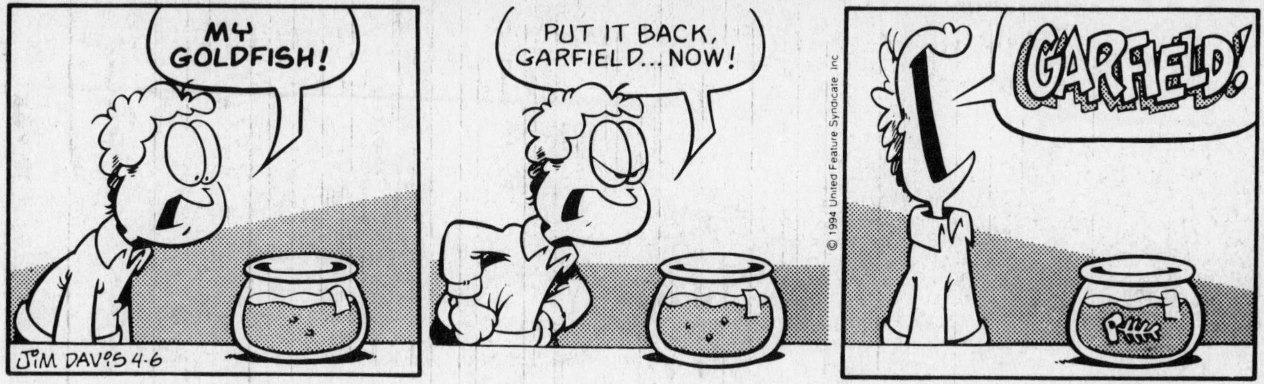
MY GOLDFISH!
JIM DAVIS 4-6
PUT IT BACK, GARFIELD... NOW!
© 1994 United Feature Syndicate Inc
GARFIELD!

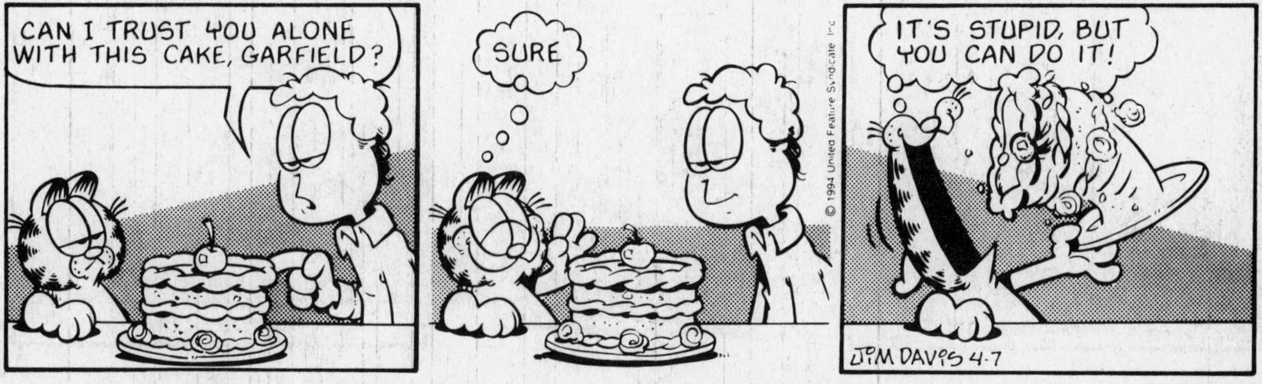
CAN I TRUST YOU ALONE WITH THIS CAKE, GARFIELD?
SURE
© 1994 United Feature Syndicate Inc
IT'S STUPID, BUT YOU CAN DO IT!
JIM DAVIS 4-7

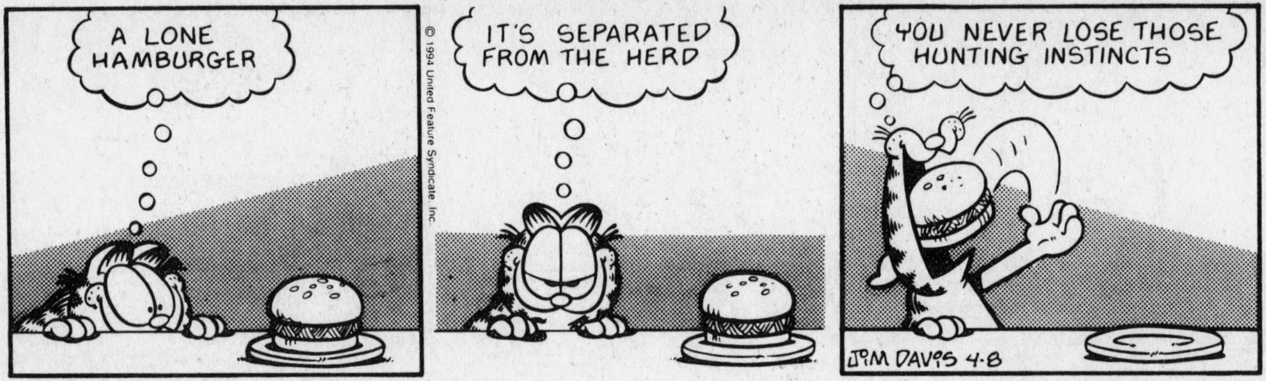
A LONE HAMBURGER
IT'S SEPARATED FROM THE HERD
YOU NEVER LOSE THOSE HUNTING INSTINCTS
JIM DAVIS 4-8
© 1994 United Feature Syndicate, Inc.

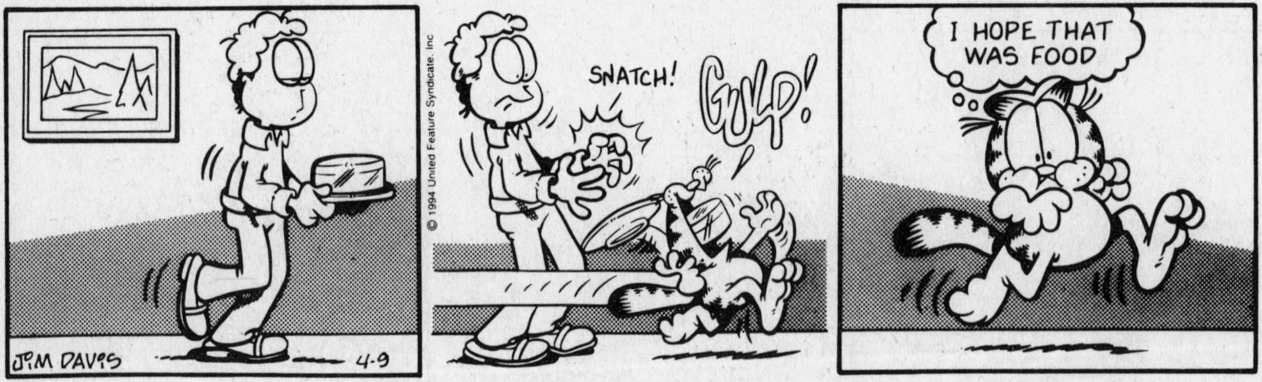
JIM DAVIS 4-9
SNATCH!
GULP!
I HOPE THAT WAS FOOD
© 1994 United Feature Syndicate, Inc.

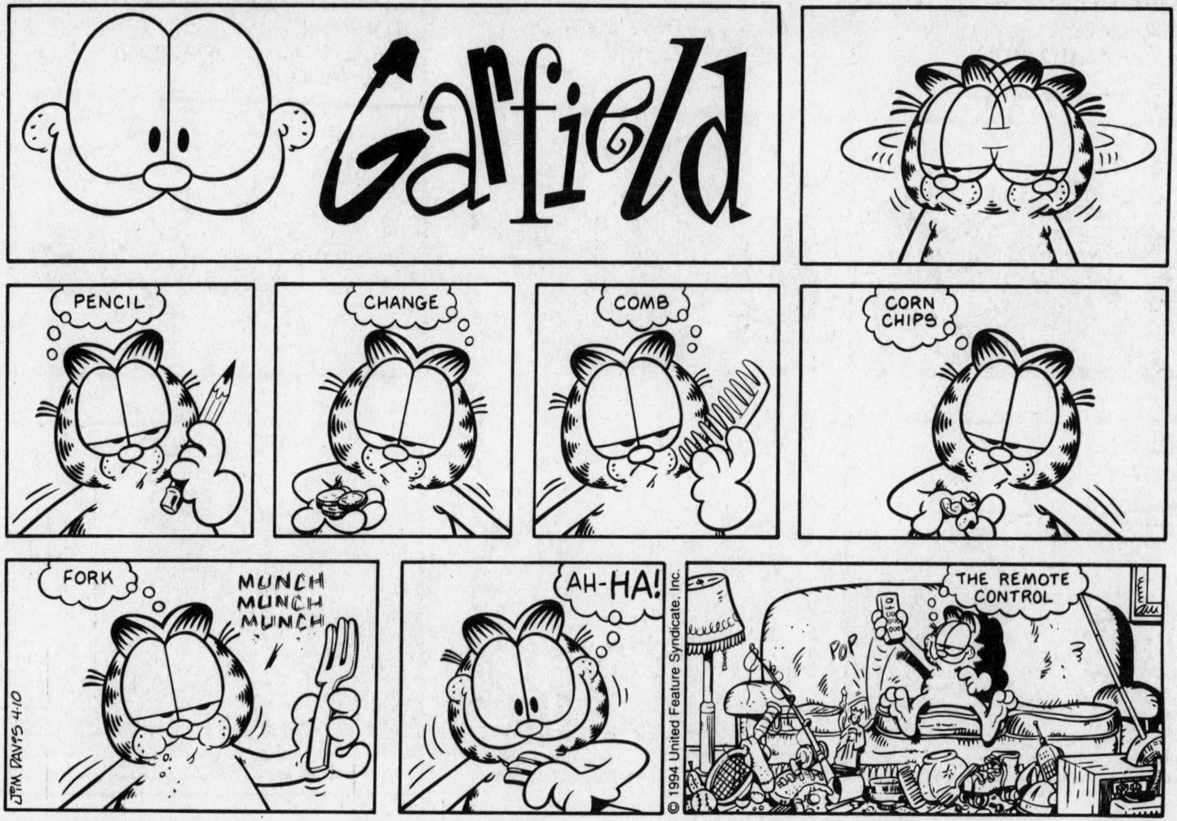
Garfield
PENCIL
CHANGE
COMB
CORN CHIPS
FORK
MUNCH MUNCH MUNCH
AH-HA!
THE REMOTE CONTROL
POP
JPM DAVPS 4·10
© 1994 United Feature Syndicate, Inc.

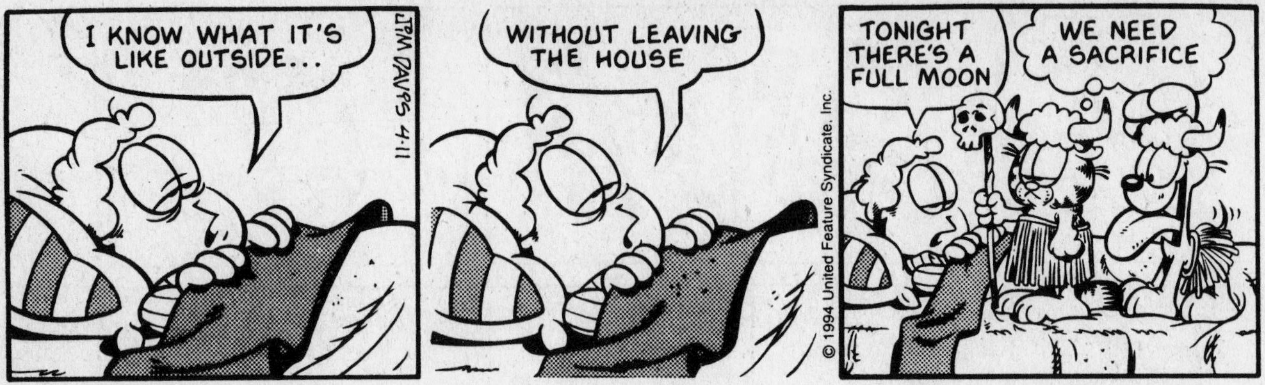
I KNOW WHAT IT'S LIKE OUTSIDE...
JIM DAVIS 4-11
WITHOUT LEAVING THE HOUSE
TONIGHT THERE'S A FULL MOON
WE NEED A SACRIFICE

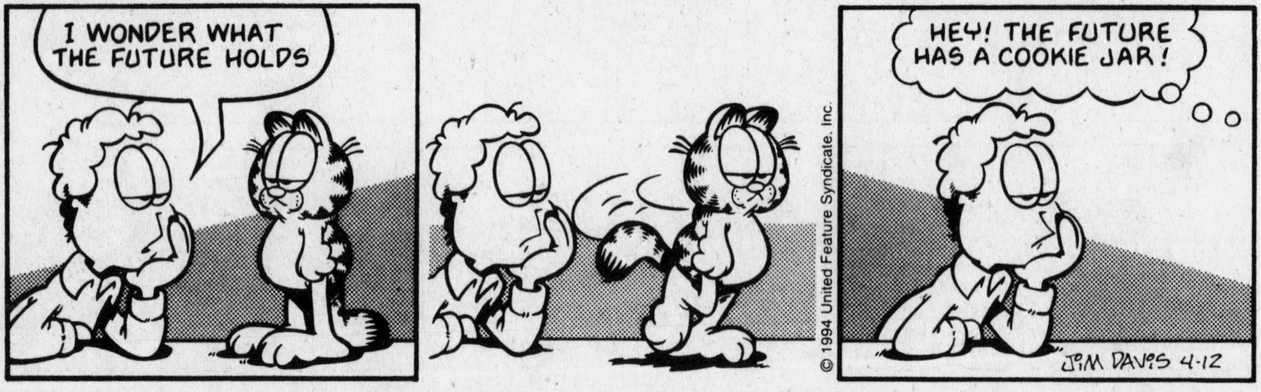
I WONDER WHAT THE FUTURE HOLDS
HEY! THE FUTURE HAS A COOKIE JAR!
JIM DAVIS 4-12

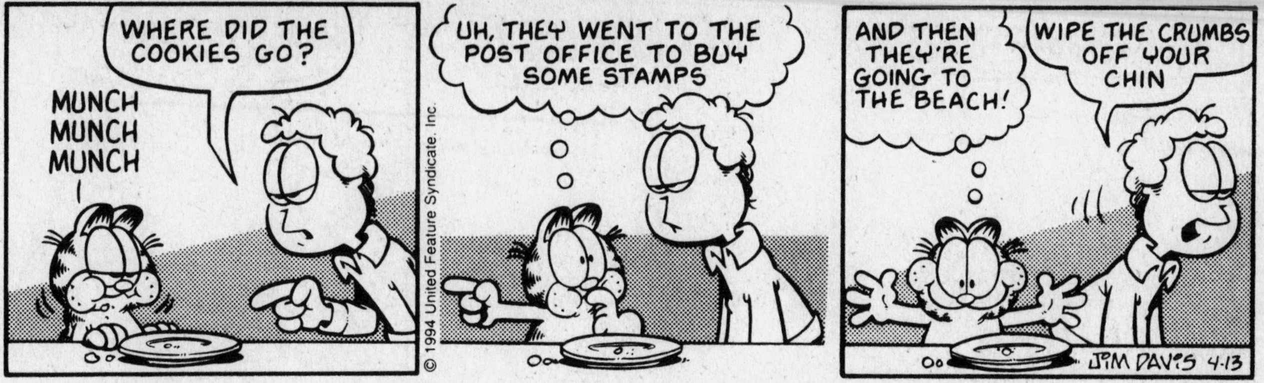
WHERE DID THE COOKIES GO?
MUNCH MUNCH MUNCH
© 1994 United Feature Syndicate, Inc.
UH, THEY WENT TO THE POST OFFICE TO BUY SOME STAMPS
AND THEN THEY'RE GOING TO THE BEACH!
WIPE THE CRUMBS OFF YOUR CHIN
JIM DAVIS 4-13

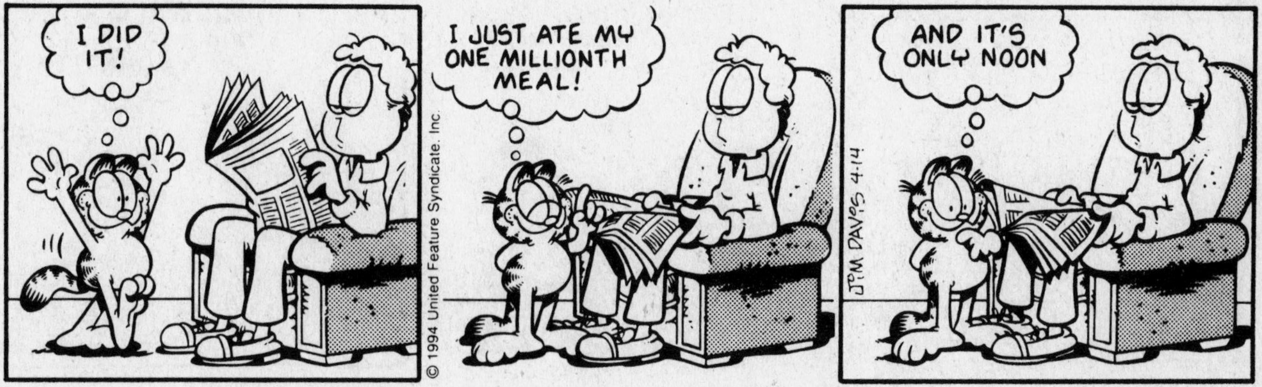
I DID IT!
© 1994 United Feature Syndicate, Inc.
I JUST ATE MY ONE MILLIONTH MEAL!
JIM DAVIS 4-14
AND IT'S ONLY NOON

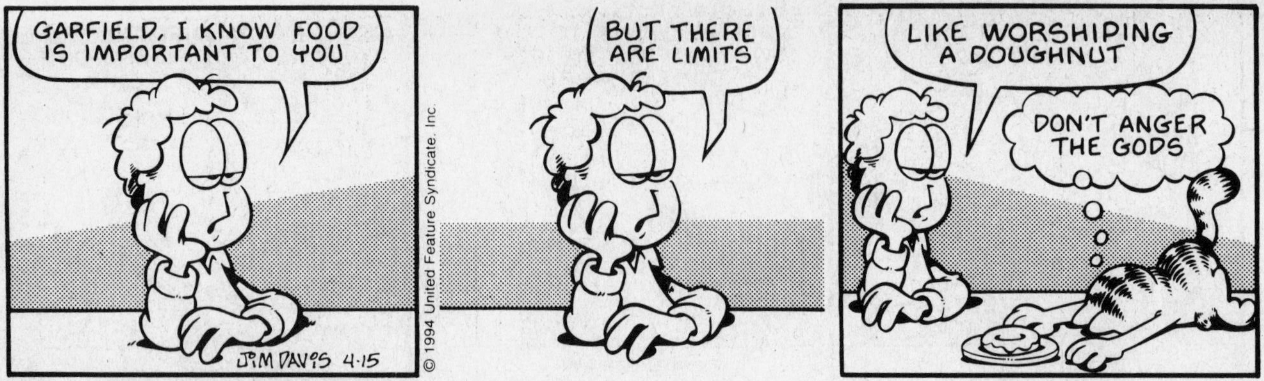
GARFIELD, I KNOW FOOD IS IMPORTANT TO YOU
JIM DAVIS 4-15
BUT THERE ARE LIMITS
LIKE WORSHIPING A DOUGHNUT
DON'T ANGER THE GODS

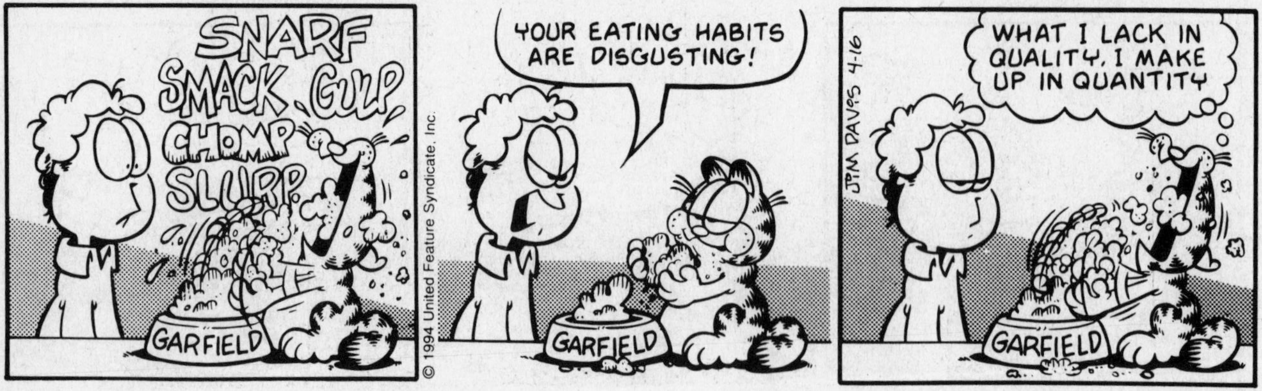
SNARF
SMACK, GULP
CHOMP
SLURP
GARFIELD
YOUR EATING HABITS ARE DISGUSTING!
GARFIELD
JIM DAVIS 4-16
WHAT I LACK IN QUALITY, I MAKE UP IN QUANTITY
GARFIELD

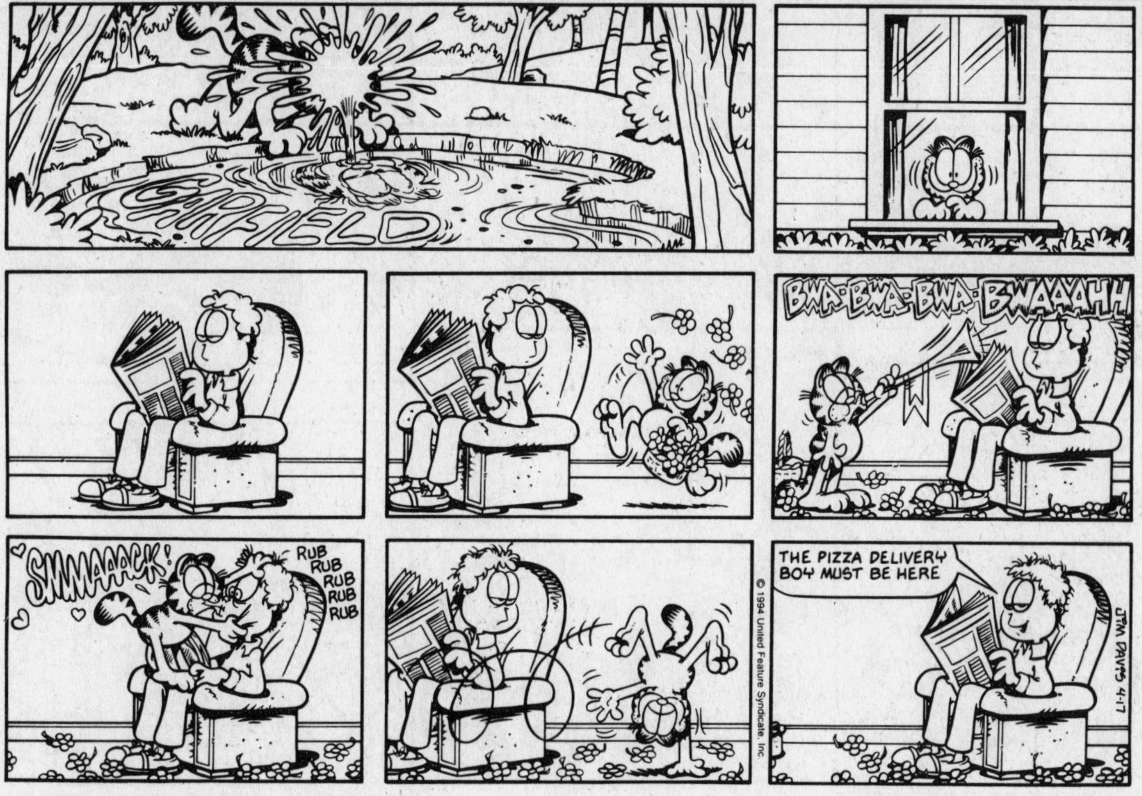
GARFIELD
BWA-BWA-BWA-BWAAAHH
SMMAAACK!
RUB
RUB
RUB
RUB
RUB
THE PIZZA DELIVERY BOY MUST BE HERE
JPM DAVPS 4-17
© 1994 United Feature Syndicate, Inc.

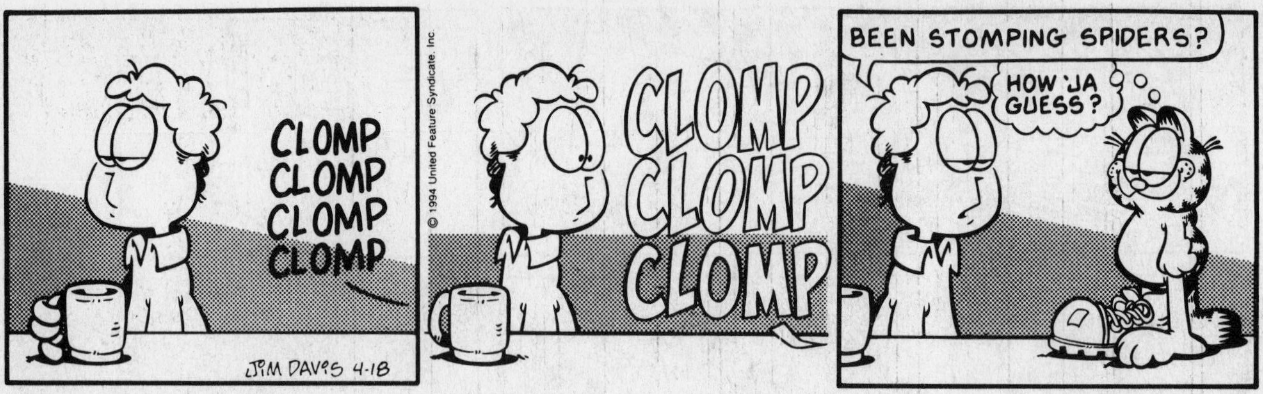
CLOMP
CLOMP
CLOMP
CLOMP
JIM DAVIS 4-18
© 1994 United Feature Syndicate, Inc.
CLOMP
CLOMP
CLOMP
BEEN STOMPING SPIDERS?
HOW 'JA GUESS?

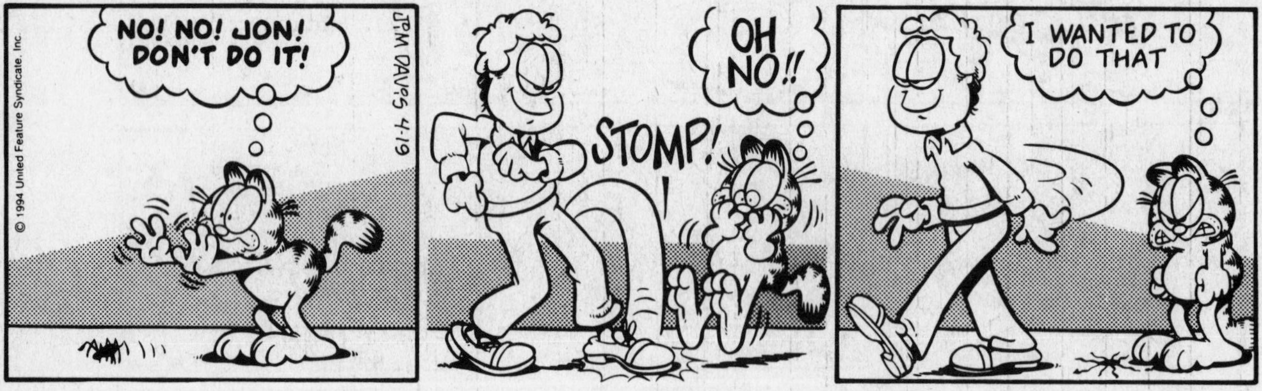
© 1994 United Feature Syndicate, Inc.
NO! NO! JON! DON'T DO IT!
JIM DAVIS 4-19
STOMP!
OH NO!!
I WANTED TO DO THAT

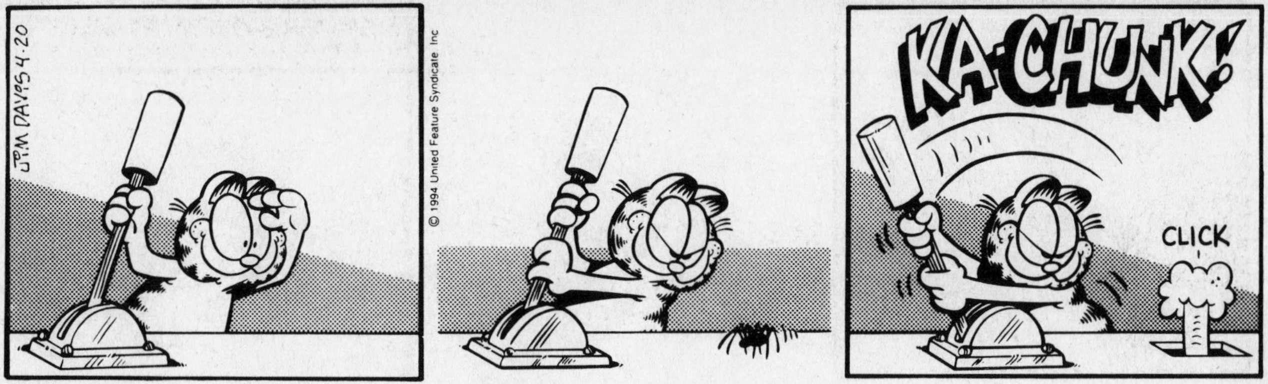
JIM DAVIS 4-20
© 1994 United Feature Syndicate Inc
KA-CHUNK!
CLICK

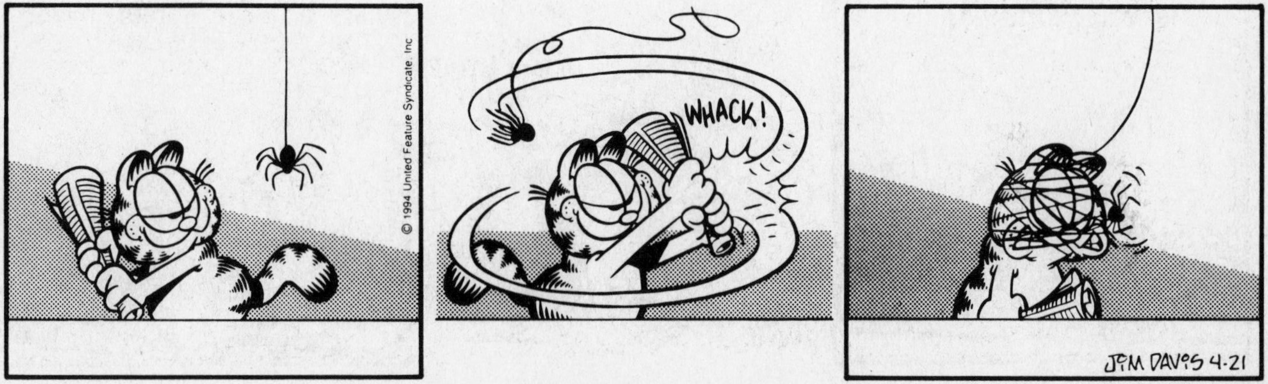
© 1994 United Feature Syndicate, Inc
WHACK!
JIM DAVIS 4-21

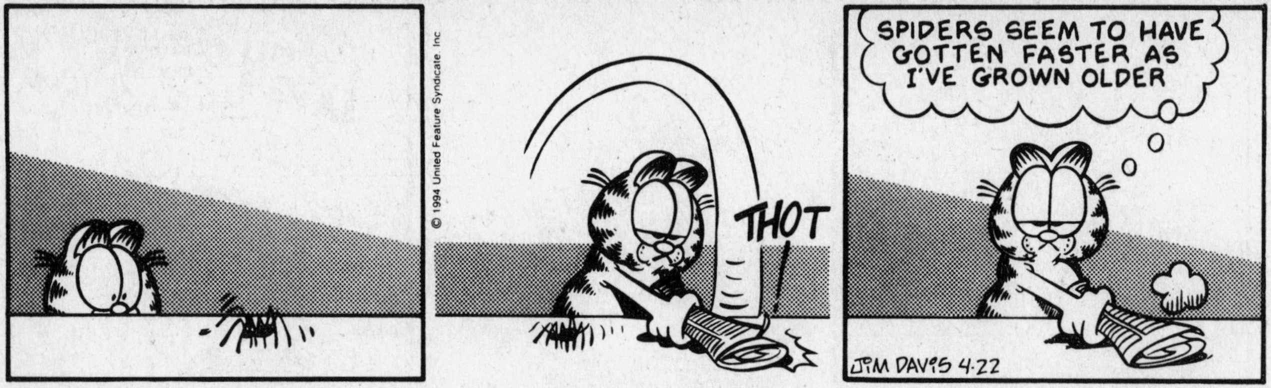
THOT
SPIDERS SEEM TO HAVE GOTTEN FASTER AS I'VE GROWN OLDER
JIM DAVIS 4·22

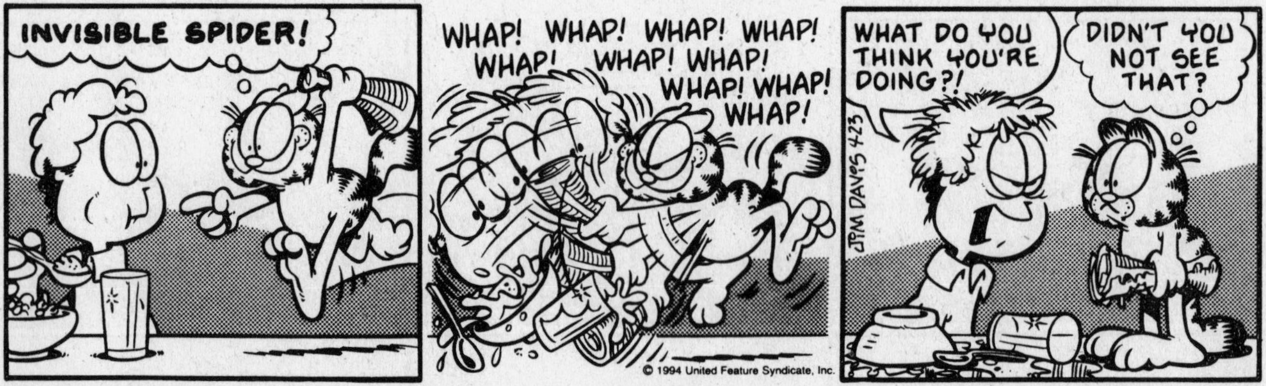
INVISIBLE SPIDER!
WHAP! WHAP! WHAP! WHAP! WHAP! WHAP! WHAP! WHAP! WHAP! WHAP!
WHAT DO YOU THINK YOU'RE DOING?!
DIDN'T YOU NOT SEE THAT?
JIM DAVIS 4·23

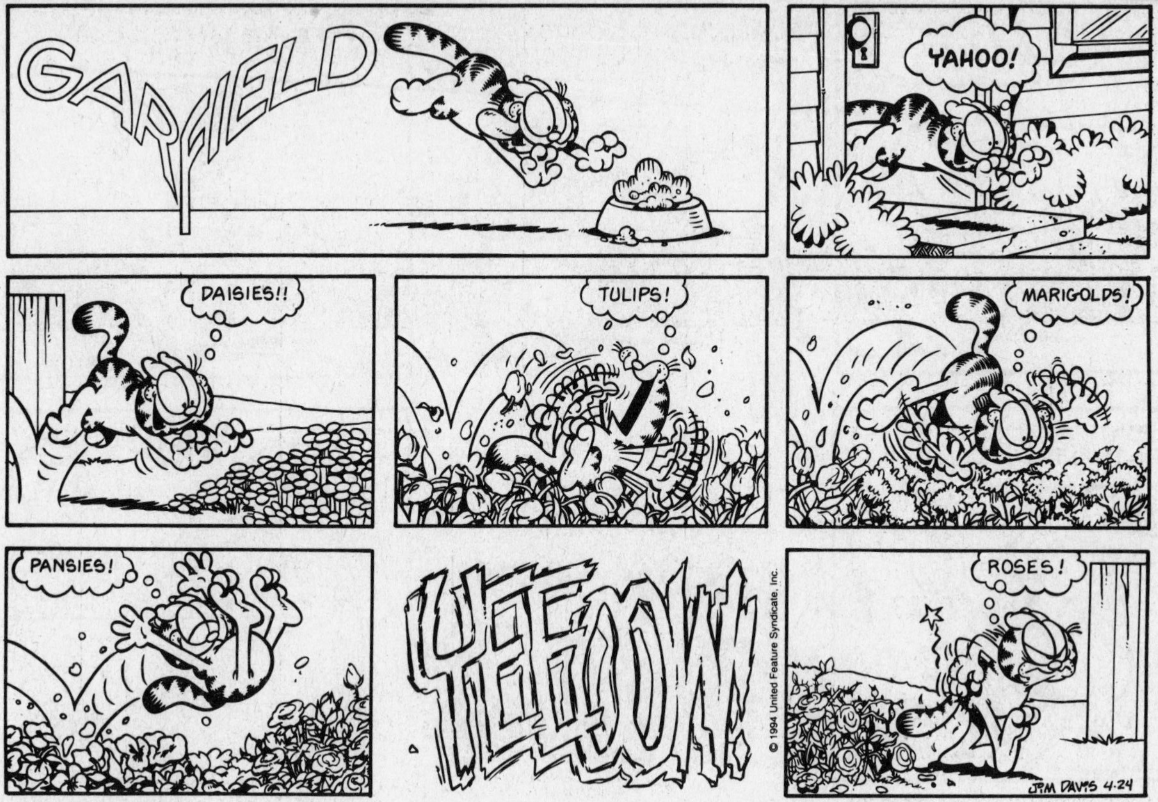
GARFIELD
YAHOO!
DAISIES!!
TULIPS!
MARIGOLDS!
PANSIES!
YEEOOW!
© 1994 United Feature Syndicate, Inc.
ROSES!
JIM DAVIS 4·24

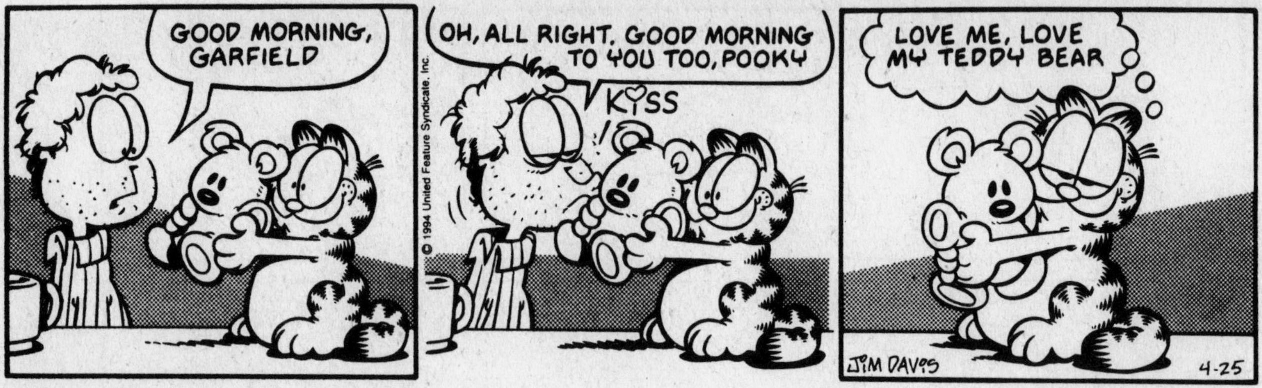
GOOD MORNING, GARFIELD
© 1994 United Feature Syndicate, Inc.
OH, ALL RIGHT. GOOD MORNING TO YOU TOO, POOKY
KISS
!
LOVE ME, LOVE MY TEDDY BEAR
JIM DAVIS
4-25

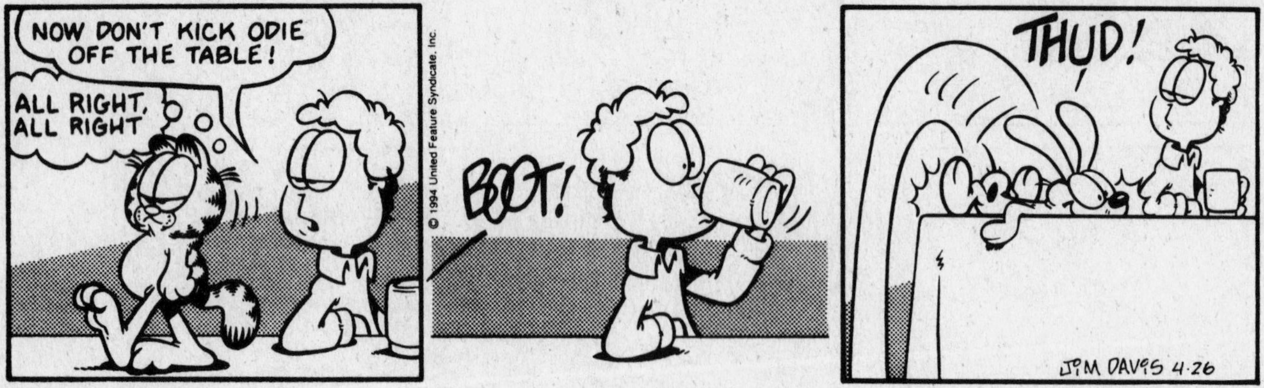
NOW DON'T KICK ODIE OFF THE TABLE!
ALL RIGHT, ALL RIGHT
© 1994 United Feature Syndicate, Inc.
BOOT!
THUD!
JIM DAVIS 4·26

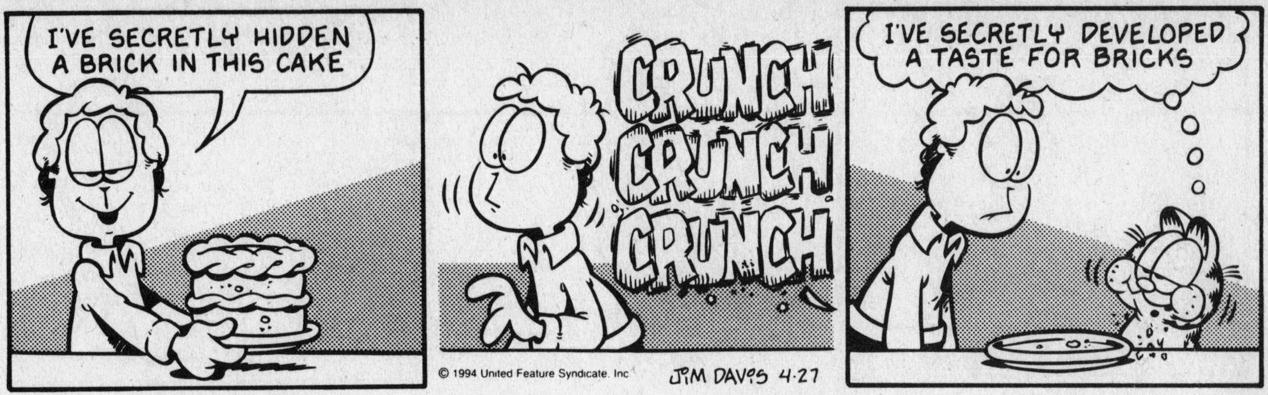
I'VE SECRETLY HIDDEN A BRICK IN THIS CAKE
CRUNCH CRUNCH CRUNCH
© 1994 United Feature Syndicate, Inc
JIM DAVIS 4·27
I'VE SECRETLY DEVELOPED A TASTE FOR BRICKS

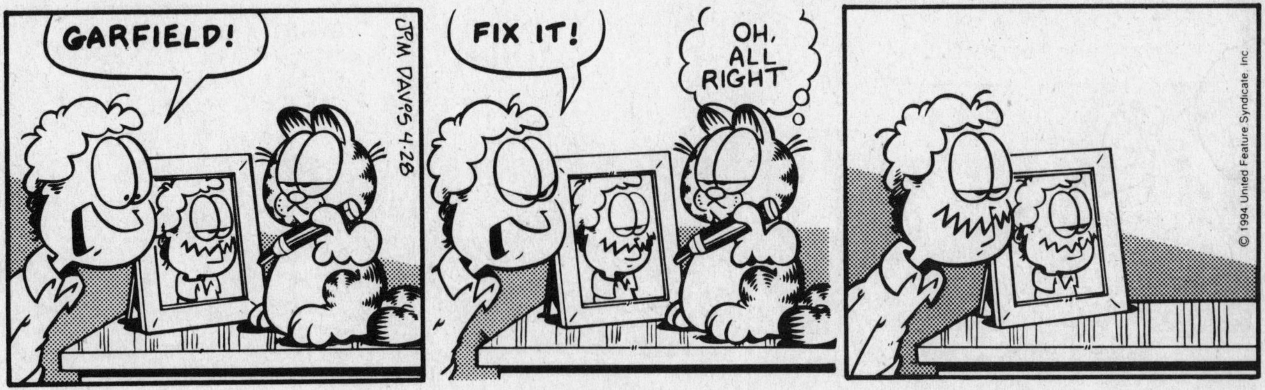
GARFIELD!
JIM DAVIS 4·28
FIX IT!
OH, ALL RIGHT
© 1994 United Feature Syndicate, Inc.

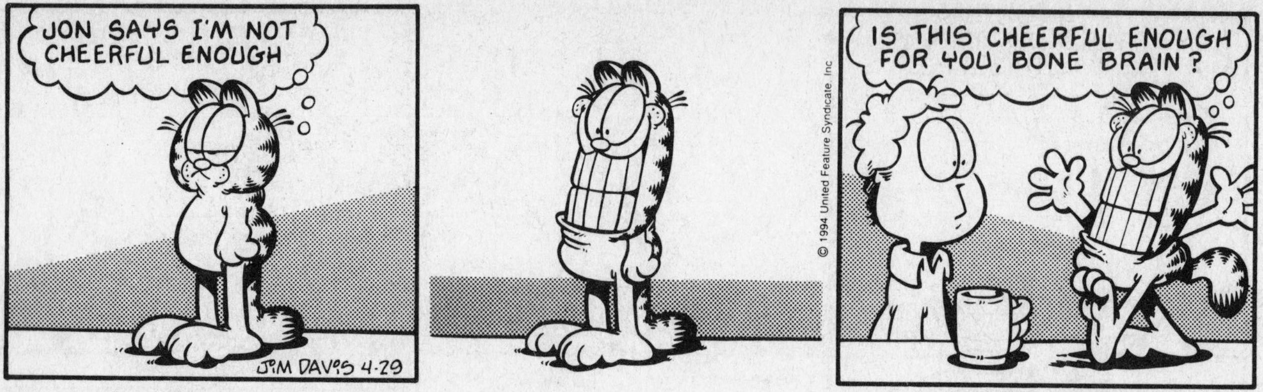
JON SAYS I'M NOT CHEERFUL ENOUGH
JIM DAVIS 4·29
IS THIS CHEERFUL ENOUGH FOR YOU, BONE BRAIN?
© 1994 United Feature Syndicate, Inc.

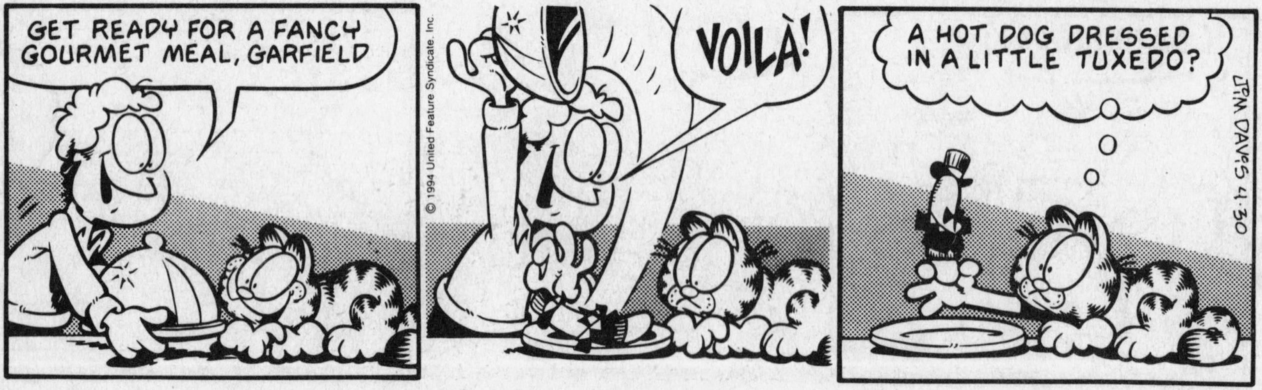
GET READY FOR A FANCY GOURMET MEAL, GARFIELD
© 1994 United Feature Syndicate, Inc.
VOILÀ!
A HOT DOG DRESSED IN A LITTLE TUXEDO?
JIM DAVIS 4·30

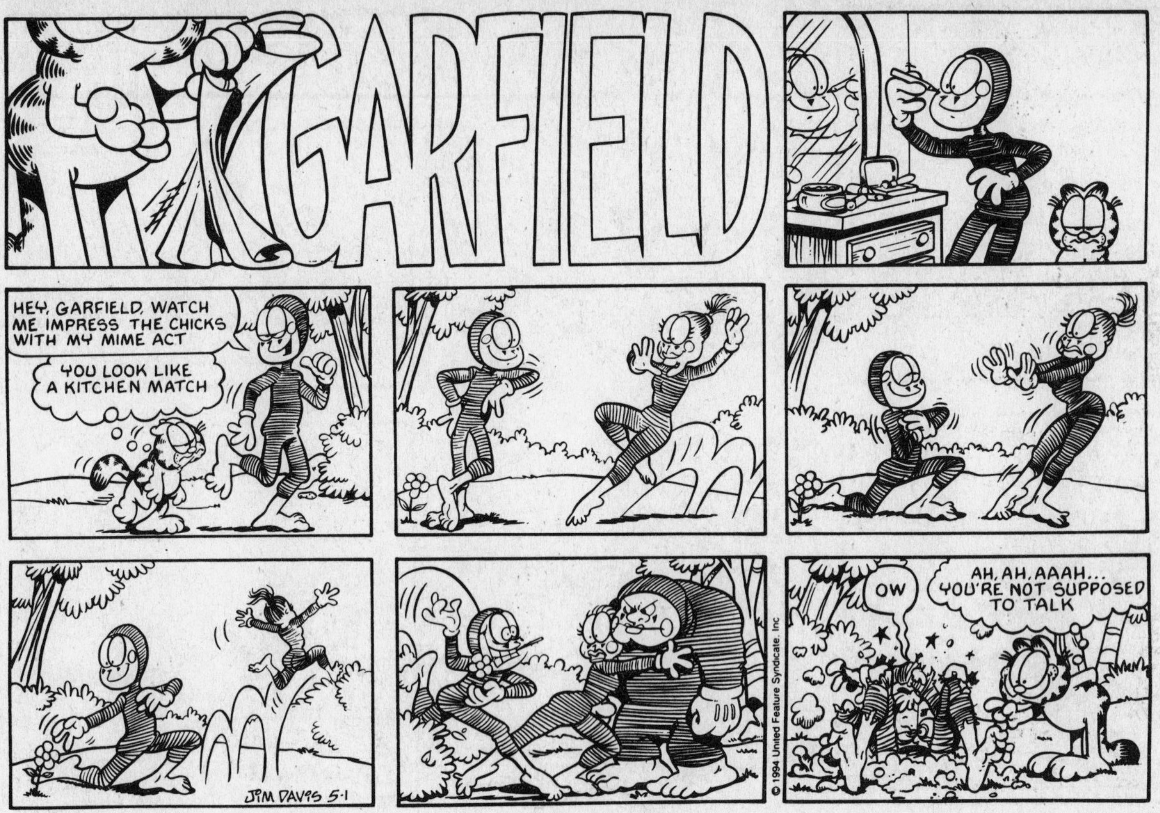
GARFIELD
HEY, GARFIELD, WATCH ME IMPRESS THE CHICKS WITH MY MIME ACT
YOU LOOK LIKE A KITCHEN MATCH
JIM DAVIS 5-1
© 1994 United Feature Syndicate, Inc.
OW
AH, AH, AAAH... YOU'RE NOT SUPPOSED TO TALK

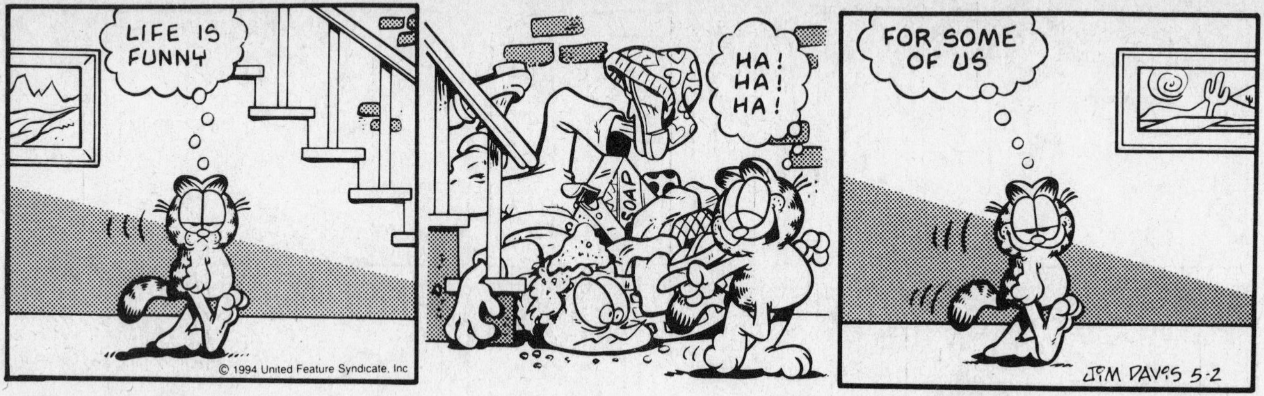
LIFE IS FUNNY
HA! HA! HA!
SOAP
FOR SOME OF US
© 1994 United Feature Syndicate, Inc
JIM DAVIS 5-2

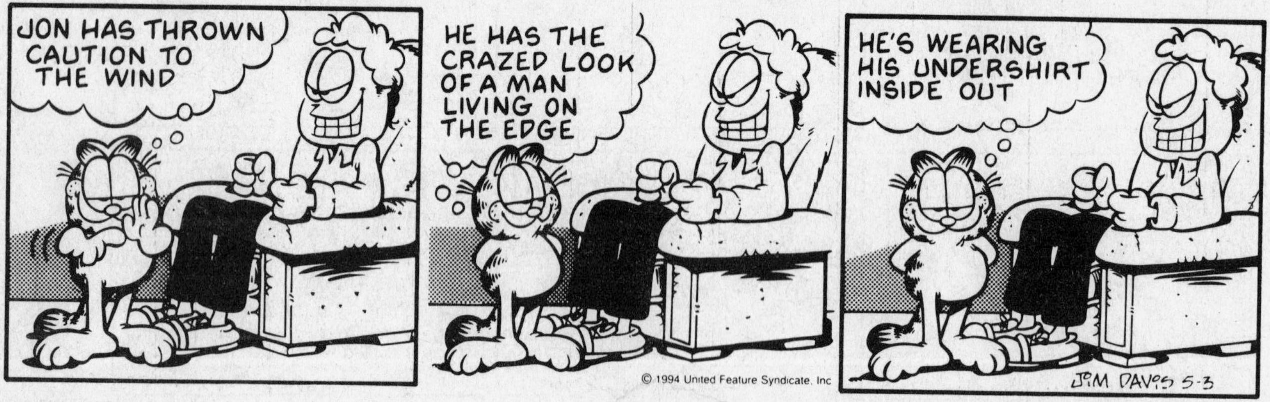
JON HAS THROWN CAUTION TO THE WIND
HE HAS THE CRAZED LOOK OF A MAN LIVING ON THE EDGE
HE'S WEARING HIS UNDERSHIRT INSIDE OUT
© 1994 United Feature Syndicate, Inc
JIM DAVIS 5-3

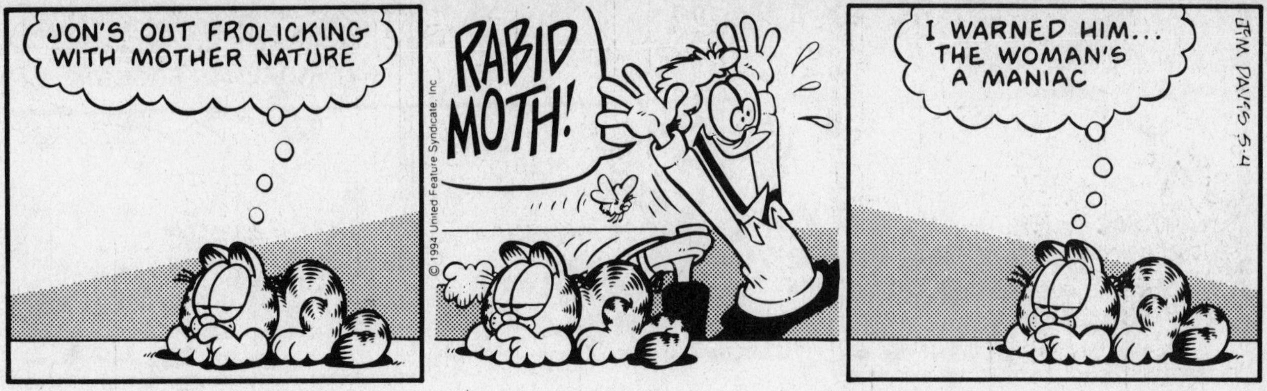
JON'S OUT FROLICKING WITH MOTHER NATURE
RABID MOTH!
I WARNED HIM... THE WOMAN'S A MANIAC
© 1994 United Feature Syndicate, Inc
JIM DAVIS 5-4

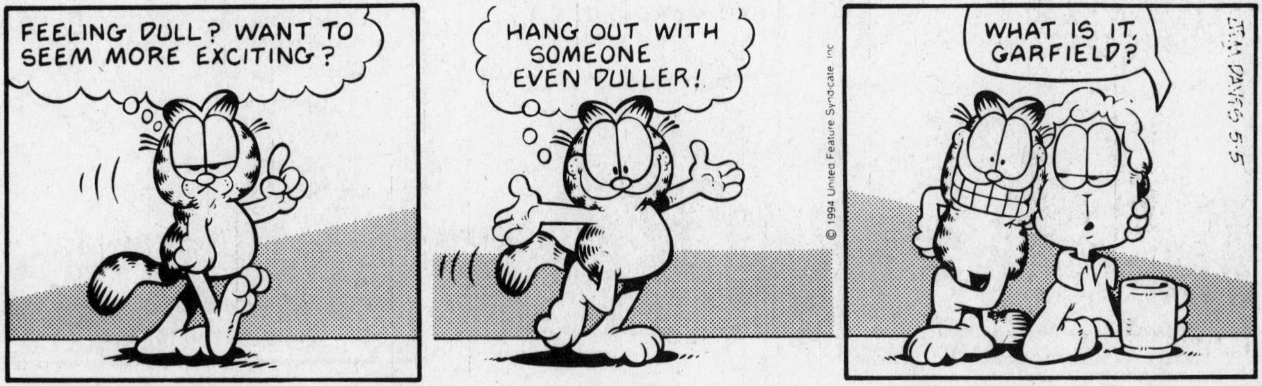
FEELING DULL? WANT TO SEEM MORE EXCITING?
HANG OUT WITH SOMEONE EVEN DULLER!
WHAT IS IT, GARFIELD?
© 1994 United Feature Syndicate, Inc
JIM DAVIS 5-5

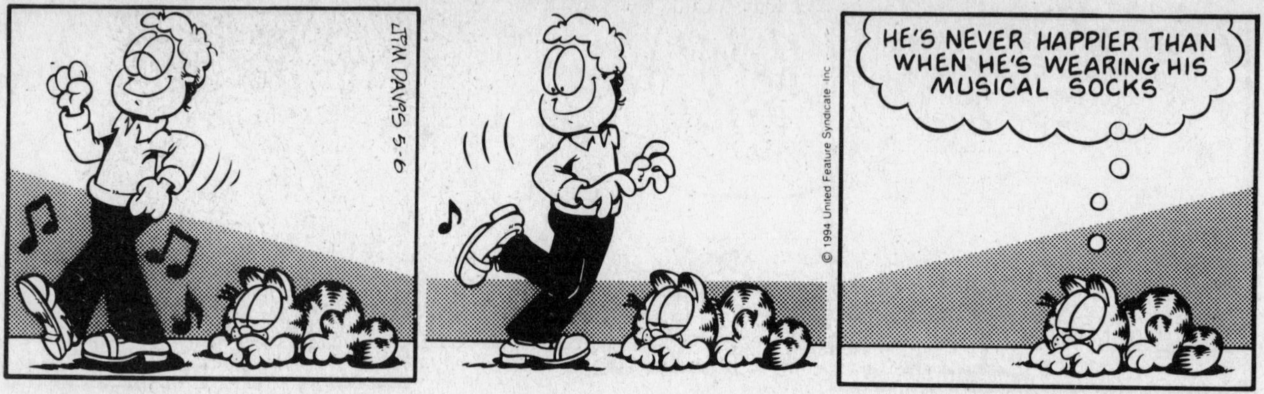
JIM DAVIS 5-6
HE'S NEVER HAPPIER THAN WHEN HE'S WEARING HIS MUSICAL SOCKS
© 1994 United Feature Syndicate, Inc

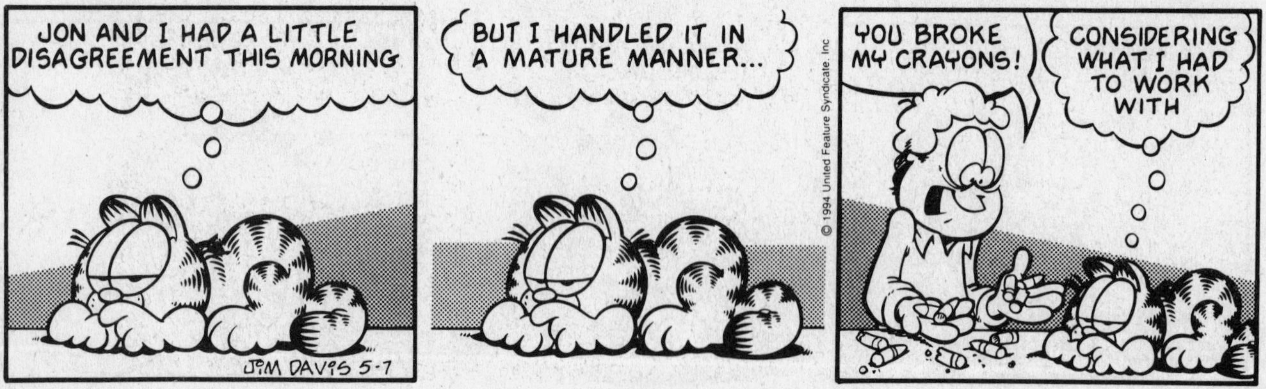
JON AND I HAD A LITTLE DISAGREEMENT THIS MORNING
JIM DAVIS 5-7
BUT I HANDLED IT IN A MATURE MANNER...
YOU BROKE MY CRAYONS!
CONSIDERING WHAT I HAD TO WORK WITH
© 1994 United Feature Syndicate, Inc

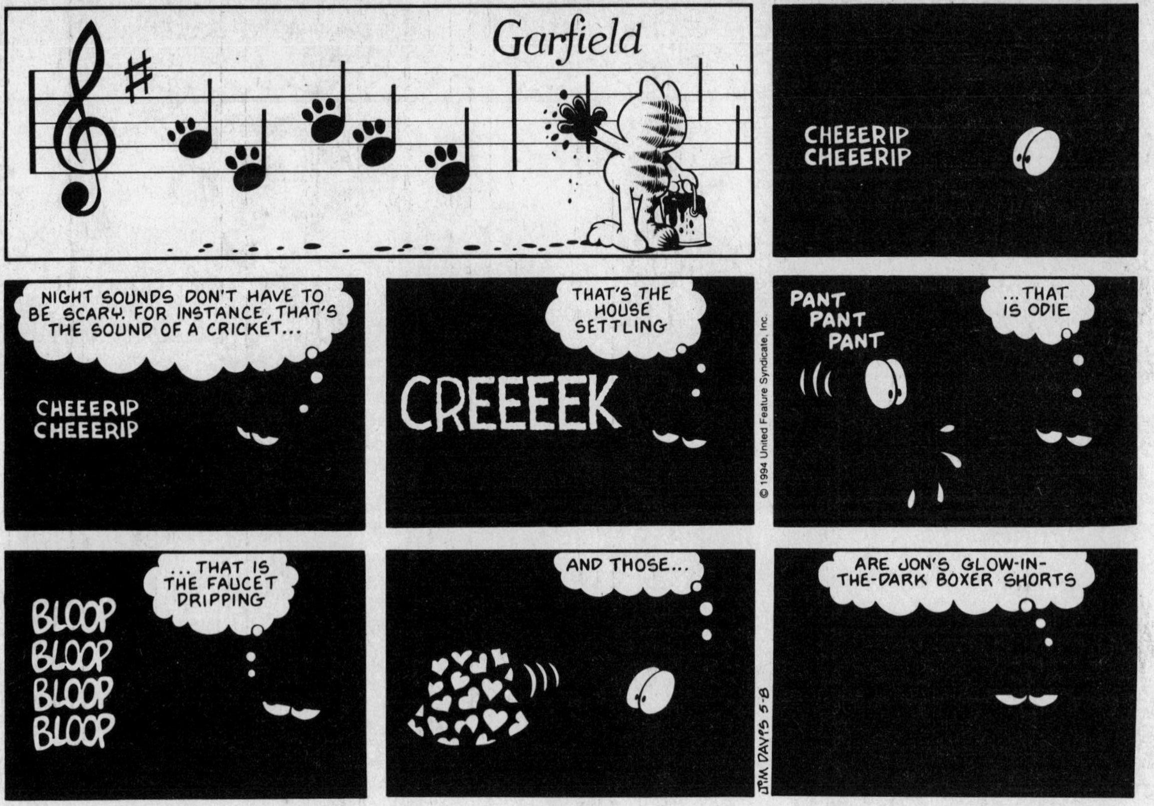
Garfield
CHEEERIP CHEEERIP
NIGHT SOUNDS DON'T HAVE TO BE SCARY. FOR INSTANCE, THAT'S THE SOUND OF A CRICKET...
CHEEERIP CHEEERIP
THAT'S THE HOUSE SETTLING
CREEEEK
© 1994 United Feature Syndicate, Inc.
PANT PANT PANT
...THAT IS ODIE
...THAT IS THE FAUCET DRIPPING
BLOOP BLOOP BLOOP BLOOP
AND THOSE...
JIM DAVIS 5-8
ARE JON'S GLOW-IN-THE-DARK BOXER SHORTS

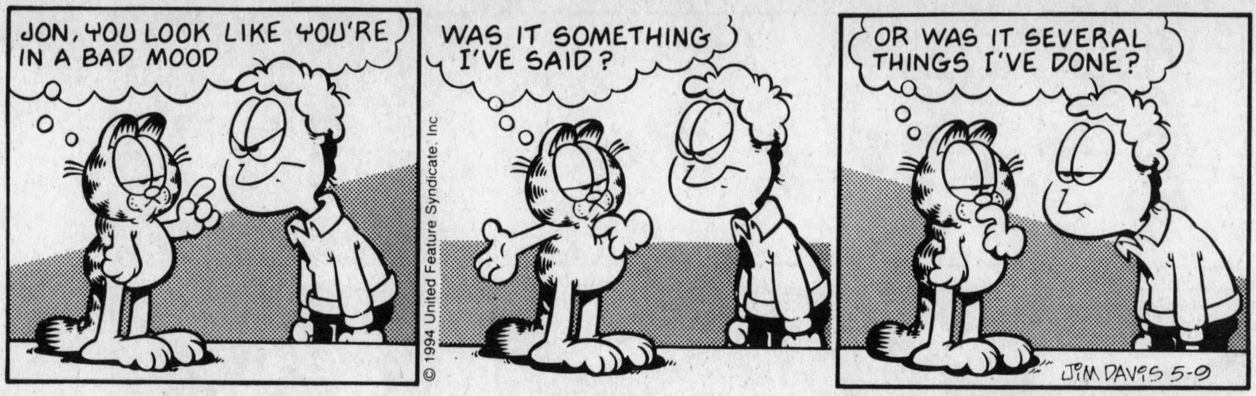
JON, YOU LOOK LIKE YOU'RE IN A BAD MOOD
WAS IT SOMETHING I'VE SAID?
OR WAS IT SEVERAL THINGS I'VE DONE?
JIM DAVIS 5-9
© 1994 United Feature Syndicate, Inc

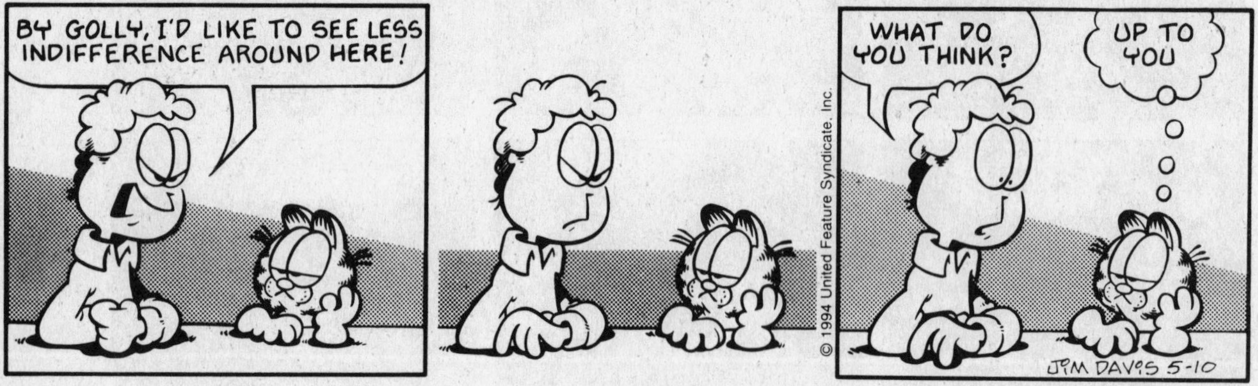
BY GOLLY, I'D LIKE TO SEE LESS INDIFFERENCE AROUND HERE!
WHAT DO YOU THINK?
UP TO YOU
JIM DAVIS 5-10
© 1994 United Feature Syndicate, Inc

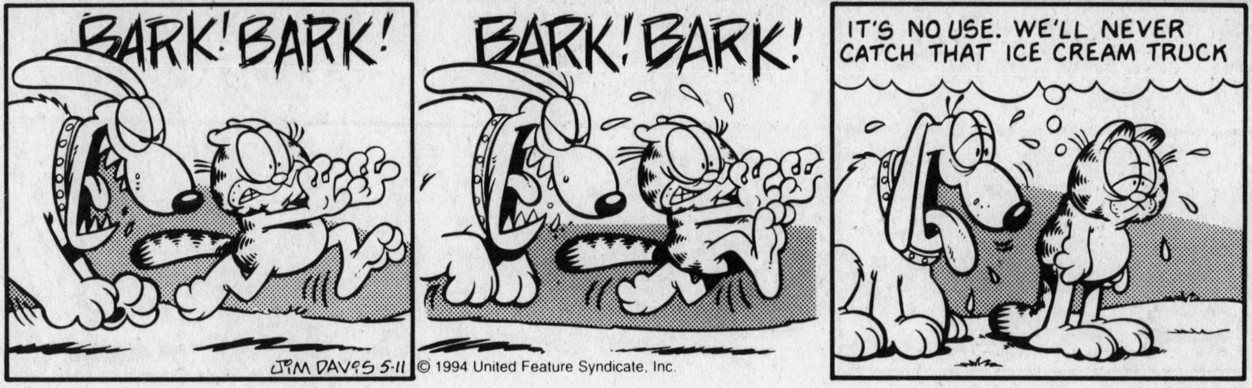
BARK! BARK!
BARK! BARK!
IT'S NO USE. WE'LL NEVER CATCH THAT ICE CREAM TRUCK
JIM DAVIS 5-11

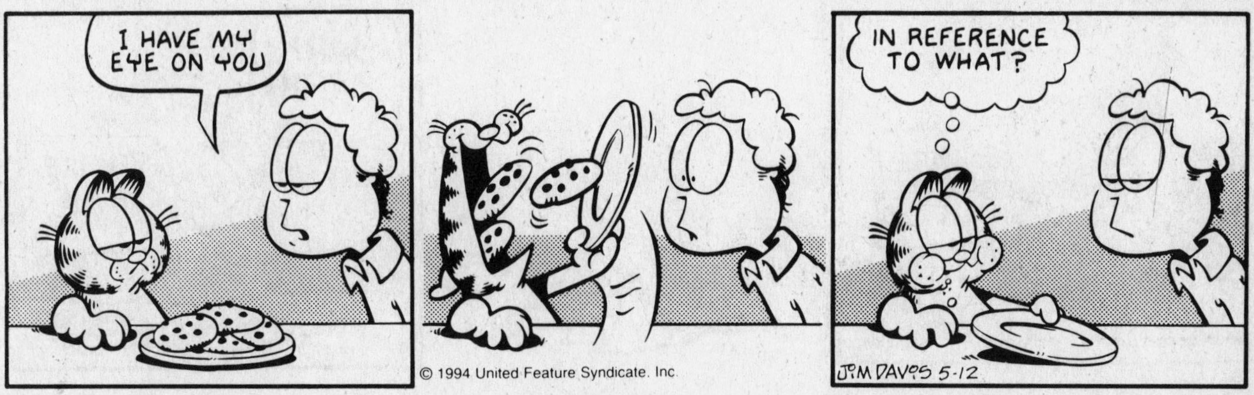
I HAVE MY EYE ON YOU
IN REFERENCE TO WHAT?
JIM DAVIS 5-12

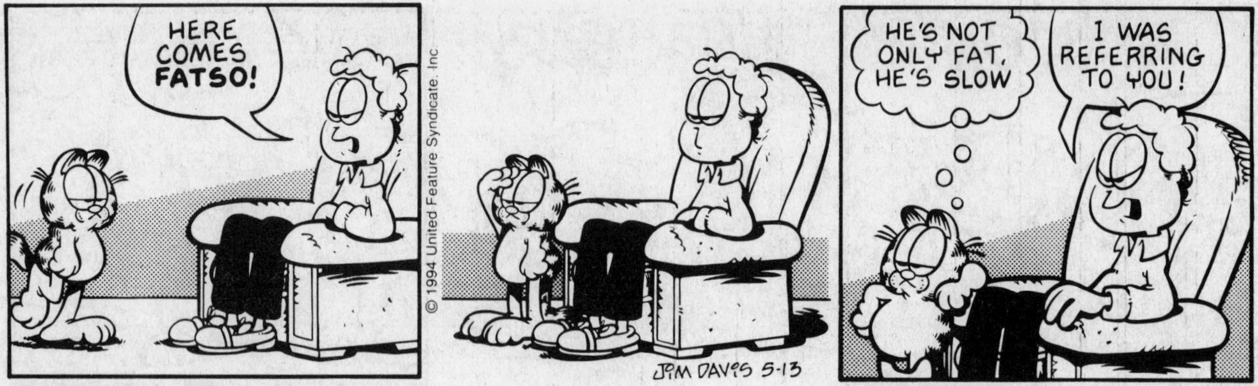
HERE COMES FATSO!
HE'S NOT ONLY FAT, HE'S SLOW
I WAS REFERRING TO YOU!
JIM DAVIS 5-13

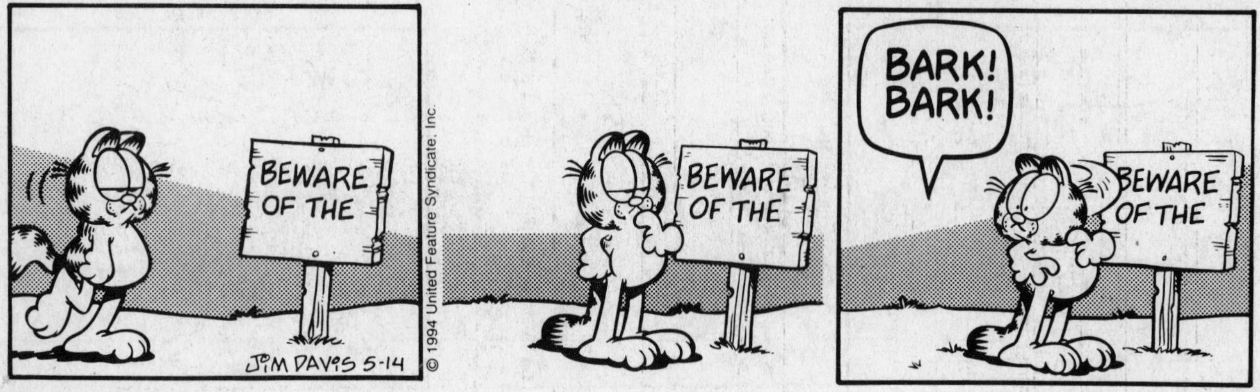
BEWARE OF THE
BEWARE OF THE
BARK! BARK!
BEWARE OF THE
JIM DAVIS 5-14

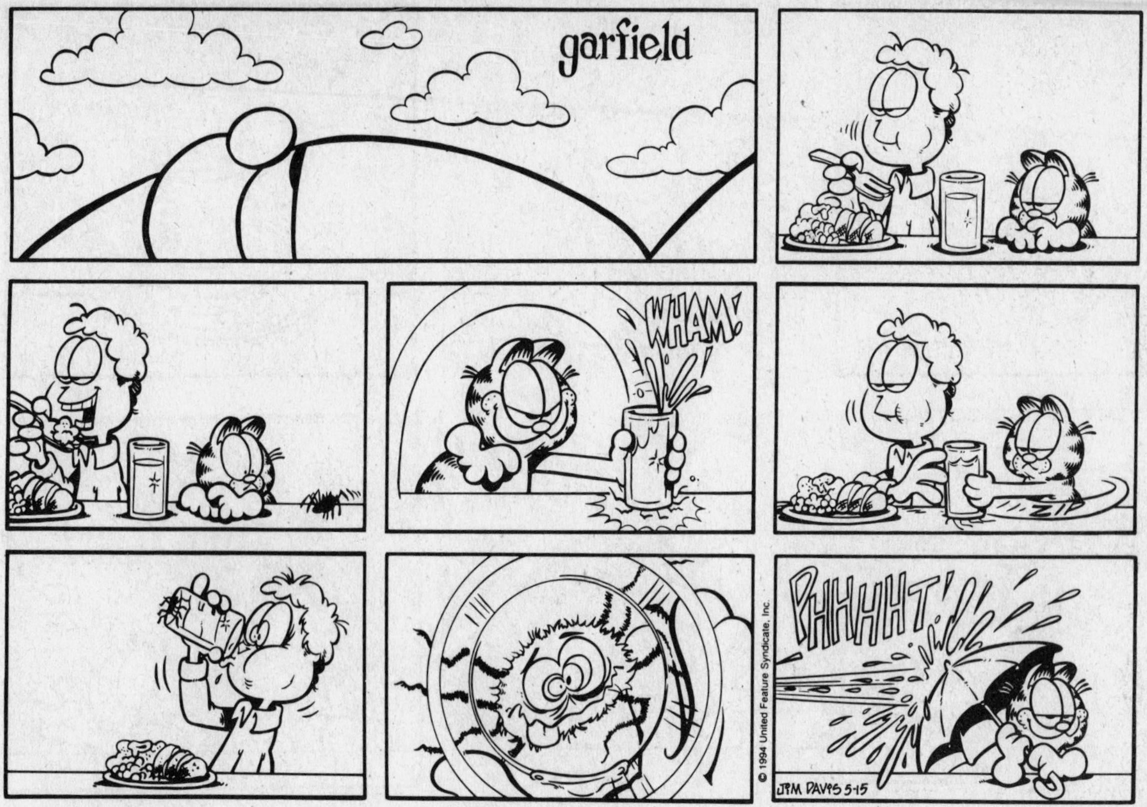

garfield
WHAM!
PHHHT!
© 1994 United Feature Syndicate, Inc.
JIM DAVIS 5-15

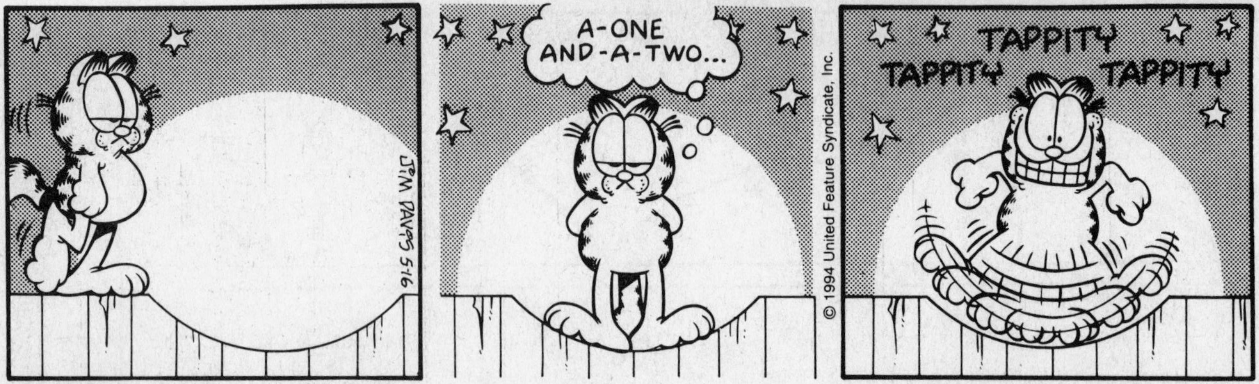
JIM DAVIS 5-16
A-ONE AND-A-TWO...
TAPPITY
TAPPITY
TAPPITY
© 1994 United Feature Syndicate, Inc.

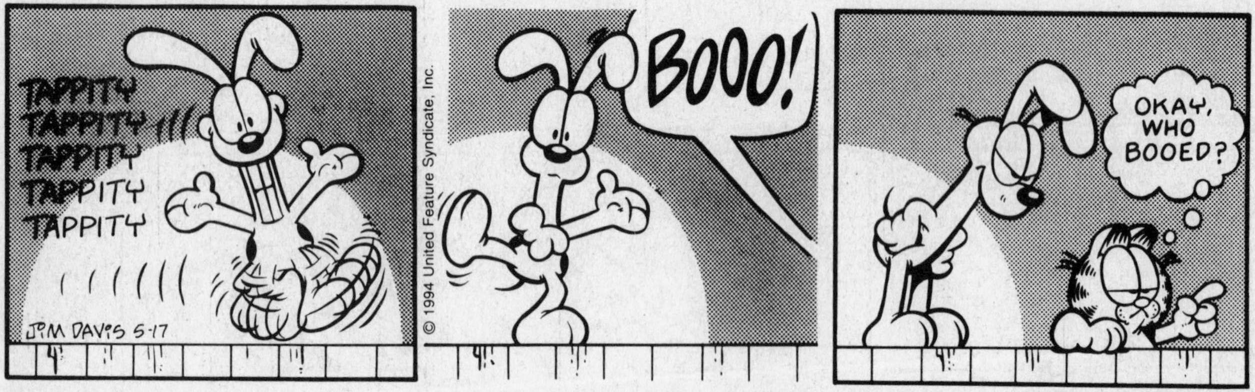
TAPPITY
TAPPITY
TAPPITY
TAPPITY
TAPPITY
JIM DAVIS 5-17
© 1994 United Feature Syndicate, Inc.
BOOO!
OKAY, WHO BOOED?

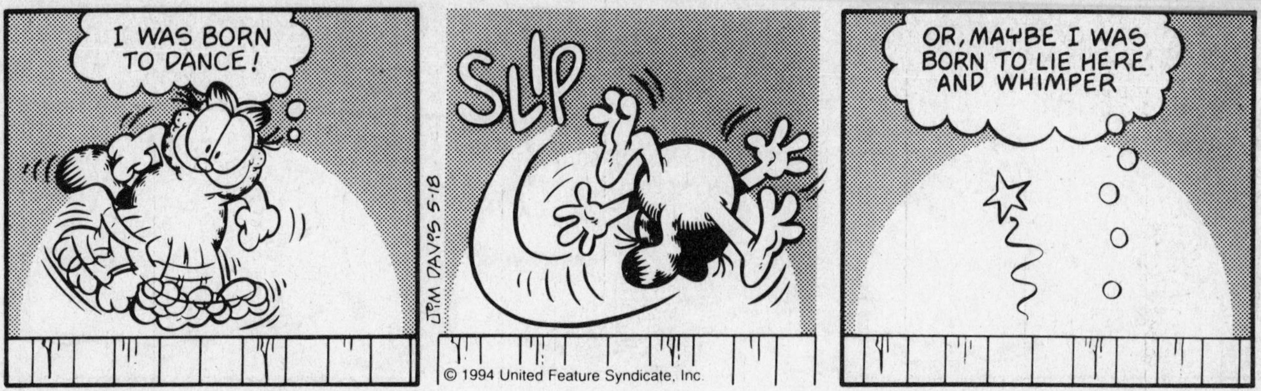
I WAS BORN TO DANCE!
SLIP
JIM DAVIS 5-18
© 1994 United Feature Syndicate, Inc.
OR, MAYBE I WAS BORN TO LIE HERE AND WHIMPER

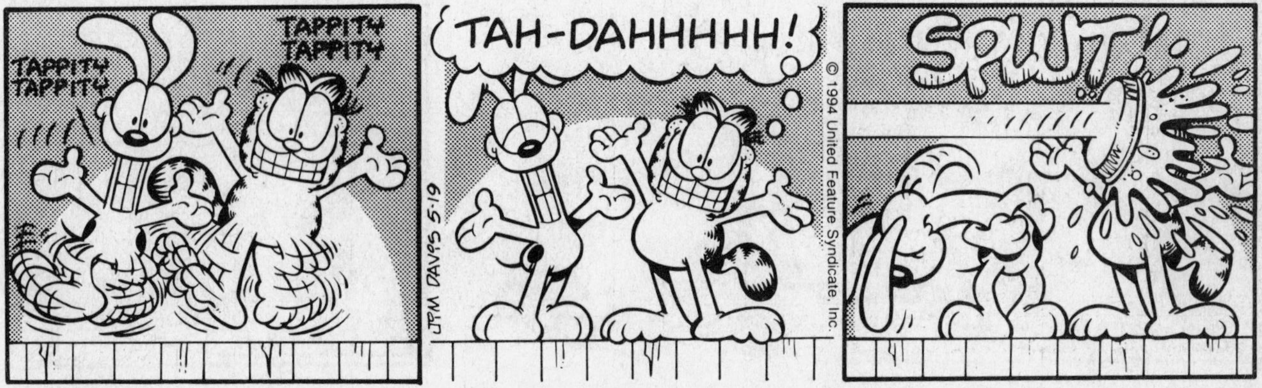
TAPPITY TAPPITY
TAPPITY TAPPITY
JIM DAVIS 5-19
TAH-DAHHHHH!
© 1994 United Feature Syndicate, Inc.
SPLUT!

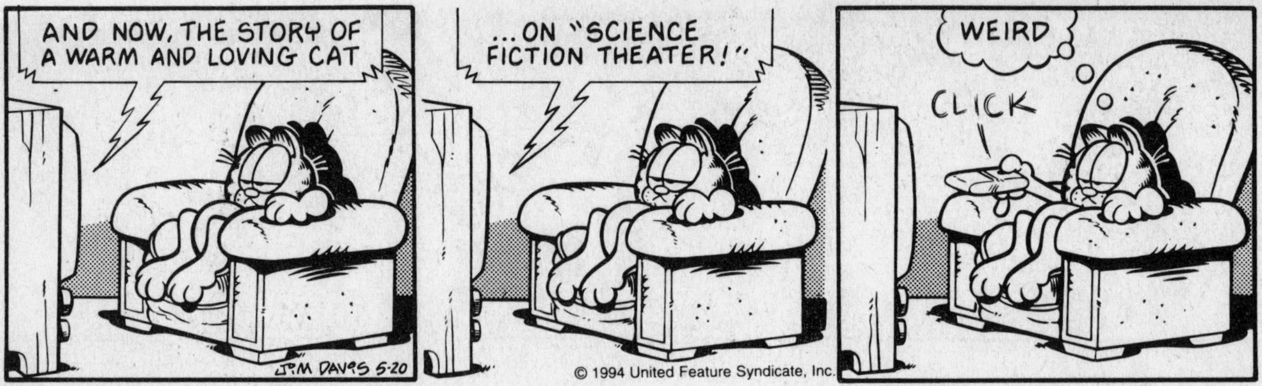
AND NOW, THE STORY OF A WARM AND LOVING CAT
...ON "SCIENCE FICTION THEATER!"
CLICK
WEIRD
JIM DAVIS 5-20
© 1994 United Feature Syndicate, Inc.

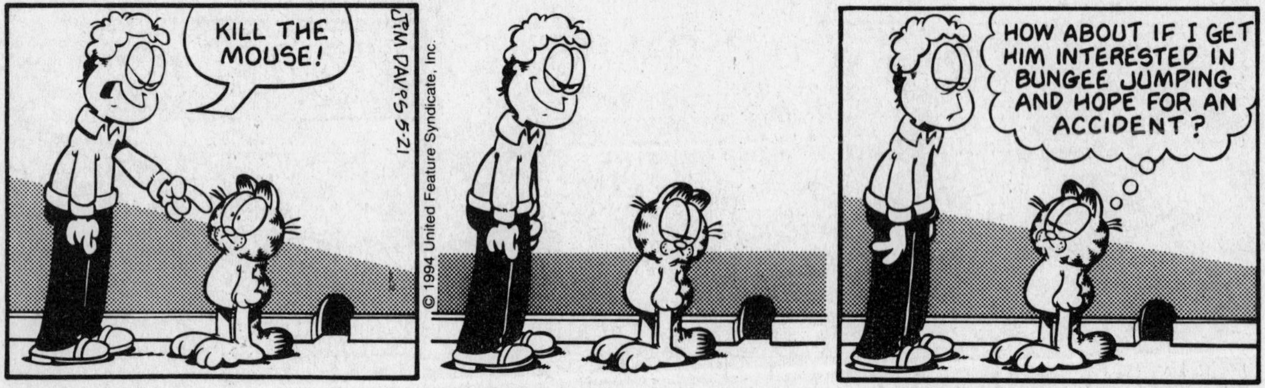
KILL THE MOUSE!
HOW ABOUT IF I GET HIM INTERESTED IN BUNGEE JUMPING AND HOPE FOR AN ACCIDENT?
JIM DAVIS 5-21
© 1994 United Feature Syndicate, Inc.

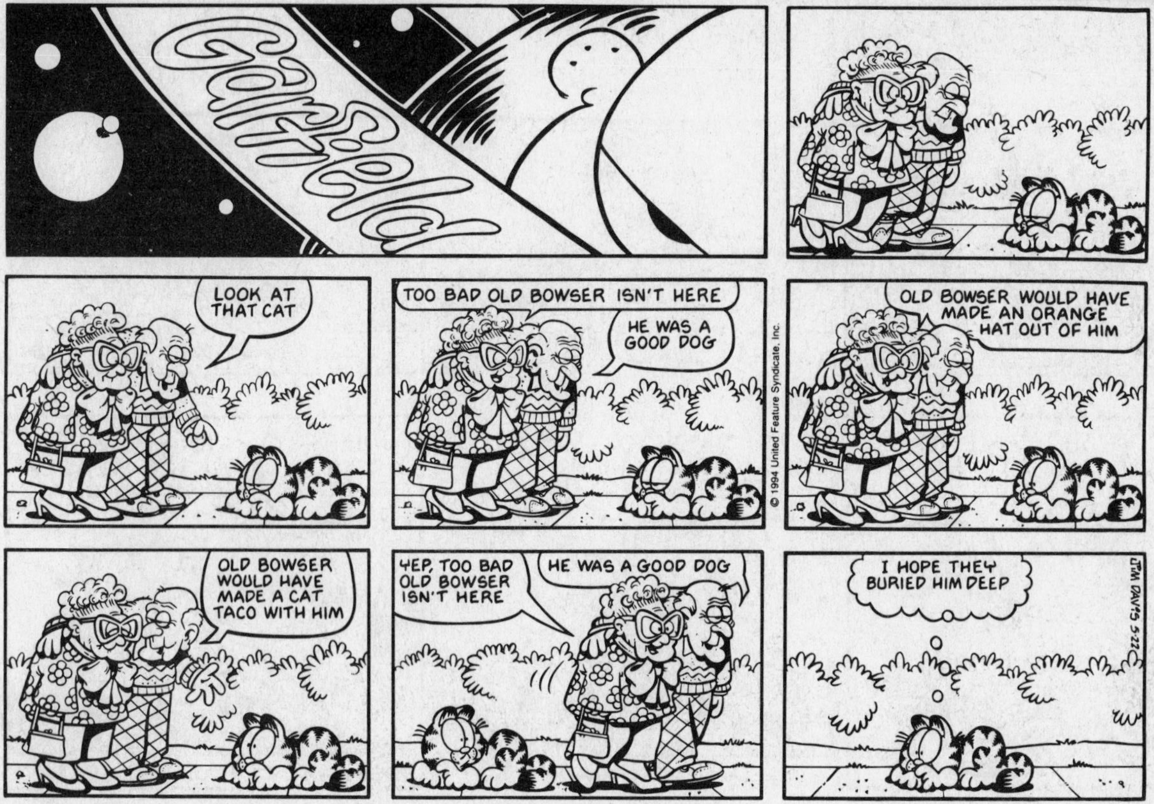
Garfield
LOOK AT THAT CAT
TOO BAD OLD BOWSER ISN'T HERE
HE WAS A GOOD DOG
© 1994 United Feature Syndicate, Inc.
OLD BOWSER WOULD HAVE MADE AN ORANGE HAT OUT OF HIM
OLD BOWSER WOULD HAVE MADE A CAT TACO WITH HIM
YEP, TOO BAD OLD BOWSER ISN'T HERE
HE WAS A GOOD DOG
I HOPE THEY BURIED HIM DEEP
JPM DAVIS 5-22

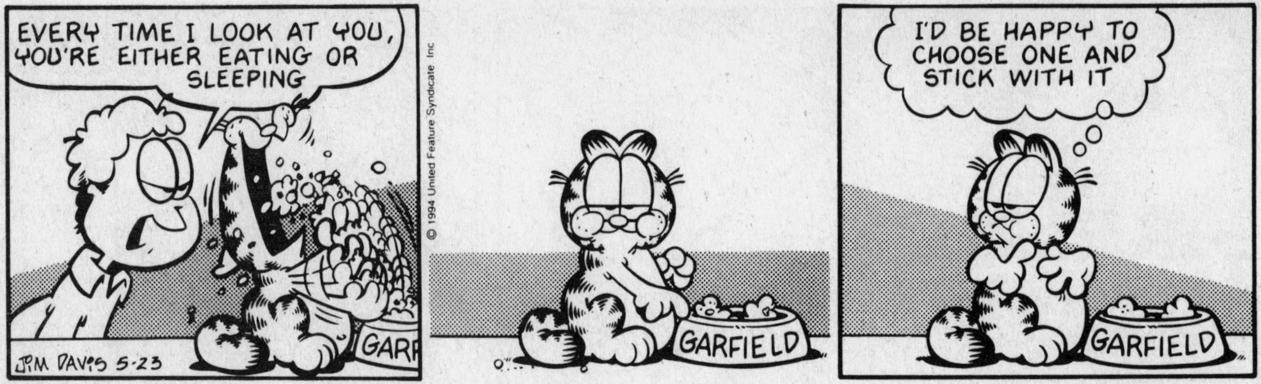
EVERY TIME I LOOK AT YOU, YOU'RE EITHER EATING OR SLEEPING
GARF
GARFIELD
I'D BE HAPPY TO CHOOSE ONE AND STICK WITH IT
GARFIELD
JIM DAVIS 5-23
© 1994 United Feature Syndicate, Inc.

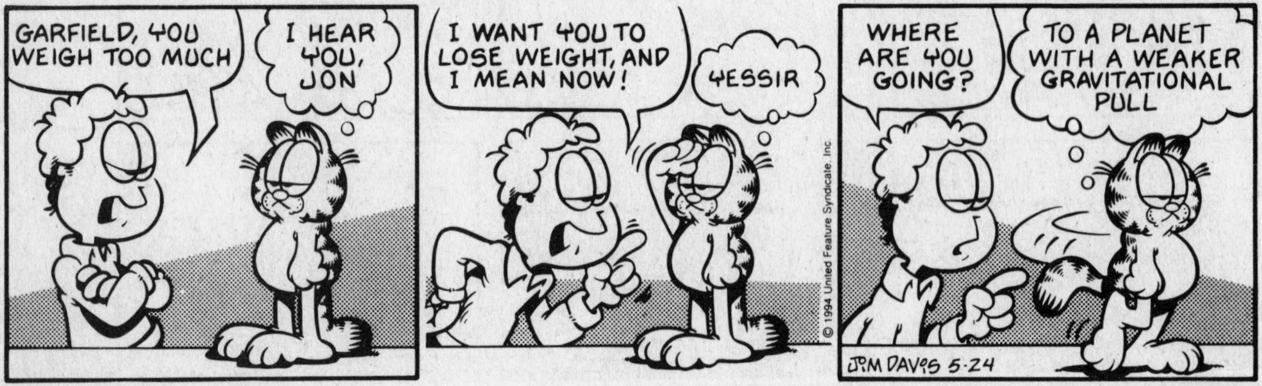
GARFIELD, YOU WEIGH TOO MUCH
I HEAR YOU, JON
I WANT YOU TO LOSE WEIGHT, AND I MEAN NOW!
YESSIR
WHERE ARE YOU GOING?
TO A PLANET WITH A WEAKER GRAVITATIONAL PULL
JIM DAVIS 5-24
© 1994 United Feature Syndicate, Inc.

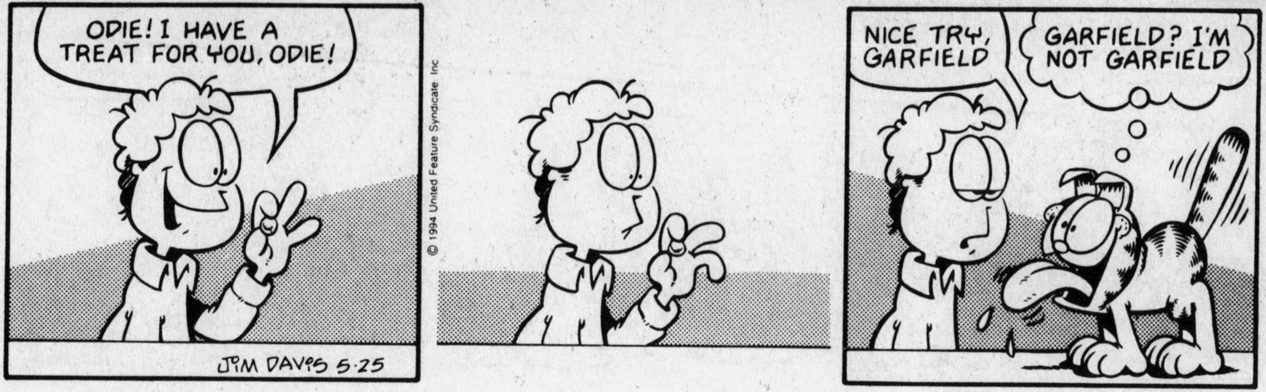
ODIE! I HAVE A TREAT FOR YOU, ODIE!
JIM DAVIS 5-25
© 1994 United Feature Syndicate, Inc
NICE TRY, GARFIELD
GARFIELD? I'M NOT GARFIELD

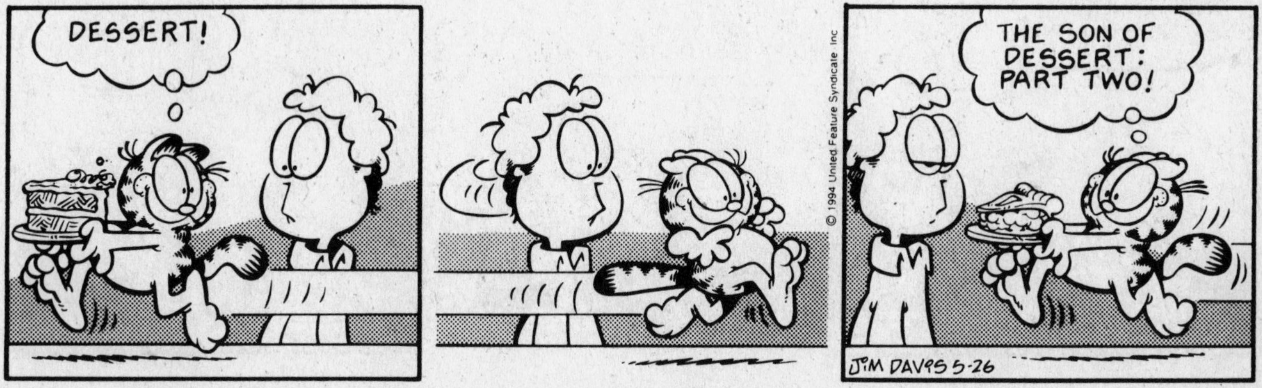
DESSERT!
© 1994 United Feature Syndicate, Inc
THE SON OF DESSERT: PART TWO!
JIM DAVIS 5-26

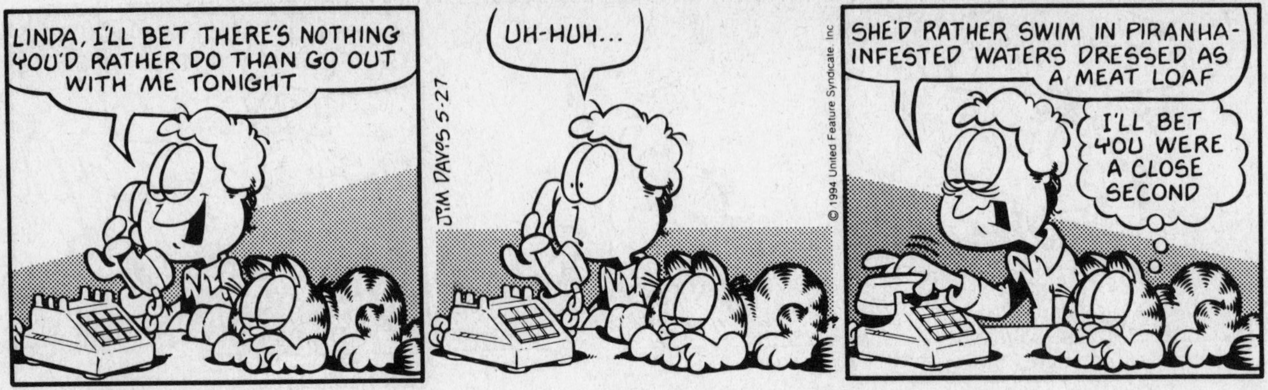
LINDA, I'LL BET THERE'S NOTHING YOU'D RATHER DO THAN GO OUT WITH ME TONIGHT
JIM DAVIS 5-27
UH-HUH...
SHE'D RATHER SWIM IN PIRANHA-INFESTED WATERS DRESSED AS A MEAT LOAF
I'LL BET YOU WERE A CLOSE SECOND
© 1994 United Feature Syndicate, Inc

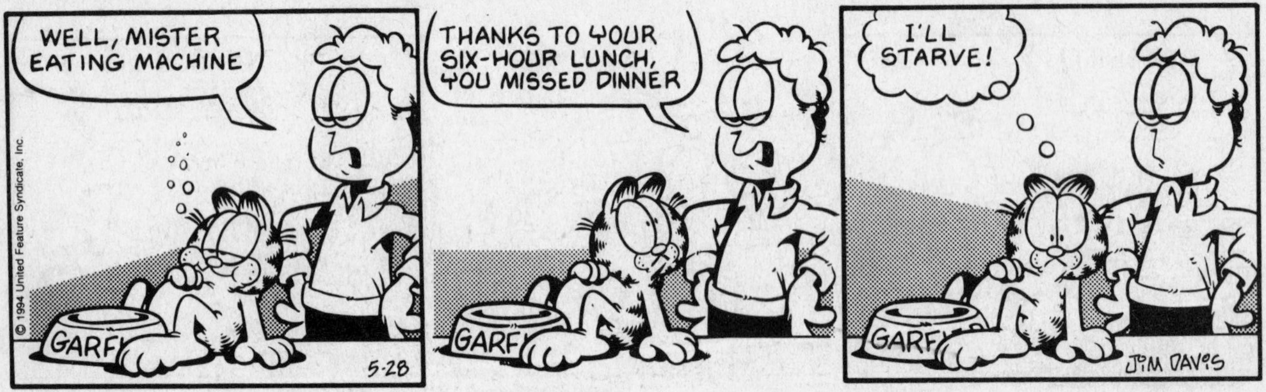
WELL, MISTER EATING MACHINE
© 1994 United Feature Syndicate, Inc.
GARF
5-28
THANKS TO YOUR SIX-HOUR LUNCH, YOU MISSED DINNER
GARF
I'LL STARVE!
GARF
JIM DAVIS

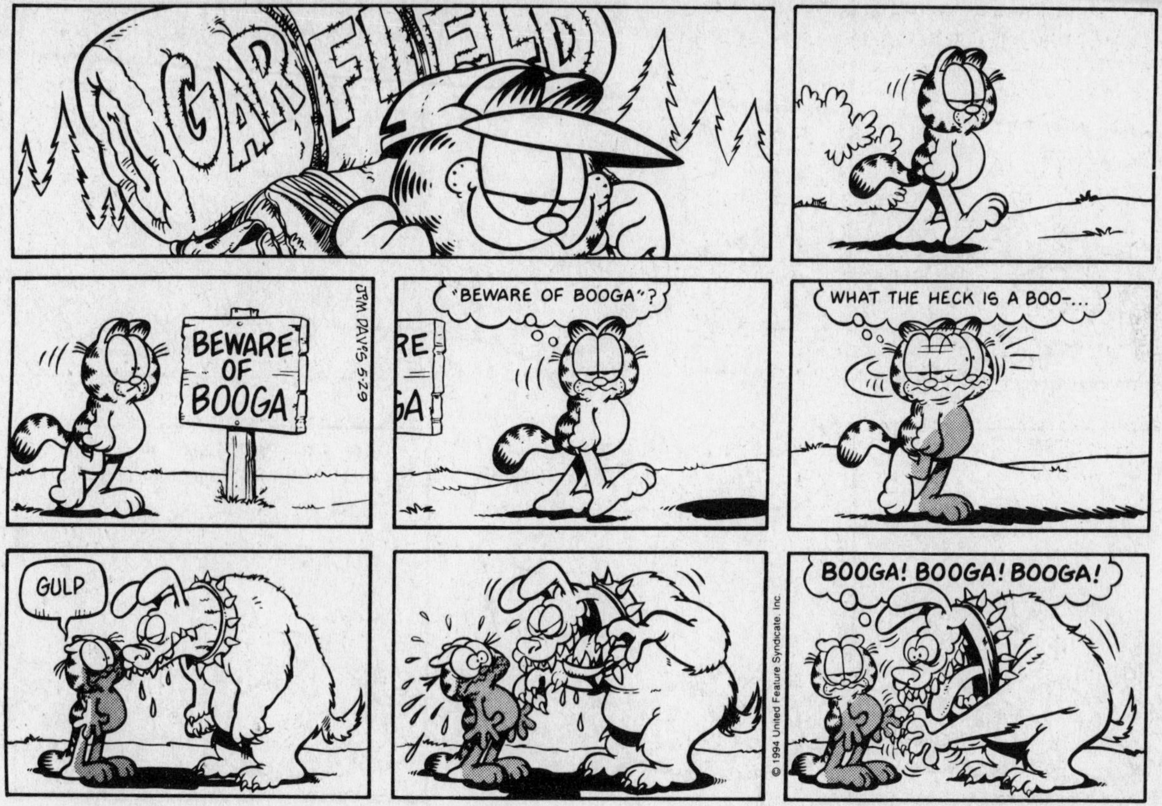
GARFIELD
BEWARE OF BOOGA
JIM DAVIS 5-29
"BEWARE OF BOOGA"?
WHAT THE HECK IS A BOO-...
GULP
© 1994 United Feature Syndicate, Inc.
BOOGA! BOOGA! BOOGA!

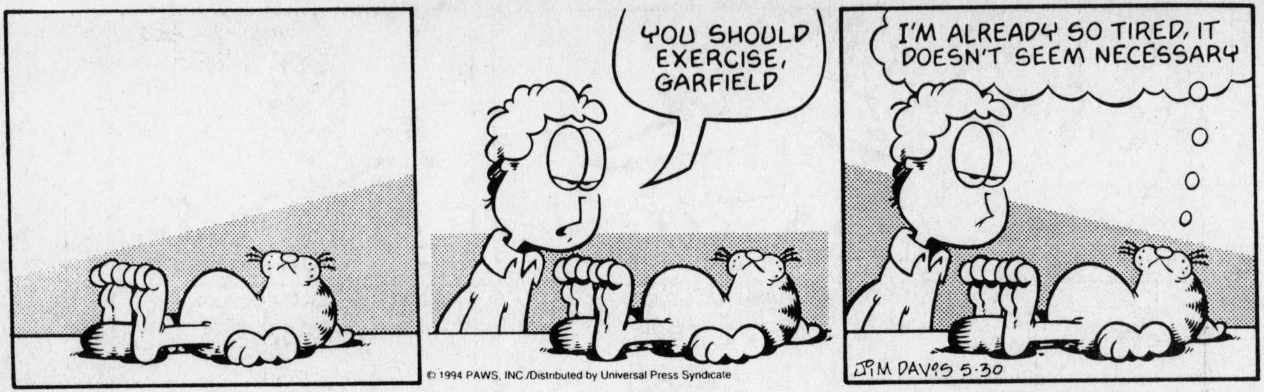
YOU SHOULD EXERCISE, GARFIELD
I'M ALREADY SO TIRED, IT DOESN'T SEEM NECESSARY
© 1994 PAWS, INC./Distributed by Universal Press Syndicate
JIM DAVIS 5-30

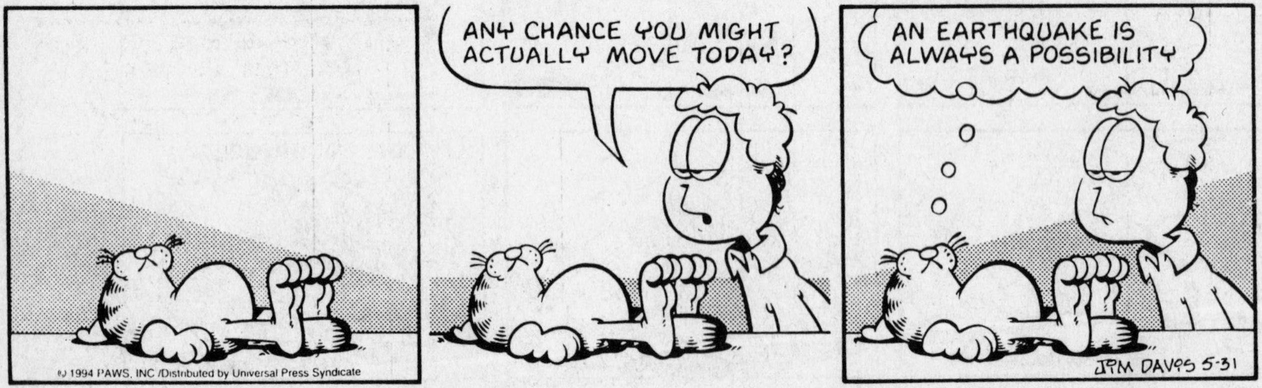
ANY CHANCE YOU MIGHT ACTUALLY MOVE TODAY?
AN EARTHQUAKE IS ALWAYS A POSSIBILITY
© 1994 PAWS, INC./Distributed by Universal Press Syndicate
JIM DAVIS 5-31

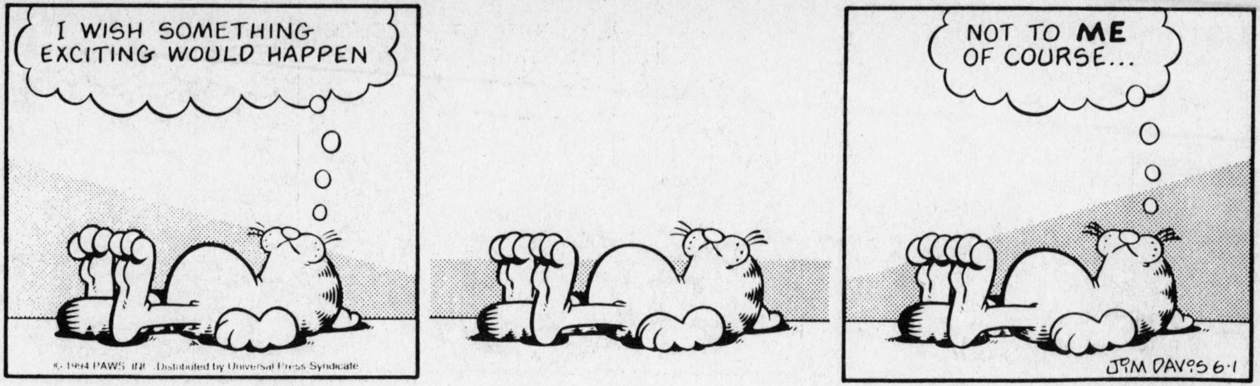
I WISH SOMETHING EXCITING WOULD HAPPEN
NOT TO ME OF COURSE...
JIM DAVIS 6-1

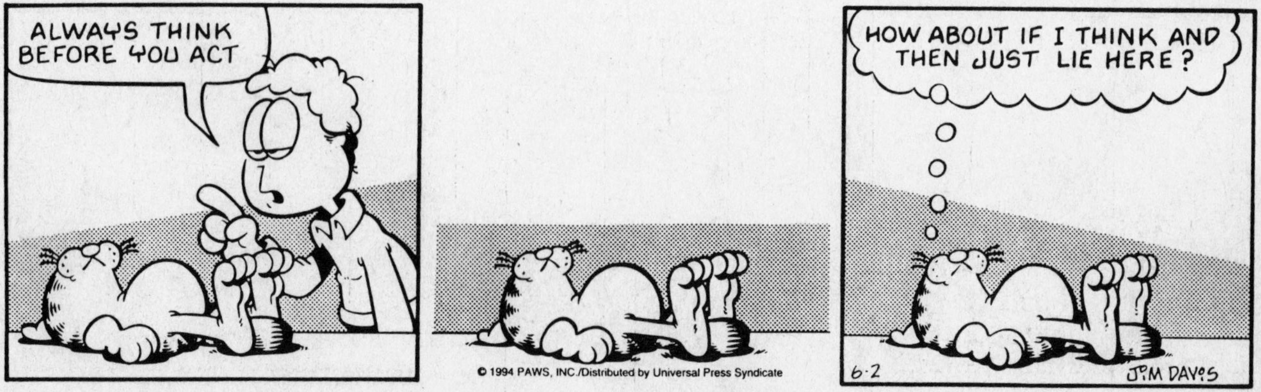
ALWAYS THINK BEFORE YOU ACT
HOW ABOUT IF I THINK AND THEN JUST LIE HERE?
© 1994 PAWS, INC./Distributed by Universal Press Syndicate
6-2
JIM DAVIS

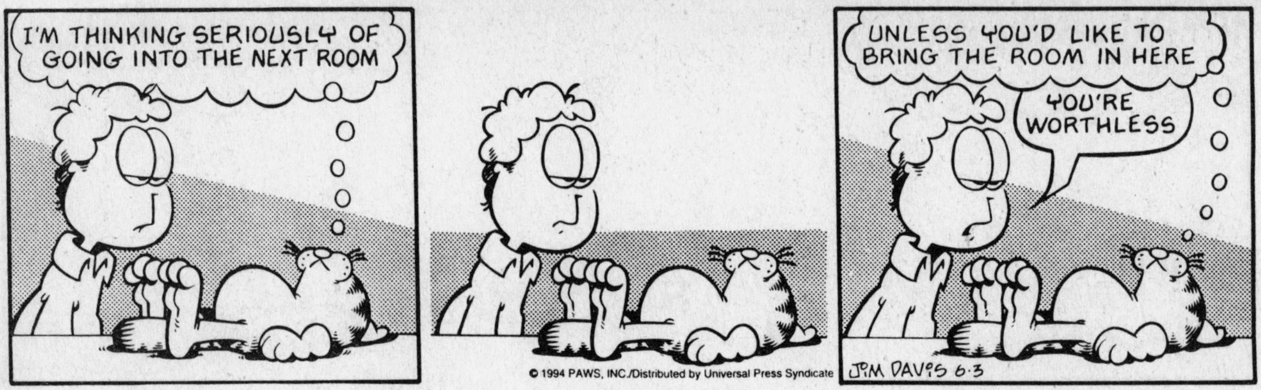
I'M THINKING SERIOUSLY OF GOING INTO THE NEXT ROOM
UNLESS YOU'D LIKE TO BRING THE ROOM IN HERE
YOU'RE WORTHLESS
© 1994 PAWS, INC./Distributed by Universal Press Syndicate
JIM DAVIS 6·3

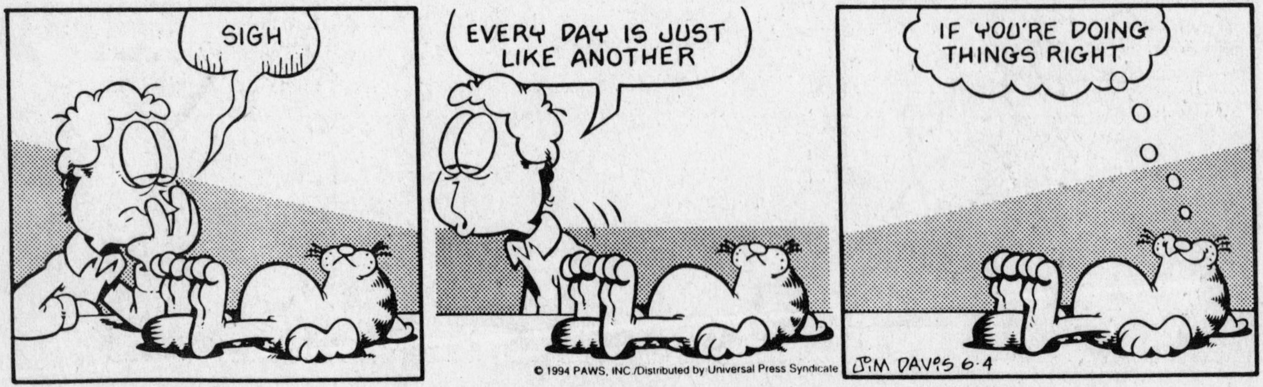
SIGH
EVERY DAY IS JUST LIKE ANOTHER
IF YOU'RE DOING THINGS RIGHT
© 1994 PAWS, INC./Distributed by Universal Press Syndicate
JIM DAVIS 6·4

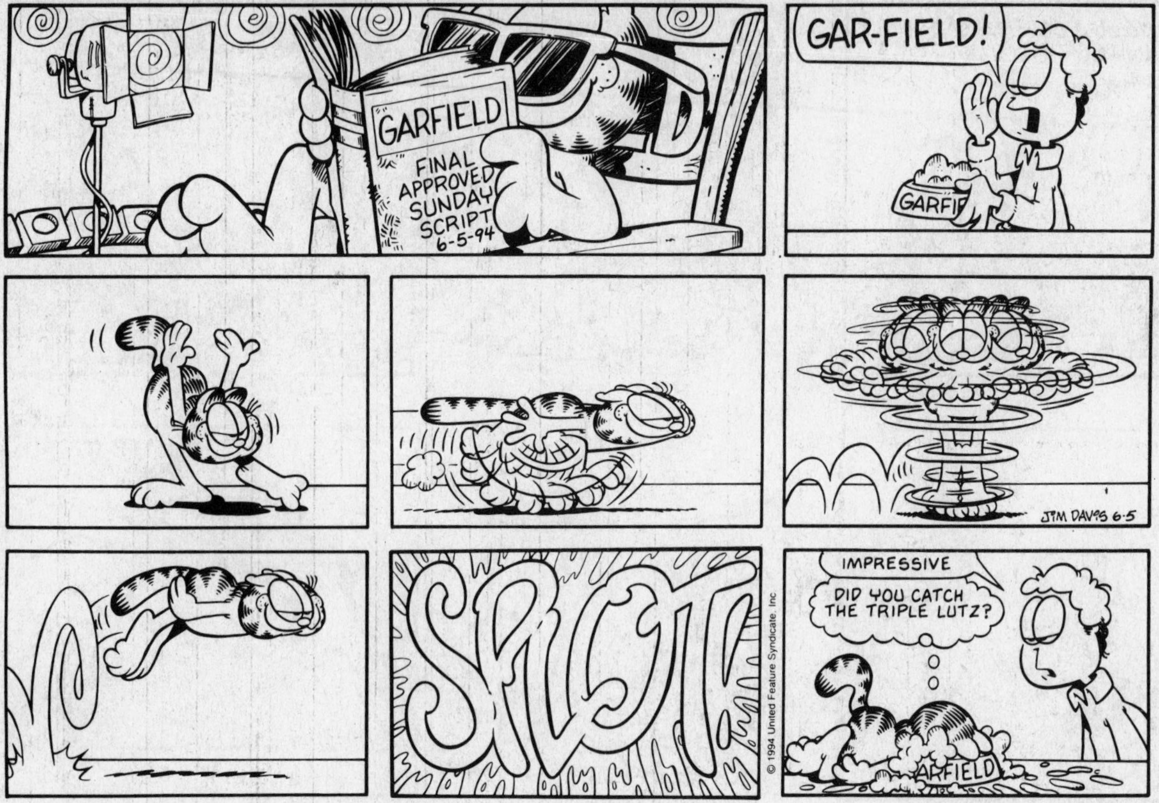

GARFIELD
FINAL APPROVED SUNDAY SCRIPT 6-5-94
GAR-FIELD!
GARFI
JIM DAVIS 6-5
SPLOT!
© 1994 United Feature Syndicate, Inc.
IMPRESSIVE
DID YOU CATCH THE TRIPLE LUTZ?
ARFIELD

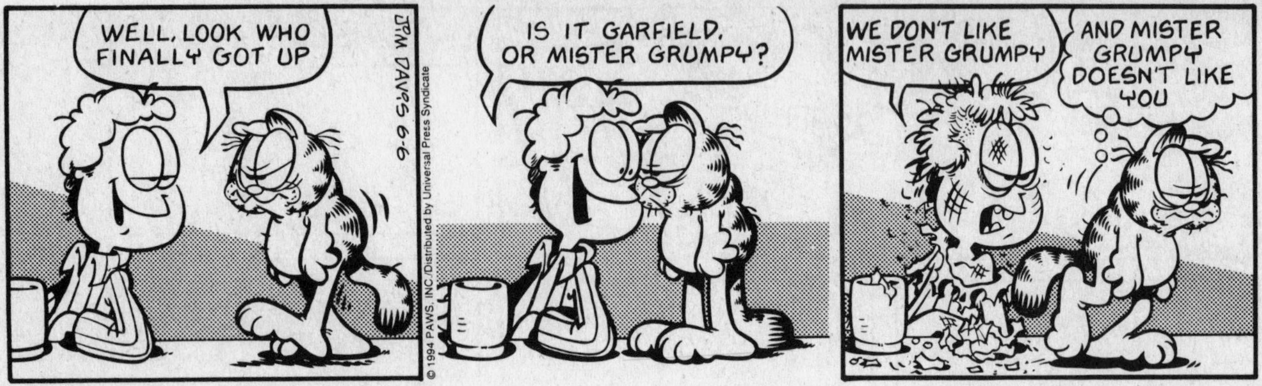
WELL, LOOK WHO FINALLY GOT UP
IS IT GARFIELD, OR MISTER GRUMPY?
WE DON'T LIKE MISTER GRUMPY
AND MISTER GRUMPY DOESN'T LIKE YOU
JIM DAVIS 6-6
© 1994 PAWS, INC./Distributed by Universal Press Syndicate

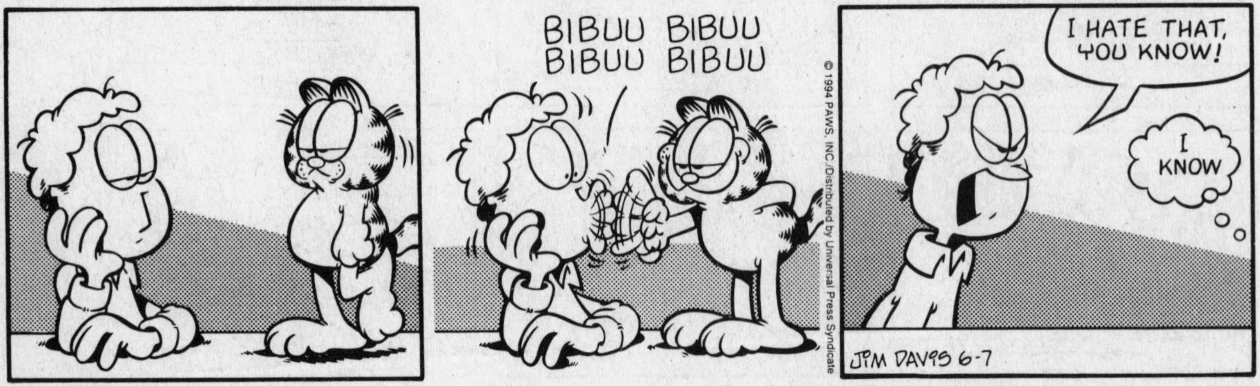
BIBUU BIBUU
BIBUU BIBUU
I HATE THAT, YOU KNOW!
I KNOW
JIM DAVIS 6-7
© 1994 PAWS, INC./Distributed by Universal Press Syndicate

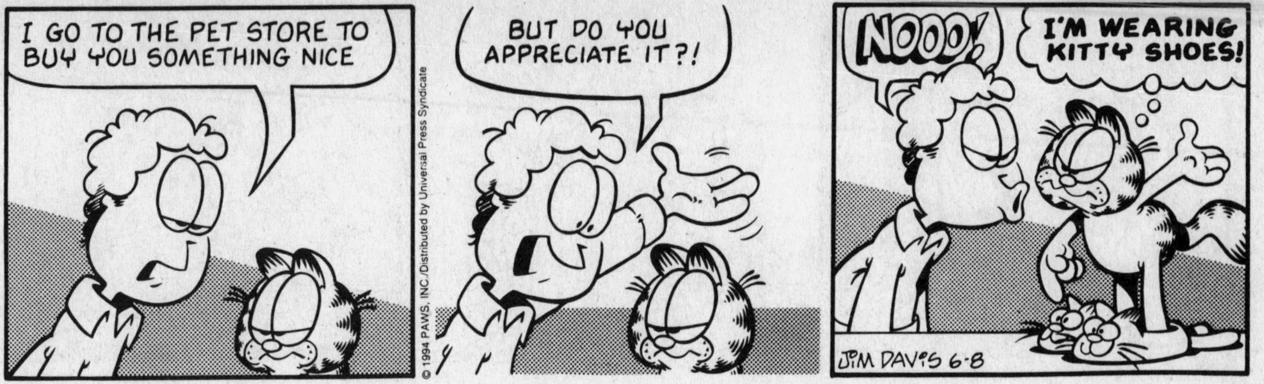
I GO TO THE PET STORE TO BUY YOU SOMETHING NICE
BUT DO YOU APPRECIATE IT?!
NOOO!
I'M WEARING KITTY SHOES!
JIM DAVIS 6-8

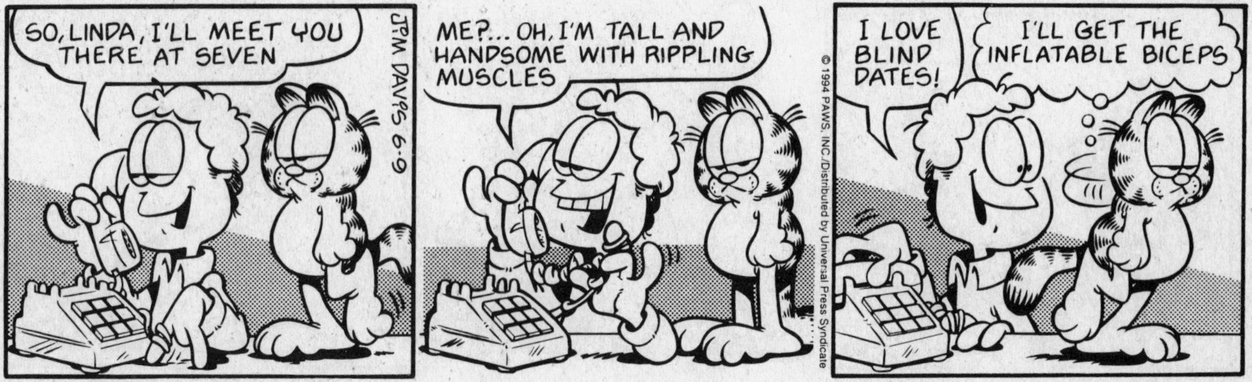
SO, LINDA, I'LL MEET YOU THERE AT SEVEN
JIM DAVIS 6-9
ME?... OH, I'M TALL AND HANDSOME WITH RIPPLING MUSCLES
I LOVE BLIND DATES!
I'LL GET THE INFLATABLE BICEPS

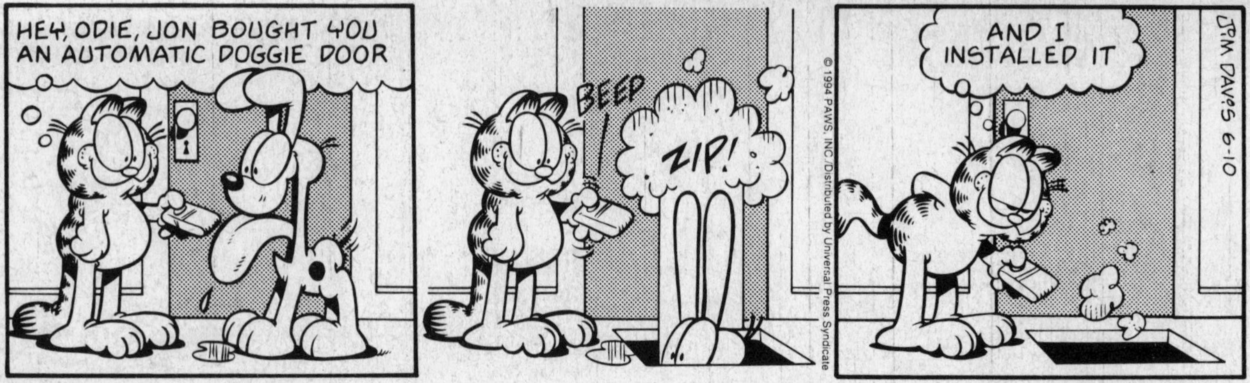
HEY, ODIE, JON BOUGHT YOU AN AUTOMATIC DOGGIE DOOR
BEEP
ZIP!
AND I INSTALLED IT
JIM DAVIS 6-10
© 1994 PAWS, INC./Distributed by Universal Press Syndicate

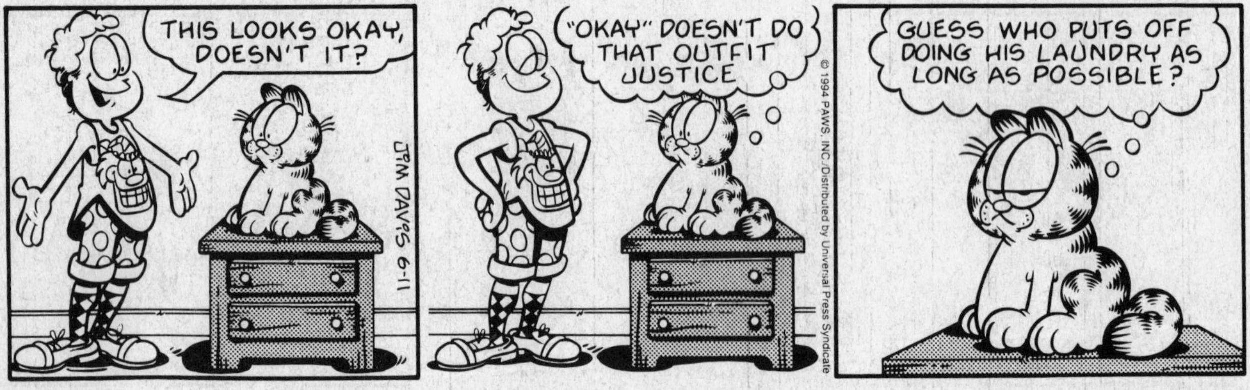
THIS LOOKS OKAY, DOESN'T IT?
JIM DAVIS 6-11
"OKAY" DOESN'T DO THAT OUTFIT JUSTICE
GUESS WHO PUTS OFF DOING HIS LAUNDRY AS LONG AS POSSIBLE?
© 1994 PAWS, INC./Distributed by Universal Press Syndicate

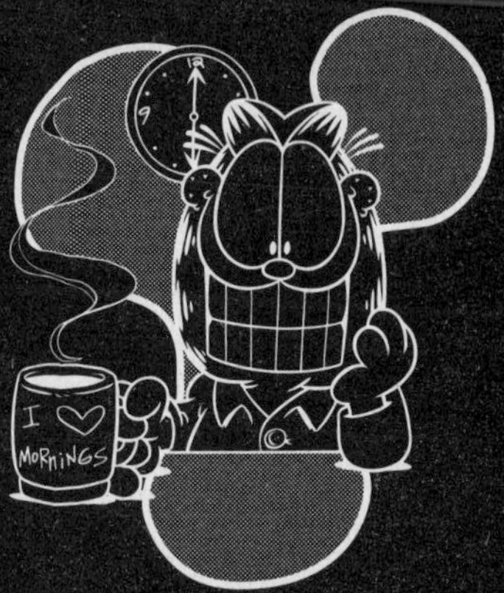
I ♥ MORNINGS

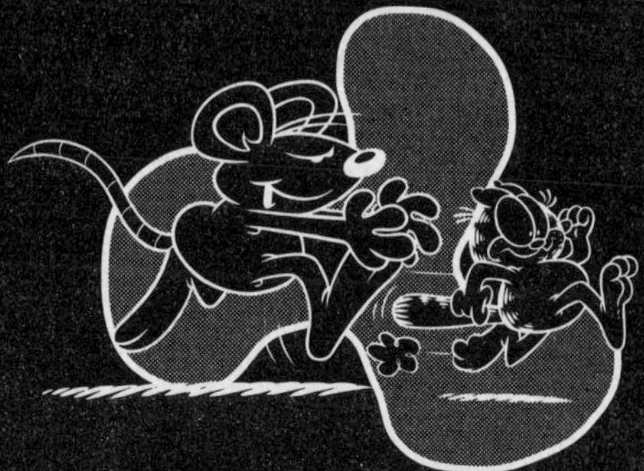

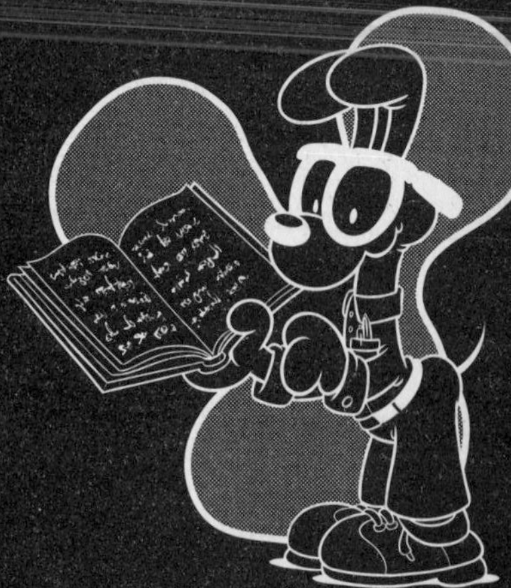

GARFIELD'S PARALLEL UNIVERSE

NIGHT IS DAY
AND BLACK IS WHITE...
BEHOLD A WORLD
OF INVERTED SIGHT!

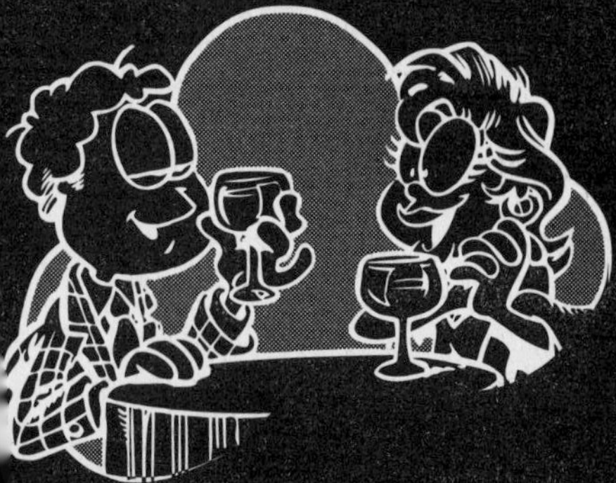

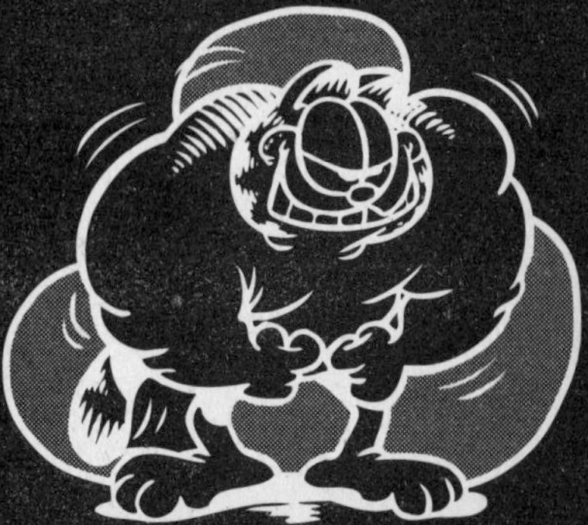